Climate Change and the Course of Global History

Climate Change and the Course of Global History: A Rough Journey presents the first global study by a historian to fully integrate the earth-system approach of the new climate science with the material history of humanity. Part I argues that geological, environmental, and climatic history explain the pattern and pace of biological and human evolution. Part II explores the environmental circumstances of the rise of agriculture and the state in the Early and Mid-Holocene, and presents an analysis of human health from the Paleolithic through the rise of the state, including the Neolithic Demographic Transition. Part III introduces the problem of economic growth and examines the human condition in the Late Holocene from the Bronze Age through the Black Death, assessing the relationships among human technologies, climatic change, and epidemic disease. Part IV explores the move to modernity, stressing the emerging role of human economic and energy systems as earth-system agents in the Anthropocene. Supported by climatic, demographic, and economic data with forty-nine figures and tables custom made for this book, *Climate Change and the Course of Global History* provides a path-breaking model for historians of the environment, the world, and science, among many others.

John L. Brooke is Humanities Distinguished Professor of History at Ohio State University, where he also directs the Center for Historical Research. His books include *Columbia Rising: Civil Life on the Upper Hudson from the Revolution to the Age of Jackson* (2010), which won the Best Book Prize from the Society of the Historians of the Early American Republic; *The Heart of the Commonwealth: Society and Political Culture in Worcester County Massachusetts, 1713–1861* (Cambridge, 1994), which won the Merle Curti Award for Intellectual History from the Organization of American Historians; and *The Refiner's Fire: The Making of Mormon Cosmology, 1644–1844* (Cambridge, 1989), which won the Bancroft Prize for American History. He has held fellowships from the Guggenheim Foundation, the National Endowment for the Humanities, the American Council of Learned Societies, the American Antiquarian Society, and the Harvard Charles Warren Center.

Studies in Environment and History

Editors

J. R. McNeill, *Georgetown University*
Edmund P. Russell, *University of Kansas*

Editors Emeritus

Alfred W. Crosby, *University of Texas at Austin*
Donald Worster, *University of Kansas*

Other Books in the Series

Climate Change and the Course of Global History

A Rough Journey

JOHN L. BROOKE

Ohio State University

CAMBRIDGE
UNIVERSITY PRESS

CAMBRIDGE
UNIVERSITY PRESS

32 Avenue of the Americas, New York NY 10013-2473, USA

Cambridge University Press is part of the University of Cambridge.

It furthers the University's mission by disseminating knowledge in the pursuit of education, learning, and research at the highest international levels of excellence.

www.cambridge.org
Information on this title: www.cambridge.org/9780521692182

© John L. Brooke 2014

First published 2014

A catalog record for this publication is available from the British Library.

Library of Congress Cataloging in Publication data
Brooke, John L., 1953–
Climate change and the course of global history / John Brooke.
pages   cm. – (Studies in environment and history)
Includes bibliographical references and index.
ISBN 978-0-521-87164-8 (hardback) – ISBN 978-0-521-69218-2 (paperback)
1. Climatic changes – History.   2. Nature – Effect of human beings on.   3. Human beings – Effect of climate on.   4. World history.   I. Title.
QC903.B76   2014
304.2'709–dc23   2013036435

ISBN 978-0-521-87164-8 Hardback
ISBN 978-0-521-69218-2 Paperback

For Sara, Matt, and Benjy, and our collective future.

Contents

Figures and Tables

The climate series in all of the figures have been displayed so that warmer and wetter conditions move up the charted figures, and colder and drier conditions down. Unless otherwise indicated, all figures are by the author.

Acknowledgments

This has been a project long in the making, running back to my undergraduate days at Cornell, and to various travels far and wide in the 1960s and 1970s. I want to thank my parents for the example of their adventuring spirit, and my undergraduate mentors at Cornell, particularly Robert Ascher, Stephen Kaplan, and the late Thomas Lynch, for their careful instruction and sage advice. After I had served for many years as an early American historian, the Tufts Environmental Studies Program got me to think again about a global perspective, and with its support in 1993 I began to teach global environmental history. A legion of undergraduates at Tufts and Ohio State have helped me think through ways to describe the long structures of the past, and I thank them for their patience and their enduring interest, and for their feedback on this manuscript as it has evolved.

I have presented chapters and general arguments around Ohio State at the Geology Sustainability Forum, the Environmental Science Graduate Program Seminar, the Global Human Health Pre-Conference, the Early Modern Seminar, the Department of History Seminar, the Byrd Polar Center Lecture Series, and elsewhere, at the University of Binghamton History Lecture Series, the University of Pennsylvania Annenberg Seminar, the University of Pittsburgh Department of Geology Speakers Series, and the American Historical Association. Thanks to all of the participants in these events who helped me sharpen and clarify my thinking.

Frank Smith listened patiently to my emerging thinking about this project for many years and carried his advocacy to higher powers at Cambridge University Press; when Frank left Cambridge, Eric Crahan lent his enthusiastic support. After Eric's departure, Deborah Gershenowitz carried this project forward with wonderful energy. After casting their sharp eyes over the entire manuscript, Donald Worster and J. R. McNeill asked me to submit to their Cambridge series "Studies in Environment and History"; I am deeply indebted to them for their encouragement and careful commentary.

Since 2005 when I started writing this book I have incurred a host of debts to colleagues near and far who have listened to my developing ideas, read innumerable chapter manuscripts, corresponded from a distance, and sent me their hard-won data. Among those who have read my manuscripts, I want to remember especially Andrew Sherratt and William Burroughs, both of whom have passed on – I hope that my efforts warrant their early support. Renée Hetherington and David Porinchu also read important parts of the manuscript for the Press, and I hope that I have done justice to their comments. Colleagues at Ohio State, Tufts, and literally around the world have provided invaluable readings, commentary, and guidance. I want to thank especially Bruce Batten, Manse Blackford, James Boone, Nick Breyfogle, Phil Brown, Bruce Campbell, Bill Childs, Barbara Hanawalt, Dan Hobbins, David Hoffman, Clark Larsen, Steve Marrone, Joy McCorriston, Chris Otter, Geoffrey Parker, Chris Reed, Jerry Rose, Nate Rosenstein, Randy Roth, Rick Steckel, the late Philip Walker, and Ying Zhang. Mark Stickle, Tim Leech, and J. R. McNeill's 2012 graduate seminar students all gave the manuscript useful readings. John Casterline and Greg Ginet provided invaluable assistance with higher math – compound growth rates and low-pass filters – at critical moments. Once again, Jim DeGrand has produced some wonderful charts and maps. Taotao Qian and David Decker helped me stumble through the challenges of building figures in IDL. Jayashree Prabhu and Ami Naramor have handled an arduous copyediting process in fine style, and Susan Cohen has produced another excellent index.

A host of climate scientists, historians, and archaeologists around the world have taken time out of their busy lives to correspond with me and send me their data: Andy Baker, Anthony Barnosky, Broxton Bird, Jean-Pierre Bocquet-Appel, Kimberley Bowes, Keith Briffa, Françoise Chalié, Fahu Chen, Hai Cheng, Francesco Cinnerella, Edward Cook, Basil Davis, Peter deMonocal, Sharon DeWitte, Carolyn Dykoski, Dominic Fleitman, Nicholas Graham, Anil Gupta, Gerald Haug, Israel Hershkovitz, Ulrike Herzschuh, Jonathan Holmes, Yetang Hong, Junfeng Ji, Willem Jongman, Mohammad Aslam Khan Khalil, Andrei Kurbatov, Matthew Lachniet, Michael Marshall, Mira Bar-Matthews, Vincent McCaulay, Ian McDougall, John Meadows, Christopher Moy, Raimund Muscheler, Jack Ridge, Charlotte Roberts, Eelco Rohling, James Russell, Frank Sirocko, Stephen J. Smith, Friedhelm Steinhilber, F. A. Street-Perrott, Faisal Saeed Syed, Liangcheng Tan, Ellen Mosley Thompson, Lucia Wick, Yongtao Yu, and Gregory Zelinsky. This list cannot do justice to their efforts, and they should take much of the credit for what I have gotten right, and none of the blame for what I have gotten wrong!! Greg Ginet was there from the beginning, conducting a mini-seminar with me all during the 1990s, crossing Mount Vernon Street every few months with armloads of well-read copies of *Scientific American* and *Science News*, and generally training me in the culture of the modern sciences.

I obviously owe a huge debt to these and many other scholars in climate science, geology, and archaeology who have gone into the field to record and then analyze and publish the mute history of the earth and humanity. Their work represents a vast treasure house of information from the sediments of time that comprises the material archive of earth history. Unfortunately I cannot cite their work adequately. Following standard practice in the historical discipline, I follow the Chicago style. For reasons of space, I restrict my footnote citations to a maximum of two authors; works produced by larger teams are cited to the lead author et al. This concession to space does not allow me to give full credit to the arduous work of a host of researchers. The bibliography lists the entire authorship of those articles from which data is used in the figures.

Sara, Matt, Benjy, and an array of old friends have patiently watched with some interest, when they were not busy with other things, as I have slowly constructed this volume. Sara, for a third of a century my love and anchor to windward, lives a life of environmental balance that often puts me to shame. Benjy at a very early age popped his head up from his drawing to articulate a simple truth – people should live their lives without disturbing the natural world. Matt started fighting the fight in the early 1990s, writing an editorial on solar power for the local paper, and – at the age of nine – conducting a heated argument with a dear but misguided relation on the validity of the science of climate change on his way to swimming at Goose Pond. May this book contribute to more such arguments, and move some minds.

Abbreviations

Abbreviations in Texts and Figures

BY	billions of years before present
ENSO	El Niño/Southern Oscillation
K-T boundary	Cretaceous-Tertiary boundary
LBK	Linear-Band-Keramik
LIA	Little Ice Age
MCA	Medieval Climate Anomaly
MIS	Marine Isotope Stage
MSA	African Middle Stone Age
MY	millions of years before present
NAO	North Atlantic Oscillation
PPN	PrePottery Neolithic
ybp	years before present
yma	moving average in years

Abbreviations for Most Frequent Citations

AER	*American Economic Review*
AHR	*American Historical Review*
AJHG	*American Journal of Human Genetics*
AJPA	*American Journal of Physical Anthropology*
AmAnth	*American Anthropologist*
AmAntiq	*American Antiquity*
ARA	*Annual Review of Anthropology*
CA	*Current Anthropology*
CArchJ	*Cambridge Archaeological Journal*
Climate Change 2007: The Physical Science Basis	Susan Solomon et al., eds., *Climate Change 2007: The Physical Science Basis. Contribution of Working Group I to the Fourth Assessment Report of the Intergovernmental Panel on Climate Change* (Cambridge and New York, 2007).

ClimCh	*Climatic Change*
ClimDyn	*Climate Dynamics*
EcolEcon	*Ecological Economics*
EconHR	*Economic History Review*
EmInfDis	*Emerging Infectious Diseases*
EnvSciTech	*Environmental Science and Technology*
EPSL	*Earth and Planetary Science Letters*
EREconH	*European Review of Economic History*
ExpEconH	*Explorations in Economic History*
GBC	*Global Biogeochemical Cycles*
GEC	*Global Environmental Change*
GPC	*Global and Planetary Change*
GRL	*Geophysical Research Letters*
HumEcol	*Human Ecology*
IJC	*International Journal of Climatology*
JAfrH	*Journal of African History*
JAmH	*Journal of American History*
JAnthArch	*Journal of Anthropological Archaeology*
JAnthRes	*Journal of Anthropological Research*
JArchRes	*Journal of Archaeological Research*
JArchS	*Journal of Archaeological Science*
JClim	*Journal of Climate*
JEArch	*Journal of European Archaeology*
JEconH	*Journal of Economic History*
JEconL	*Journal of Economic Literature*
JEconP	*Journal of Economic Perspectives*
JEEcH	*Journal of European Economic History*
JFdArch	*Journal of Field Archaeology*
JGeol	*Journal of Geology*
JGR	*Journal of Geophysical Research*
JHumEv	*Journal of Human Evolution*
JIH	*Journal of Interdisciplinary History*
JQS	*Journal of Quaternary Science*
JRA	*Journal of Roman Archaeology*
JRS	*Journal of Roman Studies*
JWH	*Journal of World History*
JWP	*Journal of World Prehistory*
MBE	*Molecular Biology and Evolution*
MedHyp	*Medical Hypotheses*
NatGen	*Nature Genetics*
NatGeosc	*Nature Geoscience*
NYT	*New York Times*
P&P	*Past and Present*
PBSRom	*Papers of the British School at Rome*

PNAS	*Proceedings of the National Academy of Sciences*
PopDevR	*Population and Development Review*
PopSt	*Population Studies*
PPP	*Palaeogeography, Palaeoclimatology, Palaeoecology*
PTRS,LB	*Philosophical Transactions of the Royal Society, London B*
QSR	*Quaternary Science Reviews*
QuatInt	*Quaternary International*
QuatRes	*Quaternary Research*
SA	*Scientific American*
SedGeol	*Sedimentary Geology*
VHAb	*Vegetation History and Archaeobotany*
WdArch	*World Archaeology*
WMQ	*William and Mary Quarterly*
YPA	*Yearbook of Physical Anthropology*

Introduction

Growth, Punctuation, and Human Well-Being

This book is a venture into history on a grand scale, a contribution to what is coming to be known variously as "big history," "deep history," and "evolutionary history."[1] I begin with a foundational question: How has the history of the earth system shaped the history of the human condition? The most cursory consideration of these histories suggests the basic outline of the story. Over the very long term, the history of a volatile and changing earth has driven biological and human evolution: it has been a rough journey, and we are products of that journey. During long epochs of organic hunter-gatherer systems and agrarian economies, humanity was fundamentally subject to natural forces of an evolving earth system; our sudden transition into fossil-fueled industrial modernity has made us an increasingly active and determining agent in that earth system.[2] Occasionally, too, hurricanes, earthquakes, or volcanic eruptions remind us that the earth is a very volatile platform for our finely balanced societies and economies.

This book, then, explores the role of nature – more precisely *natural history* – in human history. Doing so challenges a fundamental if rarely spoken tenet of my profession. We historians are extremely uncomfortable

---

[1] For key works in "big history," see David Christian, *Maps of Time: An Introduction to Big History* (Berkeley, 2004); Jared Diamond, *Collapse: How Societies Choose to Fail or Succeed* (New York, 2004); John R. McNeill and William H. McNeill, *The Human Web: A Bird's Eye View of World History* (New York, 2003); Fred Spier, *The Structure of Big History: From the Big Bang until Today* (Amsterdam, 1996); and Spier, *Big History and the Future of Humanity* (Malden, MA, 2010). For important new approaches that will reshape attitudes toward history on the grandest scale, see Daniel Lord Smail, *On Deep History and the Brain* (Berkeley, 2008); Andrew Shryock and Daniel Lord Smail et al., *Deep History: The Architecture of Past and Present* (Berkeley, 2011); and Edmund Russell, *Evolutionary History: Uniting History and Biology to Understand Life on Earth* (New York, 2011), and Daniel Lord Smail and Shryock Andrew, "History and the 'Pre," *AHR* 118 (2013), 709–737.

[2] Historians should be aware from the outset that the earth system of geological, atmospheric, and biological domains should not be confused with the "world system" theorized by Fernand Braudel, Andre Gunder Frank, and Immanuel Wallerstein.

with the idea that natural forces in some way circumscribe human agency. Fearful of being labeled "environmental determinists," we opt for a model of change in which all of the significant causal agents in historical processes are internal – or endogenous – to human culture, society, and economy. Given that most historians work on the past three to four centuries at most, this is not a completely unreasonable posture, because natural systems typically operate over much longer time frames.

But three considerations require that we set aside our avoidance of nature.[3] First, a holistic, long view of the human past, starting with evolutionary time, requires an understanding of the natural forces operating over centuries, millennia, and millions of years. Second, the short time scale of the past three to four centuries has seen both the global recovery from the Little Ice Age and the onset of rapid anthropogenic (human-induced) climate change. Third, a revolution has occurred in climate science, driven since the 1960s by an emerging understanding of the role of fossil fuel technology in altering global climate. Forty years ago, historians of another generation had no truly systematic evidence for climate history at hand, and here prudence did indeed require restraint.[4] But over the past generation the careful scientific study of chemical signatures in ice layers, lake beds, and marine sediments has established a remarkably detailed history of global environments reaching back billions of years, and of remarkable texture and resolution in the relatively recent past. One of the central purposes of this book is to introduce historians to the findings of this new global climate science. Despite recent politically driven "controversies," a massive body of incontrovertible evidence exists for the history of climate and for human-induced climate change, as this book reports in some detail.

If climate history is a central problem in this book, it shares the stage with a series of other critical questions. A big question running through my story is the shifting conditions of human well-being, as roughly measured by changes in both the size and health of populations, over the very long term of human history. Here the systematic analysis of archaeological and genetic data is beginning to radically sharpen our picture of human health in past time and to extend a chronologically shallow documentary record; I offer a tentative sketch of the ways the health evidence may suggest trends in overall societal prosperity and poverty. These involve the conditions of routine health and those of the crises of epidemics, both in their emergence and operation during the premodern agrarian epoch and their control in what is known as the epidemiological transition of the past several hundred years.

---

[3] Here see the pointed suggestions in Dipesh Chakrapbarty, "The Climate of History: Four Theses," *Critical Inquiry* 35 (2009), 197–222.

[4] For an early assessment of a pioneering climate historian, see Emanuel Le Roy Ladurie, "History without People: The Climate as a New Province of Research," in *The Territory of the Historian*, trans. Sian Reynolds and Ben Reynolds (Chicago, IL, 1979), 287–319.

Here I see a fundamentally dynamic causal interaction between disease and human agency. In the book's final section, I argue that, in addition to global empire building, an emergent understanding and practice of public health, grounded in the efforts of increasingly effective early modern nation-states, drove a declining mortality and a surge of population growth that was a critical force in the spiraling development of economic modernity.

Thus human agency itself is another central problem in this book, perhaps the central problem. If natural forces of climate, environment, and disease are indeed so powerful, how has humanity managed to arrive at its current condition of modernity? Here I take the very long view of the growth of human capacities, considering a continuum of adaptive change running from biological evolution to technological innovation and economic growth. And as this problem of human agency develops in this book, I have had to try to suppress the impulse to write a political history, but questions of the role and efficiency of the state inevitably become essential problems in this account.

If it is to examine these foundational questions, a big history necessarily must address grand theory – our inheritance from the founders of the modern social and biological sciences who established our understandings of the evolution and history of biological and human life. They were the big historians of their day, and their reach has been long and powerful.

We might well start with Benjamin Franklin, whose writings on land and population in the 1750s were powerfully influential on Adam Smith and Thomas Malthus, who in turn shaped the intellectual stage for Charles Darwin. Men of the eighteenth century, Franklin, Smith, and Malthus could not anticipate the transformation to come in the nineteenth: they were all concerned with the problem of prosperity in organic, preindustrial societies. Franklin and Malthus were more pessimistic, seeing a close, zero-sum relationship between growing populations and limited resources, and seeing a threat of the dreaded "positive check" if land – in the colonial American case – ceased to be free for the taking, or if a society failed to exert virtue in the preventive check. In his classic formulation, Malthus argued that "[t]he ultimate check to population appears ... to be a want of food, arising necessarily from the different ratios according to which population and food increase."[5] Malthus published his interpretation of populations and natural resources in 1798, and this formed part of Darwin's intellectual background when he began to develop his thinking on evolution and natural selection in the 1830s. In particular, Malthus's analysis of a steady pressure of population driving a relentless competition for resources shaped Charles Darwin's

---

[5] Thomas Robert Malthus, *An Essay on the Principle of Population: A View of Its Past and Present Effects on Human Happiness; with an Inquiry into Our Prospects Respecting the Future Removal or Mitigation of the Evils which It Occasions*, sixth edition (London: John Murray, 1826), book 1, chapter 2.

insight into how natural selection of adaptive traits formed the basic engine of biological evolution. Allied with the new gradualist geology that posed the operation of observable processes over vast stretches of time (as against Christianity's six-thousand-year history and its great dramas of Creation and the Flood), Darwin framed the concept of natural selection as a tooth-and-nail struggle for resources in a context of perpetual overpopulation.

Malthusian and Darwinian thought must be seen as inseparable intellectual frameworks. Both assume a fundamental gradualism in which a close calculus of population and resources constantly threatened individual survival. Each are oddly antihistorical, assuming that the conditions of this struggle vary within a minor and negligible range. Each posited an individual solution: Malthus's salvation lay in the preventive check of sexual restraint; Darwin's lay in the advantages accruing to individuals and evolving species from unique qualities of positive traits, later demonstrated to be operating at the genetic level by Gregor Mendel and at the molecular level by Watson and Crick.[6]

Among the classical economists, while he still only visualized gradual change in an organic economy, Adam Smith was far more optimistic than Franklin, Malthus, or Darwin. Smith posited growing prosperity per capita with an intensifying division of labor pursuing expanding markets opened by a liberal, post-mercantilist state. If energy supplies remained essentially stable, "the skill, dexterity, and judgment" of the deployment of human labor would drive the advance of human well-being.[7] In the 1950s and 1960s, Danish economist Ester Boserup formulated a restatement of this Smithian model of growth in an explicit assault on Malthus. She argued that Malthusian crises were rare events in human history because incremental innovation and intensification had generally kept population ahead of the grim reaper.[8] But Smith and Boserup shared with Malthus and Darwin basic assumptions about the

---

[6] Robert M. Young, "Malthus and the Evolutionists: The Common Context of Biological and Social Theory," *Past and Present* 43 (1969), 109–45; Silvan S. Schweber, "The Origin of the *Origin* Revisited," *Journal of the History of Biology* 10 (1977), 229–316; Sandra Herbert, "The Darwinian Revolution Revisited," *Journal of the History of Biology* 38 (2005), 51–66. For recent statements of the Darwinian synthesis, see Richard Dawkins, *The Blind Watchmaker: Why the Evidence of Evolution Reveals a Universe without Design* (New York, 1986; rev. ed., 1996); and Geerat J. Vermeij, *Nature: An Economic History* (Princeton, NJ, 2004).

[7] Adam Smith, *An Inquiry in the Nature and Causes of the Wealth of Nations* (Edinburgh, 1843), 1; Hiram Caton, "The Preindustrial Economics of Adam Smith," *JEconH* 45 (1985), 833–53.

[8] Ether Boserup, *The Conditions of Agricultural Growth: The Economics of Agrarian Change under Population Pressure* (London, 1965). Though I now dissent from important aspects of their arguments, I have learned a lot from Ronald D. Lee, "Malthus and Boserup: A Dynamic Synthesis," in David Coleman and Roger S. Scholfield, eds., *The State of Population Theory: Forward from Malthus* (Oxford, 1986), 96–103; and James W. Wood, "A Theory of Preindustrial Population Dynamics: Demography, Economy, and Well-Being in Malthusian Systems," *CA* 39 (1998), 99–216.

slow, gradual, and uniform trajectory of biological and social change. For none of these theorists is there room for sudden jolts: Malthus and Darwin saw an unremitting contest over resources by human and biological populations limited by inherently slow capacities for adaptation and change; Smith and Boserup saw those capacities as sufficient – if well enough organized – for human effort to produce significant though limited results. Running through all of these frameworks was – consciously or not – the basic principle that energy available to organic biological and economic systems is limited by an annual input of solar radiation and a product of photosynthesis. And we should remember that Adam Smith, while focusing his attention on the virtues of peaceful commerce, was well aware that the prosperity of one society might also come at the cost of another, in the "dreadful misfortunes" of those subjected to the "plundering" of conquest by expanding empires.[9]

Two quite different intellectual ventures have challenged the gradualist assumptions of the classical theorists in both economics and evolution. First, the impact of the industrial revolutions of the nineteenth and twentieth centuries exposed the limits of the perspectives developed by Smith, Malthus, and their contemporaries. Rapidly advancing technologies, designed on rigorous scientific and mathematical principles and powered by the "free" energy of fossil fuels, fundamentally challenged classical economics. Karl Marx and Frederick Engels were among the first to wrestle with the impact of the new technologies as they transformed the relationship of labor and capital. Marx's understanding of the modern capitalist economy was elaborated in the 1920s by Soviet economist Nikolai Kondratiev into a cyclical sequence of expansions and contractions, which was reformulated in the 1930s by conservative economist Joseph Schumpeter into business cycles driven by technological innovation. There is a general contemporary consensus that the modern economy is fueled by an accelerating, technology-driven Schumpeterian growth, rather than a gradual Smithian growth. Coming in unique waves rather than recurring cycles, successive technologies of increasing capacity and improving efficiency have swept through the modern economy since the early nineteenth century, overturning older systems in surges of "creative destruction."[10]

---

[9] Smith, *An Inquiry*, 258–9 (book IV, chapter 7, part 3).

[10] On Malthus, Smith, and Schumpeter, see William N. Parker, *Europe, America, and the Wider World: Essays on the Economic History of Western Capitalism* (New York, 1984), 1: 191–213; for two recent works on the Kondratiev-Schumpeter synthesis, see Carlota Perez, *Technological Revolutions and Financial Capital: The Dynamics of Bubbles and Golden Ages* (Cheltenham, 2002); and Chris Freeman and Francisco Louçã, *As Time Goes By: From the Industrial Revolutions to the Information Revolution* (Oxford, 2001). Schumpeter saw modern, technologically driven economic growth as overturning Malthus and refused to accept that population played any role in the modern economy. In Part IV of this book, I suggest that surging population growth from the early modern period, especially since the eighteenth century, provides a critical component of the demand that ultimately launched and sustained Schumpeterian growth.

A remarkably similar "catastrophism" has emerged in the arena of the natural sciences. As the first efforts to model the tectonic history of the earth were made in the 1960s, new understandings of earth history and of evolution suddenly developed, fundamentally challenging Darwinian gradualism. First fully articulated in the pioneering work of Stephen Jay Gould and Niles Eldredge, the new understanding argues that biological evolution proceeded at different rates, even in fits and starts. This punctuated equilibrium, or "pluralistic evolution," was driven by major events in earth history, in which massive geological processes –super-plume events – interrupted periods of relative stability, rupturing continents, changing sea levels suddenly, raising mountain ranges, and driving the earth's climate and environment back and forth between "greenhouse" and "icehouse" conditions. Responding to these stresses and stabilizations, one model suggests that rates of Darwinian natural selection accelerated and subsided as species, families, and phyla were subjected to mass extinctions that opened the way to equally sudden periods of speciation and expansion – the Gouldian version of Schumpeter's creative destruction.[11] An even more radical view is gaining ground, arguing that natural selection is actually a conserving force and that evolutionary breaks are biochemical responses to environmental stress, operating during the development of the embryo to establish new physical traits in the "phenotype."[12]

If the new science is mapping these processes of geological and evolutionary history since the origin of the earth, it has also mapped them in the relatively recent past, over five million years of increasingly glacial conditions of the Pliocene and Pleistocene, and over the past ten thousand years of reasonably stable and warm interglacial conditions known as the Holocene, which encompasses the entire agricultural history of humanity. The result, quite simply, is that it is now quite clear that abrupt climatic and environmental

---

[11] Niles Eldridge and Stephen Jay Gould, "Punctuated Equilibria: An Alternative to Phyletic Gradualism," in Thomas J. M. Schopf, ed., *Models in Paleobiology* (San Francisco, CA, 1972), 82–115; Stephen Jay Gould and Niles Eldridge, "Punctuated Equilibria: The Tempo and Mode of Evolution Reconsidered," *Paleobiology* 3 (1977), 115–51. The parallels between the Gould-Eldredge model of evolution and the Schumpeterian model of modern economic growth are suggested in Joel Mokyr, "Punctuated Equilibria and Technological Progress," *AER* 80 (1990), 350–4; and Vaclav Smil, *Creating the Twentieth Century: Technical Innovations of 1867–1814 and Their Lasting Impact* (New York, 2005), 5–13. It might be proposed that Malthus's inclusion of natural calamity as a "positive check" anticipated Gould and Eldredge's punctuational theory. This is not, however, the general understanding.

[12] Robert G. B. Reid, *Biological Emergences: Evolution by Natural Experiment* (Cambridge, MA, 2007); Eva Jablonka and Marian J. Lamb, *Evolution in Four Dimensions: Genetic, Epigenetic, Behavioral, and Symbolic Variation in the History of Life* (Cambridge, MA, 2005); Mary-Jane West-Eberhard, *Developmental Plasticity and Evolution* (New York, 2003); Robert G. B. Reid, *Evolutionary Theory: The Unfinished Synthesis* (Beckenham, 1985).

change has been a fundamental dimension of the long history of humanity. Trends and abrupt shifts in climate drove human evolution in Miocene-Pliocene Africa; severe glacial cycles and megadroughts episodically reduced human numbers in the Pleistocene, shaping the final evolutionary modeling of modern humanity. Even during the Holocene, milder but nonetheless significant global climatic shifts had enormous, indeed punctuating, impacts on fragile agrarian economies.

But where the Gouldian punctuation model poses a challenge to gradualism, this challenge is only to the pessimistic gradualism of Darwin and Malthus. The punctuation model posits expansionary growth as the aftermath of crisis, and not just because free resources are suddenly available. The winnowing – the creative destruction – imposed by the stresses of punctuation provides space for new adaptive strategies to take hold and to persist. In evolutionary ecology there is considerable ongoing work on the ecology of these adaptive strategies of stability and "coordinated stasis."[13] Just as there are useful analogs to be drawn between Gould-Eldredge punctuations and Schumpeterian "creative destruction," there are analogs to be drawn between this evolutionary literature on stability and stasis and the optimistic gradualism of Adam Smith, Ester Boserup, and a newly emerging literature on human resilience.[14] Increasingly, a variety of literatures are coming to an understanding that ancient and medieval/premodern populations and societies were much more stable – and resilient – than previously thought. We should not be too sanguine about the quality of life in these premodern societies; growing population density in the absence of modern public health meant shorter life spans – and shorter adult stature – than the recent modern norm. But rather than a constant story of peaking and crashing at the edge of technological capacity, long stretches of human history have been shaped by constant gradual Boserupian innovation – and occasionally even by "Smithian" economic growth. The emerging consensus here is that, within certain limits, organic economies of the past were adaptive and resilient, with the result that ancient societies lasted for enormous stretches of time, relative to the record of modernity.[15] Thus I argue throughout this

---

[13] Stephen J. Gould, *The Structure of Evolutionary Theory* (Cambridge, MA, 2002), 745–1024.

[14] Lance H. Gunderson and C. S. Holling, eds., *Panarchy: Understanding Transformations in Human and Natural Systems* (Washington, DC, 2002).

[15] Eric L. Jones, *Growth Recurring: Economic Change in World History* (Ann Arbor, MI, 2000 [1988]); Jack A. Goldstone, "Efflorescences and Economic Growth in World History: Rethinking the 'Rise of the West' and the Industrial Revolution," *JWH* 13 (2002), 323–90; Jan de Vries, "Economic Growth before and after the Industrial Revolution: A Modest Proposal," in Maarten Prak, ed., *Early Modern Capitalism: Economic and Social Change in Europe, 1400–1800* (New York, 2001), 177–94; Karl W. Butzer and Georgina H. Endfield, "Critical Perspectives on Historical Collapse," *PNAS* 109 (2012), 3628–31; Karl W. Butzer, "Collapse, Environment, and Society," *PNAS* 109 (2012), 3632–9; Patricia A. McAnamy and Norman Yoffee, eds., *Questioning Collapse: Human Resilience, Ecological Vulnerability*

book that the structure of human history is distinctly "Gouldian"/punctua-
tional, with long periods of relative stability (stasis) interrupted by well-
defined breaks best understood as episodic (not necessarily cyclical) global
climate crises – Dark Ages, perhaps – increasingly augmented and surpassed
by the eruption of epidemic disease and destructive warfare.[16]

I have not come to this nature-driven argument easily or lightly. When I
first began this project, I was very resistant to a climate-driven thesis, and I
assumed that I would be telling a fairly standard story of Malthusian sustainability crises in which episodic population growth drove both the crises
and regime shifts in human history. This argument has been most powerfully advanced in Jared Diamond's *Collapse*.[17] But, after closer consideration of the literature in a variety of fields, I have abandoned this position,
which I call the *endogenous argument*. I find a growing skepticism among
prehistoric, ancient, and medieval specialists toward rigidly theoretical
Malthusian interpretations, and among paleo-ecologists toward arguments

and the Aftermath of Empire (New York, 2010); Joseph Tainter, "The Archaeology of
Overshoot and Collapse," *ARA* 35 (2006), 59–74; Carl Folke, "Resilience: The Emergence
of a Perspective for Social-Ecological Systems Analysis," *GEC* 16 (2006), 253–67; Charles L.
Redman, "Resilience Theory in Archaeology," *AmAnth* 107 (2005), 70–7.

[16] Epidemics are certainly density dependent, requiring threshold levels of population. But they
are not necessarily density determined – it is clear that their arrival in and impact on ancient
and medieval worlds was not inexorably determined by some long-brewing Malthusian crisis of population and resources. Indeed, in many cases, simplistic as it may sound, epidemics
followed war, and war followed adverse climate change. The team led by David D. Zhang
has established this exogenous argument regarding abrupt climate change, agricultural crisis, warfare, and regime collapse for China and the Old World more broadly in the recent
past. These authors stress the inconsistency of this pattern with a traditional Malthusian
endogenous explanation of crisis. As they put it, "this view is contrary to the traditional
one of Malthus, Darwin, and many ecologists who hold land carrying capacity as a constant" (2006, 460). See David D. Zhang et al., "Global Climate Change, War, and Population
Decline in Recent Human History," *PNAS* 104 (2007), 19214–19219; "Climate Change
and War Frequency in Eastern China over the Last Millennium," *HumEcol* 35 (2007),
403–14 (esp. 413); "Climatic Change, Wars, and Dynastic Cycles in China over the Last
Millennium," *ClimCh* 76 (2006), 459–77; and Solomon M. Hsiang, et al., "Quantifying the
Influence of Climate on Human Conflict," *Science* 341 (2013), 1235367.

[17] For important recent statements of the standard Malthusian understanding of premodern
human history, which I respectfully dispute, see Diamond, *Collapse*; Christian, *Maps of
Time*; and Joachim Radkau, *Nature and Power: A Global History of the Environment*, trans.
Thomas Dunlap (New York, 2008). See also Michael Williams, *Deforesting the Earth: From
Prehistory to Global Crisis* (Chicago, IL, 2003), 37–144; Sing C. Chew, *World Ecological
Degradation: Accumulation, Urbanization, and Deforestation, 3000 B.C.–A.D. 2000*
(Walnut Creek, CA, 2001); Charles L. Redman, *Human Impact on Ancient Environments*
(Tucson, AZ, 1999); Neil Roberts, *The Holocene: An Environmental History*, second edition
(Malden, 1998), 159–206; Clive Ponting, *A Green History of the Earth* (London, 1992);
and Mark Nathan Cohen, *The Food Crisis in Prehistory: Overpopulation and the Origins
of Agriculture* (New Haven, CT, 1977). Marvin Harris laid out the fundamentals of the
"endogenous model" in *Cannibals and Kings: The Origins of Cultures* (New York, 1977).

for significant human-induced environmental degradation in premodern eras.[18] At the same time, climate scientists are finding compelling evidence for severe climate change at key periods of human crisis and transformation. I argue that until the onset of modern accelerated population growth, no premodern society of consequence occupying a reasonably adequate biome[19] suffered a purely endogenous "Malthusian crisis"; rather adversity, crisis, and collapse were fundamentally shaped by *exogenous forces*: the impacts of drought, cold, and epidemic disease drove episodic and abrupt reversals in societal complexity and the human condition. Diamond's book and many other environmental histories of the ancient past, I argue, are more jeremiads on the very real sins of modern society than descriptions of the central tendencies of past human history. Thus, to my own surprise, I argue that Malthus was wrong regarding most of human history. Contrary to the standard account, most of the human experience has not been shaped by endogenously driven overpopulation, but by a dialectic between moderately successful organic economies and the regular impact of exogenous natural forces. Only in the recent past, as we have suddenly escaped from the constraints of epidemic disease to vastly increase our numbers, has overpopulation become an earth-systemic crisis.[20]

Thus the fundamental insights informing this book are Gould's qualification of Darwin and Boserup's qualification of Malthus, with Marx and Schumpeter thrown in for good measure. In the long course of organic economies from the Paleolithic/Neolithic to the eighteenth century – during long periods of relative stability – Boserupian-Smithian processes of gradual innovation and slow cumulative economic growth on balance offset and occasionally transcended population growth. Until the onset of true Schumpeterian economic growth around the north Atlantic in the mid-nineteenth century, the human condition was governed not by a Darwinian-Malthusian synthesis of constant struggle on the razor edge of crisis and collapse, but by a combination of the Gould-Eldredge model of natural punctuation and an intervening equilibrium/stasis-Boserupian model of innovation and resilience. In sum, over the long run, human societies and

---

[18] Here compare Charles Redman's 1999 *Human Impact on Ancient Environments* with his comments in his 2005 "Resilience Theory in Archaeology."

[19] I exclude the occasional case of isolated situations such as Easter Island. But even here the Malthusian interpretation is under challenge: see Terry L. Hunt and Carl P. Lipo, "Ecological Catastrophe, Collapse, and the Myth of 'Ecocide' on Rapa Nui (Easter Island)," in Patricia A. McAnamy and Norman Yoffee, eds., *Questioning Collapse: Human Resilience, Ecological Vulnerability, and the Aftermath of Empire* (New York, 2010), 21–44.

[20] For an analysis, with ongoing commentary, of the earth system's limits on modern human populations and economies, see Johan Rockström et al., "Planetary Boundaries: Exploring the Safe Operating Space for Humanity," *Ecology and Society* 14/2/32 (2009) and "A Safe Operating Space for Humanity," *Nature* 461 (2009), 472–5. See also Will Steffen, "Observed Trends in Earth System Behavior," *WIREs Climate Change* 1 (2010), 428–49.

economies got through by getting better, but fairly regularly adverse natural forces set very bad things in motion. Only in the very recent past, when the beginnings of modern political governance, the first precursors of medical practice, and the establishment of global empires led to spreading focal points of extremely rapid population growth, did a truly Malthusian calculus begin to operate – first in England and China in the eighteenth century – and with critical transitions driven by the push of population rather than natural forcings. Paradoxically, Malthus was right – but for his own time and place, and for our own time. But before that point, population growth was not necessarily the fundamental driver of the human condition, except as it moved a gradual Boserupian process of incremental adjustment and adaptation.

Given such resilience and adaptive capacity, such gradual but effective innovation in the organic economy, fundamental crisis and collapse required a very big push, which did not come all that often. And over the course of premodern human history, when they did come, some of these exogenous impacts were simply temporary setbacks without lasting structural impacts. But others qualify as revolution drivers, Gouldian punctuations with Schumpeterian consequences. During the Pliocene and the Pleistocene, human revolutions shaped by global climate stresses included the three key junctures in human evolution: the Australopithecine divergence from advanced primates, the speciation of the genus *Homo*, and the development of modern human anatomy and cultural capacity now called the Middle Paleolithic Revolution. In the prehistoric and ancient Holocene, these moments include the origins of domestication, the rise of complex agrarian societies, the rise of the Bronze Age state, and a critical "axial" transition from Bronze Age to Iron Age polities and economies. These Iron Age structures framed the technological and sociological outlines of the entire era down to the beginnings of modernity, itself launched during an epoch of devastating natural catastrophe. Throughout each of these critical transitions in the human condition, earth systemic forces shaped an epoch of "creative destruction" leading to key departures in technology and social formation. These were bottlenecks of population, resources, and adaptive capacity/technology – but they were fundamentally shaped by abrupt climate change, not critical overpopulation.

The transition to modernity involved the launch of self-sustaining Schumpeterian growth driven by quantum leaps in technology, and is now driving an accelerating alteration of global environments and climates. It is abundantly clear that this transition necessarily involved three factors: global empires, a fruitful linkage between experimental science and artisanal technology, and cheap and accessible fossil fuels. It also followed – and was shaped by – the overlapping impacts of the Black Death and the Little Ice Age. In an age of global natural crisis perhaps more severe than anything experienced in the Holocene, the benefits of intensified organic economies and global empire accrued to certain early modern European societies. But as increasingly effective governments tipped the epidemiological balance toward rapidly growing populations, the ecological and health demands of increasingly commercialized and urbanized societies provided an essential imperative for technological change requiring massive injections of energy. Now translated to the global stage, these imperatives have driven the accelerating surges of economic growth that we collectively call the industrial revolutions and the "super-cycles" of the modern economy, as well as impacts on global environments and climates that can only be compared in scale to primal forces of the earth system itself.

Thus our modern condition has to be seen as a mushrooming complex of rapid population growth and resource and energy demands (driven by both first world "lifestyle" expectations and third world numbers), accelerating advances in science and technology, and local/regional and increasingly global environmental impacts. Living our day-to-day, year-to-year lives, we have lost sight of how extremely recently – in earth system terms and over the arc of human history – we have entered this modern condition. The fundamental question facing the world today is the simple question of sustainability: How far into the future can we sustain modern populations and standards of living? What is clear is that – natural conditions being reasonably favorable – organic societies in preindustrial times were reasonably sustainable, if not all that pleasant to live in: short individual life spans were matched by long societal chronologies. By contrast we have to wonder whether – revising the standard reading of Malthus – industrial societies have reversed this equation, in which improved conditions of health and increased life expectancy have been exchanged for an unsustainable global economy and ecology, putting the future course of our "social chronology" into some doubt. Deniers, pessimists, and pragmatists now debate this question in a global public sphere. The outcome of this debate is a matter of the greatest consequence for humanity and for the earth system. As we contemplate our uncertain collective future, it may be of some consolation to know that the entire history of humanity in the earth system has been a rough journey, and we have acquired considerable skills in navigation and travel, if only we are willing to use them.

A few words and caveats on the organization of this book are in order. Part I establishes the basic premise that there is a fundamental relationship between the dynamics of the earth's geological and atmospheric history and the evolution of biological life and of humanity over the very long term, from the first eons after earth formation to the end of the Pleistocene ice ages. The first chapter describes the new synthesis of a geological atmospheric history of stasis and crisis driving cycles of stability and punctuation in biological evolution, from earth origins down to roughly ten million years ago. Chapter 2 details the similar story of primate and human evolution, from the Miocene to the end of the Pleistocene, when modern humanity had colonized virtually the entire earth. Part II covers roughly nine thousand years, from the erratic close of the Pleistocene around 12000 BC through the peak global warmth and cooling of the Early and Mid-Holocene, in which human societies settled into postglacial environments, domesticated plant and animal species, and established stable agrarian societies and the beginnings of the state, around 3000 BC. By the end of the Pleistocene, human innovative capacities based on our anatomical and cultural modernity established by two hundred thousand years ago (in the Middle Paleolithic), were already exerting a far more significant influence on the human condition than were genetics and evolution. With the rise of the state in 3000 BC, and perhaps even with the emergence of advanced agricultural societies two thousand to three thousand years earlier, we can begin to tentatively pose the question of the shape and direction of economic growth. Part II closes with a sketch in Chapter 5 of the health and demography of ancient populations; Part III introduces the question of economic growth and the standard of living in state societies in Chapter 6. Chapters 7, 8, and 9 examine the irregular, halting pace of economic growth – and the cumulative expansions of cultural capacity – that characterized the agrarian ancient and medieval worlds from 3000 BC to the Black Death, in two long if fragmented sequences of the human experience, defined in the Old World by the Bronze Age and the long epoch of classical antiquity and "medieval" societies, interrupted by the formative crisis that launched the Iron Age. Part IV and the Coda present a new interpretation of the breakout to the accelerating, self-perpetuating economic growth of the modern world, examining the transition to modernity from the aftermath of the Black Death to our current condition of a humanity of seven billion, a significantly altered atmosphere and biosphere, a massive but sputtering global economy, and a creeping paralysis of governance.

There is also the question of global coverage. In one volume, I cannot give the entire geography of the human experience its due justice. For better or worse I have been guided by three rules of thumb: population, evidence, and environmental impact. I have focused on those parts of the world where the highest concentrations of population developed, where we have the best evidence, and where a trajectory toward state, empire, and the fossil fuel transformation seems to suggest the central problems of our human condition lie. Chapter 2 necessarily focuses on the center stage of human evolution, eastern Africa, and then the adjacent Eurasian zones of modern human dispersal. Part II on the Neolithic and transition to the early state is somewhat more selective, focusing on greater Southwest Asia/northeast Africa, and only sketching developments in India, Southeast Asia, China, and the Americas, where in many cases the archaeological data is not as fully developed. Part III, on archaic state societies, Classical Antiquity, and the Middle Ages, focuses again on Southwest Asia and to some extent China and the Americas, moving broadly into the wider eastern Mediterranean world, and from there to medieval Europe. Part IV begins with a focus on Europe and Great Britain, and moves to the United States before widening out into a global perspective of the very recent past. For better or worse, not attempting a complete global coverage provides the opportunity to examine relatively closely some well-explored sequences in world history and their place in and impact on the wider human condition.

PART I

EVOLUTION AND EARTH SYSTEMS

List of Figures for Part I: Evolution and Earth Systems

Figures

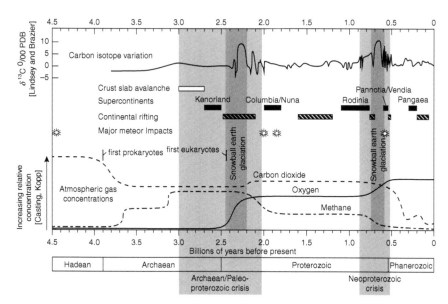

Figure I.1. Earth systems, atmosphere, and biology: paleo-crises and paleo-stasis.

The origins of life, followed by two great earth systems crises at the beginning and the end of the Proterozoic, shaped the emergence of an atmosphere that would permit terrestrial life during the Phanerozoic.

Figure by James DeGrand

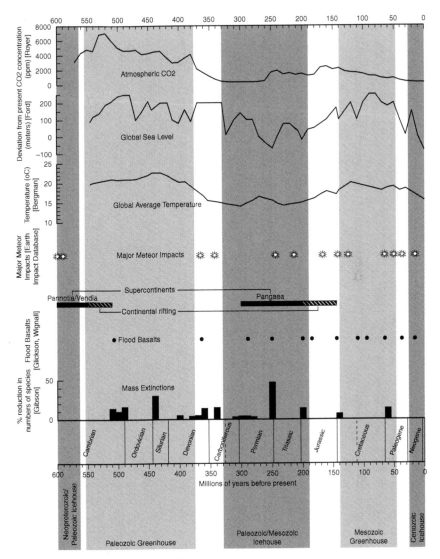

Figure I.2. Phanerozoic super-cycles.

During the last 600 million years the earth has gone through two cycles between warm Greenhouse conditions and cold Icehouse conditions. Greenhouses are characterized by rifted island continents, high atmospheric CO_2 and high sealevels; Icehouses by consolidated supercontinents, low atmospheric CO_2 and low sealevels. Though there are important exceptions, like the Permian extinction, the transitions between Greenhouse and Icehouse states may be driven by the interaction of meteor impacts and superplumes rising from the outer core.

Figure by James DeGrand

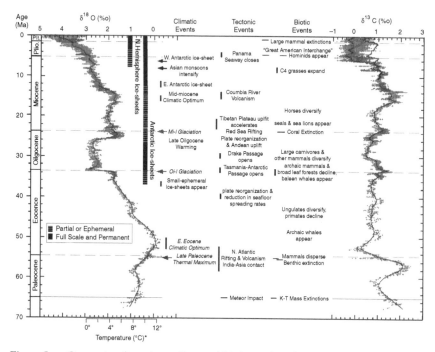

Figure I.3. Cenozoic: climatic cooling and biological evolution.

The last 65 million years, the Cenozoic, has been shaped by a long, jagged planetary cooling, as the earth has shifted into an Icehouse condition, which will culminate in tens of millions of years in a reaggregated supercontinent. This diagram by James Zachos maps the key climatic, tectonic, and biotic events against oxygen and carbon isotope proxies of global temperature. From peak temperatures at the Late Paleocene Thermal Maximum and the Early Eocene Optimum, the critical phases in this Greenhouse-Icetransition were the onset of Antarctic glaciation in the Oligocene, and Northern Hemisphere glaciation in the Pliocene.

From James Zachos, Mark Pagani, Lisa Sloan, Ellen Thomas, Katherina Billups. "Trends, Rhythms, and Aberrations in Global Climate 65 Ma to Present," Science 292 (2001), 686-93 [Fig. 2].Reprinted with permission from AAAS.

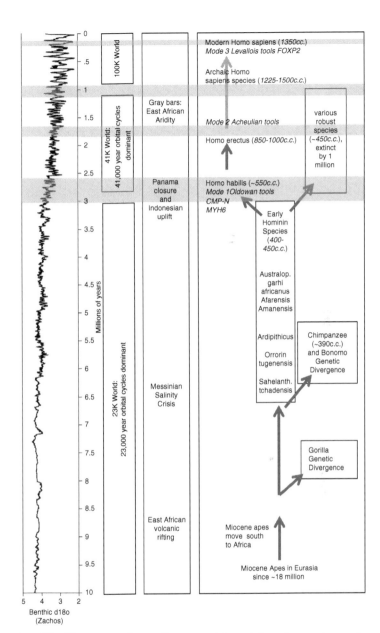

Figure I.4. The Pliocene: geology, climate, and the origins of proto-humanity.

Through the later phases of the Miocene, the Pliocene, and the Pleistocene earth climates both cooled and developed increasingly deep and regular cycles, as tectonic shifts allowed orbital forces to become increasingly dominant. Measured oxygen isotope patterns in the seafloor, these orbitally-forced cycles moved from 23,000 to 41,000 to 100,000 year patterns. Key tectonic events and episodes of severe African aridity have been associated with critical breaks in proto-human evolution. The gray bars denoting African aridity are modeled on the presentation in deMenocal, 2004; the d180 data is from Zachos, 2001. The chronology and hypothetical relationships among the "Early Hominin Species" is not indicated.

c.c. = cranial capacity, in cubic centimeters

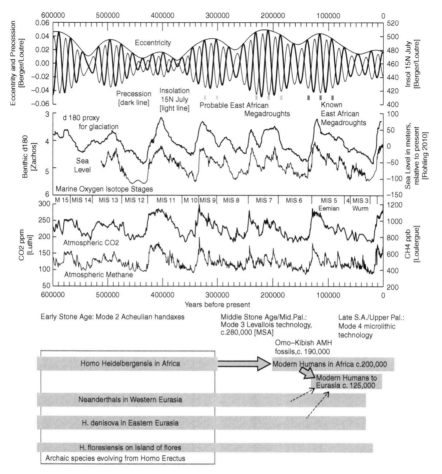

Figure I.5. The Pleistocene: the 100K world and the emergence of modern humanity. The emergence of modern humanity out of archaic homo species took place during the "100K World" of glacial and inter-glacial epochsshaped by the forces of orbital eccentricity. Extreme droughts in East Africa caused by precession extremes during interglacials MIS 9, MIS 7, and MIS 5 probably created the bottleneck conditions that drove the evolutionary leaps manifested in the transition to Levallois flaking, modern human fossils, and the exit from Africa to Eurasia. Among the various archaic species, the vast preponderance of genetic origins of modern humanity lie in Africa, but tiny genetic flows from Eurasian Neanderthals and Denisovans, descended from Homo erectus, have been detected. (Arrows indicate genetic relationships.)

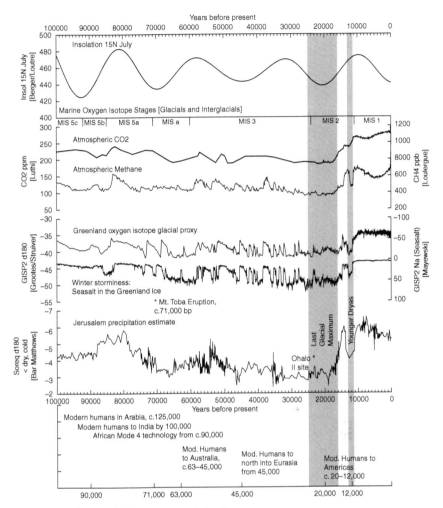

Figure I.6. The Final Pleistocene and the Younger Dryas.

The increasingly precise ice-core records have revealed the extreme variation in climatic conditions during the last Pleistocene glaciations, before the wild shifts of the Boling-Allerod warming, the cold Younger Dryas reversal, and then the sharp warming of the Early Holocene. The massive eruption of Mt. Toba at c.71,000bp aligns with one of the severe cold "Heinrich" events.

I

Geological Time

The Court Jester on the Platform of Life

Human history begins with human evolution, and human evolution is grounded in biological evolution, and this is where we must begin. Equally fundamentally, the evolution of life on earth must be seen as inexorably interwoven with its context, the earth itself, and its history. Throughout this book, we explore these interconnections, and they should be spelled out here at the outset: human history is continuous with natural history, and nature indeed has a history.

The central facts of this history are threefold. First, life and the physical constituents of the earth and the sun – a continuum running from the fiery iron of the earth's inner core out to beyond the reach of the solar wind – have been powerfully interconnected for billions of years. Second, this interaction has been complex and unstable over these billions of years; the earth has been a shifting and volatile platform for life. Third, this instability on a rough world has shaped the specific course that evolution has taken. All earthly life forms owe their very existence to a rough instability and a growing complexity that gives the planet its unique character.

This is an understanding of evolution and the planet earth that has its immediate roots in a wave of scientific advances that began in the 1960s and 1970s. During these decades, the prevailing gradualist orthodoxy gave way to a specific earth history of dramatic moments of interconnected environmental and evolutionary change. At the same time, the boundaries between scientific disciplines collapsed, as biologists, geologists, and atmospheric scientists began to work together as never before to unravel the complex story of the evolution of life and the history of its unique planetary platform, the earth itself. This chapter sketches the emerging synthesis that is developing from this intellectual revolution, but first we need to consider the revolution's central elements.

* * *

Tectonics, Asteroids, Plumes, Punctuation, Gaia:
Revolutions in Earth Science

As of the mid-1960s, roughly the time when I was finishing grade school, a gradualist model of earth history and evolution, describing evolution as an abstract mechanism marching inexorably through time, reigned supreme. This understanding was reinforced by the strict boundaries dividing the disciplines of biology, paleontology, geology, atmospheric studies, and astronomy. Early in the twentieth century, biologists had incorporated the genetic mechanisms demonstrated by Gregor Mendel into Charles Darwin's model of natural selection of advantageous traits, and, during the fifties and sixties, the discovery of the molecular structure of DNA by Rosalind Franklin, James Watson, and Francis Crick gave a powerfully concrete specificity to the process of evolution. In this "modern synthesis," evolution involved the natural selection of genetic traits advancing through time at a constant rate, driven by the imperative to reproduce themselves.[1] Geologists held a similarly "static view of the earth" in which the "planet's interior was seen as motionless and changeless except for a slow loss of heat, and, by some accounts, the contraction of the cooling globe."[2] Researchers conducted atmospheric studies without reference to biological or geological science. The fossil record, the hard evidence of the evolution of life, was relegated to dusty museum exhibits as molecular biologists occupied the "high table" of evolutionary theory.[3]

But in a few short years, between 1966 and 1973, both the mechanistic ahistoricism and the disciplinary isolation of the modern synthesis were overturned by four new perspectives that now inform the central debates in evolution. Two were substantive discoveries; two were theoretical models to be tested with further investigation. If they challenged entrenched orthodoxies, all of these new approaches were rooted in the work of earlier insurgents advanced in the 1920s and 1930s. The theories leading to *plate tectonics* were originally advanced by Alfred Wegener, Johannes Umbgrove, Arthur Holmes, and Harry Hess; understandings of *extraterrestrial impacts* by Thomas C. Chamberlain; the *Gaia-earth systems hypothesis* was grounded in ideas first proposed by James Hutton, Yevgraf Korolenko, and Vladimir Vernadsky; and the theory of *punctuated equilibrium* had its origins in models of allopatric selection advanced by Ernst Mayr and macroevolution of

[1] Julian Huxley, *Evolution: The Modern Synthesis* (London, 1942). Richard Dawkins, *The Blind Watchmaker: Why the Evidence of Evolution Reveals a Universe without Design* (New York, 1986; rev. ed., 1996) provides an excellent recent statement of the "modern synthesis."

[2] David E. Loper, "Scorched Earth: How Heat from the Core Triggers Surface Upheaval," *The Sciences* 30 (1990), 23.

[3] Niles Eldridge, *Reinventing Darwin: The Great Debate at the High Table of Evolutionary Theory* (New York, 1995).

"hopeful monsters" by Richard Goldschmidt.[4] Powerful entrenched interests resisted all four of these perspectives, but during the last third of the twentieth century they emerged as elements of a new orthodoxy broadly called the *earth systems approach* that, blending theory, history, and mountains of data, will likely stand the test of time.

First, in 1966, Allan Cox and his Berkeley associates conclusively demonstrated that the seafloor was composed of rock aligned in stripes of alternating magnetism stretching out on either side of mid-oceanic ridges, in work massively confirmed by the seabed drilling of the drill ship *Glomar Challenger*. These observations corroborated the already emerging, revolutionary understandings of plate tectonics: the crust of the earth is not inert and rigid, but is composed of thin oceanic plates rising as hot magma at mid-oceanic rifts and diving into the earth's mantle – *subducting* – at various boundaries, usually at the edge of thick and ancient continental "cratons," all driven by the rotating flow of convection currents in the earth's mantle. The theory of plate tectonics – and of continental drift – utterly reorganized the science of geology, providing dynamic and historical explanations for the vast and intractable body of geological evidence that had been accumulating since the eighteenth century. Taking introductory biology and geology courses as an undergraduate in the early 1970s, I saw firsthand the early excitement that biological evolution might have a specific history, driven by enormous transitions in global ecologies, as the earth's plates moved and collided over many, many millions of years.[5]

Seven years after the tectonics of seafloor spreading had been demonstrated, evidence for earthly instability of a very different origin began to emerge from the results of a geologist's field trip to northern Italy. In 1973, Walter Alvarez discovered a thin but dense layer of iridium in limestone deposits outside the village of Gubbio, and in 1980, he published an article that proposed that this layer marked the "K-T" boundary separating the Cretaceous and the Tertiary epochs at 65 million years ago, and that its source was a massive meteor that had devastated life on earth, bringing the Mesozoic age of the dinosaurs to a close.[6] This proposal struck a very receptive audience, because the extinctions recorded in the fossil record had recently been the subject of new research and work was under way that

[4] Kenneth J. Hsü, "Uniformitarianism vs. Catastrophism in the Extinction Debate," in William Glen, *The Mass-Extinction Debates: How Science Works in a Crisis* (Stanford, CA, 1994), 217–29; Stephen Jay Gould, "Is a New and General Theory of Evolution Emerging?" *Paleobiology* 6/1 (1980), 119–30; –, *The Structure of Evolutionary Theory* (Cambridge, MA, 2002), 451–66, 535–6; James Lovelock, *Ages of Gaia: A Biography of Our Living Earth* (New York, 1988), 9–10.

[5] Allan Cox, ed., *Plate Tectonics and Geomagnetic Reversals* (San Francisco, CA, 1973); William Glen, *The Road to Jaramillo: Critical Years of the Revolution in Earth Science* (Stanford, CA, 1982), 1–3.

[6] Glen, *Mass-Extinction Debates*, 7–9. "K-T" is the standard shorthand for the boundary between the Cretaceous and the Tertiary periods.

would define at least five massive breaks in the evolutionary record, when as much as 80 percent of the genera of marine life disappeared in a few million years.[7] Thus, just as an understanding that the internal dynamics of the earth's plates, mantle, and core tectonics might have shaped vast ecological changes in the distant history of the earth, the Alvarez team – and the impactor theory that emerged following his work – posed a countervailing model of waves of meteors driving mass extinctions of terrestrial life and opening the way for subsequent evolutionary explosions.

By the time that Alvarez ventured to Gubbio – and only a few years after Cox and company had demonstrated the dynamics of plate tectonics – inventor-scientist James Lovelock had an insight that would shatter the comfortably isolated worlds of biological, atmospheric, and geological sciences. Asked by NASA to estimate the likelihood that life existed on neighboring planets, Lovelock quickly came to the realization that, because the infrared spectrum on these planets (as observed on specially equipped telescopes) showed that their atmospheres had chemistries fundamentally different from Earth, it was highly unlikely that life could exist on Mars or Venus. By 1968 Lovelock had begun to sketch a model of the earth as "Gaia" – a global ecosystem evolving through time in which gases, rocks, and life; atmospheric conditions, tectonic geology, and terrestrial life forms – all formed an interacting and symbiotic whole. In its extreme form, Lovelock's theory was a mystical paean to a "Goddess Earth." While *mystical Gaia* became the subject of derision, Lovelock argued for an *optimizing Gaia*, in which each component of the earthly ecosystem worked to optimize the conditions of life. Out of the scientific turmoil emerged a stable (if not universally accepted) understanding known as *influential Gaia*, which posits that atmosphere, geosphere, and biosphere did indeed influence each other in profound ways, and which stands as the informal credo of a huge field of endeavor now known as *earth system science*. At the same time, biologist Lynn Margulis, who was closely involved in the formulation of the Gaia principle, was developing the equally important understanding that eukaryote cells, the building blocks of oxygen-carbon-based life forms, had their origins in the symbiotic combination of earlier and simpler prokaryote cells at an early moment in the evolution of life.[8]

* * *

[7] Norman D. Newell, "Paleontological Gaps and Geochronology," *Journal of Paleontology*. 36 (1962), 592–610; –, "Revolutions in the History of Life," *Geological Society of American Special Papers* 89 (1967), 63–91; Michael J. Benton, "Scientific Methodologies in Collision: The History of the Study of the Extinction of the Dinosaurs," *Evolutionary Biology* 24 (1990), 371–400; David M. Raup, "Taxonomic Diversity during the Phanerozoic," *Science* 177 (1972), 1065–71. J. John Sepkoski, "What I Did with My Research Career: Or How Research on Biodiversity Yielded Data on Extinction," in Glen, *Mass-Extinction Debates*, 132–44.

[8] Lovelock, *Ages of Gaia*; Stephen H. Schneider, "Debating Gaia," *Environment* 32 (1990), 5–9, 29–32. Lynn Margulis and Michael F. Dolan, *Early Life: Evolution on the Precambrian*

Evolution: From Neo-Darwinism to Complex Emergence

During these same years, a radically new understanding of the trajectory of evolution was emerging. In foundational papers published in 1972 and 1977 – and obviously influenced by the new thinking in the air – Stephen Jay Gould and Niles Eldridge proposed that the emergence of new species was not a constant process but moved in fits and starts: it was not gradual but *punctuated*.[9] Darwin and the classic geologists had assumed that what seemed to be large gaps in the fossil record were caused by the erosion of intervening layers. Such gaps posed huge problems for an understanding of evolution unfolding in a single sequence from ancient origins without some form of catastrophe, which seemingly would reopen the door to a role for divine intervention. The Gould-Eldridge concept of punctuation certainly posed no role for supernatural causes. Rather, their "punctuation" was grounded in the work of zoologist Ernst Mayr, whose "allopatric" theory of the emergence of new species, first advanced in the 1940s and restated in 1963, is now foundational to evolutionary theory.[10] Mayr argued that new species did not evolve in random fashion, but in small populations geographically isolated from the main body of an originator species, small populations that might be under stress and through which useful mutations might easily and quickly diffuse, in intergenerational "founder effects" and "genetic drift." Passing through this evolutionary "bottleneck," the result would be new bodily traits ("phenotypes") that mark a new species, traits that if particularly advantageous might allow an explosive expansion or "radiation" into other ecological space when the opportunity arises. Rather than "phyletic gradualism," Eldridge and Gould posed a model of "punctuated equilibrium," in which long periods of stasis in the fossil record of evolution would be sharply broken by waves of new species generated by allopatric processes. If in its original formulation, the theory of punctuated equilibrium hewed closely to allopatric theory and avoided any reference to drifting continents or incoming meteors, Gould, Eldridge, and Vrba quickly assimilated the new macro-environmental "forcings" as the motor driving the unsteady, punctuated beat of the evolution of life on earth.[11] The past

Earth, second edition (Boston, MA, 2002) provided a recent synthesis of Margulis's understandings. James Lovelock, *The Vanishing Face of Gaia: A Final Warning* (New York, 2009), 159–203 presents the most recent overview of the origins and debate about Gaia as an earth system theory.

[9] Niles Eldridge and Stephen Jay Gould, "Punctuated Equilibria: An Alternative to Phyletic Gradualism," in Thomas J. M. Schopf, ed., *Models in Paleobiology* (San Francisco, CA, 1972), 82–115; Stephen Jay Gould and Niles Eldridge, "Punctuated Equilibria: The Tempo and Mode of Evolution Reconsidered," *Paleobiology* 3 (1977), 115–51.

[10] Ernst Mayr, *Systematics and the Origin of Species* (New York, 1942); Ernst Mayr, *Animal Species and Evolution* (Cambridge, MA, 1963).

[11] Gould's grand statement of his approach was laid out in *The Structure of Evolutionary Theory*; for a short and powerful statement, see Gould, "The Evolution of Life on Earth,"

twenty-five years have seen a titanic struggle between the advocates of an incessant gradualist model of selection and reselection of the genetic code and proponents of a punctuated model of stasis and sudden drastic change involving genes, species, and communities interacting with vast systems of earth and atmosphere. Gould, Eldridge, and their punctuationist students, mostly dirty fossil hunters, crossed swords with the tribe of lab-coated gradualists, mostly molecular biologists, whose most notable spokesmen have been theorist Richard Dawkins, philosopher Daniel Dennett, and paleontologist Geerat Vermeij.[12]

The central problem Gould posed for the gradualists of the "modern synthesis" was that, under the right circumstances, evolution essentially stopped – or slowed to such a snail's pace during periods of stasis that it might as well have stopped – while in other circumstances it went into overdrive. This framework utterly violated the entrenched model that the fundamental driver to evolutionary change lay in the constant competition for reproductive success among competing genomes. Life is a race to simply perpetuate the gene itself, a race in which every adaptive advantage will contribute a competitive edge. Biologist Leigh Van Valen articulated this framework as a formal "law" in 1973 in the face of the emerging punctuational challenge to Darwinian orthodoxy. He described it as the Red Queen's hypothesis in a salute to Lewis Carroll, whose demented Red Queen dragged Alice through a moving countryside, running frantically just to stay in place.[13] In response to biologists' Red Queen, geologist Anthony Barnosky posed the Court Jester, an erratic, catastrophic engine of environmental forcing, the very imp of destruction. In essence, the punctuationists are saying that certain ancient ecological regimes were reasonably bountiful and balanced, while other regimes were wildly unstable. This blended approach – assuming a plurality of evolutionary contexts – is at the heart of the emerging understanding. Barnosky and others are not assuming a continual rampage of the environmental Court Jester, but the play of both the Queen and the Jester at different chronological and geographic scales; catastrophic punctuations come in waves, with long intervals of relative stability.[14] Some of

---

in *Life in the Universe: SA, A Special Issue* (New York, 1995), 53–65. Vrba's thinking was fully framed in Elizabeth S. Vrba, "Turnover Pulses, The Red Queen, and Related Topics," *AJS* 293 (1993), 414–52; and in "Mass Turnover and Heterochrony Events in Response to Physical Change," *Paleobiology* 31 (2005), 157–214.

[12] In this struggle, see most notably Eldredge, *Reinventing Darwin*; Gould, *The Structure of Evolutionary Theory*; Dawkins, *The Blind Watchmaker*; Daniel C. Dennett, *Darwin's Dangerous Idea: Evolution and the Meanings of Life* (New York, 1995); and Geerat J. Vermeij, *Nature: An Economic History* (Princeton, NJ, 2004).

[13] Leigh Van Valen, "A New Evolutionary Law," *Evolutionary Theory* 1 (1973), 1–30; Dawkins, *The Blind Watchmaker*, 183–4.

[14] Anthony D. Barnosky, "Distinguishing the Effects of the Red Queen and the Court Jester on Miocene Mammal Evolution in the Northern Rocky Mountains," *Journal of Vertebrate Paleontology* 21 (2001), 172–85; David Jablonski, "Biotic Interactions and Macroevolution:

these understandings are not so evenhanded, however. One recent analysis concluded that the Court Jester may be the dynamic actor: "If the original Red Queen model had a 'whiff' of a species running out of breath ... and then being knocked off by the next event, the interpretation we propose is different. Species do not so much 'run in place' as simply wait for the next sufficient cause of speciation to occur."[15] If the circumstances between punctuations are stable enough to suspend the "arms race" of Darwinian competition, then "equilibrium" itself is something that needs explanation, and an interconnected literature is focusing on evolutionary and ecological stasis and stability as the counterpoint to punctuation.[16]

Embedded in this new framework of different rates of evolution is the question of different mechanisms and modes of evolution. From the outset, the model of punctuated equilibrium challenged the simple Darwinianism of a single model of adaptation through natural selection. Gould, in particular, led the charge, reaching back to synthesize strands of theory suppressed by the modern Darwinian synthesis with new evidence to argue that evolution unfolded in a hierarchy of levels running from the molecule, gene, tissues, organs, and organism to the population, the species, and the "clade," or evolutionary branch. Each level of the hierarchy would respond differently to the stimuli of biotic competition and environmental change.[17] With paleontologist Elizabeth Vrba, he argued that evolution did not unfold through "adaptation," the sudden development of new, useful genetic traits when circumstances demanded them, but through "exaptation," in which useless mutations piled up in the collective genetic code until changing circumstances encouraged their expression in inheritable bodily form. This initiative was part of a wider effort to develop an evolutionary theory grounded in the understanding of complex systems and emergent structures, and the

Extensions and Mismatches across Scales and Levels," *Evolution* 62 (2008), 715–39; Seth Finnegan et al., "The Red Queen Revisited: Reevaluating the Age Selectivity Phanerozoic Marine Genus Extinctions," *Paleobiology* 34 (2008), 318–41; Michael J. Benton, "The Red Queen and the Court Jester: Species Diversity and the Role of Biotic and Abiotic Factors through Time," *Science* 323 (2009), 728–32; Thomas H. G. Ezard et al., "Interplay between Changing Climate and Species Ecology Drives Macroevolutionary Dynamics," *Science* 332 (2011), 349–51.

[15] Chris Venditti et al., "Phylogenies Reveal New Interpretations of Speciation and the Red Queen," *Nature* 463 (2010), 349–52.

[16] Steven M. Stanley, "Rates of Evolution," *Paleobiology* 11 (1985), 15–26; Carlton Brett et al., "Coordinated Stasis: An Overview," *PPP* 127 (1996), 1–20; W. A. DiMichele et al., "Long-Term Stasis in Ecological Assemblages: Evidence from the Fossil Record," *Annual Review of Ecology, Evolution, and Systematics*, 35 (2004), 285–322; Nelson G. Hairston et al., "Rapid Evolution and the Convergence of Ecological and Evolutionary Time," *Ecology Letters* 8 (2005), 1114–27; John C. Handley et al., "Probability Models for Stasis and Change in Paleocommunity Structure," *Palaios* 24 (2009), 638–49; Gould, *The Structure of Evolutionary Theory*, 745–1024.

[17] Gould, "Is a New and General Theory of Evolution Emerging?", 119–30; "Darwinism and the Expansion of Evolutionary Theory," *Science* 216 (1982), 380–7.

framing of a new theory of evolution based on the concept of "emergence" rather than "natural selection."[18]

Diehard defenders of the neo-Darwinian synthesis accused Gould and the emergence theorists of the heresy of biological heresies, Lamarckianism. A precursor to Darwin, eighteenth-century French botanist Jean-Baptiste Lamarck had proposed that in certain circumstances changes accumulated in an individual's lifetime could be transmitted to offspring, and thus that processes of change other than natural selection might have been at work. In particular, Gould seemed to have suggested that evolutionary punctuation might have involved a process of change called "saltation," a version of Lamarck's theory that proposed rapid evolutionary changes between generations.[19] Following Gould's lead, however, other evolutionary theorists have taken up the cause of both emergent complexity and of Lamarckian saltation quite cheerfully, and with growing bodies of evidence to support them. This work incorporates traditional genetic understandings with those of "epigenetics," which has demonstrated that the genetic code is regulated by a complex and fluid biochemistry and developmental biology, reconfiguring cells at the embryonic phase. Informally this fusing of evolution and development is known as "evo-devo."[20] In its more radical form, the new approach argues that natural selection, far from being the agent of change, is the means of restabilizing and then conserving a new biological form first launched in a developmental emergence shaped by fluctuations in epigenetic biochemistry. Robert Reid argues for two types of such epigenetic emergences, one involving random mutations and cellular saltations occurring continuously, and another involving "critical point emergences," when evolutionary changes cascade over thresholds. Each, he argues, is shaped variously by intrinsic/endogenous or extrinsic/exogenous conditions. In the end, however, like exaptations, such evolving features must work in the world.

[18] Stephen J. Gould and Elizabeth S. Vrba, "Exaptation – A Missing Term in the Science of Form," *Paleobiology* 8 (1982), 4–15; Bruce S. Leiberman and Elizabeth S. Vrba, "Stephen Jay Gould on Species Selection: 30 Years of Insight," *Paleobiology* 312 (2005), 113–21.

[19] Dawkins, *The Blind Watchmaker*, 229–42; Dennett, *Darwin's Dangerous Idea*, 285–9. Gould fired back with both barrels in "Darwinian Fundamentalism," *New York Review of Books*, 44, June 12, 1997, 34–7; and "Evolution: The Pleasures of Pluralism," *New York Review of Books* 44, June 26, 1997, 47–52. Gould devotes a formative section of *The Structure of Evolutionary Theory* to Lamarck's contributions to ideas about a "hierarchy of causes" in evolution, 170–92.

[20] Robert G. B. Reid, *Biological Emergences: Evolution by Natural Experiment* (Cambridge, MA, 2007), esp. 75–94, 289–328, 401–36; Eva Jablonka and Marian J. Lamb, *Evolution in Four Dimensions: Genetic, Epigenetic, Behavioral, and Symbolic Variation in the History of Life* (Cambridge, MA, 2005); Mary-Jane West-Eberhard, *Developmental Plasticity and Evolution* (New York, 2003); Gould, *The Structures of Evolutionary Theory*, 1142–78. Robert G. B. Reid, *Evolutionary Theory: The Unfinished Synthesis* (Beckenham, 1985); Nessa Carey, *The Epigenetics Revolution: How Modern Biology is Rewriting Our Understanding of Genetics, Disease, and Inheritance* (New York, 2012).

Reid argues pointedly that "to thrive they must have an emergence quality of unusual utility, or risk new environments, or find old environments that have been cleared of competition. Thus, the sense of physical movement from one environment to another is central to the concept of emergence." Fundamentally, Reid thus argues, punctuation in the geosphere is critical to evolution in the biosphere: "biological evolution … has needed the capricious clean sweeps of electro-magnetic reversals, plate tectonics, volcanic activity, glaciation, deluges, sea-level changes, and the impact of comets and asteroids. These environmental alterations were part of the substrate of progressive emergence evolution."[21]

At the core of this "ultramodern synthesis" of environmental punctuation, epigenetic emergence, and genetic stabilization lies the simple problem of *stress*.[22] Changes in circumstances create different levels of stress, whether they be in numbers competing for resources, or in the availability of those resources, shaped by the parameters of temperature and moisture that determine climate and environmental change. Stress reduces numbers and opens the way to genetic drift and evolutionary change; the release from stress allows a species to expand and flourish.[23] Such understandings underlie the entire punctuational model. New discoveries in molecular biology running back to the 1960s, a new and explosively growing body of work on "heat shock proteins," have begun to vindicate Gould's dabblings with Lamarckian saltation. Over the past decade, it has been determined that heat shock proteins (HSP) work inside eukaryote cells to control the effects of random mutations, guiding and structuring the way they fold in a sequence of DNA.[24] Under normal circumstances, the heat stress proteins

[21] Reid, *Biological Emergences*, 325, 350.

[22] Douglas M. Ruden, "The (New) New Synthesis and Epigenetic Capacitors of Morphological Evolution," *NatGen* 43 (2011), 88–9.

[23] For an early summary, see Peter A. Parsons, "The Importance and Consequences of Stress in Living and Fossil Populations: From Life-History Variation to Evolutionary Change," *The American Naturalist* 142, suppl. (1993), S5–S20.

[24] Susan Lindquist, "The Heat-Shock Response," *Annual Reviews in Biochemistry* 55 (1986), 1151–91; Suzanne L. Rutherford and Susan Lindquist, "Hsp90 as a Capacitor for Morphological Evolution," *Nature* 396 (1998), 336–42; M. E. Feder and G. E. Hoffman, "Heat-Shock Proteins, Molecular Chaperones, and the Stress Response: Evolutionary and Ecological Physiology," *Annual Review of Physiology* 61 (1999), 243–82; Christine Queiltsch et al., "Hsp90 as a Capacitor for Phenotypic Variation," *Nature* 417 (2002), 618–24; Sophie E. Jackson et al., "Hsp90: From Structure to Phenotype," *Nature Structural & Molecular Biology* 11 (2004), 1152–5; Thorsten B. R. H. Reusch and Troy E. Wood, "Molecular Ecology of Global Change," *Molecular Ecology* 16 (2007), 3973–92; Jesper G. Sørensen and Volker Loeschcke, "Studying Stress Responses in the Post-Genomic Era: Its Ecological and Evolutionary Role," *Journal of Bioscience* 32 (2007), 447–56; Randal Halfmann and Susan Lindquist, "Epigenetics in the Extreme: Prions and the Inheritance of Environmentally Acquired Traits," *Science* 330 (2010), 629–32; Daniel F. Jarosz and Susan Lindquist, "Hsp90 and Environmental Stress Transform the Adaptive Value of Natural Genetic Variation,"

are the guardians of the phenotype, blocking the expression of mutation. Thus they may possibly be literally the molecular agents of evolutionary stasis – and transformation. When severely stressed – in the case of the original experiment the stress was temperature and the species fruit flies – the HSP fails to inhibit mutation, and new traits suddenly appear, manifested in the folding and misfolding of molecular proteins. These traits may emerge in the developmental – embryonic – stages, bypassing the normal process of genetic change at the exchange of parental chromosomes. Thus they appear to be something verging on Lamarckian in their operation, an event that would occur only under the most stressful of circumstances.[25] The sequence of events would unfold on these lines:

Severe environmental stress → impact on heat shock protein/mutation threshold → expression of genetic mutations in embryonic development → new traits in populations →
accelerated natural selection for more advantageous traits → speciation → radiation

This theory is by no means fully established. But if it is, the irony will be that this research coming out of the labs once dominated by the ultra-gradualists is taking a "step toward understanding macroevolution in molecular terms," and vindicating the dirty punctuational fossil hunters at the expense of the white-coated gradualist lab men who once controlled the "high table" of evolutionary science.[26]

Thus the new synthesis argues that evolution unfolds via a variety of pathways and at wildly erratic rates shaped by the interactions of life forms and the specific punctuated history of the platform of life, the earth itself. Considerable tensions certainly exist within the camp of the new synthesis.

Science 330 (2010), 1820–4; Vamsi K. Gangaraju et al., "*Drosophila* Piwi Functions in Hsp90-Mediated Suppression of Phenotypic Variation," *NatGen* 43 (2011), 153–8.

[25] For thoughts on the wider implications of the heat shock proteins, see Ichiro Yahara, "The Role of Hsp90 in Evolution," *Genes to Cells* 4 (1999), 375–9; Anne McLaren, "Too Late for the Midwife Toad: Stress, Variability and Hsp90," *Trends in Genetics* 15 (1999), 169–71; Bob Holmes, "Ready, Steady, Evolve," *New Scientist* 175/2362 (Sept. 28, 2002), 28–31; Jesper G. Sørensen et al., "The Evolutionary Ecological Role of Heat Shock Proteins," *Ecology Letters* 6 (2003), 1025–37.

[26] An emerging body of work is looking for molecular evidence of punctuation beyond the heat shock proteins: Gregory A. Wray, "Punctuated Evolution of Embryos," *Science* 267 (1995), 1115–16; Mark Pagel, "Inferring the Historical Patterns of Biological Evolution," *Nature* 401 (1999), 877–84; Timothy G. Barraclough and Vincent Savolainen, "Evolutionary Rates and Species Diversity in Flowering Plants," *Evolution* 55 (2001), 677–83; Andrea J. Webster et al., "Molecular Phylogenies Link Rates of Evolution and Speciation," *Science* 301 (2003), 478; R. Lande, "Adaptation to an Extraordinary Environment by Evolution of Phenotypic Plasticity and Genetic Assimilation," *Journal of Evolutionary Biology* 22 (2009), 1435–46. See Katrina McQuigan and Sarla M. Sgrò, "Evolutionary Consequences of Cryptic Genetic Variation," *Trends in Ecology and Evolution* 24 (2009), 305–11 for a cautionary note calling for more research.

In their earliest days there was a certain dissonance, if not overt tension, between punctuation and Gaia. If, as optimal Gaia proposed, the earth system optimized conditions for life, it was also clear that the Gaian earth system model also suggested that explosive expansions of life suddenly drawing down CO_2 could lead to intense epochs of glaciation. The abandonment of an "optimizing" Gaia for an "influential" Gaia has gone a long way toward resolving this problem. The biosphere has complex mutual influences with the geosphere and the atmosphere, but they never have been in an "optimizing" balance.

Other tensions have not yet been resolved. In the quest for the ultimate explanation of the forces governing evolution and the earth system, an all-out war continues to rage between the adherents of internally and externally generated catastrophes, schools that we might call respectively the *geologist-plumbers* and the *astronomer-star gazers*. At stake are the explanatory rights to the great biotic transitions of the Pre-Cambrian and Cambrian, and the more recent mass extinctions that have episodically swept the evolutionary field for new ecological regimes. Geologists studying tectonic and physics of the mantle and core have arrived at increasingly sophisticated understandings of the workings – the internal plumbing – of the earth system and their role in shaping natural history on the surface.[27] Since the demonstration of plate tectonics, the geological plumbers have discovered an entire new order of volcanic stress in earth history: *superplumes* of magna rising from disturbances in the boundary between the earth's core and mantle erupt in unimaginable volumes of lava, called *continental flood basalts* and *major igneous provinces*, emitting climate-transforming quantities of CO_2 and other gases and splitting entire contents into fragments. Star-gazing astronomers and their geological allies keep identifying the sites of potential meteor or asteroid impacts and developing impressive arguments for their decisive role in driving planetary history. They have posited massive meteor impacts gouging enormous craters in the earth's surface and blasting sufficient material into the atmosphere to smother life forms in the mass extinctions. A few brave synthetic voices try to move beyond the battle for primacy between volcanist and impactor interpretations toward arguments for interactions and linked roles. And yet another line of argument gaining traction sees solar and galactic forces interacting with the earth's geomagnetic field to shape earthly climates and environments.

All of these events unfolded over vast stretches of time – vast but not indefinable. If the earth had indeed been geologically static as the mid-twentieth-century "modern synthesis" argued, this account would be mercifully short: life evolved – somehow – driven mechanically by the constant pressure of natural selection. The assiduous work of earth systems scientists since their own "big bang" three to four decades ago has produced a much

---

[27] I owe this metaphor to Loper, "Scorched Earth."

more specific story, with specific moments of profound change, real events as historians know them. Here I present a sketch of the emerging synthesis, paying attention to some of the unresolved debates that drive the scientific endeavor, but paying only lip service to the careful stratigraphic analysis and scientific dating systems that underlie this synthesis. Suffice it to say, the neo-catastrophism of the punctuated synthesis has ratified the painstaking efforts of generations of geologists to describe the epochs of the geological column and has defined the boundaries between them. As do the cultural layers in archaeological sites and the king lists of early recorded history, it turns out, these epochs so arduously learned in grade school and high school actually record real history. Behind this sequence of names lies the record of real ecosystems and the real crises that destroyed them in ancient time past, opening the way to the new. Life was born and has flourished and suffered with the vagaries of a rough world.

*   *   *

A Punctuated Earth Systems Synthesis

The essential story to be sketched here is how the basic components of the earth system – geosphere, atmosphere, hydrosphere, biosphere – interacted through time. My fundamental assumption is that the punctuated evolutionary thesis is essentially correct. Perhaps genetics (including random mutations) and natural selection – the essence of the "modern synthesis" and the story of the Red Queen – is the deep running motor of evolutionary change; perhaps it is the stabilizing conservator of epigenetic rupture. But without the complex and sometimes catastrophic infusions of energy from the earth's tectonic forces, and perhaps from incoming meteors and asteroids, the motor of natural selection would grind to a halt. As two eminent geologists have argued, "without the driving energy provided by the evolving planet the biosphere would have entered a prolonged stasis and ultimately faced extinction."[28] And it is particularly evident that these forces were indeed episodic and can be described as specific events occurring in real time. As an historian I have been particularly attracted to these new understandings of punctuation because historians – lacking strict theoretical commitments – are attracted to complex explanations that progressively tell a story unfolding in distinct events and relationships through time, if not entirely "contingent," as current historians' fashion would have it. I am happy to admit my predisposition in this fight – as an historian I am inherently, aesthetically biased toward the messy, inclusive pluralism of the

---

[28] J. F. Lindsay and M. D. Brasier, "Did Global Tectonic Drive Early Biosphere Evolution? Carbon Isotope Records from 2.6 to 1.9 Ga Carbonates of Western Australian Basins," *Precambrian Research* 114 (2002), 30.

Gouldian scenario, rather than the reductionist minimalist vision of ultra-Darwinian mathematical gradualism.

Underlying this story is the question of a prime mover – the ultimate source of energy in the global ecosystem. All ecosystems depend on flows of energy. Certainly the reasonably steady – if increasing – radiation from the sun is the fundamental energy source in the global ecosystem, mediated by the chemical layers in the atmosphere. But the internal dynamics of the earth – tectonic convection and explosive superplumes – and the intersection of the earth with the celestial system – in the impacts of meteors and asteroids – provide second-order sources of energy driving the global system. The relative role of these forces in determining the pace of change in that system is a matter of considerable debate.

Origins: The Hadean and the Archean

At its most ancient origins, the earth saw an essential transition from celestial to tectonic punctuations. Earth history began roughly 4.6 billion years ago (BY) in a coalescing ball of gases and interstellar matter gathering form and substance from an incessant bombardment of meteors that lasted about 600–800 million years before tapering off. This was what is commonly known as the Hadean, named for Hades, the hellish underworld of the ancient Greeks, a pregeological period in as much as it predated the youngest surviving rock strata. In a massive early impact hitting the earth at an oblique angle at roughly 4.5–4.45 BY, material was scoured off the emerging earth's surface to form the moon. Yet even before the impacts began to taper off two processes began to unfold, virtually in parallel.

First, a sorting of heavier and lighter elements began, with iron and nickel descending to form the molten core, lighter silicates rising to form the mantle, and the lightest gases, dominated by water and carbon dioxide, venting off to form the primitive atmosphere and precipitating to form primordial oceans. This sorting process may have been well under way quite quickly, perhaps only 50 million years after the lunar-forming impact, but it would have unfolded over several hundred million years, periodically interrupted by recurring meteorite bombardment.[29]

Second, simple organic compounds – most important, amino acids – were synthesized from inorganic chemicals, primarily water, nitrogen, and ammonia. Exactly how this happened is one of the great debates, but generally this synthesis may have begun with chemicals blasted by lightning strikes or stressed by the intensely hot conditions on the earth's surface, or at volcanic vents in the ocean floor. An intense burst of impacts at 3.9 BY might have launched this biochemical process, perhaps even delivering organic

[29] N. H. Sleep et al., "Initiation of Clement Surface Conditions on the Earliest Earth," *PNAS* 98 (2001), 3666–72.

chemistry from off-planet.[30] Protecting this early life was a *greenhouse effect* of massive proportions. Carl Sagan proposed decades ago that the early sun at 4.6BY produced 25–30 percent less radiant heat than the modern sun, which is warming toward a supernova in the very distant future. Offsetting this *weak sun* must have been a huge greenhouse effect provided by CO_2 in the atmosphere at levels perhaps 100 to 1,000 times present levels. Over time, this atmospheric greenhouse was reduced as CO_2 bonded with water and eroded exposed rocks in a process known as *chemical weathering*, and by life forms that consumed CO_2 and produced other volatile gases.[31] An earth system of interacting geological, atmospheric, hydrospheric, and biological domains was beginning to emerge in what is known as the Archean Eon.

The first linked sequence of geological change and biotic evolution may have occurred at roughly 3.5BY (see Figure I.1). First, starting around 3.6BY, a proto-continent known as Vaalbara began to form out of denser pieces of the early crust. Vast circumplanetary oceans would have surrounded this continent. Second, while arguments persist about whether microbial life forms evolved from complex chemical combinations at exactly this point, these would have been carbon-consuming, methane-producing, single-cell organisms known as *prokaryotes* and *archaeans*.

Perhaps the gradient of deeper and shallower waters around this continent shaped the environment for these early life forms. In any event, these early organisms seem to have emerged some time during this period, and gradually shaped the early atmosphere, drawing down carbon and replacing it with methane. The result was a roughly equal exchange of greenhouse gases in the earliest atmosphere, which had been warming surface temperatures since the first outgassing of CO_2, offsetting the relatively low radiation coming from the cool young sun.

The Archean/Paleo-Proterozoic Crisis

These processes were the prologue to the first great global bio-geo-atmospheric crisis, unfolding between 2.7BY and 2BY and bringing the end to the Archean age of methane-emitting prokaryotes and the onset of the Proterozoic age of oxygen-emitting eukaryotes. Primitive plate tectonics had begun to operate, as a boiling convection of the early magna ocean settled into a two-layered system consisting of a core and a mantle. A primary convection operating within the core continued the primal sorting of lighter and

[30] R. Cowen "An Early Cosmic Wallop for Life on Earth?" *Science News* 158 (2000), 357. Evidence of organic carbon dating to 3.8BY in Greenland and 3.5BY in western Australia has for the present been discounted. See Stephen Moorbath, "Dating Earliest Life," *Nature* 434 (2005), 155. For an accessible, balanced account, see Andrew H. Knoll, *Life on a Young Planet: The First Three Billion Years of Evolution on Earth* (Princeton, NJ, 2003), 16–88.
[31] William F. Ruddiman, *Earth's Climate: Past and Future* (New York, 2001), 87–102.

heavier elements, while a second convection drove currents in the mantle powering the earliest oceanic and emerging continental plates.

In a revolutionary new understanding of the dynamics of the earth's core, building upon but quite distinct from the theory of plate tectonics, geologists have several theories that explain how these "routine" two-level patterns destabilize, allowing massive superplumes of magma to cut from the core through the mantle and to erupt onto the earth's surface in vast volumes of basalt lava and clouds of CO_2. In one model, slabs of oceanic plate subducted into the mantle finally rupture the boundary between the mantle and the core, setting off plumes of magma that eventually find their way to the surface. In this understanding, the deep avalanches of subducted plate, forming vast subterranean slab graveyards, cause downwellings in the mantle that act to pull together continental fragments on the earth's surface, which combine to form *supercontinents*.[32] The second scenario revolves around the delicate conditions along the core-mantle boundary, know as the D" layer. In this model, the lighter elements convected up and away from the inner core accumulate like sand dunes along the interior, convex surface of the D" layer. Every so often, these piles collapse, causing magnetic reversals in the geodynamo operating in the earth's core. The largest slides burst the core-mantle boundary and send superplumes moving slowly through the mantle toward the surface. Meteor impacts, especially oblique ones, may send shock waves through the earth, setting off the largest of these sediment collapses along the D" layer.[33]

Whatever the fundamental cause, which remains in considerable debate, the first of these super-events had its deep origins around 3.0–2.7BY, driven by the first avalanche of crust slab through the core-mantle boundary, according to one analysis. The result was centuries or millennia of massive eruptions of volcanic material and an accelerated formation of continental crust forming the supercontinent Kenorland.[34]

These geological events at the Archean-Proterozoic boundary seem to have driven a fundamental biotic break, though there are several competing

---

[32] Patrick G. Eriksson et al., "Patterns of Sedimentation in the Precambrian," *SedGeol* 176 (2005), 17–42; Kent C. Condie, "Episodic Continental Growth Models: Afterthoughts and Extensions," *Tectonophysics* 322 (2000), 153–62; David E. Loper, "Mantle Plumes and Their Effects on the Earth's Surface: A Review and Synthesis," *Dynamics of Atmospheres and Oceans* 27 (1997), 35–54. See also Alan D. Brandson and Richard J. Walker, "The Debate over Core-Mantle Interaction," *EPSL* 232 (2005), 211–35, and Loper, "Scorched Earth."

[33] Richard A. Muller, "Avalanches at the Core-Mantle Boundary," *GRL* 29 (2002), 41-1–41-4. To avoid confusion, I call Muller's "avalanches" of light sediments "slides."

[34] Steven B. Shirey and Stephen H. Richardson, "Start of the Wilson Cycle at 3 Ga Shown by Diamonds from Subcontinental Mantle," *Science* 333 (2011), 434–6; Eriksson et al., "Patterns of Sedimentation," 29–30; John J. W. Rogers, "A History of Continents in the Past Three Billion Years," *JGeol* 104 (1996), 91–107; John J. W. Rogers and M. Santosh, "Supercontinents in Earth History," *Gondwana Research* 6 (2003), 357–68.

interpretations of the events. Both are "punctuational," but one is Gaian and the other tectonic. The Gaian argument, first proposed by James Lovelock, argues for a catastrophic interaction between the atmosphere and early life forms. Where methane-producing microbes dominated the Archean seas, James Casting and others argue that 2.7BY saw the first signs of a new kind of life form, the eukaryotes (see Figure I.1). The eukaryotes were composed of a symbiotic combination of various types of prokaryotes and archeans combining together into a new nucleus-bearing organism, first under the stress of the Archean tectonic crisis and then as conditions of their own making changed.[35] Prokaryotes had developed photosynthetic means of converting solar energy, but the new eukaryotes evolved a new water-splitting mode of photosynthesis that produced oxygen, not methane, as a byproduct. Such was the beginning of the *Great Oxidization Event.*

With the accumulation of significant amounts of oxygen in the seas and atmosphere, the first results were catastrophic. Oxygen proved toxic to the prokaryotes, and those that did not enter into the new eukaryotic symbiots were driven into shrinking anaerobic environments. Oxygen also does not have the greenhouse properties of methane, which was dropping precipitously as a component of the atmosphere.[36] It may be that there also was an accelerated drawdown of atmospheric carbon by way of the chemical weathering of rock surfaces – in which CO_2 in rainwater and snow is bound with silicates and deposited in the oceans – further contributing to the waning of the primal greenhouse. With oxygen rising and CO_2 and methane falling, the greenhouse effect that had warmed the post-Hadean earth, compensating for a weak young sun, thinned out disastrously. The outcome was the first series of major glaciations at 2.45–2.2BY, forming on the surface of the supercontinent Kenorland, or on its rifting fragments. In some accounts, this was a "snowball earth event," with the entire globe covered with ice; others doubt the spread of glaciers to equatorial regions.[37]

The Lovelock-Casting interpretation of this Paleo-Proterozoic crisis can be called "Gaian punctuational" because, in this thesis, the rise of the eukaryotes drives the first increase in oxygen. An alternative model can be called "tectonic punctuational" because it argues a massive burial of carbon with the tectonic crises of 2.7–2.2BY caused the oxidation event, which in

---

[35] Margulis and Dolan, *Early Life*, 57–81; Patrick G. Eriksson et al., eds., *The Precambrian Earth: Tempo and Events* (Amsterdam, 2004), 584.

[36] Casting and Siefert, "Life and the Evolution of Earth's Atmosphere."

[37] Colin Goldblatt et al., "Bistability of Atmospheric Oxygen and the Great Oxidation," *Nature* 443 (2006), 683–6 Robert E. Kopp et al., "The Paleoproterozoic Snowball Earth: A Climate Disaster Triggered by the Evolution of Oxygen Photosynthesis," *PNAS* 102 (2005), 11131–6, Joseph L. Kirschvink et al., "Paleoproterozoic Snowball Earth: Extreme Climatic and Geochemical Global Change and its Biological Consequences," *PNAS* 97 (2000), 1400–5. The authors in Eriksson et al., *The Precambrian Earth* are skeptical of this early snowball thesis; see 360, 440, 452, 602.

turn facilitated the emergence of eukaryote symbiots.[38] In either scenario, however, a fundamental relationship developed between evolutionary processes and the energy of the earth's tectonic system.

This was one of the few great punctuations in the Precambrian record and it was followed by a long period of relative quiet, essentially a Gouldian evolutionary stasis. The next billion and a half years or so comprised the great age of the eukaryotes, in gradual transition from single to multicellular forms, combining in thick mats called *stromatolites* in oceans where only the surfaces were significantly oxygenated. Besides the stromatolite mats, very small jellyfish-like multicellular organisms have been found in Gabon dating to 2.1BY, early and so-far lonely precursors of the complex life forms that would multiply a billion and a half years later.[39] But this was an epoch of profound stability, sometimes called the "boring billion": without the driving force of superplume tectonics the evolution of life on earth might have stalled and eventually fizzled out.[40] Geologists find two *superplume-supercontinent cycles* during this long period, one starting at roughly 1.9BY with the aggregation of the supercontinent Columbia (or Nuna) and the next at 1.2BY with the forming of Rodinia. The consolidation and then rifting of this supercontinent was bracketed by the huge Vredfort and Sudbury meteor impacts, suggesting the possibility of a celestial role in this geological cycle. The formation of Columbia may have in some way shaped the rise of oxygen in seawater, allowing an accelerated evolution of the eukaryotes. Work in regions around the globe is finding fossil and molecular evidence for the emergence of small but complex "bilaterian" worm-like forms at around 1.2BY, around the time that the supercontinent Rodinia began to assemble. Potentially, critical diversification in the direction of modern phyla occurred in these intervals, and it appears that the first colonization of land surfaces by fungi, mosses, and liverworts occurred at the time of Rodinia.[41] But these

---

[38] David J. Des Marmais, "Isotopic Evolution of the Biogeochemical Carbon Cycle during the Proterozoic Eon," *Organic Geochemistry* 27 (1997), 185–93; Lindsay and Brasier, "Did Global Tectonic Drive Early Biosphere Evolution?" 1–34; M. D. Brasier and J. F. Lindsay, "A Billion Years of Environmental Stability and the Emergence of Eukaryotes: New Data from Northern Australia," *Geology* 26 (1996), 555–8; David C. Catling and Mark W. Claire, "How Earth's Atmosphere Evolved to an Oxic State: A Status Report," *EPSL* 237 (2005), 1–20.

[39] Abderrazak El Albani et al., "Large Colonial Organisms with Coordinated Growth in Oxygenated Environments, 2.1 Gyr Ago," *Nature* 466 (2010), 100–4; see also Zhu Shixing and Chen Huineng, "Megascopic Multicellular Organisms from the 1700-Million-Year-Old Tuanshnazi Formation in the Jixian Area, North China," *Science* 270 (1995), 620–2.

[40] Lindsay and Brasier, "Did Global Tectonics Drive Early Biosphere Evolution?" 30.

[41] Gregory A. Wray et al., "Molecular Evidence for Deep Precambrian Divergences among Metazoan Phyla," *Science* 274 (1996), 568–73; Adolf Seilacher et al., "Triploblastic Animals More than 1 Billion Years Ago: Trace Fossil Evidence from India," *Science* 282 (1998), 80–2; Birger Rasmussen et al., "Discoidal Impressions and Trace-like Fossils More Than 1200 Million Years Old," *Science* 296 (2002), 1112–15; Jeffrey Levinton et al., "Simulations

Proterozoic supercontinent cycles simply set the stage for the crisis that followed, running from the end of the Neoproterozoic through the Cambrian, roughly 800 million to 500 million years ago, which brought the second major rise in atmospheric oxygen and the explosive emergence of complex hard-bodied, macroscopic life forms.

The Neoproterozoic Crisis and the Cambrian: A Snowball Earth?

The second major bio-geo-atmospheric crisis in the earth system – the Neo-Proterozoic Crisis – began with the breakup of the supercontinent Rodinia, which began to rift apart approximately 800 million years ago (MY), driven by a massive south Pacific superplume (see Figure I.1). At the same time as this continental breakup, oxygen levels in the atmosphere rose again (and may already have been rising). The result was a series of intense glaciations, at least three and possibly four, between 735MY and 580MY. At least two of these glaciations might have been global in scope, freezing the entire earth into a snowball of ice, though "thin ice" and "slushball" models are beginning to emerge.[42] Between each of these ice ages, the earth warmed into intense greenhouse conditions that further stressed life forms, which eventually flourished in blooms of productivity. The causes of this 200-million-year-long whiplash of climate are under intense debate, particularly its beginnings following the breakup of Rodinia. One proposal is that the earliest colonization on land by algae and fungi from 1.2BY reduced atmospheric CO_2 via weathering while contributing increased oxygen.[43] Another argument focused on Rodinia's location in equatorial waters and proposed that a runaway silicate weathering, stripping CO_2 from the atmosphere, was driven by this equatorial location (in recent Pleistocene times continental landmasses

of Evolutionary Radiations and their Application to Understanding the Probability of a Cambrian Explosion," *Journal of Paleontology* 78 (2004), 31–8; L. Paul Knauth and Martin J. Kennedy, "The Late Precambrian Greening of the Earth," *Nature* 460 (2009), 728–32. For the geology of the period, see Ian W. D. Dalziel, "Neoproterozoic-Paleozoic Geography and Tectonics: Review, Hypothesis, Environmental Speculation," *GSA Bulletin* 109 (1997), 16–42.

[42] Joseph L. Kirschvink, "Late Proterozoic Low-Latitude Global Glaciation: The Snowball Earth," in J. W. Schopf and C. Klein, eds., *The Proterozoic Biosphere* (New York, 1992), 51–2; Paul Hoffman et al., "A Neoproterozoic Snowball Earth," *Science* 281 (1998), 1342–6; David A. D. Evans, "Stratigraphic, Geochronological, and Paleomagnetic Constraints upon the Neoproterozoic Climatic Paradox," *AJS* 300 (2000), 347–433; Daniel P. Schrag and Paul F. Hoffman, "Life, Geology, and Snowball Earth," *Nature* 409 (2001), 306; S. Maruyama and M. Santosh, "Models of Snowball Earth and Cambrian Explosion: Synopsis," *Gondwana Research* 14 (2008), 22–32; Richard A. Kerr, "Snowball Earth Has Melted Back to a Profound Wintry Mix," *Science* 327 (2010), 1186. For an account for the nonspecialist, see Gabrielle Walker, *Snow Ball Earth: The Story of the Great Global Catastrophe That Spawned Life as We Know It* (New York, 2003).

[43] Timothy M. Lenton and Andrew J. Watson, "Biotic Enhancement of Weathering, Atmospheric Oxygen, and Carbon dioxide in the Neoproterozoic," *GRL* 31 (2004), L05202 (1–5).

covered the poles, limiting the extent of the glaciation).[44] Researchers have suggested that an unrelated change in the sulfur content of the Proterozoic oceans – or an escape of hydrogen into space – played a role in driving the rise of oxygen during this time.[45] In any event, the glaciations would have been working against the grain of the rifting of Rodinia, which must have been generated by superplumes rising from the core, and certainly was accompanied by volcanism.[46] As Paul Hoffman and his team proposed, this snowball earth punctuation scenario, with these competing systems working against each other in a series of "overshoots," may also have had a Gaian element. As each cycle of global glaciation reduced life forms to small groups of survivors, allopatric selection – and perhaps the operation of stress effects such as the masking of heat shock proteins – drove the emergence of new species. Life was driven through a series of very narrow genetic bottlenecks leading to explosions of productivity, in part feeding on the clouds of CO_2 generated by the superplume volcanoes that cyclically broke the glaciations.[47]

While the entire snowball earth scenario remains under considerable debate, it is clear that something happened: over a period of 200 million years the global system seesawed between icehouse and greenhouse conditions, oxygen levels rose, CO_2 declined, and biotic life was suddenly transformed. During the Cambrian era that followed these glaciation-greenhouse sequences (and the brief existence of a small supercontinent, Pannotia) animal and plant life jumped from microscopic single and multicellular forms to relatively large, differentiated entities, many with hard bodies. Most important for the earth system, an explosion of burrowing worms began to disturb ocean sediments, churning up carbon deposits that hitherto had been permanently withdrawn from the earthly cycle, ensuring that the extreme overshoots of this Neo-Proterozoic crisis (and of the earlier Paleo-Proterozoic crisis of 2.7–2.2BY) would not be repeated. Biotic life had survived and had fundamentally been transformed by a Gouldian macro-evolutionary punctuation and was now fulfilling one of the premises of Lovelock's optimizing Gaia: the earth system would be a much more mature, stable entity moving forward from the Cambrian explosion.[48] It would also be a far more complex place. Oceanic life diversified wildly during the Ordovician and

[44] Yannick Donnadieu et al., "A 'Snowball Earth' Triggered by Continental Break-Up through Changes in Runoff," *Nature* 428 (2004), 303–6.

[45] Catling and Claire, "How Earth's Atmosphere Evolved to an Oxic State," 14–16.

[46] Andreas Prokoph et al., "Time-Series Analysis of Large Igneous Provinces: 3500Ma to Present," *JGeol* 112 (2004), 1–22. Of the three clearly identifiable glaciations, the Sturtian and the Marinoan (735+/-5, 663–635MY) are the more contradictory, occurring during the rifting of Pangaea; the Gaskiers (580+/-MY) is less so, occurring on the Pannotia supercontinent. See later in this chapter for discussion of super-cycle ecologies.

[47] Hoffman et al., "A Neoproterozoic Snowball Earth."

[48] Nichols J. Butterfield, "Macroevolution and Macroecology through Deep Time," *Palaeontology* 50 (2007), 41–55.

Silurian, and plant life began to spread onto continental surfaces, forming massive forests in the Devonian, hosting complex communities of insects and amphibians.

Phanerozoic Super-Cycles – and Biotic Extinctions and Escalations

With the Cambrian, starting at 560MY, we enter the Phanerozoic, which encompasses a "modern" epoch in a maturing earth system (see Figure I.2). Increasingly through this epoch there is a clearer and clearer geological record because less of this younger ocean floor has been subducted into the mantle. Oceanic and atmospheric chemistry was roughly similar to contemporary patterns; life forms diversified into all of – indeed more than – the modern assemblage and the tectonic-climate interactions settled into a stable pattern. This is not to say that this was not still a rough earth, but some of the wilder edges had been rubbed off, and variation would be well inside the extremes of the Hadean, Archean, and Proterozoic. Without wanting to sound too teleological, there are grounds to argue that as it progressed through time the Phanerozoic earth system became increasingly diverse and resilient, increasingly Gaian in its self-equilibrating efficiency. But such qualities unfolded within the bounds of the supercontinent cycle, continuing to operate roughly on the terms that it had since its origins in the Archean. This super-cycle shapes the grand outlines of an oscillating global ecology marked by well-defined and sharply contrasting epochs of *Greenhouse* and *Icehouse* conditions.[49] And riding the wave of the supercontinent cycle was a series of mass extinctions, followed by equally dramatic biotic recoveries and evolutionary "escalations." At stake in a titanic struggle among geologists is the prime mover in these profound punctuations in global earth systems.

First, an overview of the super-cycles. Overall, running back to the emergence of Kenorland in the Archean, there seems to have been a total of five of these super-cycles in earth history, though their periodicity and dynamics differ somewhat.

Supercontinent	Dates Forming	Dates Rifting	Period of Rifting
Kenorland	2,700MY	2,480–2,100MY	Archean-Paleo-Proterozoic
Columbia/Nuna	2,000–1,800MY	1,600–1,200MY	Paleo-Proterozoic
Rodinia	1,100–1,000MY	850–610MY	Meso-Proterozoic
Pannotia/Vendia	600MY	540MY	Neo-Proterozoic-Cambrian
Pangaea	400–300MY	200–60MY	Jurassic-Cretaceous

---

[49] Here and subsequently, capitalized *Greenhouse* and *Icehouse* refer to the multimillion-year periods of the Phanerozoic characterized by high/low CO_2 concentrations, rifting/consolidating supercontinents, and high/low mean global temperatures. These labels obviously could be applied back to the period of the Neo-Proterozoic crisis.

Over the 600 million years since the end of the Neo-Proterozoic (in a period called the Vendian), two complete cycles of aggregation and rifted dispersion of continental plate have taken place. The supercontinent Pannotia formed around 600MY and quickly rifted in the ensuing Cambrian around 540MY. The next supercontinent, Pangaea, began to aggregate at about 400MY, at the beginning of the Devonian, and was fully formed by 300MY, during the Pennsylvanian era of the Carboniferous. Pangaea's rifting began with the massive superplume eruptions at the Triassic-Jurassic boundary around 200MY that began the long opening of the Atlantic Ocean, with final rifts appearing during the early Cenozoic around 65–60MY. Over the past 50 million years, the continents have been reaggregating toward a new supercontinent that will not be fully formed until tens of millions of years from now, but the assembly of which can be measured most dramatically in the long seismic region running from the Mediterranean to the Bay of Bengal, where the African and Indian plates have been colliding with the Eurasian plate since roughly 55 million years ago, and where devastating earthquakes have been a regular occurrence since before the beginnings of recorded history.[50]

These sequences of continental aggregation and rifting had immediate causes in the earth's tectonic rhythm. As suggested previously, there is substantial consensus among geologists that the supercontinent cycle is driven by enormous superplumes rising from the D" layer at the boundary between the core and the mantle. Broadly speaking, two cycles seem to appear in superplume activity, as reflected in the age of "mafic"/volcanic rock: one roughly at 30-million-year intervals, the other at 275-million-year

[50] Formative approaches to and synthetic overviews of these "recent" Phanerozoic super-cycles include Alfred B. Fischer, "Climatic Oscillations in the Biosphere," in M. H. Nitecki, ed., *Biotic Crises in Ecological and Evolutionary Time* (New York, 1981), 103–31; Alfred G. Fischer, "The Two Phanerozoic Supercycles," in W. A. Berggren and J. A. Van Couvering, eds., *Catastrophes in Earth History: The New Uniformitarianism* (Princeton, NJ, 1984), 129–50; R. Damian Nance et al., "Post-Archean Biogeochemical Cycles and Long-Term Episodicity in Tectonic Process," *Geology* 14 (1986), 514–18; – "The Supercontinent Cycle," *SA* 259 (July, 1988), 72–9; J. Brendan Murphy and R. Damian Nance, "Mountain Belts and the Supercontinent Cycle," *SA* 266 (April 1992), 84–91; and John J. Veevers, "Tectonic-Climatic Supercycles in the Billion-Year Plate-Tectonic Eon: Permian Pangean Icehouse Alternates with Cretaceous Dispersed-Continents Greenhouse," *SedGeol* 68 (1990), 1–16, Lawrence A. Frakes et al., *Climate Modes of the Phanerozoic: The History of the Earth's Climate over the Past 600 Million Years* (Cambridge, 1992). See also Rogers and Santosh, "Supercontinents in Earth History"; S. Rino et al., "The Grenvillian and Pan-African Orogens: World's Largest Orogenies through Geological Time, and Their Implications on the Origin of the Superplume," *Gondwana Research* 14 (2008), 51–72; R. E. Ernst et al., "Global Record of 1600–700 Ma Large Igneous Provinces (LIPs): Implications for the Reconstruction of the Proposed Nuna (Columbia) and Rodinia Supercontinents," *Precambrian Research* 160 (2008), 159–78; and A. Y. Glikson, "Milestones in the Evolution of the Atmosphere with Reference to Climate Change," *Australian Journal of Earth Sciences* 55 (2005), 125–39, esp. 125–30.

intervals.[51] While the shorter cycle resulted in periods of enhanced volcanic activity and rifting, the plumes at the 275-million-year intervals were the supercontinent busters, converting a routine double-layered convection of crust, mantle, and core into a single system, with superplumes rising and breaking through, leaving enormous flood basalts and igneous provinces in the geological record.

These events – specifically the rifting of Pannotia at 540MY and of Pangaea after 200MY – shaped two extremely warm Greenhouse epochs, lasting 150 million years and 90 million years respectively[52] (see Figure I.2). Vast eruptions would have injected huge amounts of CO_2 into the atmosphere,

---

[51] This is a simplification of the conclusions reached in Ann E. Islay and Dallas H. Abbot, "Implications of the Temporal Distribution of High-MG Magmas for Mantle Plume Volcanism through Time," *JGeol* 110 (2002), 141–58; as well as Michael R. Rampino and Ken Caldiera, "Major Episodes of Geological Change: Correlations, Time Structure and Possible Causes," *EPSL* 114 (1993), 215–27; V. Courtillot et al., "On the Causal Links between Flood Basalts and Continental Breakup," *EPSL* 166 (1999), 177–95; Kent C. Condie, "The Supercontinent Cycle: Are there Two Patterns of Cyclicity?" *Journal of African Earth Sciences* 35 (2002), 179–83. and Prokoph et al., "Time-Series Analysis of Large Igneous Provinces."

[52] The account of the Greenhouse-Icehouse supercycles in this and following paragraphs draws upon a wide array of literature, including that cited in note 50: see also James D. Hays and Walter C. Pitman, "Lithospheric Plate Motion, Sea Level Changes and Climatic and Ecological Consequences," *Nature* 246 (1973), 18–22; and Tjeerd H. Van Andel, *New Views on an Old Planet: A History of Global Change*, second edition (New York, 1994), 175–251. Note that I am presenting here one side of an argument about the role of CO_2 in ancient climates. For those advancing the role of atmospheric CO_2, see Robert A. Berner, "GEOCARBSULF: A Combined Model for Phanerozoic Atmospheric O_2 and CO_2," *Geochimica et Cosmochimica Acta* 70 (2006), 5653–64; "Inclusion of the Weathering of Volcanic Rocks in the GEOCARBSULF Model," *AJS* 306 (2006), 295–302; *The Phanerozoic Carbon Cycle* (New York, 2004); Dana L. Royer et al., "CO_2 as a Primary Driver of Phanerozoic Climate," *GSA Today* 14/3 (March 2004), 4–10; Noam M. Bergman et al., "COPSE: A New Model of Biogeochemical Cycling over Phanerozoic Time," *AJS* 304 (2004), 397–437; D. J. Beerling and D. L. Royer, "Fossil Plants as Indicators of the Phanerozoic Global Carbon Cycle," *Annual Reviews of Earth and Planetary Sciences* 30 (2001), 527–56; Gregory J. Rellaack, "A 300-Million-Year Record of Atmospheric Carbon Dioxide from Fossil Plant Cuticles," *Nature* 411 (2001), 287–90. For dissenting views, see Ján Veizer et al., "Evidence for Decoupling of Atmospheric CO_2 and Global Climate during the Phanerozoic Eon," *Nature* 408 (2000), 698–701; Daniel H. Rothman, "Atmospheric Carbon Dioxide Levels for the Last 500 Million Years," *PNAS* 99 (2002), 4167–71; Daniel H. Rothman et al., "Dynamics of the Neoproterozoic Carbon Cycle," *PNAS* 100 (2003), 8128–9; Scott C. Doney and David S. Schimel, "Carbon and Climate System Coupling on Timescales from the Precambrian to the Anthropocene," *Annual Reviews Environmental Resources* 32 (2007), 31–66. For super-cycles and ocean water chemistry, see Tim K. Lowenstein et al., "Oscillations in Phanerozoic Seawater Chemistry: Evidence from Fluid Inclusions," *Science* 294 (2001), 1086–8; and Andreas Prokoph and Jan Veiser, "Trends, Cycles, and Nonstationaries in Isotope Signals of Phanerozoic Seawater," *Chemical Geology* 161 (1999), 225–40. For changes in sea level, see Andreas Prokoph et al., "Phanerozoic Paleography, Paleoenvironment and Lithofacies Maps of the Circum-Atlantic Margins," *Marine and Petroleum Geology* 20 (2003), 249–85.

perhaps in explosive pyroclastic flows, and they may also have released sudden massive injections of gas hydrates in the atmosphere, driving runaway greenhouse effects.[53] Well before they broke through the crust, superplumes would have lifted enormous sections of continental plate. While they remained active, these upwellings – as they rifted the continents and formed new ocean floors – would have driven a sequence of oceanic "regression," as the continental plate rose and old ocean floor sank, and then "transgression," as bulging, active, new oceanic ridges raised the floor of emergent oceans and pushed water onto the newly rifted continental surfaces.[54] These were the essential conditions of the Greenhouse epochs of the Cambrian-Silurian (545–400MY) and the Jurassic-Cretaceous (200–65MY). These were extremely warm eras, with tropical or temperate conditions typically extending to the poles, caused by a greenhouse effect of the heightened CO_2 outgassing from oceanic ridges, continental margins, and plume-erupted flood basalts. The configuration of continents and oceans was important as well. The rifted and dispersed continents opened passages in the shallow oceans running around the equator: shallow waters circulating around the warmest section of the earth further contributed to the general warmth of the Greenhouse periods.

Conversely, the depletion of upwelling plumes and the aggregation of new supercontinents (Pannotia, Pangaea, and the presently emerging future supercontinent) reversed the cycle, driving the earth system into an Icehouse. Plume activity settled into occasional eruptions at hotspots (such as Reunion Island, the Azores, Iceland, or Hawaii), and oceanic ridges settled somewhat. The carbon injected into the atmosphere and biosphere trended toward deposition and burial. The weakening of the upwelling plumes allowed the countervailing downwelling forces of subducted crustal slabs – whose avalanches puncturing through the core-mantle boundary may have caused the plumes in the first place – to become the dominant tectonic force, pulling continental fragments together toward eventual supercontinents. These aggregations had two effects that then further contributed to cooling. First, the assembling continents destroyed the shallow seaways running along the equator, shutting down the warm equatorial seaways, and encouraged the emergence of deep-running north-south oceanic current systems like the modern Gulf Stream. Second, the collisions of continents raised high mountain ranges of young rock, which both reshaped the flow of wind and weather and accelerated the stripping of CO_2 from the atmosphere as this newly exposed rock rapidly weathered. Because the oceans were deeper, sea

---

[53] Paul B. Wignall, "Large Igneous Provinces and Mass Extinctions," *Earth-Science Reviews* 53 (2001), 1–33, esp. 18–20, 24–6; Morgan F. Schaller et al., "Atmospheric Pco_2 Perturbations Associated with the Central Atlantic Magmatic Province," *Science* 331 (2011), 1404–9.

[54] Anthony Hallam and Paul B. Wignall, "Mass Extinctions and Sea-Level Changes," *Earth-Science Reviews* 48 (1999), 217–50, esp. 238–42.

levels were lower, and they fell even further as glaciations locked up water at the very depths of the Icehouse.[55]

The simple effect of transitions from Greenhouse and Icehouse would obviously have profound effects on global ecosystems. The warm temperatures, vast shallow seas, and dispersed, low-lying continents of the Greenhouse eras would have hosted a great diversity of tropical communities of species, perhaps highly specialized and localized. The rifting of continents would have multiplied the evolutionary opportunities through founder effects of geographical isolation, argued in Mayr's theory of allopatric speciation. As the tropics do today, Greenhouses indeed saw a massive "escalation" in evolutionary diversity.[56] Icehouse conditions would have been more conducive to less-specialized, more migratory species. Greenhouse ecologies might have been more given to a Gaian stability; Icehouse ecologies less so. Greenhouses, with few annual extremes and weaker oceanic circulation, also saw a greater accumulation of dead plant matter. The world's great oil deposits come from the metamorphosed sediments of shallow Greenhouse seas, most important the great equatorial Tethys Sea that once stretched from the present-day Mediterranean to Indonesia. The great coal deposits are the result of the burial of huge forests in the Devonian and Carboniferous; the spread of these forests arguably accelerated the descent into the Pangaeal Icehouse by an out-of-control stripping of CO_2 from the atmosphere.[57] Enhanced oxygen (as much as 35 percent of atmospheric gases) produced by the Carboniferous forests may have spawned huge insects, but as CO_2 crashed in the descent into Pangaeal Icehouse conditions, so too did oxygen levels. Dinosaurs may have evolved highly efficient lungs during these low-oxygen (10 percent) conditions and then the return to a high CO_2–high oxygen environment may have contributed to the subsequent rise of mammals – with their less efficient lungs.[58]

* * *

[55] M. Santosh et al., "The Making and Breaking of Supercontinents: Some Speculations based on Superplumes, Super Downwelling, and the Role of the Tectosphere," *Gondwana Research* 15 (2009), 324–41; Van Andel, *New Views on an Old Planet*; Ruddiman, *Earth's Climate.*

[56] Geerat J. Vermeij, *Evolution and Escalation: An Ecological History of Life* (Princeton, NJ, 1987); "Economics, Volcanoes, and Phanerozoic Revolutions," *Paleobiology* 21 (1995), 125–52.; Van Andel, *New Views on an Old Planet*, 213–18; V. Courtillot and Y. Gaudemer, "Effects of Mass Extinctions on Biodiversity," *Nature* 381 (1996), 146–8.

[57] David J. Beerling and Robert A. Berner, "Feedbacks and the Coevolution of Plants and Atmospheric CO_2," *PNAS* 105 (2005), 1302–5; Berner, *The Phanerozoic Carbon Cycle*, 40–57; Gregory J. Retallack, "Early Forest Soils and Their Role in Devonian Global Change, *Science* 276 (1997), 583–5.

[58] J. B. Graham et al., "Implications of the Late Paleozoic Oxygen Pulse for Physiology and Evolution," *Nature* 375 (1995), 117–20; Peter D. Ward, Confirmation of Romer's Gap as a Low Oxygen Interval Constraining the Timing of Initial Arthropod and Vertebrate Terrestrialization," *PNAS* 103 (2006), 16816–22; *Out of Thin Air: Dinosaurs, Birds, and Earth's Ancient Atmosphere* (Washington, DC, 2006), 159–228.

Mass Extinctions

Clearly the changing environmental conditions that flowed from the supercontinent cycle and all of its increasingly intricate consequences were driving evolutionary change. This was not simply random change shaped by the wanderings of continents, but patterned ecosystems moving with the vast ebbs and flows of the Icehouse and Greenhouse cycle. But, hypothetically, these shifts might have been just too smooth and slow: in the long, slow transitions from one state to another, species might simply migrate ahead of the changing climates. But the reality is that the pace of evolutionary change was not smooth and slow. The work of John Seploski and David Raup has demonstrated that it was marked by enormous crises followed by sudden accelerations.[59] There were at least five moments in Phanerozoic history when great crises caused mass extinctions, and a number of other periods also saw elevated extinction. Conversely, extinctions were followed by escalations, when the open ecological space left by extinction was filled by newly evolved plants and animals.[60] Thus the great extinction at the end of the Permian decimated the Paleozoic species and opened the way for the escalation of Modern forms; the Modern escalation was interrupted by the K-T extinctions and the subsequent disappearance of most forms of dinosaurs except for birds. In layman's language, an age of amphibians gave way to an age of reptiles, and that to an age of mammals and birds.[61] It is at these extinction boundaries that geologists have gathered to struggle over an ultimate cause, the prime mover: earthly volcanic plumbing, incoming meteors, or perhaps showers of cosmic rays coming in from the galaxy.

First, we need the rough outlines of the extinction story. There is a very general relationship between the mass extinctions and the ebb and flow of the Icehouse-Greenhouse cycle. The last three turns of the Icehouse-Greenhouse cycle are roughly associated with waves of extinction: the K-T extinction, three major and lesser extinctions in the rifting Jurassic, and extinctions in the Late Devonian (see Figure I.2). Others do not quite fit. The Permian extinction occurred in the midst of the Pangaeal Icehouse, and marked no major change in global meta-ecologies. Similarly, the Ordovician-Silurian extinction occurred in the midst of the Paleozoic Greenhouse, caused by an oddball continental glaciation, when Gondwanaland drifted over the South Pole. The other three Phanerozoic major (and some minor) mass extinctions are up for grabs, and their causes have been the subject of intense debate for several decades.

---

[59] David M. Raup and John J. Sepkoski, "Mass Extinctions in the Marine Fossil Record," *Science* 215 (1982), 1501–3; "Periodicity of Extinctions in the Geological Past," *PNAS* 81 (1984), 801–5.

[60] Vermeij, *Evolution and Escalation*.

[61] "K-T" is the standard shorthand for the boundary between the Cretaceous and the Tertiary, an older term for the Cenozoic.

Though extinctions were the original markers that determined the boundaries between geological periods, interest in their scale and periodicity emerged in the late 1960s and intensified in the early 1980s with the announcement of the Alvarez impact thesis.[62] After work through the 1970s, geologists David Raup and John Sepkoski published a pivotal paper in 1982 arguing that extinctions followed a cycle of 26 million years, and within two years Alvarez had teamed up with Richard Muller to argue that there were major impacts of meteors or asteroids every 28 million years, driven by the effects of a hypothesized solar twin – which they named "Nemesis" – moving in an elliptical orbit around the sun and periodically disrupting the "Oort Cloud" of comets, sending massive objects through the solar system.[63] While the "Nemesis theory" has been discredited, a periodicity of 26–30 million years does keep reappearing in extinction patterns, and it is now understood that impacts are a real possibility in the relatively recent past.[64] Studies of microscopic glass spherules in lunar soil, formed in the explosive impacts of meteors or asteroids, indicate that impacts declined steadily from the era of Hadean bombardment to a lows running from about 2.5 BY progressively to a trough roughly encompassing the Cambrian epoch, 800–400MY, and then suddenly surging up to levels in the past 400 million years not seen since about 3 BY.[65] Adherents of the impact school focus on this recent stretch of Phanerozoic time, and in addition to the famous Chicxulub crater discovered in 1990, which seems to match up with Alvarez's iridium layer and the K-T boundary at 65MY, they see impacts linked with the series of boundary extinctions at the end of the Devonian (359MY), possibly the Permian (251MY), the Triassic (200MY), and the Jurassic (145MY) epochs.[66]

The "terrestrial" school, skeptical from the beginning, was hampered by the inherent drama of its opponent's image of an instant apocalypse, conjured up by the flash of a "deep impact" tearing into the earth, sending massive quantities of pulverized rock and soil into the atmosphere, blocking out

[62] Luis W. Alvarez et al., "Extraterrestrial Cause for the Cretaceous-Tertiary Extinction," *Science* 208 (1980), 1095–108.

[63] Raup and Sepkoski, "Mass Extinctions in the Marine Fossil Record," and Walter Alvarez and Richard A. Muller, "Evidence from Crater Ages for Periodic Impacts in the Earth," *Nature* (308 (1984), 718–20; Walter Alvarez, "Toward a Theory of Impact Crises," *Eos* 67 (1986), 649–58. The Nemesis hypothesis has been discussed at length in David M. Raup, *The Nemesis Affair: A Story of the Death of Dinosaurs and the Ways of Science* (New York, 1999; or. publ. 1986).

[64] Considerable doubt remains as to whether these events are cyclical and periodic or just random or "episodic."

[65] Timothy S. Culler et al., "Lunar Impact History from 40 Ar/39AR Dating of Glass Spherules," *Science* 287 (2000), 1785–8.

[66] Andrew Glikson, "Asteroid/Comet Impact Clusters, Flood Basalts and Mass Extinctions: Significance of Isotopic Age Overlaps," *EPSL* 236 (2005), 933–7, at 935; L. Becker, "Benout: A Possible End-Permian Impact Crater Offshore of Northwestern Australia," *Science* 304 (2004), 1469–76. The Benout impact is disputed.

the sun, and sending rank upon rank of photogenic dinosaurs to their doom. However the terrestrial school has advanced a series of telling critiques: the iridium layer is not an absolute marker of the K-T boundary, but varies from place to place, and is often found in some quantities before and after the line. It has even been argued that it is not necessarily an absolute sign of extraterrestrial origins, but can occur under certain intense volcanic conditions. At the K-T boundary, it now appears that the only indications of a total and immediate disaster are found in an impact spray zone north of the Yucatan in North America, rather than having uniform worldwide effects. And, more important, mass extinctions – especially at the K-T boundary – began well before and extended well after the dated point of impacts, suggesting a much more complicated scenario.[67] This scenario centers on the regularities of the earth's tectonic plumbing and on the problem of how disturbances to the volatile D" layer at the boundary between the core and the mantle send hot plumes up toward the surface of the earth.

At this point, a strong consensus is emerging that superplumes and the ecological impact of massive volcanic eruptions are fundamental in the ebb and flow of extinctions since the Cambrian.[68] One important analysis, done by Anthony Hallam and Paul B. Wignall, argues that extinctions occur at moments of rapid sea level change, most often in earthly "hiccups," as sea level first falls and then rises, driven first by the lifting of continental plates by rising superplumes, and then by their rifting and subsidence. As the continental surfaces subsided (and in an ensuing epoch of seafloor spreading from high, hot oceanic ridges), a surge of "anoxic" deep ocean waters flooded continental edges and surfaces, rapidly killing entire communities of life. The sudden spread of invasive species at these marine transgressions may be a corollary to the Hallam-Wignall supercontinent-hiccup theory.[69]

[67] Critiques of the impact hypothesis have been spelled out in Vincent Courtillot, *Evolutionary Catastrophes: The Science of Mass Extinction* (New York, 1999); Charles B. Officer and Jake Page, *The Great Dinosaur Controversy* (Reading, MA, 1996); William A. S. Sergeant, "The 'Great Extinction' that Never Happened: The Demise of the Dinosaurs Considered," *Canadian Journal of Earth Science* 38 (2001), 239–47; J. Phipps Morgan et al., "Contemporaneous Mass Extinctions, Continental Flood Basalts, and 'Impact Signals': Are Mantle Plume-Induced Lithospheric Gas Explosions the Causal Link?" *EPSL* 217 (2004), 263–84; and Simon Kelly, "The Geochronology of Large Igneous Provinces, Terrestrial Impact Craters, and Their Relationship to Mass Extinctions on Earth," *Journal of the Geological Society, London* 164 (2007), 923–36.

[68] Courtillot, *Evolutionary Catastrophes*; Loper, "Mantle Plumes and Their Effect"; Wignall, "Large Igneous Provinces and Mass Extinctions"; Vermeij, "Economics, Volcanoes, and Phanerozoic Revolutions"; Paul B. Wignall et al., "Volcanism, Mass Extinction, and Carbon Isotope Fluctuations in the Middle Permian of China," *Science* 324 (2009), 1179–82. Walter Alvarez concedes considerable ground in "Comparing the Evidence Relevant to Impact and Flood Basalts at Times of Major Mass Extinctions," *Astrobiology* 3 (2003), 153–61.

[69] Anthony Hallam and Paul B. Wignall, *Mass Extinctions and Their Aftermath* (New York, 1997); "Mass Extinctions and Sea-Level Changes"; Alycia L. Stigall, "Invasive Species and Biodiversity Crises: Testing the Link in the Late Devonian," *PLOS One* 5 (2010), e15584.

A competing scenario, focusing on the Permian-Triassic crisis at 250MY, argues that devastating "plume winters" shut out sunlight for perhaps millennia, launched by a double plume event. Rather than the Yucatan impact, many would point to the superplume eruptions that formed the Deccan flood basalts in southern India as the driver of the longer run K-T extinctions.[70]

The causes of the D" layer disruptions that resulted in these catastrophic surface outcomes are the subject of considerable debate. Among the "tectonic" school are advocates of drivers on the surface or in the core. Some stress the subduction of slabs of oceanic plate down through the mantle to "slab graveyards" on the D" layer; others stress the convection of the fluid molten outer core, as lighter and heavier elements continue to separate, fueling an earthly dynamo of electromagnetism. Both arguments connect periodic reversals of the earth's magnetic field with the D" layer disturbances and the rising of superplumes. In this line of thinking, the ultimate cause of extinctions would be linked to the pulsing of the earth's electromagnetic geo-dynamo and to the irregular capabilities of the D" layer to contain the volatile elements rising from the core. Strikingly, "superchrons" of tens of millions of years, in which there were few if any magnetic reversals, preceded the great extinction breaks of the Permian-Triassic and K-T boundaries that bracket the long Mesozoic Greenhouse. In these geomagnetic calms, plume activity was minimal and biotic life on the surface stabilized, and then the earth was shattered with a sudden magnetic reversal, the bursting of the D" layer, the rise of superplumes, and the rifting of earth's surface.[71]

It is a testament to the superplume-geomagnetic synthesis that it has been assimilated by William Muller, Alvarez's associate in the early impactor arguments, who recently has suggested that some – perhaps the largest – of the plume emitting disturbances of the D" layer are set off by asteroids hitting the earth at oblique angles, sending resonant waves through the earth, and plumes then rising to the surface.[72]

---

[70] Yukio Isozaki, "Integrated 'Plume Winter' Scenario for the Double-Phased Extinction during the Paleozoic-Mesozoic Transition: The G-LB and P-TB Events for a Panthalassian Perspective," *Journal of Asian Earth Sciences* 36 (2009), 459–80; Gerta Keller et al., "New Evidence Concerning the Age and Biotic Effects of the Chicxubub Impact in New Mexico," *Journal of the Geological Society, London* 166 (2009), 393–411. See also Micha Ruhl et al., "Atmospheric Carbon Injection Linked to End-Triassic Mass Extinction," *Science* 333 (2011), 430–4.

[71] Yukio Isozaki, "Illawarra Reversal: The Fingerprint of a Superplume that Triggered Pangean Breakup and the End-Guadalupian (Permian) Mass Extinction," *Gondwana Research* 15 (2009), 421–32; Vincent Courtillot and Peter Olson, "Mantle Plumes Link Magnetic Superchrons to Phanerozoic Mass Depletion Events," *EPSL* 260 (2007), 495–504; Emmanuel Dormy and Jean-Louis Le Mouël, "Geomagnetism and the Dynamo: Where Do We Stand?" *C. R. Physique* 9 9 (2008), 711–20.

[72] Muller, "Avalanches at the Core-Mantle Boundary"; Adrian P. Jones et al., "Impact Induced Melting and the Development of Large Igneous Provinces," *EPSL* 202 (2002), 551–61; Richard A. Muller and Donal E. Morris, "Geomagnetic Reversals from Impacts

The superplume theories seem compelling; the impact theories intriguing. These are being challenged, or perhaps supplemented, by the advocates of another celestial force. This leads us out to the galaxy, the Milky Way, where dying supernova emit cosmic rays that impact the solar system. As it hits the earth's atmosphere, this flux of cosmic rays is modulated by solar activity and by the earth's geomagnetic field, and the combined effect has been shown to vary closely with the formation of low-level cloudiness. The galactic generation of cosmic rays varies on several periodicities, one of which may be epochs of star formation; its advocates argue thus that two peaks and a long lull in star formation explain the hyper-glacial Paleo- and Neoproterozoic "Snowball Earth" episodes bracketing the long stability of the Proterozoic age of eukaryotes. The cosmic ray theorists then argue that episodes of continental glaciation over the past billion years has been regulated by the earth's passage through the "spiral arms" of the galaxy, each of which raises the flux of cosmic rays, generating epochs of cloudiness, cooling, and even glaciation. Over the past half billion years of the Phanerozoic, the earth and the solar system have passed through various galactic spiral arms roughly once every 140 million years, each roughly coinciding with an epoch of continental glaciation. These galactic events would have ridden on top of the supercontinent cycle, reinforcing each of the Icehouses and interrupting the Greenhouses with a shorter cold epoch.[73]

on the Earth," *GRL* 13 (1986), 177–1180; C. C. Reese and V. S. Solomatov, "Early Martian Dynamo Generation due to Giant Impacts," *Icarus* 207 (2010), 82–97. Dallas Abbott and Ann E. Islay similarly link impacts and plumes, suggesting that impacts regularly intensify plume activity, in "Extraterrestrial Influences on Mantle Plume Activity," *EPSL* 205 (2002), 53–62. A complex theory of impact-volcanic linkages has been laid out by Herbert R. Shaw in *Craters, Cosmos, and Chronicles: A New Theory of Earth* (Stanford, CA, 1994). The battle has been joined in a proposal, wickedly subversive to the "impact" agenda, that the features interpreted as impact craters have been misinterpreted. J. Phipps Morgan and his team have proposed that these "craters" are actually caused by massive gas explosions, as rising super-plumes reached a critical mass just below the crustal surface, sending blasts of carbon dioxide and sulphur – and huge blocks of pulverized crust – into the atmosphere. Labeled "verneshots" after similar ideas once proposed by Jules Verne a century ago, this catastrophic "killing mechanism" would be situated within a continuum of increasing volcanic activity that would begin before and continue long after their explosion. Morgan et al., "Contemporaneous Mass Extinctions, Continental Flood Basalts, and 'Impact Signals.'" Morgan's proposal has drawn a spirited response in Glikson, "Asteroid/Comet Impact Clusters, Flood Basalts and Mass Extinctions"; Simon Kelley, "The Geochronology of Large Igneous Provinces, Terrestrial Impact Craters, and Their Relationship to Mass Extinctions on Earth," *Journal of the Geological Society* 164 (2007), 923–36 offers a sharp critique of the impact thesis.

73 Hendrik Svensmark and Nigel Calder, *The Chilling Stars: A New Theory of Climate Change* (Thriplow, Cambridge, 2007); Vincent Courtillot et al., "Are there Connections between the Earth's Magnetic Field and Climate? *EPSL* 253 (2007), 328–39; Nir J. Sahviv, "The Spiral Structure of the Milky Way, Cosmic Rays, and Ice Age Epochs on Earth," *New Astronomy* 8 (2003), 39–77; Nir J. Shaviv and Ján Veizer, "Celestial Driver of Phanerozoic Climate?" *GSA-Today* 13 (2003), 4–10; G. N. Goncharov and V. V. Orlov, "Global Repeating Events in

It is at points such as this that the outside scholar needs to step back and renew his or her skepticism, wondering if the struggle over extinctions has become something of a competitive game of one-upmanship among its players. But it is out of such confrontational competition that science advances toward an increasingly finely tuned consensus. While it is tempting to look for a single "prime mover," changes in earthly environments and the resulting modeling and driving of biotic evolution have to be seen as coming from multiple sources. It is, however, fundamentally intriguing to consider the geomagnetics of the core dynamo, the cycles of slabs and plumes falling and rising through the mantle, the movement of continents, solar activity, waves of meteors, and galactic cosmic rays all acting to shape patterns of climate change on the surface of the earth.

But the overall lesson should be evident: while the debate about ultimate physical causes continues, the evolutionary picture is taking new form. Rather than a desperate endless race for survival by the mad Red Queen, the impulsive Court Jester occasionally takes center stage, working hard in great bursts, while in the intervals the Red Queen may simply sit around and enjoy life. Such would seem to be the best interpretation of the evidence from the geological archive, shaping the new "ultramodern" evolutionary synthesis. While a constant background of incremental evolutionary change has been operating through time, there have been dramatic moments of crisis, collapse, and acceleration in the actual history of the evolution of life, bottlenecks through which small surviving populations have emerged in new forms to perpetuate life in new ecological configurations. Whatever the exact cause, the sequence is clear: bursts of evolutionary change follow profound environmental crises through the long history of the evolving earth system.

The rest of this book is centrally concerned with ways human culture has struggled with natural punctuation in order to preserve and expand human population. If Darwin's relentless gradualism has been found wanting, so too – I argue – has Malthus's, at least for the run of history up to the edge of our modern circumstance. A single ecological model of cumulative change through recurring cycles of expansion, stability, crisis, and adaptive renewal emerges from the paleo-record of earth history, and can describe the path of humanity's subsequent rough journey.[74] This is where we turn in the following chapter.

---

the History of the Earth and the Motion of the Sun through the Galaxy," *Astronomy Reports* 47 (2003), 925–33; K. S. Carslaw et al., "Cosmic Rays, Clouds, and Climate," *Science* 298 (2002), 1732–6.

[74] Here I will be aligning evolutionary theories of punctuation and emergence with parallel theories of resilience and adaptive renewal. For a full view, see Lance H. Gunderson and C. S. Holling, eds., *Panarchy: Understanding Transformations in Human and Natural Systems* (Washington, DC, 2002).

2

Human Emergence

In the long run from 60 million years ago to 60,000 years ago, the global super-cycle moved from Greenhouse to Icehouse, from a warm, carbon-rich world in which ferns grew and dinosaurs grazed at the earth's polar extremes to a cold, carbon-depleted world, where a new humanity stood on dry equatorial African shores on the edge of a global colonization leading to our very recent past. For decades, it has been a central tenet of evolutionary studies that the human condition has its origins in this inexorable march into Icehouse conditions. Prehuman and human history over the past 15 million years has a fundamental relationship to specific tectonic events and the regular oscillations of glacial climates: as Steven Stanley has put it, we are "children of the ice age."[1] More precisely, we are the children of the

---

[1] Steven M. Stanley, *Children of the Ice Age: How a Global Catastrophe Allowed Humans to Evolve* (New York, 1996). For other leading interpretive syntheses of human evolution and climate change, see Karl W. Butzer, "Environment, Culture, and Human Evolution," *American Scientist* 65 (1977), 572–84; Robert Foley, *Another Unique Species: Patterns in Human Evolutionary Ecology* (Harlow, UK: 1987); –, "The Ecological Conditions of Speciation: A Comparative Approach to the Origins of Anatomically-Modern Humans," in Paul Mellars and Chris Stringer, eds., *The Human Revolution: Behavioural and Biological Perspectives on the Origins of Modern Humans* (Edinburgh, 1992), 298–318; Stephen M. Stanley, "An Ecological Theory for the Origin of *Homo*," *Paleobiology* 18 (1992), 237–57; Elizabeth S. Vrba et al., eds. *Paleoclimate and Evolution with Emphasis on Human Origins* (New Haven, 1995), Peter B. deMenocal, "Plio-Pleistocene African Climate," *Science* 270 (1995), 53–9; Noel Thomas Boaz, *Eco Homo: How the Human Emerged from the Cataclysmic History of the Earth* (New York, 1997); Richard Potts, *Humanity's Descent: The Consequences of Ecological Instability* (New York, 1996); William H. Calvin, *A Brain for all Seasons: Human Evolution & Abrupt Climate Change* (Chicago, 2002). For the last sections of the Pleistocene, see Brian M. Fagan, *The Long Summer: How Climate Changed Civilization* (New York, 2004); and William J. Burroughs, *Climate Change in Prehistory: The End of the Reign of Chaos* (New York, 2005); Renée Hetherington and Robert G. B. Reid, *The Climate Connection: Climate Change and Modern Human Evolution* (New York, 2010); Robert M. Hamilton et al., (NRC Committee on the Earth System Context of Hominin Evolution), *Understanding Climate's Influence on Human Evolution* (Washington, DC, 2010); Peter B. deMenocal, "Climate and Human Evolution," *Science* 331 (2011), 540–2. I have found

ice age tropics, if over time venturing into the grasslands and tundra bordering the ice itself. And it is always a shock to realize that the entirety of agriculturally based human civilization has unfolded in a brief 10,000-year interval embedded within this long sequence of glaciations, which in turn lies at the bottom of a 60-million-year descent into an Icehouse epoch. The chapters following this look with some care at this brief 10,000-year history. This chapter charts the global transition from Greenhouse to Icehouse, and then examines the emergence of humanity through the worst of the current Icehouse, between the divergence of bipedal human forbears from the arboreal great apes roughly 6 million years ago and the colonization of the entire world by modern human societies in the last phase of the Pleistocene ice ages.

As we move closer to the present, the question of vast and almost unimaginable transformations in the earth system gives way to more subtle oscillations, and the problem of the emergence of new orders of biota gives way to the problem of survival of one particular species. Biological evolution starts to share the stage with cultural evolution. If biota and earth system are inherently coupled, humanity and earth system have been progressively decoupled in this emergence of the workings of the human mind. This decoupling was limited and constrained; humanity has never been able to escape the Court Jester and the threat of punctuation by environmental forcing. Nature, acting in patterns well within the framework proposed by Stephen Jay Gould and Niles Eldridge, did not let up its grip. But increasingly – and most specifically under the stress of the Pleistocene – culture began slowly to release humanity from the stark pathways of total extinction or genetic bottleneck. The difference lies in part in the scale, if not the absolute qualities, of the environmental stresses at work. And in part the differences lie in the new capabilities for communication, problem solving, and creativity that the youngest primate brought to the struggle to survive in a rough world.

* * *

Into the Cenozoic Icehouse

Before we can begin to introduce humanity, we briefly must describe the world that produced humanity. If we are "children of the ice age," we need to understand how this "ice age" came to be. As much as we are children of the ice age, that ice age is the culmination of the long super-cyclical cooling from Greenhouse to Icehouse that separated dinosaurs in the Mesozoic Arctic from modern humans on the shore of the Pleistocene Red Sea.

Bernard G. Campbell et al., *Humankind Emerging*, ninth edition (Boston, MA, 2006) and Clark S. Larsen, *Our Origins: Discovering Physical Anthropology* (New York, 2008) particularly useful guides to human evolution.

The gradient of ecological change from late Mesozoic Greenhouse to Cenozoic Icehouse was by no means as steep as that separating the Paleozoic Greenhouse from the early Mesozoic Icehouse. In this earlier super-cyclical transition, the Paleozoic rise of early forests and forest soils combined with the slowing of tectonic rifting to depress CO_2 concentrations from perhaps 6,000 or 8,000 parts per million (ppm) at 600 million years ago (MY) to perhaps 200 ppm at 300MY. In the ensuing Mesozoic Greenhouse, CO_2 may have reached a high of about 3,500 ppm before it began to decline around 120 million years ago. By the time that an asteroid hit the Yucatan at 65MY, this decline in atmospheric CO_2 – with corresponding declines in oxygen – may have already contributed to the extinction of many of the larger species of dinosaurs.[2] After the Yucatan impact, CO_2 levels and temperatures rose again, as the North Atlantic region around Iceland rifted, reaching a final peak at the explosive "thermal maximum" at the beginning of the Eocene, around 55MY, as a super-plume ruptured the growing Atlantic at Iceland (see Figure I.3). This was followed by the first of four distinct and sharp shifts toward cooler and dryer temperatures, first during the mid-Eocene, then at the beginning of the Oligocene at 34MY, the mid-Miocene at 16MY, and finally during the Pliocene and the Pleistocene, around 5 million years ago. From the late Eocene into the early Oligocene, this global cooling was driven by a plummeting atmospheric CO_2, which fell from about 1,500 ppm to 500 ppm in 5 million years, as the long Mesozoic Greenhouse ran out of steam, rifting and volcanic activity slowed, ocean ridges deflated, and sea levels receded. At this transition to the Oligocene 34 million years ago, CO_2 fell below roughly 350 ppm, a major factor in the beginning of continental glaciation on Antarctica. In pushing CO_2 above this critical threshold in the past century, as climatologist James Hansen has stressed, we risk the catastrophic reversal of the human-friendly condition of a partially glaciated world.[3]

A second factor – the tectonically driven repositioning of continents and seas – began to play a more significant role in the Oligocene, as the declining CO_2 of the reversing super-cycle reached a key cooling threshold. At

[2] G. P. Landis et al., "Pele Hypothesis: Ancient Atmospheres and Geologic-Geochemical Controls of Evolution, Survival and Extinction," in N. MacLeod and G. Keller, eds., *Cretaceous-Tertiary Mass Extinctions: Biotic and Environmental Changes* (New York, 1996), 519–56. Dana L. Royer et al., "CO_2 as a Primary Driver of Phanerozoic Climate," *GSA Today* 14/3 (March 2004), 6.

[3] Paul N. Pearson and Martin R. Palmer, "Atmospheric Carbon Dioxide Concentrations over the Past 60 Million Years," *Nature* 406 (2000), 695–9; James Zachos et al., "Trends, Rhythms, and Aberrations in Global Climate 65 Ma to Present," *Science* 292 (2001), 686–93; Robert M. Decanto and David Pollard, "Rapid Cenozoic Glaciation in Antarctica Induced by Declining Atmospheric CO_2," *Nature* 421 (2003), 245–9; Aradna Tripati et al., "Eocene Bipolar Glaciation Associated with Global Carbon Cycle Changes," *Nature* 436 (2005); 341–6; Mark Pagani et al., "Marked Decline in Atmospheric Carbon Dioxide Concentrations during the Paleogene," *Science* 309 (2005), 600–3; James Hansen et al., "Target Atmospheric CO_2: Where Should Humanity Aim?" *The Open Atmospheric Science Journal* 2 (2008) 217–31.

34MY, open seaways emerged to separate Antarctica from South America and then from Australia, establishing circumpolar ocean currents in the southern hemisphere that accelerated global cooling. Along the equator, this northward movement of southern hemispheric continents drove the closure of warm shallow equatorial seas and passages having a similar cooling effect, as did the associated uplift of new mountain ranges. Most important, the Indian subcontinent had been on the move north since the massive "flood basalt" eruption forming the Deccan flood basalts around 65MY. By 34MY, India had collided with Asia, and was raising up the Himalayas; the weathering of these massive young mountains established a new sink for CO_2. India's movement was followed by a slow northeast rotation of Africa and Arabia, contributing to mountain building in southern Europe and the Caucasus, but also closing and eventually almost obliterating the ancient Tethys Sea, whose remnants include the Aral, Black, and Mediterranean Seas, and perhaps 60 percent of the modern world's oil supply – embedded in the carbon sediments of this shallow sea. As the Himalayas rose to heights unseen on earth since Pangaea and the moderating shallow Tethys disappeared, the Asian monsoon began to be established, erratically channeling winds and precipitation away from central Asia toward the new Ganges valley and East Africa, and desiccating the Asian interior. Finally, around 6 million years ago, as the Antarctic glaciers drew more water from the oceans, the Mediterranean dried out completely several times, further destabilizing Old World climate, and between 4.5MY and 2.5MY the equatorial seaways at Panama and in Indonesia closed, ending ancient warm-water connections between the Caribbean Sea, the Pacific, and the Indian Ocean. This would bring the beginning of northern hemisphere glaciation and the transition into the Pleistocene.[4]

* * *

The Court Jester in the Cenozoic: Debate and Three Kinds of Evidence

The operation of the environmental Court Jester – and of abrupt evolutionary emergences – on orders of land mammals during this stepped sequence of changes from Greenhouse warmth toward the Pleistocene is presently the subject of considerable debate. Since the past century, the general proposition that cooling climates gradually impelled biotic communities toward their contemporary forms has been widely accepted. From the 1920s, the key understanding of human evolution in eastern Africa has been what is known as the *savannah hypothesis*, in which a gradual but pronounced

---

[4] This quick summary is based on William F. Ruddiman, *Earth's Climate: Past and Future* (New York, 2001), 147–71; Tjeerd H. van Andel, *New Views on an Old Planet: A History of Global Change*, second edition (New York, 1994), 175–233, and the citations in notes 3 and 22.

shift from forested to savannah environments drove selection among the Pliocene great apes toward walking (or bipedalism), tool making, larger and smarter brains, and new patterns of sociability and interdependence, in essence toward humanity. In 1985, as the thesis of punctuation was taking shape, the savannah thesis was precisely stated: Elizabeth Vrba proposed that sharp climate changes resulted in widespread "turnover pulses" of species of land mammals, with increasing rates of extinction and speciation resulting in entirely new communities of animals.[5] Her particular attention was focused on what seemed to be a sharp transition at 2.5 million years ago, when continental glaciation began in the northern hemisphere, seemingly correlated with the emergence of what was called *Homo habilis*, a tool-making proto-human.

Vrba's argument for sharp and broad turnover pulses has since been challenged by analyses of some African and North American fossil records, while other work in Europe, South Asia, and Mongolia supports her turnover pulse hypothesis.[6] The difference might well be that between more stable equatorial latitudes and colder northern latitudes. But the central problem

[5] Elizabeth S. Vrba has developed her model of turnover pulses in a series of articles, most prominently "Ecological and Adaptive Changes Associated with Early Hominid Evolution," in E. Delsen, ed., *Ancestors: The Hard Evidence* (New York, 1985), 63–71; "Late Pliocene Climate Events and Hominid Evolution," in F. E. Grine, *The Evolutionary History of the "Robust" Australopithecines* (New York, 1988), 405–26; "Turnover-Pulses, the Red Queen, and Related Topics," *AJS* 293-a (1993), 418–52; "The Pulse that Produced Us," *Natural History* 102/5 (May, 1993), 47–51; "On the Connection between Paleoclimate and Evolution," and "The Fossil Record of African Antelopes (Mammalia, Bovidae) in Relation to Human Evolution," in Elizabeth S. Vrba et al., eds. *Paleoclimate and Evolution with Emphasis on Human Origins*, 24–45, 385–424; "Climate, Heterochrony, and Human Evolution," *JAnthRes* 52 (1996), 1–28; "Mass Turnover and Heterochrony Events in Response to Physical Change," *Paleobiology* 31 (2005), 157–74; Manuel Hernandez and Elizabeth S. Vrba, "Plio-Pleistocene Climatic Change in the Turkana Basin (East Africa): Evidence from Large Mammal Faunas," *JHumEv* 50 (2006), 595–626.

[6] S. R. Frost, "African Pliocene and Pleistocene Cercopithecid Evolution and Global Climatic Change," in Rene Bobé et al., eds. *Hominin Environments in the East African Pliocene: An Assessment of the Faunal Evidence* (Dordrect, 2007), 51–77; Jeffrey K. McKee, "Faunal Turnover Rates and Mammalian Biodiversity of the Late Pliocene and Pleistocene of Eastern Africa," *Paleobiology* 27 (2001), 500–11; Anna K. Behrensmeyer, "Late Pliocene Faunal Turnover in the Turkana Basin, Kenya and Ethiopia," *Science* 278 (1997), 1589–94; D. R. Prothero and T. H. Heaton, "Faunal Stability during the Early Oligocene Climatic Crash," *PPP* 127 (1996), 239–56; J. M. Harris, *Kooba Fora Research Project, Vol. II: The Fossil Ungulates: Geology, Fossil Artiodactyls and Paleoenvironments* (New York, 1991); Jan van Dam, "Long-Period Astronomical Forcing of Mammalian Turnover," *Nature* 443 (2006), 687–91; Nadin Rohland et al., "Genomic DNA Sequences from Mastodon and Woolly Mammoth Reveal Deep Speciation of Forest and Savannah Elephants," *PlosBiology* 8 (2010), e1000564; Catherine Badgley et al., "Ecological Changes in Miocene Mammalian Record Show Impact of Prolonged Climatic Forcing," *PNAS* 105 (2008), 12145–9; P. Raia et al., "Turnover Pulse or Red Queen? Evidence from the Large Mammal Communities during the Plio-Pleistocene of Italy," *PPP* 221 (2005), 293–312; Jin Meng and Malcolm C. MacKenna, "Faunal Turnovers of Palaeogene Mammals from the Mongolian Plateau," *Nature* 394 (1998), 364–7.

for human origins remains understanding the specific climatic changes in East Africa, and here Richard Potts of the Smithsonian suggested an important shift in emphasis in 1996. While not denying that a directional transition from forests to savannahs was under way, Potts is more interested in the impact of an increasing variability in climate change. In this *variability hypothesis*, the intensifying pacing and extremes of regular climate cycles, altering the landscape between moist and arid – sometimes super-arid – conditions, was impelling genetic selection in a series of punctuated bottlenecks. Bounced back and forth between wetter and drier conditions, between forest and savannah, over vast periods of time, proto-human species moved toward generalist adaptations, rather than for any particular specialization. Thus the pressures of faster and deeper climate variation shaped a species that could change its eating habits, could mentally map the landscape, and whose members could act together as a social unit. Out of these recurring, deepening, and accelerating stresses, on a long trajectory running from forest toward savannah environments, humanity would emerge.[7]

Establishing the exact relationship between climate change and human evolution takes time, analysis, and extended debate. It involves three very different kinds of evidence that are presently somewhat incompatible in their "visibility."[8] From the 1950s until the mid-1980s, the argument rested on two rather impressionistic records that had been developing since the origins of natural science in the late eighteenth century. An understanding of climate change was developed in broad outline from surface geology and the fossil record, while the record of animal and human evolution came from these same fossils and from the associated archaeological evidence of early human activity. In the past decades, however, these arduously recorded and collected physical remains of the past have been amplified by two very different kinds of records, one inscribed in cores drilled from deep geological sediments, and the other on the genetic codes that have combined and recombined in the evolutionary past and that lie in all of our living cells.

The archaeological record of human origins specifically began to emerge from scattered fossils and artifacts in South Africa in the 1920s, and then progressed in East Africa with the work of the Leakeys and then an illustrious sequence of paleontological teams. These traditional methods, now enhanced with techniques including satellite infrared surveys, ever more precise and careful recovery, and advanced dating technology, continue to uncover fundamentally important material providing absolute and direct

---

[7] Potts, *Humanity's Descent*; Richard Potts, "Variability Selection in Hominid Evolution," *Evolutionary Anthropology* 7 (1998), 81–96; –, "Environmental Hypotheses of Hominin Evolution," *YPA* 41 (1998), 93–136.

[8] For a recent prospectus of the research agendas involved, see Hamilton et al., *Understanding Climate's Influence on Human Evolution*. See also Anna K. Behrensmeyer, "Climate Change and Human Evolution," *Science* 311 (2006), 476–8.

evidence for constructing evolutionary history. Nonetheless, paleontology and archaeology are limited by the necessarily incomplete picture that they can recover: archaeological evidence can only include the subset of past activity for which evidence has survived in the ground, and the subset of that subset that scientists can find, recover, archive, and publish systematically.

Where paleontological and archaeological evidence provides focused but occasional snapshots of the past, precisely located in time and place, modern climate and genetic studies provide evidence that has very different qualities. Since the late 1960s, climate research has involved drilling and chemical analysis: cores drilled through sea beds, glaciers, and lake sediments can be carefully marked off, sampled, and chemically assayed to generate sequential series of markers of past climate that in the best of circumstances can provide an annual record of climate variability. Quite literally, the detailed understanding that modern climate studies have been able to construct over the past two decades has overwhelmed the capacities of the paleontologists and archaeologists to provide a comparable body of evidence, and it will be some time before the fossil and archaeological records can catch up with the evidence for climate history.

In the meantime, beginning in the late 1980s and now simply exploding with the decoding of the human genome, modern genetic studies have begun to make stunning contributions to an evolutionary history. Its great strength is a uniform and inclusive coverage of humanity and its ability to establish patterns of genetic proximity and distance that have suggested a strong and consistent pattern of human migrations during the Pleistocene. Its weaknesses lie in geography and chronology: genetic events can be placed only very generally in time and place, and their interpretation is complicated by how little we can know about scale of the populations from which they are drawn, and by the probability of evolutionary change unfolding at sharply different rates in epochs of equilibrium and punctuated emergence.[9]

The result is something of a mismatch, in which the archaeological, genetic, and paleoclimatic data all provide evidence of very different precision and comprehensiveness. Thus a proto-human fossil can be – in ideal circumstances – dated and placed relatively precisely in a detailed climate sequence, but its exact place in an evolutionary sequence remains in some doubt: It may be the first of its kind to have been found in a region, but was this indeed the earliest occurrence, and did its living owner evolve in this location, or somewhere else? And if it seems to be a first appearance, is that appearance related to a concurrent climate change recorded in local geology or sediment chemistry? And how might it be related to a putative branch

---

[9] Hetherington and Reid, *The Climate Connection*, 31–4. There have been only the most tentative efforts to link genetic markers with specific archaeological traditions. See, for example, Ornella Semino et al., "The Genetic Legacy of Paleolithic *Homo Sapiens sapiens* in Extant Europeans: A Y Chromosome Perspective," *Science* 290 (2000), 1155–9.

in a genetic tree? And when does a *described correlation* between climate change and new features in the archeological or genetic record merit the claim to be an *explained cause*?

I will be constructing a synthesis from these three lines of evidence, built upon the assiduous work of hundreds of specialists. But, as they would all agree, such a synthesis can only be tentative, built upon a reading of the deliberative center of the current state of the field. As I have done in the first chapter, I present what I understand to be this deliberative center: despite a debate about some of the important details, it is abundantly clear that biota in general and proto-humans in particular were shaped and reshaped by their dynamic evolutionary responses to a cooling and increasingly variable climate during the Cenozoic, as ecological change of various kinds subjected populations to stress, isolation, and resulting bottlenecks of allopatric selection and genetic drift, or perhaps epigenetic emergence. It is entirely possible that such responses might have involved the operation of heat shock proteins in embryonic development, accelerating evolutionary emergence of new species and new qualities of body and mind. It is certainly clear that at some point these emerging modern human qualities began to coalesce into the ability to progressively control a surrounding environment, to think through time and over the horizon, and to communicate these skills to others around them. From this point forward humanity began to develop the capacity to transcend climatic punctuation and to generate punctuations in its own history. Humanity began to decouple its history from climate and nature, or at least to think that such a decoupling was possible.

* * *

Miocene Apes and the Early Hominins

Paleoanthropologists are quite confident about the role of environmental change in driving the evolution of the Old World ape lineages that led toward human origins. This was a story shaped by the jolting shifts toward a cooler, Icehouse earth, driven by declining atmospheric CO_2 and the tectonic remodeling of the boundary between Africa and Eurasia during the Oligocene and Miocene epochs. By the Early Oligocene, about 32 million years ago, after the onset of glaciation in Antarctica, a series of arboreal anthropoid species, precursors of monkeys and apes, had evolved from earlier primate forms found in African or Asian forests south of the Tethys Sea.[10]

---

[10] It might be useful to review the classification of primates and some terms used here. The Primate order is divided between the Prosimians and the Anthropoids, which include New World monkeys, Old World monkeys, and the Hominoids, which include the Old World greater and lesser apes and the *Hominidae*, or the Hominids. Hominids include Orangutans, Gorillas, the *Paninae* (Chimpanzees and Bonomos), modern humanity, and its various extinct close relations. At this stage the classification is under some dispute, with competing anatomic

The first "hominoid" apes began to evolve in these forests during the warm early Miocene, 20MY, gradually developing larger brains and reduced tooth size, and replacing quadruped motion in the trees, balanced by a tail, with a swinging suspension from true hands, arms, and a fully rotating shoulder. Around 18MY, the pace of diversification among the Miocene apes accelerated, as global climate began to experience severe swings, as measured by oxygen isotopes (see Figure I.3).

There are two competing positions on where this diversification led toward humanity. The traditional understanding, as yet unsupported by fossil evidence, is that the hominoids evolved toward great apes in tropical Africa.[11] As Africa made contact with Eurasia at approximately 17–16MY, during the final epoch of the warm early Miocene, early hominoid apes joined a general mammalian movement of African mammals into the Eurasian forests north of the fragmenting Tethys Sea. These land bridges opened and closed at various intervals with variations in sea level, but it was among the transplanted and diversifying Eurasian apes that the line leading eventually to humanity evolved during the drastic and erratic cooling between 15MY and 13MY. But after 9MY, as the full effects of the Himalayan mountain building dried and cooled large stretches of Eurasia, the northern great apes either died out or tracked south with retreating woodland and forest ecosystems into Southeast Asia and back into Africa. With declining levels of atmospheric CO_2, tropical biomes soon began to change dramatically, with the spread of savannah land dominated by the C_4 grasses, which are particularly successful in low-CO_2 conditions.[12] The stage was set in East Africa for the stepped, punctuated emergence of humanity.

A series of geological and climatic stresses continued to act upon eastern Africa during the late Miocene and through the Pliocene. From 8MY, in what was apparently a small super-plume event, eastern Africa was uplifted and broken along a volcanic rift stretching from the southern Red Sea down to the central African lakes region. Simultaneously, as the general global system cooled, variation in the earth's orbit around the sun began to be manifested

---

and genetic trees, most importantly because of the close genetic relationship of humans and the *Paninae*. In this text, the term *hominin* will be used to describe the entire range of increasingly bipedal proto-human species that seem to have diverged from the *Paninae* around 7 million years ago, out of which the genus *Homo* emerged around 3–2.4 million years ago.

[11] Suzanne M. Cote, "Origins of African Hominoids: An Assessment of the Palaeobiogeographical Evidence," *Comptes Rendus Palevol* 3 (2004), 323–40.

[12] Campbell et al., *Humankind Emerging*, 140–51; David R. Begun, "Planet of the Apes," *SA* 289/2 (August 2003), 74–83; Potts, *Humanity's Descent*, 71–7; David W. Cameron, *Hominid Adaptations and Extinctions* (Sydney, 2004), 162–79, 205–10; An Zhisheng, "Evolution of Asian Monsoons and Phased Uplift of the Himalaya-Tibetan Plateau since Late Miocene Times," *Nature* 441 (2001), 62–6; Z. T. Guo et al., "Onset of Asian Desertification by 22 Myr Inferred from Loess Deposits in China," *Nature* 416 (2002), 159–63; Erika J. Edwards et al., "The Origins of C_4 Grasslands: Integrating Evolutionary and Ecosystem Science," *Science* 328 (2010), 587–91.

increasingly in cyclical effects on earth climates.[13] As a progressive cooling withdrew water from the global oceans into the growing Antarctic ice sheets, lowering sea levels, these orbital shifts compounded an underlying tectonic uplift at the Straits of Gibraltar, causing a catastrophic evaporation of the western remnants of the old Tethys Sea. With the fall of global sea levels and the rise of a shallow shelf at the straits, the Mediterranean and Black Seas were cut off from the Atlantic at 6.3 MY and completely dried out for almost a million years, in what is known as the Messinian salinity crisis. During the Messinian crisis, massive saline deposits on the evaporated Mediterranean sea floor were exposed to wind-borne erosion, and driving hot dusty winds over the surrounding regions. This event contributed to the creation of the modern Sahara desert, which had broad effects on global climate.[14]

These were the conditions in which the last common ancestors of humans and modern African great apes evolved and then diverged. Geneticists are broadly agreed that the division between humans and our closest primate cousins, the hominid gorillas and the chimpanzees, took place sometime between 9MY and 4MY, with gorillas branching off between 9MY and 6MY and chimpanzees and human precursors sometime between 7MY and 4MY; one estimate is 6.6–4.9MY[15] (see Figure I.4). French paleontologist Yves Coppen has proposed that the uplift of the Rift Valley through eastern Africa beginning around 8MY constituted the specific force that divided the ancestral great ape populations, with ancestral gorillas and chimps eventually persisting in the dense western rainforests that were fed by Atlantic rains, while new genera of proto-humans, what anthropologists are now calling *hominins*, were established across the increasingly drier and climatologically unstable eastern region, supplied by an increasingly erratic rainfall from the Indian Ocean.[16] The million-year evaporation of the Mediterranean clearly must have had a role in the conditions shaping this rupture.

[13] Peter B. de Menocal, "African Climate Change and Faunal Evolution during the Pliocene-Pleistocene," *Earth and EPSL* 220 (2004), 3–24 (8).

[14] See Jean-Marie Rouchy et al., "The Messinian Salinity Crisis Revisited," *SedGeol* 188/189 (2006), 1–8, and the articles in this special issue; Arne Michels et al., "The Late Miocene Climate Response to a Modern Sahara Desert," *GPC* 67 (2009), 193–204; Potts, *Humanity's Descent*, 76–7; Stanley, *Children of the Ice Age*, 54.

[15] For various estimates, see Sudhir Kumar et al., "Placing Confidence Limits on the Molecular Age of the Human-Chimpanzee Divergence," *PNAS* 102 (2005), 18842–7; M. A. Jobling et al., *Human Evolutionary Genetics: Origins, Peoples, Diseases* (New York, 2004), 215–17; Jinxiu Shi et al., "Divergence of the Genes on Human Chromosome 21 between Human and other Hominoids and Variation of Substitution Rates among Transcription Units," *PNAS* 100 (2003), 8331–6; for a range estimate, see R. L. Stauffer et al., "Human and Ape Molecular Clocks and Constraints on Paleontological Hypotheses," *Journal of Heredity* 92 (2001), 469–74.

[16] Yves Coppen, "East Side Story: The Origin of Humankind," *SA* 270/5 (May 1994). 88–95. For simplicity, I will refer to all bipedal potentially proto-human and human species as *hominins*, and include our hominid cousins the gorillas and the chimpanzees with the great apes.

For decades, debate over the emergence of bipedal hominins revolved around *Australopithecus*, the "southern ape," first found in south Africa in the 1920s, and then in 1959 in Kenya (now called *A. afarensis*), dating to about 4–3MY. But recently a series of fossil finds have begun to put hard evidence behind the earlier divergence suggested by the genetics, with new Australopith species (*A. anamensis*) dating back to 4.2MY, a *Kenyanthropus* dating to roughly 3.4MY, *Ardipithecus ramidus* dating between 5.8MY and 4.4MY, and two even older species, *Orrorin tugenensis* and *Sahelanthropus tchadensis*, dating from somewhere between 6MY and 7MY. The evidence suggests that before 6MY both *Sahelanthropus tchadensis* and *Orrorin tugenensis* had some walking abilities, but the consensus is that the ape-like tendency to head for the trees persisted until well after 2MY and the rise of *Homo erectus*. Fossils dated to roughly 3.4MY indicate that fully bipedal Australopiths were sharing the mosaic landscape with evolutionary cousins whose tree-climbing foot architecture was very similar to that of *Ardipithecus*.[17] There is a considerable debate about the phylogenetic relationships of these early hominin fossils, and competing arguments suggest that all of these fossils either represented a "bush" of divergent species or were various manifestations of the same general species. There are some ambiguities: the genetic differentiation between chimpanzees and proto-humans was not clear and complete until 4MY, but *S. tchadensis* and *O. tugenensis* were bipedal by 6MY: a genetic analysis suggests that the human line may have descended from a hybridization between the bipedal species and chimpanzees occurring sometime after 6MY.[18] Many of these species – including the Australopiths – may not have been true human ancestors, but part of a wider adaptive proliferation for which we have only the most scattered and fragmentary evidence (see Figure I.4). But the wider reality is becoming apparent, without worrying too much about the exact human phylogenetic lineage: a variety of early hominin forms were emerging during the ecological stressful late Miocene.

What distinguished these hominin species was a slowly evolving dental structure and an emerging ability to walk upright on two legs, perhaps useful in evading predators, perhaps adaptive in exposing less body area to the

---

[17] For overviews of these discoveries, see Campbell et al., *Humankind Emerging*, 205–13; Larsen, *Our Origins*, 282–300; Brian G. Richmond and William L. Junger, "*Orrin tugenensis* Femoral Morphology and the Evolution of Human Bipedalism," *Science* 319 (2008), 1662–5; Tim D. White, "*Ardipithecus ramidus* and the Peliobiology of Early Hominids," *Science* 326 (2009), 75–86; and Yohannes Heile-Selassie et al., "A New Hominin Foot from Ethiopia Shows Multiple Pliocene Bipedal Adaptations," *Nature* 483 (2012), 565–70. While many classifications distinguish between an African *Homo ergaster* and a Eurasian *Homo erectus*, I will for the sake of simplicity lump these together as *H. erectus*, because it is the more widely recognized label.

[18] Nick Patterson et al., "Genetic Evidence for Complex Speciation of Humans and Chimpanzees," *Nature* 441 (2006), 1103–8.

sun.[19] If they did not abandon the forest, the early hominins were capable of dealing with a patchy, mosaic environment of wooded streambeds and drier, more open upland, an environment that was increasingly characterized by instability and diversity. Such a picture of early bipedal hominins living in wooded environments comes into sharper focus in detailed paleoecological studies of various East African sites, where their fossils and those of their proposed descendants have been situated in relation to other mammalian fossils and other evidence of ancient environments.[20] But it is increasingly clear that the forces at work on the early hominins and their immediate ancestors were not so much a complete change from forest to grasslands, but an increasing variability in climate, driven by forces that were only now – as the earth approached the base of the Cenozoic Icehouse – beginning to be manifested in recurring periods of increasingly extreme climatic change. Proto-human evolution, the variability hypothesis argues, was not being shaped by a simple transition from forest to grasslands, but by the erratic oscillations of climate and terrestrial environment. We must now return to the antics of the Court Jester, the environmental forces that seem to explain the pace and sequencing of evolutionary change.[21]

* * *

Orbital Cycles: From the 23K World to the 41K World

Virtually all of the fundamental environmental forces discussed so far in this and the previous chapter have been either astronomical or tectonic in origin. The *tectonic forcings* include the vast, slow workings of *super-cycles* of continental formation, rifting, spreading, and closure, driven by the subduction of continental slabs, the geodynamics of the D" layer, and super-plumes rising from the core-mantle boundary. The subsidence of super-plumes and consequently declining CO_2 emissions had driven the Cenozoic cooling before the Oligocene. During the Oligocene and the Miocene and into the Pliocene, the dominant forces behind climate cooling involved the tectonic reshaping and consolidation of continents that mark the end of the super-cycle: the closing of the Tethys Sea, the uplift of the Himalayas, the opening of polar seaways around Antarctica, the tectonic rifting of eastern Africa, the desiccation of the Mediterranean. Two final tectonic events during the Pliocene marked a key transition. At roughly 4.5MY, continental drift began to close down two of the last remnants of the Mesozoic equatorial seaways. Paleoclimatologists

[19] Campbell et al., *Humankind Emerging*, 241–50.
[20] Tim D. White et al., "Asa Issie, Aramis, and the Origin of *Australopithecus*," *Nature* 330 (2006), 883–9; René Bobé and Anna K. Behrensmeyer, "The Expansion of Grassland Ecosystems in Africa in Relation to Mammalian Evolution and the Origin of the Genus *Homo*," *PPP* 207 (2004), 399–420.
[21] Potts, *Humanity's Descent*; Potts, "Variability Selection in Hominid Evolution."

have long pointed to the effect of the uplift of the Isthmus of Panama in closing off the Atlantic from the Pacific and establishing deep cold North Atlantic currents, beginning at 4.5MY and finally fully closing around 2.5MY and setting the stage for the beginnings of Arctic glaciation at 2.75MY. The tectonic uplift of the Indonesian region between 4MY and 3MY must have had an equally significant effect, slowing down a flow of warm, moist air into the Indian Ocean, and thus cooling and drying eastern Africa[22] (see Figure I.4).

Another set of forces were also at work on global climates, working much more rapidly and perhaps lightly, but not until tectonics had lowered global temperatures to a critical threshold at roughly 2.75MY could they begin to have serious effects of their own. These are the results of fluctuations in the relationship between the earth in its orbit and the sun itself unfolding over tens and hundreds of thousands of years, broadly known as *orbital forcings*. Specifically, these orbital variations increased and decreased the amount and seasonality of solar warmth – *insolation* – reaching the earth's upper atmosphere at different latitudes. Once a tectonic-driven threshold of global temperature had been reached, these cyclical variations began to drive the advance and retreat of continental glaciation in the northern hemisphere. To understand our world, and the world of emerging proto-humans, we need to know something about these orbital cycles.

The idea that variations in the earth's rotation and orbit might shape glaciations was first proposed more than 150 years ago, and, in the 1920s, Serbian mathematician Milutin Milankovitch established its basic premises. But not until the beginning of the modern campaign to drill and analyze cores from ocean bottoms and glaciers was the evidence to support an orbital theory of glaciation established. Three cycles of different periodicities are at work, in complex relationships with each other, with tectonic forcings, and with greenhouse gases.

The first orbital cycle involves slight variations in the orbital tilt or *obliquity* of the earth's axis in relation to its orbit around the sun. Increases in tilt expose more of the polar regions to solar warmth during the summer and less during the winter, enhancing seasonal extremes. Decreases in tilt reverse this relationship, leading to colder polar summers. Varying between 22.1° and 24.5° from vertical over the past 5 million years, the obliquity cycle runs over a peak to peak period of 41,000 years.

The second orbital cycle is driven by changes in the shape, or *eccentricity*, of the earth's annual orbit around the sun. Never a perfect circle, the earth's orbit is periodically distorted by the gravitational pull from nearby planets. Here increases in the eccentricity – or elliptical shape – of the orbit mean that

---

[22] G. Bartoli, "Final Closure of Panama and the Onset of Northern Hemisphere Glaciation," *EPSL* 237 (2005), 33–44; Mark A. Cane and Peter Molnar, "Closing of the Indonesian Seaway as a Precursor to East African Aridification around 3–4 million Years Ago," *Nature* 411 (2001), 157–62.

the earth flies a little closer to the sun on two seasonal passes, and is thus incrementally warmer. While eccentricity is manifested in a series of different cycles, the dominant one is approximately 98,500 years in length from peak to peak, with an important secondary cycle measuring 413,000 years.

Finally, the third cycle – *precession* – is itself composed of two related patterns. The first is the "wobble" or "precession of the axis," in which the entire earth wobbles like a top on its axis; the second is the "precession of the ellipse," in which the shape of the orbit itself rotates. These two cycles together make up the "precession of the equinoxes," which gradually pushes the season solstices (March 21, June 21, etc.) around the eccentric path of the orbit on cycles that measure 19,000 and 23,000 years; because the 23,000-year cycle is dominant, precession is usually measured in 23,000-year cycles. When summer and winter solstices line up at the extremes of the oval, the effect is toward a cooler earth. Obviously all of these patterns have been working simultaneously since the formation of the earth, if at gradually changing velocities. And because they are simultaneous, these cycles work in relationship with each other to create complex interactive patterns, depending on their own internal rhythms. Thus obliquity/tilt and precession can either enhance or cancel out each other's effects or the effect of eccentricity. And all of these effects only determine the degree of solar warmth that reaches the upper atmosphere as "insolation." Down on the ground, the effects of these cycles are further altered by tectonic forcings, by albedo – the proportion of incoming light reflected by a surface – and by the various biotic and geological components that shape the cycling of greenhouse gases, especially carbon dioxide and methane.[23]

As the earth descended further into the Cenozoic Icehouse, these orbital cycles increasingly began to shape global climate, and their increasing variability and scale began to shape the context of biological evolution, including proto-human evolution. When the cumulative effects of tectonic forces – the slowing of super-plume activity and the remodeling of continents and ocean basins – reached certain critical thresholds, the orbital forcings begin to independently drive the cycling of tropical monsoons and of polar continental glaciation. Evidence exists that suggests that, since at least the Oligocene-Miocene transition at about 23MY, the precession orbital pattern was shaping climate cycles. Precession directly determines the varying level of insolation (solar warmth) hitting the atmosphere, and higher and lower insolation – by differentially heating land and ocean surfaces – was already driving a cycle of stronger and weaker tropical monsoons.[24] From long before the epoch of the Miocene apes down to approximately 2.75MY,

---

[23] This quick summary is indebted to Ruddiman, *Earth's Climate*, 174–91; Martin Bell and Michael J. C. Walker, *Late Quaternary Environmental Change: Physical & Human Perspectives* (Harlow and New York, 1992), 60–3; and J. D. Hays et al., "Variations in the Earth's Orbit: Pacemaker of the Ice Ages," *Science* 194 (1976), 1121–32.

[24] James C. Zachos et al., "Climate Response to Orbital Forcing across the Oligocene-Miocene Boundary," *Science* 292 (2001), 274–8; T. Westerhold et al., "Middle to Late Oxygen

the dominant climate signal in the oxygen isotopes recovered from ocean cores is this precession signal: a 23,000-year periodicity (see Figure I.4).

Certainly the rifting of eastern Africa and the catastrophic drying of the Mediterranean during the Messinian crisis had serious regional impacts that seem to have shaped the emergence of the early hominins diverging from the great apes. But it is also clear that these species were adapted to a patchy wooded environment that did not change drastically for millions of years and – to point of fact – neither did these proto-humans. The early bipedal hominins lasted for as much as 4 million years, perhaps improving their two-legged posture and probably using twigs and the occasional rock opportunistically as tools, but maintaining a cranial capacity and the sharp difference in body size and weight between the sexes that were not radically different from that of their great ape cousins.[25] Through all these millennia, the 23,000-year, precessionally dominated orbital cycle exerted important pressures on East African climates, causing an ebb and flow of more humid and more arid conditions, but maintaining a reasonably well-forested environment.

The tectonic threshold that broke this pattern came around 3–2.5 million years ago, with the closing of the Indonesia and Panama equatorial seaways. These final major tectonically derived climate drivers cooled the global system sufficiently to set off continental glaciation in the northern hemisphere, marked by the first appearance at 2.75MY of debris carried by glaciers and "ice rafts" in the North Atlantic cores. The tectonic cooling effect set off a chain reaction that shaped the new climate regime. Once the northern glaciers were established, they accelerated the cooling of the far northern hemisphere, in part because of the increased albedo reflection of solar radiation from snow-covered surfaces, and changes in airborne dust, sea surface temperatures, and the working of the deep Atlantic currents. This accelerated cooling increased the temperature differences between the poles and the equator, and this gradient drew in more moisture that increased the snowfall and glacial ice pack. All of these forces flipped the global climate system from a "23K World" of rapid but shallow climate oscillations driven by orbital precession into a "41K World" of longer and deeper shifts defined by the 41,000-year orbital cycles of obliquity and tilt.[26]

* * *

Isotope Stratigraphy of ODP Site 1085 (SE Atlantic): New Constraints of Miocene Climate Variability and Sea-Level Fluctuations," *PPP* 217 (2005), 205–22; Xiangjun Sun and Pinxian Wang, "How Old Is the Asian Monsoon System? – Palaeobotanical Records from China," *PPP* 222 (2005), 181–222; Ruddiman, *Earth's Climate*, 194–209.

[25] Kaye E. Reed, "Paleoecological Patterns at the Hadar Hominin Site, Afar Regional State, Ethiopia," *JHumEv* 54 (2008), 743–68; Mark Collard, "Grades and Transitions in Human Evolution," *Proceedings of the British Academy* 106 (2002), 61–100.

[26] Bartoli, "Final closure of Panama"; Cane and Molnar, Closing of the Indonesian Seaway"; Ruddiman, *Earth's Climate*, 223; Maureen E. Raymo, "The Initiation of Northern

The 41K World and the Genus *Homo*

The effects of the shift to the "41K World" in eastern Africa between 3MY and
2.5MY have been described as "a profound environmental degradation."[27]
A series of changes occurred more or less simultaneously with the onset of
northern hemispheric glaciations and the establishment of the 41,000-year
climate cycle. For the first time, continental glaciers persisted for as long as
15,000–20,000 years before melting, as orbital alignments resynchronized
to bring a temporary return of solar warmth to heating of the northern
hemisphere. There were critically important changes in the tropics as well.
Ocean drilling off the African coasts has revealed a series of layers of wind-
blown dust indicating sudden shifts toward dry, arid conditions: the first of
these dust layers dates to this period, 3MY to 2.6MY (see Figure I.4). The
general consensus is that there was a movement toward savannah conditions, though they would not become the norm for another million years, at
around 1.8MY, when another surge in windborne dust in the ocean cores
lines up with a distinct shift in soil carbonates, indicating the final acceleration toward savannah grasslands. As the savannah advanced so did the
intensity of climatic variation. This blast of environmental change and climate variation in the millennia following 3MY did drive turnover in animal
populations – and the emergence of new populations of proto-humans.[28]

Hemispheric Glaciation," *Annual Reviews in Earth and Planetary Science* 22 (1994), 353–
83; "The 41 kyr World: Milankovitch's Other Unsolved Mystery," *Paleoceanography* 18
(2003), 1011–16; William F. Ruddiman, "Orbital Insolation, Ice Volume, and Greenhouse
Gases," *QSR* 22 (2003), 1597–629, at 1624. Recently there has been considerable attention
given to new estimates that atmospheric CO_2 dropped circa 3.2–2.8MY, from ~330–400
ppm to ~280 ppm. Osamu Seki et al., "Alkenone and Boron-Based Pliocene pCO_2 Records,"
EPSL 292 (2010), 201–11; Mark Pagani et al., "High Earth-System Climate Sensitivity
Determined from Pliocene Carbon Dioxide Concentrations," *NatGeosc* 3 (2010), 27–30;
Ana Christina Ravelo, "Warmth and Glaciation," *NatGeosc* 3 (2010), 672–4; William F.
Ruddiman, "A Paleoclimatic Enigma?" *Science* 328 (2010), 838–9.

[27] Bernard Wood and David Strait, "Patterns of Resource Use in Early *Homo* and *Paranthropus*,"
JHumEv 46 (2004), 119–62.

[28] DeMenocal, "Plio-Pleistocene African Climate"; deMenocal, "African Climate Change and
Faunal Evolution"; deMenocal, "Climate and Human Evolution"; Bobé and Behrensmeyer,
"The Expansion of Grassland Ecosystems in Africa in Relation to Mammalian Evolution
and the Origin of the Genus *Homo*"; Sarah J. Feakins et al., "Biomarker Records of Late
Neogene Changes in Northeast African Vegetation," *Geology* 33 (2005), 977–80; Jonathan
Guy Wynn, "Influence of Plio-Pleistocene Aridification on Human Evolution: Evidence from
Paleosols of the Turkana Basin, Kenya," *AJPA* 123 (2004), 106–18; Naomi E. Levin et al.,
"Isotopic Evidence for Plio-Pleistocene Environmental Change at Gona, Ethiopia," *EPSL*
219 (2004), 93–110. Where these studies, analyzing carbon in ancient soils, find a significant
shift to C4 grasses after 3MY and 1.5MY, studies of carbon isotopes in ungulate teeth find
an earlier shift, at 6–8MY. This earlier shift would reflect the origins of savannah grasses,
but not necessarily their dominance. Thure E. Cerling, "Global Vegetation Change through
the Miocene/Pliocene Boundary," *Nature* 389 (1997), 153–8.

As glacial patterns began to operate globally, different but increasingly linked forces were specifically at work in East Africa. In the tropics, the 23,000-year precession-insolation cycle shapes African monsoon patterns, and it is modulated by the longer 413,000-year and the shorter 100,000-year cycles of the eccentricity of the earth's orbit.[29] Uniformly, as the eccentricity of the orbit becomes more extreme, the variation of precession becomes more extreme, driving greater variations of tropical warmth, and thus greater variations in tropical monsoons. (See Figure I.5 for the pattern in the Pleistocene.) Thus the troughs and peaks of the precession respectively intensify and weaken tropical insolation and the Indian Ocean monsoon, and fill up and dry out lakes in regular succession. These patterns have been detected operating as far back as the Oligocene. But as the 41,000-year orbital obliquity/tilt cycle launched continental glaciation in the polar north, the effects of the tropical system became more extreme. The result was that, with the larger peaks of orbital eccentricity, the smaller swings in precession-controlled monsoons drove intense extremes of precipitation and hyperaridity in East Africa.[30] Precession-maximum wet periods left thick lake sediments; increasingly severe precession-minimum droughts sent up clouds of dust to be recorded in shrinking lake sediments. Swinging in wild extremes of ample rain and brimming lakes to hyperaridity and dry lake beds, these high-eccentricity epochs acted as punctuating accelerants for proto-human evolution. During droughts, hominin populations would have shrunk into isolated refuges, where the potential for the expression of emergence and resulting genetic founder effects would have greatly increased. Then, during wet periods, populations would have grown and expanded, increasing the opportunities for new species to become established.[31]

These stressful high-eccentricity epochs clearly began to drive East African evolution after 3MY (see Figure I.4). *Australopithecus anamensis*, living in patchy wooded environments, persisted until the onset of the "41K World" at about 3MY, and a period of extreme monsoon variability

---

[29] Here I am following convention in rounding up the 98,500-year cycles to 100,000.

[30] Counterintuitively, these high-eccentricity periods of extreme East African precipitation and hyperdrought were interglacial periods, when the Eurasian land mass was relatively ice free.

[31] The key recent literature on the impact of orbital eccentricity and precession on monsoon variability on East Africa includes Martin H. Trauth et al., "Trends, Rhythms, and Events in Plio-Pleistocene African Climate," *QSR* 28 (2009), 399–411; "High- and Low-Latitude Forcing of Plio-Pleistocene East African Climate and Human Evolution," *JHumEv* 53 (2007), 475–86; John D. Kingston et al., "Astronomically Forced Climate Change in the Kenyan Rift Valley 2.7–2.55 Ma.: Implications for the Evolution of Early Hominin Ecosystems," *JHumEv* 53 (2007), 487–503; Christopher J. Campisano and Craig S. Feibel, "Connecting Local Environmental Sequences to Global Climate Patterns: Evidence from the Hominin-Bearing Hadar Formation, Ethiopia," *JHumEv* 53 (2007), 515–27. This literature provides the empirical demonstration of the mechanisms behind Richard Potts's variability selection hypothesis.

in East Africa. *A. anamensis* was replaced first and briefly by *A. africanus* and *A. garhi*. Then after 2.8MY – a point of low eccentricity and low precessional stress implying moderate East African conditions – the hominin lineage divided into two stems. One would lead to evolutionary dead ends and extinctions: the various *Kenyanthropus* species (*platyops, rudolphensis*) and *Paranthropus* species (*aethiopus, robustus, boisei*). Some persisting to almost one million years ago, *Paranthropus* developed massive grinding dentition, allowing them to forage the increasingly dry savannahs virtually as generalized grazing animals, presumably with the occasional opportunistic mouse or grasshopper thrown in. More important, however, a second generalist adaptation emerged, leading to the genus *Homo*.[32]

At around 2.6MY, both northern hemispheric glaciation and another tropical high eccentricity period set in and drove a sharp acceleration in human evolution. This coincided with the first clear evidence for stone tools, in what is known as the *Oldowan tradition*, featuring round cobblestones roughly flaked to establish a sharp cutting edge. This had nothing to do with hunting. Rather, as woodland resources dwindled, some of the evolving hominins began to scavenge dead animals, probably animals killed by carnivores or the lack of water, and the primitive Oldowan choppers were the necessary means to hacking through thick hides – and smashing up bones. The goal was fat stored in bone marrow. Who first made these tools? The earliest known dates of *Homo habilis* are roughly 2.4MY, 200,000 years after the earliest dating of Oldowan tools. This would suggest the probability that under the stresses of the transition to the 41K World, broadly between 3MY and 2.5MY, late Australopiths began a behavioral transition to scavenging and very primitive stone tool production. In any event, it is clear that such early tool use and an associated set of evolutionary changes were central to the emergence of the genus *Homo*.[33]

Geneticists have proposed that a specific genetic change is the marker for the punctuation that differentiates *Homo* from its forebears and contemporaries. The first *Homo habilis* fossils date to 2.4MY, the same time as a genetic mutation suddenly reduced the size and strength of human jaw

[32] This interpretation of divergent hominin strategies is most fully expressed in Vrba, "Late Pliocene Climate Events and Human Evolution" and can be followed in Robert Foley, *Another Unique Species*, 244–55. Its characterization of *Paranthropus* as a dietary specialist has recently been challenged in Wood and Strait, "Patterns of Resource Use." Also see citations in note 37.

[33] Thomas Plummer, "Flaked Stones and Old Bones: Biological and Cultural Evolution at the Dawn of Technology," *YPA* 47 (2004), 118–64; Sileshi Semaw et al., "2.6 Million-Year-Old Stone Tools and Associated Bones from OGS-6 and OGS-7, Gona, Afar, Ethiopia," *JHumEv* 43 (2003), 169–77; Randall L. Sussman, "Hand Function and Tool Behavior in Early Hominids," *JHumEv* 35 (1998), 23–46; W. H. Kimbel et al., "Late Pliocene *Homo* and Oldowan Tools from the Hadar Formation (Kada Hadar Member), Ethiopia," *JHumEv* 31 (1996), 549–61.

muscles (known as *MYH16*).[34] Apes, early hominins, and *Paranthropus* had large muscles attaching to sagital crests on the top of their skulls, providing crushing power for jaws and teeth, but also binding the skull in a muscular vise that may have precluded any expansion in brain size. This mutation fixing was followed by a second, estimated at 2.2MY, which inactivated a gene (*CMP-N*) governing the production of acids that limit brain growth in mammals. Previously, such mutations might have been disastrous and would have been lost quickly, but in a context of emerging large-animal scavenging and tool use, they must have suddenly spread widely, marking a fundamental speciation event.[35] The result was a burst of *encephalization*: brain size increased by a fifth between the Apiths (~450 c.c.) and *Homo habilis* (~552 c.c.) and by another third with the development of *Homo erectus* (~854 c.c.) by roughly 1.8MY[36] (see Figure I.4).

Brains are useful but expensive organs, and require significantly more caloric energy than other body tissues. Thus a complex of behaviors and biological changes began to work together as *Homo* emerged from 2.4MY. The increasing ecological stresses of the "41K World transition" had encouraged late Australopiths to raid carnivore kills; encephalization allowed *Homo* to perfect the skills involved in scavenging. Descending vultures would have located nightly kills, which *Homo* bands would have exploited during the day. These raids required coordination of spotting, tracking, chasing off vultures and hyenas, and tools for quick butchering. Most of the scatter from tool manufacture is located at what would have been hillside springs or streams, or lake edges, which might have been protected by patches of woods: these seem to have been somewhat defensible home bases to which both raw stone and butchered carcasses would have been carried, and food shared in new and interdependent ways. All of this activity would have required social and technical skills, and would have produced the meat and fat that would have fed the brains that underlay those skills. A new diet and an enlarging brain required different patterns of blood circulation and a new digestive tract, and the old large gut of the apes gave way to a smaller, more

---

[34] Recently, *habilis*'s classification in the genus *Homo* has been questioned, but I keep it for the sake of simplicity. For an important recent review see Ian Tattersall and Jeffrey H. Schwartz, "Evolution of the Genus *Homo*," *Annual Reviews: Earth and Planetary Science* 37 (2009), 67–92. The dating and attribution of *Homo* has been complicated further by the discovery of an australopithecine with features leading to *Homo* at 1.95–1.78MY. This fossil might be directly ancestral to *Homo erectus*. Lee R. Berger et al., *Australopithecus Sediba*: A New Species of *Homo*-like Australopith from South Africa," *Science* 328 (2010), 195–204.

[35] Hansell H. Stedman, "Myosin Gene Mutation Correlates with Anatomical Changes in the Human Lineage," *Nature* 428 (2004), 415–18; Pete Currie, "Muscling In on Hominid Evolution," *Nature* 428 (2004), 373–4; Hsun-Hua Chou et al., "Inactivation of *CMP-N*-Acetylneuraminic Acid Hydroxylase Occurred Prior to Brain Expansion during Human Evolution," *PNAS* 99 (2002), 11636–41; Campbell et al., *Humankind Emerging*, 258. For a critique, see Hetherington and Reid, *The Climate Connection*, 17–18.

[36] Cranial capacity from Collard, "Grades and Transitions in Human Evolution," 84.

efficient gut, sending more blood to the brain. Large infant heads required new structures in the birth canal and a longer period of infant dependency. Daytime scouting on the hot savannah required a system of blood circulation that would cool the enlarging brain. These developments combined to form a mutually reinforcing feedback among activities, skills, diet, and physical structure, clearly a fundamental punctuation on the road toward humanity.[37]

Homo habilis was still a small species, at most four feet tall, and still may have retained some ape-like tree-climbing proclivities. But it had a larger brain, a new diet, and new skills, and recent discoveries suggest that it ranged much further and survived much longer than had been traditionally assumed. First, *habilis* fossils have been discovered at the Dmanisi site in the Caucasus region between the Black Sea and the Aral Sea. Dating to 1.7MY, these *habilis* individuals were not associated with a wave of African mammals, suggesting that *habilis's* special skills and diets now allowed it to spread into new ecosystems. Second, *habilis* fossils have been found in Kenya and dated to 1.44MY. This might mean that *habilis* did not disappear at 1.8MY, but may have coexisted as a parallel species with *Homo erectus* for as long as a half million years. New *erectus* finds are also suggesting that this species was much more variable in size than once thought, and may have first emerged well before its traditional emergence date of 1.9MY. One hypothesis therefore proposes that *habilis* and *erectus* were parallel species that emerged from a common ancestor as a result of the environmental disruptions of the transition from the 23K climate system to the 41K climate system, with its embedded whiplash of precession-driven East African drought and flood, around 2.5MY. On the other hand, it is entirely possible that all of these *Homo* fossils are the remains of a single, highly variable species.[38]

---

[37] Leslie C. Aiello and Peter Wheeler, "The Expensive-Tissue Hypothesis: The Brain and Digestive System in Human and Primate Evolution, *CA* (36 (1995), 199–221; Plummer, "Flaked Stones and Old Bones; Lisa Rose and Fiona Marshall, "Meat-Eating, Hominid Sociality, and Home Bases Revisited," *CA* 37 (1996), 307–38; Robert J. Blumenschine and John A. Cavallo, "Scavenging and Human Evolution," *SA* 267/4 (Oct. 1992), 90–6; Dean Falk, "Brain Evolution in *Homo*: The 'Radiator' Theory," *Behavioral and Brain Sciences* 13 (1990), 333–81; Glynn Isaacs "Aspects of Human Evolution," in D. S. Bendall, ed. *Evolution from Molecules to Men* (New York, 1983), 509–43; Glynn Isaac, "The Food-Sharing Behavior of Protohuman Hominids," *SA* 238/4 (1978), 90–138.

[38] Leo Gabunia et al., "Dmanisi and Dispersal," *Evolutionary Anthropology* 10 (2001), 158–70; David Lordkipanidze et al., "Postcranial Evidence from Early *Homo* from Dmanisi, Georgia," *Nature* 449 (2007), 305–9; F. Spoor et al., "Implications of New Early *Homo* Fossils from Ileret, East of Lake Turkana, Kenya," *Nature* 448 (2007), 688–90; Daniel E. Lieberman, "Homing In on Early *Homo*," *Nature* 339 (2007), 291–2; David Lordkipanidze et al., "A Complete Skull from Demanisi, Georgia, and the Evolutionary Biology of Early *Homo*," *Nature* 342 (2013), 326–31.

The next significant transition in East African environments at roughly 1.8MY to 1.6MY, the formal boundary between the late Pliocene and early Pleistocene, saw an intense sequence of environmental instability driving a widespread faunal change and an increase in aridity and savannah conditions. The impacts on East Africa were compounded by another high-eccentricity period, which brought wild swings in the Indian Ocean monsoon, with a sequence of wet periods and hyperdroughts that filled and dried out highland lakes and put layers of desert dust into ocean sediments.[39]

This critical climatic transition saw the development of *Homo erectus* into a species of modern human height and weight, with a brain much larger than that of *habilis*. *Erectus* was fully savannah adapted, inaugurating unquestionably modern walking and running abilities, including the distance endurance running that distinguishes humans from virtually all other species.[40] The pressures of the 1.8–1.6MY climate crisis may have pushed *erectus* out of Africa, tracking along the dry grasslands east into southern South Asia, China, and Indonesia.[41] And if they initially continued the Oldowan stone tool traditions inaugurated by late Australopiths at 2.6MY (and in use by *habilis* at Dmanisi), African *erectus* by 1.6MY had begun what is known as the *Acheulean handaxe tradition*, a remarkably uniform style of increasingly symmetrical stone tools that – among other uses – may have been thrown at game herds, as these peoples simultaneously started hunting and developing a precise hand-eye coordination.[42] The handaxe tradition did not spread out of Africa until after 780,000 years ago, and never spread east of the India-Burma border, where *erectus* peoples seem to have

[39] Gail M. Ashley et al., "Hominin Use of Springs and Wetlands: Paleoclimate and Archaeological Records from Olduvai Gorge (~1.79–1.74 Ma), *PPP* 272 (2009), 1–16; R. Bernart Owen et al., "Diatomaceous Sediments and Environmental Change in the Pleistocene Olorgesailie Formation, Southern Kenyan Rift Valley," *PPP* 269 (2008), 17–37;, Gail M. Ashley, "Orbital Rhythms, Monsoons, and Playa Lake Response, Olduvai Basin, Equatorial East Africa (ca. 1.85–1.74 Ma)," *Geology* 35 (2007), 1091–4; Trauth et al., "Trends, Rhythms, and Events"; "High- and Low-Latitude Forcing"; René Bobé et al., "Faunal Change, Environmental Variability and Late Pliocene Hominin Evolution," *JHumEv* 42 (2002), 475–97; deMenocal, "African Climate Change and Faunal Evolution"; "Plio-Pleistocene African Climate"; Bobé and Behrensmeyer, "The Expansion of Grassland Ecosystems in Africa in Relation to Mammalian Evolution and the Origin of the Genus *Homo*."

[40] Matthew R. Bennett et al., "Early Hominin Foot Morphology Based in 1.5-Million-Year-Old Footprints from Ileret, Kenya," *Science* 323 (2009), 1197–201; Dennis Bramble and Daniel E. Lieberman, "Endurance Running and the Evolution of Homo," *Nature* 432 (2004), 345–52; Fred Spoor and Bernard Wood, "Implications of Early Hominid Labyrinthine Morphology for Evolution of Human Bipedal Locomotion," *Nature* 369 (1994), 645–8; Susan C. Anton, "Natural History of *Homo Erectus*," *YPA* 46 (2003), 126–70.

[41] Susan C. Anton and Carl C. Swisher, III, "Early Dispersals of *Homo* from Africa," *Annual Reviews of Anthropology* 33 (2004), 271–96.

[42] Calvin, A Brain for All Seasons, 133–46.

used bamboo for cutting tools.[43] By 1.2MY, *erectus* had shed the last of the body hair that characterized virtually all other mammals, as its skin darkened as protection from the sun.[44] The control of fire was clearly an essential part of the new *erectus* tool kit. Early Acheulian deposits in the Wonderwerk Cave in South Africa have revealed the earliest convincing evidence for the routine use of fire at roughly a million years ago, and the first definitive fire hearth is dated to 790,000 years before present (ybp) in Israel. Richard Wrangham has argued convincingly that the shift toward modern stature and skeletal structure with *erectus* is strong circumstantial evidence that these new peoples had started to cook their food, driving the beginnings of important shifts in familial and communal organization and solidarity.[45]

Erectus peoples and the Acheulian tool kit were extremely successful and well adapted to the "41K world," as the early hominins were to the "23K World." *Erectus* lasted as a species for a million years in Africa, and – without the Acheulian – until about 40,000 years ago in isolated parts of Indonesia, where a recently discovered pygmy subspecies, *Homo floresiensis*, persisted until about 18,000 years ago![46] The Acheulian lasted 1.3 million years, longer than the Oldowan's one-million-year run. But as the "41K World" gave way to the "100K World" a new series of environmental pressures set the stage for the final transitions toward modern *Homo sapiens* – modern humanity.

* * *

[43] Naama Goren-Inbar et al., "Pleistocene Milestones on the Out-of-Africa Corridor at Gesher Benot Ya'aqov, Israel," *Science* 289 (2000), 944–7; Robert Foley and Marta Mirazón Lahr, "Mode 3 Technologies and the Evolution of Modern Humans," *CArchJ* 7 (1997), 12.

[44] Alan R. Rogers et al., "Genetic Variation at the MCIR Locus and the Time since Loss of Human Body Hair," *CA* 45 (2004), 105–8; Nina G. Jablonski, "The Evolution of Human Skin and Skin Color," *Annual Reviews in Anthropology* 3 (2004), 585–623; Nina G. Jablonski and George Chapin, "The Evolution of Human Skin Coloration," *JHumEv* 39 (2000), 57–106.

[45] Richard Wrangham, *Catching Fire: How Cooking Made Us Human* (New York, 2009); Francesco Berna et al., "Microstratigraphic Evidence of In Situ Fire in the Acheulean Strata of Wonderwerk Cave, Northern Cape Province, South Africa," *PNAS* April 2, 2012 doi:10.1073/pnas.1117620109; Naama Goren-Inbar, "Evidence of Hominin Control of Fire at Gesher Benot Ya'aqov, Israel," *Science* 304 (2004), 725–7; Nira Alperson-Afil et al., "Spacial Organization of Hominin Activities at Gesher Benot Ya'aqov, Israel," *Science* 326 (2009), 1677–80; Kristen Hawkes, "Grandmothers and the Evolution of Human Longevity," *American Journal of Human Biology* 15 (2003), 380–400.

[46] P. Brown et al., "A New Small-Bodied Hominin from the Late Pleistocene of Flores, Indonesia," *Nature* 431 (2004), 1055–61; M. J. Morwood et al., "Archaeology and Age of a New Hominin from Flores in Eastern Indonesia," *Nature* 431 (2004), 1087–91; M. J. Morwood et al., "Further Evidence for Small-Bodied Hominins from the Late Pleistocene of Flores, Indonesia," *Nature* 437 (2005), 1012–17; Kate Wong, "The Littlest Human," *SA* 292/2 (Feb. 2005), 56–65.

The 100K World: *Homo Heidelbergensis*, Archaic *Homo Sapiens*

The last break between major glacial "worlds" came roughly a million years ago, and was marked in East Africa and surrounding oceans by yet another swath of windborne dust, indicating a sudden advance of dry arid conditions. Where there had been a diversification of the hominin line at the great shift in global climates around 2.75 MY, here there was a great thinning: the last of the alternate hominin lines stemming from the Miocene apes, *Paranthropus* and probably *Homo habilis*, died out, leaving the African and Asian *H. erectus* populations to go forward into the "100K World" (see Figures I.4, I.5).

For almost 2 million years, the earth's glacial cycles had swung on 41,000-year cycles defined by orbital obliquity. Roughly a million years ago, the system began to change to a climatic cycle defined primarily by the eccentricity of the orbit. These cycles were long, deeper, and more irregular in shape, running longer than 100,000 years, with modulations at the secondary ~400,000-year eccentricity cycle. Again, like the transition to the previous "41K World," the transition to the "100K World" took place in several stages. First, around 1.2 MY, the 41,000-year cycles began to deepen and lengthen. Then, between 900,000 and 700,000 years ago, in another eccentricity-driven monsoon oscillation in eastern Africa, what is being called the "Mid-Pleistocene Revolution," an irregular 100,000-year cycle took hold, and around 450,000 years ago settled into a series of four regular deep climatic swings, on which we now ride upon the most recent upturn.[47]

These four recent and most extreme glacial cycles have strikingly similar patterns. The oxygen isotopes from ocean sediments and the CO_2 and methane gases preserved in Greenland and Antarctic ice show the same variation, a long, slow decline in temperature and an increase in ice formation followed by a plunge to a "glacial maximum" and then a sudden "termination" melt back to a rather short "interglacial." Again, a combination of forces seems to have been at work in this shift in climate regime, in which the various orbital cycles were reinforced by the general trajectory of cooling and the specific workings of greenhouse gases and the bio-geosphere. An ongoing decline in atmospheric CO_2 may have shaped both a decline in

---

[47] Mark Siddell et al., "Changes in Deep Pacific Temperature during the Mid-Pleistocene Transition and Quaternary," *QSR* 29 (2010), 170–81; Erin L. McClymont and Antoni Rosell-Melé, "Links between the Onset of Modern Walker Circulation and the Mid-Pleistocene Climate Transition," *Geology* 33 (2005), 389–92; Martin Medina-Elizalde and David W. Lea, "The Mid-Pleistocene Transition in the Tropical Pacific," *Science* 310 (2005), 1009–12; Trauth et al., "Trends, Rhythms, and Events"; deMenocal, "African Climate Change"; M. E. Raymo, "The Mid-Pleistocene Climate Transition: A Deep Sea Carbon Isotopic Perspective," *Paleoceanography* 12 (1997), 546–59; Manfred Mudelsee and Michael Schultz, "The Mid-Pleistocene Climate Transition: Onset of 100 ka Cycle Lags Ice Volume Build-Up by 280 ka," *EPSL* 151 (1997), 117–23.

sea surface temperatures and the structure of the ocean currents to drive the transition to the new regime. Then orbital precession and obliquity oscillations, working in combination with each other, either enhanced or suppressed greenhouse gases in wild but regular swings that stretched over the 100,000-year eccentricity cycles.[48]

The 100,000-year, eccentricity-dominated world had quite different impacts at the high latitudes and the equatorial latitudes, especially eastern Africa. High- and low-eccentricity epochs correlated with – and probably were the principal drivers of – interglacial and glacial episodes. Low eccentricity values are associated with the deep glaciations, manifested in lower sea levels and in lower levels of atmospheric CO_2 and methane (see Figure I.5). Despite the general lack of global moisture, with so much being drawn into the advancing continental glaciers, the eccentricity troughs actually brought relatively moderate conditions to East Africa. Low eccentricity meant relatively modest swings in precession and insolation, and thus modest swings in the tropical monsoons systems, resulting in stable East African climates. Emerging evidence suggests that during the glacial periods tropical circulation systems shifted south, with the effect of bringing more rain to East Africa, while at the same time North Africa and Southwest Asia suffered intense cold droughts and desertification. Thus during glacial periods ice would advance through the northern latitudes and the Sahara would be completely uninhabitable, while conditions would be reasonably stable and humid in East Africa.

Conversely, during high-eccentricity interglacial periods, the opposite would be the case. As in our present Holocene world, ice would retreat toward the poles and temperate ecologies would prevail across much of the middle latitudes; sea levels, CO_2, and methane would all rise together. The Sahara would become a vast savannah parkland, while the African monsoons prevailed. But the peak eccentricity pattern shaping the interglacials in these 100K cycles brought wide extremes in the peaks and troughs of the precession-insolation 23,000-year cycle, shaping extreme variability in African climate. As in the earlier environmentally unstable periods at ~2.5MY and 1.8MY, there is direct evidence from East African lake sediments for wet and dry precession cycles, complicated by tectonic shifts; the last high peak in the eccentricity cycle of 135–70K years ago very clearly drove a series of megadroughts, drying up lakes and turning semiarid landscapes into deserts.[49]

---

[48] Nicholas J. Shackleton, "The 100,000-Year Ice-Age Cycle Identified and Found to Lag Temperature, Carbon Dioxide, and Orbital Eccentricity," *Science* 289 (2000), 1897–902; William F. Ruddiman and Maureen E. Raymo, "A Methane-Based Time Scale for Vostok Ice," *QSR* 22 (2003), 141–55; Ruddiman, "Orbital Insolation, Ice Volume and Greenhouse Gases."

[49] A. G. N. Bergner et al., "Tectonic and Climatic Control on Evolution of Rift Lakes in the Central Kenya Rift, East Africa," *QSR* 28 (2009), 2804–16; Christopher A. Scholz et al.,

Because East Africa was the principal range of emerging modern humans, it seems highly likely that these eccentricity-driven oscillations of climate during interglacial times were critically important to the last stages of human evolution, as suggested by Richard Potts's variability thesis. This was the world that shaped humanity into our final form, probably in bottleneck pulses of evolution driven by extreme and abrupt climate change. This final human form, *Homo sapiens*, is distinguished primarily by our mental capacities, by a brain that lets us think in a focused, analytical manner about things that we cannot see: in the past, in the future, over the geographic horizon. It is larger than our forebears' brain, and is carried in a skull that is tall and globular, rather than relatively long and sloping, and is integrally connected to a face and throat that are our vehicle of expression and communication, and to hands that are equally involved in shaping our immediate world.

In sum, the extreme punctuations of an increasingly rough world in the mid-to-late Pleistocene brought out an extreme response: building on the hominin legacy, humanity emerged into self-consciousness and self-realization. In so doing, we stepped away from the natural world that had so shaped us. The evidence for this human emergence, in defiance of an increasingly violent Court Jester, lies literally in things shaping and shaped by the human brain: scatters of artifacts lying in the ground, fossils of the bones that encased the brains that shaped them, and increasingly the genes that we still carry with us. Each has a story to tell, a story that leads toward the dynamic relationships among human populations, technologies, and creativity that, in tension with the rough forces of the natural world, comprise the central question in the rest of this book.

These stories started slowly at the opening of the "100K World." Around one million years ago, at the same time that *Paranthropus* was going extinct with the shift toward aridity and sharper cycles, African *H. erectus* was showing some signs of change, as evidenced by a fossil skull from Eritrea dated to one million ybp, which has a higher cranium and a shorter, narrower face than the classic *erectus*.[50] The evolutionary events of the ensuing 500,000 years – roughly the transitional phase of the "100K World" – are

"East African Megadroughts between 135 and 75 Thousand Years Ago and Bearing on Early-Modern Human Origins," *PNAS* 104 (2007), 16416–21; Andrew S. Cohen, "Ecological Consequences of Early Late Pleistocene Megadroughts in Tropical Africa," *PNAS* 104 (2007), 16422–7; Martin H. Trauth et al., "East African Climate Change and Orbital Forcing during the Last 175 kyr BP," *EPSL* 206 (2003), 297–313. Given the secondary 400,000-year eccentricity cycle, the current "high-eccentricity" situation is relatively less extreme than the past three cycles.

[50] Ernesto Abbate, "A One-Million-Year-Old *Homo* Cranium from the Danakil (Afar) Depression of Eritrea," *Nature* 393 (1998), 458–9; the *erectus* described in Berhane Asfaw et al., "Remains of *Homo Erectus* from Bouri, Middle Awash, Ethiopia," *Nature* 416 (2002), 317–20 does not appear to show such signs of change.

currently under considerable debate because the next series of fossils comes from southern Europe – Italy and Spain – and date as early as 1.2MY. These fossils have been labeled *Homo antecessor* and some scholars argue that they represent the next step in the human lineage. This argument proposes a complex picture of fluctuating dispersals involving a speciation of *antecessor* in Southwest Asia, from where this species ebbed and flowed with the glacial cycles north into Europe and south into Africa. Because these earliest proto-human occupants of Europe did not carry with them the Acheulian handaxes, but only the Oldowan flake and chopper tradition, however, it is unlikely that they comprise a direct antecedent to modern humanity.[51]

The dominant position thus is that *antecessor* was an evolutionary dead end, rooted in an *erectus* dispersal from Africa during warm interglacials but driven to extinction by ensuing glaciations.[52] The fossil record in Africa in this period is sparse, but the general position is that around 850,000–800,000 years ago a new species did emerge, known as *Homo heidelbergensis*, or simply archaic *Homo sapiens*. Associated with a refined form of Acheulian technology, *heidelbergensis* had a significantly larger brain than *erectus*. These people also had regular control of fire by at least 800,000ybp, allowing them to maintain safer and more socially differentiated home bases. Ben Marwick has convincingly argued that *heidelbergensis* must have been speaking a proto-language of sorts, rather than the simple signing and signaling that the early hominins would have shared with chimpanzees and the Miocene apes. The evidence comes indirectly, from the geological signatures in stone artifacts found in various living sites. Artifacts from earlier sites came from nearby locations, which an individual could remember on his or her own within a local home range, and beyond which lay the dangerous territories of other groups. But after the rise of *heidelbergensis* stone was transported from as far as 200 kilometers away, suggesting that their acquisition might have been part of primitive boundary exchange rituals negotiated in an early form of grammatically complex language.[53]

[51] Edward Carbonell et al., "The First Hominin in Europe," *Nature* 452 465–9; Giorgio Manzi, "Human Evolution at the Matuyama-Brunhes Boundary," *Evolutionary Anthropology* 13 (2004), 11–24; J. M. Bermúdez de Castro, "The Atapuerca Sites and Their Contribution to the Knowledge of Human Evolution in Europe," *Evolutionary Anthropology* 13 (2004), 25–41; Robin Dennell, "Dispersal and Colonization, Long and Short Chronologies: How Continuous Is the Early Pleistocene Record for Hominids outside of East Africa," *JHumEv* 45 (2003), 421–40; G. Philip Rightmire, "'Human Evolution in the Middle Pleistocene': The Role of *Homo Heidelbergensis*," *Evolutionary Anthropology* 6 (1998), 218–27.

[52] Dennell, "Dispersal and Colonization"; Clive Finlayson, "Biogeography and Evolution of the Genus *Homo*," *Trends in Ecology and Evolution* 20 (2005), 457–63.

[53] Tattersall and Schwartz, "Evolution of the Genus *Homo*," 77–9; Collard, "Grades and Transitions in Human Evolution"; G. Philip Rightmire, "Brain Size and Encephalization in Early to Mid-Pleistocene *Homo*," *AJPA* 124 (2004), 109–23; Ben Marwick, "Pleistocene Exchange Networks as Evidence for the Evolution of Language," *CArchJ* 13 (2003), 67–81.

The transition to the "100K World" must have fundamentally shaped the emergence of both *antecessor* and *heidelbergensis*. Prior to the onset of the "100K World," we have spoken rather generally about changes in broad climatic and environmental regimes, but within the long and deep swings of the regime of the "100K World" – and with the fine-grained detail of the oxygen and CO_2 sequences from the ocean sediment and ice cores – we can be much more precise. Specifically, we can argue that during certain glacial cycles human populations were subjected to severe genetic bottlenecks, reducing their numbers and allowing for genes of particular "founders" to sweep through small, isolated populations. As conditions improved, these groups with newly evolved characteristics would multiply rapidly, expanding in numbers and across territory.[54] The emergence of *antecessor* and *heidelbergensis* is dated to between 1.2 million and 800,000 years ago, roughly between the first break with the 41K World and the Mid-Pleistocene Revolution, when the earth's climate settled into the strong 100K pattern. The entire period is marked by strong evidence for both extreme aridity and lake formation in East Africa, apparently the marker of the whiplash of precessional-insolation variability during a strong eccentricity period running from about 1.1MY to 850,000 years ago, followed by the first of the glacial shocks of the "100K World," 30,000 years of cold and glacial conditions between 900,000ybp and 870,000ybp (MIS 22).[55]

Marine oxygen isotope stages (MIS) are calculated from the ratios of oxygen isotopes 18 and 16 recovered in cores taken from ancient ocean sediments. Because it is lighter, O_{16} as it evaporates and freezes tends to be removed from the hydrological system of atmosphere and oceans and deposited in glacial ice. As ice sheets develop during a glaciation and O_{16} is progressively stripped from the oceans, plankton incorporate less O_{16} in their shells. Thus during glacial periods relatively less O_{16}, and more O_{18}, is deposited in ocean sediments. The result is that sediments deposited during glaciations are O_{18} enriched, and glacial sequences can be tracked by measuring very small shifts in the ratio of these two oxygen isotopes. Each of these oxygen isotope stages has been measured and numbered; generally, odd-numbered stages were warm interglacials and even-numbered stages were cold glacials. Measures of atmospheric CO_2 in polar ice running back 650,000 years mirror these stages in ocean sediments, providing further evidence that O_{16}/O_{18} ratios are a good measure of global temperature.

[54] This model had its roots in the Mayr-Gould-Eldridge allopatric-punctuation model. It has been very persuasively developed in the Pleistocene context in Marta Mirazón Lahr and Robert A. Foley, "Toward a Theory of Modern Human Origins: Geography, Demography, and Diversity in Recent Human Evolution," *YPA* 41 (1998), 137–76.

[55] Given the importance of environmental context in this account, I will be including the shorthand labels for the marine "Oxygen Isotope Stages" (oxygen isotope eighteen ratios from ocean sediments) at each important point.

We can suggest, therefore, that there would have been *very different* evolutionary consequences of these climate cycles in both East Africa and the regions to the north: North Africa and Eurasia. Strong high-eccentricity epochs drove extreme climate variability in East Africa but coincided with moderate interglacial times in the north; conversely, low eccentricity moderated East African climate change, while it drove continental glaciation in the north. Thus evolutionary pressures would intensify in the East African hearth during high-eccentricity/interglacial times, while the survivors of these bottlenecks would be drawn to the moderate northern climates. On the other hand, dispersed northern populations would be pushed south or destroyed by advancing glaciation, while low eccentricity stabilized climate in East Africa, allowing population expansion from isolated refuges. Thus interglacial times would have been periods of evolutionary stress in East Africa and species dispersion to the north; glacial times would have been times of the contraction of northern populations and the expansion of East African populations.

Here we can suggest some tentative interpretations of the northward dispersal of transitional post-*erectus* species. Perhaps the appearance of *antecessor* in southern Europe by 1.2MY was a manifestation of an early African evolutionary crisis (high eccentricity at 1.4–1.2MY) spreading into a northern frontier of the wider African bioregion not yet affected by serious glaciation. Acheulian artifacts and associated sites attributed to *heidelbergensis* on the Dead Sea in Israel are dated to 780,000 years ago, the interglacial MIS 19, and recent work has demonstrated that either *antecessor* or *heidelbergensis* had reached as far north as boreal forests in southern England during interglacial periods at either MIS 21 (866–814,000ybp) or MIS 25 (970–936,000ybp).[56] But such a northern occupation would have been intermittent, as these populations were driven to extinction or back toward southern refuges during the intensifying glacial periods of the 100K World. The Acheulian handaxe first appeared in India by 600,000ybp (interglacial MIS 15), and by 500,000ybp (interglacial MIS 13) was permanently established with *heidelbergensis* populations in southern Europe.[57]

Over the next 200,000 years it appears that we can speak of a gradual differentiation of a common proto-modern *heidelbergensis* world running from eastern Africa through southern Asia as far as India, and northwest

[56] Goren-Inbar, "Pleistocene Milestones"; Simon A. Parfitt et al., "Early Pleistocene Human Occupation at the Edges of the Boreal Zone in Northwest Europe," *Nature* 466 (2010), 229–33; –, "The Earliest Record of Human Activity in Northern Europe," *Nature* 438 (2005), 1008–12.

[57] Dennell, "Dispersal and Colonization"; Finlayson, "Biogeography and Evolution." Clive Gamble, in *Timewalkers: The Prehistory of Global Colonization* (Cambridge, MA, 1994), 135–6, suggests that the extinction of saber-toothed tigers in Europe allowed *heidelbergensis* (his term is *archaics*) back into Europe.

into Mediterranean Europe[58] (see Figure I.5). During warm, wet interglacial times – when the Sahara bloomed into a bountiful savannah and East Africa probably suffered extreme precessionary cycles of dry arid periods and wet monsoons – there would have been population expansions in the north, fed by bottleneck survivors from the south; during cold dry glacial times the deserts returned and residual northern populations would be cut off from an expanding East African hearth.[59] During this period, under the pressure of the glaciations, the European and west Asian heidelbergs gradually speciated into the cold-adapted *Homo neanderthalensis* around 500,000ybp.[60] But it was in Africa during the Saale glaciation, 280,000–240,000ybp (MIS 8), that the first evidence of a technological breakthrough appears, the first since the rise of the Acheulian almost a million and half years before. This key transition brings us to two great debates that have been raging in the past decade over the origins of modern humanity. Both of these debates have reached points of relative resolution, and in so doing have generated very useful stepping stones for thinking about human history in a rough world over the ensuing millennia.

* * *

Modern Humans in the 100K World

Together with the Neanderthals, modern humans comprised a final evolutionary pulse in the hominin line. This final transition is the subject of a series of heated debates among anthropologists. The most fundamental debate regards the time and place in which modern humans – *Homo sapiens* – first emerged. From the 1940s to the 1980s, a model of "multiregional evolution" prevailed in the explanation of modern human origins. In this understanding, there was only one dispersal from Africa, that of *Homo erectus* more than a million years ago, from which modern humans evolved in the different Old World regions. European archaeologists firmly believed

---

[58] Aurélien Mounier et al., "Is *Homo Heidelbergensis* a Distinct People? New Insight on the Mauer Mandible," *JHumEv* 56 (2009), 219–46.

[59] The idea of a Pleistocene geographic-climatological "pump" is developed in Brian M. Fagan, *The Journey from Eden: The Peopling of Our World* (London, 1990); William H. Calvin, *The Ascent of Mind: Ice Age Climates and the Evolution of Intelligence* (New York, 1991); and Philip Van Peer, "The Nile Corridor and the Out-of-Africa Model: An Examination of the Archaeological Record," *CA* 39 (1998), S115–40. I elaborate this theory based on the analysis of high-eccentricity megadroughts in Scholz et al., "East African Megadroughts"; Cohen et al., "Ecological Consequences."

[60] Richard E. Green et al., "Analysis of One Million Base Pairs of Neanderthal DNA," *Nature* 444 (2006), 330–6; James L. Bischoff et al., "The Sima de los Huesos Hominids Date to beyond U/Th Equilibrium (>350 kyr) and Perhaps to 400–500 kyr," *JArchS* 30 (2003), 275–80. For an older but useful overview of Neanderthal origins, see Campbell et al., *Humankind Emerging*, 365–9.

that the first such regional evolution occurred primarily in Europe, followed by others, with African modern emergence coming last. By the early 1980s, discoveries of transitional fossils in Africa, but not elsewhere, were bringing this Eurocentric model into question. Then, in 1987, a team of geneticists at Berkeley led by Rebecca Cann published the first sequencing of mitochondrial DNA, which indicated that all living women carry mtDNA that "coalesces" at a root origin roughly 200,000 years ago.[61] After almost two decades of controversy and intensive research, this date still stands, buttressed by an impressive array of work that has established the genetic outlines of an increasingly clear map of the origins of modern humans in Africa between 200,000ybp and 100,000ybp, and their spread around the world in a final, modern dispersal after 100,000ybp. The advocates of "multiregionalism" have retreated considerably, but evidence now suggests that there very well might have been a limited contribution of Eurasian Archaic genetics into the human modern genome.[62]

As this genetic debate moved toward resolution, a number of archaeologists began to critique the standing model of cultural and technological transformation. Since the 1920s, European archaeologists have argued that a great transformation occurred roughly 45,000 years ago in Europe, with the sudden emergence of a dramatic new array of artifacts – an explosion of new finely made tools, evidence for clothing, and symbolic art. This has been known as the "Upper Paleolithic Revolution," and has been the central evidence for radically new mental capacities that marked the beginnings of humanity as we know it. An influential school of thought has argued that this artifactual florescence must have been a product of the emergence of

---

[61] R. L. Cann et al., "Mitochondrial DNA and Human Evolution," *Nature* 325 (1987), 31–6.
[62] Among many discussions of this debate, see Michael C. Campbell and Sarah A Tishkoff, "The Evolution of Human Genetic and Phenotypic Variation in Africa," *Current Biology* 20 (2010), R166–R173; Michael DeGiorgio et al., "Explaining Worldwide Patterns of Human Genetic Variation Using a Coalescent-Based Serial Founder Model F Migration Outward from Africa," *PNAS* 106 (2009), 16057–62; Timothy D. Weaver and Charles C. Roseman, "New Developments in the Genetic Evidence for Modern Human Origins," *Evolutionary Anthropology* 17 (2008), 69–80; J. H. Relethford, "Genetic Evidence and the Modern Human Origins Debate," *Heredity* 100 (2008), 555–63; Paul Mellars, "The Impossible Coincidence: A Single-Species Model for the Origins of Modern Human Behavior in Europe," *Evolutionary Anthropology* 14 (2005), 12–27; Osbjorn M. Pearson, "Has the Combination of Genetic and Fossil Evidence Solved the Riddle of Modern Human Origins?" *Evolutionary Anthropology* 13 (2004), 145–59; Chris Stringer, "Modern Human Origins: Progress and Prospects," *PTRS,LB* 357 (2002), 563–79; John H. Relethford, *Genetics and the Search for Modern Human Origins* (New York, 2001); Shelley L. Smith and Francis B. Harrold, "A Paradigm's Worth of Difference? Understanding the Impasse over Modern Human Origins," *YPA* 40 (1997), 113–38; Gamble, *Another Unique Species*, 144–57. See also F. E. Grine, "Late Pleistocene Human Skull from Hofmeyr, South Africa, and Modern Human Origins," *Science* 315 (2007), 226–9. A genetic model has recently been applied to linguistics, and the results match the general "out of Africa" model: Quentin D. Atkinson, "Phonemic Diversity Supports a Series Founder Effect Model of Language Expansion from Africa," *Science* 332 (2011), 346–9.

modern language abilities. Under sustained attack, this understanding has been overturned in the past decade.[63]

This reassessment of modern human origins hinges on both new genetic information and a well-known artifact transition. The Oldowan and Acheulian traditions – the cobble tools and endlessly repeated handaxes of early *Homo* and *erectus* – are known in archaeological scholarship as the "Lower Paleolithic" or the "African Early Stone Age." It was during the Saale glaciation (MIS 8), after 280,000ybp, that the handaxes of the Lower Paleolithic Acheulian gave way to a "Middle Paleolithic," or "African Middle Stone Age." Here the basic processing of stone shifted fundamentally. The Oldowan and Acheulian had involved an essentially subtractive process. Stones were roughly or finely chipped away to produce a final object. The Middle Paleolithic revolved around the "Levallois" method: here a core of stone was prepared, and then flakes were struck from this core, becoming the basis of a final product. This was an entirely new thought process in the sequencing of manufacture. The result was a quantum leap in cutting edge per pound of stone, and the essential method would persist until stone tools were replaced by bronze and iron several thousand years ago.[64]

Terminology for these periods is different for different regions: the European Middle Paleolithic is comparable to the "Middle Stone Age" in Africa, and the Upper Paleolithic to the "Late Stone Age." A more universal terminology first proposed by archaeologist Grahame Clark in the 1970s has now been revived, dividing stone tool manufacture around the world into five "Modes," of which the Oldowan cobble choppers are Mode 1, the Acheulian is Mode 2, and the Levallois flake tools of the Middle Paleolithic/ Middle Stone Age are Mode 3.[65] As the genetic picture started to become clearer, and carefully excavated sites from southern and eastern Africa were published over the course of the 1990s, archaeologists began to see the new tools of Mode 3 developing after 280,000ybp as increasingly significant.

Among scholars fixated on the importance of the Upper Paleolithic transition at 45,000ybp, the new African evidence was startling. Barbed bone harpoons, tiny shell beads, and engraved stones, all evidence of art and body ornament, were emerging from sites in central and South Africa with dates running from 70,000ybp back to 95,000ybp, tens of thousands of years before their appearance in the European record. Evidence for the use of

[63] Richard G. Klein with Blake Edgar, *The Dawn of Human Culture* (New York, 2002); Ofer Bar-Yosef, "The Upper Paleolithic Revolution," *Annual Reviews in Anthropology* 31 (2002), 363–93.

[64] Grahame Clark, *World Prehistory: A New Perspective* (Cambridge, UK, 1977), 32–8; Sally McBrearty and Alison M. Brooks, "The Revolution that Wasn't: A New Interpretation of the Origin of Modern Human Behavior," *JHumEv* 39 (2000), 494–7; Robert Foley and Marta Mirazón Lahr, "On Stony Ground: Lithic Technology, Human Evolution, and the Emergence of Culture," *Evolutionary Anthropology* 12 (2003), 109–22.

[65] Clark, *World Prehistory*, 23–4; Foley and Lahr, "Mode 3 Technologies."

pigments, grindstones, and Levallois blades designed for making composite tools – all assumed to first appear in the European Upper Paleolithic – have been found in African sites dating back to at least 280,000ybp, the era of the MIS8 glaciation.[66] The result of this new work in genetics and archaeology has been to fundamentally restructure understandings of the origins of modern humanity. The European Upper Paleolithic is now downgraded in its importance; it is increasingly seen as an extremely well-studied sideshow to the main event, one moment of many in the wider dispersal of modern humans ranging out of Africa. Attention is now focused on the sequence of events unfolding in many parts of Africa between 300,000ybp and 45,000ybp.[67]

This sequence falls within a series of changes and expansions that – like those of *antecessor, heidelbergensis*, and Neanderthal – correspond quite strikingly with the sequence of glacials/interglacials–high/low-eccentricity periods between 330,000 and 70,000 years ago (MIS 9 to MIS 4), as the climate regime of the "100K World" grew increasingly extreme.

Two possible scenarios might explain the role of glaciations in the critical shift to Middle Stone Age technology around 280,000ybp, in MIS8. One model might suggest that, at the onset of the MIS8 glaciation, small, stressed populations of African *heidelbergensis* achieved a technological breakthrough.[68] But this assumes that glacial conditions were stressful in East Africa, when it appears that it was the interglacial megadroughts that were hyper-stressful. And such a glacial impact model also flies in the face of new thinking that argues that the spread of new technologies was driven by rising populations, not falling populations. When all of the evidence is in, I suspect that the records will show intensified drought conditions in East Africa during the high-eccentricity interglacials at 330,000–290,000ybp (MIS9) and 225,000–190,000ybp (MIS7) (see Figure I.5). In this perspective,

---

[66] Given the reality that small populations leave fewer artifacts and features in the record, they tend to be "archaeologically invisible." Thus it is entirely possible that Mode 3 artifacts actually were first developed before 280,000ybp, among small, bottleneck populations in the high-eccentricity period prior to the Saale MIS8 glacial period.

[67] The "African MSA" thesis has been set forth in detail in Foley and Lahr, "Mode 3 Technologies"; Lahr and Foley, "Toward a Theory of Modern Origins"; McBrearty and Brooks, "The Revolution that Wasn't"; Christopher Hensilwood and Curtis W. Marean, "The Origin of Modern Human Behavior: Critique of the Models and Their Test Implications," *CA* 44 (2003), 627–51; and the various essays in Lawrence Barham and Kate Robson-Brown, eds., *Human Roots: Africa and Asia in the Middle Pleistocene* (Bristol, 2001). The thesis was anticipated by J. Desmond Clark, in "The Middle Stone Age in East Africa and the Beginnings of Regional Identity," *JWP* 2 (1998), 235–305. See also Stringer, "Modern Human Origins: Progress and Prospects," 574–6. The Late Stone Age in East Africa is now dated to a minimum of 46,000ybp: Stanley H. Ambrose, "Chronology of the Late Stone Age and Food Production in East Africa," *JArchS* 25 (1998), 377–92.

[68] Foley and Lahr, "Mode 3 Technologies": Lahr and Foley, "Toward a Theory of Modern Origins"; McBrearty and Brooks, "The Revolution that Wasn't."

it would have been the expansion from a MIS9 bottleneck that marked the known emergence of the new stone tool technology in glacial MIS8 (~280,000ybp).

By current evidence, the ensuing MIS7 interglacial epoch between 240,000ybp and 190,000ybp was the decisive moment in the emergence of modern humans: anatomically modern *Homo sapiens* (AMH) seems to have emerged in this interval. The evidence on this critical transition has been radically changed by the redating of the anatomically modern fossils Omo-Kibish region of Ethiopia. Once thought to have been 130,000 years old, they are now dated to 195,000ybp. Another new set of fossils, from Herto in Ethiopia, have been dated to 155,000–160,000ybp.[69] Again, severe environmental fluctuations seem to have been at work. Between roughly 225,000ybp and 190,000ybp, the height of the MIS7 high-eccentricity period, with the most extreme swings in precession and insolation since 600,000ybp, there must have been a series of intense megadroughts in East Africa.[70] The dates of these Omo-Kibish fossils may reflect the expansion of post-drought populations after an intense population crash and bottleneck shaping a fundamental evolutionary emergence. The genetic evidence suggests a similar interpretation: key markers of the origins of the fixing of modern human genetic origins date from 200,000ybp and the millennia following. The approximate moment of an ancestral "mitochondrial Eve" has been established at roughly 200,000ybp. Various dates for an "Adam" – based on the male-descended Y-chromosome – tend to be somewhat younger: the oldest dates estimated are 147K +/-51K, 134K+/-45K, with outside ranges falling near the Eve date at around 195,000ybp and 180,000ybp.[71]

Modern skulls suggest modern capabilities to virtually all paleontologists. The skulls of *Homo sapiens* show a final stage in a process of enlarged cranial capacity, shortening and flattening the face and pulling it under an enlarged cranium that provided more room for a larger cerebral cortex. These were changes under way when the owner of the Omo 1 skull lived his life at 195,000ybp, and they clearly mark a fundamental transition to new mental capacities that allowed compartmentalized skills to be synthesized

[69] Tim White et al., "Pleistocene *Homo Sapiens* from Middle Awash, Ethiopia," *Nature* 423 (2003), 742–7 (Herto); Ian McDougall et al., "Stratigraphic Placement and Age of Modern Humans from Kibish, Ethiopia," *Nature* 433 (2005), 733–6 (Omo). For an overview, see Erik Trinkaus, "Early Modern Humans," *Annual Reviews in Anthropology* 34 (2005), 207–30.

[70] Megadroughts at 225,000–190,000ybp have not yet been directly demonstrated, but they have be found for the next (less severe) eccentricity period, 135,000–70,000ybp (specifically 135,000–130,000ybp and 118–90,000ybp). See Scholz et al., "East African Megadroughts"; Cohen et al., "Ecological Consequences."

[71] T. M. Karafet et al., "Ancestral Asian Source(s) of New World Y-Chromosome Founder Haplotypes," *American Journal of Genetics* 1999 (64), 817–31 (825); M. F. Hammer et al., "Out of Africa and Back Again: Nested Cladistic Analysis of Human Y Chromosome Variation," *Molecular Biology and Evolution* 15 (1998), 427–41 (434).

into an integrated intelligence. But apart from size and general shape, there is no consensus on how to read mental modernity from the inside surfaces of fossil skulls, and the debate over the origins of complex language proceeds with no end in sight. At the moment, some of the best evidence is circumstantial. Mark Collard argues that modern humans and Neanderthals comprised a final "grade" in the human lineage, distinguished from earlier species by their larger brains; a new analysis finds modern humans distinguished by a full enlargement of the parietal lobe, which governs complex integrative thought and behavior. What may have distinguished moderns from *erectus* and the archaics is a much slower rate of childhood development, as measured in growth patterns in fossil teeth. This delayed maturation is a time required to assimilate the complexities of language and culture; a shorter maturation would ready individuals for a shorter, less complex life. And Ben Marwick argues that the great distances from which modern humans acquired stone to produce artifacts, up to 400 kilometers, must have required complex systems of negotiation and exchange, and suggests that the leap from protolanguage to complex language occurred somewhere around 130,000ybp. Behind these increased capacities may lie what Thomas Wynn and Frederick Coolidge call "enhanced working memory," the ability to plot complex strategies through time and space based on remembered experience. Matt Rossano suggests that "enhanced working memory" and cognitive control would have been developed in the elaboration of repeated rituals binding parents and children and peer to peer.[72]

There is also the genetic evidence about language skills. In one set of inquiries, work is ongoing to isolate a "saltational" jump in the genetics of the organization of the brain, investigating how the asymmetries of left and right hemispheres are related to language – and to schizophrenia – which may have been launched by a shuffling of genes on the X and Y chromosomes.[73] In another promising line of work, geneticists have isolated the

[72] Daniel E. Lieberman et al., "The Evolution and Development of Cranial Form in *Homo Sapiens,*" *PNAS* 99 (2002), 1134–9; Philip Lieberman, "On the Nature and Evolution of the Neural Bases of Human Language," *YPA* 45 (2002), 36–62; Stephen Mithen, *Prehistory of the Mind: A Search for the Origins of Art, Religion and Science* (London, 1996); Collard, "Grades and Transitions in Human Evolution," 81–9; Emiliano Bruner, "Morphological Differences in the Parietal Lobes within the Human Genus," *CA* 51, Supplement 1 (2010), s77–s88; Christopher Dean et al., "Growth Processes in Teeth Distinguish Modern Humans from *Homo Erectus* and Earlier Hominins," *Nature* 414 (2001), 628–31; Marwick, "Pleistocene Exchange Networks"; Frederick L. Coolidge and Thomas Wynn, "Executive Functions of the Frontal Lobes and the Evolutionary Ascendency of *Homo* Sapiens," *CArchJ* 11 (2001), 255–60; Thomas Wyn and Frederick L. Coolidge, "Beyond Symbolism and Language: Introduction to Supplement 1, Working Memory," *CA* 51 Supplement 1 (2010), S5–S16; Matt J. Rossano, "How Our Ancestors Raised Children to Think as Modern Humans," *Biological Theory* 5 (2010), 142–53.

[73] Timothy J. Crow, "The 'Big Bang' Theory of the Origin of Psychosis and the Faculty of Language," *Schizophrenia Research* 102 (2008), 31–52; Timothy J. Crow, "Schizophrenia

uniquely human variants on the *FOXP2* gene, controlling human ability to speak in coherent and grammatical sentences. When might this mutation have occurred, and then swept through human populations? The first work posits that the fixing of the *FOXP2* variation is absolutely younger than 200,000 years old, and to have a 95 percent certainty of being younger than 120,000 years old. If so, *FOXP2* would be a trait unique to modern humans. Subsequent work found *FOXP2* in Neanderthal genetics, but the most recent analysis argues for critical distinctions between Neanderthal and modern human manifestations of the gene. This suggests that certain language capabilities were shared among the common "grade" of modern humans and Neanderthals as postulated by Mark Collard, and may have originated in a common African ancestor, but were decisively remodeled among modern humanity.[74]

At this point, we really have no idea when such critical final touches to the suite of key modern qualities could have been established in early modern human populations. But between 150,000ybp and 90,000ybp, a sequence of events seems to suggest that these new abilities were manifested in expanding modern human populations, spreading within and indeed beyond Africa. The evidence for this argument is developing rapidly, and will certainly change over the coming years.

Here a review of arguments about the spread of modern humans beyond Africa is in order. Since 1987, with the first evidence for strong African origins for modern humanity, there have been a series of competing models for exactly when, where, and how modern humans left Africa, all variously arguing that modern humans spreading out of Africa effectively replaced, or genetically "swamped" the Eurasian Heidelberg descendants of *H. erectus*. Complicating the issue, modern fossils discovered in the Levant were dated to as early 110,000ybp, but seem to have disappeared by 80,000ybp. A "multiple dispersal" model proposed in the early 1990s essentially argued for three modern "out of Africa" dispersals. First, a dispersal of Mode 3/ Middle Paleolithic moderns moved through the Sinai to the Levant around

as the Price that Homo Sapiens Pay for Language : A Resolution of the Central Paradox in the Origin of the Species," *Brain Research Review* 31(2000), 118–29; see also the essays by Crow and colleagues in Timothy J. Crow, ed., *The Speciation of Modern Homo Sapiens* (Oxford, 2002).

74 Wolfgang Enard et al., "Molecular Evolution of *FOXP2*, a Gene Involved in Speech and Language," *Nature* 418 (2002), 869–72; Jianshi Zhang et al., "Accelerated Protein Evolution and Origins of Human-Specific Features: *FOXP2* as an Example," *Genetics* 162 (2002), 1825–35; Johannes Kraus et al., "The Derived *FOXP2* Variant of Modern Humans was Shared with Neanderthals," *Current Biology* 17 (2007), 1908–12; Graham Coop et al., "The Timing of Selection at the Human *FOXP2* Gene," *MBE* 25 (2008), 1257–9; Tomislav Maricic et al., "A Recent Evolutionary Change Affects a Regulatory Element in the the *FOXP2* Gene," *MBE* 30 (2013), 844–52; Michael C. Corballis, "Mirror Neurons and the Evolution of Language," *Brain & Language* 112 (2010), 25–35; Michael C. Corballis, "The Evolution of Language," *Annals of the New York Academy of Sciences* 1156 (2009), 19–43.

110,000ybp, failed by 80,000ybp, and was followed by a second successful Mode 3/Middle Paleolithic dispersal around 60,000ybp, which crossed at the Horn of Africa into Arabia, and then followed a coastal route to South and Southeast Asia, eventually arriving in Australia by 45,000ybp. The third of these multiple dispersals carried Mode 4/Upper Paleolithic technology on a northern route up the Nile Valley to the Levant and into the Eurasia interior.[75]

Advancing studies of mitochondrial DNA and the Y chromosome complicated this scenario. First, it is now clear that there could not have been two dispersals because both the mtDNA and Y chromosome sequences indicate that all of modern humanity outside of Africa shares a single mtDNA lineage (L3) and Y chromosome mutation (M168) with northeast Africans. Such a pattern could only be the result of a single-point migration of a very small group.[76] Second, it appeared that modern humans had suffered severe population crashes – evolutionary bottlenecks – after splitting into small, genetically isolated populations, estimated by geneticists at sometimes between 100,000ybp and 70,000ybp. These bottlenecks at best estimate left 10,000 reproducing females in the entire human lineage. These small, isolated populations then grew and expanded after 50,000ybp. Scholars have argued that the cause of this bottleneck was the massive eruption of the Indonesia volcano Mt. Toba roughly 73,500ybp, blanketing South Asia with ashfall, having known impacts as far as the Arabia Sea and the South China Sea, and possibly setting off "volcanic winter" conditions globally for several years or decades.[77]

Thus the hunt for an exodus of moderns "out of Africa" has been narrowed to a single "episode," the timing of which is now a matter of great debate. If genetics imposed the constraint of a single exit, climate imposes

[75] Marta Mirazón Lahr and Robert Foley, "Multiple Dispersals and Modern Human Origins," *Evolutionary Anthropology* 3 (1994), 48–60.

[76] Peter Forster, "Ice Ages and the Mitochondrial DNA Chronology of Human Dispersals: A Review," *PTRS,LB* 359 (2004), 255–64; Vincent Macaulay et al., "Single, Rapid Coastal Settlement of Asia Revealed by Analysis of Complete Mitochondrial Genomes," *Science* 308 (2005), 1034–6; Kumarasamy Thangaraj, "Reconstructing the Origin of the Andaman Islanders," *Science* 308 (2005), 996.

[77] On Toba, see Martin A. J. Williams et al., "Environmental Impact of the 73 ka Toba Super-Eruption in South Asia," *PPP* 284 (2009), 295–314; Stanley H. Ambrose, "Late Pleistocene Human Population Bottlenecks, Volcanic Winter, and Differentiation of Modern Humans," *JHumEv* 34 (1998), 623–51; Michael R. Rampino and Stanley H. Ambrose, "Volcanic Winter in the Garden of Eden: The Toba Superexplosion and the Late Pleistocene Human Population Crash," in F. W. McCoy and G. Heiken, eds., *Volcanic Hazards and Disasters in Human Antiquity: GSA Special Paper 345* (Boulder, CO, 2000), 71–82. For critiques of the significance of the Toba eruption, see Clive Oppenheimer, "Limited Global Change to Largest Known Quaternary Eruption, Toba ~ 74kyr BP?" *QSR* 21 (2002), 1593–609; and the exchange among F. J. Gathorne-Hardy, W. E. H. Harcourt-Smith, and Stanley Ambrose, *JHumEv* 45 (2003), 227–37. See also Pearson, "Has the Combination," 146–7; and the citations in note 87.

another set of constraints. Interglacial periods with warmer northern conditions but highly erratic conditions in East Africa would draw populations north, but relatively high sea levels might block movement across the Red Sea. Hypothetically, transitional intervals of warming climate might be the best suited for such migrations, assuming that sea level rise lagged behind warmer temperatures. Such conditions might have pertained at around 60,000ybp, the beginning of the moderate warm-up of MIS3, and until recently the general favorite choice for a single modern human migration out of Africa.[78] But such conditions were much more obviously evident at the beginning of MIS5, the Eemian interglacial, at 135,000–116,000ybp. And it is here that the genetic trees – and well-dated archaeological evidence – are beginning to establish a new and integrated model for a pulse of modern human expansion.

The outlines of the division of Y-chromosome and mitochondrial DNA lineages tell the basic story of the eruption of modernity within and "out of Africa." The mtDNA sequence is longer, apparently because more men died without reproducing, truncating the Y chromosome history.[79] The possible "mtDNA Eve," or root of the branching tree of mtDNA, split into African branches Lo, L1, L2, and L3 between 140,000ybp and 80,000ybp, apparently reflecting the first surviving genetics of African divisions of the modern human lineage, at least as recorded in the genetic lineage of women, who inherit mtDNA intact from their mothers.[80] The currently estimated root of the Y chromosome tree – the "Y Adam" – is at 90,000ybp, with later splits at 82,000ybp and 68,500ybp. Again, the dates of these divisions in the Y lineage reflect the earliest known African genetic divisions. They also suggest that these divisions occurred during the demonstrated impacts of megadroughts in East Africa between 130,000ybp and 70,000ybp. These divisions apparently reflect the first diffusions of modern humans away from an East African hearth and toward the establishment of genetically isolated populations.[81]

---

[78] On MIS3, see Hetherington and Reid, *The Climate Connection*, 156, 168–9, 195–9, 223–6; on the 60,000ybp date, see discussion in Paul Mellars, "Going East: New Genetic and Archaeological Perspectives on the Modern Human Colonization of Eurasia," *Science* 313 (2006), 796–800.

[79] Spencer Wells, *The Journey of Man: A Genetic Odyssey* (Princeton, NJ, 2002), 178.

[80] See notes 62, 76, and 91; Elizabeth Watson et al., "Mitochondrial Footprints on Human Expansions in Africa," *AJHG* 61 (1997), 691–704; Antonio Salas et al., "The Making of the African mtDNA Landscape," *AJHG* 71 (2002), 1082–111; Dan Mishmar et al., "Natural Selection Shaped Regional mtDNA Variation in Humans," *PNAS* 100 (2003), 171–6.

[81] On Y chromosome patterning, see Peter A. Underhill et al., "Y Chromosome Sequence Variation and the History of Human Populations," *NatGen* 26 (2000), 358–60; Michael F. Hammer et al., "Hierarchical Patterns of Global Human Y-Chromosome Diversity," *MBE* 18 (2001), 1189–203; Peter A. Underhill et al., "The Phylogeography of Y Chromosome Binary Haplotypes and the Origins of Modern Human Populations," *Annals of Human Genetics* 65 (2001), 43–62; and Michael F. Hammer and Stephen L. Zegura, "The Human Y

These first modern dispersals seem to have moved in all directions from eastern Africa. (For context, see Figure I.6.) In southern Africa, modern human populations were producing shell beads and complex carving in a burst of advancing creativity by 77,000ybp.[82] But the more rapid movement may have been to the north and the northeast, because the first phase (MIS5e) of the very warm Eemian interglacial conditions around 135,000ybp drew Atlantic monsoons across the Sahara desert at the same time that a high-eccentricity "megadrought" completely dried out East Africa.[83] One of these earliest dispersals moved north via a recently discovered corridor of ancient rivers running through the Sahara in Libya, west of the Nile. An advanced Middle Stone Age tool tradition – the Aterian – found throughout this Sahara corridor and along the North African coast has been dated to as early as 110,000ybp.[84] To the east, shell mounds on the Red Sea shores of Eritrea mark a Middle Stone Age coastal adaptation dated to 125,000ybp. From roughly here another parallel movement of modern humans carried a related tool tradition across the Red Sea from the Horn of Africa into southern Arabia by the early Eemian. A site on the Persian Gulf has reported Mode 3/Middle Stone Age stone tools with African affinities to 127,000ybp and 123,000ybp, and a series of sites in Oman report a very well-defined cluster of MSA tools that have affinities to stonework common at the same time in the Nile Valley. The first fossils of modern humans in the Levant

Chromosome Haplogroup Tree: Nomenclature and Phylogeography of Its Major Divisions," *ARA* 31 (2002), 303–21 (314); Mark A. Jobling and Chris Tyler-Smith, "The Human Y Chromosome: An Evolutionary Marker Comes of Age," *NatGen* 4 (2003), 598–610; Peter A. Underhill and Toomas Kivisilk, "Use of Y Chromosome and Mitochondrial DNA Population Structure in Tracing Human Migrations," *Annual Review of Genetics* 41 (2007), 539–64.

[82] Francesco D'Errico et al., "*Nassarius Kraussianus* Shell Beads from Blombos Cave: Evidence for Symbolic Behavior in the Middle Stone Age," *JHumEv* 48 (2005), 3–24; Lawrence S. Barham, "Backed Tools in Middle Pleistocene Central Africa and Their Evolutionary Significance," *JHumEv* 43 (2002), 585–603; "Systematic Pigment Use in the Middle Pleistocene of South-Central Africa," *CA* 43 (2002), 181–90; John E. Yellen, "Barbed Bone Points: Tradition and Continuity in Saharan and Sub-Saharan Africa," *African Archaeological Review* 15 (1998), 173–98; McBrearty and Brooks, "The Revolution that Wasn't," 497–500, 530.

[83] On MIS5e, see Hetherington and Reid, *The Climate Connection*, 156, 160–1, 177–81, 213–14; and the somewhat conflicting positions in Scholz et al., "East African Megadroughts"; Cohen et al., "Ecological Consequences."

[84] R. N. E. Barton et al., "OSL Dating of the Aterian Levels at Dar es-Soltan I (Rabat, Morocco) and Implications for the Dispersal of Modern *Homo Sapiens*," *QSR* 28 (2009), 1914–31; Isla S. Castaneda et al., "Wet Phases in the Sahara/Sahel Region and Human Migration Patterns in North Africa," *PNAS* 106 (2009), 20159–63; Anne H. Osborne et al., "A Humid Corridor across the Sahara for the Migration of Early Modern Humans out of Africa 120,000 Years Ago," *PNAS* 105 (2008), 16444–7; Abdeljalil Bouzouggar, "82,000-Year-Old Shell Beads from North Africa and Implications for the Origins of Modern Human Behavior," *PNAS* 104 (2007), 9964–9; Elena A. A. Garcea, "Crossing Deserts and Avoiding Seas: Aterian North African-European Relations," *JAnthRes* 60 (2004), 27–53.

date between 110,000ybp and 90,000ybp. Hypothetically, modern humans would have ventured across a low-water Red Sea by the end of MIS6, roughly 135,000ybp, and then spread across Arabia as far as the Levant during the ensuing warm and humid Eemian, when the Indian Ocean monsoon would have brought precipitation far into the Arabian desert.[85]

Some of these first modern humans dispersing within and beyond Africa were not that successful, however. Modern humans in the Levant faded in the face of the advancing MIS4 glaciation by 80,000ybp, and the Aterian disappeared from a desiccating Sahara by 60,000ybp, as did the florescence of advanced Middle Stone Age cultures in southern Africa. The combination of the extreme dry conditions associated with the cold of the MIS4 glaciation, perhaps in combination with the enormous volcanic explosion of Mt. Toba in 73,500ybp, severely reduced biological net primary productivity, with a severe impact on the fortunes of modern humans.[86] On the other hand, new evidence suggests that Middle Stone Age peoples were in southern India before the Toba eruption, and survived the eruption with little cultural disruption.[87]

India might have comprised one of two oases for African-derived populations, possibly intermixing to a small degree with Asian archaic peoples. One camp sees South Asia, with its vast landmass and diverse ecosystems, as a refuge for modern human populations that had left east Africa around 130,000ybp, and which had died out in the desiccated regions of the Levant, Arabia, and the Persian-Baluchi coasts. From this as yet-hypothetical Indian refuge, modern populations spread south toward Southeast Asia, reaching Australia at some point between 63,000ybp and 45,000ybp. These southern populations comprised one of two parallel groupings that mark a great

[85] Robert C. Walter et al., "Early Human Occupation of the Red Sea Coast of Eritrea during the Last Interglacial," *Nature* 405 (2000), 65–9. The early dates in the United Arab Emirates are reported in Simon J. Armitage et al., "The Southern Route 'Out of Africa': Evidence for an Early Expansion of Modern Human into Arabia," *Science* 331 (2011), 453–6; the Oman-Nile Valley connection is reported in Jeffrey I. Rose et al., "The Nubian Complex of Dhofar, Oman: An African Middle Stone Age Industry in Southern Arabia," *Plos ONE* 6 (2011), 28239; see also Jeffrey I. Rose, "The Question of Upper Pleistocene Connections between East Africa and South Arabia," *CA* 45 (2004), 551–5. On the Levant, see Ofer Bar-Yosef, "The Role of Western Asia in Modern Human Origins," *PTRS,LB* 337 (1992), 193–200; Trenton W. Holliday, "Evolution at the Crossroads: Modern Human Emergence in Western Asia," *AmAnth* 102 (2000), 54–68. Acheulian tools recently recovered in Crete and dating to 130,000ybp might be related to this modern pulse, or could reflect movement of Neanderthals. In either event, it is evidence of early open-water transit: Thomas F. Strasser et al., "Stone Age Seafaring in the Mediterranean: Evidence from the Plakias Region for Lower Palaeolithic and Mesolithic Habitation of Crete," *Hesperia* 79 (2010), 145–90.

[86] Hetherington and Reid, *The Climate Connection*, 223–6.

[87] Michael Petraglia, "Middle Paleolithic Assemblages from the Indian Subcontinent before and after the Toba Super-Eruption, *Science* 317 (2007), 114–16; Michael Haslam et al., "The 74 ka Toba Super-Eruption and Southern Indian Hominins: Archaeology, Lithic Technology, and Environments at Jwalapuram Locality 3," *JArchS* 37 (2010), 3370–84.

division among non-African peoples, dividing those of Oceania, running from the Andaman Islands to Australia, and the peoples of all of Eurasia and the Americas. This second stream of genes and people is conjectured to have moved back from India to the Persian Gulf region and from there north (and west back into North Africa) around 45,000ybp into the tundra lands, splitting into a host of genetic branches that mark the peoples of Eurasia and the Americas.[88] By then these peoples had developed their own versions of the advanced "Mode 4" microlithic blade technologies that had appeared sporadically in Africa since 90,000ybp.

Another camp posits a different Asian refuge for modern humans. During glacial periods, the Persian Gulf would have turned into a broad valley fed by rivers and springs, a "Gulf Oasis" for bands of human descended from the first Out of Africa migrants as well as Eurasian Neanderthals. If so, the surviving archaeological record preserves evidence of interglacial occupation of regions that dried out during the glaciations, while the great body of glacial period evidence lies under the Gulf. In this model, the Gulf Oasis would have provided the source for a series of pulses of population across the southern route to Australia, north into Eurasia, and back into Africa.[89]

The archaeological evidence for modern humans in Arabia and southern India before 70,000ybp is extremely new and controversial, in great measure because no actual modern human fossil bones have been found yet in association with these artifacts. Arguments for their being made by modern humans are based on their typological properties. There is also the issue of the dating of the genetics. The mtDNA L3 marker dates to 84,000ybp, and the Mode 3 tools on the Persian Gulf date from 127,000ybp at the earliest. Generally, however, there is increasing suspicion of the coalescence dates

---

[88] This South Asian synthesis has been sketched in Michael D. Petraglia et al., "Out of Africa: New Hypotheses and Evidence for the Dispersal of *Homo Sapiens* along the Indian Ocean Rim," *Annals of Human Biology* 37 (2010), 288–311; Stephen Oppenheimer, "The Great Arc of Dispersal of Modern Human: Africa to Australia," *QuatInt* 202 (2009), 2–13; Julia S. Field et al., "The Southern Dispersal Hypothesis and the South Asia Archaeological Record: Examinations of Dispersal Routes through GIS Analysis," *JAnthArch* 26 (2007), 88–108; Ted Goebel, "The Missing Years for Modern Humans," *Science* 315 (2007), 194–6; Hannah V. A. James and Michael D. Petraglia, "Modern Human Origins and the Evolution of Behavior in the Later Pleistocene Record of South Asia," *CA* 46 (2005), S3–S27; Phillip Endicott et al., "Genetic Evidence on Modern Human Dispersals in South Asia: Y Chromosome and Mitochondrial DNA Perspectives: The World through the Eye of Two Haploid Genomes," in Michael D. Petraglia and Bridget Allchin, eds., *The Evolution and History of Human Populations in South Asia* (Dordrecht, 2007), 229–44.

[89] Jeffrey I. Rose, "New Light on Human Prehistory in the Arabo-Persian Gulf Oasis," *CA* 51 (2010), 849–83; Amanuel Beyin, "Upper Pliestocene Human Dispersal out of Africa," A Review of the Current State of the Debate," *International Journal of Evolutionary Biology* (2011), 615–94; M. V. Anikovich et al., "Early Upper Paleolithic in Eastern Europe and Implications for the Dispersal of Modern Humans," *Science* 317 (2007), 223–5; Anna Olivieri et al., "The mtDNA Legacy of the Levantine Early Upper Paleolithic in Africa," *Science* 314 (2006), 1767–70.

in genetic analysis, and its contribution is increasingly seen as establishing relationships among populations, rather than firm chronologies.[90] Thus the new single out-of-Africa dispersal to Arabia and India will be tested and challenged in the years to come.

Accounts of out-of-Africa expansions conjure up intrepid modern bands trekking vast distances across barren, empty wastelands. But a goodly portion of the Old World had been occupied – if thinly – by proto-humans, Heidelbergs, Neanderthals, and even perhaps distant descendants of *Homo erectus*. What happened when these proto-humans encountered moderns spreading out of Africa? What exactly expanded: people or genes? Did modern Africans physically move, or did their genes "move"? This question has been the subject of a great struggle among paleo-geneticists for the past decade, and a huge amount of work now suggests that, while the mtDNA and Y lineages reflect the expansion of modern characteristics out of Africa, the bearers of those genes may have mixed and hybridized with local premodern peoples, descendants of the *antecessor/heidelbergensis*, Neanderthals, and even possibly the isolated East Asian *erectus* populations occupying southern Eurasia at the time of the modern dispersal. It would appear that there may well have been some modern/premodern genetic assimilation as the transition to full global human modernity occurred.[91] What remains to be determined is how much of this premodern genetic material survived in the populations that in the late Pleistocene were filling up the world, and that comprise the basic genetic background to contemporary humanity. If the recently completed preliminary sequencing of the Neanderthal genome is any indication, this archaic assimilation was minimal: the estimate is that Neanderthals might have contributed 1 percent to 4 percent of the European

[90] For a discussion, see Phillip Endicott et al., "Evaluating the Mitochondrial Timescale of Human Evolution," *Cell: Trends in Ecology and Evolution* 24 (2009), 515–21.

[91] On the assimilation thesis, see note 62, and, among many others, Fred H. Smith et al., "Modern Human Origins," *YPA* 32 (1989), 35–68; Rosalind M. Harding, "Archaic African and Asian Lineages in the Genetic Ancestry of Modern Human," *AJHG* 60 (1997), 770–89; John Hawks et al., "Population Bottlenecks and Pleistocene Human Evolution," *MBE* 17 (2000), 2–22; Milford H. Wolpoff, "Modern Human Ancestry at the Peripheries: A Test of the Replacement Theory," *Science* 291 (2001), 293–7. Alan Templeton, "Out of Africa Again and Again," *Nature* 416 (2002), 45–51; Rosalind M. Harding and Gil McVean, "A Structured Ancestral Population for the Evolution of Modern Humans," *Current Opinion in Genetics & Development* 14 (2004) 667–74; Michael F. Hammer et al., "Heterogeneous Patterns of Variation among Multiple Human X-Linked Loci: The Possible Role of Diversity-Reducing Selection in Non-Africans," *Genetics* 167 (2004), 1841–53; Vinayak Eswaran et al., "Genomics Refutes an Exclusively African Origin of Humans," *JHumEv* 49 (2005), 1–18. For critiques, see Günter Bräuer et al., "On the Reliability of Recent Tests…," *The Anatomical Record Part A* 279A (2004), 701–7; Andrea Manica et al., "The Effect of Ancient Population Bottlenecks on Human Phenotypic Variation," *Nature* 448 (2007), 346–8 Guillaume Laval et al., "Formulating a Historical and Demographic Model of Recent Human Evolution Based on Resequencing Data from Noncoding Regions, *Plos ONE* 5 (2010), e10284.

genome. If so, this study indicates that this connection was made very early in the non-African modern human experience, somewhere in the Middle East or South Asia before the Oceania-Eurasian divergence, because all non-Africans bear marks of this Neanderthal relationship.[92]

Another recently established connection opens the door, however, to the assimilation of even further bits and scraps of archaic DNA. The genetics of a finger bone from a cave in Siberia suggests that a distinct archaic people now called the Denisovans may have occupied much of East Asia, apparently a parallel group to the western Eurasian Neanderthals, diverging perhaps 600,000 years ago. As much as 7 percent of the Melenasian genome, carried by the peoples of Papau and Bougainville in southeast Asia, may be derived from this Denisovan background. Such a connection would have happened tens of thousands of years ago somewhere in the complexities of a circulation of peoples in Asia that is now only being glimpsed. Further genetic studies are indicting that some of these small contributions of archaic human genetics to the modern genome involve the immune system, providing valuable protections against pathogens in Eurasia.[93] Certainly, then, modern humans carry tiny inheritances from the thinly scattered premodern archaic populations of Eurasia. But by far the most significant genetic human inheritance is shared with modern Africans, transferred in a single migration across the Red Sea – perhaps in the great Eemian warm-up 135,000 years ago.

* * *

[92] Richard E. Green et al., "A Draft Sequence of the Neanderthal Genome," *Science* 328 (2010), 710–22. See also David Caramelli et al., "28,000 Years Old Cro-Magnon mtDNA Sequence Differs from All Potentially Contaminating Modern Sequences," *Plos ONE* 7 (2008), e2700. The most recent estimate is that Neanderthals did not survive later than 239,000ybp: Ron Pinhasi et al., "Revised Age of Late Neanderthal Occupation and the End of the Middle Paleolithic in the Northern Caucasus," doi: 10.1073/pnas.1018938108 *PNAS* May 9, 2011. Two genetic studies reject a local *erectus* source of modern humans in East Asia: J. Y. Chu, "Genetic Relationships of Populations in China," *PNAS* 95 (1998), 11763–8; and Yuehai Ke et al., "African Origin of Modern Humans in East Asia: A Tale of 12,000 Y Chromosomes," *Science* 292 (2001), 1151–3. An indirect line of evidence from the genetics of lice suggests at least "social" contact between modern and ancient populations: David L. Reed et al., "Genetic Analysis of Lice Supports Direct Contact between Modern and Archaic Humans," *PLoS Biology* 2 (2004), e340.

[93] David Reich, "Genetic History of an Archaic Hominin Group from Denisova Cave in Siberia," *Nature* 468 (2010), 1053–60; Laurent Abi-Rached et al., "The Shaping of Modern Human Immune Systems by Multiregional Admixture with Archaic Humans," *Science* 334 (2011), 89–94. See also Wu Liu et al., "Human Remains from Zhirendong, South China, and Modern Human Emergence in East Asia," *PNAS* 107 (2010), 19201–6. The Denisovans carried a FOXP2 language gene similar to that of the Neanderthals. See Reich and Maricic et al., "A Recent Evolutionary Change."

The Modern Origins Debate and a Renewed
Understanding of Mortality

Such is the emerging resolution of the struggle between two polarized interpretations for the origins of modern humans – the Multiregional hypothesis,
positing multiple descents from scattered populations derived from *Homo
erectus*, and the Recent African Origins hypothesis. If this debate is being
settled on terms strongly favoring the Recent African Origins position, it is
worth working through one of Multiregionalists' key contributions, as it
bears on questions about humanity's rough journey that will be the central
focus of the rest of this book.

Very simply, as humanity became human over the last sections of the
Pleistocene, something new entered the equation. The Court Jester, if not
tamed, had met a worthy adversary, and Gouldian punctuation would take
on a new meaning for this new species. Armed with culture and technology, modern humans were able to push back against nature. Where nature
had driven the relationship, now culture was beginning to level the playing
field; a few thousand years later, in an instant of geological time, culture
would begin to get the upper hand. But there is one thing upon which the
two sides of the origins debate are in agreement: *prior to modernity*, isolated human societies were subject to utter extinction on a regular basis,
and – ironically – such extinctions were part of the natural process of
evolution.

In the early 1990s, as evidence for the Recent African Origins position
was beginning to take shape, a series of seminal papers established some
basic genetic parameters for modern origins. First, the *effective population* of reproductive women involved in the speciation event was extremely
small, no more than 10,000 individuals. Second, genetic loci indicated that
all human populations had experienced an evolutionary bottleneck early
in their history, followed by expansions. And third, when populations did
expand, African populations led the way, and were much larger than non-
African populations for some time after the modern dispersal into Eurasia
and points beyond.[94] Of these three points, the small "effective population
size" was the most damaging to the interests of the multiregional evolution model. In this "multiregional" interpretation, modern humans evolved
separately out of *Homo erectus* in Africa, Europe, and Asia over millions
of years, but maintained their commonality as a reproductive species by a

---

[94] Henry C. Harpending et al., "The Genetic Structure of Ancient Human Populations," *CA* 34
(1993), 483–96; Stephen T. Sherry et al., "Mismatch Distributions of mtDNA Reveal Recent
Human Populations Expansions," *Human Biology* 66 (1994), 761–75; Alan R. Rogers and
Lynn B. Jorde, "Genetic Evidence on Modern Human Origins," *Human Biology* 67 (1995),
1–36; Henry C. Harpending et al., "Genetic Traces of Ancient Demography," *PNAS* 95
(1998), 1961–7.

Brownian motion of gene flow between distant populations. An effective reproducing population size of 10,000 was simply far too few to allow for this gene flow, and the multiregional concept was in deep trouble.[95]

In defending their embattled argument, the multiregional advocates arrived at two important ideas. One is the hybridization account summarized earlier in this chapter, presented as a "wave of diffusion." Here is it is genes that move, more than people. Thus genetic modernity emerged in Africa, as suggested by the mtDNA and Y chromosome lineages, and rolled across the Old World in a genetic wave, in which local populations were transformed in a "wavefront" where modern and premodern genes were mixed into new combinations.[96] In this thesis, the observed genetic bottleneck occurred on the wavefront itself, and not in the founding population. Critics are willing to concede a certain small degree of hybridization, but the idea of the founding bottleneck has not yet been abandoned.[97]

The other idea addressed the problem of effective population size, and provides a useful opening onto the rest of human demographic history. In the midst of the 1990s, anthropologist John Relethford reconsidered an old argument about effective population sizes, developed by geneticist Sewell Wright in the 1940s. In brief, a small effective population size – as detected in genetic history – need not reflect a small *census size*, and thus a small occupied territory. Rather, the total census population – or *metapopulation* – might be much larger than the effective reproducing population (effective in the sense of leaving a genetic heritage at a later time) because of continuous small-scale population extinctions and recolonizations. Thus Relethford resurrected Wright, a venture carried on at length by his student Elise Eller, and conjured the traditional grim picture of the Pleistocene, when life was nasty, brutish, short, and subject to the entire obliteration of local populations. If the bands of hunter-gatherers in a territory were driven to extinction by climate extremes or volcanic eruptions at "time A," their territories would be recolonized by expanding adjacent groups at "times

---

[95] Relethford, Genetics and the Search for Modern Human Origins, 168–71.

[96] Vinayak Eswaran, "A Diffusion Wave out of Africa: The Mechanism of the Modern Human Revolution?" *CA* 43 (2002), 749–64; Eswaran et al., "Genomics Refutes an Exclusively African Origin of Humans."

[97] Dissenting views would include Foster, "Ice Ages and the Mitochondrial DNA Chronology"; Pearson, "Has the Combination"; Gabor T. Marth et al., "The Allele Frequency Spectrum in Genome-Wide Human Variation Data Reveals Signals of Differential Demographic History in Three Large World Populations," *Genetics* 166 (2004), 351–72; Lev A. Zhivotovsky et al., "Features of Evolution and Expansion of Modern Humans, Inferred from Genomewide Microsatellite Markers," *AJHG* 72 (2003), 1171–86; Laurent Excoffier, "Human Demographic History: Refining the Recent African Origin model," *Current Opinion in Genomics and Development* 12 (2002), 675–82; "Reconstructing the Demography of Prehistoric Human Populations from Molecular Data," *Evolutionary Anthropology* 11/S1 (2002), 166–70.

C or D," reestablishing contact across a gap, and maintaining gene flow. The multiregional evolution model was thus a possibility.[98]

Perhaps. The sum of the genetic evidence would suggest that the contribution of the regions was not an equal one, and that the advantageous modern African genes rolled over and literally buried the premodern Eurasian genes. The extinction and recolonization model has been somewhat arbitrarily applied, and fails to account for the barriers of distance and geography that separated elements of the Pleistocene proto-human metapopulation.[99]

But the general framework of extinction and recolonization is extremely helpful in conceptualizing the gradually changing circumstances of humanity during the Pliocene and the Pleistocene, circumstances that involve the well-being of human populations as technology began to contain the ravings of the environmental Court Jester. During the 1960s and 1970s, the school of cultural ecology argued persuasively that human populations during the ice ages were very small and very stable, and these low Paleolithic populations were attributed to a careful regulation of fertility by hunter-gatherers working to maintain a balanced relationship with a region's carrying capacity. These were – according to this long-established model – populations distinguished by both *low fertility and low mortality*.[100] Attuned to the environment and carefully controlling their numbers, cultural ecologists argued, Paleolithic peoples lived in an idyllic "original affluent society."[101]

Routine health of Paleolithic peoples does seem to have been reasonably good; adults grew to considerable stature compared to their agricultural Neolithic and Bronze Age descendants.[102] Certainly populations did

[98] Elise Eller, "Estimating Relative Population Sizes from Simulated Data Sets and the Question of Greater African Effective Size," *AJPA* 116 (2001), 1–12; Elise Eller, "Population Extinction and Recolonization in Human Demographic History," *Mathematical Biosciences* 177 and 178 (2002), 1–10; Elise Eller et al., "Local Extinction and Recolonization, Species Effective Population Size, and Modern Human Origins," *Human Biology* 76 (2004), 689–709; John Wakeley, "Metapopulation Models for Historical Inference," *Molecular Biology* 13 (2004), 865–75; Relethford, *Genetics and the Search for Modern Human Origins*, 171–7; Harding and McVean, "A Structured Ancestral Population." Albert Tenesa et al., "Recent Human Effective Population Size Estimated from Linkage Disequilibrium," *Genomic Research* 17 (2007), 520–6, come up with very small effective populations sizes of 2,500 to 3,000. For an earlier discussion of the importance of extinctions, see N. Takahata, "A Genetic Perspective on the Origins and History of Humans," *Annual Review Ecol. Syst.* 26 (1995), 343–72.
[99] Pearson, "Has the Combination," 147.
[100] The classic statements for population regulation in the Paleolithic were presented in the essays in Richard B. Lee and Irven Devore, eds., *Man the Hunter* (Chicago, IL, 1968); in Don E. Dumond, "The Limitation of Human Population: A Natural History," *Science* 187 (1975), 713–21; Fekri A. Hassan, *Demographic Archaeology* (New York, 1981); and Marvin Harris, *Cannibals and Kings* (New York, 1977), 11–25.
[101] Marshall Sahlins, *Stone Age Economics* (New York, 1972).
[102] Mark Nathan Cohen and George J. Armalegos, *Paleopathology at the Origins of Agriculture* (New York, 1984); Richard Steckel and Jerome C. Rose, eds., *The Backbone of History: Health and Nutrition in the Western Hemisphere* (New York, 2002). See Chapter 5 and Figure II.6.

indeed grow when people settled into villages in the warm Holocene, and
then developed agriculture, and in aggregate Paleolithic populations did not
grow significantly by comparison with what was going to come. But the
cultural ecologists' assumptions about population regulation among hunter-
gatherers and Paleolithic peoples have been challenged and rejected in the
face of new work. Studies are showing that modern hunter-gatherers can
increase their numbers quite dramatically, leading demographer Charles
Keckler to ask of the Paleolithic, "where did all the people go?" By his estimate, Paleolithic growth rates were between three and seven times *lower*
than observable modern populations of hunter-gatherers, such as the !Kung
Bushmen. Given the probable trajectories of population growth over long
periods of time, there should have been far more humans alive at the end
of the ice ages; by one estimate, given the !Kung growth rate (.7 percent),
a population of 10,000 would reach 6 billion within 1,900 years! Keckler
and others have been arguing quite effectively that Paleolithic peoples were
not restricting their fertility all that much, but that episodes of *crisis mortality* were the fundamental force at work limiting their numbers to a virtually stable population over many millennia. Recent genetic analysis suggests
that Upper Paleolithic annual growth rates were microscopic, somewhere
between .007 percent and .02 percent.[103]

Crisis mortality in Paleolithic societies probably was driven by two forces
erupting out of nature. The first is infectious disease spreading from contact
with the natural environment: an infection picked up skinning an animal

---

[103] Charles N. W. Keckler, "Catastrophic Mortality in Simulations of Forager Age-at-Death:
Where did all the Humans Go?" in Richard R. Paine, ed., *Archaeological Demography:
Multidisciplinary Approaches to Prehistoric Population* (Carbondale, 1997), 205–28; Kim
R. Hill and A. Magdelena Hurtado, *Ache Life History: The Ecology and Demography of
a Foraging People* (New York, 1996); Gary Warrick, *A Population History of the Huron-
Petun, A.D. 500–1650* (New York, 2008), 46–51. For the recent genetic estimates of popu-
lation growth, see Christopher R. Gignoux et al., "Rapid, Global Demographic Expansions
after the Origins of Agriculture," *PNAS* 108 (2011), 6044–9. For critiques of the population
regulation model and further arguments regarding the role of crisis mortality in limiting
Paleolithic numbers, see Albert J. Ammerman, "Late Pleistocene Population Dynamics: An
Alternative View," *HumEcol* 3 (1975), 219–33; W. Penn Handwerker, "The First Demographic
Transition: An Analysis of Subsistence Choices and Reproductive Consequences," *AmAnth*
85 (1983), 5–27; Lahr and Foley, "Toward a Theory of Modern Human Origins"; James
W. Wood, "A Theory of Preindustrial Population Dynamics: Demography, Economy, and
Well-Being in Malthusian Systems," *CA* 39 (1998), 121; Richard R. Paine, "If a Population
Crashes in Prehistory, and There is no Paleodemographer There to Hear It, Does It Make
a Sound?" *AJPA* 112 (2000), 181–90; Steven Shennan, "Population, Culture, and the
Dynamics of Culture Change," *CA* 41 (2000), 811–35; Stephen Shennan, *Genes, Memes,
and Human History: Darwinian Archaeology and Cultural Evolution* (London, 2002),
100–23; James L. Boone, "Subsistence Strategies and Early Human Population History: An
Evolutionary Ecological Perspective," *WdArch* 34 (2002), 6–25 (21), and John C. Caldwell
and Bruce K. Caldwell, "Pretransition Population Control and Equilibrium," *PopSt* 57
(2003), 199–215.

would have flashed through a band with often terminal results; the African savannahs may have been infested with tsetse flies carrying trypanosomiasis, the vector for sleeping sickness.[104] But the cause of variable crisis mortality in the Paleolithic must have been rooted in the extreme instability in climate. Rather than carefully restricting their fertility, Paleolithic peoples lived with the constant threat of extinction hanging over their heads, and the occasional opportunity of recolonization, expanding, and contracting with the ebb and flow of environmental conditions. During the northern glaciations or African megadroughts, some of these populations would have been devastated, with both children and adults dying at high rates, and significant local pockets would have been completely wiped out, to the degree that during these periods Paleolithic peoples were so few in number as to be virtually "archaeologically invisible," because so few sites for many of these periods have been found. During the stability of glacial periods in East Africa, or the warm northern interglacials, populations expanded dramatically with the higher carrying capacity – and became "archaeologically visible."[105] Extrapolating from the way contemporary human populations adjust to food shortages by achieving adulthood with smaller bodies, Massimo Livi-Baci, a European historical demographer, has suggested that the human populations adjusted to the constant battle with shifting climates and erratic subsistence regimes throughout the Pleistocene, not only through changing numbers of survivors, but through the changing physical size of survivors: they would have been shorter in stature and have weighed less. Thus the human capacity to survive scarcity – if at a smaller "phenotypical size" – to produce the next generation may have been part of the wider Pleistocene oscillation of which extinction and recolonization was the extreme manifestation.[106]

If the full-scale transitions between glaciations and interglacials were the sole sources of climate variability, then it is certainly possible that Paleolithic peoples might have been able to move with climate variation, especially given the typically long, slow onset of glaciations, as the earth moved into a 100K glacial period. But glacials on the scale of oxygen isotope stages were not the entire story. For the sake of simplicity I have set aside discussion of much smaller-scale variations, set within both glacials and interglacials. In

---

[104] Dorothy H. Crawford, *Deadly Companions: How Microbes Shaped Our History* (Oxford, 2007), 46–53.

[105] On the demographics of "archaeological visibility" in the African Middle Stone Age, see H. J. Deacon and J. F. Thackery, "Late Pleistocene Environmental Changes and Implications for the Archaeological Record in Southern Africa," in J. C. Vogel, ed., *Late Cainozoic Palaeoclimates of the Southern Hemisphere* (Rotterdam, 1984), 375–90; Lahr and Foley, "Toward a Theory of Modern Human Origins," 163. In general, see Keckler, "Catastrophic Mortality"; Ammerman, "Late Pleistocene Population Dynamics"; Shennan, "Population, Culture, and the Dynamics of Culture Change."

[106] Massimo Livi-Baci, *Population and Nutrition: An Essay on European Demographic History* (New York, 1991), 111–13.

the past two decades, climate scientists have discovered that climate during the 10,000 years of the post-Ice Age present, the Holocene, has been uniquely stable, almost surreally flat, compared to the jagged instabilities of the Pleistocene. Riding inside the numbered oxygen isotope stages of the Pleistocene were a myriad of smaller-scale but profoundly abrupt shifts in climate. Starting in the 1960s, evidence for such short-term variations began to emerge from Greenland ice-drilling projects and then from North Atlantic seabed drilling, and they have been carefully documented in the years following. "Heinrich events" were extreme punctuations of cold during glacial periods, lasting several hundred to several thousand years, when surging continental glaciers sent fleets of icebergs across the North Atlantic, and CO_2 levels plummeted by as much as 20 ppm. The Heinrich events were set within cycles of increasingly extreme "Dansgaard-Oeschger events," in which at ~1,470-year intervals the glacial climate warmed suddenly, and then tailed back into glacial conditions: the last 70,000 years of glacial history were punctuated by more than twenty Dansgaard-Oeschger warming spikes and at least six deep Heinrich iceboxes (see Figure I.6). These sharp and rapid patterns of climate variability – what William Burroughs has rightly called "a reign of chaos"[107] – had effects that reached around the globe.

Though the exact cause is a matter of considerable research and debate, these warm spikes and cold troughs are seen as caused by complex changes in the great conveyor belt of ocean currents running north and south through the Atlantic and east and west through the Pacific. This system is primarily driven by what is known as "thermohaline circulation," in which currents of warm water moving toward Greenland become more saline and thus denser, eventually plunging to the floor of the ocean and returning south at great depths. Pulses of fresh melt water flowing out of the Arctic or Antarctic icecaps, altering the salinity and thus the density of sea waters in the Atlantic extremes, slow or even stop this pump, leading to radically cooling global climates. During the last 100,000 years of the Pleistocene, warm D-O events may have set off the super cold Heinrich events, with a pattern of increasing intensity and cold: from 90,000 to 50,000 years ago, ten long warm D-O events were broken by two deep Heinrich events, down to about 25,000 years ago when an oscillating balance set in, with ten warm but brief D-O events broken by four deep cold Heinrichs, and finally in the Last Glacial Maximum extreme cold prevailed, with only one D-O event at 22,000ybp until the sudden warming (the final D-O event) that brought the Pleistocene to an end.[108] The D-O cycles, 1,470 years apart on average,

[107] See Burroughs, *Climate Change in Prehistory*, 37–63.
[108] Burroughs, *Climate Change in Prehistory*, 37–68 provides a summary; for other overviews, see Stefan Rahmstorf, "Ocean Circulation and Climate during the Past 120,000 Years," *Nature* 419 (2002), 207–14; Peter Clark et al., "The Role..."; Wallace S. Broecker, "The Chaotic Climate," *SA* 273/5 (Nov. 1995), 62–8; Wallace S. Broecker and George H. Denton, "What Drives Glacial Cycles?" *SA* 262/1 (Jan. 1990), 48–56.

may have been triggered by the combined effects of several cycles of solar activity.[109] The effects of these cycles embedded in this last stage of the Pleistocene were global in scope. The warm D-O events can be measured in ice cores from both the Arctic and the Antarctic; the coldest cold epochs saw ice rafts and vast fleets of icebergs in the North Atlantic, a southward shift in the equatorial Intertropical Convergence Zone, spikes of aridity in Africa (though by no means megadroughts), storms wracking the west coast of the Americas, and weakened monsoons bringing drought to southern Asia.[110] The super-eruption of the Indonesian volcano Mt. Toba adds another factor to these wild instabilities: volcanic eruptions would have powerful if typically more local impacts.

As much as the full-scale glaciations, these abrupt and steep changes in climate would have brought misery, crisis mortality, occasionally extinction, and even evolutionary bottlenecks to Paleolithic peoples, as well as the expansionary opportunities to recolonize abandoned regions and to move into new territory. One of these climate whiplash sequences might have marked an abrupt shift from Neanderthal to modern humans in Europe. In this analysis, the extreme cold of Heinrich event 5 drove Neanderthals into isolated refuges around 48,000ybp, but during the sudden warm-up that followed modern humans migrated deep into the wooded landscape and outcompeted their ancient cousins for control of Europe.[111] Thus – contrary to the understanding of the 1960s and 1970s – it would appear that humans were not children of nature living wisely in the Garden of Eden. Rather, in times of plenty they were inherently opportunistic and expansionary, and

[109] Holger Braun et al., "Possible Solar Origin of the 1,470 Glacial Climate Cycle Demonstrated in a Coupled Model," *Nature* 438 (2005), 208–11; for other approaches, see B. Staufer, "Atmospheric CO_2 and Millennial-Scale Climate Changes during the Last Glacial Period," *Nature* 392 (1998), 59–62; R. B. Alley, "Stochastic Resonance in the North Atlantic," *Paleoceanography* 16 (2001), 190–8; Andrey Ganopolski and Stefan Rahmstorf, "Abrupt Climate Changes due to Stochastic Resonance," *Physical Review Letters* 88/3 (2002), 038501; and Burroughs, *Climate Change in Prehistory*, 67–8.

[110] S. C. Fritz et al., "Millennial-Scale Climate Variability during the Last Glacial Period in the Tropical Andes," *QSR* 29 (2010), 1017–24; Rik Tjallingii et al., "Coherent High- and Low-Latitude Control of the Northwest African Hydrological Balance," *NatGeosc* 1 (2008), 670–5; and Jessica E. Tierney et al., "Northern Hemisphere Controls on Tropical African Climate during the Past 60,000 Years," *Science Express* (Sept. 1, 2008); Epica Community Members, "One-to-One Coupling of Glacial Climate Variability in Greenland and Antarctica," *Nature* 444 (2006), 195–8; Xianfeng Wang et al., "Wet Periods in Northeastern Brazil over the Past 210 kyr Linked to Distant Climate Anomalies," *Nature* 432 (2004), 740–3; Mark A. Altabet et al., "The Effect of Millennial-Scale Changes in Arabian Sea Denitrification on Atmospheric CO_2," *Nature* 415 (2002), 159–62; Lowell Stott et al., "Super ENSO and Global Climate Oscillations at Millennial Time Scales," *Science* 297 (2002), 222–6; Gerald Bond et al., "A Pervasive Millennial-Scale Cycle in North Atlantic Holocene and Glacial Climate," *Science* 278 (1997), 1257–66.

[111] Ulrich J. Müller et al., "The Role of Climate in the Spread of Modern Humans into Europe," *QSR* 30 (2011), 273–9.

repeatedly paid the price in times of want in devastating episodes of crisis mortality and local extinction.

* * *

Gould and Eldridge's Punctuation Meets Boserup's Intensification: Toward a New Understanding of the Upper Paleolithic

This understanding of crisis mortality – and the new understanding of the origins of human modernity in the African Middle Stone Age – leads to a new perspective on the Upper Paleolithic florescence of human culture, and to a wider approach to human technological and demographic history. Quite simply, growing population densities, not just modern human capabilities, led to more elaborate material culture. The Upper Paleolithic was thus less a "human revolution" than it was an "intensification" in the face of stress. For the first time in history, cultural innovation rather than genetic mutation was emerging as the fundamental human response to natural stress.

Punctuational stress had been the fundamental story behind the emergence of humanity from the Miocene apes, driven by the deepening instabilities of the Cenozoic Ice House as a moderate "23K World" climate gave way to the extremes of the "41K" and "100K" worlds. Here the motor of change was the climate ("misery") and the unit of change was the gene. But as the human mind began to blossom, a second unit of change began to gradually emerge: cultural innovation, which some count – for effect – in "memes."[112]

With the emergence of the human mind, evolutionary change accelerated: where "misery/stress" had in the natural state led to genetic change or extinction, now it might lead to cultural change – or local population collapse. Now populations might rise with something of a buffer against threats to their survival. And it is increasingly clear that – within limits that we may be now approaching in the twenty-first century – larger populations meant more cultural innovation. As archaeologist Stephen Shennan has recently argued, "it appears possible that rates of successful technological innovation may have been correlated with population sizes and densities from the origins of hominin culture to the present."[113] Escaping mortality, first and most particularly crisis mortality, brings an increasingly critical

---

[112] Shennan, Genes, Memes and Human History.

[113] Wood, "A Theory of Preindustrial Population Dynamics"; Stephen Shennan, "Demography and Cultural Innovation: A Model and Its Implications for the Emergence of Modern Culture," *CArchJ* 11 (2001), 15. See also Peter J. Richerson and Robert Boyd, "Institutional Evolution in the Holocene," in W. G. Runciman, ed., *The Origins of Social Institutions* (Oxford, 2001), 197–234. See also the references in note 117.

mass of human mind to the problem of improving the social and technological tools that shape our well-being. Here population growth was less a
crisis than an opportunity – an opportunity to accelerate cultural evolution
given a critical level of exchange among growing and interacting modern
human societies.

These "origins" do take us back a long way. This story has taken us
through the linked record of stone tools and fossil skulls to the early *Homo*
or late *Australopithecus* wielding a cobble chopper to scavenge lion-killed
game for the scraps of meat and fat that fed the first encephalization after
2.75MY, as the moderate climates of the "23K World" gave way to the
deeper instabilities of the "41K World," to the emergence of the striding,
distance-running *erectus* developing the early Acheulian handaxe as African
environments turned sharply arid at 1.8–1.6MY, and the early *heidelbergensis* refining the Acheulian sometime after the transition to the volatile climate of the "100K World." Each of these transitions improved proto-human
circumstances, but the sequence was so long and drawn out that we have to
see nature – rather than culture – as the driving force. This calculus shifted
with the train of changes that ran from 300,000 to 130,000 years ago: the
transition to the composite Levallois tools of the Middle Stone Age and
the first use of pigments and grindstones after 300,000ybp, the first known
anatomically modern people by 195,000ybp, the fixing of modern language
around 130,000ybp.

These millennia of the Middle Paleolithic now are understood as the
transformative "human revolution," the point at which nature gave way to
culture, genes began to give way to memes – and roughly the beginning of
the human condition as we know it. This a very new understanding, forged
in a short and explosive decade of discovery, analysis, and debate. It replaces
an understanding that until very recently held sway, in which the "human
revolution" was a single event that happened around 45,000 years ago,
as suddenly the rougher composite tools of the Middle Stone Age/Middle
Paleolithic gave way to the myriad complex types of the Late Stone Age/
Upper Paleolithic, and as modern human band societies began to colonize
the earth beyond Africa. Such a revision might call into question what is
meant by "punctuation" and "revolution," because we are now looking at
a series of events spread over about 100,000 years, rather than a single dramatic transition. But on the massive long-term scale of natural systems, these
100,000 years of the Middle Paleolithic were certainly revolutionary and
"punctuational": on the scale of earth history, modern humans are a sudden
appearance and their history an accelerating thrust toward the future.

So what are we to make of the Upper Paleolithic, with its explosively
complex material culture, its art, its symbol making? If this was not the
"human revolution," what was it? Decades ago, agricultural economist Ester
Boserup challenged Malthus, arguing that population growth could as often

lead to an escape through innovation as it might to a crisis of population and resources.[114] She proposed that gradual "intensification" of agricultural productivity, from slash-and-burn to various fallowing systems to annual multiple-crop systems, accommodates growing populations. Thus cultural, technological innovation is driven by the demands of growing populations. Recently, a renewed appreciation has appeared for Boserup's ideas, and an extension of them to preagricultural societies, and to the human condition as a whole. The emerging consensus is that the Upper Paleolithic was the first "Boserupian intensification" in human history. Rather than being shaped by a mortality crash and a genetic bottleneck, these Upper Paleolithic human populations – for the first time – successfully and rather quickly deployed their new cognitive powers to improve their circumstances when faced with a climate-driven clash between population and resources. In this new under-standing, the Upper Paleolithic technologies are not signs of new human capabilities, but of "intensifications" of Middle Stone Age technologies driven by growing populations endowed with existing modern capabilities encountering the effects of the final Pleistocene glaciation. This brings us back to the "miseries" of crisis mortality, and the question is that of human numbers in the Pleistocene, the beginnings of demographic history.

It has long been a truism that human population expanded dramatically with the "agricultural revolution" that followed the end of the Pleistocene Ice ages. Recently, however, geneticists have detected signs of a Pleistocene "population explosion" long before the final glaciation ended.[115] These expansions, as suggested by the evidence of Y chromosomes and mtDNA, began with bottleneck and separation of modern peoples in Africa during the megadroughts of the MIS5 interglacial (130,000–90,000ybp), growing and spreading within Africa, then out of Africa along the southern coastal route to Australia, and then north into Eurasia.

Why could these expansions occur? Were more children being born; was there an increase in fertility? Probably not. Rather, paleodemographers argue, mortality declined, specifically the crisis mortality that had previously regularly destroyed entire bands and regional populations in the face of severe and abrupt climate change. But from 130,000ybp, the record seems to be a long-range trend toward expanding populations, apparently because crisis mortality and local extinctions became less and less frequent. Certainly

---

[114] Ester Boserup's classic statements were in *The Condition for Agricultural Growth: The Economic of Agrarian Change under Population Pressure* (Chicago, IL, 1965); and Population and Technological Change: A Study of Long-Term Trends (Chicago, IL, 1981). For the most important Malthusian extensions of her argument, see Ronald D. Lee, "Malthus and Boserup: A Dynamic Synthesis," in David Coleman and Roger S. Schofield, eds., *The State of Population Theory: Forward from Malthus* (Oxford, 1986), 96–103; and Wood, "A Theory of Preindustrial Population Dynamics."

[115] These population expansions are the subject of considerable debate, but for positive summaries, see Excoffier, "Human Demographic History" and "Reconstructing the Demography."

such mortality was still a real possibility, and would take a whole new form when epidemic diseases could take hold in dense agricultural and urban populations. But in the meantime modern humans survived longer than had proto-moderns, to the point that it is being argued that grandparents began to become a reality, just as childhood lengthened.[116] As populations grew in size and density, their mobilization of language, symbol, and tool intensified. Increasingly elaborate artifacts became a vehicle for both group preservation and group definition; the elaborate blade stone tool kits of the Mode 4/Upper Paleolithic allowed for more effective subsistence and decoration that marked local identity.[117] Elders teaching children may have been a fundamental part of this new intensified social configuration, possible because of modern capabilities and the Eemian expansions, and now universal under the stresses of the final glaciations.[118]

If this account captures the rough outlines of the emergence of modern humanity, the road was not a smooth one. Certainly populations under good conditions grew, and the thickening connections among these denser populations may have driven the realization of modern human cultural potential in the scatter of increasingly complex Mode 4/Upper Paleolithic artifacts that survive in the archaeological record. But if so, it is more and more apparent that this complexity came in pulses and flickers, and adverse conditions could reduce both populations and cultural complexity. Such seems to have been the situation with modern human presence in the Levant, which appeared at roughly 110,000ybp and disappeared at 90,000ybp; and the Aterian culture of the Sahara, which eventually disappeared around 60,000ybp with the desiccation of the Sahara. Similarly, two brief and enigmatic eruptions of complexity in South Africa, the Still Bay and Howiesons

---

[116] On old age and modern humans, Catherine Driscoll, "Grandmothers, Hunters, and Human Life History," *Biology and Philosophy* 24 (2009), 665–86; Rachel Caspari and Sang-Hee Lee, "Older Age Becomes Common Late in Human Evolution," *PNAS* 101 (2004), 10895–900.

[117] Where Boone in "Subsistence Strategies and Early Human Population History," saw this intension/expansion coming with the Neolithic, the following have extended this interpretation to the Upper Paleolithic: Adam Powell et al., "Late Pleistocene Demography and the Appearance of Modern Human Behavior," *Science* 324 (2009), 1298–301; Joao Zilhao, "The Emergence of Ornaments and Art: An Archaeological Perspective on the Origins of 'Behavioral Modernity,'" *JArchRes* 15 (2007), 1–54; Shennan, "Demography and Cultural Innovation"; Lahr and Foley, "Toward a Theory of Modern Human Origins," 146–8; Foley and Lahr, "On Stony Ground," 119; McBrearty and Brooks, "The Revolution that Wasn't," 531–3, Mellars, "The Impossible Coincidence," 23. For a discussion of language families and the spread of human in the Upper Paleolithic, see Patrick Manning, "*Homo Sapiens* Populates the Earth: A Provisional Synthesis, Privileging Linguistic Evidence," *JWH* 17 (2006), 115–58. The evidence for population expansions in broad spectrum foraging will be discussed in Chapter 3.

[118] Catherine Driscoll, "Grandmothers, Hunters and Human Life History," *BiolPlos* 24 (2009), 665–86.

Poort complexes, flared briefly in two short episodes between 72,000ybp and 59,000ybp, a period of increased humidity in southwest Africa, before lapsing into archaeological invisibility or more basic Middle Stone Age technologies. And an oscillation between Middle and Upper Paleolithic technologies seems to be emerging from the archaeology of Eurasia east of western Europe, the great expanse that genetic evidence is suggesting was a critical staging ground for the diffusion of non-African modern humans.[119]

But it would seem that the potential for the autocatalytic feedback – the accelerating intensification – that characterizes human history proper began with the fixing of language and the human mind sometime between 300,000ybp and 130,000ybp.[120] Modern mental and language capabilities began to mitigate crisis mortality and local extinctions. As populations stabilized, life expectancies lengthened. Hunting territories began to fill up and to bump up against neighbors, requiring boundary maintenance and negotiation. At various points during the African Middle Stone Age and then globally during the Upper Paleolithic, the pressures and opportunities of increased population density resulted in an elaboration of culture and technology. These growing, increasingly skilled peoples would soon face a dramatic climatic punctuation that would utterly transform their world.

[119] Brian M. Chase, "South Africa Paleoenvironments during Marine Oxygen Isotope Stage 4: A Context for the Howiesons Poort and Still Bay Industries," *JArchS* 37 (2010), 1359–66; Zenobia Jacobs et al., "Ages for the Middle Stone Age of Southern Africa: Implications for Human Behavior and Dispersal," *Science* 322 (2008), 733–5; Erella Hovers and Anna Belfer-Cohen, "'Now You See it, Now You Don't' – Modern Human Behavior in the Middle Paleolithic," in Erella Hovers and Steven L. Kuhn, eds., *Transitions before the Transition: Evolution and Stability in the Middle Paleolithic and Middle Stone Age* (New York, 2006), 295–304; S. L. Kuhn et al., "The Early Upper Paleolithic and the Origins of Modern Human Behavior, in P. Jeffrey Brantingham et al., eds., *The Early Upper Paleolithic beyond Western Europe* (Berkeley, 2004), 242–8.

[120] Here I refer to Boserup, but also to Jared Diamond, *Guns, Germs, and Steel: The Fate of Human Societies* (New York, 1997), 111–12, who describes autocatalytic feedbacks beginning with the Agricultural Revolution.

PART II

DOMESTICATION, AGRICULTURE, AND
THE RISE OF THE STATE

List of Figures and Tables for Part II: Domestication, Agriculture, and the Rise of the State

Figures

Tables

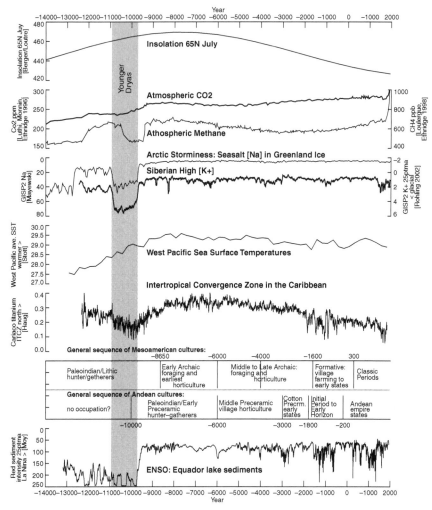

Figure II.1. The Younger Dryas, the Holocene, and early cultures in the Americas.

The arc of precession-driven solar insolation was the key force behind the great warming of the Early Holocene, with the cold melt-water reversal of the Younger Dryas registering in ice-core readings of atmospheric methane, storms in the Arctic and the strength of the Siberian High Pressure System, and in the positioning of the Intertropical Convergence Zone along the north coast of South America. The ITCZ was pulled far to the north in the warm Early Holocene between 9000 and 5000 BC. At the same time sea surface temperatures in the Western Pacific were high, and the El Niño /Southern Oscillation system stood in minimal extreme La Niña mode. As solar insolation was reduced by processional shift, the West Pacific cooled and the ITCZ moved south, and the ENSO shifted sharply toward an El Niño mode, notably following 3000 BC. The first city-states in the New World, on the Peruvian coast, were launched on this sudden burst El Niño precipitation.

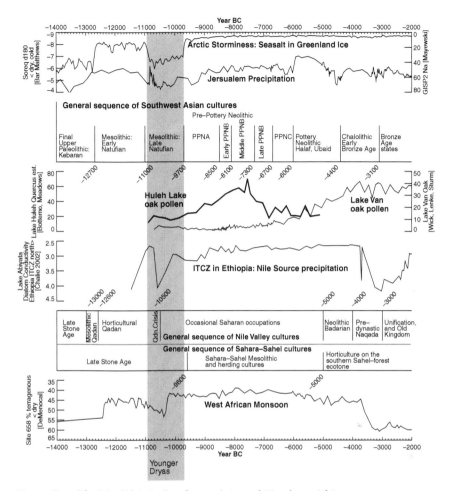

Figure II.2. The Neolithic in Southwest Asia and Northern Africa.

During the warm, humid Early Holocene early Neolithic societies developed in Southwest Asia and hunting-herding cultures occupied the Sahara savannahs. The rise and decline of oak pollen in the Hula Lake sediments (northern Israel) between 9500 and 6500 BC marks the period of the Early Holocene "megamonsoons" – the waning of this monsoon seems have shaped the decline of the Pre-Pottery Neolithic cultures. The emerging influence of the winter Atlantic westerlies, running through the Mediterranean into Anatolia and Central Sea is captured in the rising oak pollen at Lake Van from 6000 BC. In northern Africa the humid Atlantic and Indian Monsoons retreated sharply in the fourth millennium.

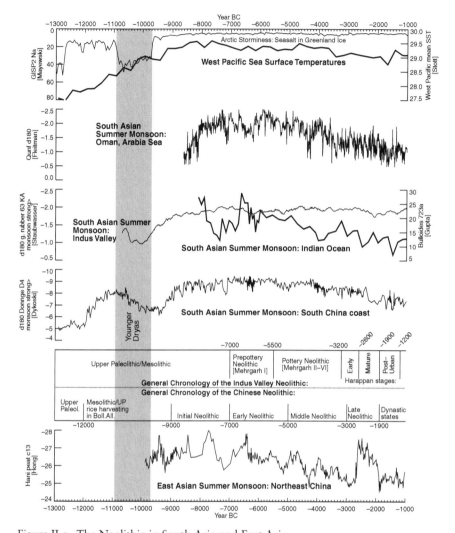

Figure II.3. The Neolithic in South Asia and East Asia.

South and East Asian Monsoon records record the impact of the Younger Dryas, the peak of Early Holocene moisture, and the general retreat of the monsoons after 600 BC, tracking the cooling of the West Pacific Warm Pool.

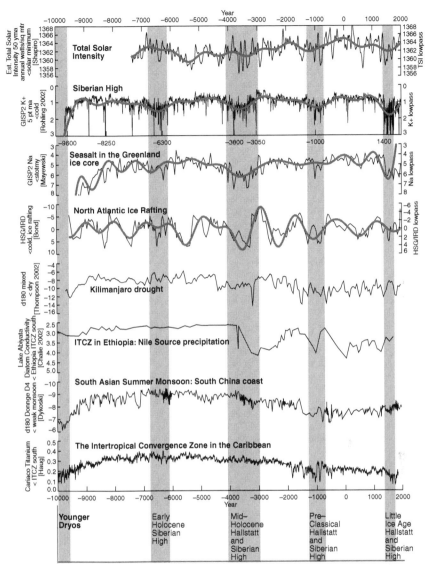

Figure II.4. The Hallstatt Cycle and the contours of the Holocene.

Over the length of the Holocene, one of the central features of the climate system has been the recurrence of cold intervals, marked by minima in the Siberian High (measured by potassium-laden dust from Siberia deposited in Greenland ice). The Siberian High event between 6700 and 6000 BC was caused by a meltwater reversal with the collapse of the Laurentian icesheet. But the next three millennial cold events were caused by "Halstatt" solar minima, in the fourth millennium BC, around 1200 BC, and around AD 1400. Solar intensity also drove the associated cycles of ice-rafting in the North Atlantic, with pulses of ice at and between each Halstatt minimum. The Halstatt events can also be detected in the records of more equatorial sites, in eastern Africa, South China, and the Caribbean coast of South America.

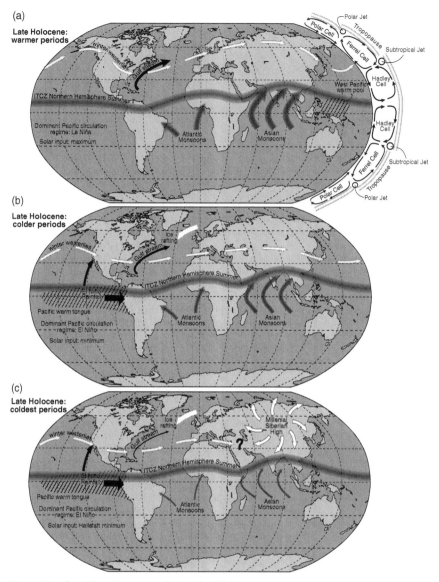

Figure II.5abc. The climate modes in the Holocene.

These diagrams roughly illustrate the global pattern of climate oscillation during the Holocene. In the Early Holocene and warmer intervals of the Late Holocene, global climates were dominated by higher solar intensity, a north-riding ITCZ, strong Asian Monsoons, a warm West Pacific, a La Niña ENSO condition, and north-running winter westerlies. With lower solar intensity, the westerlies and the ITCZ slipped south, the Asian Monsoons weakened, the West Pacific cooled, and El Niño became dominant. With the Halstatt solar minima these conditions all intensified, and the strong cold Siberian High seems to have interrupted the westerlies, setting off intense droughts in the mid-latitudes.

[Figures by James DeGrand]

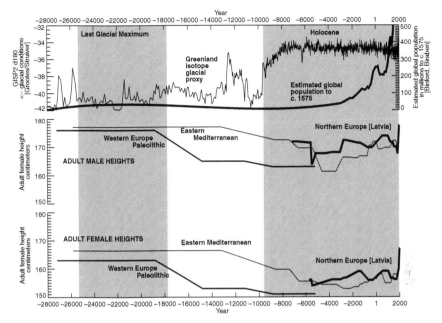

Figure II.6. Adult stature in the Mediterranean and Europe, 28,000 BC to present.

Adult stature is a very rough measure of the health status of ancient populations. Series of data for Europe suggest an inverse relationship between population size and adult stature, with Europeans losing height from the later Paleolithic into the Neolithic, oscillating around a shorter norm, and then suddenly breaking out to taller stature in the past century or so.

(The lines on this chart are created by displaying reported heights for the middle three-fifths of the reported period only, with the first and final fifths moving to the next reported height level.)

Sources: Eastern Mediterranean: Angel in Cohen and Armelagos; Western Europe Paleolithic: Formicola and Giannechini; Northern Europe [Latvia]: Gerhards.

TABLE II.I. *World population totals and increase, 9000 BC to present*

	Estimated population	Average annual growth rate (% per year)
9000 BC	7,000,000	
		.028
3000 BC	38,000,000	
		.063
AD 1	252,000,000	
		.043
AD 1500	477,000,000	
		.526
AD 2011	7,000,000,000	

Sources and note for Tables II.1, III.1a, and Figure III.1: Lewis L. Binford, Constructing Frames of Reference: An Analytical Method for Archaeological Theory Building Using Hunter-Gatherer and Environmental Data Sets (Berkeley, CA, 2001) provides quantitative modeling of primary (plant) and secondary (animal) biomass productivity in Early Holocene global biomes that establishes the best estimate of human population at the beginning of the Holocene (7 million); see 142–4. Binford estimates population in the Early Holocene at 9000 BC to be 7 million. For the period from 400 BC forward I use the figures from Jean Noël Biraben, "Essai sur L'Évolution di Nombre des Hommes," Population 34 (1979), 13–24, at p. 16. See also David Christian, Maps of Time: An Introduction to Big History (Berkeley, CA, 2004), 344–5. Between Binford's 7 million at 9000 BC and Biraben's 153 million at 400 BC, I have estimated populations assuming a .03 percent global growth rate for the Neolithic, a rough .07 percent rate for agrarian societies, and introduced two checks, at 2200–2000 BC and 1300–1100 BC. The climatic and epidemic forces behind these checks are discussed at length in Chapters 6 and 7. The Neolithic and agrarian growth rates are based on data in Christopher R. Gignoux et al., "Rapid, Global Demographic Expansions after the Origins of Agriculture," PNAS 108 (2011), 6044–9; Jean-Pierre Bocquet-Appel, "Estimates of Upper Paleolithic Meta-Population Size in Europe from Archaeological Data," JArchS 32 (2005), 1656–68; and Xiaoliang Li et al., "Increases in Population and Expansion of Rice Agriculture in Asia, and Anthropogenic Methane Emissions since 5000BP," QuatInt 202 (2009), 41–50. The results here are roughly analogous to the classic results in Robert L. Carneiro and Daisy F. Heilse, "On Determining the Probable Rate of Population Growth during the Neolithic," AmAnth 68 (1966), 177–81. More recently this argument for very slow population growth during the early Neolithic has been developed in Bruce Smith, "Low-Level Food Production," JAnthRes 9 (2001), 1–43.

TABLE 11.2. Estimates of the Neolithic Demographic Transition

	Site dates	Total sites	Skeletal sample size	Average of site NDT indices (D5-19/D5+)	# of sites with NDT index over .30	% of sites with NDT index over .30
Southwest Asia						
Early Natufian	12600–11400 BC	4	249	0.283	1	25%
Late Natufian	10500–9940 BC	2	70	0.170	0	0%
Pre-Pottery Neolithic A	9050 BC	2		0.470	2	100%
Pre-Pottery Neolithic B	8500–7500 BC	5	229	0.282	1	20%
PPNB to Pottery Neolithic*	7500–6200 BC	9	485	0.381	7	77%
Chalcolithic Samarra: Sawwan I	~5500 BC	1	29	0.552	1	
*includes three periods at Çatalhöyük, calculated at D3-19/D3+						
Europe						
Mesolithic	Pre-6000 BC	4	362	0.198	0	
Early Neolithic	6000–5000 BC	7	579	0.219	1	14%
Middle Neolithic	4999–4000 BC	6	318	0.225	1	17%
Late Neolithic	3999–3000 BC	8	834	0.271	4	50%
Late Neolithic/Early Bronze Age	2999–1950 BC	13	1350	0.252	4	31%
St. Esteve Le Port, France	700–800 AD	1	71	0.267	0	0%
Observance, Marseilles Plague pit	1722	1	172	0.256	0	0%
Eastern North America (south of the Great Lake)						
Middle Archaic	6500–3500 BC	9	1400	0.212	1	11%
Late Archaic	3000–900 BC	6	1093	0.294	3	50%
Early-Middle Woodland	500 BC–850 AD	17	2201	0.200	0	0%
Late Woodland	850–1300 AD	18	3621	0.300	8	44%
Late Woodland	1301–1500 AD	11	2025	0.236	1	9%

Note: The timing of the rise of human fertility is broadly associated with the rise of agriculture, but these indices of a "Neolithic Demographic Transition" support the position that dramatically higher fertility began not with earliest domestication and horticulture, but with the "Secondary Products Revolution" and the intensification of agriculture, in a global "Late Neolithic."

Sources: Jean-Pierre Bocquet-Appel, personal communication, August 17, 2011, revision of data originally published in: Guerrero, et al., 64-65; Bocquet-Appel (2002), 640–641; Bocquet-Appel and Naji, (2006), 343–344; Data for sites at Eynana, Netiv-Hagdud, Jericho, Abu Gosh, Çatalhöyük, Ain Ghazal and Sawwan I from Hershkovitz and Gopher, 447; Hillson, et al., Hole, 161–63; Dating of North American periods is by broad period, not specific sites, and is based on Munoz, et al.

3

Agricultural Revolutions

The origins of agriculture lay in the sudden end of the Pleistocene, as the cold, dry glacial world, after some climate oscillations, gave way to the warm, wet Holocene that has sheltered humanity ever since. After spreading thinly across African and Eurasian grasslands during the last stages of the Pleistocene, humanity suddenly settled down in villages and began to produce – rather than simply to forage for – the sustenance of survival. This was what we have called since the days of the great archaeologist V. Gordon Childe the *agricultural revolution* or the *Neolithic revolution*. This was the much debated "moment" of domestication, as plants, animals, and people themselves were transformed by a synergy of human action and natural contingency to forge a radically new configuration of human behavior and natural ecology. The result would be an accelerating growth of human numbers, and the emergence of an entirely new set of tensions between humanity and nature.

We call this a "revolution" in the human circumstance, but such terms depend on your perspective. In geological and evolutionary time, the emergence of settled life and agricultural production was certainly a revolutionary transformation. If we imagine the 5 million years of human evolutionary time as a twenty-four-hour period, the entire 300,000 years of modern humanity comprises about an hour and a half, the 135,000 years since modern humans may have left Africa comprise about a half hour, and the 12,000 years since the end of the Pleistocene and its aftershocks comprise slightly more than four minutes. Against a similar twenty-four-hour clock of the geological time of evolving earth systems since 4.6 billion years ago, these epochs are even more minute: about six seconds since the emergence of modern humanity, one second since the first successful departure from Africa, and a few nanoseconds since the end of the ice ages. Viewed from the long history of the earth system or the emergence of the human lineage, the rise of settled agriculture seems simply a single phase in the brief, explosive eruption running from the emergence of modern humans and their global colonizations and intensifications to our present high-technology, overpopulated, climatically unbalanced condition. But if we view the emergence of settled agriculture in historical time it seems excruciatingly slow. The glacial Pleistocene came to an end around 14,600 years ago, its aftershocks ended 11,600 years ago, but not until about 10,000 years ago was an agriculture based on domesticated plants and animals clearly established in the greater Levant and China, and when some of these societies were suffering their first collapse 8,000 years ago, agriculture was only at its most incipient stages in most of the rest of the world. Not until about 6,000 years ago, more than half the total time elapsed since the end of the Pleistocene, was much of humanity on a clear course toward agriculture.[1]

Thus, in human terms, the emergence of agricultural societies was a slow and complex story. Here I hope to reduce complexity to pattern. After establishing a few definitions and ecological frameworks, and sketching the basic outline of climate change between the final cycles of the Pleistocene and the middle of the Holocene epoch (roughly 14,600–5000ybp), this chapter examines the rise of agriculture in light of both the effects of climate change and the circumstances of global ecological regions. I suggest that two broad "agroecologies,"[2] inherently more and less productive, expansive, and depleting systems of food production, emerged with the warming climates of the post-Pleistocene world, shaped by climate and ecology, and profoundly shaping human conditions. The more productive and depleting of these systems, based on cereals and domesticated animals, developed in discrete hearths of domestication and spread rapidly across the semitemperate latitudes of the Old World, structuring both a precocious rise of the state and the emergence of devastating diseases. The second of these agroecological systems, various kinds of mixed horticulture developing slowly and diffusely throughout the tropics, rarely was productive enough to sustain large populations.[3] The consequences of these two trajectories out of

---

[1] Melinda A. Zeder, in "The Neolithic Macro-(R)evolution: Macroevolutionary Theory and the Study of Cultural Change," *JArchRes* 17 (2009), 1–63, esp. 45–8, arrives at the position that the Southwest Asian Neolithic was a punctuated change. Graeme Barker, *The Agricultural Revolution in Prehistory: Why did Foragers Become Farmers?* (Oxford, 2006) stresses the more gradual and diverse qualities of the global Neolithic, while putting human intellect and climate change at the center of his analysis. A note here on dating is required. Dating is an extremely complex problem from the end of the Pleistocene for both technical and cultural reasons. Through to the end of the Pleistocene I use years before present in the common sense, meaning, that is, calibrated years, not raw radiocarbon dates. In lay terms, "calibrated" dates are our best approximation of true calendar dating. Raw radiocarbon dates progressively diverge from true calendar dating. After the end of the Pleistocene I use calibrated BC/AD dating. All uncalibrated radiocarbon dates have been calibrated using the OXCAL program, version 3.10.

[2] I take this term from Donald Worster, "Transformations of the Earth: Toward an Agroecological Perspective in History," *JAmH* 76 (1990), 1087–107.

[3] Jack R. Harlan, "Agricultural Origins: Centers and Noncenters," *Science* 174 (1971), 468–74.

the Pleistocene were profound. Escaping from the burden of erratic ice age climates with the warming of the Holocene, the growing numbers of people of the major Old World cereal-animal complexes were soon resubjected to mortality crises in new forms as they locked into an agricultural economy. Conversely, the smaller numbers of peoples engaged in tropical horticulture were isolated in various ways from this disease regime, and would suffer disastrously when human global connections attenuated because the Paleolithic expansions were reestablished in recent history. Throughout this formative epoch of agriculture, the pulsing of climate change continued to frame the essential parameters of the human condition.

* * *

Energy

Considering the emergence of agriculture requires at least a brief reconsideration of the essential role of energy in natural species and ecosystems. All living species survive to reproduce themselves through an unremitting metabolic action, converting energy and nutrients into viable life. At the heart of this metabolism lies the photosynthetic process that combines solar energy with chemical resources, shared among communities of primary producers and various levels of consuming predators. Ecosystems comprise the local, regional, and global combinations of species competing for flows of energy and cycles of nutrients, contributing to or subsisting on "net primary productivity" (NPP), a fundamental measure of the total biological output, of the biota that comprise the system as a whole. Such "systems" of course are fluctuating and variable, changing in character over the entire span of earth history and conditioned by long shifts and regular cycles of solar radiation and earth climate. Thus through global time the earth as a whole varies in its net primary productivity with the waxing and waning of icehouse and greenhouse super-cycles, echoed in shorter chronologies by the orbitally driven cold glaciations and warm interglacials. And around the earth at any given time temperature and moisture shapes the global biomes of tropical rain forests, deserts and steppes, temperate and boreal forests, and tundra and polar ice fields, each generating their distinct and very different patterns of NPP. Varying in space and changing through time, the climatically determined conditions of these global biomes have driven the evolution of species and the composition of their ecological communities in which they survive.[4]

[4] Geerat J. Vermeij, *Nature: An Economic History* (Princeton, NJ, 2004); J. M. O. Scurlock and R. J. Olson, "Terrestrial New Primary Productivity – A Brief History and a New Worldwide Database," *Environmental Reviews* 10 (2002), 91–109. Lewis L. Binford, *Constructing Frames of Reference: An Analytical Method for Archaeological Theory Building Using*

The lives of proto-humans and early modern humans were fundamentally shaped by these constantly shifting conditions of net primary productivity, determining the parameters of their endless food quest, the earliest and most basic form of "energy capture."[5] As mammalian primates they were predatory consumers, and with slowly advancing cultural skills they moved up the food chain to become highly specialized high-level predators on the African savannah and the Eurasian steppes.[6] Increasingly effective skills in this food quest determined the evolutionary fate of individuals and bands. For most of this history, however, they remained simple consumers, collecting energy and nutrients from an entirely natural world, and entirely at the whim of its natural fluctuation. Survival lay in predicting this variability and adapting to it by moving with it, what is formally called *habitat tracking*. Over the past 100,000 years, as modern human capabilities began to coalesce, human societies made tentative and rudimentary steps toward overcoming ecological variability, to smooth out fluctuations in net primary productivity by moving beyond collecting to primitive forms of "cultivating." Certainly by burning grasslands, possibly by tending plots of particularly useful wild plants, such early efforts at manipulating the natural world had the goal of increasing the available useful species, in sum, useful NPP and useable energy.[7]

It seems very likely that early modern humans had mental capabilities that would have allowed them to move from collecting to producing food energy as early as the warm Eemian interglacial (MIS5e) at 135,000–116,000ybp or even possibly the previous long interglacial (MIS7) at 240,000–200,000ybp. At least one African plant may have been domesticated quite early. Genetic evidence suggests that, while bottle gourds have a global distribution, they are all African in origin, and that the division between African and Asian forms was extremely early. In its wild form the bottle gourd would be too brittle to

Hunter-Gatherer and Environmental Data Sets (Berkeley, CA, 2001) presents a quantitative system for measuring primary (plant) and secondary (animal) biomass productivity in the various terrestrial biomes; see in particular 80–113.

[5] I am very much indebted here to Ian G. Simmons, *Changing the Face of the Earth: Culture, Environment, History* (Oxford, 1989), esp. 19–23, 60–6, 128–45, 215–39; Vaclav Smil, *Energy in World History* (Boulder, CO, 1994). For recent analyses, see Stuat Rojstaczer et al., "Human Appropriation of Photosynthetic Products," *Science* 294 (2001), 2549–52; and Helmut Haberl, "The Global Socioeconomic Energetic Metabolism as a Sustainability Problem," *Energy* 31 (2006), 87–99. For the classic original statement, see Lesley A. White, "Energy and the Evolution of Culture," *AmAnth* 45 (1953), 335–56.

[6] Clive Finlayson, *Neanderthals and Modern Humans: An Ecological and Evolutionary Perspective* (New York, 2004).

[7] For a full-scale review of this argument, see Colin Tudge, *Neanderthals, Bandits, and Farmers: How Agriculture Really Began* (New Haven, CT, 1998); and Lawrence H. Keeley, "Protoagricultural Practices among Hunter-Gathers: A Cross-Cultural Survey," in T. Douglass Price and Anne Birgitte Gebauer, eds., *Last Hunters, First Farmers: New Perspectives on the Prehistoric Transition to Agriculture* (Santa Fe, NM, 1995), 243–72.

survive floating in the ocean, the established argument for its global distribution. This newest work suggests that the bottle gourd was domesticated in Africa before the out-of-Africa dispersal, selected for a thicker, more durable rind, and carried throughout the world by colonizing Upper Paleolithic peoples. A light, watertight container would have been extremely useful in the material culture of a thinly scattered, highly mobile people. More concrete evidence, in the form of starch granules on tools in Mozambique dating to roughly 100,000 years ago, indicates that Middle Stone Age peoples must have been at least occasionally harvesting wild cereals.[8] Closer in time, it appears that the first signs of landscape management and proto-cultivation in highland New Guinea and the Solomon Islands may have begun as early as 40,000ybp, roughly contemporary with the beginning of serious burning by early Australians.[9]

In so doing, early humans demonstrated one essential prerequisite for the agricultural revolution: an intellectual capacity to link cause and effect and to associate present action with future reward. But a number of other critical requirements may not have been in place. First and foremost, it is clear that productive agriculture is simply impossible during glacial epochs. During glaciations, global climates are too cool and dry to support the temperature and moisture requirements of vigorous plant growth, and, equally important, the low levels of CO_2 in the atmosphere had particularly severe impacts on the C3 plants that make up a large proportion of the key founder crops.[10] Glacial period climates were also extremely variable, so that conditions from year to year or decade to decade would have undermined the continuity of production necessary in early agriculture.

Thus we can isolate at least four key prerequisites for the emergence of agriculture, the specialized production of food energy. Agriculture is only possible when people are bright enough and the climate is warm and stable enough. In addition, agriculture is also only possible when biotic life cooperates. There may not have been many plants or animals amenable

---

[8] David L. Erickson et al., "An Asian Origin for a 10,000 Year-Old Domesticated Plant in the Americas," *PNAS* 102 (2005), 18315–20, see 18319; Deena Decker-Walters et al., "Diversity in Landraces and Cultivars of Bottle Gourd (*Lagenaria siceraria*; Cururbitaceae) as Assessed by Random Amplified Polymorphic DNA," *Genetic Resources and Crop Development* 48 (2001), 369–80; Julio Mercader, "Mozambican Grass Seed Consumption during the Middle Stone Age," *Science* 326 (2009), 1680–3. See also Eliso Kvavadze et al., "30,000-Year-Old Wild Flax Fibers," *Science* 325 (2009), 1359.

[9] Jim Allen and Peter Kershaw, "Greater Australia," in Lawrence Guy Strauss et al., eds., *Humans at the End of the Ice Age: The Archaeology of the Pleistocene-Holocene Transition* (New York, 1996), 183–5; Gifford H. Miller et al., "Ecosystem Collapse in Pleistocene Australia and a Human Role in Megafaunal Extinction," *Science* 309 (2005), 287–90.

[10] See the full review of the evidence in Laci M. Gerhart and Joy K. Ward, "Plant Responses to Low [CO_2] of the Past," *New Phytologist* 188 (2010), 674–95. The argument was first proposed in Rowan F. Sage, "Was Low Atmospheric CO_2 during the Pleistocene a Limiting Factor for the Origins of Agriculture?" *Global Change Biology* 1 (1995), 93–106.

to domestication – besides the useful bottle-gourd – in Eemian Africa. As Jared Diamond has stressed, both plants and animals must have the appropriate suite of qualities that will allow domestication. They must be reasonably productive in the wild state to attract human effort, and they must be genetically and behaviorally flexible, reproducing on an annual cycle and adaptable to different environmental conditions.[11] It turns out that such species were relatively sparsely distributed across the globe at the onset of the warm postglacial Holocene, isolated in particular regions that would develop into the various hearths of agriculture: most importantly the Fertile Crescent, northern and central China, the African Sahel, and Mesoamerica. The pull of particular biotic resources profoundly shaped the move to food production.

And then there is the fourth prerequisite: the push of necessity. The first modern human populations were tiny, on the order of tens of thousands or less, and they appear to have responded to the warm conditions of MIS5e (135,000–116,000ybp) by dispersing within Africa and perhaps into Asia: segmentation and dispersal easily solved any local scarcities. But such simple dispersals into "empty space" could not go on forever, and many Upper Paleolithic peoples in longer-settled regions were beginning to reach some of the limits of their environments. The transition to agriculture with the warming of the Holocene was also shaped by local conditions of demography, ecology, and geography. Very broadly, the pace of the transition to agriculture was governed by warming climates, the suitability of local species, and the longevity of human occupation of a given area. But even in older regions where suitable plants and animals were common, most important the Fertile Crescent, new foods and new means of acquiring them only slowly took on larger roles in a quest for subsistence predictability. The push of necessity came slowly and subtly until it suddenly took hold of humanity, as growing numbers, local degradations, and global climate shifts forced an autocatalytic intensification of the food quest in full-scale agriculture and toward the rise of the early state.

This transition to settled agriculture can be seen as a progressive intervention into the "natural" flow of energy and nutrients through regional and global ecosystems, a fundamental series of transitions in a much longer history of such energy-extracting interventions. At one extreme, we need

---

[11] Jared Diamond, *Guns, Germs, and Steel: The Fates of Human Societies* (New York, 1997), 114–75. For some of the more foundational literature, see Daniel Zohary and Maria Hopf, *Domestication of Plants in the Old World: The Origin and Spread of Plants in West Asia, Europe, and the Nile Valley*, third edition (New York, 2000); Bruce D. Smith, *The Emergence of Agriculture* (New York, 1995); David R. Harris, ed., *The Origins and Spread of Agriculture and Pastoralism in Eurasia* (Washington, DC, 1996); David R. Harris and Gordon Hillman, eds., *Foraging and Farming: The Evolution of Plant Exploitation* (London, 1989); David R. Harris, "Alternative Pathways toward Agriculture," in Charles A. Reed, ed., *Origins of Agriculture* (The Hague, 1977), 179–243.

to bear in mind that archaeologists are finding "anthropogenically" altered landscapes as far back as the control of fire, perhaps 700,000–800,000 years ago, when human populations might have appropriated .01 percent of the local net primary productivity. At the other extreme, contemporary societies extract some 30 percent of the total NPP produced on the entire earth.[12] By various estimates, crude but illuminating, this longer transition increased per capita *daily* energy consumption from about 6,000 kcal to anywhere from 160,000 kcal to 230,000 kcal. The transition to agriculture might have moved human daily consumption to 12,000 kcal/day, not much, it would appear, but more than double that of a foraging society. Such a doubling did not happen overnight, nor over a smooth continuous curve.[13] Anthropologists have devoted considerable effort to establishing the energy parameters of this transition. Their calculations revolve around balancing estimates of energy cost and energy rewards of foraging for various species with the costs and rewards of expending the effort to managing these or other species to ensure a more regular food supply, set against a backdrop of climate change and very slow population growth.[14]

[12] Jeffrey McKee, *Sparing Nature: The Conflict between Human Population Growth and Earth's Biodiversity* (New Brunswick, NJ, 2005); Donald K. Grayson, "The Archaeological Record of Human Impacts on Animal Populations, *JWP* 15 (2001), 1–68, though disputing the overkill hypothesis, reviews and synthesizes much of the anthropogenic literature; for figures, see Haberl, "The Global Socioeconomic Energetic Metabolism as a Sustainability Problem," at 91–2. On fire, see Naama Goren-Inbar et al., "Evidence of Fire Control at Gesher Benot Ya'aqov, Israel," *Science* 304 (2004), 725–7.

[13] Two roughly similar estimates of human energy consumption over the very long term have been published, one by Earl Cook in 1971, and one by Helmut Haberl in 2002.

	Cooke's estimate: Kcal/cap/day	Haberl's estimate: GJoule/cap/year	Haberl's estimate converted to Kcal/cap/day
Hunter-gatherers	5,000	10	6,548
Early agriculture	12,000		
Advanced agriculture	25,000		
Thai rice-growing village 1998		76	49,863
Early twentieth century			
Industrial economy	77,000		
Modern economy	230,000	251*	164,383*

*Austria, 1995

Earl Cook, "The Flow of Energy in an Industrial Society," *SA* 224 (1971), 135–44; Helmut Haberl, "The Energetic Metabolism of Societies, Part II: Empirical Examples," *Journal of Industrial Ecology* 5 (2002), 71–88. Cook's analysis has been widely reproduced in the literature. See Simmons, *Changing the Face of the Earth*, 24; and John W. Bennett, *Ecological Transition: Cultural Anthropology and Human Adaptation* (New York, 1976, repr. 2005), 40–3.

[14] For general overviews, see Bruce D. Smith, "Human Behavioral Ecology and the Transition to Food Production," and Robert L. Bettinger, "Agriculture, Archaeology, and Human

While there is no universally accepted "magic formula," there is good reason to suggest several incremental steps leading eventually to agriculture. These steps would include Paleolithic burning to enhance optimal grasses for hunting, clearing weeds around more useful but still wild plants, moving the plants themselves or scattering their seeds to encourage their growth, and the intentional planting of seeds of long-tended plants that would otherwise never germinate – full-scale domestication. Similarly, wild animals might be progressively corralled on a course toward domestication. Some of this might have been inadvertent, as seeds lost or excreted around caves or camps sprouted useful plants. The energy requirements of these efforts would have to be lower than those of less-interventionist hunting and gathering to make them worthwhile, though many of them would have progressively unfolded from the local gathering rounds of women, rather than the long-range hunting by men, and even from the practices of children, whose practices of play were inevitably practice for the food quest. Bruce Smith has described these stages out of foraging and into early agriculture as a continuum of "low-level food production" running from a cultivation of the wild to a small-scale horticulture of species moving toward domestication, but which might be regularly outcrossing back to wild species.[15] Full-scale agriculture comes when the domestication threshold has been crossed, which can best be described as a complete codependency in which neither humans nor the cultivated species can maintain their adaptation and numbers without the other.[16] With this dependency would come an exclusion; humans would devote their food-quest efforts to the propagation of a few highly and predictably productive domesticated species and cut their ties to the natural world.

The purpose of these efforts was to collect increasing amounts of biotically fixed energy in more concentrated locations where it could be more predictably used for subsistence. By concentrating useful species in smaller spaces, agriculture increases the net primary productivity that a given location can produce. Thus space was integral to this transition from wild to

---

Behavioral Ecology," in Douglas J. Kennett and Bruce Winterhalder, eds., *Behavioral Ecology and the Transition to Agriculture* (Berkeley, CA, 2006), 289–322; Bruce Winterhalder and Eric Alden Smith, "Analyzing Adaptive Strategies: Human Behavioral Ecology at Twenty-Five," *Evolutionary Anthropology* (2000), 51–72; Stephen Shennan, *Genes, Memes, and Human History: Darwinian Archaeology and Cultural Evolution* (London, 2002). For one important exchange, see Bruce Winterhalder and Carol Goland, "On Population, Foraging Efficiency, and Plant Domestication," *CA* 34 (1993), 710–15; K. Hawkes and J. O'Connell, "On Optimal Foraging Models and Subsistence Transition," *CA* 33 (1992), 63–6; and Robert Layton et al., "The Transition between Hunting and Gathering and the Specialized Husbandry of Resources," *CA* 32 (1991), 255–74.

[15] Bruce Smith, "Low-Level Food Production," *JAnthRes* 9 (2001), 1–43.

[16] David Rindos, "Symbiosis, Instability, and the Origins and Spread of Agriculture: A New Model," *CA* 21 (1980), 751–72.

domesticated. There was an inherent relationship between the agricultural transition and a reduction of human mobility, and the relationship may not have been one way. Intensified gathering becoming cultivation allowed people to reduce their mobility and settle down in villages. Conversely, however, the constriction of hunting territories by slowly growing populations of neighboring bands may have led to local depletions of wild resources and the growing attractiveness of early cultivation. Time was also in play. Hunting-foraging bands plotted the seasons against topography in an effort to "store" food on the landscape: moving from location to location in a seasonal round, they could with good management avoid starvation. Cultivators-becoming-farmers would avoid such mortality by storing food more locally, in their seed caches, in their herds, in their storerooms. Gradually they routinized and expanded their control of energy and nutrients, buffering themselves from the starving times that inevitably afflicted foraging peoples. Thus these changes in diet and mobility worked to increase their numbers. With an increasing predictability came increasing population. Women had more children, and more of the very young survived the weaning process. Energy captured translated into more people. With more people and prismatic impacts on local ecosystems would come the new human condition: the constant struggle to sustain through time the increasingly intensified use of larger local, regional, and global domains.

We should be careful about any population-driven arguments, however, because globally the advance of population was extremely slow. In strategically located places, however, circumstances may have been leading to surges of population, though little hard evidence exists to suggest that this was necessarily the case. Ultimately, energy in biotic systems is dependent on climate, and climate was the most powerful determinant of the agricultural revolution. Without the warming of the earth with the end of the Pleistocene, the transition to food production and the entire subsequent course of human civilization could never have unfolded. Again, if in historical terms the transition to agriculture moved slowly, in geological and human evolutionary time it was instantaneous, and its effects are still very much with us. Over about 5,000 years, beginning around 8500 BC, all of the basic founder crops that still feed human populations – wheat, barley, rice, potatoes, millet, corn/maize, sorghum, and yams – were domesticated and put to human uses.[17] Of these, all but maize, millet, and sorghum are C3 plants, which suffered in the CO_2-depleted glacial atmosphere and began to flourish when CO_2 rose with the postglacial warming. Some have argued that agriculture was "impossible during the Pleistocene but inevitable during

[17] See note 14; for overviews, see Barker, *The Agricultural Revolution in Prehistory*, 382–414; Jared Diamond, "Evolution, Consequences, and Future of Plant and Animal Domestication," *Nature* 418 (2002), 700–7; A. M. Mannion, "Domestication and the Origins of Agriculture: An Appraisal," *Progress in Physical Geography* 23 (1999), 37–56.

the Holocene."[18] Thus we must turn to a review of the earth's climate history through this critical transition.

* * *

Changing Climates: The End of the Pleistocene

The final glacial epoch of the Pleistocene began around 75,000 years ago, driven by the action of orbital cycles on solar insolation (see Figures I.6, II.1–II.4). The earth's climate moved down a long, irregular slope of increasing cold conditions, interrupted by several warm Dansgaard-Oeschger intervals until it reached the Last Glacial Maximum (LGM; MIS2), a period of almost continuous continental glaciation running from 25,000 to 14,600 years ago. The LGM began with a deep, 3,000-year-long Heinrich cold event interrupted by a warm Dansgaard-Oeschger spike at 23,400ybp, and closed with a final Heinrich cold event at 16,500–16,000ybp. Throughout the Last Glacial Maximum, methane recorded in the Greenland ice – mostly derived from the tropics now reduced by glacial droughts – fell to almost 350 ppb, less than half the modern (preindustrial) figure and the lowest level in more than 100,000 years. Atmospheric CO_2 – a fundamental driver of the climate system – stayed below 200 ppm, typical for the coldest depths of a glacial.[19] As measured by the flux of salt and dust in the Greenland ice cores, the high and middle latitudes of the northern hemisphere were wracked by recurring and intense winter storminess.

The glaciation was distantly but profoundly felt along the equatorial tropics, where the tropical convection system known as the Intertropical Convergence Zone was weakened and displaced well to the south. During the depths of the LGM, as in previous glacials, the reductions of CO_2, solar warmth, and atmospheric moisture all severely affected biotic life around the entire earth, limiting C3 plant growth and drying the tropics, where deserts expanded and rainforests shrank into relatively tiny refuges.[20] Rather than green and blue, the dominant colors of the earth were brown and white.

[18] Peter J. Richerson et al., "Was Agriculture Impossible during the Pleistocene but Mandatory during the Holocene," *AmAntiq* 66 (2001), 387–411; Gerhart and Ward, "Plant Responses to Low [CO_2] of the Past."

[19] E. J. Brooks et al., "Rapid Variation in Atmospheric Methane Concentration during the Past 110,000 Years," *Science* 273 (1996), 1087–91; J. R. Petit et al., "Climate and Atmospheric History of the Past 420,000 Years from the Vostok Ice Core, Antarctica," *Nature*, 399, 429–36; Jacqueline Flückiger et al., "High-Resolution Holocene N_2O Ice Core Record and Its Relationship with CH_4 and CO_2," *GBC* 16 (March 2002). Recent work now shows that plant life emits a considerable amount of methane, which provides a clearer picture of why methane moves so precisely with other climate variables. See Frank Keppler et al., "Methane Emissions from Terrestrial Plants under Aerobic Conditions," *Nature* 439 (2006), 187–92.

[20] William F. Ruddiman, *Earth's Climate: Past and Future* (New York, 2001), 193–209; I. Colin Prentice et al., "Mid-Holocene and Glacial-Maximum Vegetation Geography of the Northern Continents and Africa," *Journal of Biogeography* 27 (2000), 507–19.

But at the depths of the LGM, greenhouse gases began to slowly rise, and the Heinrich event at 16,500ybp – roughly 14,500 BC – was caused by a collapse of part of the eastern Canadian ice shield, hinting at changes to come.[21] The Pleistocene finally broke at 14,600ybp (12,600 BC), marked by a surge of temperatures and greenhouse gases. The overriding cause of the end of this glacial cycle was the gradual waning of the linked forcings of orbital precession and obliquity, bringing increasingly warmer winter temperatures to the winter poles. This effect was manifested in the melting of Antarctic ice and then transmitted globally through the global circulation system in a great sloshing of ocean waters: a huge collapse in the Antarctic ice sheet sent a surge of fresh water into the southern oceans, pushing warm tropical waters north and restarting the North Atlantic thermohaline pump.[22]

The effect on global climates was immediate, though slow changes had been in motion for several thousand years. Oxygen isotope readings in Greenland had been creeping up, but after 14,700ybp (12,700 BC) they jumped from a glacial −39 per mil. reading to a near modern −35 in 200 years, marking the onset of the warm interval called the Bølling-Allerød. The "Siberian High," a wintertime high-pressure system over central and northern Asia, had been extremely strong in glacial times. As measured by dust and Atlantic sea salt in the Greenland ice cores, its intensity collapsed suddenly at exactly the same time. Greenhouse gases had been rising slowly, but now they surged. Methane rose precipitously, derived both from tropical sources and melting tundra; it had risen into the 400s ppb by 18,000ybp (16,000 BC) and then jumped from the 480s around 15,200ybp to more than 660 ppb by 14,300ybp (12,300 BC). Driven by changes in oceanic chemistry that are still being worked out, as well as by several millennia of massive volcanic eruptions, atmospheric CO_2 slowly but steadily rose to modern levels by roughly 11,400ybp (9,400 BC). The renewed thermohaline circulation brought warm waters and ambient temperatures into Northern Europe, as did the inexorably advancing pattern of orbital precession and obliquity, which brought increasingly warm summers to the northern hemisphere. At the same time, sea surface temperatures in the shallow waters of the west Pacific rose, adding the force of a key tropical component to the rapid postglacial warm-up.[23]

[21] At this point in the narrative I shift from calendar years before present (ybp) to the Gregorian calendar (BC/AD) in historical work.

[22] Andrew J. Weaver, "Meltwater Pulse 1A from Antarctica as a Trigger of the Bølling-Allerød Warm Interval," *Science* 299 (2003), 1709–13; William J. Burroughs, *Climate Change in Prehistory: The End of the Reign of Chaos* (New York, 2005), 43–5.

[23] William F. Ruddiman, "Orbital Insolation, Ice Volume, and Greenhouse Gases," *QSR* 22 (2003), 1597–629; E. J. Rohling et al., "Holocene Atmosphere-Ocean Interactions: Records from Greenland and the Aegean Sea," *ClimDyn* 18 (2002), 587–93; D. Lüthi et al., "High-Resolution Carbon Dioxide Concentration Record 650,000–800,000 Years before Present," *Nature* 453 (2008), 379–82; L. Loulergue et al., "Orbital and Millennial-Scale Features of

This northern and tropical warming combined to impel the Intertropical Convergence Zone (ITCZ) to the north, as measured at the Donnge Cave on the South China coast and in the sediments in the Cariaco Basin off Venezuela. This equatorial system of rising oceanic air and falling moisture wraps around the earth at the meeting of a pair of climatic doughnuts, formally called the Hadley cells. The position of the ITCZ relative to the equator is fundamentally determined by the influence of orbital precession in warming the postglacial northern hemisphere. As had happened at the end of previous glacial periods, the north-riding ITCZ of the Early Holocene brought with it strong monsoonal summer rains to North Africa, the Mediterranean and Southwest Asia, India, and China. Under the force of this enhanced global monsoon system, the tropics bloomed and temperate biomes began to advance north, displacing taiga forests and the tundra steppe.[24]

This warming was, however, a false start. Its formal name is the "Bølling" interstadial, and though interrupted by a colder "Older Dryas" interval, it continued into the "Allerød" for 1,400 years (12,600–11,000 BC). The Older Dryas was a harbinger of some serious postglacial hiccups, however. After 10,900 BC, a serious cooling set in, intensifying into about 1,200 years of

Atmospheric CH4 over the Past 800,000 Years," *Nature* 453 (2008), 383–6; Shaun A. Marcott et al., "A Reconstruction of Regional and Global Temperature for the Past 11,300 Years," *Science* 339 (2013), 1198–201; P. A. Mayewski et al., "Major Features and Forcing of High-Latitude Northern Hemisphere Atmospheric Circulation Using a 110,000-Year-Long Glaciochemical Series. *JGR* 102 (1997), 26345–66; Gregory A. Zeilinski et al., "A 110,000 Yr Record of Explosive Volcanism from the GISP2 (Greenland) Ice Core," *QuatRes* 45 (1996), 109–18; –, "Volcanic Aerosol Records and Tephrochronology of the Summit, Greenland, Ice Cores," *JGR* 102 (1997), 26, 525–40; C. U. Hammer et al., "50,000 Years of Recorded Global Volcanism," *ClimCh* 35 (1997), 1–35. Peter deMenocal et al., "Coherent High- and Low-Latitude Climate Variability during the Holocene Warm Period," *Science* 288 (2000), 2198–202; G. H. Miller et al., "Temperature and Precipitation History of the Arctic, *QSR* 29 (2010), 1679–715; Lowell Stott, "Decline of Surface Temperature and Salinity in the Western Tropical Pacific Ocean in the Holocene Epoch," *Nature* 431 (2004), 56–9.

24 Dirk C. Leuschner and Frank Sirocko, "The Low-Latitude Monsoon Climate during Dansgaard-Oeschger Cycles and Heinrich Events," *QSR* 19 (2000), 243–54; Carrie Morrill et al., "A Synthesis of Abrupt Changes in the Asian Summer Monsoon since the Last Deglaciation," *The Holocene* 13 (2003), 465–76; Larry C. Peterson and Gerald H. Haug, "Variability in the Mean Latitude on the Atlantic Intertropical Convergence Zone as Recorded by Riverine Input of Sediments to the Cariaco Basin (Venezuela)," *PPP* 234 (2006), 97–113; Conrad A. Hughen et al., "Abrupt Tropical Vegetation Response to Rapid Climate Changes," *Science* 304 (2004), 1955–9; E. C. Pielou, *After the Ice: The Return of Life to Glaciated North America* (Chicago, IL, 1991); Carolyn A. Dykoski et al., "A High-Resolution, Absolute-Dated Holocene and Deglacial Asia Monsoon Record from Dongge Cave, China," *EPSL* 233 (2005), 71–86; and Dominik Fleitmann et al., "Holocene ITCZ and Indian Monsoon Dynamics Recorded in Stalagmites from Oman and Yemen (Socotra)," *QSR* 26 (2007), 170–88. For an overview, see Ruddiman, *Earth's Climate*, 301–19.

near-glacial cold. This event, the "Younger Dryas," is named for a tundra flower common in the ice ages that once puzzled European paleo-scientists because its pollen reappears in European sediment cores twice after the seeming end of the Pleistocene. Climates throughout the world fell back into their glacial mode and pushed the ITCZ south to the equator, weakening the monsoon systems that water Africa and southern Asia. Methane, fundamentally a product of tropical environments, seems to have been delayed in its response, dropping sharply about 800 years after the cold onset and recovering 400 years after the sudden polar warm-up. The causes of the Younger Dryas are now in some debate. The established explanation has been that warming temperatures melted North American sheets, and then the impounded melt water suddenly released into the Labrador Sea shut down the North Atlantic thermohaline pump. Recently, evidence has suggested that this melt water pulse was driven northwest, into the Arctic Ocean along Canada's McKenzie River. This thesis has been amplified by evidence for a low-atmospheric explosion of a meteor or comet over North America, which would have decimated life across the continent and released the melt water pulse driving the Younger Dryas.[25]

In any event, the Younger Dryas was the final major event of glacial cold. It abated suddenly in the century following 9700 BC. The Younger Dryas would not be the last aftershock of the Pleistocene: two other shorter melt water reversals – the "Preboreal Oscillation" and the "Laurentine Crisis" at 8200 BC and 6200 BC respectively – brought cold temperatures to the North Atlantic. But the Early Holocene that followed the cold Younger Dryas was a particularly warm epoch. Lasting for more than 4,000 years, the Early Holocene was the warmest period the earth had seen for at least 100,000 years, and warmer than it has been since.[26] This era has traditionally been called the "Holocene Optimum" or the "Holocene Megathermal," and in the terms of an older climate science includes all of the "Boreal" and

---

[25] The original melt water thesis was developed in Wallace S. Broecker et al., "Routing of Melt Water from the Laurentine Ice Sheet during the Younger Dryas Episode," *Nature* 341 (1989), 318–21. More recently see Julian B. Murton et al., "Identification of Younger Dryas Outburst Flood Path from Lake Agassiz to the Arctic Ocean," *Nature* 464 (2010), 740–3. The impact theory is developed in R. B. Firestone et al., "Evidence for an Extraterrestrial Impact 12,900 Years Ago That Contributed to the Megafaunal Extinctions and the Younger Dryas Cooling," *PNAS* 104 (2007), 16016–21; Douglas J. Kennett et al., "Shock-Synthesized Hexagonal Diamonds in Younger Dryas Boundary Sediments," *PNAS* 106 (2009), 12623–8. For a critique, see Wallace S. Broecker et al., "Putting the Younger Dryas Event into Context," *QSR* 29 (2010), 1078–81.

[26] The boundary between the Younger Dryas and the Early Holocene has recently been calculated to be 11,700ybp, or 9700 BC. Mike Walker et al., "Formal Definition and Dating of the GSSP (Global Stratotype Section and Point) for the Base of the Holocene Using the Greenland NGRIP Ice Core, and Selected Auxiliary Records," *JQS* 24 (2009), 3–17. OIS 11, roughly 400,000 years ago, may have had a long warm period similar to the Holocene. See Chapter 6 (discussion of the Ruddiman thesis).

"Atlantic I." In the northern hemisphere, the boundary between coniferous and deciduous forests was several hundred miles north of its current latitude. As the northern landmasses warmed, drawing the ITCZ north, regular monsoons watered the entire region from East Asia to the Sahara, which reverted to a green steppe grassland. Around 5000 BC, at the beginning of the Mid-Holocene, these ideal warm conditions would begin to abate; for 2,000 years, various markers indicate the return to cooler more unstable climates, culminating in the Mid-Holocene Crisis of roughly 3000 BC. But the Early Holocene Optimum, and before it the Bølling-Allerød warming and the cold, dry Younger Dryas itself, would be the context in which humans in a few critical locations around the world would begin to settle in, to cultivate local landscapes, and begin to produce food through farming.

* * *

New Climate Science, New Archaeological Science

We know these things because a technological revolution unfolding in climate science over the past decade is revealing an increasingly detailed picture of the Pleistocene deglaciation and the character of climate variation in the Holocene.[27] Ancient CO_2 and methane gases extracted from dated layers in the polar ice cores provide the foundational evidence. Scientists are making major efforts to recover ice core records from tropical glaciers threatened by global warming.[28] Traditional geological materials derived from ocean cores, simple sediments as well as various chemical signals, are providing a detailed picture of the ebb and flow of tropical monsoon systems, as are chemical signals in layers of ancient corals, seashells, and the limestone "speleothems" (*stalactites* in common parlance) that precipitate in caves.[29]

---

[27] For overviews of the paleoclimate revolution, see Eugene Linden, *The Winds of Change: Climate, Weather, and the Destruction of Civilizations* (New York, 2006); Tim Flannery, *The Weather-Makers: How Man Is Changing the Climate and What It Means for Life on Earth* (New York, 2005); and Burroughs, *Climate Change in Prehistory*, 26–31; and for an important statement of the implications of new scientific approaches to the past, see Michael McCormick, "History's Changing Climate: Climate Science, Genomics, and the Emerging Consilient Approach to Interdisciplinary History," *JInterdH* 42 (2011), 251–73.

[28] Lonnie G. Thompson et al., "Kilimanjaro Ice Core Records: Evidence of Holocene Climate Change in Tropical Africa," *Science* 298 (2002), 589–93; –, "A 25,000-Year Tropical Climate History from Bolivian Ice Cores," *Science* 282 (1998), 1858–64.

[29] Gerard Bond et al., "A Pervasive Millennial-Scale Cycle in North Atlantic Holocene and Glacial Climates," *Science* 278 (1997) 1257–66; Christopher M. Moy, "Variability of El Niño/Southern Oscillation Activity at Millennial Timescales during the Holocene Epoch," *Nature* 420 (2002), 162–5; Miryam Bar-Matthews et al., "Sea-Land Oxygen Isotopic Relationships from Planktonic Foraminifera and Speleothems in the Eastern Mediterranean Region and Their Implications for Paleo-Rainfall during Interglacial Times," *Geochimica et Cosmochimica Acta* 67 (2003), 3181–99.

Carbon-14 has long been a means of dating ancient organic materials, but it has been carefully corrected through a calibration with the tree rings of ancient California bristle-cone pine. Variations in the calibrated carbon-14 scale provide a proxy for the rate of insolation arriving at the top of the atmosphere, and thus a measure of solar forcing of climate.[30] Ancient tree rings themselves provide both exact dating and a biotic record of climate change, as do the sediments in lakes and bogs.[31]

A parallel technological revolution has been under way in the archaeological analysis of domestication and early agriculture. While a generation ago we learned in introductory courses that this transition would remain forever obscure because organic materials were invisible in the archaeological record, the past two decades has seen an all-out effort to render them visible, if through the microscope, building on established methods of the analysis of pollen recovered from lake and bog sediments. The study of domestication has taken an enormous leap forward with the discovery that many plants, but primarily grasses, produce their own fingerprints in microscopic "stones": microscopic structures of silica called *phytoliths* unique to each species develop in leaves and stems. Just as phytoliths can be harvested from archaeological soils, so too species-unique grains of ancient starch can be isolated on the surface of grinding implements. Methods have recently been developed to detect the isotopic signatures of milk and beer on archaeological pot sherds, and of terrestrial or marine species diet in human bone. Such work follows an older method of studying the surfaces of flints for the distinctive gloss that develops when they are used to harvest grasses, determined by experiment with reproduction tools. More directly, the now routine fine screening of archaeological deposits, and running samples through floatation machines, has produced a huge volume of organic material that older methods would have lost. Seeds from these collections are being sectioned and microscopically examined to determine whether they show signs of domestication, usually in the thickness of their husks. On the consumption side, broad categories of diet – marine versus terrestrial – produce chemical signatures that survive in bones, and new work is under way

[30] Maura Vonmoos et al., "Large Variations in Holocene Solar Activity: Constraints from 10Be in the Greenland Ice Core Project Ice Core," *JGR* 111 (2006), A10105; Raimund Muscheler et al., "Geomagnetic Field Intensity during the Last 60,000 Years based on ¹⁰Be and ³⁶Cl from the Summit Ice Cores and ¹⁴C," *QSR* 24 (2005), 1849–60; K. Hughen et al., "¹⁴C Activity and Global Carbon Cycle Changes over the Past 50,000 Years," *Science* 303 (2004), 202–7; Raimund Muscheler, personal communication, May 5, 8, 9, 2006.

[31] M. G. L. Baillie, *A Slice through Time: Dendrochronology and Precision Dating* (London, 1995); Peterson and Haug, "Variability in the Mean Latitude on the Atlantic Intertropical Zone"; Y. T. Hong, "Inverse Phase Oscillations between the East Asian and Indian Ocean Summer Monsoons during the Last 12,000 Years and Paleo-El-Niño," *EPSL* 231 (2005), 337–46; Dmitri Mauquoy et al., "Changes in Solar Activity and Holocene Climatic Shifts Derived from 14C Wiggle-Match Dated Peat Bogs," *The Holocene* 14 (2004), 45–52.

to assess these isotopic signatures in prehistoric skeletal material. Equally importantly, though usually more macroscopically, the stresses of life – diet, work routine, disease, and violence – produce their signatures on the skeletal anatomy, and increasingly ambitious projects are under way to interpret the long-term history of human health from systematically recorded skeletal collections.

Finally, there is genetics, both of plants and of humans. Just as the exploding work in genetic history is providing new structure to the history of human emergence, it is bringing increasingly precise detail to our understanding of the shape of the huge expansions of population that followed the Pleistocene and the emergence of agriculture. The historical analysis of the genetics of modern populations is increasingly supported by a parallel analysis of genetic material from archaeological skeletons. The genetic analysis of plant and animal species is providing yet another set of information on the process of domestication.[32] And finally the refined recalibration of carbon-14 dating is giving an ever-sharper picture of how archaeological deposits around the world align in time, both with each other and with the signals of climate change in the archives of sedimentary layers that detail the natural history of the earth.[33] All of these efforts comprise the basis of our understanding of the human condition in the Early Holocene. Given limitations of space in the following account, I will only be able to summarize the findings and implications of these methodologies, and not be able to do justice to the nuances and caveats that their practitioners bring to their arduous work.

*   *   *

Human Adaptation at the Bølling-Allerød Warming: The Mesolithic

Warmer climates are easier to survive than are glacial ones. Such is the simplest perspective on the great post-Pleistocene warm-up, and the implication of an effort to measure the size of populations of Upper Paleolithic peoples

[32] Melinda A. Zeder et al., eds., *Documenting Domestication: New Genetic and Archaeological Paradigms* (Berkeley, CA, 2006); Jean D. Meunier and Fabrice Colin, eds., *Phytoliths: Applications in Earth Sciences and Human History* (Lisse, 2001); B. D. Smith *The Emergence of Agriculture*, 35–48; Martin Jones and Terry Brown, "Agricultural Origins: The Evidence of Modern and Ancient DNA," *Holocene* 10 (2000), 769–76; M. P. Richards, "Stable Isotope Evidence of Diet at Neolithic Çatalhöyük, Turkey," *JArchS* 30 (2003), 67–76; Richard H. Steckel and Jerome C. Rose, eds., *The Backbone of History: Health and Nutrition in the Western Hemisphere* (New York, 2002); Clark Spencer Larsen, *Bioarchaeology: Interpreting Behavior from the Human Skeleton* (New York, 1997); Mark Nathan Cohen and George J. Armelagos, eds., *Paleopathology at the Origins of Agriculture* (New York, 1984).
[33] Paul Mellars, "A New Radiocarbon Revolution and the Dispersal of Modern Humans in Eurasia," *Nature* 439 (2006), 931–5.

in Europe, through the Last Glacial Maximum and into the Bølling-Allerød. Nothing in these estimates would suggest a late Paleolithic population crisis. Between the arrival of Upper Paleolithic peoples in Europe around 45,000 years ago and the Last Glacial Maximum, European populations probably hovered near a total of around 5,000 people. This tiny population only slowly and incrementally grew, but on the other hand did not disappear in the face of brutal conditions. Then with the warming conditions after 17,000 BC that accelerated with the onset of the Bølling-Allerød at 12,600 BC, European populations may have risen by a factor of five, spreading out to the north as the glaciers retreated. Though much of this population growth resulted from the availability of new territories, population densities may have almost tripled with the warming climates.

Bocquet-Appel's estimate of Western European population at the end of the Pleistocene

		Average Greenland Methane	Average estimated European populations	Average estimated population density per 100 km²
Aurignacian	40–31,000 BC	494 ppb	4,424	0.168
Gravettian	31–23,000 BC	430 ppb	4,776	0.183
Solutrean-Magdelanian (LGM)	23–17,000 BC	406 ppb	5,885	0.257
Magdalenian-Mesolithic	17–11,000 BC	591 ppb	28,736	0.722

Sources: Population estimates from Jean-Pierre Bocquet-Appel, "Estimates of Upper Paleolithic Meta-Population Size in Europe from Archaeological Data, JArchS 32 (2005), 1656–68; methane from data supporting Brooks et al., "Rapid Variation in Atmospheric Methane Concentration during the Past 110,000 Years."

Europe is uniquely amenable to such estimates because it is the most carefully surveyed region in the world, but this leaves the rest of the world uncounted. There is a range of estimates for human population numbers, though they may have stood at roughly 7 million people at the end of the Pleistocene, and it is certainly reasonable to suggest that this number climbed significantly as climates warmed.[34] The figures for Europe may indicate that the warming of late glacial and Bølling-Allerød times brought a sudden release from Pleistocene mortality crises and a consequent population explosion.

But the ecological changes that came with these warmer climates created their own problems as well. With the three-step jolt of the Bølling-Allerød

[34] Binford, *Constructing Frames of Reference*, 142–4; Mark Nathan Cohen, in *The Food Crisis in Prehistory: Overpopulation and the Origins of Agriculture* (New Haven, CT, 1977), 54, argued that the total could be as high as fifteen million.

warming, the Younger Dryas cooling, and the early Holocene rewarming, biomes that had been in a relatively stable cool and dry glacial mode began to change significantly. In the tropics, dry forest and scrubland gave way to rainforest, and deserts turned into shifting savannahs. In the mid-latitudes, from Europe and Southwest Asia to China and North America, dry steppes gave way to various temperate forest types, governed by the flow of rain-bearing winds. Global terrestrial net primary productivity probably roughly doubled between the LGM and the Holocene Optimum.[35] Adjusting to this bounty, however, was not easy, because by early in the Holocene the "packaging" of the easily useable NPP had changed considerably. Upper Paleolithic peoples, particularly outside of sub-Saharan Africa, found that the big game that had provided the big "protein packages" in their diet for hundreds of thousands of years was disappearing.

The causes of the megafaunal extinctions are a matter of considerable debate. What is clear is that larger species of herbivores, and carnivores as well, went extinct in the Americas, in Australia, and across Eurasia. Only in Africa, where humans and their prey had lived together for millions of years, did the megafauna survive, perhaps a suggestion that human hunting did have a hand in their demise elsewhere. The overkill hypothesis, advanced most vigorously by Paul S. Martin, posits that the sudden impact of highly skilled big-game hunters, or simply ecologically disruptive human populations, moving into unoccupied regions during the global colonization after 60,000ybp, played a key role in the disappearance of the megafauna. The contrary position finds little hard evidence, and argues for the impact of the end of the last glaciation: the overkill theorists quite justifiably retort that the earth had moved through at least nine such cycles in the past million years without such a die-off. Adding complexity to this debate, the advocates of a Younger Dryas meteor impact see that event as critical to both megafaunal collapse and the sudden end of the North American Paleoindian Clovis point tradition, a marker of wide-ranging hunting peoples.[36]

---

[35] A simulation estimates NPP in China was 208 g/m²·a at the LGM, 409 g/m²·a at the Mid-Holocene, and 355 g/m²·a at the present. He Yong, "The Terrestrial NPP Simulations in China since Last Glacial Maximum," *Chinese Science Bulletin* 50 (2005), 2074–9.

[36] Ross D. E. MacPhee, ed., *Extinctions in Near Time: Causes, Contexts, and Consequences* (New York, 1999); G. H. Miller et al., "Ecosystem Collapse in Pleistocene Australia"; J. Stuart et al., "Pleistocene to Holocene Extinction Dynamics in Giant Deer and Mammoth," *Nature* 431 (2004), 684–9; Gary Haynes, "The Catastrophic Extinction of North America Mammoths and Mastodonts," *WdArch* 33 (2002), 391–416; for a contrary view, see Grayson, "The Archaeological Record of Human Impacts on Animal Populations," 34–45, who argues that extinction models for continents are based erroneously on island histories. For the impact theory, see Firestone et al., "Evidence for an Extraterrestrial Impact 12,900 Years Ago." Yet another proposal is that dogs migrating with Paleolithic bands carried diseases that might have jumped to some of the megafauna. Stuart J. Fiedel, "Man's Best Friend – Mammoth's Worst Enemy? A Speculative Essay on the Role of Dogs in Paleoindian Colonization and Megafaunal Extinction," *WdArch* 37 (2005), 11–25; Carl Zimmer,

When all of the evidence is in, two basic points will probably emerge. First, it seems most likely that a confluence of causes was at work, with species weakened by the end of the glacial climates done in by the fire-making, hunting people appearing in their midst for the first time. Second, it will be equally clear that the megafaunal extinctions really have only a tangential bearing on the origins of agriculture. The major extinctions can be dated to around 45,000–50,000 years ago in Australia, 11,000 years ago in the Americas, and as late as 5,000 years ago in remote northern Siberia. In none of these areas are these extinctions followed immediately by a sudden transition from mobile hunting to sedentary proto-food production.

The reality was a bit more prosaic. While the great dramas of megafaunal extinction were taking place at the cutting edge of human expansion, peoples in longer-occupied regions were experiencing a more general change in local biogeography, as the postglacial warming changed steppe regions into forests of various kinds. More than the great extinctions, this simple biotic transition reduced the numbers of the herd animals that had ranged on the open grasslands of glacial times. At the same time, rising sea levels and increased rainfall began to flood the continental shelves, creating entirely new hotspots of net primary productivity in estuaries, swamps, and marshlands. Very simply, useable NPP shifted from steppe toward wetland, but it required an entirely new technology and social scheduling to exploit. And across this sequence of biotic change two other variables were coming into play. Longer-settled regions, some now with quite ancient settlement histories, may have been filling up with foraging bands with increasingly competitive claims to territory, and in some of these regions the constraints of topography on the distribution of NPP-rich resources imposed boundaries to further expansion. Archaeologist Lewis Binford describes this moment as the "*packing threshold*," when the ratio between population and NPP pushed people into an *intensifying* trajectory toward food production. It would be in these areas of *circumscription*, if appropriate food species were available, that the transition toward food production would begin with the Bølling-Allerød warming. Alternatively, however, it has been proposed that living for the first time in warm, wet environments, post-Pleistocene peoples would have struggled to maintain their numbers against an onslaught of new waterborne disease, and this "exogenous" natural force would have led to new demands for more predictable sources of food.[37]

"Carriers of Extinction," *Discover* 16/6 (July 1995), 28–9. For a critique, see David J. Meltzer and Vance T. Holliday, "Would North American Paleoindians have Noticed Younger Dryas Climate Changes?" *JWP* 23 (2010), 1–41.

[37] Binford, *Constructing Frames of Reference*, 363–472. The term *circumscription* was first used in the formative essay by Robert Carneiro, "A Theory of the Origin of the State," *Science* 169 (1970), 733–8; Les Groube, "The Impact of Diseases upon the Emergence of Agriculture," in Harris, ed., *The Origins and Spread of Agriculture and Pastoralism in Eurasia*, 101–29.

Pervasively, then, across Eurasia, China, northern Africa, and the Americas, the end of the Pleistocene saw the end of the Upper Paleolithic. Driven by biotic change, human populations shifted toward a more sedentary settlement pattern and toward the exploitation of smaller, more numerous species, toward plant gathering, toward freshwater and marine resources.[38] Lewis Binford first noticed this pattern in the 1960s, and in 1969 Kent Flannery labeled it the "broad spectrum revolution"; Mark Nathan Cohen described it as the transition from first-choice to second-choice foods; food production would bring the final transition to third-choice foods.[39] Their technology shifted toward the material culture required to harvest this spectrum of more numerous, more productive, but small and faster prey: nets, traps, bows and arrows, baskets. The formal labels for this epoch in human history vary from region to region; in much of Eurasia it is called the Mesolithic, in Southwest Asia the Epipaleolithic, in the Americas the Archaic, and in Africa it is broadly continuous with the Late Stone Age. I will call them all *mesolithic* as a shorthand.

If the European estimates are even a vague approximation of the demographics of the wider transition, populations increased everywhere with the release from glacial climates. Population densities might have increased as mesolithic peoples settled for longer seasons at particularly favorable sites on the postglacial landscape. But only in a very few specific locations is there evidence for an immediate transition to an intensive plant food collection that suggests a form of proto-horticulture, the beginnings of Bruce Smith's "low-level food production." For China, a series of recent studies have found phytolith evidence for the sudden appearance of species of wild rice during the Bølling-Allerød warming, in a core from a flooded estuary, and from a cave site in the middle reaches of the Yangtze Valley. The evidence seems to suggest both that rice was very sensitive to changes in temperature and CO_2, and that peoples in the region turned quickly to harvesting wild rice at the first warming.[40] Along the Nile, increasing monsoonal rainfall at

---

[38] M. P. Richards et al., "Isotope Evidence for the Intensive Use of Marine Foods by Late Upper Paleolithic Humans," *JHumEv* 49 (2005), 390–4 (and literature there cited).

[39] Lewis R. Binford, "Post-Pleistocene Adaptations," in S. R. Binford and L. R. Binford, eds., *New Perspectives in Archaeology* (Chicago, IL, 1968), 313–41; Kent V. Flannery, "Origins and Ecological Effects of Early Domestication in Iran and the Near East," in Peter J. Ucko and G. W. Dimbley, eds., *The Domestication and Exploitation of Plants and Animals* (Chicago, IL, 1969), 73–100; Cohen, *The Food Crisis in Prehistory*; Brian Hayden, "Research and Development in the Stone Age: Technological Transition among Hunter-Gatherers," *CA* 22 (1981), 519–45; for the most recent review, see Mary C. Stiner, "Thirty Years on the "Broad Spectrum Revolution" and Paleodemography," *PNAS* 98 (2001), 6993–6.

[40] Houyuan Lu et al., "Rice Domestication and Climatic Change: Phytolith Evidence from East China," *Boreas* 31 (2002), 378–85; Zhijun Zhao and Dolores R. Piperno, "Late Pleistocene/ Holocene Environments in the Middle Yangtze Valley, China and Rice (*Oryza sativa* L.) Domestication: The Phytolith Evidence," *Geoarchaeology* 15 (2000), 203–22; Charles Higham and Tracy L.-D. Lu, "The Origins and Dispersal of Rice Cultivation," *Antiquity*

its equatorial headwaters brought catastrophic floods downstream, a period called the Wild Nile, eliminating a wide valley floor where Paleolithic peoples had lived off herds of wild cattle and hartebeest. In response, local Qadan hunter-gatherers focused on fishing and, where possible, the roots of marsh plants, processed with grindstones to reduce their toxicity.[41]

But the best-documented shift toward plant use came in the southern Levant of the Southwest Asian Fertile Crescent. Here, with the onset of significantly increased rainfall at the opening of the Bølling-Allerød, the local Paleolithic Kebaran peoples settled into seasonal hamlets of pit houses, base camps in their wider subsistence circuit, living off collecting grass seed, acorns, and gazelles harvested in increasingly sophisticated drives. These villages – if never as large as later Neolithic settlements – are evidence of locally dense settlements of people living amongst the debris and burials of numerous generations and generating a far more complex cultural life than their predecessors. If the most recent DNA analysis is right, this was the point when dogs were domesticated from local wolf populations; we can imagine packs of village dogs feeding on garbage and providing an early warning system for the settlement.[42] This was the Early Natufian, and it lasted for about 1,500 years, until the summer rains faded and the Younger Dryas set in.[43] Natufian exploitation of plant resources had origins running back to the preceding Upper Paleolithic (Kebaran) period, as demonstrated

[72] (1998), 867–70; and Zhao Zhijun, "The Middle Yangtze Region in China is One Place Where Rice Was Domesticated: Phytolith Evidence from the Diaotonghuan Cave, Northern Jiangxi," *Antiquity* 72 (1998), 885–97.

[41] Joel J. Shiner, "The Cataract Tradition," and Fred Wendorf, "Summary of Nubian Prehistory," in Fred Wendorf, ed., *The Prehistory of Nubia*, vol. 2 (Dallas, TX, 1968), 564–629, 1050–1, 1056; Barbara E. Barich, *People, Water, and Grain: The Beginnings of Domestication in the Sahara and the Nile Valley* (Rome, 1998), 33–7; Angela E. Close, "Plus Ça Change: The Pleistocene-Holocene Transition in Northeast Africa," in Strauss et al., *Humans at the End of the Ice Age*, 44–54; Steven Mithen, *After the Ice: A Global Human History, 20,000–5000 B.C.* (Cambridge, MA, 2004), 451–2.

[42] Bridgett M. von Holdt et al., Genome-Wide SNP and Haplotype Analyses Reveal a Rich History Underlying Dog Domestication," *Nature* 464 (2010), 898–902. For work that suggests earlier dog domestication, see Adam R. Boyko et al., "Complex Population Structure in African Village Dogs and Its Implications for Inferring Dog Domestication History," *PNAS* 106 (2009), 13903–8; Carles Vilas et al., "Multiple and Ancient Origins of the Domestic Dog," *Science* 276 (1997), 1687–9; Martin Jones, "Issues of Scale and Symbiosis: Unpicking the 'Agricultural Package,'" in Peter Bellwood and Colin Renfrew, eds., *Examining the Farming/Language Dispersal Hypothesis* (Cambridge, 2002), 371–2. For a review, see Rodney L. Honeycutt, "Unravelling the Mysteries of Dog Evolution," *BMC Biology* 8 (2010).

[43] For recent reviews, see Ofer Bar-Osef, "The Natufian Culture in the Levant, Threshold to the Origins of Agriculture," *Evolutionary Anthropology* 6 (1998), 161–7; Marc Verhoeven, "Beyond Boundaries: Nature, Culture and a Holistic Approach to Domestication in the Levant," *JWP* 18 (2004), 231–40; Mithen, *After the Ice*, 29–45; Brian F. Byrd, "Reassessing the Emergence of Village Life in the Near East," *JArchRes* 13 (2005), 231–90; and Brian Boyd, "On 'Sedentism' in the Later Epipaleolithic (Natufian) Levant," *WdArch* 38 (2006), 164–78.

by the dramatic discovery of a waterlogged habitation site in the northern Jordan Valley, filled with evidence of grass seed exploitation, dating to 23,500–22,500ybp.[44] While this Ohalo II site has been presented as evidence for a continuous pattern of plant gathering in the Levant through the Last Glacial Maximum, it dates exactly to the period of the brief warm Dansgaard-Oeschger Event 2, dated at 23,400ybp, and the highest carbon-13 reading in the Soreq Cave speleothems – a hint of marginally better growing conditions for C3 plants – for the entire period between 35,000ybp and 18,000ybp.[45] Thus the Ohalo II site might well record a very brief flash of warm climate and intensive plant exploitation in the longer postglacial times, broken again with the Bølling-Allerød, when a second and longer climate-driven trajectory toward a plant-based diet had more enduring results starting with the Early Natufian.

Rice phytoliths in the Yangtze region, sickles and grinding stones along the Nile, the dense Early Natufian settlements in the Levant: these comprise the sum total of the earliest *known* beginnings of horticulture in the first warm epoch following the Last Glacial Maximum. It is certainly possible that there were slow trajectories in motion in the Old World tropics that archaeological studies as yet have failed to detect, and despite ever-increasing efforts such early evidence has not been found for the New World. The archaeology of the earliest moves toward agriculture in the Americas is complicated by the fact that there is not even a solid consensus that human populations arrived before 12,000 years ago, after the Bølling-Allerød warming and in the middle of the cold Younger Dryas. On the other hand, arguments have been made for earlier colonizations, as early as 20,000ybp, along coastal routes from Siberia, and even possibly along the ice front from Europe. In any event, however, the western hemisphere, particularly the Mesoamerican New World hearth, was too thinly settled – and the plant life too resistant to domestication – for the beginnings of agriculture to date to 10,000 BC.[46]

---

[44] Ehud Weiss et al., "The Broad Spectrum Revisited: Evidence from Plant Remains," *PNAS* 101 (2004), 9551–5; Dolores Piperno et al., "Processing Wild Cereals in the Upper Paleolithic Revealed by Starch Grain Analysis," *Nature* 430 (2004), 670–3.

[45] This point is based on the GISP2 record and the data associated with Bar-Matthews et al., "Sea-Land Oxygen Isotopic Relationships"; see also Miryam Bar-Matthews and Avner Ayalon, "Climatic Conditions in the Eastern Mediterranean during the Last Glacial (60–10 ky bp) and Their Relations to the Upper Paleolithic in the Levant: Oxygen and Carbon Isotope Systematics of Cave Deposits," in A. Nigel Goring-Morris and Anna Belfer-Cohen, eds., *More than Meets the Eye: Studies on Upper Paleolithic Diversity in the Near East* (Oxford, 2003), 13–18.

[46] Alan G. Fix, "Rapid Deployment of the Five Founding Amerind mtDNA Haplogroups via Coastal and Riverine Colonization," *AJPA* 128 (2004), 430–6; Bruce Bradley and Dennis Stanford, "The North Atlantic Ice-Edge Corridor: Possible Paleolithic Route to the New World," *WdArch* 36 (2004), 459–78; Dolores R. Piperno and Deborah M. Pearsall, *The Origins of Agriculture in the Lowland Neotropics* (New York, 1998), 12.

What do the three earliest trajectories toward plant dependence share in common? Each had a resource that was amenable to intensive exploitation, though only in China and the Levant did this lead to successful domestication. Each was in an area long occupied by modern humans, the Nubian Nile since 60,000ybp, the Levant since 40,000ybp, and China from perhaps 30,000 years ago. Each was located in the mid-latitudes, rather than the tropics, though the Nubian Nile was considerably south of the latitude of the Levant and the Yangtze. Each also was in some way *bounded geographically and environmentally*: the Yangtze sites are caves into dry limestone hills that surround moist swamps, lakes and river valleys, the Nubian Nile a ribbon of braided channels and alluvium set between desert escarpments, the Levant a narrow strip of well-watered hills between desert to the east and the Mediterranean to the west, a sea that was precipitously rising and flooding once-inhabited shores during the Bølling-Allerød.[47] These were places where there were bountiful resources, but from which there was little room for expansion. These were regions where – in the warm climates of the postglacial Bølling-Allerød – it was easier to develop complexity in place than to evade scarcity by moving, the ancient strategy of early humans.

If a transition toward the mesolithic broad spectrum of foraging was beginning throughout the world, these three regions were places where local peoples took this intensification of the food quest to a new height. The stresses on the people in the Levant have been detailed in a series of studies measuring the changing qualities of animal diet consumed by Kebaran and Early Natufian peoples. Looking at the animal bones preserved at archaeological sites, Natalie Munro has demonstrated that Early Natufians progressively consumed far more small game than did the Paleolithic Kebaran peoples, a sign that the depletion of resources was demanding new, more intensive subsistence strategies. Her conclusion is that "human population packing and territorial circumscription undoubtedly characterized the cultural context of the Early Natufian Levant. Clearly, this was a period in which environmental carrying capacity was effectively raised to a new level." Here it seems clear that pressures on the land stemmed from the relatively dense populations of the Natufian hamlets. It would seem entirely likely that populations did grow in an unprecedented way during the Early Natufian, setting the stage for a new crisis.[48]

* * *

[47] These ideas are informed broadly by Andrew Sherratt's "Plate Tectonics and Imaginary Prehistories: Structures and Contingency in Agricultural Origins," in Harris, ed., *The Origins and Spread of Agriculture and Pastoralism in Eurasia*, 130–40.
[48] Natalie D. Munro, "Zooarchaeological Measures of Hunting Pressure and Occupation Intensity in the Natufian," *CA* 45 (2004), S5–S33, quote at S20. See also Mary C. Stiner et al., "Paleolithic Population Growth Pulses Evidenced by Small Animal Exploitation," *Science* 283 (1999), 190–4; Simon Davis, "Why Domesticate Animals? Some Zoo-Archaeological

The Younger Dryas and the Early Holocene: Cereal Domestication in the Northern Mid-Latitudes

The warm, wet weather of the Bølling-Allerød lasted no more than 1,400 years, from 12,600 BC to roughly 11,200 BC, when the cold glacial Younger Dryas set in, as melt waters slowed and stopped the North Atlantic thermohaline pump, and altered climates throughout the world. Though climate scientists can measure the impact of the Younger Dryas on the tropics, its effects seem to have been particularly significant – or observable – in the three circumscribed mid-latitude regions that had made such precocious strides toward a sedentary plant-dependent subsistence.[49]

Along the Yangtze River in China, rice phytoliths totally disappear from the record between roughly 11,000 BC and 9500 BC, before reappearing in increasingly domesticated forms (see Figure II.3). Apparently either increasing cold or changes in seasonality radically diminished the growth of wild rice.[50] As the Younger Dryas set in, the peoples of the Nile in Nubia (present-day northern Sudan) seemed to have suffered the first recorded resource war. A Nubian cemetery excavated in 1968 shows signs of extreme and systematic violence; at least 40 percent of the fifty-nine recovered individuals died violent deaths, and many were buried in joint graves. Evidence for interpersonal, and probably communal, violence during this epoch has been found in Algeria and among the Natufian in the Levant. Along the Nile, the mesolithic population seems to have entered a downward spiral; the culture associated with the violence-ridden cemetery, the Qadan, disappeared in the middle of the Younger Dryas around 10,000 BC. Until 8000 BC, parts of the Nile Valley were virtually abandoned[51] (see Figure II.2).

Evidence from the Levant," *JArchS* 32 (2005), 1408–16; and Donald O. Henry, "Models of Agricultural Origins and Proxy Measures of Prehistoric Demographics," in R. T. J. Cappers and S. Bottema, eds., *The Dawn of Farming in the Near East* (Berlin, 2002), 15–25. These results vindicate the approach developed by Cohen, *The Food Crisis in Prehistory*, 80–1, and his analysis of the Natufian, 132–8.

[49] Peterson and Haug, "Variability in the Mean Latitude on the Atlantic Intertropical Zone"; Hughen et al., "Abrupt Tropical Vegetation Response"; Piperno and Pearsall, *The Origins of Agriculture in the Neotropics*, 104–5.

[50] Zhao, "The Middle Yangtze Region," 894 and Lu et al., "Rice Domestication and Climatic Change," 384 attribute gaps in the rice phytolith record to the impact of the Younger Dryas.

[51] Close, "Plus Ça Change," 44–54; Fred Wendorf, "A Nubian Final Paleolithic Graveyard near Jebel Sahaba, Sudan," in Wendorf, *The Prehistory of Nubia*, 954–94. See also Fanny Bocquentin and Ofer Bar-Yosef, "Early Natufian Remains: Evidence for Physical Conflict from Mt. Carmel, Israel," *JHumEv* 47 (2004), 19–23; L. Bachechi, "An Arrow-Caused Lesion in a Late Upper Paleolithic Human Pelvis," *CA* 38 (1997), 135–40; Vered Eshed, "Has the Transition to Agriculture Reshaped the Demographic Structure of Prehistoric Populations? New Evidence from the Levant," *AJPA* 124 (2004), 315–29, at 326; Arthur Ferrill, *The Origins of War: From the Stone Age to Alexander the Great*, rev. ed. (Boulder, CO, 1997), 23–4.

The cold Younger Dryas brought a similar but better-documented decline to the Levant, where rainfall shifted from summer to winter around 11,700 BC, suggesting the retreat of the warm African and Indian Ocean summer monsoon and the intensification of the Atlantic westerlies, bringing some winter rain to these regions (see Figure II.2). Very rapidly, the dense Early Natufian settlements of round, stone-lined huts were abandoned, and the Late Natufians returned to a small-scale migratory subsistence, spreading out of the southern Levant north to the Euphrates and south into the Negev desert. It seems clear that population dropped significantly, apparently because the plant resources that the summer rains had supported – acorns, wild wheat, and barley – were severely reduced. Natalie Munro found that the Late Natufians shifted from small game back to larger animals, suggesting that hunting pressures reduced as populations declined, either through attrition and local crisis mortality or by out-migration into a very meager existence in the desert. Many of the aspects of the flourishing material culture of the Early Natufian disappeared, but one important feature indicates a cultural continuity: the Late Natufians used the Early Natufian village sites for graveyards, where they gathered perhaps annually to rebury their dead from scattered locations.[52]

In these three regions, the glacial Younger Dryas had a serious impact on early food-gathering peoples; to the north across Eurasia, mesolithic peoples moved back into Paleolithic ways for the duration of this millennium of glacial cold.[53] To the south, in the tropics, there is no clear indication that there were serious adverse impacts, but at the same time there is also no indication that tropical peoples were moving rapidly and precipitously toward agriculture. Rather it would be in the Yangtze and the greater Fertile Crescent, both long-occupied, circumscribed regions in the northern mid-latitudes with plants and animals amenable to domestication, where the rebound from the Younger Dryas into the warming Holocene would bring the most rapid trajectories toward agriculture.

Archaeologists have argued for some years that the stresses of the Younger Dryas led directly to domestication by the Late Natufians, building on a long history of climate stress models. The first was the "oasis thesis" proposed by V. Gordon Childe, who argued that agriculture developed in isolated wet locations in a general desiccation of the Mid-East at the end of the Pleistocene. This approach was rejected in the 1950s when scientists learned that the region got wetter, not drier, with the Holocene. In the 1960s, Lewis Binford proposed a model in which population growth forced excess

[52] Bar-Osef, "The Natufian Culture in the Levant"; Munro, "Zooarchaeological Measures"; Verhoeven, "Beyond Boundaries," 241–3; Brian F. Byrd and Christopher M. Monahan, "Death, Mortuary Ritual, and Natufian Social Structure," *JAnthArch* 14 (1995), 251–87; Mithen, *After the Ice*, 46–54.

[53] See the essays in Strauss et al., ed., *Humans at the End of the Ice Age*, 83–170.

populations into marginal areas, where they developed agriculture: this approach was undermined as it became clear that domestication developed in favorable, not marginal, areas. The Younger Dryas thesis was developed in the late 1980s and 1990s, as it became clear that post-Pleistocene climate change was more convoluted than previously thought. In essence, it revives Childe's "oasis model," now transferred to the cold, dry conditions of the Younger Dryas. It proposes that the enlarged sedentary populations of the Early Natufian took two routes when faced with the stresses of the Younger Dryas: back to mobile hunter-gathering subsistence or forward into domestication, bringing wild wheat and barley into domestic cultivation quite rapidly, becoming farmers under the lash of a climate reversal.[54]

Unfortunately, recent work has considerably undermined this elegant thesis. First, Natalie Munro argues that her evidence for a shift in Natufian hunting back to larger game indicates that the Late Natufian population was much smaller during the Younger Dryas, and shows no evidence of a pressure toward agriculture. If cereal plants could potentially be domesticated in a relatively short period, perhaps 200 biotic generations, the evidence indicates that the real process was much slower, on the order of 2,000 to 3,000 years. Mark Nesbitt has done a careful review of the earliest dates of known domesticated plants, and has concluded that domestication did not take place until after 8500 BC, almost 1,000 years after the end of the Younger Dryas, in what is called the Early Phase of Pre-Pottery Neolithic B (PPNB), arguing that, while Late Natufians might well have cultivated wild plants, they did not domesticate them. Most recently, there has been a recalculation of the dating of the pollen profile from Lake Huleh in Israel, based on a new understanding of the carbon content of modern waters affecting the C14 dating. The old dating of the Huleh core indicated an expansion of cereal pollen around 11,500 BC, right at the beginning of the Late Natufian. The new dating of the Huleh core shifts this cereal onset

---

[54] Here I follow the literature review in Verhoeven, "Beyond Boundaries," 192–9. There are many statements of variants of the Younger Dryas argument, including A. M. T. Moore and G. C. Hillman, "The Pleistocene to Holocene Transition and Human Economy in Southwest Asia: The Impact of the Younger Dryas," *AmAnth* 57 (1992), 482–94; Ofer Bar-Yosef and Richard H. Meadow, "The Origins of Agriculture in the Near East," in Price and Gebauer, eds., *Last Hunters, First Farmers*, 39–95; Andres Garrand et al., "The Emergence of Crop-Cultivation and Caprine Herding in the "Marginal Zone of the Southern Levant," in Harris, ed., *The Origins and Spread of Agriculture and Pastoralism in Eurasia*, 204–26; Andrew Sherratt, "Climatic Cycles and Behavioural Revolutions: The Emergence of Modern Humans and the Beginning of Farming," *Antiquity* 71 (1997), 271–87; Robert Layton, "The Human Evolutionary Time-Scale and the Transition between Hunting and Gathering, and Farming," in John Bintliff, ed., *Structure and Contingency: Evolutionary Processes in Life and Human Society* (London, 1999), 102–17; Bar-Yosef, "The Natufian Culture in the Levant"; and Ofer Bar-Yosef and Anna Belfer Cohen, "Facing Environmental Crisis: Societal and Cultural Changes at the Transition from the Younger Dryas to the Holocene in the Levant," in Cappers and Bottema, *The Dawn of Farming in the Near East*, 55–66.

by 4,000 years, placing it at 7500 BC, in the Middle Phase of the PPNB[55] (see Figure II.2).

The current consensus broadly suggests a series of adaptive cycles, and the peoples of the Levant responded to the sequence of climatic change in an oscillation between low-density foraging and higher-density sedentism and proto-agriculture. During the Late Natufian, under the stress of the Younger Dryas, the peoples of the southern Levant dispersed from their settled hamlets, but retained knowledge of plant exploitation and developed a burial cult linked with the old settlements. The last several hundred years of the Younger Dryas (10,000–9700 BC) were particularly severe, shattering the Late Natufian peoples into a thin jumble of refugee groups in the Jordan valley.[56] Then, as the climate warmed with the true onset of the Holocene around 9700 BC, peoples throughout the western Fertile Crescent from the Levant up into Anatolia settled into new and larger villages, again with round or oval structures, situated on spring-fed alluvial fans where barley and wheat stands may have grown more thickly. This was the Pre-Pottery Neolithic A, but as yet the "Neolithic" component was pretty minimal. These were sedentary hunter-gatherers much like the Natufians, but without the pottery that typically is a marker of the Neolithic, and cultivating wild plants rather than controlling domesticated plants. The PPNA and the ensuing Early PPNB, running from 9600 BC to roughly 8200 BC, were the truly transitional cultures in the emergence of agriculture in Southwest Asia. The PPNA people of the Levant, cultivating wild barley, wheat, and rye in an early form of flood-water farming, increasingly learned its ecology, while contemporary peoples to the north in Anatolia began to edge wild goats and sheep into domestication. True agricultural dependence advanced only after a short climate deterioration at perhaps 8300–8200 BC that led to the

[55] Munro, "Zooarchaeological Measures," S20–S21; Natalie Munro, "Small Game, the Younger Dryas, and the Transition to Agriculture in the Southern Levant," *Mitteilungen der Gesellschaft für Urgeschichte* 12 (2003), 47–71; Ken-Ichi Tannio and George Wilcox, "How Fast Was Wild Wheat Domesticated?" *Science* 311 (2006), 1886; Dorian Q. Fuller, "Contrasting Patterns in Crop Domestication and Domestication Rates: Recent Archaeolbotanical Insights from the Old World," *Annals of Botany* 100 (2007), 903–24; Mark Nesbitt, "When and Where Did Domesticated Cereals First Occur in Southwest Asia?" in Cappers and Bottema, eds., *The Dawn of Farming in the Near East*, 113–32; John Meadows, "The Younger Dryas Episode and the Radiocarbon Chronologies of the Lake Huleh and Ghab Valley Pollen Diagrams, Israel and Syria," *The Holocene* 15 (2005), 631–6; George Willcox et al., "Late Pleistocene and Early Holocene Climate and the Beginnings of Cultivation in Northern Syria," *Holocene* 19 (2009), 151–8.

[56] Nigel Goring-Morris and Anna Belfer-Cohen, "The Articulation of Cultural Processes and Late Quaternary Environmental Changes in the Cisjordan," *Paléorient* 32/2 (1998), pp. 82–4. For an analysis of the Natufian-PPN sequence from a resilience perspective, see Arlene M. Rosen and Isabel Rivera-Collazo, "Climate Change, Adaptive Cycles, and the Persistence of Foraging Economies during the Late Pleistocene/Holocene Transition in the Levant," *PNAS* 109 (2012), 3640–5.

abandonment of the PPNA villages and a period of refugee migration.[57] The ensuing Early PPNB was a brief period of consolidation and reaggregation, unifying the proto-domestic flood-water farming of the Levant with the herded goats and sheep of Anatolia into the beginnings of an "agro-pastoral synthesis," supporting larger villages with – for the first time – rectangular structures.[58] It seems clear that the shift from oval to rectangular houses is an almost universal marker of the transition to agriculture, and it seems to be associated with the need to define measured space and to protect property. They also began the process of controlling herded animals, rather than simply hunting them, domesticating goats and sheep.[59]

The geography of this transition to domestication and rectilinear villages was much broader than the Natufian, and the near millennium of slow transition appears to suggest that domestication was not really a concerted effort to improve production. Rather it appears to have been almost an "accidental" by-product of a system of trade and exchange, what archaeologists call a *interaction sphere*, in which peoples in an extensive region circulated far and wide in the context of an ongoing burial cult derived from the Late Natufian. Seeds exchanged on what appear to have been pilgrimages to sacred sites, such as the apparent temple at Gobelki Tepe in southern Anatolia, seem to have been the vehicle for distributing increasingly viable domesticates over a wide region.[60]

[57] Goring-Morris and Belfer-Cohen, "The Articulation of Cultural Processes," 85–6. This break between PPNA and PPNB seems to line up with Bond Event 7, at 8430–8230 BC, marked by ice rafting in the North Atlantic and the first wave of Holocene El Niños, and a sharp spike in the GISP2K+ marker of the cold Siberian High. For a complete analysis, see Bernhard Weninger et al., "The Impact of Rapid Climate Change on Prehistoric Societies during the Holocene in the Eastern Mediterranean," *Documenta Praehistorica* 36 (2009), 7–59, at 14–30.

[58] David R. Harris, "Development of the Agro-Pastoral Economy in the Fertile Crescent during the Pre-Pottery Neolithic Period," in Cappers and Bottema, eds., *The Dawn of Farming in the Near East*, 67–83; Andrew Sherratt, "Diverse Origins: Regional Contributions to the Genesis of Farming," in S. Colledge and J. Conolly, eds., *The Origins and Spread of Domestic Plants in Southwest Asia and Europe* (Walnut Creek, CA, 2007), 1–29; Verhoeven, "Beyond Boundaries," 241–57; Ian Kuijt and Nigel Goring-Morris, "Foraging, Farming, and Social Complexity in the Pre-Pottery Neolithic in the Southern Levant: A Review and Synthesis," *JWH* 16 (2002), 367–87; Byrd, "Reassessing the Emergence of Village Life," 262–8.

[59] Kent V. Flannery, "The Origins of the Village Revisited: From Nuclear to Extended Households," *AmAntiq* 67 (2002), 417–33; A. Nigel Goring-Morris and Anna Belfer-Cohen, "A Roof over One's Head: Developments in Near Eastern Residential Architecture across the Epipaleolithic-Neolithic Divide," in Jean-Pierre Bocquet-Appel and Ofer Bar-Yosef, eds., *The Neolithic Demographic Transition and Its Consequences* (New York, 2008), 239–86.

[60] K. Schmidt, "Göbekli Tepe, Southeastern Turkey: A Preliminary Report on the 1995–1999 Excavations," *Paléorient* 26 (2001), 45–54; Trevor Watkins, "Supra-Regional Networks in the Neolithic of Southwest Asia," *JWP* 21 (2008), 139–71; Mithen, *After the Ice*, 64–9; Sherratt, "Diverse Origins." The wider thesis of an "ideological origin" of the agricultural revolution has been most powerfully advanced by Jacques Cauvin, in *The Birth of the Gods and the Origins of Agriculture*, Trevor Watkins, trans. (New York, 2000), who stresses the

The outcome would be fully apparent in the Middle Pre-Pottery Neolithic B epoch, when the Lake Huleh pollen profile, as currently redated, begins to register significant amounts of cereal pollen settling into the lake sediments, and the ensuing Late PPNB. Their villages grow in size and complexity, as do their plastered houses with elaborate two-floor plans and warrens of storage rooms. Supporting these villages were not only domesticated grains, but increasing numbers of goats and sheep, followed by pigs and cattle after about 6800 BC, again circulated through trade patterns that linked the entire region. These were places where the "agro-pastoral transition" had taken place, and with it a revolution in predictability and continuity in food resources. Grains could be stored and grown from seed; animals could be herded and preserved for the future, a guaranteed supply for daily sustenance and a hedge against hard times. The results in numbers were quite startling, though we can only estimate the size of the largest villages and guess at the growth of total populations:

Estimates of settlement size, Levant, 15,000–6000 BC

		Estimated population per settlement
Geometric Kebaran	15,400–13,000 BC	18–22
Early Natufian	13,000–11,500 BC	
Late Natufian	11,500–9600 BC	60
PPNA	9600–8500 BC	330
Early PPNB	8500–8100 BC	
Middle PPNB	8100–7300 BC	760
Late PPNB	7300–6700 BC	3,300
Final PPNB (C)	6700–6200 BC	
Pottery Neolithic	6200 BC→	400

Sources: Ian Kuijt, "People and Space in Early Agricultural Villages: Exploring Daily Lives, Community Size, and Architecture in the Late Pre-Pottery Neolithic," JAnthArch 19 (2000), 75–102; and Henry, "Models of Agricultural Origins."

These were places where the wild had been domesticated and transformed; buffered from the more immediate uncertainties of nature, people increasingly fixated on the problem of life. And an elaborate ritualism of mortality prevailed, running back to the Late Natufian, with burials saturating the floors and alleyways of these villages, and the decorated skulls

dualistic fertility cult of "the woman and the bull." For comprehensive overviews of the Natufian and the Pre-Pottery Neolithic, see Alan H. Simmons, *The Neolithic Revolution in the Near East* (Tucson, AZ, 2007), 46–174; Barker, *The Agricultural Revolution in Prehistory*, 104–81 stresses the possibility of more diffuse and parallel processes of domestication from the Levant to South Asia.

of household patriarchs watching over households from ritual niches and shrines.[61]

This Near Eastern intensification of cultivation, transition to domestication, and florescence of early agriculture unfolded over three millennia of the warmest climate of the Holocene (see Figures II.1 and II.2). Methane readings in the Greenland ice cores, which had fallen back to almost 450 ppb, rebounded to more than 700 ppb by 9600 BC. CO_2 reached 260 ppm by 9400 BC, virtually the norm for the preindustrial Holocene. Throughout the world, the climate was warmer and moister than it has been since, with powerful thermohaline circulation and the northward-tracking Intertropical Convergence Zone bringing intense summer monsoon rains across mid-latitude Asia, northern Africa, and the tropical Americas – what are being called *mega-monsoons*.[62] During these centuries of good weather, agriculture began to emerge in several hearths around the world. This was a slow and incremental process, not a sudden explosion, at least when measured in historical time. If it took almost a millennium from the end of the Younger Dryas for the peoples of the Fertile Crescent to arrive at the first approximation of an agricultural economy, in most other places it took considerably longer for either a local domestication or for local people to adopt agricultural practices spreading out from hearths of domestication. Again, the types of local species, and the particular pressures on local populations, shaped the chronology of the wider transition to agriculture.

The Chinese transition to agriculture shared many of the same characteristics as that in the Fertile Crescent, and followed roughly the same chronology (see Figure II.3). At the end of the Younger Dryas, a strong East Asian monsoon pattern was reestablished, bringing warm, wet conditions as far north as the Yellow River to regions that had been cold and dry during glacial times. Broadly speaking, the emergence of agriculture in China can be divided into a cultivating "Initial Neolithic" of 9000–7000 BC, perhaps analogous to the Natufian or the transitional PPNA in the Fertile Crescent, and a domesticated "Early Neolithic" of roughly 7000–5000 BC, with an economy of villages growing rice or millet, with domesticated pigs and chickens, roughly equivalent to the PPNB, equivalent except that in China this Neolithic was not "pre-pottery"! In the north in the Yellow River Valley, where millet was domesticated by 7000 BC, the earliest known village site dates to roughly 8500 BC, and reveals evidence of grinding implements,

[61] Harris, "Development of the Agro-Pastoral Economy"; Verhoeven, "Beyond Boundaries," 249–59; Kuijt and Goring-Morris, "Foraging, Farming, and Social Complexity," 387–413; Ian Kuijt, "People and Space in Early Agricultural Villages: Exploring Daily Lives, Community Size, and Architecture in the Late Pre-Pottery Neolithic ," *JAnthArch* 19 (2000), 75–102.

[62] Peterson and Haug, "Variability in the Mean Latitude on the Atlantic Intertropical Zone"; Gerald Haug et al., "Southward Migration of the Intertropical Convergence Zone through the Holocene," *Science* 293 (2001), 1304–8; Basil A. S. Davis and Simon Brewer, "Orbital Forcing and the Role of the Latitudinal Insolation/Temperature Gradient," *ClimDyn* 32 (2009), 143–65.

pottery, and the possible domestication of dogs and pigs as early as 11,000–10,500 BC, roughly the period of the Younger Dryas.[63] In the Yangtze Valley, evidence for rice exploitation reemerges in the wake of the Younger Dryas, with half of the phytoliths suggesting domestication by 7500 BC. The details of how village life might have begun in the intervening two millennia is unknown, as the first site in the Yangtze, in the Hupei basin at Pengtoushan, dates to about 7500 BC; another early site just north of the Yangtze at Jiahu in the Huai River valley dates at the earliest to 7000 BC. The Pengtoushan site reveals large square houses with associated ash pits and burials and a well-developed pottery tradition: pottery developed before domestication in China because pots provided an effective means for boiling rice.[64]

The rise of agriculture in China mirrored that in Southwest Asia in many ways. Both were mid-latitude regions in which shifts in rainfall had severe regional impacts; in both regions domestication took place in relatively circumscribed corridors hemmed in by desert, mountains, or sea. These were areas where the Younger Dryas had severe but not debilitating impacts on incipient cultivators of wild grasses; these were areas in which the "packing" of populations on the landscape contributed to the gradual search for new foods and subsistence practices. And both domesticated particular species of seed-bearing C3 grasses, which grew poorly in the reduced CO_2 of the glacial atmosphere, and which bloomed in the elevated CO_2 of the Holocene. The grasses are particularly susceptible to domestication if harvested with a sickle rather than by hand. Seeds are attached to the grass stem by a short "rachis": in the wild state the rachises in an individual mature from the top down, turning brittle and allowing the seeds to fall off in a sequence over several weeks, ensuring a diversity of germination times. If the seeds are stripped off by hand, the harvester collects all of the seeds in a mixture, but if she or he strikes the stems with a sickle, the more brittle rachises break and the seeds are lost: the harvester is left with the stems and the seeds with the tougher rachises. Then the selection at harvesting would be complemented by a selection at sowing, when particularly large seeds would be favored for planting. Thus seeds are relatively easy to manipulate, and are genetically "plastic," meaning that they adopt and hold new genetic structures

[63] Tracy L.-D. Lu, "Some Botanical Characteristics of Green Foxtail (Setara Viridis) and Harvesting Experiments on the Grass," *Antiquity* 72 (1998), 902–7; Barker, *The Agricultural Revolution in Prehistory*, 182–205; Li Liu, *The Chinese Neolithic: Trajectories Toward Early States* (New York, 2004), 24–5; B. D. Smith, *The Emergence of Agriculture*, 133–40.

[64] Zhao, "The Middle Yangtze Region," 892–5; Higham and Tracy, "The Origins and Dispersal of Rice Cultivation," 870–1; Gary W. Crawford and Chen Shen, "The Origins of Rice Agriculture: Recent Progress in East Asia," *Antiquity* 72 (1998), 858–66; Zhang Juzhong and Wang Xiangkun, "Notes on the Recent Discovery of Ancient Cultivated Rice at Jiahu, Henan Province: A New Theory Concerning the Origin of *Oryza Japonica* in China," *Antiquity* 72 (1998), 897–901; B. D. Smith, *The Emergence of Agriculture*, 128–33; Mithen, *After the Ice*, 364–9.

relatively easily because they are self-propagating, rather than outcrossing with wild varieties.[65]

* * *

Early Holocene Warming and Tropical Domestications

Southwest and East Asian crops would spread far and wide across Eurasia and northern Africa, and then invade the New World at the hand of colonizing Europeans and Africans; by the high point of classical antiquity they fed between them perhaps 75–80 percent of a global population of somewhere between 170 million and 225 million people. Beyond these mid-latitude hearths, however, domestications moved somewhat more slowly, either because of the space offered by non-circumscribed ecologies in an epoch of beneficent climate, or because of the difficulties of domesticating root crops like potatoes, yams, and manioc, or the primitive grass ancestral to maize/corn, all of which had a strong tendency to outcross to the wild stock.[66] Eventually these would join wheat, barley, millet, and rice among the great Holocene Neolithic founder crops that feed us to this day.

These more diffuse domestications tended to be in the tropics. In the New World tropics, the warming of the Holocene altered the subsistence patterns of Paleolithic peoples; as the forests closed in, the work required to raise sufficient sustenance apparently led extremely quickly to a cultivation of productive wild plants (see Figure II.1). Concurbita squash may have been domesticated in Ecuador by relatively sedentary peoples engaged in broad-spectrum foraging at perhaps 10,000 BC.[67] Squash would have been domesticated at many places, perhaps roughly simultaneously, in a widespread "non-center" pattern identified by botanist Jack Harlan more than thirty years ago. So too would have been manioc or cassava, a fundamentally important food source in the tropical Americas, which had a chronologically unknown origin in the southern Amazon region, reaching Panama by perhaps 6000 BC, the earliest dated evidence for its human use.[68] Maize/

[65] Gordon C. Hillman and M. S. Davies, "Measured Domestication Rates in Wild Wheats and Barley under Primitive Cultivation at Abu Hureyra on the Euphrates," *JWP* 4 (1990), 157–222.

[66] Harris, "Alternative Pathways toward Agriculture," 179–243.

[67] Dolores Piperno and Karen Stothert, "Phytolith Evidence for Early Holocene *Cucurbita* Domestication in Southwest Ecuador," *Science* 299 (2003), 1054–7. For a synthesis, see Barker, *The Agricultural Revolution in Prehistory*, 231–72.

[68] Harlan, "Agricultural Origins"; Dolores Piperno et al., "Starch Grains Reveal Early Root Crop Horticulture in the Panamanian Tropical Forest," *Nature* 407 (2000), 894–7; Kenneth M. Olsen and Barbara A. Schaal, "DNA Sequence Data and Inferences on Cassava's Origin and Domestication," in Zeder et al., *Documenting Domestication*, 123–33.

corn apparently was domesticated in a "center," the Balsas Valley in Mexico, where its tendency to outcross with wild species made its domestication an extremely slow process: genetic evidence suggests a division with wild stock around 8500–8000 BC; maize starch has been dated to at least 6700 BC, maize pollen at 5100 BC, and actual cobs at 4250 BC, which suggests the rough sequence of domestication.[69] Broadly speaking, throughout the Neotropics and into Mexico, it would appear that wild-plant experimentation long preceded the establishment of settlements larger than several families in a small hamlet; if large villages first appeared in the Valdiva culture of coastal Ecuador after 4500 BC, they were not evident in Mexico until after 1800 BC, and in coastal Panama around 800 BC.[70]

This chronology would date the emergence of agriculture and village life in the American tropics roughly 3,000–4,000 years later than the parallel sequence in the Fertile Crescent or China. In the High Andes, the transition to agriculture came around 2000 BC. In a relatively well-defined region north of Lake Titicaca, llamas, alpacas, guinea pigs, the grain quinua, and – most important – the potato were all domesticated in a coherent complex by 2000 BC.[71] In North America, the beginnings of domestication were delayed until about 2000 BC, when four floodplain weeds – sunflowers, squash, marsh elder, and chenopod – were cultivated in the interior region of the Mississippi and Ohio Valleys. This cultivation intensified after 500 BC, several hundred years after the beginnings of the Adena "interaction sphere," a ritual exchange system focused on mortuary mounds and reaching throughout the Ohio Valley, not unlike the burial cult that shaped the PPNA in the Fertile Crescent 8,000 years before. Not until after AD 800 would maize/corn derived from Mexico displace these domesticated native plants in most of North America.[72]

* * *

[69] Dolores Piperno et al., "Starch Grain and Phytolith Evidence for Early Ninth Millennium B. P. Maize from the Central Balsas River Valley, Mexico," *PNAS* 106 (2009), 5019–24; Anthony J. Ranere et al., "The Cultural and Chronological Context of Early Holocene Maize and Squash Domestication in the Central Balsas River Valley, Mexico," *PNAS* 106 (2009), 5014–18.

[70] Piperno and Pearsall, *The Origins of Agriculture in the Lowland Neotropics*, 14–15, 167–8, 14–15, 253–4, 286, 295–6, 305, 309, 312–15, 318; Dolores R. Piperno, "The Origins of Plant Cultivation and Domestication in the Neotropics: A Behavioral Ecological Perspective," in Kennett and Winterhalder, *Behavioral Ecology and the Transition to Agriculture*, 137–66.

[71] B. D. Smith, *The Emergence of Agriculture*, 170–81; Peter Bellwood, *First Farmers: The Origins of Agricultural Societies* (Oxford, 2005), 158.

[72] B. D. Smith, *The Emergence of Agriculture*, 184–201; Bruce D. Smith, "Seed Plant Domestication in Eastern North America," in Price and Gebauer, *Last Hunters, First Farmers*, 193–214.

Into the Mid-Holocene: Final Domestications and First Dispersals

The New World trajectory toward agriculture carries us far beyond the beneficent climate of the Early Holocene Optimum, however. By 6000 BC, when slash-and-burn agriculture began to support the beginnings of agricultural villages in Mesoamerica, this Holocene Optimum was beginning to wane. And when agriculture developed in or spread to other global regions in the ensuing millennia, it was in the context of a slow but relentless deterioration of global climate conditions. The following chapter discusses the establishment of the "modern" climate system at some length, but this transition needs to be briefly sketched here, because it was fundamental to the basic story of global domestications.

Fundamentally, the Mid-Holocene transition was driven by the inevitable peaking and decline of solar radiation reaching the earth's atmosphere, as shaped by the inexorable mathematics of orbital precession cycle. This "insolation" peaked between 8500 BC and 7000 BC, and then began a long decline, as the tilting of the earth's northern hemisphere away from the sun started the long shift toward a 20,000-year precessional minimum (see Figures I.6, II.1). The proxy measures of modern climate science provide an increasingly precise picture of the ensuing deterioration. Methane, a very precise barometer of global climate, after hitting an early peak of 700–730 ppb between 9600 and 8900 BC, had hovered in the 670s and 680s down to about 7000 BC, when it started a slow decline that hit a minimum of 550 ppb around 3300 BC, in the closing centuries of what is known as the Early-to-Mid-Holocene transition crisis, in which global climates were radically reorganized into a cooler, drier system.[73] This deterioration would shape the most recent 5,000 years of human history, as societies shifted from village- to state-based societies.

Other forces would be at work as well, as the warm Early Holocene began to fade. The first of these were two postglacial melt water events that slowed the north Atlantic thermohaline pump driving the Gulf Stream; one at roughly 8200 BC, and another at 6200 BC, when the Laurentian ice shield in Canada collapsed, sending a melt water surge through Hudson's Bay into the North Atlantic. This event was embedded in a longer cooling between 6700 BC and 6000 BC that reached into the monsoonal tropics.[74] Exactly what shaped this longer cooling is unclear, but the next three events on this scale seem to have been shaped by the recurring 2,200-year

---

[73] Loulergue et al., "Orbital and Millennial-Scale Features of Atmospheric CH4"; Flückiger et al., "High-Resolution Holocene N_2O Ice Core Record."

[74] Richard B. Alley et al., "Holocene Climate Instability: A Prominent, Widespread Event 8200 yr Ago," *Geology* 25 (1997), 483–6; Christopher R. W. Ellison, Surface and Deep Water Interactions during the Cold Climate Event 8200 Years Ago," *Science* 312 (2006), 1929–32; Helga Flesche Kleiven et al., "Reduced North Atlantic Deep Water Coevel with the Glacial Lake Agassiz Freshwater Outburst," *Science* 319 (2008), 60–4.

"Hallstatt" solar cycle, during which solar output declined significantly for several centuries. These sharp and centuries-long coolings, what I call *millennial Siberian Highs*, brought particularly cold stormy winters to the northern latitudes and aridity to mid-latitudes for periods of several centuries. Including the event between 6700 BC and 6000 BC, four of these millennial Siberian Highs occurred between the Early Holocene and the present[75] (see Figure II.4).

When the seventh-millennium BC cooling event was over, the global climate returned to its previous condition, indeed warmer and more humid in many locations. The transition toward permanently colder and drier climates took hold after the second millennial Siberian High, roughly 4000–3000 BC. Driven by the waning of orbital warming, the Intertropical Convergence Zone (ITCZ), governing rainfall throughout the tropics and into the temperate mid-latitudes, gradually moved south after roughly 5700 BC, bringing the Early Holocene mega-monsoon period to an end, reducing the South Asian Monsoon, and abruptly ending the African Monsoon that had kept the Sahara in grass and influenced the Mediterranean, around 3700 BC (see Figures II.2, II.3). At the close of the fourth millennium, with its cold north and increasingly arid Old World mid-latitudes, the modern El Niño pattern suddenly activated, bringing periods of intense precipitation to the west coast of the Americas and intensifying aridity across the Pacific in South and Southeast Asia. From this point forward, a post-Optimum "Late Holocene" regime set in, with cooler and drier climate oscillating in regular unison in a rough two-millennial cycle, shaping conditions for better or worse of growing and fragile agricultural societies throughout the world.[76]

---

[75] F. Steinhilber et al., "Interplanetary Magnetic Field during the Past 9300 Years Inferred from Cosmogenic Radionuclides," *JGR* 115 (2010), A01104; Gianluca Marino et al., "Early and Middle Holocene in the Aegean Sea: Interplay between High and Low Latitude Climate Variability," *QSR* 28 (2009), 3246–62; Eelco J. Rohling and Eike Pälike, "Centennial-Scale Climate Cooling with a Sudden Cold Event around 8,200 Years Ago," *Nature* 434 (2005), 975–9; Rohling et al., "Holocene Atmosphere-Ocean Interactions"; Loren D. Meeker and Paul A. Mayewski, "A 1400-Year High-Resolution Record of Atmospheric Circulation over the North Atlantic and Asia," *Holocene* 12 (2002), 257–66.

[76] See the citations in note 28 and the following: Paul A. Mayewski et al., "Holocene Climate Variability," *QuatRes* 62 (2004), 243–55; Weninger et al., "The Impact of Rapid Climate Change on Prehistoric Societies," 9–17, 30–4; Lonnie G. Thompson et al., "Late Glacial State and Holocene Tropical Ice Core Records from Huascarán, Peru," *Science* 269 (1995), 46–50; Thompson et al., "Kilimanjaro Ice Core Records"; Camilo Ponton, "Holocene Aridification of India," *GRL* 39 (2012), L03704; Harunur Rashid et al., "Late Glacial to Holocene Indian Summer Monsoon Variability Based upon Sediment Records Taken from the Bay of Bengal," *Terrestrial, Atmospheric, and Oceanic Sciences* 22 (2011), 215–28; deMenocal, "Coherent High- and Low-Latitude Climate Variability during the Holocene Warm Period"; Hong, "Inverse Phase Oscillations between the East Asian and Indian Ocean Summer Monsoons"; Yongjin Wang et al., "The Holocene Asian Monsoon: Links to Solar Changes and North Atlantic Climate," *Science* 308 (2005), 854–7; Yongtao Yu et al., "Millennial-Scale Holocene

The Early-to-Mid-Holocene transition marked an important climatic driver in the story of the emergence of agriculture. It would seem that in the New World the environmental context of the earliest experimental cultivation of the tropical forest was the Early Holocene Optimum, and the trend toward an intensifying slash-and-burn corn- and/or manioc-based agriculture was in part a response to the slowly unfolding decline into the Mid-Holocene Crisis.[77] Such was also the case across much of the Old World tropics.

The earliest domestications and horticulture in the last great hearth, a huge "non-center" region spanning the Sahara and the fringes of the savannah Sahel, were also shaped by this long decline in the Holocene climate (see Figure II.2). During the 3,000 to 4,000 years of the Holocene Optimum, with the ITCZ riding well north of the equator, the Sahara turned into a green but variable savannah. Hunter-gatherer groups spread out from various refuges, including parts of the Nile Valley, living a migratory life among the great lakes in the Sahara that drew their moisture from the Optimum Atlantic monsoon. Here, animal domestications – not sedentary villages or wild plant cultivation – seem to have come first. Saharan hunter-gatherers may have begun to domesticate wild cattle (*bos primigenius*) as early as 9000–8000 BC, as part of a strategy to improve the predictability of food supply in a patchy and variable ecosystem where savannah frequently shifted with more arid conditions.[78] A herding economy intensified as the Holocene Optimum waned, and the Sahara gradually reverted to desert after 4000 BC, forcing people east and south toward more dependable water. These migratory hunter-gatherers/herders exploited wild seeded grasses, pearl millet, sorghum, and African rice. Wild millet was harvested by 8500 BC, and millet and sorghum may have been domesticated in parts of Sudan by 5000 BC, but solid evidence for domestication comes from after 2000 BC, well after villages had to coalesce along the Sahel south of the desert Sahara.[79]

Climate Variability in the NW China Drylands and Links to the Tropical Pacific and the North Atlantic," *PPP* 233 (2006), 149–62; and Fagan, *The Long Summer*, 107–13.

[77] Piperno and Pearsall, *The Origins of Agriculture in the Neotropics*, 313.

[78] Fiona Marshall and Elizabeth Hildebrand, "Cattle before Crops: The Beginnings of Food Production in Africa," *JWP* 16 (2002), 99–143; Bellwood, *First Farmers*, 104–5; Olivier Hanotte, "African Pastoralism: Genetic Imprints of Origins and Migrations," *Science* 296 (2002), 336–99. The more traditional consensus is that Asian cattle (*Bos taurus*) was introduced from the Fertile Crescent after 6000 BC. For a review leaning toward introduction, see Diane Gifford-Gonzales and Olivier Hanott, "Domesticating Animals in Africa: Implications and Archaeological Findings," *JWP* 24 (2011), 1–23.

[79] Barker, *The Agricultural Revolution in Prehistory*, 278–310; Barich, *People, Water, and Grain*, 121–33; Kathleen Nicoll, "Recent Environmental Change and Prehistoric Human Activity in Egypt and Northern Sudan," *QSR* 23 (2004), 561–80.

The shifting climate at the Mid-Holocene drove cultural change in many other global regions. In eastern North America, it marks the boundary between the Middle and Late Archaic, essentially a shift from mobile hunting-gathering in a warm, moist ecology to increasingly intense local exploitation and sedentism, in the direction of the Mesolithic Natufian of the Levant, with incipient horticulture. In South America, in the lowlands of the La Plata in Uruguay, the Mid-Holocene brought a decisive emergence of cultivation and villages. In South Asia, where the Southwest Asian crops reached Rajasthan around 4000 BC, the climate stress of the Mid-Holocene seems to have driven the further dispersal of this complex as well as local domestications of millets, rice, and pulses (beans and peas), and coalescence of village traditions. In Australia, the Mid-Holocene explosion of El Niño at roughly 3000 BC similarly increased aridity, making the interior more susceptible to fire. The result was a change in the hunting strategy among Australian peoples and a dramatic rise in population.[80]

Saharan Africa and probably South Asia saw a process of agricultural emergence in the context of a climate-driven dispersal of peoples. Elsewhere, such dispersals carried agriculture with them. A major debate has unfolded over the past decade as to whether the spread of agriculture from centers of domestication was by the diffusions of species and practices "down the line" of mesolithic cultures or by the "demic diffusion" of actual peoples carrying with them agro-pastoral systems – and languages – in colonizing expansions. The reality appears to have been something of both, and the current debate is over which played the greater role. But clearly agriculture expanded, carried by small colonizing movements that left signatures buried in the geography of the human genome and that probably built the basic linguistic structure of the modern world. I present the case for a restrained "farming/language dispersal" hypothesis because I think that best explains the evidence of modern human diversity. It also suggests that the Neolithic saw a series of powerful expansions of peoples, cultures, and agricultural practices, in many but not all cases overlaying and transforming the earlier peoples of the Paleolithic "out-of-Africa" dispersals of 65,000–40,000ybp. And as were these Paleolithic expansions,

---

[80] Manuel E. Munoz et al., "Synchronous Environmental and Cultural Change in the Prehistory of the Northeastern United States," *PNAS* 107 (2010), 22008–13; José Iriarte et al., "Evidence for Cultivar Adoption and Emerging Complexity during the Mid-Holocene in the La Plata Basin," *Nature* 432 (2004), 614–17; Dorian Q. Fuller, "Agricultural Origins and Frontiers in South Asia: A Working Synthesis," *JWP* 20 (2006), 1–86, at 61–2; Chris S. M. Turney and Douglas Hobbs, "ENSO Influences on Holocene Aboriginal Populations in Queensland, Australia," *JArchS* 33 (2006), 1744–8. For a complete global discussion, see Nick Brooks, "Cultural Responses to Aridity in the Middle Holocene and Increased Social Complexity," *QuatInt* 151 (2006), 29–49.

the Neolithic dispersals were shaped by climate forces, most importantly the Mid-Holocene deterioration.

What do we know of these dispersals?[81] We must start with the Near East, as the spread of agriculture from this core began the earliest and reached the farthest, in what has been called the "great exodus" of the Pre-Pottery Neolithic.[82] The earliest agricultural dispersals were carried by small groups of colonizers moving considerable distances over land and sea to settle very specific kinds of alluvial soils. Then agricultural practices spread slowly to the indigenous mesolithic foragers, sometimes after considerable resistance.[83] As the zone of the earliest proto-agricultural PPN communities in the western Fertile Crescent began to expand, Cyprus was colonized some time after 8500 BC. As part of the same expansion, the Early PPNB spread into Anatolia between 8300–8000 BC, and its influences as far east as the Iranian Zagros Mountains by perhaps 8000 BC. By 7000 BC, agricultural villages growing Southwest Asian crops had spread to the edge of the Indian subcontinent in Beluchistan, and had been established on Crete[84] (see Figure II.3).

It is possible that the colonization of Cyprus and perhaps Anatolia coincided with a century or two of ice rafting in the North Atlantic and drought in South Asia around 8200 BC; it is more likely that these initial expansions were shaped by the following bubble of good climate conditions prevailing in the Early Holocene, which apparently allowed the populations of the Middle PPNB communities of the Fertile Crescent to reach rather amazing

---

[81] The literature on farming dispersals, genetics, and language is now quite extensive, and I only skim the surface here. For important useful summaries and landmark works, see Bellwood, *First Farmers*, 67–96, 106–10, 122–45, 180–279; the collected essays in Bellwood and Renfrew, eds., *Examining the Farming/Language Dispersal Hypothesis*; Luigi Luca Cavalli-Sforza, *Genes, Peoples, and Languages*, Mark Seielstad, trans. (New York, 2000); Luigi Luca Cavalli-Sforza and Francesco Cavalli-Sforza, *The Great Human Diasporas*, Sarah Thorne, trans. (Menlo Park, NJ, 1995); Albert J. Ammerman and Luigi Luca Cavalli-Sforza, *The Neolithic Transition and the Genetics of Populations in Europe* (Princeton, NJ, 1984); Jared Diamond and Peter Bellwood, "Farmers and Their Languages: The First Expansions," *Science* 300 (2003), 597–603; Jared M. Diamond, "The Language Steamrollers," *Nature* 389 (1997), 544–6; Colin Renfrew, "World Linguistic Diversity," *SA* (January 1994), 116–23; Luigi Luca Cavalli-Sforza et al., "Demic Expansions and Human Evolution," *Science* 259 (1993), 639–46.

[82] Catherine Perlès, *The Early Neolithic in Greece* (New York, 2001), 62.

[83] This "leap-frogging" model was developed as a refinement of Cavalli-Sforza's "demic wave of advance." See Tjeerd H. van Andel and Curtis N. Runnels, "The Earliest Farmers in Europe," *Antiquity* 69 (1995), 481–500; and Staso Forenbaher and Preston T. Miracle, "The Spread of Farming in the Eastern Adriatic," *Antiquity* 79 (2005), 514–28.

[84] Simmons, *The Neolithic Revolution in the Near East*, 229–62; Edgar Pelternberg and Alexander Wasse, eds., *Neolithic Revolutions: New Perspectives on Southwest Asia in Light of Recent Discoveries on Cyprus* (Oxford, 2004); Sherratt, "Diverse Origins"; Bellwood, *First Farmers*, 64, 71–2, 84–5; Fuller, "Agricultural Origins and Frontiers in South Asia," 20–35; Perlès, *The Early Neolithic in Greece*, 38–63.

sizes. The best measure of regional climate may be the redated Huleh pollen profile, which shows a long rise of deciduous oak pollen from the late stages of the Younger Dryas to a peak during the Middle PPNB, around 7550 BC[85] (see Figure II.2). This oak peak was followed by a long decline to a minimum around 6600 BC, coinciding with the first peak of a double-headed ice-rafting episode in the North Atlantic, and with the increased levels of sea salt and potassium dust in the Greenland ice cores, evidence of an intensified Siberian High. During this period, the volume of oak pollen remained low, but the region was blasted by intense rainfall coming in explosive storms that caused massive erosion, which left distinct anaerobic sediments in the Mediterranean Sea bottom, known as the *sapropel condition*.[86] Well after this pattern set in, a final melt water crisis took place when the vast glacial lake Agassiz in Canada ruptured the Laurentian ice sheet, with huge volumes of fresh water shutting down the Gulf Stream and sending Europe and the Middle East into perhaps two centuries of intense dry cold around 6200 BC.[87]

These declining climate conditions added insult to injury in the emerging agricultural regions of the PPN Fertile Crescent, compounding a human-induced degradation of local environments that had been building for hundreds of years. The huge Middle PPNB village communities destroyed

---

[85] Here I reinterpret the descriptions in Sytze Bottema, "The Use of Palynology in Tracing Early Agriculture," in Cappers and Bottema, eds., *The Dawn of Farming in the Near East*, 27–38, in light of the redating of the Huleh profile presented in Meadows, "The Younger Dryas Episode." See Figure II.2.

[86] Miryam Bar-Matthews et al., "The Eastern Mediterranean Paleoclimate as a Reflection of the Regional Events: Soreq Cave, Israel," *EPSL* 166 (1999), 85–95, see p. 91; Arie S. Issar and Mattanyah Zohar, *Climate Change: Environment and Civilization in the Middle East* (Berlin, 2004), 61–2, 65–6.

[87] Marino et al., "Early and Middle Holocene in the Aegean Sea"; Kleiven et al., "Reduced North Atlantic Deep Water." There has been an extended argument since 1996 as to whether the Laurentine melt water pulse flooded the Black Sea, driving Neolithic farmers northwest into Europe. First proposed in William B. F. Ryan et al., "An Abrupt Drowning of the Black Sea Shelf," *Marine Geology* 31 (1997), and developed in William B. F. Ryan et al., "Catastrophic Flooding of the Black Sea," *Annual Review of Earth and Planetary Science* 31 (2003), 525–54 and Fagan, *The Long Summer*, 107–13, the theory has been challenged in Valentina Yanko-Hombach et al., "Controversy over the Great Flood Hypotheses in the Black Sea in Light of Geological, Paleontological, and Archaeological Evidence," *QuatInt* 167–8 (2007), 91–113. More recent work supports the flood hypothesis, but on a more limited scale than first proposed: Liviu Giosan et al., "Was the Black Sea Catastrophically Flooded in the Early Holocene?" *QSR* 28 (2009), 1–6; G. Lericolais et al., "High Frequency Sea Level Fluctuations in the Black Sea since the LGM," *GPC* 66 (2009), 65–75; Chris S. M. Turley and Heidi Brown, "Catastrophic Early Holocene Sea Level Rise, Human Migration and the Neolithic Transition in Europe," *QSR* 26 (2009), 2036–41. G. Soulet et al., "A Revised Calendar for the Last Reconnection of the Black Sea to the Global Ocean," *QSR* 30 (2011), 1019–26 presents evidence that the last flooding of the Black Sea from the Mediterranean occurred roughly around 7000 BC, well before the Laurentine melt water event.

enormous quantities of timber for construction, for household fires, and for kiln firing the massive volume of lime plaster that coated their houses. Their growing flocks of goats and sheep overgrazed the fragile soils; the circuits around the PPNB villages would have been brown and dusty where they once had been green. The result of the combination of resource stress and climate change was the general crisis of the Pre-Pottery Neolithic, the first collapse of a civilization. One of the Anatolian settlements, Çatalhöyük, was totally abandoned for several hundred years following the Laurentine melt water crisis; the town of 'Ain Ghazal apparently filled with refugees (during the PPNC) before collapsing. Population in the Fertile Crescent crashed and then recoalesced in much smaller village settlements, more focused on herding than before. This new cultural and settlement pattern is known as the *Pottery Neolithic* in the Levant and the *proto-Hassuna* in northern Mesopotamia, what is now Syria and Iraq.[88]

This sequence of climate decline and ecological crisis was the general context of a second wave of dispersals out of the Fertile Crescent core. Between 6500 BC and 6200 BC, the Near Eastern package of agriculture spread to mainland Greece and southeast Europe, the Caucasus Mountains, and the Nile Valley; in each case it would appear that colonies of migrants played a significant role. By 6000 BC, agriculture had spread to southern Italy in the west and Turkmenistan in the northeast. The Italian Early Neolithic, known as the *Cardial culture* from their pottery, would suddenly spread west in a series of colonizations along the Mediterranean to Portugal around 5400 BC. And around 5600 BC, longhouse-building agricultural peoples, known from their pottery as the *Linear-Band-Keramik* (or LBK) began to move up the Danube and within 500 years had spread to France.[89]

[88] Simmons, *The Neolithic Revolution in the Near East*, 175–97; Gary O. Rollefson, "The Neolithic Devolution: Ecological Impact and Cultural Compensation at 'Ain Ghazal, Jordan," in Joe E. Seger, ed., *Retrieving the Past: Essays on Archaeological Research and Methodology in Honor of Gus W. Van Beck* (Mississippi State, 1996), 219–30; Gary O. Rollefson et al., "Neolithic Cultures at 'Ain Ghazal, Jordan," *JFdArch* 19 (1992), 433–70; Verhoeven, "Beyond Boundaries," 259–63; Kuijt, "People and Space in Early Agricultural Villages," 96–7.

[89] Bellwood, *First Farmers*, 71–96; Perlès, *The Early Neolithic in Greece*, 52–120; João Zilhão, "Radiocarbon Evidence for Maritime Pioneer Colonization at the Origins of Farming in West Mediterranean Europe," *PNAS* 98 (2001), 14180–5; Detlef Gronenborn, "A Variation on a Basic Theme: The Transition to Farming in Southern Central Europe," *JWP* 13 (2003), 123–210; Sue Colledge et al., Archaeobotanical Evidence for the Spread of Farming in the Eastern Mediterranean, *CA* 45 (2004), S34–S58; Ron Pinhasi and Mark Pluciennik, "A Regional Approach to the Spread of Farming in Europe," *CA* 45 (2004), S59–S82; Bernhard Weninger et al., "Climate Forcing due to the 8200 cal yr BP Event Observed at Early Neolithic Sites in the Eastern Mediterranean," *QuatRes* 66 (2006), 401–20; Charles Keith Maisels, *Early Civilizations of the Old World: The Formative Histories of Egypt, The Levant, Mesopotamia, India, and China* (New York, 1999), 124–5, 132–5, 147, 150–2.

Such was the reach of the Fertile Crescent agriculture that, by 5000 BC, it had already reached India and over the next 2,000 to 3,000 years it moved west from Egypt along the North African coast, northwest to the British Isles, north into the Russian steppes, and as far as China, carried by small but strategic groups of colonists.[90] Genetic markers in modern populations track these paths of dispersal in sudden expansions that take the shape of rakes or starbursts in diagrams, indicating the rapidity of their spread. Sometimes these trails can be faint, because they have been obscured to different degrees by subsequent movements, and because Near Eastern colonists mixed with local populations. Geneticists have estimated that 20 percent of the genetic markers of Europeans can be traced to Near East migrations, with the rest inherited from the mesolithic peoples of the Paleolithic dispersal, many of whom fiercely resisted the progress that agriculture would bring. Genetics suggest that the LBK colonists coming up the Danube were predominantly men, who intermarried with local mesolithic women.[91] Then there is the question of language. While there is considerable debate over these arguments, it seems increasingly possible that these Neolithic farming dispersals imposed new languages on these widespread regions: one model that has considerable support argues for a potentially Natufian or PPN root to a series of families of languages spreading with

[90] On China, see Xiaoqiang Li, "Early Cultivated Wheat and Broadening of Agriculture in Neolithic China," *Holocene* 17 (2007), 555–60.

[91] Here I am radically compressing the enormous and growing literature on genetics and the early farming dispersals. For overviews, see Bellwood, *First Farmers*, 252–72; Spencer Wells, *The Journey of Man: A Genetic Odyssey* (Princeton, NJ, 2002), 146–80. More recent, see Martin Richards, "The Neolithic Invasion of Europe," *Annual Reviews in Anthropology* 32 (2003), 135–62; R. Alexander Bentley, "The Neolithic Transition in Europe: Comparing Broad Scale Genetic and Local Scale Isotopic Evidence," *Antiquity* 77 (2003), 63–6; Ornella Semino et al., "Origin, Diffusion, and Differentiation of Y-Chromosome Haplogroups E and J: Inferences on the Neolithization of Europe and Later Migratory Events in the Mediterranean Area," *AJHG* 74 (2004), 1023–34; Wolfgang Haak, "Ancient DNA from First European Farmers in 7500-Year-Old Neolithic Sites," *Science* 310 (2005), 1016–18; B. Bramanti et al., "Genetic Discontinuity between Local and Hunter-Gatherers and Central Europe's First Farmers," *Science* 326 (2009), 137–40; T. Kivisild et al., "The Genetic Heritage of the Earliest Settlers Persists Both in Indian Tribal and Caste Populations," *AJHG* 72 (2003), 313–32; Sanghamitra Sengupta et al., "Polarity and Temporality of High-Resolution Y-Chromosome Distributions in India Identify Both Indigenous and Exogenous Expansions and Reveal Minor Genetic Influence of Central Asian Pastoralists," *AJHG* 78 (2006), 202–21. On conflict in the Mesolithic-Neolithic transition, see Peter Rowley-Conwy, "How the West Was Lost: A Reconsideration of Agricultural Origins in Britain, Ireland, and Southern Scandinavia," *CA* 45 (2004), S83–S113; Gronenborn, "A Variation on a Basic Theme"; Marek Zvelebil, "The Agricultural Frontier and the Transition to Farming in the Circum-Baltic Region," in Harris, ed., *The Origins and Spread of Agriculture and Pastoralism in Eurasia*, 323–46; and Bruce Bowers, "Cultivating Revolutions," *Science News* 167 (Feb. 5, 2005), 88–92.

early agriculture out of the Fertile Crescent: Afroasiatic, Elamo-Dravidian, and Indo-European.[92]

Elsewhere at later dates there would be equally dramatic expansions of peoples and agricultures. Around 3500 BC, a seaborne migration began on the coast of China opposite Taiwan that would carry a rice-growing and fishing culture with its Austronesian languages into Southeast Asia and the South Pacific, reaching both Hawaii and Madagascar by AD 500. These Polynesians voyagers may have used the east-moving winds of the strong El Niño periods to drive their migrations.[93] In China, Han-speaking rice growers moved south during the early part of the Zhou dynasty, 1100–221 BC, absorbing or sweeping aside a wide number of local peoples and languages.[94] In the Americas, clear farming dispersals occurred in Central America and southern Mexico soon after the maturation of a slash-and-burn corn agriculture around 2500 BC, and indigenous seed horticulture and then corn farming seem to have driven a series of linguistic expansions in eastern North America.[95] In Africa, the Nilo-Saharan languages seem to have spread after 9000 BC with the early herding peoples of the Sahara, while the huge Bantu language family had its roots in a yam-growing people who began to spread out of tropical Cameroon around 2000 BC. Protected by evolving immunities to the malaria that developed as they cleared rainforest for yam cultivation, the Bantu peoples eventually incorporated cattle into their economy and swept down through eastern Africa.[96] And a recent analysis suggests that agriculture was introduced into the British Isles by a "large influx" of Neolithic settlers early in the fourth millennium, the opening centuries of the mid-Holocene transition.[97]

Thus, by 5000 BC, the world was broadly divided among three great subsistence strategies. Some peoples, typically in ecologically increasingly

---

[92] See the citations in note 91, especially the recent summary of the Southwest Asian dispersal in Bellwood, *First Farmers*, esp. 201–17; and Mehmet Özdiğan, "An Alternative Approach in Tracing Changes in Demographic Composition: The Westward Expansion of the Neolithic Way of Life," in Bocquet-Appel and Bar-Yosef, eds., *The Neolithic Demographic Transition and its Consequences*, 139–78. For an influential early statement of superfamily dispersal from Southwest Asia, see Colin Renfrew, "Language Families and the Spread of Farming," in Harris, ed., *The Origins and Spread of Agriculture and Pastoralism in Eurasia*, 70–92. One linguistic term for this Natufian or PPN root is *proto-Nostradic*. Barker, *The Agricultural Revolution in Prehistory* is critical of Neolithic migration theories, but see 413–14.

[93] Diamond, *Guns, Germs, and Steel*, 334–76; Atholl Anderson et al., "Prehistoric Maritime Migration in the Pacific Islands: An Hypothesis of ENSO Forcing," *The Holocene* 16 (2006), 1–6.

[94] Diamond, *Guns, Germs, and Steel*, 322–33; Bellwood, *First Farmers*, 222–7.

[95] Bellwood, *First Farmers*, 237–50.

[96] Ibid., 217–22; Diamond, *Guns, Germs, and Steel*, 376–401. On the role of a malarial "immunological gradient" in the Bantu dispersal, see James L. A. Webb, Jr., "Malaria and the Peopling of Early Tropical Africa," *JWH* 16 (2005), 269–91, esp. 285–90.

[97] Mark Collard et al., "Radiocarbon Evidence Indicates that Migrants Introduced Farming into Britain," *JArchS* 37 (2010), 866–70.

extreme and marginal places, carried on the mesolithic foraging strategies, some down to the edge of the contemporary world. Others, particularly in the tropics, blended mesolithic foraging with small-scale horticulture evolving widely and slowly across great regions, blending cultivation of domesticates with management of the wild. But those peoples distributed across the semiarid to temperate mid-latitudes became dependent on the cereal-animal complex in its several varieties, emerging quickly from discrete centers of domestication. From these centers spread great dispersals of agricultural practices, carried by small but strategic venturing colonists.

The great Neolithic farming dispersals shared an essential commonality: all of them were expansions of peoples carrying either seed crops or domesticated animals. In sharp contrast, the diffusion of the outcrossing tropical root crops, erratically moving toward domestication in many locations, spread "down the line" from hamlet to hamlet, leaving transitional foraging-horticultural societies in place and intact. But agriculture based on a various combinations of cereals and animals had an inherently expansionary dynamic. As an efficient "energy trap," the Old World agrarian synthesis produced more useable calories independently of the wild ecosystem, and thus fed a more rapid population growth. These cereal-animal farming populations thus were poised to migrate, and had the means of migration in their agriculture. Both dry, storable seeds and self-propelling beasts of burden would allow the movement of peoples and their practices to new regions, where the growth and expand cycle could begin again. By the year AD 1, the peoples of the Old World regions of cereal-animal agriculture may have comprised 80 percent of the world's total population, claiming at the very most 23 percent of the world's total land surface[98] (see Figure III.2).

Bound up in this expansion was a fundamental ecological problem. These growing populations and their cereals and animals would through time not just fill up but also degrade their local ecologies, depleting soils and using up timber; societies would respond by further intensifying their land use. In decades past, this sequence of intensification and degradation has been seen as the primary environmental motor in the post-Neolithic condition, but recently it has become clear that the "joker" of climate change played a powerful role.[99] This was not the force of grand super-cycles and super-plumes and meteorite strikes that drove biological evolution over the long term, or even the long glacial swings of the "100K world" that put the final touches on human speciation. Relatively slight and shallow movements in

---

[98] Populations from in Jean-Nöel Biraben, "Essai sur l-Évolution du Nombre des Hommes," *Population* 34 (1979), 13–24; and Colin McEvedy and Richard Jones, *Atlas of World Population History* (New York, 1978).

[99] Marvin Harris, *Cannibals and Kings: The Origins of Cultures* (New York, 1977) is a classical and enduring statement.

the Holocene climate, regular episodes of Arctic cooling shaped by periodic fluctuations in solar radiation, the oscillation of El Niño and La Niña, the occasional serious volcanic eruption, could bring crisis mortality to newly enlarged populations, peoples who in normal times could manage the year-to-year flow of sustenance reasonably effectively. Such will be the primary problem considered in the following chapters.

4

The Mid-Holocene, the Late Neolithic, and the Urban-State Revolution

During the millennia following the Younger Dryas, human populations around the world crossed a fundamental boundary, reshaping their access to the earth's primary productivity through domestication and the opening of the agricultural revolution. If this occurred in a geological instant, it was also, as we have seen, an uneven process when viewed in historical time. The earliest centers of agriculture were focused in environmentally bounded mid-latitude regions where genetically malleable plants and animals were available for domestication. Elsewhere, particularly across the tropics, much more diffuse and extended domestications unfolded as human populations responded to climatic change and subtle tensions between their numbers and the wild resources around them. Across wide stretches of the semiarid and temperate Old World, the Neolithic agricultural package that developed in the Levant and Anatolia spread east and west.

The transition to more complex social forms and to the rise of the city and the earliest states was embedded in this uneven story of the Neolithic, and it is the central problem for this chapter. We may define this complexity as the hierarchical and interdependent practices and institutions of civil society and the state that, in derivative forms, persist into the contemporary world. Most important, these involve the economic and political arrangements that allow large populations to live together in relative harmony in cities and their associated hinterlands, bounded and governed by legal systems enforced by a polity wielding sufficient force to keep the peace and protect the people from external harm. But we shall see that they also involve an earlier emergence of village-based hierarchies of households defining themselves one against another in material productivity and the accumulation and transmission of property.

Just as did early domestication, the rise of village and of city-state complexity had a history shaped and constrained by climate change. Ecological conditions certainly do not totally explain these departures: we need to remember that they were exactly that – the framing *conditions* in which human societies mobilized to change their circumstances. The first part of this chapter sketches the general outlines of global climate change between 7500 BC and 3000 BC, and serves as a baseline for further discussions of modern global climate, between the onset of the late Holocene around 3000 BC and the onset of modern human-induced climate change around AD 1870. The major part of this chapter examines the ways powerful forces of climate change shaped the emergent complexities of village and city. The earliest development and spread of agriculture occurred during the very warm Holocene Optimum, during which global temperatures were, if not necessarily stable, much warmer than in the recent past. The progressive collapse of this climate regime, culminating at roughly 3000 BC, helped to push humanity across the threshold into complex state societies. Here there is necessarily some overlap with the story told in the previous chapter, because agricultural emergence and trajectories toward social hierarchy and the state occurred simultaneously in various parts of the world.

* * *

The Emergence of Modern Global Climates: The Mid-Holocene Transition

Before we can consider the rise of complexity in human societies, we must review the environmental context. It bears repeating that the climate of the Holocene world was not static; it had a dramatic history of its own. But roughly 5,000 years ago, it settled into what is known as the Late Holocene, a global pattern that governed the wider circumstances of human life until the first serious impacts of anthropogenic change during the past several centuries. The following section thus comprises something of a baseline for the postglacial world, describing in broad brush the structure of that Late Holocene system and its evolution, both out of the glacial Pleistocene but also out of the exaggerated warmth of the postglacial Early Holocene, and suggesting some of the critical features of episodic and abrupt change that it has undergone over these millennia.

Global climate can very broadly be described in terms of horizontal cells and vertical oscillations (see Figure II.5). Most fundamentally, a series of atmospheric circulation systems, or cells, operate horizontally around the earth, shaped by the gradient between a warm equator at the earth's median bulge and cold poles at the northern and southern extremes, and separated by jet streams and the Intertropical Convergence Zone (ITCZ). Given the geometry and dynamics of a spinning earth as well as solar influences, each has different dominant surface wind patterns, each moving east or west but also circulating up to the top of the troposphere at low-pressure zones, laterally as upper-level winds, and down to the surface at high-pressure zones. At the poles, the polar cells encompass the reach of extreme seasonal cold, expanding toward the equator with each winter. Their easterly surface winds (running east to west) are generally contained by the east-flowing westerly polar jet stream separating the polar cells from the Ferrell cell, which operates roughly between 60° and 30° north and south latitudes, and which is bounded on the south by the subtropical jet stream. The winds in the Ferrell cells are east-flowing westerlies, particularly strong in the winter as the polar jets shift toward the equator. Around the equatorial tropics, between the Ferrell cells, the earth is encircled by the Hadley cells, a double doughnut of inversely rotating circulation that meets at the Intertropical Convergence Zone. The Hadley cells are dominated by the trade winds, running northeast to southwest and southeast to northwest on either side of the system and meeting at the ITCZ, where converging wind flow and solar heating pushes massive volumes of warm air and moisture aloft, driving essentially daily precipitation in the equatorial tropics. Just as the polar cells expand with every winter, the ITCZ and the Hadley cells annually are pulled north of the equator by the summer warming of the northern continents, and then south of the equator by summer warming in the southern hemisphere.[1] Easterly trade winds fundamentally govern the summer monsoons in the equatorial tropics, from the western Pacific to Asia, Africa, and South and Central America, which together comprise a large volume of the Hadley cell circulation, and have been called *the global monsoon*.[2] The boundaries between these circulation systems are defined not only by jet streams and the ITCZ, but by patterns of atmospheric pressure and precipitation. Rising air causes low surface pressure and in pushing moisture aloft sets off precipitation; falling air causes high pressure but drier conditions. The polar front and the ITCZ are somewhat similar in having rising air masses, low pressure, and considerable precipitation; the subtropical front, or the horse latitudes, has falling air masses, high pressure, and less precipitation.

But here the wild card of vertical oscillations comes into play. If the earth had no continents, it might have continuous belts of high and low pressure running around the earth at 60°, 30°, and the equator. But land masses – colder in winter and hotter in summer than the surrounding oceans – are a potent climate force of their own. Especially in the northern hemisphere, heating during the summer months confuses the horizontal cells. The result is that the patterns of high and low pressure along these boundaries are clumped into locations of pressure extremes, semipermanent highs and lows that wax and wane – and even move – with the seasons. In the southern

[1] This and the following paragraph are indebted to Edward Aguado and James E. Burt, *Understanding Weather and Climate*, fourth edition (Upper Saddle River, NJ, 2007); C. Donald Ahrens, *Meteorology Today: An Introduction to Weather, Climate, and the Environment*, ninth edition (Belmont, CA, 2009); and Robert V. Rohli and Anthony J. Vega, *Climatology*, second edition (Sudbury, MA, 2012).

[2] Kevin E. Trenberth et al., "The Global Monsoon as Seen through the Divergent Atmospheric Circulation," *JClim* 13 (2000), 3969–93.

hemisphere, the picture is reasonably simple; a regular series of highs located along the subtropical horse latitudes in the south Atlantic, the Indian Ocean, summertime Australia, and the southeast Pacific are roughly matched in "dipoles" with lows along the coast of Antarctica. In the northern hemisphere, the picture is more confusing: a strong wintertime Aleutian Low oscillates with a strong summertime Hawaiian High; the winter Icelandic Low weakens and moves west in the summer, while the paired Azores High strengthens and move north. Across Asia, the pattern is reversed: a strong Siberian High pressure cell – interacting with the winter Aleutian Low and comprising the continental sibling of the high-pressure cell over the north pole – forms in the winter as the north Asian landmass becomes extremely cold. During cold winters, the Siberian High sends blasts of cold winds into the mid-latitudes. During the summer, it weakens as southern Asia warms, strengthening its seasonal dipole – the Tibetan Low.

Two of these oscillating systems are particularly important to the chapters following, because they impacted peoples across Eurasia and the world at large. Actually, they need to be seen as operating as a northern triad, as two systems budding off from the low pressure on the edge of the polar front, which intensifies in winter (and develops wave structures of ridges and troughs) in relation to the band of northern subtropical highs in what is known as the *Arctic Oscillation* (AO). This Arctic Oscillation operates in tandem with the *North Atlantic Oscillation* (NAO), defined by the shifting relationship between the Icelandic Low and the Azores High. The positive and negative modes of the NAO determine the path and power of the winter westerly winds in the Ferrell cell, directing the flow of winter precipitation from the Atlantic into Eurasia.[3] In the multiannual positive NAO mode, with a stronger winter Azores High and weaker Icelandic Low, the winter westerlies and associated storms are pushed north, bringing mild but wet winters to northern Europe and dry conditions to the Mediterranean and Anatolia. In the multiannual negative NAO mode, with a stronger winter Icelandic Low and weaker Azores High, the westerlies and their storms track south through the Mediterranean – somewhat complicated by swirling cyclones in the eastern Mediterranean and other patterns – resulting in a dry, cold winter in northern Europe, but bringing precipitation to a swath of territory running from the Mediterranean into Central Asia. The Asian dipole broadly linked with the Arctic polar cell is equally important. Centered near Lake Baikal, the winter Siberian High sends cold, dry winter winds south across Asia with powerful effects on the intensity of both

---

[3] My general understanding of the NAO is grounded on James W. Hurrell, "Decadal Trends in the North Atlantic Oscillation: Regional Temperatures and Precipitation," *Science* 269 (1995), 676–9. For authoritative approaches to the NAO in less than millennial timescales, see the essays in James W. Hurrell et al., eds., *The North Atlantic Oscillation: Climatic Significance and Environmental Impact* (Washington, DC, 2003).

Eurasian and global winters. Conversely, the strength of the summer Tibetan Low, shaped by the summer warming of the Tibetan plateau, is one of two forces fundamental to the strength of the Asian summer monsoons, in which precipitation drawn off cooler ocean waters by a warmer continent waters vast stretches of South and Southeast Asia.[4]

Two other critical enduring systems involve ocean currents and atmospheric circulation, to varying degrees, and each has a school of advocates for their primary role in regulating global climate, the North Atlantic and Tropical schools. One of these systems has been introduced in some detail in preceding chapters: the thermohaline pump operating off the coast of Greenland, in which evaporation from the north-running Gulf Stream increases the saline density of the water to the point that it plunges to the oceanic abyss, forming a south-running cold current that may drive much of the global oceanic current system. Pulses of fresh water spilling off melting continental glaciers can slow and even stop this system, by diluting the dense saline waters that drive the thermohaline pump.[5]

The second system, the El Niño/Southern Oscillation (ENSO), running horizontally across the tropical Pacific, has only been mentioned briefly, and needs further explanation.[6] If the thermohaline pump off Greenland

---

[4] Matthew D. Jones, "A High-Resolution Late Holocene Lake Isotope Record from Turkey and Links to North Atlantic and Monsoon Climate," *Geology* 34 (2006), 361–4; Michael S. Mann, "Large-Scale Variability and Connections with the Middle-East in Past Centuries," *ClimCh* 55 (2002), 287–314; Heidi M. Cullen et al., "Impact of the North Atlantic Oscillation on Middle Eastern Climate and Streamflow," *ClimCh* 55 (2002), 315–38; Heidi M. Cullen and Peter B. deMenocal, "North Atlantic Influence on Tigris-Euphrates Streamflow," *IJC* 20 (2000), 853–63; Thomas Felis, "A Coral Oxygen Isotope Record from the Northern Red Sea Documenting NAO, ENSO, and North Pacific Teleconnections on Middle East Climate Variability since the year 1750," *Paleoceanography* 15 (2000), 679–94; T. P. Barnett et al., "The Effect of Eurasian Snow Cover on Global Climate," *Science* 239 (1988), 54–7; George H. Denton et al., "The Role of Seasonality in Abrupt Climate Change," *QSR* 24 (2005), 1159–82.

[5] Some of the more influential statements of the North Atlantic school include Wallace S. Broecker, "Thermohaline Circulation, the Achilles Heel of Our Climate System: Will Man-Made CO_2 Upset the Current Balance?" *Science* 278 (1997), 1582–8; Wallace S. Broecker and G. H. Denton, "What Drives Glacial Cycles?" *SA* 262/1 (Jan. 1990), 48–56; and Gerard Bond et al., "Persistent Solar Influence on North Atlantic Climate during the Holocene," *Science* 294 (2001), 2130–6.

[6] The Tropical school thesis centering on ENSO dynamics has been advanced in Mark A. Cane, "A Role for the Tropical Pacific," *Science* 282 (1998), 59–61; Mark A. Cane and Michael Evans, "Do the Tropics Rule?" *Science* 290 (2000), 1107–8; Amy C. Clement et al., "An Orbitally Driven Tropical Source for Abrupt Climate Change," *JClim* 14 (2001), 2369–75; Richard A. Kerr, "The Tropics Return to the Climate System," *Science* 292 (2001), 660–1; and Dirk C. Leuscher and Frank Sirocko, "Orbital Insolation Forcing of the Indian Monsoon – a Motor for Global Climate Changes?" *PPP* 197 (2003), 83–95; Julien Emile-Geay et al., "El Niño as a Mediator of the Solar Influence on Climate," *Paleoceanography* 22 (2007), PA3210. For a spirited account of the contest between the North Atlantic and Tropical schools, see Mark Bowen, *Thin Ice: Unlocking the Secrets of Climate in the World's Highest Mountains* (New York, 2005), esp. 247–311.

comprises one particularly powerful force in the global climate system, the West Pacific Warm Pool comprises the second. Lying along the equator northeast of Indonesia, the West Pacific Warm Pool is the warmest body of ocean waters in the world, and may comprise the "pump" for the ENSO system. As it has functioned in "modern times," the ENSO essentially involves an oscillation of warm and cooler waters between the West Pacific Warm Pool and the eastern Pacific off South America, interacting with circulation in the tropical Hadley cells. ENSO variation between La Niña and El Niño extremes – and a normal "La Nada" – is determined by the strength of the Hadley cells, particularly the high-level Walker circulation that drives the east-to-west pattern of the trade winds in the Hadley cells. In "normal" years, the Walker circulation is strong, and the surface trade winds running out of the east from the Caribbean and the Atlantic push warm Pacific waters to the west, allowing an upwelling of cold subsurface waters. This is the "normal ENSO" condition, with high pressure in the late summer and autumn on the western American coasts shaping warm, dry conditions, while the rising moisture in a low-pressure system at the West Pacific Warm Pool Low fuels the monsoons that water Australia, South and Southeast Asia, and southern China, with influences reaching as far as Arabia and parts of eastern Africa. The ENSO operates in an annual and multiannual cyclical variation around this "La Nada norm" between "La Niña" and "El Niño." The La Niña condition, which brings severe drought to the Pacific lowlands of South America and to the southern half of North America, is an intensification of these "normal" conditions. The converse condition is El Niño, which is shaped by the weakening of the Hadley cell and the Walker circulation. In these years, the easterly trade winds fail, anomalous westerlies (running from west to east) develop, pushing a "warm tongue" of the West Pacific Warm Pool waters into the central and eastern Pacific. On South American coasts, this El Niño pattern brings sometimes catastrophic Pacific storms to the lowlands; with the easterly trade winds blocked, the high Andes and much of Amazonia suffers from drought. It would appear that ENSO oscillation is driven by variations in solar heating, strengthening and weakening the trans-Pacific Walker circulation.

There is an important ENSO connection with the Asian monsoons, which also feed off the warm waters of the West Pacific Warm Pool. Typically, in the past several thousand years, the two systems have operated inversely. (Compare Figures II.5a and b.) When the western Pacific is relatively warm, ENSO is in a quiet La Niña mode and the Asian monsoons are relatively strong, as the summer warming of the Asian interior (with the Tibetan Low) draws the monsoon off cooler ocean waters. Conversely, when the eastern Pacific is warm, ENSO is in the stormy El Niño mode and the Asian monsoon systems are typically weak. A general relationship also exists between ENSO and the North Atlantic: cold conditions in the North Atlantic (negative NAO) are associated with stronger El Niño; warmer conditions in the

North Atlantic (positive NAO) are associated with La Niña or La Nada. The result is an enduring three-point pattern: warm north, La Niña conditions, strong Asian monsoons, and its obverse, cold north, El Niño conditions, and weak Asian monsoons.[7]

Obviously, all of these systems were not static, but evolving and shifting through time, most powerfully forced by orbital cycles that govern the solar input to the earth system. During the glacial periods of the Pleistocene, the global cell system would have been compressed by expanding fronts of the Polar and Siberian Highs, which during the northern winter might have reached as far south as southern Portugal. As the polar cells were strengthened in glacial periods, the Ferrell and Hadley cells were compressed and weakened, and the north-south movements of the ITCZ minimized. (Compare Figures II.5a, b, and c.)

The weakened Hadley cells seem to have also meant a weakened Walker circulation and a stronger El Niño during glacial periods. In fact, it appears that ENSO has evolved dramatically over the past 2.5 million years. During the warm preglacial Pliocene, with the North Pole still ice free, the Hadley cell system was presumably very broad but also weak and unstructured. Apparently, the modern Walker circulation had not developed; a permanent El Niño condition existed in the eastern Pacific. As increasingly glacial conditions in the polar north began around 2.5 million years ago, evidence for an oscillation of El Niño and La Niño conditions begins to appear, suggesting that the Hadley cell strengthened and the Walker circulation started. Ironically, however, ENSO apparently responded to global glacial conditions in a Goldilocks fashion: some cooling was a good thing; too much was too much. The full ENSO variability between El Niño and La Niña operated during the Pleistocene, with a stronger La Niña associated with interglacials and a stronger thermohaline pump in the North Atlantic. But where during the warm Pliocene the tropical Hadley cells had been too big and weak to generate La Niña conditions, now, during Pleistocene glacial periods, they were too small and weak, so glacial periods saw permanent El Niños.[8]

[7] For an overview of ENSO, see Mark A. Cane, "The Evolution of El Niño, Past and Present," *EPSL* 230 (2005), 227–40. On the "Warm Pool," see Michael K. Gagan et al., "Post-Glacial Evolution of the Indo-Pacific Warm Pool and El Niño-Southern Oscillation," *QuatInt* 118–19 (2004), 127–43; and J. M. Brijker, "ENSO Related Decadal Scale Climate Variability from the Indo-Pacific Warm Pool," *EPSL* 253 (2007), 67–82.

[8] For permanent El Niño-like conditions during the warm Pliocene, see Ana Christina Ravelo et al., "Regional Climate Shifts Caused by Gradual Global Cooling in the Pliocene Epoch," *Nature* 429 (2004), 263–7; A. V. Federov et al., "The Pliocene Paradox (Mechanisms of a Permanent El Niño)," *Science* 312 (2006), 1485–9; J. Etourneau et al., "Intensification of the Walker and Hadley Atmospheric Circulations during the Pliocene-Pleistocene Climate Transition," *EPSL* 297 (2010), 103–10; Alexey V. Federov, "Tropical Cyclones and Permanent El Niño in the Early Pliocene Epoch," *Nature* 463 (2010), 1067–70. For the argument for strong ENSO oscillation during the Pleistocene, see Lowell Stott, "Super ENSO and Global Climate Oscillations at Millennial Time Scales," *Science* 297 (2002), 222–6;

These conditions obviously reversed when the present interglacial began around 12,000 years ago, with the wild oscillation of the warm Bølling-Allerød, the cold Younger Dryas, and the warming of the Early Holocene. Here the arc of a single orbital-glacial cycle (governing the volume of solar input), interrupted by a massive melt water event at the Younger Dryas, has driven the shape of global climates over the past 12,000 years (see Figure II.1). During the Early Holocene, between roughly 9500 and 7000 BC, the earth's tilt gave maximum possible exposure of the poles to the sun exactly at the same time that the orbital precession brought earth in summer to the closest possible distance from the sun. This was the peak of the earth's postglacial solar exposure, with the height of the interglacial warmth occurring over the next few millennia. The earth's exaggerated tilt brought an extreme seasonal variability to the northern latitudes, making Early Holocene summers in the northern hemisphere particularly warm and winters cold and stormy. After 7000 BC, this solar exposure progressively declined, to the point that today the regions along the 60° north latitude line receive about 7 percent less solar radiation during the summer than they would have 10,000 years ago. The far northern winters warmed with the gradual orbital changes, while the northern summers cooled somewhat, meaning a decline in seasonal extremes. Along the equator, a long-term cooling of the West Pacific Warm Pool started around 8000 BC, which would have a powerful effect on the general tropical monsoon system.[9]

The rise and decline of this pattern of Early Holocene warmth changed the shape and structure of global atmospheric circulation. During the Early Holocene, the warm northern summers strengthened both the Ferrell and Hadley cells, lifting the ITCZ well north of the equator. The north-riding Early Holocene ITCZ brought the summer mega-monsoons that watered North Africa, Arabia, the eastern Mediterranean, the Indian subcontinent, and southern China.[10] So much fresh water was introduced into the eastern

Athanasios Koutavas et al., "El Niño-Like Pattern in Ice Age Tropical Pacific Sea Surface Temperature," *Science* 297 (2002), 226–30; and the literature reviewed in Amy C. Clement and Larry C. Peterson, "Mechanisms of Abrupt Climate Change of the Last Glacial Period," *Reviews in Geophysics* 46 (2008), RG4002, esp. 10–12. See also Marie Alexandrine Sicre et al., "A 4500-Year Reconstruction of Sea Surface Temperature Variability at Decadal Time-Scales off North Iceland," *QSR* 27 (2008), 2041–7 for a discussion of the linkages between ENSO and the North Atlantic thermohaline system.

9   William F. Ruddiman, *Earth Climate: Past and Future* (New York, 2001), 313–21; A. Berger and M. F. Loutre, "Insolation Values for the Climate of the Last 10 Million Years," *QSR* 10 (1991), 297–317; G. H. Miller et al., "Temperature and Precipitation History of the Arctic," *QSR* 29 (2910), 1679–715; Lowell Stott, "Decline of Surface Temperature and Salinity in the Western Tropical Pacific Ocean in the Holocene Epoch," *Nature* 431 56–9.

10 In a vast literature, see Gerald H. Haug et al., "Southward Migration of the Intertropical Convergence Zone through the Holocene," *Science* 293 (2001), 1304–8; Peter deMenocal, "Abrupt Onset and Termination of the African Humid Period: Rapid Climate Responses to Gradual Insolation Forcing," *QSR* 19 (2000), 347–61; Lonnie G. Thompson et al., "Kilimanjaro Ice Core Records: Evidence of Holocene Climate Change in Tropical Africa," *Science* 298 (2002), 589–93; Françoise Gasse, "Hydrological Changes in the African Tropics

Mediterranean from direct monsoon rainfall and indirectly from East Africa via the Nile River flow that an anoxic condition called a *sapropel* formed, manifested in a black layer of organic deposits.[11] Conversely, the north-riding ITCZ weakened the southern Hadley cell, and thus the South American monsoon coming off the south Atlantic, which waters virtually all of South America to the Andean summits: South America was thus fundamentally dry during the Early Holocene. At the same time, the ENSO system – the preponderance of evidence suggests – was suppressed into a long "normal" with only minimal La Niña/ El Niño variation, matching the strong monsoons in the northern hemisphere. Here the warm Early Holocene West Pacific Warm Pool played a key role in driving the summer Asian monsoons and limiting the ENSO system. The result strengthened the monsoons in Asia, while further contributing to dry conditions in Early Holocene South America.[12]

since the Late Glacial Maximum," *QSR* 19 (2000), 189–211; Dominik Fleitmann et al., "Holocene ITCZ and Indian Monsoon Dynamics Recorded in Stalagmites from Oman and Yemen (Socotra)," *QSR* 26 (2007), 170–88, esp. 170–1, 179, 180; Carolyn A. Dykoski et al., "A High-Resolution, Absolute-Dated Holocene and Deglacial Asian Monsoon Record from Dongge Cave, China," *EPSL* 233 (2005), 71–86.

[11] E. J. Rohling et al., "The Marine Environment: Present and Past," in Jamie C. Woodward, ed., *The Physical Geography of the Mediterranean* (Oxford, 2009), 33–68, esp. 48–58, summarizes several decades of research. See also Martine Rossignol-Strick, "The Holocene Climate Optimum and Pollen Records of Sapropel 1 in the Eastern Mediterranean, 9000–6000 BP," *QSR* 18 (1999), 515–30; Miryam Bar-Matthews et al., "The Eastern Mediterranean Paleoclimate as a Reflection of Regional Events: Soreq Cave, Israel," *EPSL* 166 (1999), 85–95.

[12] On the South American monsoon, see Broxton W. Bird et al., "Holocene Tropical South American Hydroclimate Revealed from a Decadally Resolved Lake Sediment $\delta^{18}O$ Record," *EPSL* 310 (2011), 192–202. The weight of the scholarship argues for low ENSO variation during the Early Holocene. See also Luc Ortieb et al., "Marine Radiocarbon Reservoir Effect along the Northern Chile-Southern Peru Coast (14–24°S) throughout the Holocene," *QuatRes* 75 (2011), 91–103; Jessica L. Conroy et al., "Holocene Changes in Eastern Tropical Pacific Climate Inferred from a Galápagos Lake Sediment Record," *QSR* 27 (2008), 1166–80; Michael A. Gagan and Lonnie G. Thompson, "Evolution of the Indo-Pacific Warm Pool and Hadley-Walker Circulation since the Last Deglaciation," in Henry F. Diaz and Raymond F. Bradley, eds., *The Hadley Circulation: Past, Present, and Future* (Dordecht, 2004), 289–312; Xavier Rodó and Miquel-Angel Rodriguez-Arias, "El-Niño-Southern Oscillation: Absent in the Early Holocene?" *JClim* 17 (2004), 423–6; Koutavas et al., "El Niño-Like Pattern in Ice Age Tropical Pacific Sea Surface Temperature"; Donald T. Rodbell et al., "An ~15,000-Year Record of El-Niño-Driven Alluviation in Southwestern Ecuador," *Science* 283 (1999), 516–520; Christopher M. Moy, "Variability of El Niño-Southern Oscillation Activity at Millennial Timescales during the Holocene Epoch," *Nature* 420 (2002), 162–5. On the other hand, there has been a competing school of thought for a stronger ENSO pattern during the Early Holocene, based on Peruvian records: Bert Rein et al., "El Niño Variability off Peru during the Last 20,000 Years," *Paleoceanography* 20 (2005), PA403, 1–17; Mattieu Carré et al., "Strong El-Niño Events during the Early Holocene: Stable Isotope Evidence from Peruvian Sea Shells," *The Holocene* 15 (2005), 42–7. All of the ENSO studies concur on a weak ENSO during the Mid-Holocene and the starting of the modern ENSO variation around 3000 BC.

The new dynamics of the Early Holocene set up another diagnostic pattern in the North Atlantic Oscillation/Arctic Oscillation (NAO/AO). Exactly how the NAO/AO operated in glacial conditions is not clear, but presumably it lay in some sort of super-negative mode, with intense polar winters pushing winter westerlies far south.[13] Then with the warm-up of the Early Holocene, the NAO/AO shifted suddenly toward a strongly positive mode, bringing winter precipitation to northern Europe. This entire global system of a warm north, positive NAO/AO, minimal ENSO variation, north-riding ITCZ, and strong Asian and African monsoons persisted until the Mid-Holocene[14] (see Figure II.5a).

At the Mid-Holocene transition, roughly 5000 BC to 3000 BC, this entire system began to shift in important if perhaps subtle ways. As the earth changed its precessional seasonality and wobble, summer insolation declined in the northern hemisphere and rose in the southern hemisphere, and with it the entire array of climate systems shifted south, ending the Early Holocene epoch of mega-monsoons (see Figures II.1–II.3). The West Pacific Warm Pool began to cool and the ITCZ and associated Asian monsoons gradually withdrew from their northernmost reach in the summers, bringing a slow reduction of summer precipitation to much of Asia. Across equatorial Africa, the Atlantic monsoon weakened, drying out the Sahara and reducing the flow to the Nile. At the same time, the NAO/AO patterns shifted from predominantly positive to predominantly negative. The result was that, progressively through the Mid-Holocene, winter westerlies began to carry moisture through the Mediterranean and into central Asia, somewhat counterbalancing the loss of summer monsoon rain.[15] As the ITCZ moved south permanently, it strengthened the South American monsoon off the south Atlantic, bringing rising precipitation and humidity to all of South America up to the eastern side of the Andean summits. Simultaneously, – influenced by the cooling West Pacific Warm Pool – ENSO variation began

---

[13] Duri Florineth and Christian Schlüchter, "Alpine Evidence for Atmospheric Circulation Patterns in Europe during the Last Glacial Maximum," *QuatRes* 54 (2000), 295–308.

[14] After roughly 7000 BC, the East Asian monsoon began to vary inversely with ENSO and the South Asian monsoon because of influences from Siberia. Y. T. Hong, "Inverse Phase Oscillations between the East Asian and Indian Ocean Summer Monsoons during the Last 12,000 Years and Paleo-El Niño," *EPSL* 231 (2005), 337–46.

[15] Françoise Chalié and Françoise Gasse, "Late-Glacial-Holocene Diatom Record of Water Chemistry and Lake Level Change from the Tropical East African Rift Lake Abiyata (Ethiopia)," *PPP* 187 (2002), 259–83; Nick Marriner et al., "ITCZ and ENSO-Like Pacing of Nile Delta Hydro-Geomorphology during the Holocene," *QSR* 45 (2012), 73–84; N. Rimbu et al., "Arctic/North Atlantic Oscillation Signature in Holocene Sea Surface Temperature Trends as Obtained from Alkenone Data," *GRL* 30 (2003), 1280, 13: 1–4; N. Rimbu et al., "Holocene Climate Variability as Derived from Alkenone Sea Surface Temperature and Coupled Ocean-Atmosphere Model Experiments," *ClimDyn* 23 (2004), 215–27; Elena N. Aizen et al., "Precipitation and Atmospheric Circulation Patterns as Mid-Latitudes of Asia," *IJC* 21 (2001), 535–56.

to strengthen around 3000 BC, establishing the modern, trans-Pacific oscillation between the El Niño pattern of South American coastal rains and Asian drought and the La Niña pattern of South American coastal drought and Asian monsoon rain. But where there had been mega-monsoons during the Early Holocene, there would be megadroughts during the Late Holocene, periods of a century or more with reduced rainfall in wide rain-dependent regions.[16]

Such has been the general shape of global climate history through the Holocene, shaped by the cycles of orbital forces and the resulting influence of the sun on the earth's surface. But there are two other critical forces at work that had shorter, more episodic influences on global climate. Just as orbital forcings are not as strong as super-cyclical tectonic forcings, volcanic action and solar variation have weaker and shorter-lived influences than does orbital variation. But from the point of view of a human society extracting biomass on the surface of the earth, these more subtle solar and volcanic variations have been extremely significant, making the difference between sufficiency, dearth, and even starvation. Volcanic eruptions, occurring in a relatively unpatterned way at various velocities, can have a variety of local, regional, and global effects. Besides the direct destruction of lava and pyroclastic flow, the cooling effects of sulphur ejected in these eruptions generally overwhelm the warming effects of volcanic CO_2. Sulphur traces in the ice core record suggest that an enormous number of volcanic eruptions occurred during the Early Holocene down to roughly 4500–3500 BC, eruptions that may have been set off as the continental surfaces rebounded with the melting of the massive Pleistocene ice sheets. Enormous eruptions at later dates may well have played important roles in triggering shifts in global climate.[17]

The sun is a more pervasive and variable climate factor, however. While the earth's orbital relationship to the sun moved through broad arcs of several thousand years, the output of the sun itself flickers on periodicities that can be measured in decades, centuries, and millennia. The most familiar of these solar variations is the eleven-year sun-spot cycle, which regularly sends

---

[16] Cullen et al., "Impact of the North Atlantic Oscillation on Middle Eastern Climate and Streamflow"; Mann, "Large-Scale Climate Variability and Connections with the Middle East in Past Centuries"; M. Jones et al., "A High-Resolution Late Holocene Lake Isotope Record from Turkey"; Ulrike Herzschuh, "Palaeo-Moisture Evolution in Monsoonal Central Asia during the Last 50,000 Years," *QSR* 25 (2006), 163–75; Thomas Felis and Norel Rimbu, "Mediterranean Climate Variability Documented in Oxygen Isotope Records from Northern Red Sea Corals – a Review," *GPC* 71 (2010), 232–41. For a synthesis stressing the Mid-Holocene rise of ENSO and a shift toward negative NAO/AO, see Heinz Wanner et al., "Mid- to Late Holocene Climate Change: A Review," *QSR* 27 (2008), 1791–828. On megadroughts, see Ashish Sinha et al., "A Global Context for Megadroughts in Monsoon Asia during the Past Millennium," *QSR* 30 (2011), 47–62.

[17] Gregory A. Zielinski et al., "A 110,000-Yr. Record of Explosive Volcanism from the GISP2 (Greenland) Ice Core," *QuatRes* 45 (1996), 109–18.

waves of solar particles that damage and destroy orbiting satellites. Less well known, but more important for our purposes here, are the great maxima and minima in solar output, here the most famous is the Maunder Minimum of the late seventeenth century, during which the River Thames froze solid at London, and the Dutch are supposed to have invented skating. These grand minima have been estimated to come in waves roughly 2,300 years apart, known as Hallstatt cycles.[18] Between the eleven-year cycles and the great solar maxima and minima of the 2,300-year Hallstatt cycle is a series of solar cycles on intermediate scales (see Figures II.4, III.3). As has been suggested in earlier chapters, it may well be that rather than solar output per se, the key global influence lies in the interaction of solar output with cosmic ray flux coming from galactic sources, which during solar minima may increase global cloudiness and thus drive waves of cooling.[19]

Periods of higher and lower solar output have been a fundamental force in global climate history in a number of ways, but here it is sufficient to pick out two patterns that seem particularly important. In the early 1990s, a team of scientists led by the late Gerard Bond revealed a recurring pattern of sedimentary deposits in the North Atlantic that indicate that flotillas of ice rafts have floated out from Greenland eight times since the Younger Dryas. Mirroring the 1500-year glacial Dansgaard-Oeschger cycles, these iceberg flotillas – known as *Bond events* – then brought cooling conditions to Europe, and may have had global influences through the thermohaline circulation system. These ice raft events, coming roughly every 1,500 years, have been convincingly attributed to solar variation.[20] A broad connection also exists between solar variation, the North Atlantic Oscillation, and the summer reach of the Intertropical Convergence Zone. Strong solar insolation moves the ITCZ farther north in the summer and strengthens high

---

[18] I am illustrating (Figure II.4 and following) solar strength with the estimate of total solar intensity (annual watts/square meter of land surface) developed in A. I. Shapiro et al., "A New Approach to Long-Term Reconstruction of the Solar Irradiance Leads to Large Historical Forcing," *Astronomy and Astrophysics* 529 (2011), A67. This data set provides a 9,000-year, annual-scale estimate of solar activity; it is based on that by F. Steinhilber et al., "Total Solar Irradiance during the Holocene," *GRL* 36 (2009), L19704; "Interplanetary Magnetic Field during the Past 9300 Years Inferred from Cosmogenic Radionuclides," *JGR* 115 (2010), A01104; the Shapiro estimate finds a stronger amplitude of solar variation than does that by Steinhilber and colleagues. See also Jürg Beer and Ken McCracken, "Evidence for Solar Forcing: Some Selected Aspects," in T. Tsuda et al., *Climate and Weather of the Sun-Earth System (CAWSES): Selected Papers from the 2007 Kyoto Symposium* (Tokyo, 2009), 201–16; P. E. Damon and J. L. Jirikowic, "The Sun as a Low-Frequency Harmonic Oscillator," *Radiocarbon* 34 (1992), 199–205.

[19] See Chapter 1, note 73.

[20] The foundational articles describing the ice-rafting events are Gerard Bond et al., "A Pervasive Millennial-Scale Cycle in North Atlantic Holocene and Glacial Climates," *Science* 278 (1997), 1257–66; and Bond et al., "Persistent Solar Influence." On solar influences, see also A. Mangini et al., "Persistent Influence of North Atlantic Hydrography on Central European Temperature during the Last 9000 Years," *GRL* 34 (2007), L02704.

pressure at the Azores, thus shaping a positive NAO and pushing winter precipitation north out of the Mediterranean and into Northern Europe[21] (see Figures II.4, II.5a–c).

Solar variation on a very large scale also seems to be behind another more powerful series of cooling events that have influenced the entire northern hemisphere, at least since the Mid-Holocene transition. Potassium found in the Greenland ice cores, derived from dust from Asian deserts, seems to measure the intensity of the Siberian High. Since the beginning of the Holocene, there have been four obvious peaks in the Siberian High: at roughly 6900–6000 BC, 4000–3000 BC, 1200–600 BC, and AD 1300–1700; each coincides with a Bond ice-rafting event and brackets an intervening one. These events, which we shall call *millennial Siberian Highs*, had simultaneous and direct impacts across the entire northern hemisphere, and indirect effects on the southern hemisphere, as monsoon and even ENSO dynamics were affected by a cold north (see Figures II.4, II.5c, III.3).

The last three of these events line up reasonably well with the 2,300-year Hallstatt solar cycle, and it is a reasonable hypothesis that after 4000 BC and the onset of the Mid-Holocene transition the Hallstatt events are responsible for the millennial Siberian Highs. The cold event at 6900–6000 BC and the Hallstatt at roughly 5800–5000 BC are obviously not in synch. The cold event was in part shaped by a postglacial melt water event at 6200 BC slowing the thermohaline pump in the North Atlantic, but this does not explain the long-term cooling beginning at 6900. Conversely, the effect of the early Hallstatt at 5800–5000 BC may have been masked by the continuing influence of the orbitally shaped Early Holocene warmth in the northern hemisphere. But after the onset of the Mid-Holocene, the Hallstatt cycle and the millennial Siberian High clearly work together to shape the essential pulse of global climate history. That history looks like a slowly descending arc of orbitally driven cooling, notched by cold, stormy millennial highs and intervening ice rafting events, and their global climatic reverberations in the midlatitudes and the tropics. This history had enormous consequences over these millennia for populations – perhaps three-quarters of humanity – concentrated in the Old World along the mid-latitudes from the Mediterranean to East Asia, and along the west coast of the Americas from Mexico to Chile.[22]

---

[21] L. J. Gray et al., "Solar Influences on Climate," *Reviews of Geophysics*, 48 (2010), at 17, 22; B. Vannière et al., "Circum-Mediterranean Fire Activity and Climate Changes during the Mid-Holocene Environmental Transition, (8500–2500 cal B.P.)," *Holocene* 21 (2011), 57; Julian P. Sachs et al., "Southward Movement of the Pacific Intertropical Convergence Zone AD 1400–1850," *NatGeosc* 2 (2009), 519–25. On the Pleistocene megadroughts, see Chapter 2. Very broadly, it would appear from work done on the past two millennia that the Atlantic ice rafting record is a general index for larger shifts in the North Atlantic Oscillation: less ice correlating with a positive NAO mode, more ice with a negative NAO mode. See Figure III.5a.

[22] S. R. O'Brien et al., "Complexity of Holocene Climate as Reconstructed from a Greenland Ice Core," *Science* 270 (1995), 1962–4 provided an early road map of this pattern of 2,300-

With all of these global climate patterns briefly sketched, we can explore some of the details of the Mid-Holocene transition. The first hints of this long transition came during the 6900–6100 BC cooling event that culminated in the dramatic melt water event of 6200 BC, when the North American Laurentine ice sheet finally collapsed. This cooling has been detected in paleo-records from Peru to the North Atlantic to the China coast.[23] In the Levant and in adjacent parts of the Mediterranean, which had been watered by cyclonic circulation shaped since the Younger Dryas by north-rising African and Indian Ocean spring and summer monsoonal rains, a sharp and permanent decline of oak pollen deposited in lake sediments suggests that the Indian Ocean summer monsoon retreated from the Levant around 7000 BC[24] (see Figure II.2). Similarly, the monsoon retreated in South Asia itself, though it would return, and the subcontinent would remain relatively humid and well watered for several thousand years. In Central Asia, at a particularly sensitive intersection of Pacific and Atlantic influences, the Indian Ocean Monsoon had its optimum influence for about 3,000 years, but began its permanent withdrawal around 5700 BC.[25]

year millennial cooling events. Since then, the formative articles on this topic are Paul A. Mayewski et al., "Major Features and Forcing of High-Latitude Northern Hemisphere Atmospheric Circulation Using a 110,000 Year-Long Glaciochemical Series," *JGR* 102 (1997), 26345–66; Eelco J. Rohling et al., "Holocene Atmosphere-Ocean Interactions: Records from Greenland and the Aegean Sea," *ClimDyn* 18 (2002), 587–93; Anders J. Noren et al., "Millennial-Scale Storminess Variability in the Northeastern United States during the Holocene Epoch," *Nature* 419 (2002), 821–4; Paul A. Mayewski et al., "Holocene Climate Variability," *QuatRes* 62 (2004), 243–55; Gianluca Marino et al., "Early and Middle Holocene in the Aegean Sea: Interplay between High and Low Latitude Climate Variability," *QSR* 28 (2009), 3246–62; Bernhard Weninger et al., "The Impact of Rapid Climate Change on Prehistoric Societies during the Holocene in the Eastern Mediterranean," *Documenta Praehistorica* 36 (2009), 7–59; Heinz Wanner et al., "Structure and Origin of Holocene Cold Events," *QSR* 30 (2011), 3109–23; Mads Faurschou Knudsen et al., "Evidence of Sues Solar-Cycle Bursts in Subtropical Speleothem $\delta^{18}O$ Records," *Holocene* 22 (2011), 597–602.

[23] Weninger et al., "The Impact of Rapid Climate Change," 30–4; Mayewski et al., "Holocene Climate Variability," 251; Eelco J. Rohling and Heiko Pälike, "Centennial-Scale Climate Cooling with a Sudden Cold Event around 8,200 Years Ago," *Nature* 434 (2005), 975–9; L. G. Thompson et al., "Late Glacial Stage and Holocene Tropical Ice Core Records from Huascarán, Peru," *Science* 269 (1995), 46–50; Bond et al., "Persistent Solar Influence." Rohling and Pälike argue for a solar influence shaping the 6900–6000 BC Siberian High.

[24] John Meadows, "The Younger Dryas Episode and Radio-Carbon Chronologies of the Lake Huleh and Ghab Valley Pollen Diagrams, Israel and Syria," *Holocene* 15 (2005), 631–6; Willem van Zeist et al., "Holocene Palaeoecology of the Hula Area, Northeast Israel," in Eva Kaptijn and Lucas Petit, eds., *A Timeless Vale: Archaeological and Related Essays on the Jordan Valley in Honour of Gerrit van der Kooij on the Occasion of his Sixty-Fifth Birthday* (Leiden, 2009), 29–64, figure 5; Rossignol-Strick, "The Holocene Climate Optimum."

[25] The South Asian monsoon has been described in a number of recent articles, including Anil K. Gupta et al., "Abrupt Changes in the Asian Southwest Monsoon during the Holocene and Their Links to the North Atlantic Ocean," *Nature* 421 (2003), 354–7; Ulrich von Rad et al., "A 5000-yr Record of Climate Change in Varved Sediments from the Oxygen Minimum Zone off Pakistan, Northeastern Arabian Sea," *QuatRes* 51 (1999), 39–53; Dykoski et al., "A

Strikingly, as the Indian summer monsoon began to withdraw to the south, the Atlantic winter westerlies shifted toward a more southerly pattern, from a track predominantly across northern Europe to one that increasingly flowed across the Mediterranean and Central Asia. This was the effect of the shift of the NAO/AO from a more positive to a more negative state, as solar irradiance declined and global climate systems shifted south. The arrival of the Atlantic westerlies seems to explain the expansion of oaks around Lake Van in eastern Anatolia beginning at roughly 6100 BC, and then perhaps 1,000 years later at Lake Zeribar in the Iranian Zagros Mountains.[26] The reach of the winter westerlies peaked in central Asia between 6400 BC and 5400 BC, surpassed the declining Indian Ocean monsoon and – after 4000 BC – the East Asian monsoon to become the most significant source of precipitation in Central Asia down to the present[27] (see Figure II.2).

The second phase of the Holocene transition began around 4500 BC, roughly with the first waning of the post-Pleistocene volcanic eruptions. Increasing aridity registered at Mount Kilimanjaro between 4600 BC and

... Monsoon Record from Dongge Cave, China"; Yangjin Wang et al., "The Holocene Asian Monsoon: Links to Solar Changes and North Atlantic Climate," [Dongge DA] *Science* 308 (2005), 854–7; Junfeng Ji et al., "Asian Monsoon Oscillations in the Northeastern Qinghai-Tibet Plateau since the Late Glacial as Interpreted from Visible Reflectance of Qinghai Lake Sediments," *EPSL* 233 (2005), 61–70; and Y. T. Hong, "Correlation between Indian Ocean Summer Monsoon and North Atlantic Climate during the Holocene" [Hongyuan], *EPSL* 211 (2003), 371–80. It has recently been demonstrated in Ming Tan, "Climatic Differences and Similarities between Indian and East Asian Monsoon Regions of China over the Last Millennium: A Perspective Based Mainly on Stalagmite Records," *International Journal of Speleology* 36 (2000), 75–81 that the Dongge Cave records as well as others in southern China and Tibet were shaped by the South Asian monsoon. The Dongge DA and D4 records thus provide the best-detailed sequences for the South Asian monsoon. For Central Asia, see Herzschuh, "Palaeo-Moisture Evolution in Monsoonal Central Asia."

[26] Lucia Wick et al., "Evidence of Lateglacial and Holocene Climatic Change and Human Impact in Eastern Anatolia: High-Resolution Pollen, Charcoal, Isotopic and Geochemical Records from Laminated Sediments of Lake Van, Turkey," *Holocene* 13,2 (2003), 665–73, figure 5; L. R. Stevens et al., "Proposed Changes in Seasonality of Climate during the Late Glacial and Holocene at Lake Zeribar, Iran," *Holocene* 11 (2001), 747–55, figure 3; see also Huw I. Griffiths et al., "Environmental Change in Southwestern Iran: The Holocene Ostracod Fauna of Lake Mirabad," *Holocene* 11 (2001), 75–64, esp. 761–2. Neil Roberts, in "Did Prehistoric Landscape Management Retard the Post-Glacial Spread of Woodland in Southwest Asia," *Antiquity* 76 (2002), 1002–10, argues that Neolithic burning slowed the advance of oak in eastern Anatolia and the Zagros, but he does not explain why such burning did not slow the earlier oak growth in the Levant nor does he consider the timing of monsoonal and westerly precipitation.

[27] Herzschuh, "Palaeo-Moisture Evolution in Monsoonal Central Asia." See also Philippe Sorel et al., "Climate Variability in the Aral Sea Basin (Central Asia) during the Late Holocene Based on Vegetation Changes," *QuatRes* 67 (2007), 357–70; Michel Magny et al., "Contrasting Patterns of Hydrological Changes in Europe in Response to Holocene Climate Cooling Phases," *QSR* 22 (2003), 1589–96; and Yongtao Yu et al., "Millennial-Scale Holocene Climate Variability in the NW China Drylands and Links to the Tropical Pacific and the North Atlantic," *PPP* 233 (2006), 149–62.

4000 BC, a marker of the retreat of the Intertropical Convergence Zone that also can be seen in records from equatorial Africa, Oman, and south China[28] (see Figures II.3, II.4). By the middle of the fourth millennium (4000–3000 BC), the Asian monsoon was retreating from Central Asia, and the Indian Ocean monsoon was weakened to the point that India itself was moving from humid to arid, as was the Sahara, with the African monsoon in retreat.[29] The decline of tropical moisture also registered in the global decline of atmospheric methane, which dropped from a maximum of 700 ppb just after the Younger Dryas (9700–8800 BC) to a Holocene minimum of 550 ppb around 3300 BC.

As these structural shifts unfolded, the fourth millennium brought a wild and final reversal to the North Atlantic. A cluster of deep solar minima in a long fourth millennium between roughly 4300 and 2900 BC would not be replicated for more than 2,000 years. In the North Atlantic itself there is evidence of an onslaught of icebergs and of an accelerated cycling of deep ocean waters, and the cold conditions registered at least as far south as the Aegean Sea. Sediments in the North Atlantic starting around 4300 BC indicate that vast fleets of icebergs moved off Greenland, and at 3500 BC and then again at 3000 BC there were deep minimums in the turnover of warm surface waters that suggest the worst failure of the thermohaline circulation system since the Younger Dryas.[30] At 3900 BC, the millennial Siberian High took hold; readings of salt, dust, and potassium deposited in the Greenland ice suggest an epoch of intense winter storms (see Figures II.4, III.3).

These events culminated in a final crisis to the stormy fourth millennium, running from 3200 BC to 2900 BC. At Mount Kilimanjaro in Kenya and Soreq Cave at Jerusalem, oxygen isotope proxies indicate a sharp cooling at roughly 3200 BC; conditions at Kilimanjaro became increasingly dusty, while small spikes of dolomite and calcium in sediment cores from the Gulf of Oman indicate similar dry dusty conditions in Southwest Asia. In central Turkey, Lake Tecer – after hundreds of years of humid conditions – completely dried up into a desiccated basin, a condition that lasted for two centuries. At exactly the same time (3195 BC), extremely narrow tree rings in Irish oaks indicate an extreme cold event in northwest Europe. In the Tyrolean Alps, glacial advance rapidly covered a Neolithic shepherd, now known as the "Iceman," who died in the mountains at ~3200 BC; in Peru,

[28] Thompson et al., "Kilimanjaro Ice Core Records"; deMenocal, "Abrupt Onset and Termination of the African Humid Period"; Fleitmann et al., "Holocene ITCZ and Indian Monsoon Dynamics"; Dykoski et al., "A … Monsoon Record from Dongge Cave, China."

[29] Herzschuh, "Palaeo-Moisture Evolution in Monsoonal Central Asia"; Hong et al., "Correlation between Indian Ocean Summer Monsoon and North Atlantic Climate"; Peter deMenocal, "Coherent High and Low-Latitude Climate Variability during the Holocene Warm Period," *Science* 288 (2000), 2198–202.

[30] Rohling et al., "Holocene Atmosphere-Ocean Interactions"; Daniel W. Oppo et al., "Deepwater Variability in the Holocene Epoch," *Nature* 422 (2003), 277–8; Bond et al., "Persistent Solar Influence."

the Quelccaya glacier similarly advanced over plants dating to ~3100 BC.[31] In the Nile Valley, the Levant, and in the greater Mesopotamia drainage, evidence exists of severe reductions in precipitation, river flow, and thus serious droughts around 3200–3000 BC[32] (see Figure III.3). This snap of extreme cold, dry conditions probably lasted no more than a couple of centuries at most, but it established permanently cooler and drier conditions that would not be reversed until the recent decades of twentieth-century global warming, when both the Tyrolean "Iceman" and the Peruvian plants emerged from melting glaciers at opposite ends of the earth, after being buried in the ice for 5,000 years.

These Mid-Holocene events were imbedded in a strange negative NAO couplet. As the icebergs and the ITCZ moved south from 4300 BC, so too apparently did the winter westerlies, as evidenced by high lake levels in the Mediterranean and central Europe, markers of strong precipitation brought by a strengthened negative mode of the North Atlantic Oscillation. But the onset of the Siberian High at 3900 BC interrupted this sequence of high lake stands – and the best explanation is that the cold, dry blasts of the Siberian High simply blocked the flow of negative NAO westerlies into the Mediterranean. (See Figure II.5c for a conjectural reconstruction of the global impact of a millennial Siberian High.) The high lake levels returned around 3750 BC, but were interrupted again by the cold event at 3200 BC, when the high lake stands disappeared in several hundred years of intense aridity; finally, after 2900 BC, a strong negative NAO was restored, and with it the winter westerly rains. This erratic play of negative NAO and the Siberian High had a powerful impact on the trajectory of societies from Egypt to India.[33]

[31] Most of the vast literature summarized in part here has recently been synthesized in Lonnie G. Thompson et al., "Abrupt Tropical Climate Change: Past and Present," *Proceedings of the National Academy of Sciences* [PNAS] 103 (2006), 10536–43, esp. 10541–2. See also Neil Roberts et al., "The Mid-Holocene Climatic Transition in the Mediterranean"; Neil Roberts et al., "Climatic, Vegetation and Cultural Change in the Eastern Mediterranean during the Mid-Holocene Environmental Transition"; Miryam Bar-Matthews and Avner Ayalon, "Mid-Holocene Climate Variations Revealed by High-Resolution Speleolthem Records from Soreq Cave, Israel and the Correlation with Cultural changes"; Catherine Kuzucuoğlu et al., "Mid- to Late-Holocene Climate Change in Central Turkey: The Tecer Lake Record," all in *Holocene* 21 (2011), 3–13, 147–62, 163–71, 173–88, at 181, 185. Issue 21/1 of *Holocene* is a special series on the impact of the Mid-Holocene transition on the Mediterranean and Southwest Asia.

[32] Karl W. Butzer, "Environmental Change in the Near East and Human Impact on the Land," in Jack M. Sasson, et al., eds., *Civilizations of the Ancient Near East* (Peabody, MA, 1995), 123–151, esp. 133, 135–7; Christopher E. Bernhardt et al., "Nile Delta Vegetation Response to Holocene Climate Variability," *Geology* 40 (2010), 615–18; Migowski et al., "Holocene Climate Variability and Cultural Evolution in the Near East from the Dead Sea Sedimentary Record," *QuatRes* 66 (2006), 421–31.

[33] C. Giraudi et al., "The Holocene Climatic Evolution of Mediterranean Italy: A Review of the Continental Geological Data," *Holocene* 21 (2011), 105–15, Michel Magny, "Holocene

It was in this context that the El Niño/Southern Oscillation began to reappear, around 3700 BC according to lake sediments in Ecuador, around 3200 BC according to marine sediments off Peru. Then, in the century following 3000 BC, as the millennial cooling event subsided and the NAO/AO settled into a long-term generally negative mode, the ENSO record exploded; the evidence from Ecuador suggests twenty-three years of strong El Niños in this century followed by fifteen in the next[34] (see Figure III.1). The ENSO system had been gradually reasserting itself in conjunction with the decline in solar warming, the southern migration of the ITCZ, and the waning of the African and Asian monsoons. But the global instability at 3200–3100 BC may have jolted the El Niño/La Niña variation into a particularly strong pattern, exactly as the NAO system shifted away from its strong Early Holocene positive mode, which had held warmth and winter precipitation on a northern track. And the Indian Ocean monsoon, which had lingered over the Persian Gulf and the southern Mesopotamian alluvium after retreating from the Levant around 7000 BC, now retreated out to sea, setting off significantly drier and dustier conditions in this important region.[35]

This crisis marked a fundamental shift in global climates. From 3000 BC, the earth system stabilized in a system fundamentally shaped by cooler northern summers, with regular epochs of global climate stress. The North Atlantic Oscillation generally stood in a negative mode, with a cold, dry north and a warmer, moister south, propagating weak westerlies on a southern track along the northern Mediterranean into Eurasia. With the weaker surface heating during cooler summers, the northern continents no longer dragged the ITCZ/monsoon system as far to the north, and the weakened monsoons began to dance in oscillation with El Niño rains and La Niña droughts that now struck the Pacific American coasts with near clocklike regularity.[36] Rather than any long-term directionality, Late Holocene climate would stand in this configuration on a fairly permanent basis. But in recurring intervals it would break into an abrupt reversal to colder and drier temperatures, crises that would have a profound effect on human civilizations, where slowly but inexorably growing populations depended on limited, fragile agricultural systems.

* * *

Climate Variability as Reflected by Mid-European Lake-Level Fluctuations and Its Probable Impact on Prehistoric Human Settlements," *Quaternary International* 113 (2004), 65–79.

[34] Moy, "Variability of El Niño-Southern Oscillation."

[35] Frank Sirocko, "Century-Scale Events in Monsoonal Climate over the Past 24,000 Years," *Nature* 364 (1993), 322–4; Guillermo Algaze, "Initial Social Complexity in Southwestern Asia," *CA* 42 (2001), 202–3.

[36] Here I describe global climate patterns as controlled by the global north, but there are good reasons to see the south as the driver, with the action of solar forcing working on the ENSO system as the driver. See note 6.

The Mid-Holocene Crisis and the Rise of the State

The previous chapter argued that the development of tropical horticulture and the onset of the dispersals of Southwest Asian and Chinese agricultural systems were set in motion by this Mid-Holocene climatic transition, described more fully in the previous section of this chapter. Here our problem is the rise of complexity in this context of profound climatic change. What is particularly striking is the *simultaneity* of these changes. Certainly, the "state" did not sprout "from Athena's brow" everywhere at exactly the same time, but the coincidences are striking. The wider Mid-Holocene transition, and its crisis at 3200–2900 BC, saw a significant intensification of human economies – and the restructuring rationalization that defines the transition from kin-based village societies to bureaucratic states, and to the high civilizations perpetuated by systems of artificial memory, writing and monumental symbolism, mobilized by new cultural and political elites.[37] In sum, and in its constituent parts, these events marked a fundamental moment of punctuated change in the human condition, a punctuation in the sense suggested by Gould and Eldridge in their classic formulation.

The relationship between the specific dynamics of the Mid-Holocene transition and the rise of complex society can be traced in all of the global hearths of civilization as we classically know them.[38] On the western coasts of South America, it appears that the strengthening of the Atlantic monsoon and the beginning of the Holocene El Niño sequence launched the rise of agro-ritual complexity that would lead eventually to the cultural and imperial systems of Chavin, Moche, and the Inca. Previously dry deserts, the narrow coastal zone and adjacent interior valleys of north Peru were transformed by rising precipitation from the Atlantic and the increasing frequency of El Niño storms at the end of the fourth millennium. The oceanic impacts of the El Niño shift brought bountiful shoals of anchovies and sardines to this coast, while increasing rains made the desert bloom and opened the opportunities for both early agriculture and collective organization leading to the proto-state. The result was a sudden transformation of the local Archaic hunter-gathering-fishing societies into what is known as the Cotton Pre-Ceramic: large settlements with platform mounds and sunken plazas began to appear on the coast and in the valleys around 3000 BC, supported by irrigated farming of squash and beans, and fish and mollusks gathered in La Niña years (see Figure II.1). These settlements may have combined ritual authority with a specialization in growing and processing cotton, perhaps

---

[37] Bruce G. Trigger, *Understanding Early Civilizations: A Comparative Study* (New York, 2003), 43–8.

[38] Nick Brooks, "Cultural Responses to Aridity in the Middle Holocene and Increased Social Complexity," *QuatInt* 151 (2006), 29–49. Daniel H. Sandweiss et al., "Transitions in the Mid-Holocene," *Science* 283 (1999), 499–500 and Thompson et al., "Abrupt Tropical Climate Change" provide comprehensive enumerations.

trading textiles and fishing line and nets to smaller coastal centers. There are estimates that population grew by a factor of somewhere between fifteen and thirty.[39]

The general southward shift of the Intertropical Convergence Zone and the monsoons watering the Old World tropics was compounded by both the Siberian High running from 4000–3000 BC and the sudden surge of ENSO variation around 3000 BC. While the Indian Ocean monsoon had been fading slowly in the greater eastern Mediterranean for several thousand years, now the cold northern conditions of the Siberian High seem to have blocked the Atlantic winter westerlies, bringing pervasive drought from the Mediterranean into Central Asia (see Figures II.4, II.5c). Then the explosion of El Niño undermined the residual influence of the Asian and African monsoons.

The effects of the Mid-Holocene Crisis, particularly its chaotic end, were particularly apparent in predynastic Mesopotamia and Egypt (see Figure II.2). In southern Mesopotamia, the process – for reasons detailed later in this chapter – was particularly elongated. The origins of the Uruk cultures of the Mesopotamian Plain date to roughly 4200 BC, and in less than a millennium the Uruk were constructing the first true city-states, whose imperial and commercial extensions influenced Naqada Egypt. In Mesopotamia, the Mid-Holocene collapse of winter precipitation undermined spring runoff into the Tigris and Euphrates systems: the Uruk cities collapsed, followed by a transitional Jemdet Nasr period of 200 years, during which a league of cities developed. Then, after 3000 BC, the early Bronze Age warrior dynasties began a recurring cycle of imperial expansion.[40]

[39] James B. Richardson and Daniel H. Sandweiss, "Climate Change, El Niño, and the Rise of Complex Society on the Peruvian Coast during the Middle Holocene," and Paul Roscoe, "Catastrophe and the Emergence of Political Complexity: A Social Anthropological Model," in Daniel H. Sandweiss and Jeffrey Quilter, eds., *El Niño, Catastrophism, and Culture Change in Ancient America* (Washington, DC, 2008), 59–100; Jonathan Haas and Winifred Creamer, "Crucible of Andean Civilization: The Peruvian Coast from 3000 to 1800 BC," *CA* 47 (2006), 745–75; Peter Bellwood, *First Farmers: The Origins of Agricultural Societies* (Malden, MA, 2005), 159–64; Dolores R. Piperno and Deborah M. Pearsall, *The Origins of Agriculture in the Lowland Neotropics* (San Diego, CA, 1998), 271–80. The dating of the Peruvian Cotton Pre-Ceramic has been established by Jonathan Haas et al., "Dating to Late Archaic Occupation of the Norte Chico Region in Peru," *Nature* 432 (2004), 1020–3; and Ruth Shady Solis et al., "Dating Caral, a Preceramic Site in the Supe Valley on the Central Coast of Peru," *Science* 292 (2001), 723–6. For the consequences of the increased ENSO variability, see Daniel Sandweiss et al., "Variations in Holocene El Niño Frequencies: Climate Records and Cultural Consequences in Ancient Peru," *Geology* 29 (2001), 603–6; and Daniel H. Sandweiss et al., "Geoarchaeological Evidence from Peru for a 5000 Years B. P. Onset of El Niño," *Science* 272 (1996), 1531–3. Haas and colleagues reject the ~3710 BC dates that lead Daniel Sandweiss and colleagues to argue (in "Variations in Holocene El Niño Frequencies") for the origins of the Cotton Pre-Ceramic at that date. For the significance of cotton, see Jeffrey Quilter et al., "Subsistence Economy of El Paraíso, an Early Peruvian Site," *Science* 251 (1991), 277–83.
[40] Frank Hole, "Environmental Instabilities and Urban Origins," in Gil Stein and Mitchell S. Rothman, eds., *Chiefdoms and Early States in the Near East: The Organizational Dynamics*

Along the Nile, where Southwest Asian agriculture had been introduced early in the Mid-Holocene deterioration at roughly 5000 BC, the Early Neolithic Badaran cultures after 4000 BC evolved into the more populated, stratified, and expansive Naqada. It may be that the reduction of Nile flow after 4000 BC actually reduced marshy conditions along the river, encouraging an expansion of agriculture. Then around 3200 BC, at the culmination of the 500-year transition of the Sahara from savannah grassland into desert and with a sudden drastic decline in Ethiopian rainfall that severely reduced the Nile river flow, the first identifiable kings emerged in Upper Egypt (near the present border with Sudan). These kings may have managed an expanding system of irrigation, and they certainly drove the conquest of the Nile delta that unified Upper and Lower Egypt, establishing the basic pattern for the ensuing Early Dynastic and the Old Kingdom periods[41] (see Figure III.3).

Across the Asian steppes, the cooling of the Mid-Holocene disrupted early agricultural societies and set off a sequence of competitive nomadism. To the south and east the sharp transition to state forms was similar to southwest Asia, if somewhat delayed. In the Indus Valley, 3200 BC saw the beginnings of Early Harappan culture, with the city-states of the Mature Harappan taking shape after a distinct disruption around 2600 BC (see Figure II.3). Where it has long been argued that Harappan civilization developed and thrived in a humid climate, it now appears that it was pre-Harappan village societies that developed in the humid peak in South Asia, between 6000 BC and roughly 3500 BC. The earliest Harappan period emerged after a long-term trend toward aridity in South Asia had begun, and its increasingly mature phases developed in the face of an increasing dry condition, as the ITCZ and the monsoon system retreated further to the south.[42]

of Complexity (Madison, WI, 1994), 121–51; Roger J. Matthews, "Jemdet Nasr: The Site and the Period," *Biblical Archaeologist* 55 (1992), 196–202.

[41] Maisels, *Early Civilizations of the Old World*, 44–65; Béatrix Midant-Reynes, *The Prehistory of Egypt: From the First Egyptians to the First Pharaohs* (Malden, MA, 1992), 231–50; A. J. Spencer, *Early Egypt: The Rise of Civilization in the Nile Valley* (Norman, OK, 1993), 48–62; Marriner et al., "ITCZ and ENSO-Like Pacing of Nile Delta Geo-Morphology"; Robert C. Allen, "Agriculture and the Origins of the State in Ancient Egypt," *ExpEconH* 34 (1997), 135–54; Alexander H. Joffee, "Egypt and Syro-Mesopotamia in the 4th Millennium: Implications of the New Chronology," *CA* 41 (2000), 113–23; Steven H. Savage, "Some Recent Trends in the Archaeology of Predynastic Egypt," *JArchRes* 9 (2001), 101–55. The late fourth millennium East African-Nile drought may have been an effect of the beginning of a general warming transition out of the Mid-Holocene crisis, in which the Nile drought correlated with the sudden reduction of North Atlantic sea ice, while the winter Siberian High signal remained strong. See Figure III.3.

[42] Frank Schlütz and Frank Lehmkukh, "Climatic Change in the Russian Altai, Southern Siberia, Based on Palynological and Geomorphological Results, with Implications for Climatic Teleconnections and Human History since the Middle Holocene," *VHAb* 16 (2007), 101–18; Glen McDonald, "Potential Influence of the Pacific Ocean on the Indian Summer Monsoon and Harappan Decline," *QuatInt* 229 (2011), 140–8; Marco Madella and Dorian Q. Fuller, "Palaeoecology and the Harappan Civilization of South Asia: A Reconsideration,"

In East Asia, the Pacific monsoon remained strong far longer than did the African and South Asian monsoons, allowing a long fluorescence of Neolithic societies. Where the African and South Asian monsoons began to decline from roughly 5500 BC and 4700 BC, the East Asian monsoon weakened somewhat around 4500 BC, but saw a real crisis only around 2400–2000 BC, manifested in massive flooding, followed by a significantly weaker, more erratic monsoon (see Figures II.3, III.3, III.4). But before that crisis the long Holocene Optimum seems to have extended the life of the Middle Neolithic, in which Chinese agrarian systems were consolidated at the village level, giving way along the Yellow River to the Late Neolithic Longshan, in the northeast to the Hongshan, and in the south to the Liangzhu. The Chinese Late Neolithic cultures can be compared with the Ubaid in southern Mesopotamia and the Naqada in Egypt, and perhaps the pre-Harappan villages in the Indus valley, in which dense, hierarchical networks of villages competed for territory and resources. If we accept the foundational mythology in the Chinese tradition, the first state emerged in China in the wake of the flooding that marked the final end of the East Asian optimum. The Xia state was probably one of many small polities, and some doubt its existence, but it has been identified with an extensive archaeological tradition focused on the site of Erlitou, which was clearly a political center. Xia is traditionally dated from 2100 BC, but the Erlitou site has its origins at 1900 BC. Japan saw a trajectory broadly analogous to China's Late Neolithic, with the rise of the Early Jomon settlements around 5000 BC, preagricultural but with elaborate ceramic traditions, grading into the classic Middle Jomon after 3000 BC, and going into decline after 2000 BC, with the fading of the East Asian optimum.[43]

QSR 25 (2006), 1283–301. For a climate skeptic, see Greg Possehl, *The Indus Civilization: A Contemporary Perspective* (Walnut Creek, CA, 2002), 29, 40–51; Greg Possehl, "The Transformation of the Indus Civilization," *JWP* 11 (1997), 425–72. See note 25 for citations on South Asian monsoon proxies.

[43] Li Liu, *The Chinese Neolithic: Trajectories to Early States* (New York, 2004), 25–7, 30–1, 163–8, 235; Kwang-Chih Chang, "China on the Eve of the Historical Period," in Michael Loewe and Edward L. Shaughnessy, eds., *The Cambridge History of China: From the Origins of Civilization to 221 B.C.* (Cambridge, 1999), 65–73; Gina L. Barnes, *The Rise of Civilization in East Asia: The Archaeology of China, Korea, and Japan* (London, 1999), 24–5, 92–118; Kwang-Chih Chang, *The Archaeology of Ancient China*, fourth edition (New Haven, CT, 1986), 234–316; Charles K. Maisels, *Early Civilizations of the Old World: The Formative Histories of Egypt, The Levant, Mesopotamia, India and China* (London, 1999), 291–313; Anne P. Underhill, "Current Issues in Chinese Neolithic Archaeology," *JWP* 11 (1997), 103–60; Anne P. Underhill and Junko Habu, "Early Communities in East Asia: Economic and Sociopolitical Organization at the Local and Regional Levels," in Miriam T. Stark, ed., *Archaeology of Asia* (Malden, MA, 2006), 134–40; Andrew Lawler, "Beyond the Yellow River: How China Became China," *Science* 325 (2009), 930–43; Jing Tao et al., "A Holocene Environmental Record from the Southern Yangtze River Delta, Eastern China,"

Such is a very brief account of the Mid-Holocene collapse of advanced Neolithic societies and the rise of the earliest states. Traditionally, running back to Durkheimian sociology, the state is seen as a more complex social form than the kinship-based village societies that it displaced. But recent thinking has turned this truism around, arguing that the bureaucratic and legal forms were a drastic simplification of the organic ritual and familial complexities of Neolithic societies.[44] And of course the "state" did not entirely replace these ancient complexities, but had to work over time to superimpose itself upon them, more and less successfully. But the rise of the state was indeed a "rise," an "emergence," of urban and court elites who – other than the monarch – were chosen for their skills and not necessarily their kinship, and who "traded" their ritual, military, and managerial services for a sustenance produced by householders-becoming-peasants. At the center of the skills and services lay the artificial memory systems of writing and monumental symbolism that recorded accounts, histories, and mythologies – and required experts to interpret. These memory systems would be the vehicle of "civilizations" that would endure through time, encompassing the state polities that would rise and fall in the ensuing 5,000 years of "history," facilitating their reestablishment after points of collapse.[45]

PPP 230 (2006), 204–29; Hong, "Inverse Phase Oscillations"; Carrie Morrill et al., "A Synthesis of Abrupt Changes in the Asian Summer Monsoon since the Last Deglaciation," *Holocene* 3 (2003), 465–76; Zhisheng An, "Asynchronous Holocene Optimum of the East Asian Monsoon," *QSR* 19 (2000), 743–62. Tropical south China had a smoother gradient toward the Late Holocene because its precipitation was shaped by the South Asian monsoon system.

[44] C. R. Hallpike, *The Principles of Social Evolution* (Oxford, 1986), 138–45, 268–83; Norman Yoffee, *Myths of the Archaic State: Evolution of the Earliest Cities, States, and Civilization* (New York, 2005), 91–112. For a theoretical proposition on the state and simplification, see James Scott, *Seeing Like a State: How Certain Schemes to Improve the Human Condition Have Failed* (New Haven, CT, 1998).

[45] Trigger, *Understanding Early Civilizations*, 585–625; Bruce G. Trigger, "Going Still Further?" *CArchJ* 15 (2005), 256–8. There has been some discussion of the possibility of genetic correlates to the rise of hierarchical and state societies. One recent study proposed that a variant of a gene (*ASPM*) regulating brain size, with a strong regional distribution in the Middle East, appeared 5,800 years ago, or roughly 3800 BC, which the authors suggested was aligned with the chronology of "the rapid expansion of population associated with the development of cities and written language 5000 to 6000 years ago around the Middle East." Nitzan Mekel-Bobrov et al., "Ongoing Adaptive Evolution of *ASPM*, a Brain Size Determinant in *Homo Sapiens*," *Science* 309 (2005), 1720–2. This Bronze Age dating was immediately critiqued as based on methods that could also support an argument for Paleolithic timing (Mathias Currat et al., "Comment on 'Ongoing Adaptive Evolution of *ASPM*, a Brain Size Determinant in *Homo Sapiens*' and 'Microcephalin, a Gene Regulating Brain Size, Continues to Evolve Adaptively in Humans," *Science* 213 (2006), 172a). Two years after their first claim, the authors of the original *ASPM* article published another presenting data that *ASPM* was in no way linked to IQ. Nitzan Mekel-Bobrov et al., "The

The relationship between the rise of the earliest states and civilizations and the climatic crises of the Mid-Holocene transition strongly argues for treating this as a punctuational event, in the sense Gould and Eldridge first proposed for the fossil record. The rise of the city and the state was not, recent work suggests, a long, slow process, but a short, dramatic event. Norman Yoffee, in *Myths of the Archaic State*, has argued that – contrary to generations of thinking – that "cities crystallized, at some point, rapidly ... as phase transitions ... almost as supernovas."[46] In one elaboration of his argument, Katherina Schreiber writes that "ancient societies did not follow a series of steps, moving holistically in lock step from one to the next, in order to arrive at the top of the ladder, the state. Rather, states exploded nova-like from beginnings much more humble: simple tribal or village societies."[47] Recently, new dating for the emergence of temple ritual in precontact Hawaii suggests how "nova-like" these events might be: assumed by archaeologists to have taken 250 years, the new dating indicates that the construction of a sequence of thirty temples on southeast Maui took place over a sixty-year period between 1580 and 1640. Confounding the gradualists, this redating confirms native Hawaiian accounts of a mythic leader who forged the temple system. Joyce Marcus and Kent Flannery report another tight chronology, if not as tight as this: new dates suggest that, in the Mexican Oaxaca Valley, 1,300 years separated the construction of the first ritual men's house and the emergence of the Zapotec military state.[48] Similarly, Greg Anderson has argued that the development of the Athenian polis was not a centuries-long process running through the late Iron Age, but unfolded very rapidly during a forty-year period between 520 BC and 480 BC.[49] Such examples strongly suggest that "history" actually happened in "prehistory," in real, short, punctuated – indeed political – time.

These punctuations in historical time leading to "pristine state formation" occurred in particular ecological circumstances. Thirty-five years ago, Robert Carneiro proposed that the origins of the state lay in population

Ongoing Adaptive Evolution of *ASPM* and Microcephalin Is Not Explained by Increased Intelligence," *Human Molecular Genetics* 16 (2007), 600–8. See also the extended discussions of the possibility of recent genetic selection for intelligence in Gregory Cochran and Henry Harpending, *The 10,000 Year Explosion: How Civilization Accelerated Human Evolution* (New York, 2009), 100–28, and for medieval–early modern England, Gregory Clark, *A Farewell to Alms: A Brief Economic History of the World* (Princeton, NJ, 2007), 6–10, 112–44.

[46] Yoffee, *Myths of the Archaic State*, 230, 214.

[47] Katherina Schreiber in "Old Issues, New Directions," *CArchJ* 15 (2005), 265.

[48] Patrick V. Kirch and Warren D. Sharp, "Coral ^{230}Th Dating of the Imposition of a Ritual Control Hierarchy in Precontact Hawaii," *Science* 307 (2005), 102–4. Joyce Marcus and Kent V. Flannery, "The Coevolution of Ritual and Society: New ^{14}C Dates from Ancient Mexico," *PNAS* 101 (2004), 18257–61.

[49] Greg Anderson, *The Athenian Experiment: Building an Imagined Political Community in Ancient Attica, 508–490 B.C.* (Ann Arbor, MI, 2003).

pressures in contexts of environmental "circumscription": village populations living in locally bountiful circumstances but hemmed in by hostile
deserts, mountains, or nomadic tribes, moved to the establishment of state
political authority to gain protection and predictability in a dangerous
world.[50] I have suggested that such a framework helps to explain the origins
of agriculture. Carneiro's model – particularly a simplified version suggesting that population growth led inexorably to state formation – has been subjected to considerable critique over the past years.[51] Without reviewing all
of these critiques, I would suggest that Carneiro's model of circumscription
continues to have considerable merit, particularly if it is somewhat relaxed
and extended.[52] Populations that were in some way circumscribed by ecological gradients through space *and* time often accepted, or were forced to
accept, the superimposition of ritual and military elites over the basal stratum of Neolithic village life. By *space* we mean the ecological variability of
geography, by *time* the ecological variability of climate. In general terms, it
is safe to argue that early states could only emerge where there was sufficient
net primary productivity to support their energy demands and subsequent
growth. Such were the circumstances of the El Niño coast of Peru, and the
great valleys of the Nile, the Tigris-Euphrates, the Indus, and the Yellow
Rivers. But these hearths of early civilization were also located in a wider
context of relatively arid mid-to-tropical latitudes. These were well-watered
regions bounded by more dry and hostile biomes; of these the Nile was the
most circumscribed, the Yellow River the least. Early polities did *not* emerge
in broad reaches of temperate western Europe or eastern North America,
in the tropical Amazon basin, or on the plains of northern Mesopotamia.
They took the most time to develop in China, where the ecologies of the
great river systems may have been the least circumscribed among the early
hearths.[53] Additionally, located in these more arid biomes, each of the early
hearths was particularly susceptible to climate change and fluctuation: a
regional bounty might suddenly be overwhelmed by more generally hostile circumstances. The Neolithic peoples of these hearth regions were thus
poised on a climatic hair trigger.

---

[50] Robert L. Carneiro, "A Theory of the Origin of the State," *Science* 39 (1970), 733–8.

[51] Henry T. Wright and Gregory A. Johnson, "Population, Exchange, and Early State Formation
in Southwestern Iran," *AmAnth* 77 (1975), 267–89; Andrew Sherratt, "Reviving the Grand
Narrative: Archaeology and Long-term Change," *JEArch* 3 (1995), 1–32, esp. 17–24.
Sherratt is among the more important of these critics, arguing that early city-states were
forged on the resource differentials that drove early trade. This argument, which bears a
relationship to ideas of ecological circumscription in the sense of ecological differentiation,
will be addressed later in this chapter.

[52] For other arguments supporting the central elements of Carneiro's position, see Hallpike,
The Principles of Social Evolution, 252–68; Allen, "Agriculture and the Origins of the State
in Ancient Egypt"; and Michael Mann, *The Sources of Social Power. Vol. I: A History of
Power from the Beginning to A. D. 1760* (New York, 1986), 75–6, 98–101.

[53] Liu, *The Chinese Neolithic*, 169–91.

The trigger seems to have been the Mid-Holocene Crisis, as variously manifested. Here the new climate history allows us to take a step beyond Carneiro and invoke real historical events. In each case, abrupt climate change played a formative role. Rather than population pressure in circumscribed regions leading by itself to competition, warfare, and state formation, all of these trajectories were set within a gradual constriction and deterioration driven by the waning of the Holocene Optimum. But with only the exception of Harappa in the Indus Valley, where the process was more gradual, the immediate origins of the early state lay in a sharp crisis that was probably measured in decades, perhaps a couple of centuries.[54] The trigger was a discrete natural catastrophe, droughts in Egypt and Mesopotamia, floods in China and Peru, that led to *population collapse and cultural crisis*. Such epochs of natural catastrophe undermined the integrity of local Neolithic societies through mass calamity: people died in huge numbers, villages were emptied, local gods discredited, ancient memories lost.[55] Out of such ashes rose the first states, Yoffee's super-novas, led by charismatic leaders, in which a new caste of priests monopolized and routinized ritual supplication, and a new caste of warriors armed with new bronze weapons monopolized and routinized collective violence.[56] In this scenario of natural catastrophe and population crash, an obvious case can be made for an explosive cultural punctuation, as the new elite stratum formulated new authoritative cultures from the flotsam of the shattered village traditions, now preserved in the amber of writing and monumental sculpture.[57]

[54] The Harappan exception may prove Carneiro's rule. Thomas J. Thompson has proposed that Harappa was unique in its lack of any evidence for defense or war. He argues that a lack of circumscription in the wider India Valley allowed the Harappans to channel their efforts into commerce rather than conflict. Here the slow, steady, noncatastrophic retreat of the South Asian monsoon also provides a significant point of contrast with the emergence of warlike states in Egypt, Mesopotamia, and China. See "An Ancient Stateless Civilization: Bronze Age India and the State in History," *The Independent Review* 10 (2006), 365–84; and also the similar arguments, focusing on stratification, in Maisels, *Early Civilizations of the Old World*, 254–9, 342–59.

[55] Here one might draw an analogy to the cultural disruptions that followed the intrusions of Europeans into the New World and the subsequent mass death of native peoples by war and disease.

[56] I take this formulation from Hole, "Environmental Instabilities and Urban Origins"; Liu, *The Chinese Neolithic*, 235; and Wright and Johnson, "Population, Exchange, and Early State Formation." For a similar catastrophe-refugee-cultural restructuring argument for the early PPNA and early PPNB, see N. Goring-Morris and A. Belfer-Cohen, "The Articulation of Cultural Processes and Late Quaternary Environmental Changes in Cisjordan," *Paléorient* 32 (1998), 71–93, at 83–5.

[57] Here I ignore Karl Wittfogel's hydraulic hypothesis, because it has already been made very clear that mass irrigation was a consequence of the state, rather than a cause. Robert McC. Adams, *The Evolution of Urban Society: Early Mesopotamia and Prehistoric Mexico* (Chicago, IL, 1966), 66–78; Hallpike, *The Principles of Social Evolution*, 260–6; Mann, *The Sources of Social Power*, 1: 94–8.

There is no question that the populations of early states grew explosively. But it would appear plausible that their *beginnings* lay in periods of disaster and depopulation. Such *de*populations imply reasonably large *pre-crisis* populations; conversely, the rapid *re*population of the territories of new states suggests that both ecological potential and established human skills were at work. If the state-creating Mid-Holocene disasters of drought and flood undermined agricultural productivity, conditions returned to stability sufficiently rapidly to allow populations to regrow. And it is safe to say that these populations grew – under (or despite) the ritual and military "management" of the early state – on the foundation laid by the agricultural skills and capacities developed over the several millennia of the Holocene Optimum. Thus we need to sketch the outlines of the "Second Neolithic Revolution" that set the stage for the explosive emergence of high civilization. All of this requires that we look again at the question of energy flows in early human societies.

* * *

Neolithic Intensification: The Secondary Products Revolution

Quite simply, it is increasingly clear that early domestication and the "agricultural revolution" as commonly conceived was not nearly sufficient to establish the ecological and economic base – the flow of energy – upon which fundamentally successful high civilizations would emerge and thrive as pristine original roots of subsequent history. Among others, Bruce Smith has argued particularly cogently that the early domestication of wild food plants was only the beginning of a very long and slow road leading to full-scale farming, and that it could not have supported a truly significant expansion of populations.[58] Early Neolithic peoples were essentially limited to a somewhat stabilized and slightly expanded flow of biomass and energy from an exploited landscape, and their numbers grew extremely slowly and incrementally. For a number of years, however, archaeologists have posited a "Second Neolithic Revolution," in which the meager foundations of the "First Neolithic Revolution" were amplified into full-scale farming. Andrew Sherratt launched this argument in the early 1980s with his proposal that this second revolution, what he called a "Secondary Products Revolution," involved the domestication of important new plants and animals and the development of agrarian technologies that have persisted in remote parts of the world into recent living memory.[59] Thinking in terms of energy, this

---

[58] Bruce Smith, "Low-Level Food Production," *JAnthRes* 9 (2001), 1–43.

[59] These essays are collected in revised form in Andrew Sherratt, *Economy and Society in Prehistoric Europe: Changing Perspectives* (Princeton, NJ, 1997), 155–248. Haskel J. Greenfield, "The Secondary Products Revolution: The Past, Present, and Future," *WdArch* 42 (2010), 29–54 presents a positive reappraisal of the concept.

transition from horticulture to full-scale agriculture might well have doubled human energy consumption, from perhaps 12,000 Kcal per person per day to 25,000.[60]

Very broadly, these developments out of the limited horticulture of the early Neolithic toward what we call *peasant farming*, and then the incremental improvements to that farming through the ancient and medieval periods, fall within the framework of "intensification" that economist Ester Boserup proposed. Critiquing an extreme version of the Malthusian theory of technological limits in premodern societies, she argued that constant modest improvements in the energy outputs of agriculture and technology manage to feed inexorably growing human populations.[61] We last saw a technological "intensification" at work in the elaboration of skill among Upper Paleolithic hunter-gatherers dealing with rising populations in the era of modern human dispersal, and in the shift toward horticulture following the end of the Pleistocene and the Younger Dryas. Following this shift toward the domestication of plants and animals in the wake of the Younger Dryas, Boserup's agricultural intensification has remained a central feature in the human circumstance. As manifested in the Late Neolithic agrarian transition, we might even want to consider it a very early manifestation of Adam Smith's model of growth through the specialization and division of labor, so-called Smithian growth.

While a version of Boserup's "intensification," or of Sherratt's "secondary products revolution," certainly unfolded in the New World, it was more obvious and productive in the Old World, where it revolved around the expanding use of animals for purposes beyond the direct, primary consumption of the domesticated prey: milk, wool, and, most important, traction. In sum, this incorporation of cattle, sheep, goats, pigs, and eventually donkeys, horses, and camels into Old World agrarian systems cumulatively increased the energy brought into human economies in the form of food, textiles, and motive power.[62] Here obviously lay the root advantage of Old World societies over those in the Americas. Human beings no longer had to use simply their own muscle power to gain a subsistence, but could multiply their time input with animal energy.

From this intensifying incorporation of animal power flowed a series of important outcomes. Making the energy output of a beast of burden more efficient required a technological revolution in the invention of wheeled carts and plows, the central implements of Eurasian agriculture down into modern

[60] See discussion in Chapter 3, note 13.

[61] Ester Boserup, *The Conditions of Agricultural Growth: The Economics of Agrarian Change under Population Pressure* (London, 1965); Peter J. Richerson and Robert Boyd, "Institutional Evolution in the Holocene," in W. G. Runciman, ed., *The Origins of Social Institutions* (Oxford, 2001), 197–234.

[62] Vaclav Smil, *Energy in World History* (Boulder, CO, 1994), 39–49.

times. Carts and plows may well have been central to a series of fundamental changes to the structure and workings of families and communities. First, they may have worked to reshape the gendered division of labor, from an early Neolithic world in which women controlled horticulture while men hunted and herded. Animals hitched to plows and carts seem to have brought men into agriculture and moved women toward the household, where they lost their now ancient horticultural role, but unburdened women of the chore of firewood collection, universally a female task in prefarming societies.[63]

Then there is the impact on collective work and reciprocity that these new technologies would have had. Jack Goody proposes that the traditional agrarian world has been divided between cultures of the hoe and the plow, with profound legal and sociological implications.[64] The construction of a plow or a cart was a complex and expensive investment, and if it originally was shared around a village, subsequent history suggests that it soon became the property of a given household, as did the surplus product of its labor enhancement. Thus the intensifications of Sherratt's "secondary products revolution" – it has been suggested – drove the general social reorganization of society from the foraging band to the village of households, and the resulting emergence of familial and individual claims to property.[65] In late Neolithic intensification lay the seed of social inequality.

---

[63] Peter Bogucki, *The Origins of Human Society* (Malden and Oxford, 1999), 227–9; Peter Bogucki, "Animal Traction and Household Economies in Neolithic Europe," *Antiquity* 67 (1993), 492–503. See also Margaret Ehrenberg, *Women in Prehistory* (London, 1989), 99–107; Autumn Stanley, "Daughters of Isis, Daughters of Demeter: When Women Sowed and Reaped," *Women's Studies International Quarterly* 4 (1989), 289–304; and Cheryl Calaasen, "Mothers' Workloads and Children's Labor during the Woodland Period," in Sarah Milledge Nelson and Myriam Rosen-Ayalon, eds., *In Pursuit of Gender: Worldwide Archaeological Approaches* (Walnut Creek, CA, 2002), 225–34.

[64] Jack Goody, *Production and Reproduction: A Comparative Study of the Domestic Domain* (New York, 1976).

[65] Kent V. Flannery, "The Origins of the Village Revisited: From Nuclear to Extended Households," *AmAntiq* 67 (2002), 417–33; Bogucki, *The Origins of Human Society*, 205–16. Strikingly, Charles I. Jones, in a modeling simulation of population and economy since the Pleistocene, argues that the "property reward" for ideas and innovations spiked in an epoch running from 6000 BC to 4000 BC, and again since AD 1700, roughly bracketing the social-legal reorganizations of the late Neolithic and the industrial revolutions. The onset of Jones's Neolithic surge roughly correlates with the Pottery Neolithic and Chalcolithic cultures in Southwest Asia (6000 BC), and the Middle Neolithic in China (5000 BC), which saw the emergence of large agricultural villages in both Old World core regions. Jones's model rests solely, however, on elaborate quantitative speculation on the basis of very slim evidence about population growth rates since the end of the Pleistocene, and does not factor in climate change, which might well explain some of his shifts in population growth rates. But almost analogous peaks in his model marking Sherratt's "secondary products revolution" and the early modern–modern industrial revolution are nonetheless intriguing. Charles I. Jones, "Was an Industrial Revolution Inevitable? Economic Growth in the Very Long Term," *Advances in Macroeconomics* 1/2/article 1(2001), 1–43.

The "secondary products revolution," the "late Neolithic intensification": these are not part of the common parlance of world history. Here I should make my point as plain as possible, in two particulars. First, the elaboration of late Neolithic cultures was a salient event in post-Pleistocene world history; second, it must be seen as an *energy revolution*, one of five such energy revolutions that I am stressing in this book. Each of these revolutions reorganized humanity's assembly of natural primary productivity for human consumption. And each followed an epoch of abrupt climate change: each energy revolution was in some measure a response to the stresses, depopulation, and cultural reorganization driven by an abrupt pulse in climate well beyond our commonsense framework of understanding. The first of these energy revolutions was domestication, a long, slow process following the Younger Dryas. The next two such energy revolutions, the late Neolithic solidification of village agriculture and the rise of the state, cannot be understood outside of the rubric of the two millennial cooling events – at 6900–6100 BC and 4000–3000 BC – that bracket the transition from the Early Holocene Optimum and the Mid-Holocene Crisis. I have sketched the role of the Mid-Holocene Crisis on the rise of the state; in the final section of this chapter I explore the early dynamic of the 6900–6000 BC climate event and the launching of the secondary products revolution.

* * *

China and Mesopotamia in the Neolithic–Bronze Age Transition

Among the high civilizations developing in the longer ancient world after the Mid-Holocene transition, only two were truly successful: Southwest Asia-Egypt and China. *Successful* is a loaded and perhaps pejorative term, but it has a basis in reality. Each generated massive population growth; neither was ever completely destroyed by an utter collapse. Each would have permanent cultural and political legacies. Chinese civilization would endure in place with reasonable continuity from the rise of the first states around 2000 BC down to the present day; Southwest Asian civilization, most powerfully in its Mesopotamian and Egyptian manifestations, would endure for several millennia as its essential traditions were grafted onto Mediterranean, North African, and South Asian societies. In the New World, high civilizations developed more slowly, and in the end could not withstand the brutal shock of global reunification that marked the beginning of the modern world. High civilization in both China and Southwest Asia rested in eminently successful Neolithic intensifications. Of these we know far more of Southwest Asia, and we also are beginning to have a picture of the human demographic patterns in Southwest Asia that suggest the outlines of a long-term history of human welfare. Thus in the brief account that follows I focus my attention there.

Robert Carneiro's argument that ecological circumscription shaped the rise of the pristine state has obvious parallels in Ester Boserup's model of population pressure driving intensification; in effect Carneiro's state is an extreme manifestation of Boserup's intensification. But if Carneiro's model of circumscription – enhanced by climate change – may help to explain the rise of the state, it does not seem to have had a role in the rise of Late Neolithic agricultural economies in either central China or in northern Mesopotamia. In both of these situations a relatively well-watered, wide expanse of territory provided the ground upon which gradual and incremental improvements to agricultural technology brought a significant growth of population, dispersing and segmenting into ramifying networks of relatively similar, relatively prosperous village communities. The formative intensification and maturation of agrarian systems took considerable time, free of climate shocks, in environments that could absorb considerable human impact. But in Southwest Asia it is clear that there was a powerful discontinuity in the seventh millennium, with the climate-driven disruption and collapse of the Pre-Pottery Neolithic paving the way for the long intensifications of the ensuing two millennia.[66]

In central China, such unshocked, uncircumscribed conditions lasted for a very long period of time. During the long peak of the Holocene Optimum East Asian monsoon, from immediately following the Younger Dryas to roughly 2500 BC, the central Chinese Neolithic moved slowly toward a more fully formed dry rice/millet agriculture. This development culminated in the wide dispersal of villages in the Middle Neolithic, around 5000–3000 BC, becoming significantly more stratified and violent as the monsoon system began to wane, leading to the Late Neolithic cultures like the Longshan[67] (see Figure II.3). A recent find is a testament to both the sophistication achieved by the end of the Chinese Neolithic and the power of the natural forces that snapped it into an Early Bronze Age state. At a Late Neolithic village on the Yellow River (Lajia), archaeologists have recovered a bowl of millet noodles under a three-meter layer of floodplain silt; the noodles were preserved when the massive flood that destroyed this village around 2000 BC flipped the bowl bottom-up off a table and onto the floor, and into the archaeological record.[68]

This noodle bowl, miraculously unbroken, can stand as a metaphor for the long continuities that built the foundations of Chinese village agriculture. The floods for which its stands as evidence also have a central place in the

---

[66] Liu, *The Chinese Neolithic*; Allen, "Agriculture and the Origins of the State in Ancient Egypt," 150–1 has some trenchant thoughts on the gradient of circumscription shaping the rise of the earliest pristine states, which I have found particularly useful.

[67] See citations in note 42.

[68] Houyuan Lu et al., "Millet Noodles in Late Neolithic China," *Nature* 437 (2005), 967–8; Wu Wenxiang and Liu Tungsheng; "Possible Role of the 'Holocene Event 3' on the Collapse of the Neolithic Cultures around the Central Plain of China," *QuatInt* 117 (2004), 153–66.

foundations of Chinese history: tradition recounted how the perhaps mythical founder of the Xia dynasty, "Yu the Great," tamed the floods by organizing drainage systems along the Yellow River.[69] The prehistory of Southwest Asia was not so continuous and unbroken, and it was similarly shaped by floods and flood myths. But for perhaps 2,000 years, the wide reaches of the upper Euphrates in Syria, Iraq, and Turkey served as the hearth of a fundamental maturation of an agrarian economy.

This Late Neolithic economy certainly had its roots in the achievements of the Pre-Pottery Neolithic B communities scattered thinly across the Levant and into this northern Mesopotamian region. But a climatic crisis separated the PPN cultures from the advanced north Mesopotamian agrarian societies. The Mid-Holocene climatic decline had its first manifestations in this region by the end of the eighth millennium BC (~7400 BC) when the summer monsoon rains coming off the Indian Ocean began to falter, as measured distantly by a decline in oak pollen in the sediment cores at Lake Hula in northern Israel, and in rising levels of dust and dolomite coming from desert soils recorded in Arabian Sea sediments(see Figure II.2). Occasional winter downpours from the Atlantic westerlies that were beginning to move into the region eroded the soil and gullied the hillsides in the dry Levant.[70] It was in these conditions – compounded by human impacts on local environments through deforestation and overgrazing, and capped by the advance of the 6900–6100 BC millennial cooling event culminating in the disastrous century-long drought following the Laurentine melt water event in 6200 BC – that the Pre-Pottery culture of the Levant eventually collapsed. If the record of fortifications and massive fires at a series of sites in southwest Anatolia is any indication, the climate degradation in these centuries led to strife and warfare analogous to that among the Mesolithic Qadan peoples along the Nile during the glacial Younger Dryas.[71]

---

[69] Liu, *The Chinese Neolithic*, 105, 235; Chang, "China on the Eve of the Historical Period," 65–73.

[70] S. De Rijk et al., "Eastern Mediterranean Sapropel S1 Interruptions: An Expression of the Onset of Climatic Deterioration around 7ka BP," *Marine Geology* 153 (1999), 337–43; Arie S. Issar and Mattanyah Zohar, *Climate Change: Environment and Civilization in the Near East* (Berlin, 2004), 65–6.

[71] On the end of the PPN cultures and the beginnings of the Pottery Neolithic, once called the *Hiatus Palestinien*, see Alan H. Simmons, *The Neolithic Revolution in the Near East* (Tucson, AZ, 2007), 175–227; Marc Verhoeven, "Beyond Boundaries: Nature, Culture and a Holistic Approach to Domestication in the Levant," *JWP* 18 (2004), 259–63; Peter M. M. G. Akkermans and Glenn M. Schwartz, *The Archaeology of Syria: From Complex Hunter-Gatherers to Early Urban Societies, (ca. 16,000–300 BC)* (New York, 2003), 99–115; Alan H. Simmons, "Villages on the Edge: Regional Settlement Change and the End of the Levantine Pre-Pottery Neolithic," in Ian Kuift, ed., *Life in Neolithic Farming Communities: Social Organization, Identity, and Differentiation* (New York, 2000), 211–34; Gary O. Rollefson, "The Neolithic Devolution: Ecological Impact and Cultural Compensation at 'Ain Ghazal, Jordan," in Joe D. Seger, ed., *Retrieving the Past: Essays on Archaeological Research and*

Simultaneous with the decline and collapse of the PPN cultures centered on the Levant coast, new developments were brewing in the interior, in the upper drainage of the Tigris River. Here – out of the local PPNB peoples – the Pottery Neolithic cultures known as Hassuna and Samarra were evolving, the foundations of the copper-using Chalcolithic societies that followed.[72] The origins of these cultures, in a manifestation called Proto-Hassuna, featured orderly planned sites, coarse pottery differentiating it from its Pre-Pottery antecedents, and a mixed hunting-herding economy.[73] Proto-Hassuna might have had its origins as early as 7500 BC and might have graded into Hassuna by 7100 BC, the tradition differentiating into the Samarra as it spread south along the Tigris into central Mesopotamia.[74]

It is possible that these north Mesopotamian cultures benefited from the first continental winter rains brought by the emerging southern track of the westerlies driven by the North Atlantic Oscillation in its new negative mode, shifting south as the summer monsoons retreated (see Figure II.5b). Such would be the hinge of the Mid-Holocene transition in Southwest Asia, as the Intertropical Convergence Zone and the southern summer monsoon withdrew, the influence of the Atlantic expanded, mediated by a winter storm track that ran through the northern Mediterranean, the Aegean and into

---

Methodology in Honor of Gus W. Van Beck (Mississippi State, 1996), 219–30. For the evidence for terminal PPNB warfare, see Lee Clare et al., "Warfare in Late Neolithic/Early Chalcolithic Pisidia, Southwestern Turkey: Climate Induced Social Unrest in the Late 7th Millennium calBC," *Documenta Praehistorica* 35 (2008), 65–92.

[72] The absolute dating of Mesopotamian cultures has been complicated by more than two decades of warfare in the region and a necessary hiatus of archaeological work. Here I follow a chronology shaped by points of agreement among the following authorities: Yoffee, *Myths of the Archaic State*, 199; Henry T. Wright and E. S. A. Rupley, "Calibrated Radiocarbon Age Determinations of Uruk-Related Assemblages," in Mitchell S. Rothman, ed., *Uruk Mesopotamia & Its Neighbors* (Santa Fe, NM, 2001) 85–122; Maisels, *Early Civilizations of the Old World*, 125, 135; Edith Porada et al., "The Chronology of Mesopotamia," in Robert W. Ehrlich, ed., *Chronologies of Old World Archaeology*, third edition (Chicago, IL, 1992), 80–8, 92, 100, 103; Trevor Watkins and Stuart Campbell, "The Chronology of the Halaf," and Joan Oates, "Ubaid Chronology," in Olivier Aurenche et al., *Chronologies du Proche Orient/Chronologies in the Near East: Relative Chronologies and Absolute Chronology, 16,000–4,000 B.P.* (Oxford, 1987), 427–65, 473–82; Joan Oates, "Ubaid Mesopotamia Reconsidered," in T. Cuyler Young, ed., *The Hilly Flanks and Beyond: Essays on the Prehistory of Southwest Asia* (Chicago, IL, 1983), 251–81. With the exception of the first two citations, radiocarbon dates in these studies have been recalibrated using OxCal 3.10. Among these studies the most significant discrepancy is the dating of the end of Ubaid and the beginning of Uruk during the fifth millennium. See further discussion of dating in note 99.

[73] Roger Matthews, *The Early Prehistory of Mesopotamia:500,000 to 4,500 bc* (Turnhout, 2000), 57–63.

[74] My dating here follows Yoffee, *Myths of the Archaic State*, 199. For a map of the geography of these cultures, see Norman Yoffee and Jeffery J. Clark, eds., *Early Stages in the Evolution of Mesopotamian Civilization: Soviet Excavations in Northern Iraq* (Tucson, AZ, 1993), 264.

Anatolia, watering the catchment basin of the Euphrates and the Tigris systems that ran through Mesopotamia.[75] But the pollen profiles from the river Delphinos in Crete and Lake Van in Turkey show significantly increased oak pollen for the millennia only after roughly 6200 BC, suggesting that the Atlantic westerlies did not arrive until the era of the Laurentine event, or perhaps until after the end of the 6900–6100 BC cooling epoch.[76] By the time that there is clear evidence of the arrival of the NAO-driven westerlies, the Hassuna had faded (by 6600/6300 BC); the winter westerlies would have had more of an influence on the Samarra and the ensuing Chalcolithic Halaf and Ubaid cultures.

These north Mesopotamian cultures thus emerged depending on these new winter rains, expanding as the Pre-Pottery cultures centered on the Levant disappeared. While there are certainly well-planned settlements among their remains, the tendency was toward smaller, more widely distributed locations, small villages distributed across a dry landscape taking advantage of local water sources. Unlike the isolated beehive concentrations of the PPNB-C peoples at places like Çatalhöyük and 'Ain Ghazal, which could be as large as twelve to thirteen hectares, the Hassuna-Samarra-Halaf settlements were widely distributed in a ramifying network of small villages each of one to five hectares spread across the north Mesopotamia plains. Small as they were, these dry-country cultures seem to have been the focus of fundamental changes in the Southwest Asian farming systems, and launched the beginning of the intensification, Sherratt's secondary products revolution, that would lay the foundations for the urban civilizations to come.[77]

Their most obvious technical innovation lay in the pottery that defined them as archaeological entities, coarse wares in the Proto-Hassuna period but increasingly refined and elaborately painted, incised, and burnished

[75] See citations in note 4 and the discussion on pp. 160, 166, 171–76 on the role of winter and Atlantic-westerly-derived precipitation on Anatolia and thus greater interior Southwest Asia.

[76] Sytze Bottema and Anaya Sarpaki, "Environmental in Crete: A 9000-Year Record of Holocene Vegetation History and the Effect of the Santorini Eruption," *Holocene* 13 (2003), 733–49; Wick et al., "Evidence of Lateglacial and Holocene Climatic Change and Human Impact in Eastern Anatolia." Arlene Miller Rosen, in "Early to Mid-Holocene Environmental Changes and Their Impact on Human Communities in Southeastern Anatolia," in Arie S. Issar and Neville Brown, eds., *Water, Environment, and Society in Times of Climatic Change* (Dordrecht, 1998), at 234–5, sees a moister phase in the seventh millennium, drier conditions in the sixth millennium, and moister conditions in the fifth millennium, patterns that do not seem to match the Lake Van data.

[77] Simmons, *The Neolithic Revolution in the Near East*, 215–16; Sherratt, *Economy and Society in Prehistoric Europe*, 92, 183–8, 224, 230; Andrew M. T. Moore, "The First Farmers in the Levant," in Young, ed., *The Hilly Flanks and Beyond*, 91–112; Petr Charvát, *Mesopotamia before History* (London, 2002), 57–89; Patricia L. Fall et al., "Agricultural Intensification and the Secondary Products Revolution along the Jordan Rift," *HumEcol* 30 (2002), 445–82.

wares in the succeeding eras. Pots were fired in open hearths in the Hassuna and Samarra and in more advanced up-draft kilns, reaching temperatures of 950 degrees centigrade, in the Halaf and Ubaid. By this time pottery production had become a professionalized craft, perhaps controlled by powerful elite households, and part of a regional system of exchange that transcended local and ethnic boundaries in a wide interaction sphere.[78] The development of the skills and secrets of transforming earth by fire was obviously a momentous transition in the history of energy and technology, as the relatively massive burning of wood and charcoal led to fundamental improvements in human ecology. The kiln firing of clay to make pottery and the chemical experiments that led to early glazing led reasonably directly to the first systematic metallurgy, which began with small, hammered, copper ornaments during the Pottery Neolithic and progressed to full-scale smelting and casting during the Chalcolithic.[79]

Technological changes launched during the Late Neolithic were matched by the beginnings of a profound sociological change. Over the long term in the human condition, bands of hunter-gathers, in which the equalizing force of collective identity and reciprocal obligation was paramount, was giving way to a segmented and hierarchical mode of social existence that we still inhabit today.[80] For better and worse, the immediate bonds of kinship and experience of the band were dissolved, to be reformulated into the autonomy of the family as an affective and economic unit, eventually to be governed by abstract understandings of law in a civil society protected and enforced by a state.

In the wider Southwest Asian sequence some of this sociological change had unfolded between the transition from the Mesolithic Natufian bands of the Younger Dryas and the great PPNB communities of the Holocene Optimum, where round huts in circled formations had given way to virtual apartment complexes of living and storage rooms in great sprawling square buildings. But there were continuities between the Natufian and the

[78] Charvát, *Mesopotamia before History*, 19, 29–30, 65–6; N. Ya. Merpert and R. M. Munchaev, "Yarim Tepe I," and Norman Yoffee, "Mesopotamian Interaction Spheres," in Yoffee and Clark, eds., *Early Stages*, 87–114, 257–69; Yoffee, *Myths of the Archaic State*, 204–5.

[79] Ceramic kilns are curiously neglected in two recent overviews of the history of energy: Alfred W. Crosby, *Children of the Sun: A History of Humanity's Unappeasable Appetite for Energy* (New York, 2006), and Smil, *Energy in World History*. See discussions in Charvát, *Mesopotamia before History*, 29–30. On early copper metallurgy, see Charvát, *Mesopotamia before History*, 17–18, 30, 67–8; N. Ya. Merpert and R. M. Munchaev, "The Earliest Evidence for Metallurgy in Ancient Mesopotamia," in Yoffee and Clark, eds., *Early Stages*, 241–8. By roughly 500 BC, the first signs of air pollution from copper smelting were beginning to register in polar ice. Sungmin Hong, "History of Ancient Copper Smelting Pollution during Roman and Medieval Times Recorded in Greenland Ice," *Science* 272 (1996), 246–9.

[80] Bogucki, *The Origins of Human Society*, 205–18.

PPNB, most importantly in the ritual treatment of the dead as ancestors, in which the skulls of the elders were reexcavated, decorated, and set up in ritual alcoves in given households, in a pattern that suggests the operation of a uniform collective ritual of unity connecting the living and the dead through time and space. Indeed it might be suggested that the failure of the PPNB was rooted at least in part in a collapse of ancient and brittle institutions of ritual equality manifested in the skull cult. Notably, this skull cult disappeared in the small dispersed settlements of the Pottery Neolithic and Chalcolithic, where there is reason to argue that local men of note were emerging as leaders, superseding great councils of priest/elders of the PPNB super-villages. Other more variable mortuary rituals, and traditions of ritual circle dancing, certainly must have worked to perpetuate a version of the ancient corporate unities.[81]

But with the late Neolithic Hassuna and Samarra in the seventh millennium BC the material manifestations of unequal familial power and accumulation began to emerge in new house forms and settlement patterns. At the beginnings of the sequence at Tell Hassuna, well after the dense human beehive settlements of the PPNB had been abandoned, house forms were small and compact three-room constructions that only could have accommodated a nuclear family. Within several hundred years, however, such small, isolated houses had been abandoned – or expanded into – haphazard, open compounds of two to three domestic units arranged around a common courtyard, sharing some ovens and storage rooms. To this day in the agricultural Middle East such courtyard compounds house extended families, and they would be a logical means by which family labor might be pooled to conduct more extended agriculture.[82] In certain sites, this elaboration of domestic architecture was associated with the mixture of Samarra pottery into a Hassuna context, and apparently with an important elaboration of the agricultural economy.[83] It was in the Samarra sites located toward the

[81] Ian Kuijt, "Keeping the Peace: Ritual, Skull Caching, and Community Integration in the Levantine Neolithic," in Kuijt, ed., *Life in Neolithic Farming Communities*, 137–62; Ian Kuijt, "People and Space in Early Agricultural Villages: Exploring Daily Lives, Community Size, and Architecture in the Late Pre-Pottery Neolithic," *JAnthArch* 19 (2000), 97–9; Matthews, *The Early Prehistory of Mesopotamia*, 61, 65, 67, 74, 81, 110, 119; N. Ya. Merpert and R. M. Munchaev, "Burial Practices in the Halaf Culture," in Yoffee and Clark, eds., *Early Stages*, 207–24; Yosef Garfinkel, *Dancing at the Dawn of Agriculture* (Austin, TX, 2003).

[82] Flannery, "The Origins of the Village Revisited," 423–9; Charvát, *Mesopotamia before History*, 85–6, 88; Brian F. Byrd, "Households in Transition: Neolithic Social Organization within Southwest Asia," in Kuijt, ed., *Life in Neolithic Farming Communities*, 63–102. See also Thomas E. Levy, "Archaeological Sources for the Study of Palestine: The Chalcolithic Period," *Biblical Archaeologist* 49 (1986), 82–108; and Isaac Gilead, "The Chalcolithic Period in the Levant," *JWP* 2 (1988), 397–443.

[83] Matthews, *The Early Prehistory of Mesopotamia*, 67, 73–4, 81; Merpert and Munchaev, "Yarim Tepe I," 84, 100–4.

south, at or just below the line of regular rainfall running across northern Mesopotamia, that archaeologists argue that irrigated agriculture must have been developed by approximately 6000 BC, judging from the presence of water-dependent crops such as flax in an otherwise excessively dry region, and an actual water channel at the Samarra site of Choga Mami.[84]

Early irrigation may well have been the key to the survival of the Samarra, which lasted at least 400 years beyond the end of Hassuna, and spreading toward the south might have had a role in the crystallizing of the Ubaid, which would flourish in the southern Mesopotamian lowlands. The Hassuna faded sometime during the second half of the seventh millennium. Though the dating is vague, there was a clear break between the Hassuna and the Chalcolithic Halaf that followed it, marked by a period of aridity that might have been caused by the Laurentine crisis of 6200 BC, the nadir of the seventh millennium decline, when the advance of the NAO westerlies had not yet compensated for the retreat of the southern monsoons.[85] In such a circumstance it makes sense that irrigated agriculture supported the Samarra for several hundred more years. To the north the conical houses of the emerging Chalcolithic Halaf may have been an adaptation to hotter, drier conditions: roughly similar houses are still built from Turkey into Afghanistan.[86] The Halaf was eminently a dry-country adaptation that never extended south of the rainfall line north of the Euphrates, but the advance of the NAO winter westerlies, as measured by pollen in Crete and Lake Van, must have ameliorated their circumstances considerably in the sixth millennium (5000s).[87]

Spread thinly across the northern Mesopotamian landscape, Halaf villages typically occupied virgin soils never previously inhabited. The Ubaid peoples of the southern Gulf similarly appear on new lands in the archaeological record at about the same time in the seventh millennium. But there are suspicions that their origins run in a totally different direction; their sites appear at the head of the Persian Gulf, reasonably well developed. It seems likely that the origins of the Ubaid lie lost under the waters of the Persian Gulf, covered by rising postglacial sea levels.[88] As their skein of small villages thickened, the Halaf and the Ubaid peoples launched a network of formal exchange literally marked by the clay seals with which household owners marked their packages before sending them beyond their sight. And

[84] Charvát, *Mesopotamia before History*, 21, 26; Matthews, *The Early Prehistory of Mesopotamia*, 76, 80.

[85] Matthews, *The Early Prehistory of Mesopotamia*, 108; Yoffee, *Myths of the Archaic State*, 199.

[86] Akkermans and Schwartz, *The Archaeology of Syria*, 103–6.

[87] Bottema and Sarpaki, "Environmental in Crete"; Wick et al., "Evidence of Lateglacial and Holocene Climatic Change and Human Impact in Eastern Anatolia."

[88] Jeffrey I. Rose, "New Light on Human Prehistory in the Arabo-Persian Gulf Oasis," *CA* 51 (2010), 849–83.

driving this expansion of villages, and the population occupying them, was a fundamental increase in the husbandry of cattle and pigs. The increasing number of pigs – and the increasing evidence for orchards of olives and date palms – suggests that these Chalcolithic societies were increasingly fixed in place, because pigs (and orchards) do not migrate easily the distances required by regular seasonal transhumance.[89] Petr Charvát sees a fundamental connection between this final "sedentarization," the population growth driving the expanding numbers of small Halaf and Ubaid villages, and the intensification required to maintain those numbers. The result – Charvát argues – was a profound break with the past:

> By releasing an irreversible trend of population growth, sedentarization must have resulted in economic intensification if all the new mouths were to be fed.... [T]his necessity of catering for the needs of more humans than before must have led to systematic and profound assessments of the economic potential of landscapes inhabited by human groups and to environmental exploitation far more intense than before. All of a sudden, whole landscapes clad themselves in settlements and, while in the Neolithic you were delighted to live with neighbors you only saw once every six months or so, in the Chalcolithic you had them permanently "on the other side of the hill."[90]

In these more crowded landscapes, people sought ways to add to their energy intake, and cattle provided the most fundamental contribution. The increasing herds of cattle in Halaf and Ubaid villages provided more meat, and presumably milk, important for children as a weaning food. The earliest use of milk in western Eurasia has now been identified through the analysis of isotopic residues of fatty acids on pottery sherds: the hearth of milk consumption seems to have been northwestern Turkey between 6500 BC and 5500 BC.[91] At the same time, these people put animals to work for the first time, driving single oxen in a circle to thresh grain. Cattle hooves were soon supplemented with weighed sledges, often embedded with sharp flint, dragged behind the rotating ox: these implements both threshed chaff from grain and chopped the straw. We can imagine a role for priests and collective in the first circular deployment of cattle on the threshing floor. Beginning sometime in the fifth millennium, sheep were used as pack animals, replaced later with donkeys derived from Africa. This was a key moment: the fusion

[89] Akkermans and Schwartz, *The Archaeology of Syria*, 139–41; Charvát, *Mesopotamia before History*, 60, 62, 72–3, 86–8; Matthews, *The Early Prehistory of Mesopotamia*, 97; Joan Oates, "A Prehistoric Communications Revolution," *CArchJ* 6 (1996), 165–76; Bogucki, *The Origins of Human Society*, 231.

[90] Charvát, *Mesopotamia before History*, 95, see also 76; Akkermans and Schwartz see much less population growth in the northern Halaf, at least in Syria; see *The Archaeology of Syria*, 120.

[91] Richard P. Evershed et al., "The Earliest Date for Milk Use in the Near East and Southeastern Europe Linked to Cattle Herding," *Nature* 455 (2008), 528–31; Mithen, *After the Ice*, 438–9; Matthews, *The Early Prehistory of Mesopotamia*, 109.

of wood and leather technology with the bio-energy of another living creature to extend human abilities to alter natural things, a beginning of an energy revolution that gradually lifted the direct burden of work from human muscle and bone.[92] As Charvát argues, the "[w]holesale application of traditional inventions and deliberate efforts at maximization of the energy output (more cattle) must have brought in economic returns considerably surpassing those traditional subsistence modes."[93] Across the board the Halaf and Ubaid peoples of the sixth millennium tinkered, improved, innovated, and intensified: pottery, metallurgy, detailed inlaid stonework, and the pack trains and even small boats sailing on the rivers and Gulf that supported the increasingly dense and regulated exchanges that brought these goods hither and yon across the region.[94]

These were, as Norman Yoffee has put it, people and places of "emergent properties." They stood between the long and perhaps uncertain beginnings of the earlier Neolithic and the explosive super-novas of the first centralized city-states. Relationships between communities were reasonably peaceable, and relations within communities were governed in a reasonably equalitarian fashion by councils of elders representing extended households and larger kin groups.[95] If there was an epoch in the prehistoric past when Adam Smith's model of economic growth – increasing intensification and specialization of production leading to incremental improvements in human well-being – the Late Neolithic here and in China may be candidates.

If the entire span from the beginning of Hassuna to the end of Ubaid ran more than 2,000 years, such an Edenic world could not last forever. If the endogenous, depleting effects of an intensifying exploitation of the landscape did not bring this world to an end, the exogenous effects of natural forces would do the job. Contrary to so much of our recent emphasis in the study of the environmental history of ancient and medieval societies, nature

[92] Andrew Sherratt, "La traction animale et la transformation de l'Europe néolithique," in P. Pétrequin et al., eds., *Premiers chariots, premiers araires. La diffusion de la traction animale en Europe pendant les IVe et IIIe millénaires avant notre ére* (Paris, 2006): 329–60 (PDF file of the English text: "Animal Traction and the Transformation of Europe," posted at http://www.archatlas.dept.shef.ac.uk/people/ASherratt.php, accessed August 8, 2012); Charvát, *Mesopotamia before History*, 61–2, 72; Sherratt, *Economy and Society in Prehistoric Europe*, 209–10; Albano Beja-Pereira et al., "African Origins of the Domestic Donkey," *Science* 304 (2004), 1781.

[93] Charvát, *Mesopotamia before History*, 73–4.

[94] Nicole Boivin and Dorian Q. Fuller, "Shell Middens, Ships and Seeds: Exploring Coastal Subsistence, Maritime Trade and the Dispersal of Domesticates in and around the Ancient Arabian Peninsula," *JWP* 22 (2009), 113–80, at 126–9; Oates, "A Prehistoric Communications Revolution"; Charvát, *Mesopotamia before History*, 57–97; Susan Pollock, *Ancient Mesopotamia: The Eden that Never Was* (New York, 1999), 81–92.

[95] Yoffee, *Myths of the Archaic State*, 203–14; Bogucki, *The Origins of Human Society*, 208–9, 232–6.

was more damaging than humanity as Mesopotamia began to make the transition toward cities and states.

The sequence of archaeological cultures provides the outline of this story. The Ubaid had been restricted to the head of the Persian Gulf in southern Mesopotamia since its origins around 6000 BC. At around 5200 BC, two things began to happen. First, the reach of Ubaid settlement in southern Mesopotamia began to decline, with many regions being abandoned, while certain key locations grew larger. Second, Ubaid influence began to appear throughout the region, from Syria to Iran and down along the Arabian coast of the Persian Gulf. To the north, in the greater arc of the upper Euphrates, the Halaf cultures waned, disappearing by 5000 BC, replaced by the northern extension of Ubaid, either by emulation or imposition.[96] Here and to the south and southeast into Iran there appear to have been both Ubaid colonies and trading posts. At the ancient Ubaid center, and at some of the new places of the Ubaid diaspora, a new social configuration took shape, comprised of elaborate central-hallway house forms, collective cemeteries, and expanded canal construction; temples, present in modest forms in the Early Ubaid, now became more prominent and ubiquitous.[97]

How long this classic Ubaid culture lasted seems to be a matter of some difference: one school sees it running down to 4250 BC, another ending at roughly 4600–4700 BC.[98] Whether you have a long "Late Ubaid" or a long "Early Uruk," however, the general story seems clear: the fifth millennium was one of instability and abandonment, extensions and transformation. Over the long term, the Uruk culture displaced the Ubaid, though the pace and timing varied considerably from region to region. The Uruk was characterized by a series of departures from the past. Elaborately painted

---

[96] Hole, "Environmental Instabilities and Urban Origins," 130; Akkermans and Schwartz, *The Archeology of Syria*, 154–7.

[97] Joan Oates, "Trade and Power in the Fifth and Fourth Millennia BC: New Evidence from Northern Mesopotamia," *WdArch* 24 (1993), 403–22; Roger Matthews, *The Archaeology of Mesopotamia: Theories and Approaches* (London, 2003), 102–8; Akkermans and Schwartz, *The Archaeology of Syria*, 154–80; Frank Hole, "Patterns of Burial in the Fifth Millennium," in Elizabeth F. Henrickson and Ingolf Thuesen, eds., *Upon This Foundation: The 'Ubaid Reconsidered* (Copenhagen, 1989), 178–9; Bogucki, *The Origins of Human Society*, 233–6; Yoffee, *Myths of the Archaic State*, 209–11. The new excavations by Gil Stein at the Ubaid Tell Zeidan, Syria, a Ubaid town overlying a long Halaf background, will provide new detail on this Ubaid expansion. See John Noble Wilford, "In Syria, a Prologue for Cities," *NYT*, April 5, 2010; Gil J. Stein, Tell Zeidan, *2008–2009 Annual Report of the Oriental Institute*, University of Chicago, 126–37; "Tell Zeidan, 2009–2010," *2010 Annual Report of the Oriental Institute*, University of Chicago, 105–18.

[98] Frank Hole, in "Environmental Instabilities and Urban Origins," follows Joan Oates's dating of the end of the Ubaid 4600/4700 BC ("Ubaid Chronology"). Wright and Rupley's more recent article ("Calibrated Radiocarbon Age Determinations of Uruk-Related Assemblages") puts the beginning of diagnostic Uruk assemblages at 4250 BC. Given the apparent flux in fifth-millennium Mesopotamia, finding an absolute transitional date between the social forms involved in Ubaid and Uruk is probably pointless.

pots reflecting regional and local traditions were abandoned for undecorated bowls mass produced on potters' wheels. The elaborate burial traditions that had been evolving since the Natufian preagricultural villages were completely abandoned, and burials simply disappear from the archeological record until Dynastic times. Settlements grew from a maximum of 10 hectares – several hundred people – in Ubaid times to the massive cities of 250 hectares – perhaps 20,000 people – of the Late Uruk between 3400 and 3100 BC. Temple complexes with massive granaries grew with the settlements and cities and suggest that a managerial priesthood governed the Uruk, planning canal construction, storing and distributing grain, propitiating the gods, and perhaps directing the defense of the cities and the expansion of their influence. In one of his last major publications, the late Andrew Sherratt presented a powerful argument for the adoption of the plow as part of an expansion of agriculture to support this Uruk "urban revolution." Here the sledges used for threshing were turned into plows drawn in a straight line by two oxen, perhaps particularly to cut furrows to channel water for an expanding irrigation system. The adoption of the plow would have been led by wealthier households and priestly authorities; both extended the role of nonhuman energy in the agrarian economy but also deepened a now decided stratification of society.[99] The Uruk city-states built in other ways on Ubaid foundations, expanding an imperial reach up the rivers to the north and along the Gulf to the south. Much of this was recorded on the world's first writing system, the Late Uruk pictorial inscriptions on clay tablets that must have had their roots in the property seals of the Halaf and Ubaid, which evolved into the cuneiform script of Dynastic Mesopotamia.[100] Not yet the monarchical absolute despotisms of the coming ages, Petr Charvát describes the Uruk as a strange utopian amalgam of the ancient past and coming future, a "huge and essentially equalitarian Leviathan" that "represented the final stage of the evolution of traditional society" but which mobilized men and resources on an utterly unprecedented massive scale.[101]

Why did this happen? What was the role of natural forces? And how might an ecological model of circumscription help to explain the unraveling of the Ubaid and the rise, triumph, and collapse of the Uruk? In regard to the long transition between Ubaid/Halaf and the Uruk, it would appear

---

[99] Sherratt, "La traction animale." Linking the plow with irrigation, Sherratt left open the possibility (not discussed) that the plow originated among the Samarra, who were irrigating from roughly 6000 BC. Sherratt's earlier work suggests the possibility of a fifth millennium origin of the plow. See Sherratt, *Economy and Society in Prehistoric Europe*, 92–3, 96, 224; and Matthews, *The Early Prehistory of Mesopotamia*, 108.

[100] Matthews, *The Archaeology of Mesopotamia* 102–26; Charvát, *Mesopotamia before History*, 98–159; Yoffee, *Myths of the Archaic State*, 210–12; Bogucki, *The Origins of Human Society*, 337–42; Trigger, *Understanding Early Civilizations*, 588–90.

[101] Charvát, *Mesopotamia before History*, 150, 159. See also Yoffee, *Myths of the Archaic State*, 211–14.

that the lack of water was not the issue. Indeed there was probably too much water, and in the wrong places. Water came from three directions, in a unique confluence in the narrow channel running between Arabia and Iran: Mesopotamia and the Persian Gulf. From the north, the Atlantic westerlies had moved far enough south by 6000–5500 BC to drive the spread of oaks in eastern Anatolia and the Zagros Mountains, suggesting that there was winter precipitation sufficient to maintain a strong springtime flow of river water in the Euphrates and the Tigris.[102] From the south, while the summer monsoons had retreated from the Levant by 7000 BC and Arabia at perhaps 6200 BC,[103] they lingered over the Gulf and the southern reaches of Mesopotamia, bringing summer rains to a lush, well-watered region.[104] The third source was global: the final postglacial rise in sea level, a process that had been under way since the end of the Pleistocene. In Central China, rising sea levels would contribute to the shifting and braiding channels and the massive flooding along the Yellow River that would drive the collapse of the Late Neolithic and the origins of the Xia/Erlitou state around 1900 BC, and they played a central role in the demise of the Ubaid and the transition to the Uruk.

During the fifth millennium, and as early as 5200 BC, a "marine transgression" spread inland at the head of the Persian Gulf. Where the head of the Gulf stood on a line with present-day Basra around 6000 BC, by 4000 BC it had advanced northwest to present-day Nasiriyya, and the sites of the ancient cities of Uruk, Ur, Eridu, and Larsa. In this transgression, the invading Gulf waters and the combined precipitation of the westerlies and the monsoon conspired to turn the river courses of the Euphrates and the Tigris into wildly erratic monsters, thrashing across a wet, marshy landscape, shifting from year to year, and repeatedly devastating Ubaid villages with disastrous floods.[105] In the 1920s, archaeologist Leonard Woolley, in excavating the lower levels of the city of Ur, found a twelve-foot layer of flood-borne silt overlying an Ubaid settlement. While he thought that he had discovered direct evidence of the biblical flood, the reality was that there were many floods in these centuries, some massive enough to have shaped myths of great destruction. Accounts of Mesopotamian floods – perhaps a massive flood at the end of the Mid-Holocene Crisis at 2900 BC – passed down in Sumerian tradition certainly were the root of the biblical story.[106] The effects of these

[102] Wick et al., "Evidence of Lateglacial and Holocene Climatic Change and Human Impact in Eastern Anatolia"; Stevens et al., "Proposed Changes in Seasonality of Climate."

[103] Meadows, "The Younger Dryas Episode"; Sirocko, "Century-Scale Events."

[104] Sirocko, "Century-Scale Events"; Algaze, "Initial Social Complexity," 202–3.

[105] Hole, "Environmental Instabilities and Urban Origins"; Adnan A. M. Aqrawi, "Stratigraphic Signatures of Climate Change during the Holocene Evolution of the Tigris Euphrates Delta, Lower Mesopotamia," *GPC* 28 (2001), 267–83. See also Algaze, "Initial Social Complexity," 201.

[106] Charles Leonard Woolley, *Ur Excavations. Volume IV: The Early Periods* (Philadelphia, PA, 1955), 2–6, 15–22, 68–9; *Excavations at Ur: A Record of Twelve Years' Work* (London,

disasters that so prismatically assailed southern Mesopotamia, archaeologist Frank Hole argues, were at the root of the long emergence, consolidation, expansion, and demise of the Uruk. As entire regions were devastated, surviving refugees were set in motion, crowding into settlements in more favored locations. Leading households in those places evolved into temple compounds, becoming the focus of emerging cities. At these temples, raised on tells above the periodic floods, men of particular ability spoke to the gods, gathered in and parceled out grain from granaries, and managed swarms of refugee labor for public works and war as needs be in dark, uncertain times. They began to mobilize cattle and plows to expand irrigation to feed these growing numbers. In these conditions, smaller villages of a hectare or so gave way to larger towns of ten to fifteen hectares, while the total population probably fell or stagnated, and some number ventured forth, up the rivers and down the gulf, seeking new lands and trading opportunities.[107]

Thus the relentless pressure of the gulf marine transgression seems to explain the transformation of the Ubaid. If the general consensus that Uruk began toward the end of the fifth millennium is right, it is possible that a sudden drought at the onset of the 4000–3000 BC cooling event, manifested in the coldest temperatures on Mount Kilimanjaro (4400–4100 BC) since the Younger Dryas and a slight increase in the desert dust reaching the Arabian Sea, may have been the tipping point.[108] But with the onset of the fourth millennium the transgression up the Gulf came to a halt and began to reverse. Since this reversal, over the past 6,000 years the head of the Persian Gulf has retreated gradually about 200 kilometers, to well south of Basra. As of 4000 BC, however, the end of the Gulf transgression left the great Ubaid-becoming-Uruk settlements situated on the northern shores of the gulf, entrepôts between the ocean waters and the interior rivers, and in command of the richest, best-watered alluvial soils in all of southwest Asia. If the recurring floods of the transgression or a searing drought at the end of the millennium were the context for the emergence of the austere Uruk sociology, the improving conditions of the beginnings of the regression was the context for the emergence of Uruk urbanization and proto-state building. Trade and apparently expansive war emerged in the Middle Uruk after 3800 BC, followed by the explosion of cities and writing in late Uruk in 3400 BC.

Here there is a great debate about trade and empire, circumscription and opportunity among the contemporary students of the Uruk. All would agree with Guillermo Algaze's account of the unique ecological advantages at the head of the Gulf in the fourth millennium. While catastrophic flooding

1954), 27–36; M. E. L. Mallowan, "Noah's Flood Reconsidered," *Iraq* 26 (1964), 62–82; Samuel N. Kramer, "Reflections on the Mesopotamian Flood: The New Cuneiform Data and the Old," *Expedition* 9/4 (1967), 12–18.

107 Hole, "Environmental Instabilities and Urban Origins."
108 Thompson et al., "Kilimanjaro Ice Core Records"; Sirocko, "Century-Scale Events."

receded, the rivers brought enough water and silt in the spring to make the southern landscape particularly bountiful and the region fantastically productive in agricultural resources. The rivers and the shallow Gulf provided the means of waterborne transportation running hundreds of miles from the Straights of Oman to the Assyrian plain. And they would also agree that southern Mesopotamia was also devoid of a host of the essentials of ancient material life: metal ores, valuable stone, certain kinds of timber, and various precious exotics.[109] The lower alluvial plain was so resource poor in this regard that the Ubaid peasantry had to resort to making sickles and other tools out of hard-fired clay.[110] What southern Mesopotamia had was people and farm products. During the later part of the Ubaid and throughout the Uruk, the two would be combined into a valuable line of exports. Women were recruited and managed by the temple households to produce textiles in vast quantities – in what has been described as a "fiber revolution" – that became the basis of trade with regions beyond the Uruk core.[111]

This expansive engine of production and trade, Andrew Sherratt has argued, drove the next great event in the unfolding energy revolution: the mass application of the wheel. Southern Mesopotamia had no real need for better transportation, given the web of waterways at the head of the Gulf that provided friction-free transit. But as Uruk colonies spread to the dry plains of northern Mesopotamia, this advantage disappeared. He suggests that the wheel evolved quickly in these northern outposts from a roller that had begun to appear under the threshing sledges. Two wheeled carts and four wheeled wagons emerged extremely quickly in mountain and flat-lying regions, and then spread – with the plow – across western Eurasia in the course of a very short 200 years, between 3500 BC and 3300 BC. These innovations were initially the possessions of elites, and they leapfrogged from center to center across the steppes and then Europe, before diffusing down the social scale to more ordinary households. The result of this rapid adoption of the wheel and the plow across Europe would provide the basis of the region's hierarchy and stability for thousands of years to come. The technology of mixed farming that lay at the root of Europe's economy through the Industrial Revolution would sort its people into wealthier and

---

[109] Guillermo Algaze, *The Uruk World System: The Dynamics of Expansion of Early Mesopotamian Civilization*, second edition (Chicago, IL, 2005); Algaze, "Initial Social Complexity." Algaze has expanded his thesis to Mesoamerica, the Indus, and Egypt in "Expansionary Dynamics of Some Early Pristine States," *AmAnth* 95 (1993), 304–33.

[110] Pollock, *Ancient Mesopotamia*, 84–5; Charvát, *Mesopotamia before History*, 59, 68; Trigger, *Understanding Early Civilizations*, 280.

[111] Algaze, *The Uruk World System*, 4–5, 74–5, 118; Joy McCorriston, "The Fiber Revolution: Textile Extensification, Alienation, and Social Stratification in Ancient Mesopotamia," *CA* 38 (1997), 517–49; Oates, "Trade and Power in the Fifth and Fourth Millennia BC"; Boivin and Fuller, "Shell Middens, Ships and Seeds," 136–48.

poorer, but in combination with young glacial soils and temperate climate, it would build a powerful and enduring cultural matrix.[112]

In Mesopotamia, the rising prosperity of Uruk, scholars agree, rested on the dynamics of complementary resources between regions linked by increasingly good transportation. But here the consensus breaks down. One group of scholars would stress peaceable relations between centers linked by transportation routes, in which goods flowed between northern Mesopotamia and the Uruk cities on the Gulf to mutual benefit.[113] But Algaze has convincingly argued that this was an asymmetric relation, in which Uruk was the core to a wide circuit of peripheries, its advantage grounded on the mobilization of labor for the production of textiles, and that the relationship was in some measure imperial rather than simply commercial. This was, he argues, a "world system" of extraction on the periphery for the benefit of a powerful center, a framework first developed by Immanuel Wallerstein to describe the imperial economies of the early modern world. His case has recently been bolstered with the excavation of the northern site of Tell Hammoukar that clearly had been besieged and overrun by Uruk warriors at roughly 3500 BC.[114] And Algaze's application of a world system model is strengthened by his argument for a multiplicity of city-states in the fourth millennium Uruk core, city-states, often within sight of each other, which competed (like early modern European states) for control of resource-rich peripheries beyond the head of the Gulf. Commercial and military competition between city-states, and between factions within city-states, would explain the various manifestations of Uruk expansions: merchant settlements, military outposts, exile refugee communities.[115]

---

[112] Sherratt, "La traction animale"; Bogucki, "Animal Traction and Household Economies."

[113] Among the critics of the Algaze thesis, see Gil J. Stein, *Rethinking World Systems: Diasporas, Colonies, and Interaction in Uruk Mesopotamia* (Tucson, AZ, 1999); Glenn M. Schwartz, "Syria and the Uruk Expansion," and Marcella Fragipane, "Centralization Processes in Greater Mesopotamia: Uruk 'Expansion' as the Climax of Systematic Interactions among Areas of the Greater Mesopotamian Region," in Rothman, ed., *Uruk Mesopotamia & Its Neighbors*, 233–64, 307–48. See the rebuttals in Algaze, *The Uruk World System*, 144–9, and Algaze, "The Prehistory of Imperialism: The Case of Uruk Period Mesopotamia," in Rothman, ed., *Uruk Mesopotamia & Its Neighbors*, 27–84; and the commentary on this controversy in Matthews, *The Archaeology of Mesopotamia*, 114–26; Yoffee, *Myths of the Archaic State*, 212–13; Pollock, *Ancient Mesopotamia*, 114; and Akkermans and Schwartz, *The Archaeology of Syria*, 203–5.

[114] John Noble Wilford, "Archaeologists Unearth a War Zone 5,500 Years Old," *NYT*, December 16, 2005, A16; John Noble Wilford, "Ruins in Northern Syria Bear Scars of a City's Final Battle," *NYT* January 16, 2007, D2.

[115] Gregory A. Johnson, "Late Uruk in Greater Mesopotamia: Expansion or Collapse?" *Origini* 14(1988–9), 595–611 presents an argument that the expanding Uruk presence beyond the southern alluvium was a function of refugee exile communities. Given that many things can be happening over a 500-year period, there is every reason to suspect that some of these outlying Uruk settlements were indeed refugee communities.

While I tilt toward the world system model here, all of these explanations bear a relationship to Robert Carneiro's now venerable model of circumscription and the rise of the state. His model may not survive in all its particulars. Thus a circumscription shaped by a simple pressure of simple population growth on local resources (carrying capacity) seems to be not an absolutely necessary driver, or more necessary than a circumscription stemming from gradual or abrupt environmental and climate change or even the "circumscription" of the competitive marketplace, driven by human aspirations for bright and shiny things. But all would agree that the southern alluvium attracted huge numbers of migrant peoples over the course of these two millennia, either as refugees, or as transhumant peoples looking for better land. At the same time, all would agree that it was in some measure resource poor and that, one way or another, this combination of factors led to an unprecedented mobilization of labor to advance the fortunes of the Uruk cities. In this mobilization there was a settling down, a "social caging," as Michael Mann argues in *The Sources of Social Power*, that comprised a circumscribing force of its own, a limiting of options to an elaboration of the new order, and the loss of the most ancient means of avoiding adversity: segmentation and dispersal.[116] Recurrently, the collapse of great sociopolitical systems, usually under the duress of powerful natural forces, would allow generations of people to escape the state into the freedom of tribal herding societies.[117] But there seems to be every reason to think, judging by the relative constrictions of the Mesopotamia alluvium, the Egyptian Nile, and the Peruvian coastal valleys, and the relatively open terrain of northern Mesopotamia, the Indus Valley, and the Chinese Yellow River, that boundaries and gradients in geography and climate, in space and time, form the essential root condition of circumscription that shape the timing of the pristine emergence of the state. Open, reasonably bountiful regions, without sharp environmental boundaries between high and low potential for net primary productivity, were not the places where states first formed, unless these boundaries moved through time in the form of sharp and abrupt, but temporary climate reversals.[118]

---

[116] Mann, *The Sources of Social Power*, 1: 37–40, 46–9, 67–9, 75–6, 98–102, 105–27.

[117] Robert McC. Adams, "Strategies of Maximization, Stability, and Resistance in Mesopotamian Society, Settlement, and Agriculture," *Proceedings of the American Philosophical Society* 122 (1978), 329–35; Fall et al., "Agricultural Intensification and the Secondary Products Revolution along the Jordan Rift."

[118] Allen, "Agriculture and the Origins of the State in Ancient Egypt," 150–1; Thompson, "An Ancient Stateless Civilization." Melinda A. Zeder has suggested that prohibitions against the pig have their roots less in ecological concerns (as argued in Marvin Harris, *Cannibals and Kings: The Origins of Cultures* [New York, 1977]) as in the freedom from centralized authority that pig husbandry offered to individual households because pigs were difficult to regulate by urban hierarchies – thus pigs were a vehicle of autonomy for the marginal that the early state elites needed to suppress. See "The Role of Pigs in Near Eastern Subsistence: A View from the Southern Levant," in Seger, ed., *Retrieving the Past*, 297–312.

Such an abrupt reversal struck the southern Mesopotamian alluvium, and the entire world, suddenly and sharply as the fourth millennium cooling event came to a close. Between 3200 and 2800 BC, the North Atlantic Oscillation settled into a negative mode while ENSO storms and droughts began to develop. The Indian monsoon weakened and retreated further south. A burst of cold, dry weather at 3200 BC registered in the high mountains around the world from the Alps to Kilimanjaro to the Andes, as the waning of the South Atlantic monsoon finally completed the transition to a desert Sahara; the Nile, the Dead Sea, and the Tigris-Euphrates all sank to catastrophically low levels.[119] This was the final transition to the Late Holocene, a global regime of colder, drier climate that would follow a pulse of its own. And in this context certain societies around the world suddenly changed shape and scale, lurching through this crisis into new forms, from the coasts of Peru to the Nile valley – and the southern reaches of Mesopotamia (see Figure III.3).

Here the collapse of the Uruk around 3100 BC, during a century or so of intense drought, was marked by a sudden end to the far-flung connections of the cities with hinterlands and peripheral regions, by interruptions in writing systems and accounting practices. In the great city of Uruk itself, the temple complex was destroyed and rebuilt. As they recovered, urban centers actually grew, flooded with refugees from the countryside, fleeing "invasions and social upheavals," and with peoples settling in the alluvium from outlying regions, perhaps driven by drought.[120] After perhaps 200 years of disintegration and recovery, the outlines of the new order, the Early Dynasties of Ur, began to emerge around 2900 BC. The priestly managers of the great temples began to share authority with new actors. War leaders perhaps elected by councils in times of crisis gradually assumed political powers and monarchical legitimacy that they passed on to their offspring; they resided in new great places – the first court palaces. Reliefs and monumental sculptures, absent in the Uruk, began to record and glorify dynastic names and deeds. Throughout society the emergence of ranked burial ritual marked the weakening of temple authority and the rise of new social hierarchies. By 2400 BC, kings absorbed the temples' property holding and declared themselves divine.[121]

It was such a warrior-king – or series of warrior-kings – who inspired the Sumerian Epic of Gilgamesh, one of the great texts preserved in the Babylonian tradition. He is described as "heroic offspring of Uruk ... mighty floodwall, protector of his troops ... restorer of holy places that the deluge

---

[119] See note 31.
[120] Quote from Marc van de Mieroop, *A History of the Ancient Near East, ca. 3000–323 BC* (Malden, MA, 2004), 37–8; see also Pollock, *Ancient Mesopotamia*, 67–8.
[121] Van De Mieroop, *A History of the Ancient Near East*, 43–5; Pollock, *Ancient Mesopotamia*, 181–92.

has destroyed, founder of rites for teeming peoples." Gilgamesh did battle with the minions of the god Enlil, who assailed men with calamity upon calamity: flood, drought, and disease. Enlil sought to defend a great cedar forest in the mountains with the monster Humbaba, whose "cry is the roar of a deluge, his maw is fire, his breath is death!" Killing the monster and chopping down the cedar forest, Gilgamesh made a great door "six times twelve cubits high" for the temple at Nippur. Next Gilgamesh did battle with the "Bull of Heaven," which came down as a drought upon Uruk: "it dried up the groves, reedbeds, and marshes, it went down to the river, and lowered the river by seven cubits."[122]

Here then, in one of the oldest texts surviving in the human tradition, we have articulated the great paradox of the human condition: the struggle between humanity and the nature from whence it came. Nature strikes in terrible calamity; humanity strikes back to transform natural bounty into the material structures of great, walled cities. For hundreds of millennia nature had the advantage, in the Court Jester's hard hand of environmental change, driving cycles of crisis mortality, and even local extinctions. Here, at the dawn of civilization, humanity was asserting itself, but in its understanding of divine natural power, devastating disease was associated with flood and drought. At this point, as people were first experiencing the devastation of epidemics, it is useful to review what little we now know – or can conjecture – about the evolving condition of human demography and human health between the end of the Paleolithic and the rise of the state. From this foundation will flow much of the analysis in the second half of this book.

---

[122] Benjamin R. Foster, trans. and ed., *The Epic of Gilgamesh: A New Translation, Analogues, Criticism* (New York, 2001), 4 (Tablet I), 18 (Tablet II), 45 (Tablet V), 49 (Tablet VI).

5

Human Well-Being from the Paleolithic to the Rise of the State

What then of human welfare? How did humans fare during the millennia between the end of the Pleistocene, and the close of great eons of a hunter-gatherer existence, and the rise of civilizations during the Mid-Holocene transition? And, in particular, how did the transition to agriculture affect human fortunes? Here we need to start with human numbers and human health, the fundamental measures of the human condition in historical time. Working out this demographic history of ancient peoples from archaeological remains is no easy matter, and the labors of numerous scholars have established only the outlines of working hypotheses. This chapter explores these hypotheses and proposes a tentative synthesis.[1]

* * *

Human Health in the Paleolithic

The first part of this story must necessarily be sketched only lightly. The conditions of health during the Paleolithic, and indeed back into the roots of the genus *Homo*, are the subject of considerable speculation, based on slim but improving archaeological and genetic information.[2]

---

[1] The foundational studies of human health from the Paleolithic to the Neolithic are in three collections: Mark Nathan Cohen and George Armelagos, eds., *Paleopathology at the Origins of Agriculture* (New York, 1984); Mark Nathan Cohen and Gillian M. M. Crane-Kramer, eds., *Ancient Health: Skeletal Indicators of Agricultural and Economic Intensification* (Gainesville, FL, 2007); and Jean-Pierre Bocquet-Appel and Ofer Bar-Yosef, eds., *The Neolithic Demographic Transition and Its Consequences* (New York, 2008). For an essential review of the primary evidence, see Clark Spencer Larsen, *Bioarchaeology: Interpreting Behavior from the Human Skeleton* (New York, 1997).

[2] Here and later in this chapter, I rely on the excellent review by Mark Nathan Cohen and Gilliam Crane-Kramer, "The State and Future of Paleoepidemiology," in Charles L. Greenblatt and Mark Speigelman, eds., *Emerging Pathogens: The Archaeology, Ecology, and Evolution of Infectious Disease* (New York, 2003), 79–91, esp. 82–7; and George J. Armelagos and Kristin

Very broadly speaking, the health of proto-human and early human pop-ulations was shaped by their ecological circumstances. As climate began to swing toward widening extremes from the late Pliocene into the Pleistocene, small, isolated bands of opportunistic primate foragers and predators were pushed from tropical forest environments toward increasingly dry savannah grasslands. These conditions contributed not only to changes in their diet, but to their exposure to disease. Contact with hunted animals or hand-grubbed soils would have exposed early humans to various viral and bacte-rial infections and insect and worm parasites, just as they would have any other similar animal species. Perhaps both their low population densities and their trajectory into dry savannah grasslands would have reduced the cumulative impact of this disease exposure. But spread thinly across belts of open territory in Africa and across Eurasia, early humans would have been continuously exposed to small, sharp, local surges of disease that would have decimated the peoples of discrete territories before they burned out. Sleeping sickness and tapeworms are among the afflictions now thought to date from earliest human origins. Sleeping sicknesses of different virulence are caused by various species of trypanosomes carried by tsetse flies from cattle and wild ungulate herds; native to eastern Africa, *T.b. gambiense* is found in the forests west of the Rift Valley, while the more dangerous *T.b. rhodesiense* is endemic to the savannahs to the east. As *australopithecines* and early *Homo* moved out into the open savannah they might have been protected briefly by *gambiense* immunities, but that the more deadly *rho-desiense* would have taken a serious toll on small bands, restraining the growth of population and literally driving evolving humans "out of Africa."[3] Tapeworms are traditionally seen as a disease of domestication, passed from domesticated animals to humans during the Neolithic. This understanding has been overturned by genetic studies, which find a deep commonality between human tapeworms and those of African hyenas and big cats: lions and cheetahs. Here it appears that humans began to share tapeworms with these carnivores as *Homo* began to compete with hyenas to scavenge the remains of kills brought down by the cats. The irony is that it seems that humans passed the tapeworm back to animals when they domesticated the animals during the Neolithic.[4] It also appears that human tuberculosis was

N. Harper, "Genomics at the Origins of Agriculture, Part Two," *Evolutionary Anthropology* 14 (2005), 114–15. See also Mark Nathan Cohen, *Health & the Rise of Civilization* (New Haven, CT, 1989), 32–8; and, for a classic account, William H. McNeill, *Plagues and Peoples* (New York, 1977), 14–30.

[3] Susan C. Welburn et al., "Sleeping Sickness: A Tale of Two Diseases," *Trends in Parasitology* 17 (2001), 19–24; Dorothy H. Crawford, *Deadly Companions: How Microbes Shaped Our History* (Oxford, 2007), 47–53.

[4] Eric P. Hoberg, "Phylogeny of *Taenia*: Species Definition and Origins of Human Parasites," *Parasitology International* 5 (2006), S23–S30; Eric P. Hoberg et al., "Out of Africa: Origins of the *Taenia* Tapeworms in Humans," *Proceedings of the Royal Society, London B* 268 (2001),

transferred from animals in East Africa well before domestication – with the earliest evidence consisting of lesions on a 500,000-year-old *Homo erectus* skeleton. TB would certainly have intensified during the Neolithic, but it now is ranked among a growing group of confirmed Paleolithic diseases.[5]

Human migration also shaped early human physiology and its integral role in human health. While Australopithecines and early *Homo* species were probably hairy and pale skinned, the aggressive savannah adaptation of *Homo erectus* roughly a million and a half years ago likely launched the transition toward relative hairlessness, as body hair would have contributed to overheating in a fast-moving, wide-ranging species. The second effect in this transition would have been to select for dark skin that would protect against damage from ultraviolet solar radiation, to sweat glands, and to the regulation of folate, a nutrient essential to reproduction.[6] The thinning of body hair would have reduced the primate practice of mutual grooming, which would have decreased the amount of infected body lice passed between individuals. It is possible that living on dry savannah lands would have limited exposure to mosquito-borne malaria. The Middle Stone Age geographic expansions in tropical Africa that are now recognized as marking the emergence of anatomically modern humans around 100,000ybp may have reexposed populations to malaria, an argument suggested by the spread of a mutation called "Duffy negativity," which conveyed resistance to vivax malaria. This protection only extended to modern humans who remained in sub-Saharan Africa, indicating that it developed after the first African modern human divisions. These Middle Stone Age expansions are also congruent with recent estimates of East African origins and spread of leprosy with the out of Africa diaspora.[7]

781–7; Jessica M. C. Pearce-Duvet, "The Origin of Human Pathogens: Evaluating the Role of Agriculture and Domestic Animals in the Evolution of Human Disease," *Biological Reviews* 81 (2006), 369–82, at 374–6.

[5] See the recent review in Helen D. Donoghue, "Human Tuberculosis – an Ancient disease, as Elucidated by Ancient Microbial Biomolecules," *Microbes and Infections* 11 (2009), 1156–62; M. Cristina Gutierrez et al., "Ancient Origin and Gene Mosaicism of the Progenitor of *Mycobacterium Tuberculosis*," *PLoS Pathogens* 1(1) (2005): e5; R. Brosch et al., "A New Evolutionary Scenario for the *Mycobacterium Tuberculosis* Complex," *PNAS* 99 (2002), 3684–9.

[6] Nina G. Jablonski and George Chapin, "The Evolution of Human Skin Coloration," *JHumEv* 39 (2000), 57–106; Nina G. Jablonski, "The Evolution of Human Skin and Skin Color," *Annual Reviews in Anthropology* 3 (2004), 585–623, see 598–600. See also Heather L. Norton et al., "Genetic Evidence for the Convergent Evolution of Light Skin in Europeans and East Asians," *MBE* 24 (2007), 710–22.

[7] Richard Carter and Kamini N. Mendis, "Evolutionary and Historical Aspects of the Burden of Malaria," *Clinical Microbiology Reviews* 15 (2002), 562–94, see 572–4. James L. A. Webb, "Malaria and the Peopling of Early Tropical Africa," *JWH* 16 (2005), 269–91, esp. 270–9, provides the modern historical synthesis; see also James L. A. Webb, *Humanity's Burden: A Global History of Malaria* (New York, 2009), 18–41. On leprosy, see Marc Monot et al., "On the Origin of Leprosy," *Science* 308 (2005), 1040–2.

Upper Paleolithic peoples of tropical African genetic origins who populated the rest of the globe after 65,000ybp were exposed to other stresses.
Early Upper Paleolithic peoples in Europe were particularly tall, apparently
an expression of both tropical origins and better-quality food during an
interglacial. By the depths of the Late Glacial Maximum, these peoples had
shrunk in stature and were suffering larger numbers of stress lesions on their
teeth and bones.[8] Skin color also may have changed. Dark-skinned tropical
peoples moving north and then encountering glaciations would have had
significant difficulties synthesizing vitamin D from reduced northern solar
radiation, a problem that would have been particularly acute during glacial epochs. Thus geneticists have argued that modern racial distinctions
of skin color are the result of the progressive fading of skin color among
populations spreading into the north, a process that would have accelerated in the tiny refuge populations surviving the Late Glacial Maximum.
Vitamin D deficiencies cause rickets, a crippling deformity in the pelvis and
long bones. A different mutation conferring an enhanced biological ability
to accumulate iron and thus avoid iron deficiencies developed in Europe at
the end of the Pleistocene, and is now concentrated in parts of the northern
hemisphere.[9] A diet rich in fish and marine mammals, a good source of vitamin D, may have contributed to the persistence of darker skin by essentially
Mesolithic peoples of the farthest north, around the Arctic Circle.[10]

* * *

The Neolithic Demographic Transition

These were the basic conditions of health that set the stage for the demographic explosions associated with the agricultural revolution. The scale of
demographic change is readily evident in a very bold estimate of total human
population across the Holocene (Table II.1). (For details, see Table III.1a.)

Clearly, in raw figures, humanity has been very successful during the
Holocene, multiplying its Early Holocene population by a factor of thirty-
six during the first 9,000 years and then by a factor of twenty-seven during
the past 2,000 years. But equally clearly that "success" in the growth of
numbers is massively weighted to the past 500 years, and indeed to the past

---

[8] Brigitte M. Holt and Vincenzo Formicola, "Hunters of the Ice Age: The Biology of Upper
   Paleolithic People," *YPA* 51 (2008), 70–99; Vincenzo Formicola and Monica Giannecchini,
   "Evolutionary Trends of Stature in Upper Paleolithic and Mesolithic Europe," *JHumEv* 36
   (1999), 319–33; Christopher B. Ruff et al., "Body Size, Body Proportions, and Mobility in
   the Tyrolean 'Iceman,'" *JHumEv* 51 (2006), 91–101.

[9] S. Distante et al., "The Origin and Spread of the *HFE*-C282Y Heamochromatis Mutation,"
   Human Genetics 115 (2004), 269–79.

[10] Jablonski and Chapin, "The Evolution of Human Skin Coloration"; Jablonski, "The
   Evolution of Human Skin and Skin Color," 606–9.

60 years, during which global population has almost tripled. By contrast, population can be estimated to have grown at an infinitesimal annual rate of .03 percent per year during the long Neolithic running down to 3000 BC, when annual growth rates increased to a broad ancient-medieval plateau of something like .07 percent. Ancient-medieval growth was in turn less than a tenth of the total early modern–modern growth since AD 1500. And if Neolithic population growth was slow, perhaps almost continuous with rates during the Paleolithic and the Mesolithic, it suggests that agriculture in its earliest forms was not a revolutionary transformation but a stop-gap measure, as small populations struggled to adjust to changing ecologies.[11]

This is obviously a very rough estimate, and it leaves unaddressed the timing and the geography of this growth. Where, when, and how did population grow over these millennia? "Where" is probably the easiest question for which to suggest an answer. The estimates of the distribution of population at the height of the ancient world (roughly the year AD 1), suggest that more than 80 percent of the human population, perhaps 200 million people, was concentrated in the belt of Old World civilizations and cultures running from Europe and North Africa into Southwest Asia, India, and China, a region comprising (generously) 25 percent of the inhabited surface of the earth.[12]

Thus the great weight of population was concentrated around the generally dry, low-to-mid north latitude Old World centers of domestication from which agricultural packages of cereals, animals, and intensified agriculture had dispersed into neighboring regions. Conversely, population densities were far lower in the tropical, temperate, or polar regions where human communities continued to follow foraging or horticultural subsistence patterns. Obviously the sequence of population growth in these highly populated Old World regions is of particular importance.

The "when" and "how" of these questions of Neolithic population growth are much more complicated. But if the evidence is slim, the problem is being cracked. Accounting for population growth, of course, classically means accounting for the addition to and subtraction from human numbers, births

---

[11] Thus we can accept in spirit Mark Nathan Cohen's classic understanding of population pressure leading to domestication, while adjusting it to argue that the "pressure" came as much from changing climate and regional ecologies as from "Paleolithic overpopulation." See Mark Nathan Cohen, *The Food Crisis in Prehistory: Overpopulation and the Origins of Agriculture* (New Haven, CT, 1979); Binford, *Constructing Frames of Reference*; and Robert Bates Graber, *A Scientific Model of Social and Cultural Evolution* (Kirksville, MO, 1995).

[12] The estimates of population for the Old World Core of Southwest Asia, South Asia, East Asia, North Africa, and non-Russian Europe in Biraben, "Essai sur l-Évolution du Nombre des Hommes" and Colin McEvedy and Richard Jones, *Atlas of World Population History* (New York, 1978). The figures in McEvedy and Jones are lower than those in Biraben (166 million versus 252 million), but in both estimates the Old World Core comprised about 83 percent of the total world population.

and deaths, fertility and mortality. Over the past fifty years, demographers have worked out the changing dynamics of fertility and mortality for the recent "modern demographic transition," which over the past 500 years has driven a fourteen-fold increase in human population, from under 500 million to 7 billion. In its most simple form, the modern demographic transition is a story of mortality decline followed by fertility decline. Premodern agrarian societies are understood to have had high birth rates and death rates, each more or less balancing each other out, producing a slowly growing population. In the modern demographic transition, mortality fell first, allowing high birth rates to drive enormous population increases before fertility was restrained, leading to a new balance of low birth and death rates and low population growth.[13]

As this model was being confirmed for the recent past, a matching and now much debated model was developed for a demographic transition from the Paleolithic to the Neolithic. Here – in a framework that modeled the Upper Paleolithic as the first affluent society – the early assumption was that migratory Paleolithic peoples had both low levels of mortality and fertility, and that they self-consciously restricted their fertility to maintain a low level of population growth. Then, with domestication and the agricultural revolution, according to this account, fertility rose as foraging bands settled into agricultural villages, where women – relieved of the stresses of migration – had shorter birth intervals and thus more children, children who could be put to work in the routines of village life. Thus by this model population would have grown rapidly until this high fertility was balanced out by an equivalent increase in mortality with the onset of epidemics and routine disease caused by high population densities. This new high fertility–high mortality regime would have settled in with the emergence of cities and early states, and endured down to the modern demographic transition.[14]

Though it is not without its supporters, several considerations have challenged this classic model of a fertility-driven Neolithic demographic transition. Increasingly, there are questions about the ability of Paleolithic populations to keep their birth rates in check, and that under the right conditions they too experienced relatively high rates of fertility and infant mortality. Such conditions would include the expansion during beneficent interglacial times of modern humans into new territories lightly populated by Neanderthals or other archaic humans.[15]

[13] Jean-Claude Chesnais, *The Demographic Transition: Stages, Patterns, and Economic Implications: A Longitudinal Study of Sixty-Seven Countries Covering the Period 1720–1984* (Oxford, 1992) provides the modern synthesis of the modern demographic transition.

[14] For example, see Ansley Coale, "The History of Human Population," *SA* (Sept. 1974), 41–51; Brian Hayden, "Population Control among Hunter-Gatherers," *WdArch* 4 (1972), 205–21; Don E. Dumond, "The Limitation of Human Population: A Natural History, *Science* 187 (1975), 713–21.

[15] James L. Boone, "Subsistence Strategies and Early Human Population History: An Evolutionary Ecological Perspective," *WdArch* 34 (2002), 6–25; John C. Caldwell and Bruce

If Paleolithic populations could expand quickly, they also could collapse quickly. Such is the position of a group of archaeological demographers who argue that any increases in population during the early Neolithic were caused primarily by reductions in the frequency and scale of crisis mortality. In this model, the *predictability of controlled food production*, however much it might have narrowed the range of nutrients, and the storage of food – whether grains in special structures or in the protein on the hoof embodied in domesticated animals – buffered the impact of subsistence crises. This nutritional predictability allowed individuals, families, and communities to survive through longer periods of time, in particular through droughts or other environmental adversity. As the frequency of mortality crises waned, greater numbers survived, especially some of the most vulnerable, the very young and the very old.[16]

This crisis mortality thesis has an insidious corollary in the survival benefits of social hierarchy. In this argument the egalitarian structure and ethos of band-like communities, in which food was shared equally, exacerbated crisis mortality: in times of bounty all shared equally, and when the food ran out all died equally. Conversely, as property distinctions began to segment communities into wealthier and poorer households, crisis mortality killed the poor while the better off survived. The result would be an ongoing culling of the poor, in both fertility and mortality. Studies of family demography in recent centuries may have some application in the ancient past, with implications of epigenetic influences leapfrogging through generations via subtle alterations in the biochemistry that regulates the genetic code. Studies of early modern demography have shown that higher-status families had higher fertility, better childhood survival, and larger completed families. The poor had fewer opportunities to marry, and fewer children when they

---

K. Caldwell, "Pretransition Population Control and Equilibrium," *PopSt* 57 (2003), 199–215; John C. Caldwell and Bruce K. Caldwell, "Was there a Neolithic Mortality Crisis?" *Journal of Population Research* 20 (2003), 153–68.

[16] Boone, "Subsistence Strategies and Early Human Population History"; Stephen Shennan, *Genes, Memes, and Human History: Darwinian Archaeology and Cultural Evolution* (London, 2002), 100–37; James W. Wood, "A Theory of Preindustrial Population Dynamics: Demography, Economy, and Well-Being in Malthusian Systems," *CA* 39 (1998), 99–135; Richard R. Paine and Jesper L. Boldsen, "Linking Age-at-Death Distributions and Ancient Population Dynamics," in Robert D. Hoppa and James W. Vaupel, eds., *Paleodemography: Age Distribution of Skeletal Samples* (New York, 2002), 169–80; Richard R. Paine, "If a Population Crashes in Prehistory, and There is No Paleodemographer There to Hear It, Does It Make a Sound," *AJPA* 112 (2000), 181–90; Charles N. W. Keckler, "Catastrophic Mortality in Simulations of Forager Age-at-Death: Where Did All the Humans Go?" and Jesper L. Boldsen, "Estimating Patterns of Disease and Mortality in a Medieval Danish Village," in Richard R. Paine, ed., *Integrating Archaeological Demography: Multidisciplinary Approaches to Prehistoric Population* (Carbondale, 1997), 205–41; Peter Rowley-Conwy, "How the West Was Lost: A Reconsideration of Agricultural Origins in Britain, Ireland, and Southern Scandinavia," *CA* 45 (2004), s83–s113. W. Penn Handwerker, "The First Demographic Transition: An Analysis of Subsistence Choices and Reproductive Consequences, *AmAnth* 85 (1983), 5–27 argued for reduced mortality, but not especially crisis mortality.

did. And when famine struck, the poor not only died disproportionately, but reproduction among the poor was reduced, for decades. Thus in eighteenth-century Finland poor children who survived famines had fewer offspring than did either the more wealthy or the poor who did not endure childhood famines. Evidence from Sweden, Holland, and Finland in the nineteenth century and during World War II famines indicates that the stresses of poverty and malnutrition have a host of health impacts that can be passed from generation to generation, a long-reaching influence shaped by the biochemistry regulating the genetic code. Thus deprivation had a cascading impact on the health of generations of the poor in times past. Most fundamentally, however, the weight of poverty drove diminishing numbers on a series of fronts, while property brought a modicum of security and continuity.[17]

* * *

Civilizational Stresses in the Neolithic

There is a rising consensus that the Neolithic was not a period of happy, healthy people, but one of severe health stress and morbidity, as a species long adapted to hunting and gathering suddenly settled down and developed an agricultural economy. The impact of warmer, wetter climates, new diets, new routines of work, and new population densities between the Paleolithic and the Neolithic all contributed to a primal "epidemiological transition," a decline in health that is being described as "civilization stress."[18]

---

[17] Boone, "Subsistence Strategies and Early Human Population History," 13–14; Ian J. Rickard et al., "Food Availability at Birth Limited Reproductive Success in Historical Humans," *Ecology* 91 (2010), 3515–25; Vegard Skirbekk, "Fertility Trends by Social Status," *Demographic Research* 18 (2008), 145–80; J. G. Eriksson, "Epidemiology, Genes and the Environment: Lessons Learned from the Helsinki Birth Cohort Study," *Journal of Internal Medicine* 261 (2007), 418–25; R. C. Painter, "Transgenerational Effects of Prenatal Exposure to the Dutch Famine on Neonatal Adiposity and Health in Later Life," *JBOG: An International Journal of Obstetrics and Gynaecology* (2008), 1243–9; Bastiaan Heijmans et al., "Persistent Epigenetic Differences associated with Prenatal Exposure to Famine in Humans" [Netherlands], *PNAS* 105 (2008), 17046–9; Tessa A. Roseboom et al., "Hungry in the Womb: What Are the Consequences? Lessons from the Dutch Famine," *Maturitas* 70 (2011), 141–5; Marcus E. Pembrey et al., "Sex-Specific, Male-Line Transgenerational Responses in Humans" [Sweden], *European Journal of Human Genetics* 14 (2006), 159–66; Susan J. Scott and C. J. Duncan, "Interacting Effects of Nutrition and Social Class Differentials on Fertility and Infant Mortality in a Pre-Industrial Population," *PopSt* 54 (2000), 71–87; see also James L. Boone "Status Signaling, Social Power, and Lineage Survival," in Michael Diehl, ed., *Hierarchies in Action: Qui Bono?* (Carbondale, 2000), 84–110; and Nessa Carey, *The Epigenetics Revolution: How Modern Biology is Rewriting Our Understanding of Genetics, Disease, and Inheritance* (New York, 2012).

[18] Armelagos and Harper, "Genomics at the Origin of Agriculture, Part Two," 109–21, esp. 113–17; George J. Armelagos et al., "Evolutionary, Historical and Political Economic Perspectives on Health and Disease," *Social Science & Medicine* 61 (2005), 755–65; Ronald

Studies of Neolithic skeletal remains from around the world indicate the new stresses that human populations were undergoing. Adult human stature is an accepted proxy for general health, an indicator in particular of childhood malnutrition, disease, and excessive work.[19] Where statistics are available, height rose and fell with climate among hunter-gatherers, but then fell decisively with the turn to the Neolithic. Upper Paleolithic peoples in Europe were particularly tall: men around 5'9" (176cm) and women around 5'5" (164cm). Mesolithic people may have been about three quarters of an inch (2cm) shorter in general, and Neolithic populations another inch to an inch and a quarter (3–4 cm) shorter still (see Figure II.6). Almost uniformly, Neolithic populations show a higher frequency of tooth decay – dental caries – caused by the acidic destruction of tooth enamel by the sugars in the carbohydrates that made up such a large fraction of the agricultural diet. Malnutrition becomes more frequent in Neolithic skeletons, with indicators including stress lines on teeth (dental hypoplasia), iron-deficiency anemia (porotic hyperstosis), and reduced bone mass: the evidence comes from the Levant, the Persian Gulf, India, Southeast Asia, China, Peru, the North American Atlantic coast, and Europe. New work routines – women grinding grain, men working with heavy tools – left distinct and severe signatures on Neolithic skeletons as well as frequent indications of generative joint disease: osteoarthritis.[20]

A critical source of the generalized stress revealed in this recent work in paleobiology was an intensifying level of diseases, some new, some established but transformed by the ecology of Neolithic settlement. A host of *zoonotic diseases* either spread from newly domesticated animals into human populations during the Neolithic, or intensified as human and animal densities increased, with devastating impacts and long-lasting symbioses. Generally, if direct and immediate transfer from animal hosts at domestication is not quite so obvious now, it is clear that the new densities and ecologies of villages and cities provided a new platform for the transmission

---

Barrett et al., "Emerging and Re-Emerging Infectious Diseases: The Third Epidemiological Transition," *ARA* 27 (1998), 247–71.

[19] Richard H. Steckel, "Stature and the Standard of Living," *JEconL* 33 (1995), 1903–40.

[20] Clark S. Larsen, "The Agricultural Revolution as Environmental Catastrophe: Implications for Health and Lifestyle in the Holocene," *QuatInt* 150 (2006), 12–20 provides a recent synthesis. See the articles in Cohen and Armelagos, eds., *Paleopathology at the Origins of Agriculture*; and Cohen and Crane-Kramer, eds., *Ancient Health*; Vered Eshed et al., "Paleopathology and the Origin of Agriculture in the Levant," *AJPA* 143 (2010), 121–33; Anastasia Papathanasiou, "Health Status of the Neolithic Population of Alepotypa Cave, Greece," *AJPA* 126 (2005), 377–90; Clark Spencer Larsen, "Post-Pleistocene Human Evolution: Bioarchaeology of the Agricultural Transition," in Peter S. Ungar and Mark F. Teaford, eds., *Human Diet: Its Origins and Evolution* (Westport, 2002), 19–36; Larsen, *Bioarchaeology*; Theya Molleson, "The Eloquent Bones of Abu Hureyra," *SA* 271/2 (August 1994), 70–5; and Cohen, *Health & the Rise of Civilization*, 105–22.

and intensification of diseases of animal origins.[21] Evolving over thousands of years in the increasingly dense Neolithic and Bronze Age settlements, as villages morphed into cities, these animal-transmitted zoonotic diseases would have oscillated in their impact, from epidemics devastating "virgin soil" populations to endemic loads of misery burdening a humanity growing in numbers and developing various natural resistances and tolerances.

Pertussis – whooping cough – may go back to the Paleolithic past, but several strains are clearly linked to sheep and pigs. Chicken pox and influenza are particularly associated with pigs and poultry. Measles has traditionally been seen as deriving from dog distemper, but modern genetic studies link it with cattle rinderpest; it probably did not become endemic until the rise of urban populations. Genetic studies suggest that while malaria was an endemic background disease during the Upper Paleolithic, distributed globally by the modern human expansion out of Africa, it expanded and evolved into the more virulent *Plasmodium falciparum* form in the new warm, wet ecologies of the early Holocene, apparently spread by the disturbances caused by early slash-and-burn agriculture, most importantly the cultivation of yams in tropical West Africa. This intensified malaria was met by a human genetic response, the sickle-cell trait that alternatively protects its bearers from malaria or subjects them to devastating sickle-cell anemia.[22] If tapeworms similarly had a Paleolithic origin, domestication passed them to domesticated animals, establishing a new transmission vector. The beginnings of irrigated agriculture in Mesopotamia, Egypt, and China would have begun the cyclical transmission of schistosomatic parasites between snails and humans, as farmers waded barefoot through field waters continuously reinfected by human "night soil." Tuberculosis also had clear Paleolithic origins, and was present in Pre-Pottery Neolithic villages in the

---

[21] For recent reviews, see Harald Brüssow, "Europe, the Bull, and Minotaur: The Biological Legacy of a Neolithic Love Story," *Environmental Microbiology* 11 (2009), 2778–88; F. E. G. Cox, "History of Human Parasitology," *Clinical Microbiology Reviews* 15 (2002), 595–612; Pearce-Duvet, "The Origin of Human Pathogens," 378–9. The argument for the particularly Neolithic spread of zoonotic diseases has been sketched in Jared Diamond, *Guns, Germs, and Steel: The Fate of Human Societies* (New York, 1997), 195–214; Arno Karlen, *Man and Microbes: Disease and Plagues in History and Modern Times* (New York, 1995), 36–41; and McNeill, *Plagues and Peoples*, 36–53, but, given new genetic evidence, these accounts should be treated with care. For a review of zoonotic vectors with a modern focus, see Mich Greger, "The Human/Animal Interface: Emergence and Resurgence of Zoonotic Infectious Diseases," *Critical Reviews in Microbiology* 33 (2007), 243–99.

[22] Deirdre A. Joy et al., "Early Origin and Recent Expansion of *Plasmodium falciparum*," *Science* 300 (2003), 318–21; Sarah A. Tishkoff, "Haplotype Diversity and Linkage Disequilibrium at Human *G6PD*: Recent Origin of Alleles that Confer Malarial Resistance," *Science* 293 (2001), 45–62. For a recent synthesis, see Webb, "Malaria and the Peopling of Early Tropical Africa," 280–90, and Webb, *Humanity's Burden*, 42–65. One recent genetic analysis claims to show that the *p. falciparum* form was endemic in pre-out-of-Africa modern human populations, but was not carried to the Americas: Kazuyuki Tanabe et al., "*Plasmodium falciparum* Accompanied the Human Expansion out of Africa," *Current Biology* 20 (2010), 1–7.

Levant. But – with leprosy – TB apparently did not become biologically endemic until the rise of the city during the Uruk and Dynastic periods: an allele conveying some protection against both diseases dates from urbanization, not cattle domestication.[23] And finally, smallpox has been traditionally associated with cattle and cowpox, but genetic studies now demonstrate that smallpox has a close common ancestor with camelpox in various rodent diseases. The new understanding then is that humans and camels would have developed their species-specific "poxes" at roughly the same time from a common rodent origin. Camels and dromedaries were domesticated in southern Arabia, Somalia, and Turkmenistan sometime at the end of the increasingly arid Mid-Holocene, and it was the new cities of the early Bronze Age that were first struck by smallpox epidemics.[24]

The uneven spread of agricultural practices in the Neolithic and ensuing epochs left a mosaic of tolerances and intolerances to domesticated foods among modern populations. These include varying tolerances to alcohol and gluten intolerances – so-called celiac disease – that are particularly concentrated in Ireland, where wheat agriculture was extremely late in developing.[25] Migrating Neolithic peoples had exposures to animal influences of a different kind. The earliest consumption of milk in the greater Mediterranean has now been located near the Sea of Marmora in northwest Turkey, around 6500–5500 BC. Most members of humanity, including East Asians, Native Americans, and most Africans, are lactose intolerant, meaning that they cannot digest fresh cow milk after roughly the age of two, having not had a long or particularly close exposure to cattle. Three groups have recently been identified as having genetic bases for adult lactose tolerance. Each of these derives from small groups of migratory peoples, herding cattle away from the Middle East, among whom the capacity of adults to digest milk was of great survival value. In Africa these include the Berbers of the Atlas Mountains and east Africans in parts of Kenya and Tanzania, who would have migrated west and south from the Upper Nile region at roughly 5000 BC and after 3000 BC.[26] In Europe, adult lactose tolerance is strongly

[23] Pearce-Duvet, "The Origin of Human Pathogens," 370–1; Israel Hershkovitz et al., "Detection and Molecular Characterization of 9000-Year-Old *Mycobacterium tuberculosis* from a Neolithic Settlement in the Eastern Mediterranean," *PLoS ONE* 3 (2008), e3426; Ian Barnes et al., "Ancient Urbanization Predicts Genetic Resistance to Tuberculosis," *Evolution* 65 (2010), 842–8.

[24] Caroline Gubser and Geoffrey L. Smith, "The Sequence of Camelpox Virus Shows It Is Most Likely Related to Variola Virus, the Cause of Smallpox," *Journal of General Virology* 83 (2002), 855–72; Pearce-Duvet, "The Origin of Human Pathogens," 371–3.

[25] Armelagos and Harper, "Genomics at the Origins of Agriculture, Part Two," 116–17; and Cornelius C. Cronin and Fergus Shanahan, "Why is Celiac Disease so Common in Ireland?" *Perspectives in Biology & Medicine* 44 (2001), 342–52.

[26] Richard P. Evershed et al., "The Earliest Date for Milk Use in the Near East and Southeastern Europe Linked to Cattle Herding," *Nature* 455 (2008), 528–31; Sarah A. Tishkoff et al., "Convergent Adaptation of Human Lactase Persistence in Africa and Europe," *NatGen*

focused on the north German plain, in a region occupied by the Neolithic LBK Linear-Band Ceramic and then the TRB "Funnel Beaker" peoples, but broadly diffused across northern Europe and the Eurasian plains.[27] In each of these cases, adult lactose tolerance would have spread rapidly through the genetic bottlenecks of small migrating groups, one of several examples of very recent human evolution revealed by the mapping of the human genome. More generally, hidden from our view are the immediate consequences for ancient peoples of the impact of dietary change at the opening of the Neolithic. Long-term genetic change would have been the result of short-term suffering for individuals whose bodily constitutions could not tolerate the wider shift away from a diet rich in proteins toward a more plant-based and sometimes dairy-based diet filled with unfamiliar toxins.[28]

* * *

(Advance online publication, December 10, 2006); Sean Myles et al., "Genetic Evidence in Support of a Shared Eurasian-North African Dairying Origin," *Human Genetics* 17 (2005), 34–42.

[27] Michela Leonardi et al., "The Evolution of Lactase Persistence in Europe: A Synthesis of Archaeological and Genetic Evidence," *International Dairy Journal* 22 (2012), 88–97; Pascale Gerbault et al., "Evolution of Lactase Persistence: An Example of Human Niche Construction," *Philosophical Transactions of the Royal Society B* 366 (2011), 863–77; Joachim Burger et al., "Absence of Lactase-Persistence-Associated Allele in Early Neolithic Europeans," *PNAS* 104 (2007), 3736–41; Todd Bersaglieri et al., "Genetic Signatures of Strong Recent Positive Selection at the Lactase Gene," *AJHG* 74 (2004), 1111–20; Albano Beja-Pereira, "Gene-Culture Coevolution between Cattle Milk Protein Genes and Human Lactase Genes," *NatGen* 35 (2003), 311–13. For variants on the migration thesis, see also Ruth Mace, "Testing Evolutionary Hypotheses about Human Biological Adaptation Using Cross-Cultural Comparison," *Comparative Biochemistry and Physiology, Part A* 136 (2003), 85–94. William H. Durham, *Coevolution: Genes, Culture, and Human Diversity* (Stanford, CA, 1991), 226–86 argues that a more general lack of local vitamin D sources across northern Europe and into Eurasia may have shaped the broad distribution of lactose tolerance.

[28] For a useful general comment on the new toxins in the Neolithic diet, see Tony McMichael, *Human Frontiers, Environments and Diseases: Past Patterns, Uncertain Futures* (Cambridge, 2001), 64–74. There may well have been long-range consequences of the genetic shift allowing lactose tolerance and the consumption of dairy fats. For the past forty years, scientists have been developing the theory that a "thrifty gene" allows humans to survive in extremely marginal circumstances by maximizing the absorption of fats from food. This same genetic predisposition, it is argued, then backfires when people bearing this thrifty gene begin to eat high-fat modern diets and become susceptible to obesity and type 2 diabetes. Broadly speaking, peoples who have until recently pursued foraging and horticultural economies are so disposed, as are East Asians dependent on rice agriculture. It also has been proposed that there is a link between lactose tolerance and diabetes resistance that may run back to the Neolithic. Northern Europeans are both lactose tolerant and diabetes resistant, as is, strikingly, a sample of Tanzanians of cattle-herding traditions (diabetes resistance has apparently not been measured among the Berbers). Hypothetically, such small, cattle-dependent populations would have had their own type 2 diabetes crisis in prehistoric times and emerged somewhat protected. For a review of diabetes, see Leslie Sue Lieberman, "Dietary, Evolutionary, and Modernizing Influences on the Prevalence of Type 2 Diabetes," *Annual*

Fertility and Mortality in the Neolithic

Both paleopathology and the emerging evolutionary history of disease suggest that the Neolithic was thus the point at which a "civilizational stress" mounted in the human condition. This thesis is a matter of considerable debate and controversy. There is the unsettling issue of determining the actual meaning of lesions and infirmities found on archaeological skeletons. In what has been labeled the *osteological paradox*, it has been argued that evidence of poor health inscribed in skeletal bone may actually suggest that the affected individuals were living long enough to suffer these manifestations of disease, rather than dying more quickly. Thus the appearance of these lesions would suggest a healthier population on average.[29] This paradox of the meaning of the bones is only one of many contradictory pieces of the complex puzzle of how we unravel the way populations changed and grew in the Early to Mid-Holocene, and the practices of horticulture and then a more intensified agriculture took hold. The positions that I have laid out so far, rising fertility, rising morbidity, waning crisis mortality, and the osteological paradox, are not all in mutual contradiction. Very broadly, they can be divided into two camps. The critique of the paleopathologists articulated in the osteological paradox is a central premise of the school that sees improving food production and technology suppressing crisis mortality. And, on the other hand, if mortality was rising, the paleopathologists have an ally in the fertility model, because it is clear that eventually population did rise, and more death would have to be offset by much more birth.

The classical fertility model is thus being revived, and its revival is rooted in the debates about the meaning of old bones, excavated from hundreds of sites over the past century. One issue involved the apparently shorter life spans, estimated as mean age at death, for Neolithic compared to Paleolithic excavated skeletons. After some debate, paleo-demographers agreed that the average age of death of recovered skeletons was a problematic figure, obscuring the difference between *growing populations with high fertility rates*, and

---

Review of Nutrition 23 (2003), 345–77; for a critique, see Daniel Benyshek and James T. Watson, "Exploring the Thrifty Genotype's Food-Shortage Assumptions: A Cross-Cultural Comparison of Ethnographic Accounts of Food Security among Foraging and Agricultural Societies," *AJPA* 131 (2006), 120–6. For the lactose tolerance/diabetes connection, see John S. Allen and Susan M. Cheer, "The Non-Thrifty Genotype," *CA* 37 (1996), 831–42. For an alternate view, which stresses the abatement of subsistence crises in early modern Europe, see Jared Diamond, "The Puzzle of Diabetes," *Nature* 423 (2003), 599–602.

[29] James W. Wood et al., "The Osteological Paradox: Problems from Inferring Prehistoric Health from Skeletal Samples," *CA* 33 (1992), 343–70; Lori E. Wright and Cassady J. Yoder, "Recent Progress in Bioarchaeology: Approaches to the Osteological Paradox," *JArchRes* 11 (2003), 43–78. For critiques, see Mark Nathan Cohen, "The Osteological Paradox Reconsidered," *CA* 35 (1994), 629–37; and "Does Paleopathology Measure Community Health? A Rebuttal of 'The Osteological Paradox' and Its Implications for World History," in Paine, ed., *Integrating Archaeological Demography*, 242–60.

declining populations with low fertility rates. Assuming a general uniformity in medical practice across the entire premodern epoch, growing populations with many infants and children – a broad base to the age pyramid – would have a high proportion of infant and child deaths, and thus a lower average age at death. A declining population with a low birth rate would have fewer children, and thus a higher average age at death. Counterintuitively, then, the population with the lower average age at death might have been a healthier, more rapidly growing population.[30]

   This resolution to this debate has given the classical fertility model a new impetus. Exploiting this new understanding that growing premodern populations with high fertility left a disproportionately high number of children's skeletons in the archaeological record, archaeological demographer Jean-Pierre Bocquet-Appel has collated large samples of estimated ages at death for skeletons from large series of excavated cemeteries from Neolithic Europe and Archaic-Woodland North America.[31] Because the skeletons of infants and small children are poorly preserved in the archaeological record, he restricted his sample to skeletons with estimated ages at death of five years and older, and constructed a simple "Neolithic Demographic Transition" (NDT) ratio of "(5 to 19)/(all over 5)": all sub-adults dying between the ages of five and nineteen as a proportion of all individuals dying at or over the age of five. A ratio of .16-.18 seems to be equivalent to "zero population-growth," a ratio of ~.26-.28 may be a typical premodern replacement plus rate, while a ratio in the .40s or .50s would result in rapid growth and villages overrun with children.[32] Dating these sites from putative points

---

[30] Lisa Sattenspiel and Henry Harpending, "Stable Populations and Skeletal Age," *AmAntiq* 48 (1983), 489–98; G. R. Milner et al., "Pattern Matching of Age-at-Death Distributions in Paleodemographic Analysis," *AJPA* 80 (1989), 49–58; see reviews in Robert McCaa, "Paleodemography of the Americas: From Ancient Times to Colonialism and Beyond," in Richard Steckel and Jerome C. Rose, eds., *The Backbone of History: Health and Nutrition in the Western Hemisphere* (New York, 2002), 95–9; and Jane E. Buikstra, "Paleodemography: Context and Promise," in Paine, ed., *Integrating Archaeological Demography*, 367–80. These issues are explored in Hoppa and Vaupel, eds., *Paleodemography*.

[31] Jean Pierre Bocquet-Appel, "Paleoanthropological Traces of a Neolithic Demographic Transition," *CA* 43 (2002), 637–50; and Stephan Naji, "Testing the Hypothesis of a Worldwide Neolithic Demographic Transition: Corroboration from American Cemeteries," *CA* 47 (2006), 341–65. See also James S. Bandy, "New World Settlement Evidence for a Two-Stage Neolithic Demographic Transition," *CA* 46 (2005), S109–15; and Jane E. Buikstra et al., "Fertility and the Development of Agriculture in the Prehistoric Midwest," *AmAntiq* 51 (1986), 528–46. Most recent, see Jean-Pierre Bocquet-Appel, "When the World's Population Took Off: The Springboard of the Neolithic Demographic Transition," *Science* 333 (2011), 560–1.

[32] My guesses at the behavioral implications of the NDT ratio is from Peter Bellwood and Marc Oxenham, "The Expansions of Farming Societies and the Role of the Neolithic Demographic Transition," in Bocquet-Appel and Bar-Yosef, eds., *The Neolithic Demographic Transition and Its Consequences*, 24; and calculations from data in Silvia Bello et al., "Age and Sex Bias in the Reconstitution of Past Population Structures," *AJPA* 129 (2006), 24–38 (an eighth-

of agricultural origins, he argues that the sequence of derived $(5-19)/(5+)$ ratios reveals "the signal of a major demographic change characterized by a relatively abrupt increase in the proportion of immature skeletons" between the Mesolithic and the Neolithic. This work seems to demonstrate that – if we set aside the possibility of a large drop in adult deaths – the Neolithic saw a significant rise in fertility, and perhaps a 600–800-year period of population growth, sometime soon after the adoption of agriculture. It also suggests a decline in fertility just before the adoption of agriculture, suggesting resource stress among late Mesolithic hunter-gatherers.

When Bocquet-Appel's heroic intervention was tested in papers covering contexts from around the world, however, a series of caveats and qualifications began to emerge.[33] The "NDT signal" has been confirmed in a number of settings, and augmented by relatively straightforward counts of sites by archaeological period and radiocarbon dates. There clearly was a moment of fertility expansion and population growth, but the problem of when that moment occurred has reemerged. Recent work distinguishes between the hearth and dispersal zones of agriculture: adoption is not the same thing as invention. Most of Bocquet-Appel's European Neolithic sites are less than 5,500 years old, and most of his North American sites are less than 1,000 years old, and they contain evidence for peoples adopting agricultural practices developed earlier elsewhere (see Table II.2). By contrast, Old World domestication dates to 9500–9000 BC, and New World domestication in Mesoamerica to 5000–4000 BC. Thus while Bocquet-Appel's first analyses certainly suggest that fertility did increase substantially with the *adoption* of agriculture in temperate Europe and North America, his data does not necessarily tell us anything about the demographic consequences of the *origins* of agriculture in Southwest Asia, China, or the Americas. A major direction in current thinking is now positing slow demographic transitions in zones of agricultural origin and fast transitions in zones of agricultural diffusion.[34]

Another body of data on fertility, coming from the demography of quantified "premodern" populations, supports the model of slow and fast transitions.[35] Looking mostly at various historical and recent Old World

---

century Iron Age site and a Marseilles plague pit, 1721; both have a $(5-19/(5+)$ ratio of approximately .26).

[33] Bocquet-Appel and Bar-Yosef, eds., *The Neolithic Demographic Transition and Its Consequences*.

[34] Bellwood and Oxenham, "The Expansions of Farming Societies and the Role of the Neolithic Demographic Transition," 13–34, esp. 13, 21–3. Slow and fast demographic transitions during the Neolithic have their equivalent in the modern demographic transition. See Chesnais, *The Demographic Transition*, 221–79.

[35] K. L. Campbell and J W. Wood, "Fertility in Traditional Societies: Social and Biological Determinants," in P. Diggory et al., *Natural Human Fertility: Social and Biological Mechanisms* (London, 1988), 39–69; Gillian R. Bentley et al., "The Fertility of Agricultural and Non-Agricultural Societies," *PopSt* 47 (1993), 269–81; "Is the Fertility of Agriculturalists Higher than that of Non-Agriculturalists?" *CA* 34 (1993), 778–85; Daniel W. Sellen and

societies, these studies ask whether fertility rates differ among foraging societies, horticultural societies, and intensive agricultural societies. Horticulture, it should be remembered, involves a limited gardening form of production, usually pursued by women while men continue hunting; intensive agriculture involves a total commitment to agrarian systems, in the Old World involving the use of animal power, a fundamental part of Andrew Sherratt's "Secondary Products Revolution." The result is quite striking: foraging and horticultural societies have quite similar fertility rates, while agricultural societies have somewhat higher fertility.

Total fertility rates of subsistence groups
(the Bentley et al. 1993 sample)

	Mean Fertility rate	N
Foragers	5.6	12
Horticulturalists	5.4	14
Agriculturalists	6.6	31
Total sample	6.1	57

Summarizing these studies, James Boone argues that garden horticultural subsistence requires considerable female labor, reducing the time and energy women have to give to reproduction and child rearing, while men hunt and engage in ritual and warfare. In intensive agriculture, men perform more useful labor, including firewood collection. Relieved of the most stressful outdoor labor and with an increasingly predictable, carbohydrate-rich diet, women would have reduced intervals between childbirth, the primary vehicle of increased fertility.[36]

One could, of course, construct a variety of scenarios from these models and the evidence under debate. The Bocquet-Appel model is of increasing stress and population decline during the Mesolithic (perhaps in some cases driven by the cold climates of the Younger Dryas) followed by the adoption of agriculture and a burst of fertility and population growth. The paleopathologists would add the caveat that this fertility would have to overcome the signs of increased stress and morbidity. Indeed there is room for a fertility-mortality standoff position during much of the Neolithic. The crisis mortality school would certainly advocate such a standoff, adding the stipulation that the gradual accumulations of human innovation, the

Ruth Mace, "Fertility and Mode of Subsistence: A Phylogenetic Analysis," *CA* 38 (1997), 778–85.

[36] Boone, "Subsistence Strategies and Early Human Population History," 17–20; Karen L. Kramer and James L. Boone, "Why Intensive Agriculturalists Have Higher Fertility: A Household Energy Budget Approach," *CA* 43 (2002), 511–17.

manifestations of Sherratt's "secondary production revolution," would have laid the foundations for a fertility signal, and for rapid population growth coming late in the transition to agriculture. Along the way one might envision perhaps two disease expansions: a slow development of a Neolithic village disease regime, and then an explosive emergence of an urban epidemic regime with the rise of Chalcolithic and Bronze Age cities. And here we could also posit possible "epidemiological optimums" coming during the intervals between the establishment of new social ecologies and the emergence of a consequent new disease ecology.

Scenarios remain just that until they are tested. The pages following explore the dynamic of agricultural and demographic transition in Southwest Asia in some detail, and then review such evidence as is available for the rest of the world.

* * *

Fertility, Mortality, and the Origins of Complex Societies: The Case of Southwest Asia

Looking at the transitions in Southwest Asia, we may start with a generalized picture of Paleolithic demography, grounded less in evidence than in current archaeological thinking. Upper Paleolithic peoples, spread relatively thinly on the hunting territories, were isolated from communicable disease and survived by extremely strenuous activity. If they survived to adulthood they were quite tall, robust, and healthy; they frequently died by violence, accident, or infection. There was no effective conscious effort to restrain fertility, but fertility was indeed reduced from its "natural" potential by the effects of the arduous routines of camp life and seasonal movement on women's reproductive systems. Infant mortality might have been quite high. Individual survival was protected by the ancient ethic of sharing within the Paleolithic band. And at regular intervals subsistence crises and occasional outbreaks of animal-vector disease devastated these bands as isolates or across certain regions.[37] From this Paleolithic baseline let us follow the evidence, such as it is, among the settled Natufian foragers, the various phases of the Pre-Pottery Neolithic communities of the Levant, the Late Neolithic and Chalcolithic villages of Mesopotamia, and the complex transition to the earliest cities and state (see Table II.1).

---

[37] This quick sketch relies on Boone, "Subsistence Strategies and Early Human Population History"; Caldwell and Caldwell, "Pretransition Population Control and Equilibrium"; and the data in J. Lawrence Angel, "Health as a Crucial Factor in the Changes from Hunting to Developed Farming in the Eastern Mediterranean," in Cohen and Armelagos, eds., *Paleopathology at the Origins of Agriculture*, 51–73.

Compared with the Upper Paleolithic people at the Ohalo II site (21,000 BC), the Early Natufians were somewhat shorter, suggesting the effects of territorial crowding. But despite their close quarters in semipermanent settlements of pithouses, the Early Natufians were healthier than they would become in the Late Natufian, when the Younger Dryas again brought cold glacial-influenced conditions to the Levant, and the Late Natufians reverted to the nomadic foraging of the Paleolithic. And as measured by Bocquet-Appel's NDT age 5–19/5+ ratio, the sedentary Early Natufians had somewhat higher fertility than did the more nomadic Late Natufians of the Younger Dryas. Late Natufian adult males were somewhat shorter than their Early Natufian counterparts.[38] Thus it would seem that fertility was higher in the more settled Early Natufian, and life was harder on Late Natufian boys and men during the cold, dry conditions of the Younger Dryas. Some of this stress may have been due to violence, but the little evidence here bears on the entire Natufian, and suggests that these foraging peoples had to defend their territories from competitors.[39] Their teeth tell a similar story. Throughout the period, Natufians had high rates of tooth decay (dental caries) and abrasion, reflecting the important of stone-ground cereals in their diet. Again there are signs of stress in the Late Natufian, where children were more likely to have lost some of their molars.[40] And then there was the condition of the Natufian settlements. It appears that Early Natufians, settling into permanent villages for the first time, had not yet worked out issues of garbage disposal and probably sanitation. Compared to the often very neat and even well-swept conditions reflected in the archaeology of later Neolithic villages, the archaeology of the Natufian settlements indicates that garbage was strewn everywhere, in the pattern of mobile hunter-gatherers who are constantly on the move. There are thus real questions about the possibility of severely unsanitary conditions in the Natufian villages.[41]

As the cold Younger Dryas waned, and the Levant region re-warmed during the Early Holocene around 9600 BC, Late Natufians began to settle into new semipermanent villages, situated on or adjacent to well-watered alluvial fans, and began to cultivate wild legumes and grasses. After 1,000 years, and

---

[38] Anna Belfer-Cohen et al., "New Biological Data for the Natufian Populations of Israel," in Ofer Bar-Yosef and Francois R. Valla, eds., *The Natufian Culture in the Levant* (Ann Arbor, MI, 1991), 411–24, see 413 and 421–2.

[39] Fanny Bocquentin and Ofer Bar-Osef, "Early Natufian Remains: Evidence for Physical Conflict from Mt. Carmel, Israel," *JHumEv* 47 (2004), 19–23; Ofer Bar-Yosef and Anna Belfer-Cohen, "Facing Environmental Crisis: Societal and Cultural Changes at the Transition from the Younger Dryas to the Holocene in the Levant," in R. T. J. Cappers and S. Bottema, eds., *The Dawn of Farming in the Near East* (Berlin, 2002), 61.

[40] Patricia Smith, "The Dental Evidence for Nutritional Status in the Natufians," in Bar-Yosef and Valla, eds., *The Natufian Culture in the Levant*, 425–32, see 429–31.

[41] Tania Hardy-Smith and Philip C. Edwards, "The Garbage Crisis in Prehistory: Artifact Discard Patterns at the Early Natufian Site of Wadi Hammeh 27 and the Origin of Household Refuse Disposal Strategies," *JAnthArch* 23 (2004), 253–89.

perhaps a major crisis, these "Pre-Pottery Neolithic" peoples had domesticated these plants, and, by 8000 BC and the development of the Middle Pre-Pottery Neolithic B, they were living in large villages and had begun to add domesticated sheep and goats to domesticated legumes and cereal grasses. Five hundred years later, with the Late PPNB, they were living in much larger villages of up to 3,300 people, occupying complex dwellings with second-story living areas built over a rabbit warren of tiny storage rooms. Pigs and cattle were domesticated; with an ever-advancing dependence on herds rather than hunting the people began to bury some of their dead with sheep and goats as grave goods. By 6700 BC, in the Final PPNB, their numbers clearly were waning, as overexploitation of resources combined with the beginnings of the Mid-Holocene climatic transition turned the Levant into a dry and dusty country. With the mini-glaciation of the Laurentine crisis at 6200 BC the Pre-Pottery Neolithic tradition was close to extinguished.[42]

Such is the trajectory of the rise and fall of the Pre-Pottery Neolithic cultures over 3,000 years, one of the two earliest contexts of domestication and early agriculture. What were the health circumstances of these earliest farming peoples? Certainly they learned to live together in large concentrations, and to keep their villages reasonably clean, increasingly painted with huge amounts of lime-based whitewash. Their populations must have increased to a degree, but there is considerable agreement that the size of their settlements reflected as much concentration of numbers as their overall growth.[43]

Assuming that Pre-Pottery Neolithic populations did grow somewhat, when did fertility increase? The record is somewhat ambiguous as to where these rising numbers came from: increased fertility or decreased mortality. In 1990, an early study by Israel Hershkovitz and Avi Gopher indicated that child burials (0–14 years) increased from 23 percent in the Natufian to about 32 percent in the Pre-Pottery Neolithic B. They were particularly emphatic, however, that population did not rise rapidly, and was subject to continuing mortality crises: during the entire PPN period "sharp fluctuations in population size occurred during this period as a result of various factors such as drought and epidemics." Such collapses are, they argue, virtually invisible in the archaeological record because they were short in duration.[44] More

---

[42] Synthesis based on Ian Kuijt and Nigel Coring-Morris, "Foraging, Farming, and Social Complexity in the Pre-Pottery Neolithic of the Southern Levant: A Review and Synthesis," *JWP* 16 (2002), 361–440; and Marc Verhoeven, "Beyond Boundaries: Nature, Culture and a Holistic Approach to Domestication in the Levant," *JWP* 18 (2004), 179–282, animals in burials: 258–9.

[43] Peter M. M. G. Akkermans and Glenn M. Schwartz, *The Archaeology of Syria: From Complex Hunter-Gatherers to Early Urban Societies, (ca. 16,000–300 BC)* (New York, 2003), 58; Ian Kuijt, "People and Space in Early Agricultural Villages: Exploring Daily Lives, Community Size, and Architecture in the Late Pre-Pottery Neolithic," *JAnthArch* 19 (2000), 97–9.

[44] Israel Hershkovitz and Avi Gopher, "Paleodemography, Burial Customs, and Food-Producing Economy at the Beginning of the Holocene: A Perspective from the Southern

recently, reviewing the entire Levant record carefully, they conclude that there was "no major demographic shift" separating the Natufian and the Pre-Pottery Neolithic: they stress that the story of population growth in the Levant Neolithic was a "bumpy road." Combining their data with sites covered by the Bocquet-Appel team (who also concludes that the NDT in the Levant was a slow, complex process), the bumps in the road seem to have been primarily climatic and developmental[45] (see Table II.2). Fertility was higher in the Early Natufian, lower in the nomadic Late Natufian, higher in the resedentizing PPNA, then lower in the PPNB to about 7500 BC, as larger villages and animal domestication took hold. Evidence for consistently higher fertility only developed in the PPNB sites dating after 7500 BC. But at the great tell at Çatalhöyük, measures of fertility at Early, Middle, and Late levels over almost 1,000 years of occupation suggest a massive surge of fertility in the Middle occupation, around 6600–6200 BC, with significantly lower rates in the earlier and later levels.[46]

The picture in general seems ambiguous, indeed murky, which may indeed be the nature of the situation. The Pre-Pottery Neolithic was a long proto-agricultural experiment evolving from Natufian hunter-gatherer traditions. The evidence from teeth surviving in burials provides as much evidence for continuities in diet between the Natufians and the Pre-Pottery peoples as it does of change.[47] The Pre-Pottery Neolithic put increasing efforts into the subsistence predictability offered by domesticated plants, herds of sheep and goats, and storage, but despite these efforts these people were probably subject to mortality crises that periodically slashed their numbers. On

---

Levant," *Mitekufat Haeven: Journal of the Israel Prehistoric Society* 23 (1990), esp. 35–9; see also Shennan, *Genes, Memes, and Human History*, 129–34.

[45] Quotes from Israel Hershkovitz and Avi Gopher, "Demographic, Biological, and Cultural Aspects of the Neolithic Revolution: A View from the Southern Levant," in Bocquet-Appel and Bar-Yosef, eds., *The Neolithic Demographic Transition and its Consequences*, 471–5. The data in Table II.2 is in part a synthesis of data in Hershkovitz and Gopher, "Demographic, Biological, and Cultural Aspects," 447; with that originally published in Emma Guerrero et al., "The Signal of the Neolithic Demographic Transition in the Levant," in Bocquet-Appel and Bar-Yosef, eds., *The Neolithic Demographic Transition and its Consequences*, 57–80, at 64–5, subsequently revised and supplied by Jean-Pierre Bocquet-Appel, personal communication, August 17, 2011.

[46] Simon W. Hillson et al., "The Human Remains I: Interpreting Community Structure, Health, and Diet in Neolithic Çatalhöyük," in Ian Hodder, ed., *Humans and Landscapes of Çatalhöyük* (Los Angeles, CA, in press).

Çatalhöyük levels:	D3–19	D3+	D3–19/D3+
Early (7000–6370 BC)	2	7	.286
Middle (6610–6250 BC)	37	80	.462
Late (6410–6150 BC)	15	51	.294

[47] Vered Eshed, et al., "Tooth Wear and Dental Pathology at the Advent of Agriculture: New Evidence from the Levant," *AJPA* 130 (2006), 145–59; Patrick Mahoney, "Dental Microwear from Natufian Hunter-Gatherers and Early Neolithic Farmers: Comparisons within and between Samples," *AJPA* 130 (2006), 308–19.

the other hand, fertility could surge to extremely high rates in the growing PPNB great towns.

If fertility did not rise consistently before 7500 BC it may be for the same reasons that James Boone and others have suggested about horticultural societies. The Pre-Pottery Neolithic subsistence was a stable and enduring form of horticulture, in which women probably played a key role in working the fields while the men continued to hunt while the game survived, and then turned increasingly to herding. Men also must have been the central players in the communal rituals manifested in the decorated skull cult that left such a mark in the archaeology of the PPN sites. It has been suggested that this increasingly elaborated ritual was a vehicle of community cohesion that reinforced an egalitarian social structure, effectively a complex elaboration of the Paleolithic and Natufian band.[48]

Disease patterns were also clearly shifting during the Early Neolithic. It would appear that there was a significant increase in the rate of inflammatory and infectious disease – and perhaps malaria – between the Natufian and the Pre-Pottery Neolithic, but this increase seems to have come late, at the very end of the period.[49] One analysis finds a broad oscillation in health circumstances: poor nutrition explaining poor health in the Late Natufian and PPNA, relatively good health in the Middle PPNB, and then declining health in the Late PPNB/PPNC coming from infectious disease, including tuberculosis, which has actually been isolated in a PPNC skeleton. The incipient conditions for the transfer and transmutation of zoonotic disease were established clearly for the first time with the early domestication of sheep and goats in the Middle PPNB, but they must have reached a critical mass in the Late PPNB – when settlements reached into the thousands, when burials of people with animals are reported in numbers, and when skeletal evidence for infectious disease begins to be very significant.[50]

[48] Ian Kuijt, "Negotiating Equality through Ritual: A Consideration of Late Natufian and Prepottery Neolithic A Period Mortuary Practice," *JAnthArch* 15 (1996), 313–36; Nigel Goring-Morris, "The Quick and the Dead: The Social Context of Aceramic Neolithic Mortuary Practices as Seen from Kfar HaHoresh," and Ian Kuijt, "Keeping the Peace: Ritual, Skull Caching, and Community Integration in the Levantine Neolithic," in Ian Kuijt, ed., *Life in Neolithic Farming Communities: Social Organization, Identity, and Differentiation* (New York, 2000), 103–64.

[49] Vered Eshed et al., "Paleopathology and the Origin of Agriculture in the Levant," *AJPA* 143 (2010), 121–33; Vered Eshed et al., "Has the Transition to Agriculture Reshaped the Demographic Structure of Prehistoric Populations? New Evidence from the Levant," *AJPA* 124 (2004), 315–29; Hershkovitz and Gopher, "Demographic, Biological, and Cultural Aspects," 453; I. Hershkovitz and G. Edelson, "The First Identified Case of Thalassemia?" *Human Evolution* 6 (1991), 49–54.

[50] Patricia Smith and Liora K. Horwitz, "Ancestors and Inheritors: A Bioanthropological Perspective on the Transition to Agropastorialism in the Southern Levant," in Cohen and Crane-Kramer, eds., *Ancient Health*, 206–22, at 218–21; Hershkovitz et al., "Detection and Molecular Characterization"; Liora K. Horowitz, and Patricia Smith, "The Contribution of

Thus it seems that these late Pre-Pottery Neolithic circumstances saw the first serious impact of emerging zoonotic diseases, probably wiping out entire villages of un-immunized, "virgin soil" populations before settling into a pattern of childhood and adolescent disease, from which the survivors emerged with immunizing antibodies and even genetic resistance.[51] These local epidemics were interwoven with the weight of environmental degradation, climate change, and an inflexible social structure where all lived and died equally, and may have played a role in the decline and collapse of the Pre-Pottery Neolithic peoples.

Here abrupt climate change cannot be emphasized enough. During the centuries of the millennial Siberian High of 6900–6100 BC, culminating in the 6200 BC Laurentine melt water crisis, the climate of the Levant turned increasingly arid, with the withdrawal of the Indian Ocean and African monsoons, and apparently the periodic interruption of the increasingly critical Atlantic winter westerlies. In the context of cold, dry winters, and in a pattern that would reappear again in several subsequent epochs, Neolithic people would have closed themselves and their animals into the poorly ventilated close quarters of the PPNB great towns. The result was clearly a catastrophic rise in infectious disease that contributed to the collapse of the Pre-Pottery Neolithic cultures.[52]

As the Pre-Pottery Neolithic went into decline in the Levant new cultural configurations began to emerge in northern Mesopotamia, in the wider Pottery Neolithic, and the ensuing Late Neolithic/Chalcolithic cultures of Hassuna, Samarra, Halaf, and Ubaid, described in some detail in the previous chapter. In contrast to the huge villages and egalitarian social order of the PPNB, aspects of Late Neolithic settlement and sociology stand out as adaptive responses to ecological stress. These societies were established across a scatter of very small villages where collective traditions of the Pre-Pottery Neolithic gave way to a household-focused sociology, which by the Hassuna clearly encompassed several generations.

This new configuration had several advantages over the great PPN villages. First, small scattered villages would have been much more resistant

Animal Domestication to the Spread of Zoonoses: A Case Study from the Southern Levant," *Anthropozoologica* 31 (2000), 77–84.

[51] The question of increased childhood and adolescent death in the Neolithic complicates the NDT model, which assumes that increased sub-adult skeletons in sites is a reflection of heightened fertility. But the possibility of age-specific illnesses may explain the large numbers of adolescent burials noted in the Pre-Pottery Neolithic cemeteries studied by Hershkovitz, Gopher, and Eshed. A similar pattern of adolescent death has been found for Europe, rising with the Neolithic and peaking in the Bronze and Iron Ages, and is also ascribed to the impact of childhood epidemics. Hershkovitz and Gopher, "Paleodemography, Burial Customs, and Food-Producing Economy," 24–5; Eshed, "Has the Transition," data on p. 320; Paine and Boldsen, "Linking Age-at-Death Distributions and Ancient Population Dynamics."

[52] Smith and Horwitz, Ancestors and Inheritors," 220–1.

to epidemics, and it seems likely that it was in these contexts that some of the early animal-vector diseases were brought under immunological control. Second, the new primacy of household and lineage over community would have led to social and economic inequalities. Quite simply, concentrations of wealth paradoxically allowed more people to survive subsistence crises. Wealthier households accumulated wealth, property, and strength in labor; poorer households slipped behind. Wealthier households produced more surviving children, poor households fewer. The ancient collective traditions of sharing rooted in the hunting-gathering band began to give way to the family patterns of property. When crisis hit, rather than all sharing alike in feast or famine, each household would fend for itself. Those with larger surpluses stored within their walls would be more likely to survive.[53] It would have been in these marginally wealthier households that Andrew Sherratt's "secondary products revolution" would have started to develop, as a truly intensified agriculture began to emerge, with cattle used for threshing grain, new plant domesticates adopted, and pottery made for the first time. Mortality crises would certainly not have disappeared, but the intensification of agriculture during the sixth millennium (6000–5000 BC) probably was more effective than the horticultural economies of the Pre-Pottery Neolithic in building defenses against dearth.[54]

Late twentieth-century geopolitical conditions have meant that the skeletal evidence for this important period and region has not been studied systematically. But scraps and hints of evidence suggest that it was during these Late Neolithic and Chalcolithic cultures that fertility would have risen. Some of the evidence rests in the human teeth found in the tell at abu Hureyra in northern Syria. The grinding surfaces of molars in Pre-Pottery Neolithic skeletons were heavily pitted, apparently from the abrasion of bits of stone mixed with the grain ground on mortars. With the adoption of pottery after 6000 BC these abrasions disappear, suggesting that grains were now more frequently boiled whole in pots set on the fire. With this culinary revolution, observable in other contexts as well, infants could be fed something other than breast milk, and could be weaned at a younger age, meaning that pregnancies could begin sooner, and birth intervals shortened. The result was apparent in the burials at abu Hureyra, which was part of a group of sites with significantly higher (5–19)/(5+) NDT ratios. If we include infants with children to the age of twelve, the numbers of the very young jumped from

[53] Boone, "Subsistence Strategies and Early Human Population History"; Peter Bogucki, *The Origins of Human Society* (Malden and Oxford, 1999), 210–16.
[54] Ian Kuijt sees the Late PPNB increases in fertility as grounded in the effects of better food storage, rather than domestication. See Kuijt, "Demography and Storage Systems during the Southern Levantine Neolithic Demographic Transition," in Bocquet-Appel and Bar-Yosef, eds., *The Neolithic Demographic Transition and its Consequences*, 287–314.

about 40 percent of the total recovered burials in the Pre-Pottery Neolithic to 65 percent in the Pottery Neolithic.[55]

The burial evidence from subsequent cultures is so weighted toward children that it seems suspect: sites across northern Mesopotamia in the Hassuna and Samarra produced such extremely high proportions of infant and child burials that it would appear that adults were mostly buried in cemeteries beyond the villages, and not yet excavated – if they ever will be. But one Samarra context, Level I of the site of Sawwan (ca. 5500 BC), may reflect something approximating an entire burial population, producing eighty-four identifiable burials.[56] Of these thirteen were adults, sixteen were adolescents, and fifty-five (65.5 percent) were infants. The Sawwan numbers for adults and adolescents produce an NDT ratio of .55, similar to both the high-growth middle level at PPNB Çatalhöyük and the Pottery Neolithic at abu Hureyra. These child burials, we should remember, are not evidence of extreme infant mortality, but of average mortality in villages now teeming with children. As in the Pottery Neolithic at abu Hureyra, improvements in material life during the Chalcolithic "secondary products revolution" may have affected the birth rate. In particular the significant increase in cattle during the Halaf era (6500–5500 BC) may have begun to provide milk, yogurt, and cheese, adding fats to the diets of both infants and women. Cow milk would have provided an early weaning food for infants, reducing the birth interval for women among whom dairy fats would have affected menstruation and ovulation cycles.[57] Despite the paleodemographic orthodoxy that infant mortality was stable, one has to wonder whether dairy fats would increase the possibility of childhood survival as well, providing a key driver – besides fertility – to population growth.[58]

---

[55] Theya Molleson et al., "Dietary Change and the Effects of Food Preparation on Microwear Patterns in the Late Neolithic of Abu Hureyra, Northern Syria," *JHumEv* 24 (1993), 455–68.

[56] The Sawwan Level I burials are listed and discussed in Frank Hole, "Burial Patterns in the Fifth Millennium," in Elizabeth F. Henrickson and Ingolf Thuesen, eds., *Upon This Foundation: The 'Ubaid Reconsidered* (Copenhagen, 1989), 161–3; and Stuart Campbell, "Death for the Living in the Late Neolithic in North Mesopotamia," in Stuart Campbell and Anthony Green, eds., *The Archaeology of Death in the Ancient Near East* (Oxford, 1995), 29–34; for summaries of the burials in Chalcolithic sites, see Roger Matthews, *The Early Prehistory of Mesopotamia:500,000 to 4,500 BC* (Turnhout, 2000), 61, 65, 81, 90, 110, 119. See also the comments on the Chalcolithic cemetery at Peqi'in in Hershkovitz and Gopher, "Demographic, Biological, and Cultural Aspects," 474.

[57] Matthews, *The Early Prehistory of Mesopotamia*, 109; Steven Mithen, *After the Ice: A Global Human History, 20,000–5000 B.C.* (Cambridge, MA, 2004), 438–9. Andrew Sherratt, *Economy and Society in Prehistoric Europe: Changing Perspectives* (Princeton, NJ, 1997), 174–80; Frederick J. Simoons, "The Antiquity of Dairying in Asia and Africa," *Geographical Review* 61 (1971), 431–9.

[58] For arguments supporting increased infant survival, see Renee L. Pennington, "Did Food Increase Fertility? Evaluation of !Kung and Herero History," *Human Biology* 64 (1992), 497–521; Renee L. Pennington, "Causes of Early Human Population Growth," *AJPA* 99 (1996), 259–74.

Thus it would seem that it was in the networks of scattered villages of the Pottery Neolithic and the Chalcolithic – more than 3,000 years after the earliest beginnings of agriculture – that the real Neolithic demographic transition occurred. Thus it was not the *domestication* of plants and animals, but the *intensification* of agriculture, that allowed the consistent rise in fertility that set off significant and sustained population growth. Ironically, epidemic disease may have actually *preceded* a dramatic increase in fertility in southwest Asia, the reverse of accepted understanding. Rather than this Neolithic demographic transition being comprised of a single increase in fertility followed by a rise in mortality, it is entirely possible that small increases in fertility competed with pulses of mortality in the various stages of the Pre-Pottery Neolithic down to the PPN collapse. Then a new settlement pattern, a new sociology, and a gradual intensification of agriculture and material life – the secondary products revolution – allowed fertility to rise consistently above mortality during the Pottery Neolithic and the Chalcolithic Hassuna, Samarra, Halaf, and Ubaid, those societies of – as Norman Yoffee has put it – "emergent properties." They might even be candidates as some of the first societies to experience a hint of Smithian economic growth.

The labor and milk of cattle thus played a fundamental role in expanding the available energy resources of a growing population on the edge of the urban revolution. Cattle may have had a greater, long-range impact on much smaller groups expanding away from the Middle East. Apparently, if modern medical surveys can be extrapolated into the distant past, the peoples of Mesopotamia never developed the biological capacity to digest fresh milk as adults. Instead they remained relatively lactose intolerant, after the universal human trait of milk digestion in infancy wore off, and would have consumed milk in a fermented form, in a form of yogurt. Even if children were more likely to survive infancy and particularly the weaning transition, their health prospects were not particularly good. Limited evidence from teeth excavated at a site in Israel suggests that – despite the advances of the "secondary products revolution" – the Chalcolithic peoples, particularly children, were subject to either a poor diet or waves of debilitating disease, and probably both.[59] Rising numbers of domesticated cattle may have played a role in the spread of tuberculosis in the Chalcolithic settlements. While current evidence indicates that tuberculosis spread from wild animals to humans during the Paleolithic, the consensus is that it intensified in the

[59] N. Lev-Tov et al., "Dental Evidence for Dietary Practices in the Chalcolithic Period: The Findings from a Burial Cave in Peqi'in (Northern Israel)." *Paléorient* 29 (2003), 121–34. Rathbun suggests from scattered evidence from Iraq and Iran that the frequency of Harris lines increased from 10 percent in the Neolithic to 69 percent in the Chalcolithic to 92 percent in the Bronze and Iron Ages. Ted A. Rathbun, "Skeletal Pathology from the Paleolithic through the Metal Ages in Iran and Iraq," in Cohen and Armelagos, eds., *Paleopathology at the Origins of Agriculture*, 137–67, at 147.

growing agricultural towns of the fourth millennium; one estimate is that the first epidemic of tuberculosis in Southwest Asia might have occurred around 3500 BC, another, as we have seen, finds the emergence of TB-resistant alleles in Southwest Asia at the opening of this urban revolution.[60]

The archaeology of Southwest Asia provides the most detailed picture that we have of the Neolithic demographic transition in a hearth of agriculture. The evidence for China is limited to site counts based on intensive surveys, but also suggests a slow demographic transition in a "zone of origin." Surveys of Neolithic sequences from throughout China – including one of more than 11,000 recorded sites – suggest a marked population increase in the late Neolithic after 3000 BC, rather than at a putative point of millet or rice domestication in the early Neolithic, around 7000 BC. The earliest pulse of population growth seems to have come in the Miaodigou phase of the Middle Neolithic Yangshao, between 4000 BC and 3500 BC, in the millet-growing regions of Shaanzi in North China. Generally, however, Chinese expansion in the Neolithic dates from the Longshan culture and other Late Neolithic equivalents starting between 3500 BC and 2500 BC, in a tenfold site increase with many densely populated centers.[61] As this population grew rapidly in these increasingly sophisticated agrarian villages and town, so too did the evidence for poor health: after the late Neolithic transition to the Longshan, populations were shorter and showed higher skeletal signs of stress, including anemia.[62]

Then there is the issue of spread zones, regions where agriculture moved after its origins elsewhere. Bocquet-Appel used two such zones, Europe and North America, to develop his original analysis of the Neolithic demographic transition. Here, some suggest, his results indicate that the transition could have come reasonably quickly after the adoption of the agricultural package. But even in these locations, the pattern seems to be one of a slow start and then a sharp rise associated with the equivalent of the "secondary products revolution." For Europe, Bocquet-Appel measured a distance of a site from a wave front of agricultural diffusion beginning with the Linear-

---

[60] Israel Hershkovitz and Avi Gopher, "Is Tuberculosis Associated with the Domestication of Cattle: Evidence from the Levant," in György Pálfi et al., *Tuberculosis: Past and Present* (Budapest, 1999), 445–9; Barnes et al., "Ancient Urbanization Predicts Genetic Resistance to Tuberculosis."

[61] Bellwood and Oxenham, "The Expansions of Farming Societies and the Role of the Neolithic Demographic Transition," 23; Li Lui, *The Chinese Neolithic: Trajectories Toward Early States* (New York, 2004) 26–8, 180, 194, 208–9; Zhang Chi and Hsiao-Chun Hung, "The Neolithic of Southern China – Origin, Development, and Dispersal," *Asian Perspectives* 47 (2008), 299–329, at 316–17; Li et al., "Increases in Population and Expansion of Rice Agriculture in Asia."

[62] Ekaterina A. Pechenkina et al., "Diet and Health Changes at the End of the Chinese Neolithic: The Yangshao/Longshan Transition in Shaanxi Province," *AJPA* 117 (2002), 15–36; "Diet and Health in the Neolithic of the Wei and Middle Yellow River Basins, Northern China," in Cohen and Crane-Kramer, eds., *Ancient Health*, 255–72.

Band Ceramic (LBK) and parallel cultures, mostly beginning around 5500 BC.[63] But if his site list is ranked by a simple grouping by millennia, a different pattern emerges (see Table II.1.). The Early Neolithic (5–19)/(5+) ratio between 6000 BC and 5000 BC differs only marginally from estimates for the Mesolithic, but the highest fertility rates seem to have come in the Late Neolithic, after 4000 BC, in the millennium when Andrew Sherratt saw the profound and rapid impact of the plow and other elements of a Southwest Asia secondary products complex across Europe.[64] The Mesolithic level of European fertility may have been a shade higher than zero population growth; the earliest Neolithic period – dominated by the LBK villages – and the middle Neolithic were not much better. The Late Neolithic/Early Bronze Age (2999–2000 BC) had a ratio (~.25), not unlike at least two medieval and early modern sites (~.26), suggesting that these were the ratios typical of slow growth in archaic societies.[65]

In the American Southwest, where maize farming was adopted first around 2000 BC, the (5–19)/(5+) ratio suggests a fertility expansion about 1,200 years later, then a contraction, and finally a second decisive expansion, roughly at AD 500, at what was a wider transition to an intensive use of maize, rather than its first introduction.[66] In Mexico and the Yucatan, while maize begins to show signs of domestication around 6000 BC, the emergence of large villages. significant maize cultivation, and presumably a fertility pulse did not occur until around 1500 BC in the Early Formative, followed by a much more dramatic pulse of growth with the rise of states and cities around 500 BC.[67] On the Peruvian coast, the dramatic expansion of the Pre-Ceramic settlements suggests a fertility pulse after 3000 BC.

A reanalysis of Bocquet-Appel's data for eastern North America suggests two fertility expansions, not unlike the Levant, Mesoamerica, and the American Southwest. Both of these fertility expansions line up with estimates of expanded population based on the frequencies of radiocarbon

---

[63] Data originally published in Bocquet-Appel, "Paleoanthropological Traces of a Neolithic Demographic Transition," 640–1, subsequently revised and supplied by Jean-Pierre Bocquet-Appel, personal communication, August 17, 2011.

[64] Andrew Sherratt, "La traction animale et la transformation de l'Europe néolithique," in P. Pétrequin et al., eds., *Premiers chariots, premiers araires. La diffusion de la traction animale en Europe pendant les IVe et IIIe millénaires avant notre ère* (Paris, 2006): 329–60 (PDF file of the English text: "Animal traction and the transformation of Europe," posted at http://www.archatlas.dept.shef.ac.uk/people/ASherratt.php, accessed August 8, 2012). It is possible that Europe saw another fertility spike in the Iron Age.

[65] Bello, "Age and Sex Bias," table 8, p. 30.

[66] Timothy A. Kohler and Matt Glaude, "The Nature and Time of the Neolithic Demographic Transition in the North American Southwest," in Bocquet-Appel and Bar-Yosef, eds., *The Neolithic Demographic Transition and its Consequences*, 81–105.

[67] Richard G. Lesure, "The Neolithic Demographic Transition in Mesoamerica? Larger Implications of the Strategy of Relative Chronology," in Bocquet-Appel and Bar-Yosef, eds., *The Neolithic Demographic Transition and its Consequences*, 107–38.

dates. One spike of high fertility (manifested in the three sites in the Ohio Valley) seems to be related to the first successful Late Archaic cultivation of local domesticates such as goosefoot or marsh elder, successfully cultivated from 3000 BC. The Late Archaic is known to have been a period of relatively good climate in North America, and sites and radiocarbon counts suggest a peak of population. This Late Archaic spike of fertility and numbers was followed by a long period of low fertility indices and low population for Early and Middle Woodland sites throughout eastern North America between 500 BC and AD 850. Then the late arrival of corn cultivation after AD 800 drove a pulse of fertility throughout Late Woodland North America at sites dating to between AD 850 and AD 1300, followed by a decline. Of any of the world regions for which we have estimates, the impact of corn on North American fertility comes the closest to the model of an immediate Neolithic fertility transition, but here we might consider its impact analogous to the secondary products revolution on a population long involved in low-grade horticulture.[68]

All of this evidence strongly suggests that human populations remained very small through much of the Neolithic, and did not expand significantly until critical transitions toward full-scale agriculture and proto-urbanism. If we use a generalized Old World sequence, the trajectory of health and population might look something like this. A standoff of fertility and mortality running deep into the Paleolithic extended into the Mesolithic and early Neolithic, with a few minor oscillations, and perhaps a tendency of both rates to rise slightly. The Middle Neolithic may have seen a slight "fertility optimum" driving the rise of larger villages, followed quickly by the first crisis of the diseases of domestication, intensified by climate downturn. A second and more significant fertility optimum arrived in the Late Neolithic and early metal-using cultures, as intensified agriculture underwrote a significant bubble of population growth. There may well have been several hundred years of population expansion, which was the real Neolithic burst of growth. But this bubble was followed by a second intensification of disease, here perhaps in the mid-Holocene Siberian High, probably expressed in waves of epidemics brewed in the new ecologies of early cities. When these people emerged from this experience they were locked into the classic demography of the archaic world that ran down to modernity: high fertility

---

[68] Data used here was originally published in Bocquet-Appel and Naji, "Testing the Hypothesis," 343–4, subsequently revised and supplied by Jean-Pierre Bocquet-Appel, personal communication, August 17, 2011. See the comments by Andrew T. Chamberlain and Gary Warrick, following Bocquet-Appel and Naji, "Testing the Hypothesis," 351–2, 355. See also Gary Warrick, *A Population History of the Huron-Petun, A.D. 500–1650* (New York, 2008), 154–84. Population estimates from Samuel E. Munoz et al., "Synchronous Environmental and Cultural Change in the Prehistory of Northeastern United States," *PNAS* 107 (2010), 22008–13.

just barely offsetting a high mortality that varied significantly with powerful waves of epidemic disease.

* * *

In reality, our understanding of the conditions of disease during the rise of cities and early civilizations is just beginning to get beyond educated guesses. Studies of the origins of disease typically cover the thousands of years between domestication and the rise of the city-state in a single paragraph, even a single sentence. In great measure this is a reflection of how little we know. But the outlines of the onset of routine and epidemic disease can be minimally sketched, using Southwest Asia as a template.

First, it was not an "onset." Disease outbreaks had been part of the periodic onslaught of crisis mortality with the Paleolithic, and had – as I suggested earlier – probably played a role in the collapse of the great Pre-Pottery Neolithic towns. The subsequent dispersal of settlement in Southwest Asia may indeed have been a defensive flight from the horrors of epidemics. But the trajectory of new evidence suggests that human diseases had long and complex histories that began long before the urban revolution.

Second, if diseases were old, the conditions for their qualitatively different impact changed fundamentally in the fifth millennium BC (5000–4000 BC), as erratic climate change shattered the stable geography of Ubaid settlement in lower Mesopotamia. Towns, villages, and entire regions were destroyed by floods and ravaged by drought. Populations fell precipitously, but also aggregated, as favored locations attracted refugees. By the end of the Uruk period at 3200 BC, Mesopotamian cities could have up to 20,000 inhabitants, while in Egypt the Naqada capital at Hierakonpolis held perhaps 10,000. It was in such densities and concentrations of people that the sporadic village diseases of the Neolithic and Chalcolithic must have transmuted into truly endemic forms. By William McNeill's classic account in *Plagues and Peoples*, these densities would have initiated the transition of various crowd diseases from occasional epidemics to endemic childhood diseases, for those populations for whom exposure led to immunological and genetic defenses. But as Guillermo Algaze has stressed, these were centers of commerce and empire, through which commodities and armies flowed to and from the periphery.

Concentrations of people in cities and armies would have been susceptible to new diseases, such as smallpox, sometime after 3000 BC.[69] Urban populations would be susceptible to incoming infections, and their armies would carry with them outgoing infections, shaping what McNeill described as dead zones on the edges of empire, as urban diseases swept into unprotected

---

[69] Pearce-Duvet, "The Origin of Human Pathogens," 371–3.

marginal peoples.[70] As was the case in later epochs, the source of population growth would have been in scattered agricultural villages where the basic domesticated diseases had been "tamed," but were buffered by distance and some minimal isolation from the direct impact of urban epidemiology. But realistically we have virtually no information about these events during the fundamentally transitional millennia between the secondary products revolution and the urban revolution, when the world's first texts tell us, in the Epic of Gilgamesh, of a divinely ordained monster whose "roar is of a deluge, his maw is fire, his breath is death!"

If we know little about the conditions of health and well-being in Southwest Asia in the 6,000 years between domestication and the rise of the state, we know less about the rest of the world. But considerably more is known about the past 5,000 years, as prehistory turned into history. It is to this epoch that we now turn, or more precisely to the epoch of the ancient and medieval worlds running from the Mid-Holocene Crisis to the Black Death and the onset of the Little Ice Age. For this 4,400-year stretch, the bulk of humanity remained suspended in an enduring condition, in an agrarian world perpetually poised on the brink of crises that might come at the hands of climate or disease.

---

[70] McNeill, *Plagues and Peoples*, 55–63; Guillermo Algaze, *The Uruk World System: The Dynamics of Expansion of Early Mesopotamian Civilization* (Chicago, IL, 1993, 2005). James Webb has recently argued for a similar "epidemiological gradient" in which malaria-resistant Bantu cultivators spread east and south into tropical forests where populations lacking immunities died away. Webb, "Malaria and the Peopling of Early Tropical Africa," 285–90.

ANCIENT AND MEDIEVAL AGRARIAN SOCIETIES

List of Figures and Tables for Part III: Ancient and Medieval Agrarian Societies

Figures

Tables

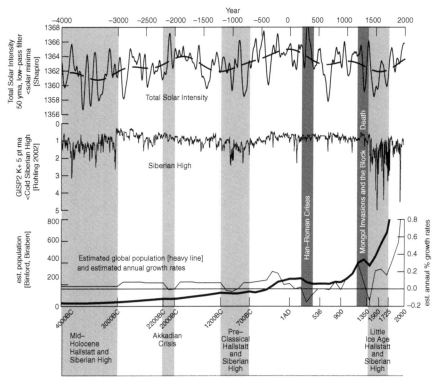

Figure III.1. A model of the conditions of global population growth, 4000 BC–present.

If human populations had grown without interruption since the Early Paleolithic the earth would have filled to beyond capacity long since. Thus crisis mortality – severe reductions in annual growth rates – have to have been a powerful determinant of human total population, which suddenly has multiplied by a factor of ten in the past three hundred years. This conjectural figure sets generally accepted population figures back to 400 BC and my guestimates before that against the major climatic and disease events of the Late Holocene. My guestimates before 400 BC assume a population of seven million in the early Holocene, modestly higher growth rates (~.08%) during the Bronze Age Optimum and Early Iron Age, and lower growth rates during the Accadian Crisis (0.0%) and the Bronze Age Crisis after 1200 BC (~.025%).

See Tables II.1 and III.1A.

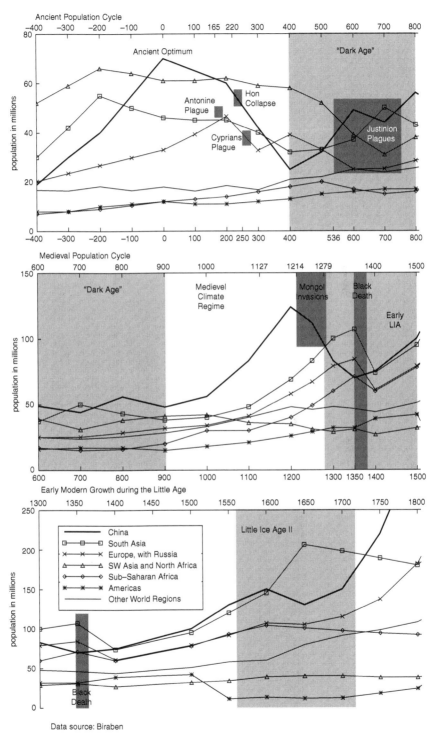

Figure III.2. Estimated global populations by world regions, 400 BC–AD 1800.

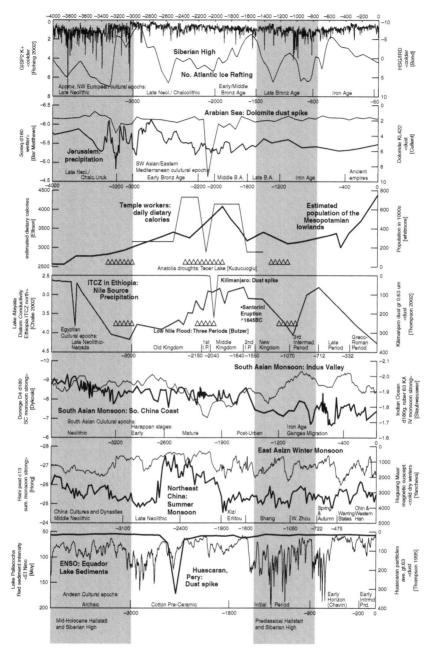

Figure III.3. Climatic change and state formations, 4000 BC–AD 1.

The Mid-Holocene Halstatt (40000–3000 BC), the Akkadian Event (2200–200 BC), and the Preclassical Hallstatt (1400–700 BC) shaped the material conditions of human societies in Eurasia, Africa, and the Americas.

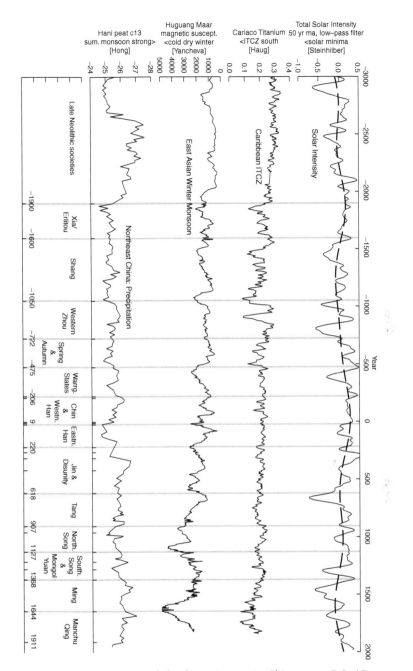

Figure III.4. Climatic change and the dynastic state in China, 3000 BC–AD 1911.

Downturns in the East Monsoon system, shaped by solar intensity and broadly analogous to the position of the ITCZ in the southern Caribbean, are remarkably associated with dynastictransitions in China since the second millennium BC. The major exception is the consolidation of the Chin at the ends of the Warring States period. See also Figure III.5c.

249

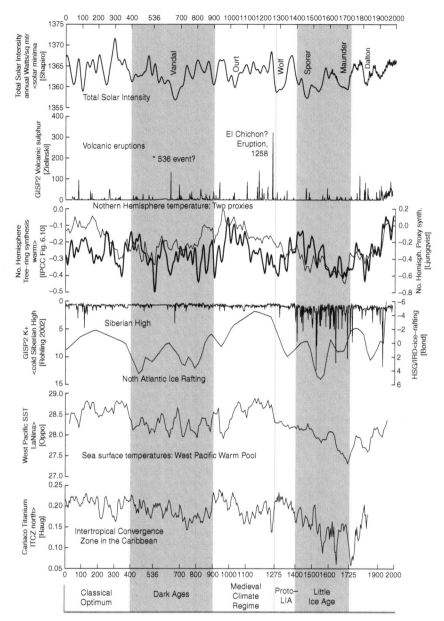

Figure III.5a. Climatic change, AD 1–2000: Forcings, Northern Hemisphere, and the Pacific.

The climate history of the last two millennia can be described as two-thirds of a solar Halstatt cycle, with Little Ice Age being the most recent Halstatt minimum, and the Dark Ages the half-cycle solar downturn. Generally, solar intensity, northern Hemisphere temperatures, North Atlantic ice rafting, West Pacific sea-surface temperature, and the position of the ITCZ on the north coast of South America all moved together, as did the Bay of Bengal Monsoon (Figure III.5.b).

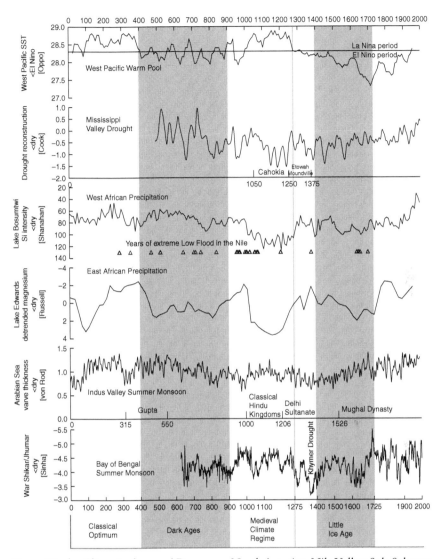

Figure III.5b. Climatic change, AD 1–2000: North America, Nile Valley, Sub-Saharan Africa, and South Asia.

The transition from the Dark Ages to the Medieval Climate Regime brought drought to North America and Africa, with slightly different timing. The advancing medieval droughts seem to have struck Africa first, causing catastrophic low floods in the Nile between the 950s and the 1070s. Advancing drought in the middle of North America shaped the emergence of the Cahokia city-state, which was destroyed by three intense mega droughts between 1150 and 1250. Conversely, the monsoons that water South Asia were stronger in the Middle Ages and weaker in the Little Ice Age. Sources for Nile Valley Droughts: Ellenblum; Hassan; G. Parker.

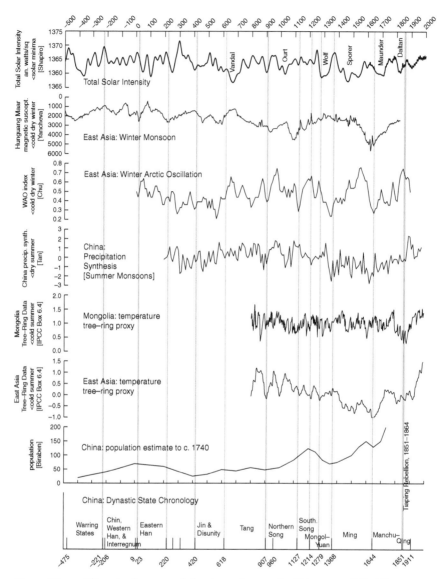

Figure III.5c. Climatic change and the dynastic state in China, 475 BC–AD 1911.

Again, dynastic crises in China align with climatic downturns, which were manifested in erratic summer monsoons, flooding and especially cold and dry winter monsoons from Siberia.

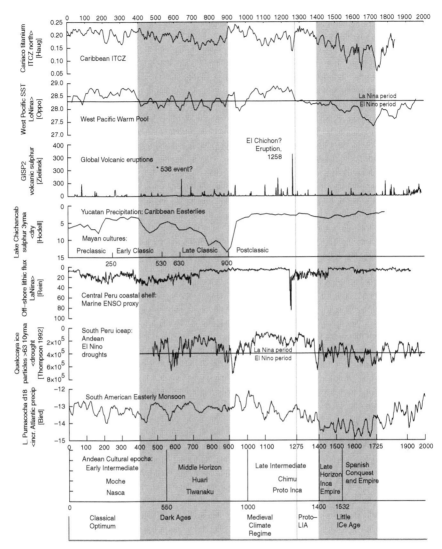

Figure III.5d. The El Niño/Southern Oscillation, Central America, and the Andes, AD 1–2000.

Floods and droughts driven by ENSO variation shaped the contours of Andean imperial state history down to the Spanish conquests. The Mayan crisis of 760–900 was shaped by one of these El Nino episodes, which suppressed the easterly Caribbean summer rains that water the Yucatan. The spikes in the Cariaco ITCZ, the GISP2 volcanic, and off-shore Peruvian records all may mark the Chichon eruption at 1258, which might have been aphase trigger for the Little Ice Age. Sea surface temperatures in the Western Pacific provide the best general proxy or general La Niña/El Niño conditions over the last two millennia.

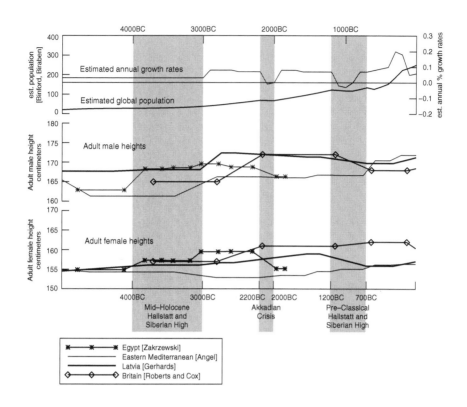

Figure III.6. Adult stature in the Mediterranean and Europe, 5000 BC–AD 1.

Stature from series from the Ancient Mediterranean and Europe suggests that adult height often varied with the broader climate history, improving in optima and declining with crises.

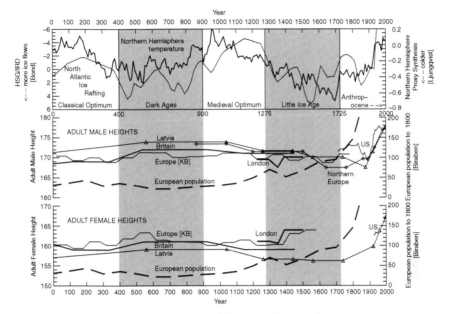

Figure III.7. Adult stature in Europe and the United States, AD 1–2000.

More detailed records of adult heights from the last two millennia suggest a pattern linked more with population scale and patterns of state formation. Between the Roman era and the Dark Ages, populations fell and heights increased, suggesting that isolation from imperial disease circulation and improved land/labor ratios offset the impact of colder, wetter climates. A similar pattern may be apparent as medieval populations, surviving the Black Death, entered the Early Little Ice Age, but the extreme conditions of the final Little Ice Age may have impacted height and health.

Sources: Latvia: Gerhards; Britain: Roberts and Cox, in Cohen and Crane-Kramer;

Europe [KB]: Koepke and Baten; European population: Biraben; London: Museum of London Center for Bioarchaeology: Spital Square, East Smithfield, and St, Mary Graces cemeteries, London [See Chapter 9, note 60] Northern Europe: Steckel, 2004.

US: Steckel, Historical Statistics [Bd653–67].

Except for the decadal US data, reported heights displayed for the middle three-fifths of period only; otherwise free-floating.

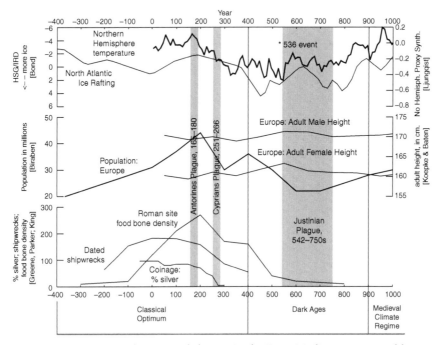

Figure III.8. Economy, climate, and disease in the Euro-Mediterranean world, 400 BC–AD 1000.

Estimates of population and economic indicators chart the trajectory of the economic vitality of the Roman Empire, undermined after the mid-2nd century by epidemic disease, climate change, and political failures. Strikingly, adult heights may have improved as the population shrank and the economy faltered.

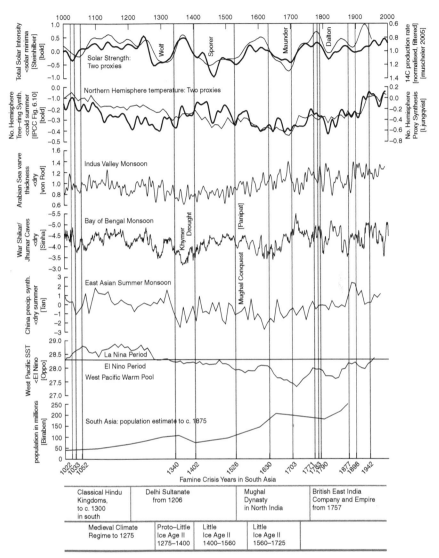

Figure III.9. Climate and famine in South Asia, AD 1000–2000.

As in the history of dynastic collapse in China, the sequence of recorded famines in India aligns broadly with the climatic record, most obviously in the apparent absence of recorded famines during the better part of the Medieval Climate Anomaly, when a dominant La Nina pattern in the Pacific shaped strong monsoons in South Asia. The early eleventh-century famines may have been part of the general crisis that struck from Egypt to Iran. Sources for South Asian famines: See Chapter 10, Notes 71 and 73.

257

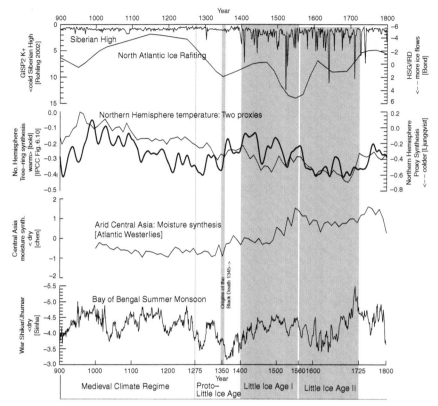

Figure III.10. The Little Ice Age and the Black Death.

The climatic preconditions of the Black Death are a matter of some debate. It appears that Northern Hemispheric temperatures had been dropping for several centuries, and that ice had started to form in the North Atlantic around 1260. The South Asian Monsoon had been declining since the 1250s, heading toward the extremes of the Khymer Drought in the 1360s. As the global system cooled and shifted south, the North Atlantic Oscillation shifted from positive toward a negative mode, increasing winter precipitation from the Atlantic westerlies through the Mediterranean and into Central Asia, which had been particularly arid during the Medieval Climate Regime. The first impact of enhanced rainfall on the steppes may have launched the Black Death, as rodent and flea populations bearing the bubonic plague bacillus would have expanded sharply with rising humidity.

TABLE III.IA. Estimated global population growth rates, 9000 BC–AD 2030

	Population in millions at		Elapsed Years	Annual Growth Rate
	Opening Date	Closing Date		
Global: 9000–3000BC	7.0	38.0	6,000	0.03%
3000–2000	38.0	68.0	1,000	0.06%
2000–1000	68.0	118.0	1,000	0.06%
1000–500	118.0	139.0	500	0.03%
500–400	139.0	153.0	100	0.10%
400–300	153.0	187.0	100	0.20%
300–200	187.0	225.0	100	0.18%
200–100	225.0	237.0	100	0.05%
100BC–AD 0	237.0	252.0	100	0.06%
AD 0–100	252.0	252.0	100	0.00%
100–200	252.0	257.0	100	0.02%
200–300	257.0	222.0	100	−0.15%
300–400	222.0	206.0	100	−0.07%
400–500	206.0	207.0	100	0.00%
500–600	207.0	208.0	100	0.00%
600–700	208.0	206.0	100	−0.01%
700–800	206.0	224.0	100	0.08%
800–900	224.0	222.0	100	−0.01%
900–1000	222.0	253.0	100	0.13%
1000–1100	253.0	299.0	100	0.17%
1100–1200	299.0	400.0	100	0.29%
1200–1250	400.0	417.0	100	0.04%
1250–1300	417.0	431.0	100	0.03%
1300–1340	431.0	442.0	40	0.06%
1340–1400	442.0	380.0	60	−0.25%
1400–1500	380.0	477.0	100	0.23%
1500–1550	477.0	539.5	50	0.25%
1550–1600	539.5	618.0	50	0.27%
1600–1650	618.0	619.3	50	0.00%
1600–1700	619.3	667.5	50	0.15%
1700–1750	667.5	776.3	50	0.30%
1750–1800	776.3	954.0	50	0.41%
1800–1850	954.0	1245.0	50	0.53%
1850–1900	1245.0	1641.0	50	0.55%
1900–1950	1641.0	2536.0	50	0.87%
1950–2000	2536.0	6050.0	50	1.74%
2000–2011	6050.0	7000.0	11	1.33%
2011–2030	7000.0	8174.0	19	0.82%

Sources: see note for Table II.1, Biraben, Maddison.
Compare with Figure III.1.

TABLE III.1B. Estimated population growth rates, selected world regions, 400 BC–AD 2000

	Population in millions at		Elapsed Years	Annual Growth Rate
	Opening Date	Closing Date		
China 400BC–AD 0 (Biraben)	19.0	70.0	400	0.33%
Mediterranean World 400BC–AD 200 (McEvedy and Jones)	28.0	50.0	600	0.10%
Italy 400BC–AD 0 (McEvedy and Jones)	4.0	7.0	400	0.14%
Song China 1000–1200 (Biraben)	58.0	124.0	200	0.38%
England 1205–1315 (Clark MPL data)	3.3	6.1	110	0.56%
China 1700–1850 (Biraben)	150	435	150	0.71%
Europe (excluding Russia) 1700–1850 (Biraben)	95	209	150	0.53%
United Kingdom and Ireland 1700–1850 (Madisson)	8.6	27.2	150	0.77%
All other Europe 1700–1850 (Biraben)	86.4	181.8	150	0.50%
United States 1700–1850 (Hist Stat)	0.25	23.6	150	3.03%
Europe and United States 1700–1850	95.25	232.6	150	0.60%
Global 1700–1850 (Biraben)	667.5	1245	150	0.42%
China, Europe, United States 1700–1850 (Biraben)	245.25	667.6	150	0.67%
All other 1700–1850 (Biraben)	422.25	577.4	150	0.21%
China 1850–2000	435	1262	150	0.71%
Europe (excluding Russia) 1850–2000	209	514	150	0.60%
United States 1850–2000	23.6	282	150	1.65%
Europe and the United States 1850–2000	232.6	796	150	0.82%
Global 1850–2000	1245	6050	150	1.05%
China, Europe, United States 1850–2000	667.6	2058	150	0.75%
All other 1850–2000	577.4	3992	150	1.29%

6

Stasis and Growth in the Epoch of Agrarian Empires

Getting Ahead, Running in Place, Falling Behind

Around 3000 BC, driven by the abrupt final crisis of the Mid-Holocene transition, the state organization of society suddenly began to emerge in particular locations in the Old World, first in Mesopotamia and Egypt, then the Indus Valley, and the Yellow River Valley of China. Now, in the early twenty-first century, we look back over 5,000 years of "history," defined as such by the bureaucratic organization of the state and the writing systems that support it. Even within those 5,000 years, however, our modern condition emerged only yesterday, grounded in an industrial transition to fossil fuel that began only 300 years ago, on a world economy of center and periphery that emerged only 500 years ago with the rise and spread of early modern European empires. These 500 years encompass the early modern and modern transformations that will be the subject of Part IV of this book. Part III examines the forty-four centuries that intervened between the rise of the state and the opening of the crises that would lead eventually to global modernity. More precisely, I close my account of premodernity around AD 1350, after New World societies had been severely impacted by medieval droughts and as Old World societies were feeling the first manifestations of the Little Ice Age and facing the devastation of the grievous mortality of the Black Death.

What then of the ancient and medieval worlds that occupied the global stage between "prehistory" and "modernity"? The rise of modernity, with its global reach, massive population and economic growth, and energy revolutions can make these worlds look paltry by comparison, a long, flat-line epoch of stagnant agrarian economies governed by unchanging autocratic states. From this perspective, ancient and medieval societies simply were bound in a "Malthusian trap" of the limits of the organic economy. Economic growth was limited to either additive territorial expansion of growing populations to new territories – increasingly by imperial violence – or by an equally additive intensification of commerce, labor, and organic technologies, so-called

Smithian growth. Economists and demographers seeking to unravel the origins of modernity contrast these forms of extensive and intensive growth against the sustained Promethean or "Schumpeterian" growth of modern economies, driven by accelerating cycles of advanced technological innovation in a fossil-fueled, mineral-based economy. For these scholars, the central problem of world history involves explaining the forces and factors that would allow strategic populations to break out of the Malthusian trap and onto the road to modern sustained economic growth, in a punctuation as powerful and far more rapid than those Niles Eldridge and Stephen Jay Gould proposed for the paleo-past.[1]

These are indeed important questions, and I attend to them in Part IV. But the economists' focus on the immediate origins of the modern world obscures the character of human experience during the four and a half millennia preceding. In this and the next three chapters I look at the Bronze Age, Iron Age, antiquity, and the Middle Ages in a compression that violates historical conventions (and historians' sensibilities), and which perhaps concedes too much to the economists' flat-line view of the archaic world. But my purpose is to achieve a more nuanced perspective on the natural and human forces at work between the end of prehistory and the dawn of modernity.[2]

My arguments here are heretical to some schools of thought – but supported by others. First I stand – in pretty good company – in quiet critique

---

[1] For an influential sample of this important literature, see most recently, Gregory Clark, *From Alms to Riches: A Brief Economic History of the World* (Princeton, NJ, 2007); and Jacob L. Weisdorf, "From Stagnation to Growth: Revisiting Three Historical Regimes," *Journal of Population Economics* 17 (2004), 455–72; Niles-Peter Lagerlof, "From Malthus to Modern Growth: Can Epidemics Explain the Three Regimes?" *International Economic Review* 44 (2003), 755–77; Charles I. Jones, "Was an Industrial Revolution Inevitable? Economic Growth over the Very Long Run," *Advances in Microeconomics* 1 (2001), 1–43; Oded Galor and David N. Weil, "Population, Technology, and Growth: From Malthusian Stagnation to the Demographic Transition and Beyond," *AER* 90 (2000), 806–28; Michael Kremmer, "Population Growth and Technological Change: One Million B.C. to 1990," *Quarterly Journal of Economics* 108 (1993), 681–716. On punctuations in economic history, see Joel Mokyr, "Punctuated Equilibria and Technological Progress," *AER* 80 (1990), 350–4; and "Evolution and Technological Change: A New Metaphor for Economic History?" in Robert Fox, ed., *Technological Change: Methods and Themes in the History of Technology* (Amsterdam, 1996), 63–83.

[2] Across these forty-four centuries, human societies can be divided into two broad categories. On one hand, large world populations in the "monsoon belt" running from a European fringe through North Africa, Southwest, South, and East Asia, and organized in tribute and military empires and petty kingdoms, had agroecologies based on grain monocrops and domesticated animals, which provided not only food but traction power. On the other hand, a substantial minority of global populations distributed across the global tropics and the Americas were variously grounded on mixed horticultures and varying forms of hunting and gathering. Very broadly, these have been described as the worlds of the plow and hoe; they can also be described as societies with higher and lower population densities and societal rates of energetic metabolism. Given the much larger impact of the societies of the plow, they will be the focus of most of the following chapters.

of those who dismiss completely the epoch of the archaic agrarian state as a stagnant, utterly Malthusian world. My company here is a group of world historians and historians of ancient and medieval economies. World historians of the likes of William H. McNeill, John R. McNeill, David Christian, and Fred Spier organize their interpretations around similar constructs of evolving systems of complexity. Christian and Spier carry their approach to systems complexity back into the evolutionary past, and situate a growing human social complexity in relation to a base of biological complexity. With the McNeills they also see a cumulative development of interaction, organization, and innovation emerging over the four ancient and medieval millennia that were the essential foundation for the explosive breakout to modernity in the past 500 years.[3] Victor Lieberman also has stressed the cumulative force in state formation, in his model of Bronze Age primary or pristine state empires, secondary Iron Age and classical empires, and medieval secondary monarchal states, to which we might add tertiary post-Columbian nation-states. Ian Morris takes a similarly cumulative approach in an important assessment of the long-term fortunes of China and the West.[4] These world historians take a long, developmental view for good reason; sustained modern economic growth did not and could not erupt out of the palace economies of the Bronze Age, any more than it could out of the Neolithic. Thus these historians focus on the cumulative development of human intellectual, technological, and sociopolitical capacities as forging a springboard for modernity.

A quite different school, the Marxian world system historians, has developed a comprehensive model of economic and political development running back from the early modern world to the beginnings of the Bronze Age. These world system historians propose that economic and political systems have ebbed and flowed over the past five millennia, and they seek to explain these oscillations in terms of system dynamics. If I do not follow the explanatory framework that the world system historians have developed, their chronology of cumulative expansion and contraction of economies provides a useful counterpoint to the flat-line view of the economists. And, with Victor Lieberman, I pay particular attention to "strange parallels" – the simultaneous ebb and flow of premodern economies over these millennia.[5]

---

[3] John R. McNeill and William H. McNeill, *The Human Web: A Bird's Eye View of World History* (New York, 2003); David Christian, *Maps of Time: An Introduction to Big History* (Berkeley, CA, 2004); Fred Spier, *The Structure of Big History: From the Big Bang until Today* (Amsterdam, 1996); and *Big History and the Future of Humanity* (Malden, MA, 2010).

[4] Victor Lieberman, *Strange Parallels: Southeast Asia in Global Context, c. 800–1830. Vol. II: Mainland Mirrors: Europe, Japan, China, South Asia and the Islands* (New York, 2009), 91, 108; Ian Morris, *Why the West Rules – For Now: The Patterns of History, and What They Reveal about the Future* (New York, 2010).

[5] The world systems historians have developed a sequence of "A" and "B" phases that summarizes broad patterns of ancient and medieval economies, grounded in the work of Annaliste

And many historians argue that several of these expansions involved real economic growth: specifically that classical antiquity and the Middle Ages saw not only effective innovative intensification in the face of growing numbers, but actual per capita improvement of conditions in those societies. Eric Jones, in an analysis of "growth recurring" since ancient times, defines premodern growth as both "extensive" and "intensive." His extensive growth is more Boserupian, as technologies and economies run in place with growing populations; his intensive growth is more Smithian, as that growth begins to lift the average standard of living. For Jones, the long-term operation of both of these modes of growth is essential in building the platform for Schumpeterian or "Promethean" growth of modern economies.[6] Jack Goldstone's very similar conception of "efflorescences" of growth is equally useful. Rather than simply dividing history into a flat line of stagnant, archaic regimes followed by a progressive modernity, Goldstone proposes a model of alternating *efflorescence* and *crisis* in premodernity: an

---

economic historian Francois Simiand, who described the early modern economy in terms of a series of 200-year expansionary "A-phases" and contracting "B-phases." Barry K. Gills and Andre Gunder Frank have expanded his sequence to reach back to the origins of the city and the state, at roughly 3000 BC, most recently in "The Five Thousand Year World System in Theory and Praxis," in Robert A. Denemark et al., eds., *World System History: The Social Science of Long-Term Change* (London and New York, 2000), 3–24. While I am agnostic on their cyclical world systems theory, their summary of 5,000 years of economic history is very useful. It has been tested in part by two other scholars, David Wilkinson and Andrew Bosworth, using city-size data from Tertius Chandler, *4000 Years of Urban Growth: An Historical Census* (Lewiston, 1987). I for the most part concur with the Wilkinson/Bosworth revisions of the Gill/Frank sequence, which do considerable violence to the idea of 200-year cycles in the ancient world. See David Wilkinson, "Decline Phases in Civilizations, Regions, and Oikumenes," in *Comparative Civilization Review* 33 (1995), 33–78; and Barry K. Gills and Andre Gunder Frank, "World System Cycles, Crises, and Hegemonial Shifts, 1700 B.C. to 1700 A.D.," *Review* 15 (1974), 621–87, in which they summarize Bosworth's critique on pp. 680–1. See also the essays in Stephen K. Sanderson, *Civilizations and World Systems: Studying World-Historical Change* (Walnut Creek, CA, 1995); Andre Gunder Frank and Barry K. Gills, *The World System: Five Hundred Years or Five Thousand?* (London, 1993); and Andre Gunder Frank, "Bronze Age World System Cycles," *CA* 34 (1993), 383–429; Andrew Sherratt, "What Would a Bronze-Age World System Look Like? Relations between Temperate Europe and the Mediterranean in Later Prehistory," *JEArch* 1 (1993), 1–57; and Guillermo Algaze, *The Uruk World System: The Dynamics of Early Mesopotamian Civilization*, second edition (Chicago, IL, 2005); Andre Gunder Frank and William R. Thompson, "Afro-Eurasian Bronze Age Economic Expansion and Contraction Revisited," *JWH* 16 (2005), 115–72; Philippe Beaujard, "The Indian Ocean in Eurasian and African World-Systems before the Sixteenth Century," *JWH* 16 (2005), 391–410; Philippe Beaujard, "From Three Possible Iron-Age World Systems to a Single Afro-Eurasian World-System," *JWH* 21 (2010), 1–44. On synchronous patterns in Old World history, see Lieberman, *Strange Parallels*, II: 77–92.

[6] Eric L. Jones, *Growth Recurring: Economic Change in World History* (Ann Arbor, MI, 2000 [1988]). On extensive, Smithian, and Schumpeterian growth, see also Jan de Vries, "Economic Growth before and after the Industrial Revolution: A Modest Proposal," in Maarten Prak, ed., *Early Modern Capitalism: Economic and Social Change in Europe, 1400–1800* (New York, 2001), 177–94, esp. 178–89.

efflorescence brought "a relatively sharp, often unexpected upturn in significant demographic and economic indices, usually accompanied by political expansion and institution building and cultural synthesis and consolidation." Goldstone's efflorescences combine elements of territorial expansion with Boserupian intensification and Smithian growth, shaped by hard work and the division of labor without any necessarily fundamental technological change. Goldstone's crises reversed most of these advances, but after the emergence of systems of writing a crisis might not erase all of the cultural and institutional paradigms developed in efflorescences, allowing the slow, irregular, cumulative advance stressed by the world historians.[7]

I will not argue, however, that the conditions of life for the great majority of humanity improved more than incrementally over the very long term of the premodern epoch. If occasionally certain fortunate populations may have indeed "gotten ahead" in short, "efflorescent" bursts of real if limited economic growth, most of the energy benefits of the technological innovation that occurred over these millennia was consumed by population growth that significantly surpassed that of the Neolithic.[8] We should also recognize that one society's growth through "territorial expansion" was another society's loss. Adam Smith wrote in *The Wealth of Nations* about the "dreadful misfortunes" that befell the societies of the New World after Columbus's arrival, and we need to consider the role of plunder and conquest in shaping the economic fortunes of ancient empires, as well as more modern states.[9] Imperial ventures did not necessarily contribute to the sum of human well-being. More generally, the Malthusian trap of organic economies may well have shaped a pervasive "running in place," with societies gradually innovating and intensifying simply to maintain life as it had been known in the past. And while many societies, particularly large, powerful empires, were able to maintain large populations in reasonably good conditions for many decades, even many hundreds of years, the axe inevitably fell. Populations and economies did "fall behind," often catastrophically so, collapsing in civilizational disasters that tore the fabric of history.

But *why* did ancient societies fall behind? Why did ancient civilizations collapse in ruins? My second heretical proposition is one that I have come to

7   Jack A. Goldstone, "Efflorescences and Economic Growth in World History: Rethinking the 'Rise of the West' and the Industrial Revolution," *JWH* 13 (2002), 323–90, see esp. 323–7, 333–4, and 379. See also Jack A. Goldstone, "Neither Late Imperial nor Early Modern: Efflorescences and the Qing Formation in World History," in Lynn A. Struve, ed., *The Qing Formation in World-Historical Time* (Cambridge, MA, 2004), 242–302.

8   Ronald D. Lee, "Malthus and Boserup: A Dynamic Synthesis," in David Coleman and Roger S. Scholfield, eds., *The State of Population Theory: Forward from Malthus* (Oxford, 1986), 96–103; James W. Wood, "A Theory of Preindustrial Population Dynamics: Demography, Economy, and Well-Being in Malthusian Systems," *CA* 39 (1998), 99–216.

9   Adam Smith, *An Inquiry into the Nature and Causes of the Wealth of Nations* (Edinburgh, 1843), 258–9 (book IV, chapter 7, part 3).

gradually, after much puzzlement. Here we need to untangle the Malthusian *trap* from the Malthusian *crisis*. For the past four decades, since the rise of the environmental movement, the new school of environmental history has argued that intensification of premodern agricultural economies inevitably led to degradation, further intensification, and eventual collapse. Modeling its interpretation of the ancient and medieval past on the environmental critique of modern economies, a dominant school of environmental historians has consistently argued that human populations – in their multiplication and day-to-day will to survive – have always been the fundamental root cause of their own demise. Human history has thus been in this account a tale of recurring Malthusian *crises of sustainability*, a tale that has been mobilized as an object lesson for our contemporary global circumstance.[10] I call this the *endogenous model* – endogenous in the sense that all of the significant factors at play were structurally *internal* to societies of the archaic agrarian world. Nature "acts" only as it is passively degraded. This endogenous model in environmental history is obviously a corollary of the economists' Malthusianism. Both share a primary explicit premise that archaic technological development could not keep up with archaic population growth. Thus growing populations pushed societies beyond the limits of economic and ecological sustainability, leading to inevitable "collapse." Such is the title of an important and influential book by Jared Diamond, who has most recently advanced this argument. Such degradations did take place and, as Diamond and others show, this dynamic did lead to the collapse of archaic societies – in isolated and ecologically delicate situations. "Ecologically delicate situations" is the operative phrase. But I argue that there is no evidence that intensification or degradation – or a condition of Malthusian stalemate – led independently to the collapse of a large civilization in the Old World or the New.

Thus my second heresy is related to my first. Despite the Malthusian assumptions of the economists I posit that – all things being equal, and on the basis of good evidence – ancient and medieval societies in *reasonably robust ecological situations* were sustained for considerable periods of time without running into fundamental constraints of technology. Incremental gains in population were matched by slow technological innovation; if

---

[10] Jared Diamond, *Collapse: How Societies Choose to Fail or Succeed* (New York, 2005); Sing C. Chew, *World Ecological Degradation: Accumulation, Urbanization, and Deforestation, 3000 B.C.–A.D. 2000* (Walnut Creek, CA, 2001); Charles L. Redman, *Human Impact on Ancient Environments* (Tucson, AZ, 1999); Clive Ponting, *A Green History of the World* (London, 1992). Marvin Harris laid the fundamentals of the "endogenous model" in *Cannibals and Kings: The Origins of Cultures* (New York, 1977). David Christian, in *Maps of Time*, follows this argument in his account of Malthusian cycles of human history. For other important statements of the endogenous model, see Michael Williams, *Deforesting the Earth: From Prehistory to Global Crisis* (Chicago, IL, 2003), 37–144; Neil Roberts, *The Holocene: An Environmental History*, second edition (Malden, MA, 1998), 159–206.

minor shifts in rainfall brought localized famine and minor outbreaks of disease brought elevated mortality, societies soon rebounded. Contrary to the Malthusian assumptions of many environmental historians I posit a corollary: all things being equal, archaic human societies did achieve a *reasonably sustainable condition* in the "second nature" that human societies wove with the "first nature" of the preagricultural landscape.[11]

But all things were not equal. Neither the economists nor the ecologists have factored in the role of severe exogenous natural forces. Nature mattered, whether a society was standing pat in a Malthusian deadlock, advancing with some signs of economic growth, or sliding into endogenous degradation. Abrupt climate change was real, and had powerful impacts on the fate of premodern human societies. Agricultural and timbering practices certainly degraded soils and watersheds, but it was generally in a trajectory of deteriorating climate that these practices led to civilizational crises. So too new diseases striking unaccustomed ancient and medieval populations were fundamentally destructive. Certainly many of the disease vectors in the archaic world were "domesticated" and essentially endogenous, circulating recurrently around the large population centers in the Old World. But before they were "domesticated," they were "wild": and it was the new disease emerging at random out of the natural world and striking "virgin soil populations" that had the most civilizationally damaging impacts. Populations did not crash and civilizations did not topple at every minor ripple in the climate or local outbreak of smallpox. But when they did, serious large-scale climate change and virgin soil epidemics – both *exogenous forces* operating at a scale *beyond the imagination and control of these societies* – have been at work. Civilizational crises in the ancient and premodern world, Goldstone's premodern crises, may have been *conditioned* by endogenous degradation of sustainability, but they were fundamentally driven by natural forces *exogenous* to human society.[12]

Both the Goldstone/Jones model of "efflorescences recurring" and my stress on exogenous forces can be assimilated to the new model of ecological

---

[11] The framework of humanity's "second nature" was developed most notably in William Cronon, *Nature's Metropolis: Chicago and the Great West* (New York, 1991), 56–7, 265–9; and fundamentally informs Simon Schama, *Landscape and Memory* (New York, 1995).

[12] Here see Solomon M. Hsiang et al., "Quantifying the Influence of Climate on Human Conflict," *Science* 341, (2013), DOI:10.1126/science.1235367; David D. Zhang et al., "The Causality Analysis of Climate Change and Large-Scale Human Crisis," *PNAS* 108 (2011), 17296–301; Harry F. Lee et al., "Climatic Change and Chinese Population Growth Dynamics of the Last Millennium," *ClimCh* 88 (2008), 131–56; David D. Zhang et al., "Global Climate Change, War, and Population Decline in Recent Human History," *PNAS* 104 (2007), 19214–19; "Climate Change and War Frequency in Eastern China over the Last Millennium," *HumEcol* 35 (2007), 403–14, esp. 413; "Climatic Change, Wars, and Dynastic Cycles in China over the Last Millennium," *ClimCh* 76 (2006), 459–77. See also Zhibin Zhang et al., "Periodical Climate Cooling Enhanced Natural Disasters and Wars in China during AD 10–1900," *Proceedings of the Royal Society B* 277 (2010), 3745–53.

resilience, which posits that natural and social systems evolve through adaptive cycles of expansion, crisis, and reorganization, with long-range cumulative trajectories. Resilience theory had its origins in the efforts of ecologists to think historically about ecosystems in an earth systems context, and in fact much of the discussion in this book to this point can be understood in its terms. But new forces come increasingly into play. Proto-human and early human societies were almost as directly impacted by natural crises as were animal and plant populations, but human-ness itself introduces new variables of the coordinating power of culture and then the state. Indeed it is an essential quality of humanity to remember and to predict, and to act to avert or at least deflect exogenous impacts, to extend and even transform the adaptive cycle. This approach is driving an emerging critique of Jared Diamond's popular model of "collapse," stressing the resilient reformation of social, cultural, and political forms in the face of serious challenges. Most important, these forms involved increasingly sophisticated varieties of the state.[13]

Part III explores the human condition of ancient and medieval societies in the wide space between the natural world and the state. But it is worthwhile thinking through the implications of the two interpretive pairings that I have here proposed. It is clear that the economists' stagnation model is inherently associated with the environmental historians' endogenous degradation model: both assume a closed circle of causation: population growth inevitably transcends technological abilities and local environments. Conversely, the world historian's "slow and episodic growth/cumulative knowledge model" and the natural scientist's exogenous "rough world" model share wild card factors. The world historians take human culture seriously, and the physical scientists take nature seriously. On the surface, these two understandings are in tension: the cumulative growth of knowledge – and of economies – was episodically and savagely interrupted by the natural forces of drastic climate shift and "wild" pandemic. But perhaps one explains the other. Human capacities meant that ancient and medieval societies with slowly rising populations at least "ran in place" and often even inched "ahead"; natural forces were the fundamental cause when they "fell

---

[13] On resilience theory, see the essays in Lance H. Gunderson and C. C. Holling, eds., *Panarchy: Understanding Transformations in Human and Natural Systems* (Washington, DC, 2002); Carl Folke, "Resilience: The Emergence of a Perspective for Social-Ecological Systems Analysis," *GEC* 16 (2006), 253–67; Charles Redman, "Resilience Theory in Archaeology," *AmAnth* 107 (2005), 70–7. For increasingly sophisticated applications to long-term history, see Glenn M. Schwartz and John J. Nichols, eds., *After Collapse: The Regeneration of Complex Societies* (Tucson, AZ, 2006), 137–43; Patricia A. McAnamy and Norman Yoffee, eds., *Questioning Collapse: Human Resilience, Ecological Vulnerability and the Aftermath of Empire* (New York, 2010); Joseph Tainter, "The Archaeology of Overshoot and Collapse," *ARA* 35 (2006), 59–74; and Karl W. Butzer, "Collapse, Environment, and Society," *PNAS* 109 (2012), 3632–9.

behind." And, in the terms of the resilience theorists, civilizational structures rarely completely disappeared, but continually reemerged to reform expanding societies.

These relationships between cultural capacity and natural forcings seem to have operated in two contradictory ways. The first of these explanations is grounded in the understandings developed for the Paleolithic past by James Boone and Stephen Shennan, and for the recent condition by Robert Fogel.[14] Severe crisis mortality limited the curve of technological development, sharply reversing both the human capital and the population demands that have driven such directional change. A possible technological trajectory may have been emerging in ancient Rome, China's Sung epoch, and late medieval Europe, but in each case crisis truncated a possible "efflorescent" path toward the future. Escaping a mortality crisis between 1500 and 1800 with the first rudiments of public health, the capture of primary productivity in imperial extraction, and the shift to fossil fuel, northwest Europe launched itself into that future at the turn of the nineteenth century. Conversely, however, civilizational crisis could sometimes play a role of creative destruction, clearing out cultural roadblocks that stood in the way of fundamental and cumulative change. Thus a prior crisis – that of the Black Death – and an ongoing stress – that of the Little Ice Age – played formative roles in Europe's trajectory out of the Middle Ages.

In the chapters that follow I test the case for and against the endogenous model of human stagnation in the face of population growth, and the exogenous model of human trajectories cut short by unimaginable natural crises. To set the stage, we need to briefly sketch the broad parameters of population growth, climate change, disease, and social and technological innovation over these four and a half millennia between the first rise of the state and the devastation wrought by the Black Death.

* * *

Population Growth and Dark Ages

A casual glance at our shaky understanding of global population growth since the end of the Pleistocene ice ages provides a good starting point for our discussion.[15] Three points stand out. Global population during the

---

[14] James L. Boone, "Subsistence Strategies and Early Human Population History: An Evolutionary Ecological Perspective," *WdArch* 34 (2002), 6–25; Stephen Shennan, "Demography and Cultural Innovation: A Model and Its Implications for the Emergence of Modern Human Culture," *CArchJ* 11 (2001), 5–16; Robert Fogel, *The Escape from Hunger and Premature Death, 1700–2100: Europe, America, and the Third World* (New York, 2004).

[15] The following analysis is based on two estimates that come to roughly similar conclusions, if differing somewhat in detail: Colin McEvedy and Richard Jones, *Atlas of World Population*

Neolithic certainly grew faster than during the Paleolithic, but the age of the archaic state brought a surge of population growth: the Bronze Age doubled the Neolithic rate, and periods of the Iron Age might have more than doubled that again (see Figure III.1, Table III.1a). By AD 200, world population had reached a total of roughly 250 million, and the height of the Middle Ages saw more than 400 million people on earth. Thus the first point is obvious: *ancient global population growth was tied to the emergence of the archaic state.* The second point is equally obvious, and is the staple of the Malthusian economists' approach: *ancient and medieval populations and growth rates were miniscule compared to the exponential proliferation of peoples that began around 1750,* and resulted in the surge to one billion total global population by 1820 and the present 7 billion level less than 200 years later.

The third point is less obvious, particularly if one assumes a simple, smooth curve of population growth. *But population growth rates between 3000 BC and AD 1800 could not possibly have followed a smooth curve.* Rather, growth rates were interrupted by devastating reversals: the population reversals of the Black Death of the 1300s and of the plagues at the end of the ancient world have been measured with some rough degree of accuracy; earlier reversals can only be guessed at. These reversals fundamentally deflected population growth trajectories. If population had grown at the Bronze Age rate of .07 percent per year, it would have only slightly exceeded the actual increase through roughly 1600; a .1 percent annual increase would have brought the world's people to the one billion threshold by AD 1200, rather than in 1820. Combining these rates – with a .07 percent annual increase from 5000–1000 BC followed by a .1 percent annual increase – would have produced global populations almost twice the actual size after AD 800, and reached the one billion threshold around 1700. Obviously this hypothetical trajectory misses the mark by hundreds of years. World population increased incrementally before 1700, and then exploded, with a massive acceleration during the twentieth century. And rather than smoothly growing through time, human populations – particularly those in the high-population, high-energy metabolism Old World societies running from the Mediterranean and its hinterlands east to India and China – were periodically reduced by devastating setbacks. Such a model of a rising and falling line of global population growth rates would reflect

History (New York, 1978), and an alternative slightly higher set of numbers presented in Jean-Noël Biraben, "Essai sur l'Evolution do Nombre des Hommes," *Population* 34 (1979), 13–24, though the growth rates are roughly similar. Biraben's numbers are considerably more variable than those in McEvedy and Jones, and he presents the case for serious mortality crises governing the trajectory of the growth of human populations adopted here. The baseline of 7 million at 9000 BC is from Lewis L. Binford, *Constructing Frames of Reference: An Analytical Method for Archaeological Theory Building Using Hunter-Gatherer and Environmental Data Sets* (Berkeley, CA, 2001), 142–4 (see Chapter 5, note 11).

at least seven setbacks – the Mid-Holocene transition, the "Akkadian" crisis of 2200–2000 BC, the terminal Bronze Age crisis of 1200–1000 BC, the Homeric solar minimum of 700–500 BC, the collapse of the ancient world at AD 300–500 and the impact of the climatic Dark Ages through 900, and the mid-fourteenth-century Black Death and the Little Ice Age crisis of the seventeenth century (see Figure III.1.)[16] It is a much more realistic picture than any smooth and gentle curve of population growth.

This model of a series of cycles of population growth and collapse probably best describes the most fundamental pulse of the human condition in the era of the Late Holocene. As I have argued for the Paleolithic, mortality crises that slowed or reversed the rate of population growth had powerful cumulative effects. While certainly not as catastrophic as the local extinctions that severely curtailed Paleolithic populations, these demographic reversals limited the cumulative expansion of population down to the very dawn of the modern era.

With the exception of the Mayan collapse around AD 900, none of these massive setbacks feature in the standard list of civilization collapses typically discussed by environmental historians, who dwell on the unique dramas of tiny island isolates like the Greenland Norse or the Easter Islanders.[17] But archaeologists and historians of many schools have broadly described these as "Dark Ages," and despite its hyperbolic quality this term is a useful one.[18] During these periods – usually spanning several centuries – famine,

---

[16] My estimation of global population in Figure III.1 is obviously highly speculative. It is bracketed by Binford's estimate of 7 million hunter-gatherers in an optimum Early Holocene world and Biraben's figure of 153 million at 400 BC. I posit 38 million total at 3000 BC (which is probably high), a global population stabilization at 2200–2000 BC, and ~9 percent decline at 1200–1000 BC, and otherwise interpolate. Biraben's data indicated a drop in population at AD 900, driven by reversals in China, India, and Mesoamerica.

[17] See in particular Diamond, *Collapse*; Ponting, *A Green History of the World*; and Redman, *Human Impact on Ancient Environments*.

[18] The literature informing the expansion/efflorescence versus Dark Age/crisis framework that I use in this chapter is vast. Among the work that has been particularly influential in my thinking I would include Goldstone on "efflorescences"; the world systems literature cited in note 5; Patrick R. Galloway, "Long-Term Fluctuations in Climate and Population in the Preindustrial Era," *PopDevR* 12 (1986), 1–24; Reid A. Bryson, "Civilization and Rapid Climate Change," *Environmental Conservation* 15 (1988), 7–15; Karl W. Butzer, "Environmental Change in the Near East and Human Impact on the Land," in Jack M. Sasson, ed., *Civilizations of the Ancient Near East*, vol. 1 (Farmington Hills, MI, 1995), 123–51; M. G. L. Baillie, "Extreme Environmental Events and the Linking of Tree-Ring and Ice-Core Events," in Jeffrey S. Dean et al., eds., *Tree Rings, Environment, and Humanity: Proceedings of the International Conference, Tucson, Arizona, May 17–21, 1994* (Tucson, AZ, 1996), 703–11; Joyce Marcus, "The Peaks and Valley of Ancient State: An Extension of the Dynamic Model," in Gary M. Feinman and Joyce Marcus, *Archaic States* (Santa Fe, NM, 1998), 59–94, as qualified by Roger Matthews, *The Archaeology of Mesopotamia: Theories and Approaches* (London, 2003), 100–1; Benny J. Peiser et al., *Natural Catastrophes during Bronze Age Civilizations: Archaeological, Geological, Astronomical and Cultural Perspectives* (Oxford, 1998); Harvey Weiss and Raymond S. Bradley, "What Drives Societal

epidemics, rebellions, and invasions singly and in "perfect storm" disrupted societies, destroyed ancient polities, and reduced and scattered populations. In the interval economies, societies, polities, and populations restructured and recovered, usually restoring a prior status quo, occasionally forging a significantly new configuration of culture and economy. Time and again, these reversals define the boundaries between long-established periods in the archeological and historical record. These "Dark Ages" can be visualized as punctuations in the sense proposed by Niles Eldridge and Stephen J. Gould, the historical and cultural equivalents of the great environmental punctuations in geological time that drove biological evolution.

The elements of this story are the fundamental forces of nature and culture, locked in a contest that we in the modern era seem to think – or thought until very recently – that culture had finally won. Certainly culture in the form of agricultural improvement and modern medicine has allowed us to dodge global famine and devastating epidemic since the 1960s, in the form of the Green Revolution and the campaign against AIDS. Our ancient and medieval forbears had less to work with, and suffered the consequences. But as the world historians stress, their cumulative efforts laid the ground for modernity, and gradually improved – within severe limits – the odds of their survival against the onslaught of natural forces.

* * *

Endogenous Degradations?

The collapse of ancient civilizations has been a topic of particular attention of environmental historians for the past several decades, and until relatively recently there has been a dominant interpretation: intensification of human economies led to ecological degradation of local and regional environments, setting the stage for civilizational crises. Such certainly makes sense from our commonsense observations of the modern world, and the histories of ancient peoples and places seem to provide a cautionary tale for our present condition.[19] Certainly such degradations did take place: forests were cut

Collapse?" *Science* 291 (2001), 609–10; Peter B. deMenocal, "Cultural Responses to Climate Change during the Late Holocene," *Science* 292 (2001), 667–73; Sing C. Chew, "Globalization, Ecological Crisis, and Dark Ages," *Global Society* 16 (2002), 333–56; Chew, *World Ecological Degradation*; Chew, *The Recurring Dark Ages: Ecological Stress, Climate Changes, and System Transformation* (Lanham, MD, 2007); Roger Matthews, "Zebu: Harbingers of Doom in Bronze Age Western Asia?" *Antiquity* 76 (2002), 438–46; Marc van de Mieroop, *A History of the Ancient Near East, ca. 3000–323 B.C.* (Malden, MA, 2004), 37–8, 67–70, 115–17, 179–94; Kristian Kristianson and Thomas B. Larrson, *The Rise of Bronze Age Society: Travels, Transmissions, and Transformations* (New York, 2005), 105–6; Claudia Migowski et al., "Holocene Climate Variability and Cultural Evolution in the Near East from the Dead Sea Sedimentary Record," *QuatRes* 66 (2006), 421–31.

[19] Harris, *Cannibals and Kings: The Origins of Cultures*; I. G. Simmons, *Changing the Face of the Earth: Culture, Environment, History* (Malden, MA, 1989); Ponting, *A Green*

down, soils were lost or salinized, water tables were depleted. And certainly human activity contributed to change in regional ecologies as measured in pollen stratigraphy and sedimentation, for example. But these human "signals" – as much as they altered natural environments – did not necessarily mark the crisis points of human existence. As Israeli archaeologists Arie Issar and Mattahyah Zohar have recently put it, a general swinging of the interpretive pendulum is under way. In the face of new and precise studies by paleoecologists, profound ecological changes that until very recently were ascribed to the impacts of human activity are now understood as much more complicated processes in which gradual or abrupt climate change played the more significant role.[20]

In the following chapters, I consider the classic cases where human degradation has traditionally been seen as causing the collapse of ancient civilization. The evidence for Mesopotamia, the Indus, and the Mayan Yucatan suggests that – at best – human action interacted with climatic change. In China and along the Peruvian coast, while deforestation was certainly a problem, no scholar has ever proposed that human action contributed to the collapse of civilization.

The debate over the relative roles of human and natural forces in the fate of ancient landscapes has been particularly heated in regards to the ancient Mediterranean world from the Bronze Age through the end of the Roman empire, and this literature is worth reviewing here. The environmental history of the Mediterranean was long dominated by two controversial figures, Claudio Vita-Finzi and Donald Hughes, both of whom saw the hand of humanity in a decline of Mediterranean landscapes and ecologies. In the late 1960s, Vita-Finzi, a geologist, proposed that the sedimentary geology of the Mediterranean was dominated by two massive features, an

---

History of the World; Roberts, *The Holocene: An Environmental History*; Redman, *Human Impact on Ancient Environments*; Michael Williams, "Dark Ages and Dark Areas: Global Deforestation in the Deep Past," *Journal of Historical Geography* 26 (2000), 28–46; Chew, *World Ecological Degradation*; Michael Williams, *Deforesting the Earth: From Prehistory to Global Crisis*; Diamond, *Collapse*. For a global survey, see Patrick V. Kirch, "Archaeology and Global Change: The Holocene Record," *Annual Reviews in Environmental Resources* 30 (2005), 409–40.

[20] Arie S. Issar and Mattanyah Zohar, *Climate Change – Environment and Civilization in the Middle East* (Berlin, 2004), 1–12, 137–8. For candid admissions of shifts from endogenous cultural to exogenous climate explanations in Mid-Eastern archaeology, see Bernhard Weninger et al., "Climate Forcing due to the 8200 cal yr BP Event Observed at Early Neolithic Sites in the Eastern Mediterranean," *QuatRes* 66 (2006), 401–20, at 418; Matthews, *The Archaeology of Mesopotamia*, 100–1, critiquing (in 2003) Marcus's 1998 interpretations that ignore climate change ("Peaks and Valleys") (full cites in note 14). For critiques, see Arlene Miller Rosen, *Civilizing Climate: Social Responses to Climate Change in the Ancient Near East* (Lanham, MD, 2007), 1–16; Paul Coombes and Keith Barber, "Environmental Determinism in Holocene Research: Causality or Coincidence?" *Area* 37 (2005), 303–11. For a theoretical perspective, see Wood, "Theory of Preindustrial Population Dynamics," 117–18. Charles Redman, having argued strongly for a degradation model, is taking a more neutral position: see "Resilience Theory in Archaeology," 74–6.

Older Fill deposited during the ice ages, and a Younger Fill, sediments set loose by human action from the late Roman empire to the Middle Ages. Hughes, an ancient historian, worked from literary texts to describe environmental decline at the hands of ancient peoples; most recently he has focused in *Pan's Travail* on the Greeks and Romans and the decline of the Mediterranean.[21] Both of these interpretations have been challenged in the past several decades.

A team led by geologist Tjeerd van Andel set out in the late 1970s to test the Vita-Finzi thesis of the Younger Fill in the Greek Argolid region. The team refocused attention on the Bronze Age, where it argues that a series of erosional episodes can be detected. While the team's conclusion was that "human activity" played a "predominant role" in laying down these sediments, it also added a new, perhaps counterintuitive, explanation. Van Andel argued that as much as the expansion of settlement, the decline of settlement also caused erosion. Thus the clearing of forest by agrarian households may have loosened soil deposits, but conversely the abandonment of carefully constructed hillside terrace systems in a context of depopulation would have had even greater effect.[22] John McNeill's examination of the mountainous regions of the Mediterranean similarly finds evidence for ecological change with the spread of agricultural societies, but no fundamental degradation in ancient times unless populations – and thus labor to maintain field systems – was cut drastically by war or epidemic disease. Recent work in Highland Mexico and in the Bronze Age Levant has arrived at similar conclusions, that soil erosion followed the collapse of large, socially complex populations, rather than their emergence.[23]

Two major works published in 2000 and 2001, *The Corrupting Sea*, by Peregrine Horden and Nicholas Purcell, and *The Nature of Mediterranean Europe*, by A. T. Grove and Oliver Rackham, have challenged Vita-Finzi and Hughes point by point. In the place of their human actors, these authors – as do a host of recent paleoecological scientists – argue for broad continuities

[21] Claudio Vita-Finzi, *The Mediterranean Valleys: Geological Changes in Historical Times* (Cambridge, 1969); J. Donald Hughes, *Ecology in Ancient Civilizations* (Albuquerque, NM, 1975); J. Donald Hughes, *Pan's Travail: Environmental Problems of the Ancient Greeks and Romans* (Baltimore, MD, 1994). See Fernand Braudel, *The Mediterranean and the Mediterranean World in the Age of Philip II*, Siân Reynolds, trans., 2 vols. (New York, 1972).

[22] Tjeerd H. van Andel et al., "Five Thousand Years of Land Use and Abuse in the Southern Argolid, Greece," *Hesperia* 55 (1986), 103–28; –, "Land Use and Soil Erosion in Prehistoric and Historical Greece," *JFdArch* 17 (1990), 379–96.

[23] John R. McNeill, *The Mountains of the Mediterranean World: An Environmental History* (New York, 1992), 68–86; Christopher T. Fisher, "Demographic and Landscape Change in the Lake Pátzcuaro Basin, Mexico: Abandoning the Garden," *AmAnth* 107 (2005), 87–95; Patricia Fall et al., "Environmental Impacts of the Rise of Civilization in the Southern Levant"; Charles L. Redman et al., *The Impact of Humans on Their Environment* (Washington, DC, 2004), 141–57.

in the ecologies of the Mediterranean, hinging on a "great aridification," corresponding to the Mid-Holocene transition of 4000–3000 BC. In their reconstructions, in addition to the Mid-Holocene global climate, unstable tectonics on the boundary between Eurasia and Africa provide the primary explanation for a recent sedimentary history of sudden soil movement and sea level change.[24]

The episodic and local manifestations of soil erosions in the Mediterranean also speak against a general crisis set off by simultaneous crises of population and degradation. John Bintliff, once an ardent supporter of Vita-Finzi, now argues with many others for a more subtle approach, in which human action would have accentuated trajectories set off by shifting climate patterns. He is emphatic that it is unlikely that "Bronze Age populations were ever high enough in southern Greece to have lost social stability by soil nutrient collapse." In another review of the literature, with an eye toward modern conservation efforts, Harriet D. Allen summarizes a common consensus among paleoecologists that an older "ruined landscape" argument for a dry, sparse Mediterranean must be abandoned; rather than human action, natural forces have shaped the Mediterranean world.[25]

There is no question that the advance of ancient human economies can be read in the geological and sedimentary record. But visibility is not necessarily terminal degradation. There is a growing consensus among a new generation of scientific scholars that until recently these economies were of less significance than natural forces in shaping both landscapes and the ecological fate of human societies. Barring great exogenous catastrophes, ancient peoples in aggregate were able to maintain a reasonable balance with the natural world in which they lived their daily lives, meeting small losses with small improvements. But nature occasionally could act outside these limits, and the results were devastating to the human condition.

* * *

---

[24] Peregrine Horden and Nicholas Purcell, *The Corrupting Sea: A Study of Mediterranean History* (Malden, MA, 2000), 298–341; A. T. Grove and Oliver Rackham, *The Nature of Mediterranean Europe: An Ecological History* (New Haven, CT, 2001), esp. 288–311; see also Oliver Rackham, "Ecology and Pseudo-Ecology: The Example of Ancient Greece," in Graham Shipley and John Salmon, eds., *Human Landscapes in Classical Antiquity: Environment and Culture* (New York, 1996), 16–43; and Robert Sallares, *The Ecology of the Ancient Greek World* (London, 1991), 372–3.

[25] John Bintliff, "Time, Process and Catastrophism in the Study of Mediterranean Alluvial History: A Review," *WdArch* 33 (2002), 417–35, quote at 430. Harriet D. Allen, "Response of Past and Present Mediterranean Ecosystems to Environmental Change," *Progress in Physical Geography* 27 (2003), 358–77. See also R. S. Shiel, "Refuting the Land Degradation Myth for Boeotia," in G. Bailey et al., eds., *Human Ecodynamics* (Oxford, 2000), 55–62; Jesse Casna, "Mediterranean Valleys Revisited: Linking Soil Erosion, Land Use and Climate Variability in the Northern Levant," *Geomorphology* 101 (2008), 429–42. For further scholarship that emphasizes balancing natural and anthropogenic forces, see Chapter 8, note 61.

Late Holocene Climate Reversals

The first among equals among these exogenous natural forces was that of climate. With the near complete dependence on agriculture emerging from the global late Neolithic secondary products revolution, the threat of crop failure hung over human societies. In years of good, predictable rainfall, the people of villages and cities fared well and accumulated surpluses. But when harvests fell short these surpluses were consumed and hoarded by the more prosperous; the poor faced scarcity and then starvation if the reach of the polity could not distribute grain among affected regions. If crop failures were general and persisted for as few as three years, even the prosperous would be reduced to eating their seed grain and slaughtering the last of their livestock; before mass famine took hold rebellions and insurrections could shake and even bring down ruling elites.

Thus climate mattered in these ancient and medieval societies. There were of course recurrent patterns of harvest plenty and crop failure. Studies have indicated that the eleven-year solar cycle affected the price of grain in medieval Europe and that there is a close correlation between major volcanic eruptions, whose sulphuric emissions can force cool and wet conditions globally for a few years, and crop failure and famine.[26] On the grander scale, the archaic agricultural economies contended with a global climate shaped by cooler and drier northern summers than had been the case before the Mid-Holocene Crisis. Indeed the trend toward cooler and drier conditions may have reinforced dependence on agriculture, as reduced primary productivity made a gathering economy increasingly tenuous if not totally impossible across much of the temperate and semiarid northern hemisphere.

As the Late Holocene opened around 3000 BC, global climate had been reshaped by the retreat of the orbital precession cycle from its Early Holocene peak, as the shift in the orbit and tilt of the earth drew the focus of summer solar "insolation" away from the northern hemisphere and toward the equator. This shift had two broad results affecting the emerging human majority, along the tropics and in the northern latitudes. First, as the West Pacific Warm Pool cooled and the Intertropical Convergence Zone (ITCZ) and its surrounding Hadley cells moved south, influence of the summer monsoons on the northern mid-latitudes was reduced; from the Sahara to China conditions became increasingly arid. After 3000 BC, the southward retreat of the ITCZ strengthened the Walker circulation in the Hadley cell, reviving the El Niño-Southern Oscillation (ENSO) system, with variable episodes of El Niño and La Niña bringing rain and drought alternatively to

---

[26] L. A. Pustilnik and G. Yom Din, "Space Climate Manifestation in Earth Prices – From Medieval England up to Modern U.S.A.," *Solar Physics* 224 (2004), 472–81. For a general statement on the causes of famines during the premodern epoch, see Cormac Ó'Gráda, *Famine: A Short History* (Princeton, NJ, 2009), 13–39.

American coasts and the wider Indo-Pacific rim. In the north, the balance of the northern high- and low-pressure systems known as the North Atlantic Oscillation and the Arctic Oscillation (NAO/AO) shifted from a more "positive" pattern of weaker low pressure at Iceland and the pole and stronger high pressure at the Azores and along the equator to a reversed more "negative" pattern. The result was that winter westerlies in the Ferrell cell weakened and shifted south into the northern mid-latitudes, bringing winter rain and snowfall to a line running from the northern Mediterranean into Central Asia, offsetting to a small extent the decline of the Early Holocene mega-monsoons (see Figure II.5a–b).

Thus from 3000 BC the "modern" Late Holocene climate system was characterized typically by a south-tracking ITCZ; an ENSO cycling between El Niño, La Niña, and intermediate "normal" mode, linked to the ebb and flow of the Asian monsoons; and a generally "negative" NAO/AO pattern. Over these past 5,000 years, the topic of the rest of this book, the weight of climate science suggests that global climate moved around a general mean condition between two extremes, characterized respectively by – on one hand – lower solar irradiance, a south-slumping ITCZ, a colder north, high ENSO variability, and weak monsoons and – on the other hand – a higher solar irradiance, a north-riding ITCZ, a warmer north, lower ENSO variability, and strong monsoons. The actual documentation of these patterns through time is well developed, if not without some dispute and certain gray areas. The fundamental drivers behind these shifts in climate mode are a matter of great debate among historical climate scientists, involving complex atmospheric movements of moisture, the impact of solar variation, and volcanic outbursts. Sorting these out is probably best left in their hands. As of now it would appear that all three were at work, though the tropical mechanisms are in particular debate. Generally, it seems increasingly clear that cycles of the two extremes of warm (cold) north, weak (strong) ENSO variability, and strong (weak) Asian monsoons since 3000 BC are driven by solar activity, with major volcanic activity providing an occasional triggering effect.

Cycles in northern temperature – shaped by solar variation – are a fundamental part of this pattern. The Bond ice raft cycle (measured by layers of debris dropped by icebergs in the North Atlantic) operates on roughly 1,500-year periodicities, a pale reflection of the much more pronounced Dansgaard-Oeschger cycles of the later Pleistocene. The Bond cycles were weaker than the 2,500-year cycle of the millennial Siberian High, which from the Mid-Holocene forward is clearly and directly linked to the solar Hallstatt cycle. These "millennial Siberian Highs" have occurred four times since the end of the glacial Younger Dryas: 7000–6000 BC, 4000–3000 BC, 1300–700 BC, and AD 1400 to the nineteenth century. Each millennial Siberian High overlapped with a Bond ice-rafting event off Greenland, and there was one ice-rafting event intervening between each of the millennial

Siberian Highs. We have considered the first two of these major global events, what we can call the Early Neolithic and Mid-Holocene Crises, discussed in the preceding chapters. The history of the next 5,000 years of human history would be shaped by the next two, which we can call the "Preclassical" and Little Ice Age Crises[27] (see Figures II.4, III.3).

The Hallstatt-driven millennial Siberian High events had powerful effects across the entire northern hemisphere, bringing cold "outbursts" across Asia and Europe as far south as the Red Sea. These mini-glacial events also shaped climate in the tropics. (See my reconstruction in Figure II.5c.) Resonances of the millennial Siberian High can be seen in monsoon proxies from Oman and in the Cariaco sediments off Venezuela, and indicate that during these strong northern coolings the ITCZ moved to the south.[28] At the same time, the Pacific Walker circulation apparently weakened; strong evidence suggests that El Niños intensified with the strong Siberian High. Stronger El Niños contributed to the failure of the Asian monsoon as did the winter Siberian High itself: deep snows on the Tibetan plateau would have shortened the continental summer heating that pulls the monsoons off the oceans and over the Asian lowlands. Stronger El Niños and a south-riding ITCZ both seem to have been at work in reducing precipitation to the headwaters of the Nile.[29] And across Eurasia the millennial Siberian High pushed the North Atlantic winter westerlies south and then blocked them altogether, bringing erratic precipitation and then cold drought conditions to the semi-arid lands supporting the majority of global ancient and medieval populations, running from North Africa to China.[30]

The pacing of the strong Siberian High and human history is particularly powerful. Starting with the melt-water-associated events of the Younger Dryas and 7000–6000 BC, the millennial Siberian Highs – with their ensuing

---

[27] In the absence of an obvious name for the Hallstatt solar cycle–driven millennial Siberian High of 1300–700 BC, I will call it the *Preclassical Crisis*.

[28] Dominik Fleitmann et al., "Holocene ITCZ and Indian Monsoon Dynamics Recorded in Stalagmites from Oman and Yemen (Socotra)," *QSR* 26 (2007), 170–88; Gerald H. Haug et al., "Southward Migration of the Intertropical Convergence Zone through the Holocene," *Science* 293 (2001), 1304–8; Julian P. Sachs et al., "Southward Movement of the Pacific Intertropical Convergence Zone AD 1400–1850," *NatGeosc* 2 (2009), 519–25.

[29] E. J. Rohling et al., "Holocene Ocean-Atmosphere Interactions: Records from Greenland and the Aegean Sea," *ClimDyn* 18 (2002), 587–93; Heiko Lars Legge and Jörg Mutterlose, "Climatic Changes in the Northern Red Sea during the Last 22,000 Years as Recorded by Calcareous Nannofossils," *Paleoceanography* 21 (2006), PA 1003; Nick Marriner et al., "ITCZ and ENSO-like Pacing of Nile Delta Hydro-Geomorphology during the Holocene," *QSR* 45 (2012), 73–84.

[30] Matthew Jones et al., "A High-Resolution Late Holocene Lake Isotope Record from Turkey and Links to the North Atlantic and Monsoon Climate," *Geology* 34 (2006), 361–4; Ulrike Herzschuh, "Palaeo-Moisture Evolution in Monsoonal Central Asia during the Last 50,000 Years," *QSR* 25 (2006), 163–75; Heidi M. Cullen et al., "Impact of the North Atlantic Oscillation on Middle Eastern Climate and Streamflow," *ClimCh* 55 (2002), 315–38.

climate optimums – line up with critical passages in human material history. Victor Lieberman has called attention to these "strange parallels" as they operated in the medieval and early modern Old World, but I propose a wider and longer pattern:

12,200–9600 BC The Younger Dryas
  9600–7000 BC The Early Holocene Optimum and Early Domestication
7000–6000 BC The Early Neolithic Crisis
  6000–4000 BC The Late Neolithic Optimum
4000–3000 BC The Mid-Holocene Crisis and the Rise of the State
  3000–1300 BC The Bronze Age Optimum
1300–700 BC The Preclassical Crisis
  700 BC–AD 1400 The Ancient and Medieval Optimums
AD 1400–1700 The Little Ice Age and Imperial Globalization
  AD 1700– The Industrial Revolution and the Modern Anthropocene

Other climate reversals would intervene, including a mystery event at 2200 BC, volcanic-driven events at approximately 1645 BC, AD 536, AD 1258, and the often synchronous impact of the Bond cycle and important variations in the El Niño/Southern Oscillation. At the risk of being labeled an environmental determinist, I would venture that these major climate events shaped "strange parallels" of global reach, driving the very different circumstances in which premodern peoples worked to maintain and develop their societies. The following chapters set out the evidence for this proposition. But climate shared the stage with disease, sometimes in tandem, and we need to sketch the trajectory of the human microbial story during ancient and medieval times.

* * *

Disease and Epidemics

By the time that the Gilgamesh epics were first written down, and probably well before they were first told, epidemic disease was deeply entrenched in aggregating agricultural and proto-urban societies. Three decades ago, William McNeill laid out the dynamics of epidemic disease in early state societies in an account that has not been fundamentally improved upon.[31]

Disease vectors that moved from animal to human populations required certain thresholds to develop into epidemics infecting large numbers of hosts, but not killing them off entirely. The need of a parasite to maintain a host population – and the ability of that host population to develop limited biological defenses led to the taming, the domestication of "wild" disease.

---

[31] William H. McNeill, *Plagues and Peoples* (New York, 1977).

Disorders that probably destroyed entire villages in the Pre-Pottery Neolithic increasingly became childhood experiences, and pools of resistance to certain pathogens began to develop.

Then, as isolated village societies became regional societies with emerging urban centers, the first of a sequence of *disease confluences* developed. Peoples brought together from different places in early cities brought with them their local diseases, and until the rise of modern public health in the late nineteenth century the city became a glittering palace of death, as urban newcomers brought new disorders and died of established vectors of disease. The growing numbers in these early cities provided the thresholds for new disease mutations to take hold. A second confluence followed the lines of trade out from the emerging cities: when the communications that had worked to homogenize a disease pool within a civilization reached out into neighboring and further-flung centers, it merged civilizational disease pools with mutually devastating results.

There were at least three rising tides of such disease confluence in the archaic Old World through the fourteenth century: launched by the evolving linkages among Bronze Age polities, linkages destroyed in the early Iron Age and then redeveloped in more elaborate form in classical antiquity, and again collapsing in the Dark Ages and then revived by medieval societies when the Black Death struck in the fourteenth century. As much as by trade, perhaps even more, epidemics spread with warfare. This was a two-way street. As McNeill stressed in *Plagues and Peoples*, the garrisons on the edges of empire, as much as the communities of traders, spread the diseases of the centers of empire out to the margins and into the periphery, presumably decimating previously isolated communities of farmers, herders, and even residual hunter-gatherers. Conversely, military campaigns against distant centers repeatedly brought deadly exotic diseases across the boundaries of empire. We can indeed think about a suite of miseries – drought, epidemic, war, and armed migrations – consuming humanity during certain unfortunate epochs.[32]

Of course how much epidemic disease contributed to the first few crises of the Old World population is an open question because systematic evidence for disease in antiquity is extremely slim. But disease was certainly the fundamental agent of population collapses at the end of antiquity and during the fourteenth century, and in neither case does climate seem to have played a fundamentally determining role. Very broadly, we can suggest that during classical antiquity disease emerged as the primary driver of civilizational crisis, and climate change receded somewhat in importance. To some degree, this was a result of "short" human histories being set within "long" climate cycles: classical antiquity and the Middle Ages both unfolded within

---

[32] Ibid., 61–4, 87–93; Andrew T. Price Smith, *Contagion and Chaos: Disease, Ecology, and National Security in the Era of Globalization* (Cambridge, MA, 2009), 159–88.

the broad "optimum" between millennial Siberian Highs starting in roughly 600 BC and ending around AD 1300.[33] But, when these two conditions returned in the early modern era, the resulting crisis during the seventeenth century – devastating as it was – marked something new: certain Eurasian societies had developed new means of maintaining their numbers by enlarging their share of the global economic pie, and by beginning to curtail their mortality from disease. This is a story to be told in a subsequent chapter, but it reminds us of the human response to the forces of nature.

* * *

Energy: Innovation, Labor, and Slavery

While the economists dismiss them out of hand, important sequences of innovation by ancient and medieval peoples allowed the support of incrementally growing populations. We have already seen in epochs in prehistory – the Upper Paleolithic, domestication in early Neolithic center hearths of agriculture, and Late Neolithic "secondary products" intensification – when rising populations set off relatively slow but nonetheless important phases of enduring "Boserupian" advance. After the rise of the state, such population-driven innovations may have sparked relatively long and sustained "efflorescences," some of which lasted longer than the entire history of the modern economy. Thus we need to follow the world historians here and consider the essential features of technological and organizational innovation in these archaic societies.

Trade and the state require various forms of soft technology, most importantly systems of information and organization. Larger numbers of people and things need to be managed and mobilized. The earliest writing systems in the Mesopotamian lowlands evolved from the seals that mercantile households applied to their goods sent into regional trade. These evolved into the accounts of temples and from there to the records of early states, tracking the production and compensation of labor, the raising of taxes and of armies. By the time of the Akkadian empire around roughly 2300 BC, the management of empire had generated a bureaucratic division of authority in which power was delegated in fractions by a monarch to administrators. These administrators, in turn, managed the cult that guaranteed their place in the world: the construction of the permanent monumental architecture that recorded the deeds of the king and the glories of the state.[34] And if some

---

[33] This "optimum" was interrupted by a Dark Age Bond ice-rafting event and enhanced ENSO between roughly AD 300 and AD 700.

[34] McNeill and McNeill, *The Human Web*, 55–60; Bruce G. Trigger, *Understanding Early Civilizations* (New York, 2003), 541–625; Jared Diamond, *Guns, Germs and Steel: The Fate of Human Societies* (New York, 1997), 215–38.

have seen the early state as a macro-parasite, feeding off the surplus of an overtaxed peasantry, an alternative perspective suggests that life in an extensive and well-managed empire was somewhat more predictable, stable, and secure than life outside. By the time of classical antiquity, the legal and coercive reach of the empire ensured that regional markets functioned within its domain, with the result that there may have been shortages of food, but rarely total dearth and famine.[35]

Trade and writing were global universals in the rise of civilization, common to the New World as well as the Old. But three key features of complex societies were unique to the Old World, and each brought an advantage that can be measured in energetic terms. Metals, horses, and rotary power would all be fundamental to Old World economies in ancient and medieval times. The long-term consequences of these advantages took millennia to unfold.

If the pictographic writing systems that recorded the details of monarchical power in Mesopotamia and Egypt had evolved from merchants' seals, the bronze metallurgy that sealed the power of the early state evolved from the ceramic glazes developed in the advanced potteries controlled by those elite families. Metals were an absolutely fundamental departure from the technology of the past. If metal weapons were more impressive than stone weapons, metal tools were more efficient. The efficiency of hand tools can be measured in their capacity to cut or maul a quantity of natural materials in a given period of time, and experiments with stone, bronze, and iron axes indicate that metal is significantly more efficient in at least one task, felling trees.[36] Thus, while metal paved the way for mass warfare, it also improved the energetic ratio involved in work. Less physical effort per unit of work meant that the same unit of food could generate more work, and the same unit of work involved a reduced wear on the body. Thus metal tools must have brought something like an energy revolution to the human condition, where our unit of energy is still the human engine. As the production of bronze was perfected at the end of the third millennium, another energy revolution unfolded on the Pontic steppes of Russia, with the domestication of the horse. Even if simply used as a draft animal, the horse is potentially twice as powerful and twice as fast as oxen, so here as the secondary

[35] Compare William H. McNeill's argument on the early state as a "macro-parasite" in *The Human Condition: An Ecological and Historical View* (Princeton, NJ, 1980) with Peter Garnsey, *Famine and Food Supply in the Greaco-Roman World* (Cambridge, 1988) and –, *Food and Society in Classical Antiquity* (Cambridge, 1999). See also David Kessler and Peter Temin, "The Organization of the Grain Trade in the Early Roman Empire," *EconHistR* 60 (2007), 313–32 and Peter Temin, "A Market Economy in the Early Roman Empire," *JRS* 91 (2001), 169–81. For a broad review, see Michael E. Smith, "The Archaeology of Ancient State Economies," *ARA* 33 (2004), 73–102.

[36] James R. Mattieu and Daniel A. Mayer, "Comparing Axe Heads of Stone, Bronze, and Steel: Studies in Experimental Archaeology," *JFdArch* 24 (1997), 334–51.

products revolution proceeded there was another significant injection of energy into the Old World economic system.[37]

Of course, when we think of bronze and horses we think of chariot-mounted warriors. The Bronze Age was a particularly hierarchical world, one in which the sudden invention of hierarchy after eons of a relatively equalitarian human condition led to certain extremes. Relying on tin and copper ores traded from distant and different regions, its production was tightly tied to royal palaces that controlled that commerce. Only in the last centuries does it appear that bronze began to replace stone for the cutting needs in agricultural households, and the crises that overturned these palace economies around 1200 BC also undermined the production of the noble metal. Over the next five or six centuries, iron production slowly rose to fill the space occupied by bronze, and to fill a host of practical needs for which bronze had not been practical. If iron is more difficult to work than bronze, and in its cruder forms no more efficient, iron ores were much more widely distributed, and any centralized political control of metal was from henceforth impossible. Iron thus universalized metal in Old World economies, though given its rapid decomposition in the earth, and the massive recycling of used scrap, we will never know for sure when this happened. But iron clearly became the "democratic metal," the metal of the workshop, the ploughshare, and the massed formation of plebeian infantry. With only a little experimentation, iron could be transformed into the cruder varieties of steel, giving an even more durable surface and edge.[38] If we give credit to copper and bronze as the conceptually revolutionary transition in technology, like the conceptual revolution of earliest domestication, the development and spread of iron was analogous to the Late Neolithic secondary products revolution, when the full consequences of domestication had been realized. Just as the Late Neolithic saw the full realization of agriculture, the Iron Age saw the full realization of metals: these were the truly revolutionary moments in these earliest economies. And exactly when the Iron Age ended is a matter for debate. Formally, it ended with the establishment of the classical civilizations of high antiquity. But for the ordinary household, the

---

[37] Vaclav Smil, *Energy in World History* (Boulder, CO, 1994), 40–9; Marsha Levine et al., eds., *Late Prehistoric Exploitation of the Eurasian Steppe* (Cambridge, 1999); David W. Anthony and Dorcas R. Brown, "Eneolithic Horse Exploitation in the Eurasian Steppes: Diet, Ritual and Riding," *Antiquity* 74 (2000), 75–86.

[38] The term *democratic metal* was first used in Samuel Lilley, *Men, Machines, and History: The Story of Tools and Machines in Relation to Social Progress*, revised edition (New York, 1965), 25–41. For the recent literature on the transition to iron, see Theodore A. Wertime and James D. Muhly, eds., *The Coming of the Age of Iron* (New Haven, CT, 1980) and Vincent C. Pigott, ed., *The Archaeometallurgy of the Asian Old World* (Philadelphia, PA, 1999). My thinking about metals and economic growth has been stimulated by Karl G. Persson, *Pre-Industrial Economic Growth: Social Organization and Technological Progress in Europe* (Oxford, 1988). 21–4.

age of iron may not have truly started until the Middle Ages, and lasted until the Industrial Revolution of the eighteenth and nineteenth centuries.

The spread of iron – and certainly steel for special purposes – in the first millennium BC must have contributed to an industrial revolution of its own time. Rotary action is a fundamental principle of all modern technologies. If its earliest use was the wheel, it seems that rotary power did not spread beyond transport until the first millennium. The first application seems to have been the rotary quern, a system of round stones turned by hand that replaced the reciprocating (back and forth) action of traditional grindstones, which date securely to the fifth century BC, roughly the point at which iron had spread widely in ancient societies. Iron and more particularly steel tools, with their increasingly precise cutting and sawing capacities, must have played a role in the translation of the rotary quern into a wide array of rotary machinery. During the third century BC, an explosion of technical experimentation, a veritable scientific revolution, in Hellenistic Alexandria produced a host of rotary and hydraulic devices that relatively quickly made their way around the Mediterranean and east to China.[39] Manifested most importantly in irrigation systems (like the Archimedean screw, the *saqiya*) and in water-powered grist mills, the spread and elaboration of rotary power in ancient times was an energy revolution in its own right, certainly enabling the rapid rise of Mediterranean and Asian populations, and probably contributing to an "efflorescence" of several centuries of "economic growth" for certain favored peoples.[40]

One has to wonder whether the per capita iron production of late medieval Europe was fundamentally higher than that of Iron Age and classical societies, and indeed whether medieval economies really improved upon the classical standards in many areas. Given the skills of classical metallurgists and inventors, one has to wonder what would have happened if Greece, Egypt, or Italy had been endowed with quantities of accessible coal.[41] However, classical Old World economies – as would be the medieval economies that followed – were indeed trapped in an organic energy source; there was a rigid upper limit on their developmental potential.[42] Within these limits, the

---

[39] On rotary power and its connections to the ancient scientific revolution, see Orjan Wikander, ed., *Handbook of Ancient Water Technology* (Leiden, 2000); M. J. T. Lewis, *Millstone and Hammer: The Origins of Water Power* (Hull, 1997); Lucio Russo, *The Forgotten Revolution: How Science Was Born in 300BC and Why It Had to Be Reborn*, Silvio Levy, trans. (Berlin, 2004).

[40] Andrew Wilson, "Machines, Power and the Ancient Economy," *JRS* 92 (2002), 1–32; Kevin Greene, "Technological Innovation and Economic Progress in the Ancient World: M. I. Finley Re-Considered," *EconHistR* 53 (2000), 29–59.

[41] See Russo, *The Forgotten Revolution*, 95–141.

[42] Willem Jongman, "The Rise and Fall of the Roman Economy: Population, Rents and Entitlement," in Peter F. Bang et al., eds., *Ancient Economies, Modern Methodologies: Archaeology, Comparative History, Models and Institutions* (Bari, 2006), 243–61.

cumulative benefits of innovation were not insignificant. The aggregate of innovations of governance and markets, metal and rotary power provided for the citizens and subjects of empire a certain freedom from the absolute pressures of weather and disease faced by the people of the small Stone Age societies from which they had recently emerged.

Freedom is a critical and loaded word here, however. If metals and rotary power relieved some of the burden of labor, empire shifted that burden in other ways. Empires ancient, medieval, and early modern were places of violently coerced land and labor, and conquest and slavery were the most severe of Adam Smith's "dreadful misfortunes." Some forms of slavery probably dated back to the Neolithic, but it is most clearly associated with imperial states. Ironically, slavery begins to be visible in the Iron Age, when a cheap "democratic metal" was available to literally forge its fetters. Slavery would not be abolished until after the rise of steam power in the mid-nineteenth century, and very broadly the replacement of one by the other suggests critical questions about the energy budgets of certain human economies. Evidence for servitude and slavery in various forms can be detected deep into the past, perhaps as far back as late Neolithic stratified societies. In the Roman Empire, it would appear that about a quarter of the labor force was enslaved, in Italy mostly descended from war captives reduced to slavery during the burst of empire building during the last two centuries BC. Estimating the energy input of the sheer muscle power of slaves would be a difficult task, complicated by the fact that they would have to be fed by the controlling society. But it is obvious that work in preindustrial contexts involved hands, and the more muscle-driven kinetic energy one could control the more benefit would accrue. In any case, the mobilization of enslaved human energy must be seen as an inherent part of the ecological history of archaic societies. One society's efflorescence was often grounded in another's destruction, in a near zero-sum game.[43]

* * *

Punctuations

On aggregate, people of the ancient and medieval worlds did reasonably well with moderate challenges posed by climate, and they may well have

---

[43] Timothy Taylor, "Believing the Ancients: Quantitative and Qualitative Dimensions of Slavery and the Slave Trade in Later Prehistoric Eurasia," *WdArch* 33 (2001), 27–43; H. D. Baker, "Degrees of Freedom: Slavery in Mid-First-Millennium BC Babylon," *WdArch* 33 (2001), 18–26; essays by Daniel C. Snell, Dimitris J. Kyrtatas, David Braund, Walter Scheidel, and Cam Grey, in Keith Bradley and Paul Cartledge, eds., *The Cambridge World History of Slavery, Vol. I: The Ancient Mediterranean World* (Cambridge, 2011); Jean-François Mouhot, "Past Connections and Present Similarities in Slave Ownership and Fossil Fuel Usage," *ClimCh* 105 (2011), 329–55.

resisted the ravages of routine "domesticated" diseases. These were societies in stasis, but not in perpetual crisis. They were, however, seriously set back by abrupt climatic change beyond the scale of routine memory, and by diseases to which they had never been exposed. Exogenous traumas, rather than inherent endogenous failings, laid waste to these societies.

Two propositions by noted scientists help to stitch together the millennia of interaction of natural forces and human agency that I have summarized here and in several of the preceding chapters. The first is provided by a dissident climatologist, now retired from an eminent career. Here the causal arrow moves from culture to climate. In 2003, William Ruddiman published a widely read and provocative article in which he argues that while climate certainly deteriorated around 3000 BC, it *did not do what it was scheduled to do*: it did not continue to cool into the next glacial period of the Pleistocene. Ruddiman contends that, given the orbital precessional trajectory toward cooler global climates, the relatively warm climate of the past 5,000 years is an anomaly that only can be explained by elevated levels of atmospheric CO_2 and methane emissions detected in ice cores (see Figures I.5, II.1). He maintains that if orbitally forced climate patterns had followed the example of most previous interglacials, the period from 9000–7000 BC would have seen a maximum in levels of methane and CO_2, and that these greenhouse gases should have not only declined as they did until 3000 BC, but continued to decline until the present, as the earth settled into the first stages of the next glacial period. Ruddiman's central and still controversial thesis is that the enhanced CO_2 and methane appearing in the climate record can only have come from the spread of early farming. In his earliest account, Ruddiman attributed the rise of methane and CO_2 to the first emergence of Neolithic farming; he has since refined his argument to see this increase coming with growing populations shaped by the Late Neolithic and the rise of the Bronze Age state, especially in China, where rice paddy farming would have released increasing volumes of methane.[44] Literally, his argument suggests that we should connect the fertility pulse population growth of the Late Neolithic with the first impact of anthropogenic greenhouse

---

[44] William F. Ruddiman, "The Anthropogenic Greenhouse Era Began Thousands of Years Ago," *ClimCh* 61 (2003), 261–93. Ruddiman has published a popular version of this argument in *SA* 292 (March 2005), as well as a tradebook version: *Plows, Plagues, and Petroleum: How Humans Took Control of Nature* (Princeton, NJ, 2005). For Ruddiman's response to his critics, who see an analogy between the methane curve of Holocene and OI Stage 11 (~400k ybp), see pp. 106–14. For a recent review, see M. James Salinger, "Agriculture's Influence on Climate during the Holocene," *Agricultural and Forest Meteorology* 142 (2007), 96–102. On the population, emissions, and the late Neolithic and early Chinese state, see William F. Ruddiman et al., "Early Rice Farming and Anomalous Methane Trends," *QSR* 27 (2008), 1291–5 and Xiaoliang Li et al., "Increases in Population and Expansion of Rice Agriculture in Asia, and Anthropogenic Methane Emissions since 5000BP," *QuatInt* 202 (2009), 41–50.

gases. Thus the climate since 3000 BC has been altered by human activity, placing us in the Anthropocene since the secondary products revolution and the rise of the state. Ruddiman's analysis has been forcibly made and defended, and it is gaining ground among many climate scientists.[45]

Our second proposition is the familiar argument for punctuated change put forward by Stephen J. Gould and Niles Eldridge. Joel Mokyr has suggested that the Eldridge/Gould punctuation model can be useful in modern economic history, and here I suggest that it helps explain the broad contours of human economies throughout the Holocene.[46]

In broad overview, it is striking how punctuations in climate and culture have followed one upon the other since the end of the Pleistocene. First, Early Neolithic domestication in the Levant and in central China followed the stresses of the Younger Dryas neoglaciation. Then, following the cold Siberian High conditions of the seventh millennium, culminating in the glacial spike at 6200 BC, the secondary products revolution in Southwest Asia diversified and intensified the agricultural economy. The Mid-Holocene Crisis of the fourth millennium was followed by the consolidation of the early Bronze Age state. The next truly major crisis and the third epoch of a Siberian High – between 1200 BC and 600 BC – launched a technological revolution in the rise of iron and rotary power. Such is the central pivot of the next two chapters. In the book's final chapters I – with certain real caveats – make another such argument: the emergence of the modern global industrial economy was grounded in the fourth epoch of the Siberian High, the Little Ice Age that started in 1400.

While I may be condemned for crude determinism, a strong case can be made that natural forces were a crucial part of the causal mix that repeatedly shattered the coherence of ancient systems of culture, clearing the way for new systems in cosmic acts of creative destruction. In the next three chapters, I discuss the sequence of these expansions and crises between the Mid-Holocene Crisis and the Black Death, and make the case that on balance exogenous punctuations, rather than endogenous contradictions, provide the explanation for the overarching pattern of the human condition.

---

[45] Ruddiman has summarized the state of the argument in a new afterword to the 2010 edition of *Plows, Plagues, and Petroleum*. A recent analysis suggests that the rising values of greenhouse gases around 3000 BC can be attributed to the stabilization of oceanic systems, most importantly to the influence of thermohaline circulation, but that human influences explain rising methane and CO_2 after 500 BC. M. Debret et al., "Evidence from Wavelet Analysis for a Mid-Holocene Transition in Global Climate Forcing," *QSR* 28 (2009), 2675–88.

[46] See Mokyr, "Punctuated Equilibria and Technological Progress"; "Evolution and Technological Change: A New Metaphor for Economic History?"; and the essays in John D. Bintliff, *Structure and Contingency: Environmental Processes in Life and Human History* (London, 1999).

7

Optimum and Crisis in Early Civilizations, 3000–500 BC

The two and a half millennia from 3000 BC to 500 BC, one half of recorded human history, can be described in terms of a long global climatic optimum – and another global climatic crisis driven by a Hallstatt solar minimum. During this enormous span of time, and despite their apparent diversity, world cultures marched in generally common patterns, striking in their evolutionary similarities. Many of these similarities were shaped by a common global experience of long stretches of relatively stable climate optimum – and then roughly simultaneous abrupt climate change. If New World societies did not develop agriculture – and epidemic diseases – at quite the same pace as did those in the Old World, the pulse of the global Bronze Age optimum and then the Preclassical Crisis moved global societies along surprisingly similar tracks.

* * *

The Old World Bronze Age: Expansions and Crises, 3000–1000 BC

The Bronze Age encompassed at least the first two millennia of urban civilization in the Old World. During this long sweep of time, Old World societies in the Middle East, the eastern Mediterranean, India, and China developed amazingly enduring patterns of power and economy. With the apparent exception of Harappan India, these were societies of strict hierarchy, based on concepts of sacred kingship. Here the priests did not speak in the temple with the gods in the name and interest of the people; the king became a god and was the focal point of all things. Rather than evolving and changing, the Bronze Age systems simply intensified, becoming ever more elaborated and involuted. Their fate was in great measure decided by their environmental context. In India, a slow fading of the monsoons would equally slowly undermine the Harappan cities, as their peoples gradually abandoned them for a dispersed village life. In China, where a great crisis of flooding forged the beginnings of an early state, a broadly stable structure of the monsoon regime meant that the essential form of the Bronze Age polity would endure to the dawn of modernity. In most of Southwest Asia and the Mediterranean, however, the Bronze Age system eventually cracked and crashed, and a world with fundamentally new and different features emerged. Let us begin with this greater Mediterranean world.

The chronologies of the Bronze Age of Mesopotamia, Egypt, and adjacent regions are remarkably tightly linked[1] (see Figure III.3). Very broadly, scholars traditionally divide these chronologies into three sections: an Early Bronze Age running to roughly 2000 BC, a Middle Bronze Age running to 1600 BC, and a Late Bronze Age running to 1200 BC. Each of these periods has clear manifestations in the various regions. In Egypt they were the Old Kingdom, the Middle Kingdom, and the New Kingdom; the Egyptian Early Dynastic transition from the Late Neolithic was complete by 2650 BC, launching the Old Kingdom, in which the cult of the pharaoh was fully established, manifested in the great pyramids at Giza, built by 2500 BC. In Mesopotamia, an Early Dynastic of multiple competing Sumerian city-state monarchies was not consolidated until roughly 2330 BC, when the conquests of Sargon established the Akkadian empire. The grand monuments that legitimated these regimes were based on the command of labor by a palace household, a command that reached into the management of the economy at large. The royal palaces governed the irrigation schedules for much of the agricultural production, and levied taxes in kind and in labor as tribute to the sacred person of the king.[2] The royal households also managed long-distance trade as a form of gift exchange among a brotherhood of monarchs; merchants involved in distant trade were royal officials whose purpose was to acquire exotic goods for the king and his dependents. Such trade involved a range of luxury commodities drawn in long lines of trade with distant sources, such as lapis lazuli from Afghanistan, tin from Anatolia, or amber from the Baltic. But it also involved the now ancient

---

[1] It is also increasingly precisely dated, though not without some continuing controversy. See Manfred Bietak and Ernst Czerny, eds., *The Synchronisation of Civilisations in the Eastern Mediterranean in the Second Millennium B.C.*, Vols. I and II (Vienna, 2000, 2003); Sturt W. Manning, *A Test of Time: The Volcano of Thera and the Chronology and History of the Aegean and East Mediterranean in the Mid Second Millennium BC* (Oxford, 1999); Christopher B. Ramsey et al., "Radiocarbon-Based Chronology for Dynastic Egypt," and Hendrick J. Bruins, "Dating Pharaonic Egypt," *Science* 328 (2010), 1554–7, 1489–90; and Sturt W. Manning et al., "Anatolian Tree-Rings and a New Chronology for the East Mediterranean Bronze-Iron Age," *Science* 294 (2001), 2532–5. For a recent world systems analysis of the Old World Bronze Age, see Andre Gunder Frank and William R. Thompson, "Afro-Eurasian Bronze Age Economic Expansion and Contraction Revisited," *JWH* 16 (2005), 115–72.

[2] Susan Pollock, *Ancient Mesopotamia: The Eden that Never Was* (Cambridge, 1999), 149–95; Daniel C. Snell, *Life in the Ancient Near East, 3100–332 B.C.E.* (New Haven, CT, 1997), 11–29.

exchange between these two neighboring centers, and by 2600 BC small kingdoms were emerging in the Levant along the trade route between Egypt and Mesopotamia, and then north across Anatolia.[3]

These trade networks would be elaborated in the Middle Bronze Age, but it was in the Late Bronze Age after 1600 BC that they reached a florescence, moving considerable cargoes, increasingly along the Mediterranean coast. In a northern maritime extension of this system of trading polities, Minoan Crete emerged as an important power in the Middle Bronze Age, while Mycenae emerged as the first important state on the coast of Europe in the Late Bronze Age, around 1500 BC. In Anatolia, the Hittite kingdom emerged around 1650 BC, and quickly became a major power, sacking Aleppo and Babylon in the 1590s. The Late Bronze Age thus saw the establishment of a multipolar international trading system backed up by the competition of expansive empires. Previously, the king's soldiers had concentrated on defending the polity from nomadic intruders, and incorporating small neighboring regions with promising resources into the realm; Mesopotamian rulers since the Uruk had engaged in such frontier defense and conquest. But the Hittite raids at the opening of the Late Bronze Age anticipated a cycle of aggressive imperial warfare to control the space between the empires in the Levant. By the 1400s, the Egyptian New Kingdom had launched empire-building efforts that led it to the borders of Anatolia and the headwaters of the Euphrates, in what was the first long-distance sustained mobilization of armies of conquest.[4]

Thus the key elements of the contest for strategic power among formidable states were established during the Late Bronze Age of the greater Mediterranean. Commerce and warfare linked a network of states, each seeking to gather exotic resources and to set the terms of their distribution. If a core and periphery "world system" had been first launched by the Uruk around the Mesopotamia lowlands, it now extended over a vast terrain. Diverse societies were involved in the extraction, production, and trade in commodities that established for the first time something like a market

---

[3] Leon Marfoe, "Cedar Forest to Silver Mountain: Social Change and the Development of Long-Distance Trade in Early Near Eastern Societies," and Mario Liverani, "The Collapse of the Near Eastern Regional System at the End of the Bronze Age: The Case of Syria," in Michael Rowlands et al., eds., *Centre and Periphery in the Ancient World* (New York, 1987), 25–35, 66–73; Peter M. M. G. Akkermans and Glenn M. Schwartz, *The Archaeology of Syria: From Complex Hunter-Gatherers to Early Urban Societies (ca. 16,000–300 BC)* (New York, 2003), 352–3; Andrew Sherratt, "What Would a Bronze-Age World System Look Like? Relations between Temperate Europe and the Mediterranean in Later Prehistory," *JEArch* 1 (1993), 1–57; Andrew Sherratt and Susan Sherratt, "From Luxuries to Commodities: The Nature of Mediterranean Bronze Age Trading Systems," in N. H. Gale, *Bronze Age Trade in the Mediterranean* (Jonsered, 1991), 351–86.

[4] Arther Ferrell, *The Origins of War: From the Stone Age to Alexander the Great*, rev. ed. (Boulder, CO, 1997), 44–60; Marc van de Mieroop, *A History of the Ancient Near East, ca. 3000–323 B.C.* (Malden, MA, 2004), 135–7.

economy. The hierarchies of these trading systems were interwoven with those of this new economy's organization and of its productive base. Long-distance trade was conducted by royal households, and production was managed from the palace.[5] Indeed that production was carried on with little or no significant innovation, essentially on the technological base inherited from the Late Neolithic-Chalcolithic secondary products revolution. The world of the palace and the world of the peasant were radically separated, with little or no communication between the two other than to extract the surplus. If the *shaduf,* a weighted pivoting pole that lifts water buckets out of wells or rivers, may have been a Bronze Age innovation, metal made its way into the ordinary household only very slowly, in the Late Bronze Age at best; flint sickles were in use in Syria and the Levant throughout the period. By the last centuries of the Late Bronze Age, at least in parts of Syria, exploitation of a bound peasantry was reaching a breaking point, and communities were fleeing as refugees into the wastelands to become nomads.[6]

Thus, indeed, there are reasons to suggest that internal endogenous factors were at work when Near Eastern/Mediterranean Bronze Age societies collapsed, which they did – spectacularly – on three occasions. These might seem to have been classic crises of sustainability, in which ancient economies overran their resources. But the problem for an endogenous interpretation is that these collapses were simultaneous and universal, and there is ample reason to argue that they were fundamentally shaped by abrupt climate shifts toward cold and dry conditions.

After the Mid-Holocene climatic transition ended in perhaps two centuries of severe drought, the dawn of the Near Eastern Bronze Age had been blessed with several centuries of remarkably good weather. Indeed these good conditions of a Bronze Age Optimum provided the stable platform upon which the new states established their claims to legitimacy and power: the new kings called for sun and rain, and it was so. The Mid-Holocene Crisis of 3200 BC to 3000 BC had seen intense drought from Kilimanjaro to the Nile and the Levant, a final cold outburst from the Siberian High, and apparently the reigniting of El Niño variability. In the centuries following, the climate stabilized considerably. Evidence for centuries of good rainfall has been found at Kilimanjaro, the Oman coast, Jerusalem, the Dead

[5] Sherratt and Sherratt, "From Luxuries to Commodities," 370–3; Liverani, "The Collapse of the Near East Regional System," 66–9; Van de Mieroop, *A History of the Ancient Near East,* 121–35; Akkermans and Schwartz, *The Archaeology of Syria,* 327–58.

[6] Vaclav Smil, *Energy in World History* (Boulder, CO, 1994), 50–1; Akkermans and Schwartz, *The Archaeology of Syria,* 333, 353; Steven A. Rosen, *Lithics after the Stone Age: A Handbook of Stone Tools from the Levant* (Walnut Creek, CA, 1997), 142–3; Arlene Miller Rosen, "The Social Response to Environmental Change in Early Bronze Age Canaan," *JAnthArch* 14 (1995), 26–44; Arlene Miller Rosen, *Civilizing Climate: Social Responses to Climate Change in the Ancient Near East* (Lanham, MD, 2007), 1–16, 140–3; Liverani, "The Collapse of the Near Eastern Regional System," 69.

Sea: the entire Middle East saw a distinct moderation of climate.[7] It was in these bountiful circumstances that the first monarchs established their rule in the Mesopotamian city-states and along the Nile (see Figure III.3).

These conditions lasted for a remarkably long time. But when they broke around 2200 BC, the effects were catastrophic, in *a general crisis that marks the boundary between the Early and Middle Bronze Ages*. The chronology is clearly marked in the region's traditional chronologies and king lists. In Egypt, the breaks are conveniently labeled the *Intermediate Periods*, periods of famine, rebellion, or invasion, and the breakdown of pharaonic rule. Egypt's First Intermediate Period is dated very precisely to 2150–2040 BC, ninety years that saw four dynasties and as many as thirty-six pharaohs. Drought conditions recorded in both geological sediments and ancient texts indicate that this was no normal event, but a "Dark Age." Sediments from Italy to the Arabian Sea mark the 2200 BC event as wildly abnormal. In the Arabian Sea, various markers for windborne dust from the Persian Gulf region spike up and off the charts; an enormous volume of dust was deposited on Mount Kilimanjaro in east Africa. Water levels in the Dead Sea dropped to levels not seen since the 3200 BC crisis. Lakes in Anatolia again dried up – in one case for 450 years – and Anatolian drought reduced the flow of water in the Tigris-Euphrates systems. Stream flow in the Nile dropped precipitously, matching accounts of drought and famine in Egypt's First Intermediate Period. The event has even been connected to a band of narrow oak tree rings in Ireland, though at a date of 2354 BC.[8] Famine

---

[7] Lonnie G. Thompson et al., "Kilimanjaro Ice Core Records: Evidence of Holocene Climate Change in Tropical Africa," *Science* 298 (2002), 489–593; Dominik Fleitmann et al., "Holocene ITCZ and Indian Monsoon Dynamics Recorded in Stalagmites from Oman and Yemen (Socotra),"*QSR* 26 (2007), 170–88; Mira Bar-Matthews and Avner Ayalon, "Mid-Holocene Climate Variations Revealed by High-Resolution Speleothem Records from Soreq Cave, Israel and the Correlation with Cultural Changes," *Holocene* 21 (2011), 163–71; Karl W. Butzer, "Environmental Change in the Near East and Human Impact on the Land," in Jack M. Sasson, ed., *Civilizations of the Ancient Near East*, Vol. 1 (Farmington Hills, MI, 1995), 123–51; Claudia Migowski et al., "Holocene Climate Variability and Cultural Evolution in the Near East from the Dead Sea Sedimentary Record," *QuatRes* 66 (2006), 421–31.

[8] For the key works, see H. Weiss et al., "The Genesis and Collapse of Third Millennium North Mesopotamia Civilization," *Science* 261 (1993), 995–1004; the essays in H. Nüzhet Dalfes et al., eds., *Third Millennium BC Climate Change and Old World Collapse* (Berlin, 1993), esp. Gerry Lemcke and Michael Sturm, "⊠[18]o and Trace Element Measurements as Proxy for the Reconstruction of Climate Changes at Lake Van (Turkey): Preliminary Results," 653–78; H. M. Cullen, "Climate Change and the Collapse of the Akkadian Empire: Evidence from the Deep Sea," *Geology* 28 (2000), 379–82; Peter B. DeMenocal, "Cultural Responses to Climate Change during the Late Holocene," *Science* 292 (2001), 667–73; Thompson et al., "Kilimanjaro Ice Core Records"; Arie S. Issar and Mattanyah Zohar, *Climate Change – Environment and Civilization in the Middle East* (Berlin, 2004), 132–7; Russell Drysdale et al., "Late Holocene Drought Responsible for the Collapse of Old World Civilizations Recorded in an Italian Cave Flowstone," *Geology* (2006), 101–4; Jean-Daniel Stanley et al., "Short Contribution: Nile Flow Failure at the End of the Old Kingdom, Egypt: Strontium Isotopic and Petrologic Evidence," *Geoarchaeology* 18 (2003), 395–402; Yehouda Ensel

spread throughout the region and apparently revolts broke out; powerful dynasties fell, and for several centuries power was dispersed among successions of local rulers. Entire districts in northern Mesopotamia and the Zagros Hills were abandoned, and refugees flooded into the southern lowlands, where rations supplied to temple workers were cut dramatically.[9] The recently consolidated Akkadian empire was overrun in 2154 BC by the Guttians from the Zagros foothills, after the Akkadians had attempted to stem a tide of nomads and drought refugees with a long fortified wall called the "Repeller of the Amorites." When the Guttians were deposed and local power restored in the Third Dynasty of Ur, the nomadic Amorites emerged again to conquer and hold Sumeria. In the Levant and Upper Mesopotamia, the Early Bronze Age towns were abandoned, and for several hundred years scattered village farmers abandoned wheat and olives for barley and increased pastoralism.[10]

In Lower Mesopotamia, one of the great degradations of agricultural land began to unfold. Traditionally, archaeologists have ascribed the salinization of the ancient Sumerian farmlands to increasing irrigation driven by

et al., "Late Holocene Climates of the Near East Deduced from Dead Sea Level Variation and Modern Winter Rainfall," *QuatRes* 60 (2003), 263–73; Migowski et al., "Holocene Climate Variability ... from the Dead Sea Sedimentary Record"; Helge W. Arz et al., "A Pronounced Dry Event Recorded around 4.2ka in Brine Sediments from the Northern Red Sea," *QuatRes* 66 (2006), 432–41; Michael Staubwasser and Harvey Weiss, "Holocene Climate and Cultural Evolution in Late Prehistoric-Early Historic West Asia," *QuatRes* 66 (2006), 372–87; Catherine Kuzucuoğlu et al., "Mid- to Late-Holocene Climate Change in Central Turkey: The Tecer Lake Record," *Holocene* 21 (2011), 181, 184–5; Christopher E. Bernhardt et al., "Nile Delta Vegetation Response to Holocene Climate Variability," *Geology* 40 (2010), 615–18; and Karl W. Butzer, "Collapse, Environment, and Society," *PNAS* 109 (2012), at 3633–4.

9 Barbara Bell, "The Dark Ages in Ancient History I: The First Dark Age in Egypt," *American Journal of Archaeology* 75 (1971), 1–26; Rosen, "The Social Response to Environmental Change in Early Bronze Age Canaan"; Fekri A. Hassan, "Nile Floods and Political Disorder in Early Egypt," and Harvey Weiss, "Late Third Millennium Abrupt Climate Change and Social Collapse in West Asia and Egypt," in Dalfes et al., *Third Millennium BC Climate Change and Old World Collapse*, 1–24, 711–24; Harvey Weiss, "Beyond the Younger Dryas: Collapse as Adaptation to Abrupt Climate Change in Ancient West Asia and the Eastern Mediterranean," in Garth Bawden and Richard M. Reycraft, eds., *Environmental Disaster and the Archaeology of Human Response* (Albuquerque, NM, 2000), 75–98; Patricia L. Fall et al., "Agricultural Intensification and the Secondary Products Revolution along the Jordan Rift," *HumEcol* 30 (2002), 445–82; Akkermans and Schwartz, *The Archaeology of Syria*, 282–7; Van de Meiroop, *A History of the Ancient Near East*, 67–9; Rosen, *Civilizing Climate*, 128–49; Issar and Zohar, *Climate Change*, 132–53. Calorie lists for Mesopotamia from Rosemary Ellison, "Diet in Mesopotamia: The Evidence of the Barley Ration Tests (c. 3000–1400 BC)," *Iraq* 45 (1981), 35–45; –, "Some Thoughts on the Diet of Mesopotamia from c. 3000–600BC," *Iraq* 45 (1983), 146–50.

10 deMenocal, "Cultural Responses"; Issar and Zohar, *Climate Change*, 144–5. See also Robert McC. Adams, *Land behind Baghdad: A History of Settlement of the Dyala Plains* (Chicago, IL, 1965), 42–5.

overpopulation. As irrigation water evaporates, salts build up in the soil. But the advancing salinization in the Mesopotamian lowlands was caused – it now appears – by a combination of refugee-driven overpopulation and the aridification of the landscape, both of which increased the volume of irrigation. The impact of this crisis can actually be quantified in grain produced and calories consumed. Salinization forced a total shift to salt-tolerant barley and a sharp decline in output of barley per hectare.[11] The Babylonian barley ration list, recorded over 1,600 years, suggests that during both the 2200 BC crisis and the subsequent 1600 BC crisis temple workers received about two-thirds of the food allotment that they had during non-crisis centuries[12] (see Figure III.3).

Why did this widespread drought at 2200 BC occur? There is no consensus. While it coincided with a Bond ice-rafting event, it was off cycle relative to the millennial Siberian High. Climate scientists have suggested that the 2200 BC crisis involved a massive El Niño event; evidence from the Andes and the ocean off Peru points to a massive El Niño event around 2450 BC, which would have shocked the Asian monsoon systems, bringing drought to the western Pacific and southern Asia.[13] While there are no clear indications of El Niño activity closer to 2200 BC, there clearly were droughts from east Africa into Anatolia and climate impacts in North America and on the China coast. If ice rafting off Greenland is a reasonable proxy for the North Atlantic Oscillation, then this would have been a period of negative NAO, which generally weakens the Atlantic westerlies and pushes them south, as suggested by high lake levels in the Mediterranean and Central Europe. But if the westerlies were in the Mediterranean, they were deflected away from Anatolia and the Levant. Somehow global forces would have lined up to

[11] The salinity thesis was developed most formatively in Thorkïld Jacobsen, *Salinity and Irrigation Agriculture in Antiquity* (Malibu, CA, 1982), esp. 52–6, focusing on the period 2600–1400 BC, encompassing the crisis of 2200–2000 BC. For the most recent critique, see Issar and Zohar, *Climate Change*, 137–8. It should be noted that Jacobsen did not ascribe the general crisis of the period to salinity, but to nomadic invasion and endemic warfare (pp. 72–4).

[12] Ellison, "Diet in Mesopotamia."

[13] Bert Rein et al., El Niño Variability off Peru during the Last 20,000 Years," *Paleoceanography* 20 (2005), PA403, 1–17; Lonnie G. Thompson, et al., "Ice-Core Paleoclimate Records in the Glacial South America since the Last Glacial Maximum," *JQS* 15 (2000), 377–94, at 379; Donald Rodbell et al., "An ~15,000-Year Record of El Niño-Driven Alluviation in Southwestern Ecuador," *Science* 283 (1999), 516–20; Y. T. Hong et al., "Inverse Phase Oscillations between the East Asian and Indian Ocean Summer Monsoons during the Last 2,000 Years and Paleo-El Niño," *EPSL* 231 (2005), 337–46, at 344. Unfortunately this event is not reflected in the Cariaco sediments. A massive meteor strike or even the close passing of a comet have been proposed: Weiss et al., "The Genesis and Collapse of Third Millennium North Mesopotamia Civilization," 1001–2; Mike Baillie, *Exodus to Arthur: Catastrophic Encounters with Comets* (London, 1999), 201–2. Butzer dissents from the model of a global climatic crisis, however, especially in regard to the Akkadian crisis: see "Supporting Information" for "Collapse, Environment, and Society."

bring severe drought to large parts of the global northern mid-latitudes.[14] Whatever the explanation, the reality is the same. The Middle East and points beyond were subjected to a devastating two-century drought, far beyond the scale of any routine event. But the reassertion of the ancient patterns is equally real: by 2000–1900 BC the climate had stabilized, and centralized rule returned to the societies of the greater Near East, broadly labeled the *Middle Bronze Age* by generations of archaeologists.

The year 2200 BC was also a critical turning point for centers of Old World civilization lying to the east, China, Japan, and Harappan India. In China, the 2200 BC crisis was manifested as a huge surge of flooding as the East Asian monsoon stalled over the central plain and the Yellow River: legend has it that China's earliest Bronze Age state was launched by the success of "Yu the Great" in managing the control of these waters[15] (see Figure III.4). This catastrophic flooding may have been linked to a sudden shift in the East Asian winter monsoon, which brings cold, dry winds out of Central Asia across China and Japan. Strong during the fourth millennium BC Mid-Holocene transition, the winter monsoon had waned during the third millennium BC, analogous to the Early Bronze Age optimum in southwest Asia. This third millennium optimum had underwritten both the florescence of Longshan and other Late Neolithic cultures in China, as well as the pre-Neolithic pottery-using middle Jomon culture in Japan. Around 2000 BC it turned sharply colder, as China shifted toward the dynastic state, and putting the Jomon into a long decline that would end with the arrival of the rice-cultivating Yayoi around 300 BC.[16]

[14] C. Giraudi et al., "The Holocene Climatic Evolution of Mediterranean Italy: A Review of the Continental Geological Data," *Holocene* 21 (2011), 105–15; Michel Magny, "Holocene Climate Variability as Reflected by Mid-European Lake-Level Fluctuations and Its Probable Impact on Prehistoric Human Settlements," *Quaternary International* 113 (2004), 65–79; Robert K. Booth et al., "A Severe Centennial-Scale Drought in Mid-Continental North America 4200 Years Ago and Apparent Global Linkages," *Holocene* 15 (2005), 321–8; Cheng-Bang An et al., "Climate Change and Cultural Response around 4000 cal yr B.P. in the Western Part of Chinese Loess Plateau," *QuatRes* 63 (2005), 347–52; Wu Wenxiang and Liu Tungsheng, "Possible Role of the 'Holocene Event 3' on the Collapse of the Neolithic Cultures around the Central Plain of China," *QuatInt* 117 (2004), 153–66; Yongtao Yu et al., "Millennial-Scale Holocene Climate Variability in the NW China Drylands and Links to the Tropical Pacific and the North Atlantic," *PPP* 233 (2006), 149–62, see esp. 160.

[15] Wenxiang and Tungsheng, "Possible Role of the 'Holocene Event 3'"; Li Liu, *The Chinese Neolithic: Trajectories to Early States* (Cambridge, 2004), 235–6.

[16] Carrie Morril et al., "A Synthesis of Abrupt Changes in the Asian Monsoon since the Last Deglaciation," *Holocene* 13 (2003), 465–76; Gergana Yancheva et al., "Influence of the Intertropical Convergence Zone on the East Asian Monsoon," *Nature* 445 (2007), 74–7; Gina L. Barnes, *The Rise of Civilization in East Asia: The Archaeology of China, Korea, and Japan* (London, 1999), 69–91, 108–30; William Wayne Farris, *Daily Life and Demographics in Ancient Japan* (Ann Arbor, MI, 2009), 8–9. South China had a somewhat smoother climatic descent, given the influences of the South Asian monsoon. See Chapter 4, note 25.

The story in Harappan India was somewhat different (see Figure III.3). The Bronze Age village and urban societies of the Indus Valley are something of an anomaly, in that archaeologists have found little indication of local defense and regional warfare. It would seem that the bountiful monsoon rainfall of the Early to Mid-Holocene had forged a condition of plenty for all, and that competitive energies were channeled into commerce rather than conflict. Scholars have long argued that these rains shaped the origins of the urban Harappan societies, which emerged from Neolithic villages around 2600 BC. It now appears that this rainfall began to slowly taper off in the third millennium, at just the point that the Harappan cities began to develop. Thus it seems that this "first urbanization" in South Asia was the initial response of the Indus Valley peoples to the beginning of Late Holocene aridification. These cities were maintained for 300 to 400 years and then gradually abandoned as the Harappan peoples resettled in scattered villages in the eastern range of their territories, into the Punjab and the Ganges Valley. It would appear that a South Asian manifestation of the 2200 BC event, if it indeed occurred, would have played a significant role in this abandonment.[17]

In Southwest Asia and the Eastern Mediterranean, the recovery from the 2200 BC crisis would be relatively brief. Climate in the Levant stabilized after the 2200–2000 BC crisis in a drier mode, with less volatility but less rainfall.[18] The interval running for roughly 400 years to around 1600 BC is known as the *Middle Bronze Age*. It would be disrupted in the eastern Mediterranean and surrounding regions by a cataclysmic volcanic eruption, setting off a *second general crisis* that marked the opening of the Late Bronze Age. Exploding the island of Santorini in 1623 BC+/- 25, the eruption destroyed the maritime civilization of Thera located there. The effects of this eruption were felt throughout the eastern Mediterranean. A tsunami rushing out from the eruption decimated settlements around the Aegean, and a region from eastern Crete to the Nile Delta and the Sinai was blanketed with a thick coat of heavy ash. This heavy ash traveled southeast in the lower troposphere, but at the upper stratospheric levels the prevailing westerlies carried a high cloud of aerosols and small volcanic particles to the

---

[17] Liviu Giosan et al., "Fluvial Landscapes of the Harappan Civilization," *PNAS* 102 (2012), E1688–E1694; Camilo Ponton, "Holocene Aridification of India," *GRL* 39 (2012), L03704; Harunur Rashid et al., "Late Glacial to Holocene Indian Summer Monsoon Variability Based upon Sediment Records Taken from the Bay of Bengal," *Terrestrial, Atmospheric, and Oceanic Sciences* 22 (2011), 215–28; Marco Madella and Dorian Q. Fuller, "Paleoecology and the Harappan Civilization of South Asia: A Reconsideration," *QSR* 25 (2006), 1283–301. Compare with the very different interpretations in Gregory L. Possehl, *The Indus Civilization: A Contemporary Perspective* (Lanham, MD, 2002), 237–45 and Michael Staubwasser et al., "Climate Change at the 4.2 ka BP Termination of the Indus Valley Civilization and Holocene South Asian Monsoon Variability," *GRL* 30 (2003), 1425.

[18] Bar-Matthews and Avner Ayalon, "Mid-Holocene Climate Variations."

east, over Anatolia. The people of Thera were obliterated and the Minoans on Crete suffered massive destruction. Where the Minoans had controlled the Aegean during the Middle Bronze Age, the Mycenaeans to the north-west – free and clear of most of the effect of the volcano – would take up this role in the coming centuries. To the east in Anatolia, the volcanic aerosol clouds – one geologists has recently suggested – blocked the sun to the extent that crops failed and tree growth faltered. Perhaps it panicked the Hittites, recently forged into a new kingdom. In any event, soon after the Santorini eruption, Hittite armies began raiding to the south, sacking Aleppo and then Babylon by 1595.[19]

The Santorini eruption and the Hittite raids were only two manifestations of a wider disorder during the last decades of the Middle Bronze Age. Other groups of nomadic tradition, the Kassites, the Hurrians, the Hyksos, and the Hebrews, were also on the move. The Hittites sacked but did not occupy Babylon, and soon thereafter the tribal Kassites took control in Upper Mesopotamia and later moved south. The Hurrians had emerged from the southern Caucasus mountains in Iran around 2500 BC, and had established small kingdoms in northern Syria by 1725 BC. Credited with bringing the horse and light chariot to the Near East from the Pontic steppes, Hurrian war making in the mid-1600s seems to have pushed groups of Semitic warriors, merchants, and shepherds – among them the Hyksos and Hebrew peoples – south into Egypt, where the Middle Kingdom pharaohs, possibly weakened by droughts and famine, failed to keep them out. The establishment of Hyksos kingdoms in the Delta around 1640 marked the onset of the Second Intermediate Period, which ended a century later when Egyptian armies from Thebes to the south pushed the Hyksos back into Palestine, inaugurating the aggressive war making of the New Kingdom.[20] To the north, the disruptions of Hittite and Hurrian campaigns had repercussions in the ancient chain of trade running up to the Baltic via the Black Sea and

[19] Floyd W. McCoy, "The Late-Bronze Age Explosive Eruption of Thera (Santorini) Greece: Regional and Local Effects," in Floyd W. McCoy and Grant Heiken, eds., *Volcanic Hazards and Disasters in Human Antiquity* (Boulder, CO, 2000), 43–69; William J. Broad, "It Swallowed a Civilization: Scientists Revisit an Aegean Eruption Far Worse Than Krakatoa," *NYT*, October 21, 2003, D1–2, citing research by Floyd W. McCoy. Siro Igino Trevisanato, "Six Medical Papyri Describe the Effects of Santorini's Volcanic Ash, and Provide Egyptian Parallels to the So-Called Biblical Plagues," *MedHyp* 26 (2006), 187–90; the dating of the eruption of Santorini is highly controversial. For the most recent dating, see Walter F. Friedrich et al., "Santorini Eruption Radiocarbon Dated to 1627–1600 B.C.," *Science* 312 (2006), 548. Mt. Vesuvius erupted in 1780 BC, perhaps a precursor to the Santorini eruption: Giuseppe Mastrolorenzo et al., "The Avellino 3780-yr-B.P. Catastrophe as a Worst-Case Scenario for a Future Eruption at *Vesuvius*," *PNAS* 103 (2006), 4366–70.
[20] See Van de Mieroop, *A History of the Ancient Near East*, 115–17, 125–9, 142–5, 161–9; Robert Chadwick, *First Civilizations: Ancient Mesopotamia and Ancient Egypt* (London, 2005), 70–2, 168–71; and Issar and Zohar, *Climate Change*, 138–53; 152 for Middle Kingdom weakness deriving from a low Nile.

the Danube Valley. With contacts shattered, this trade closed down, and when it reopened it was situated farther to the west, on a new line running from the Aegean to the head of the Adriatic and over the Alps. This was a departure that would eventually lead to the rise of Rome.[21]

Disease must have moved with this swirling violent movement. Certainly epidemic disease was a great horror for peoples of Southwest Asia and the eastern Mediterranean well before this, probably since the time of the chaos of the fourth millennium. Then disease would have certainly followed commerce, as traders moved goods over long distances from center to center. But during the crisis period of 1700–1500 BC we start to get bits of evidence in the surviving record. Sometime before 1600 BC the black rat and the bubonic plague are said to have arrived in Egypt from India, apparently following a chain of maritime linkages that probably originated in China.[22] Then – in a contested chronology – there are the biblical plagues associated with the Hebrews in Egypt; one has been identified tentatively as tularemia, a virulent rabbit-born infection to which a herding people might have been immune, but apparently not the Egyptians.[23]

We have to assume a low-grade regional transmission of disease, perhaps with devastating consequences, but limited by the small scale of contacts, from the Early Bronze into the Middle Bronze Age. Then the increasing volatility of movement during the crisis decades of 1650–1500 BC brought together peoples from greater distances in greater numbers, and with them a larger load of exotic disease. But it would be in the Late Bronze Age (1500–1200 BC), after conditions improved and order had been restored, that systemic international commerce and aggressive imperial war making would have significantly increased the circulation of new diseases. The case linking rising disease and Late Bronze Age trade is merely hypothetical, based on what would happen in centuries to come. The case for disease and war is based on the next flurry of surviving accounts of epidemics. During the mid-fourteenth century BC, infected Egyptian prisoners of war are said to have set off an epidemic – bubonic plague? smallpox? – among the Hittites

---

[21] Sherratt, "What Would a Bronze-Age World System Look Like?" 31–3.

[22] Eva Panagiotakopulu, "Pharaonic Egypt and the Origins of Plague," *Journal of Biogeography* 31 (2004), 269–75. This reputed Egyptian bubonic plague of 1600 BC is not clearly manifested in the most recent genetic analysis, but it is not necessarily refuted by it either. This analysis put the root of *y. pestis* emerging from *y. psuedotuberculosis* in China or adjacent parts of Asia sometime between 2,603 and 28,646 years ago: Giovanna Morelli et al., "*Yersinia Pestis* Genome Sequencing Identifies Patterns of Global Phylogenetic Diversity," *NatGen* 42 (2010), 1140–3.

[23] Siro I. Trevisanato, "Did an Epidemic of Tularemia in Ancient Egypt Affect the Course of World History?" *MedHyp* 63 (2004), 905–10; Mary Ellen Snodgrass, *World Epidemics: A Cultural Chronology of Disease from Prehistory to the Era of SARS* (Jefferson, NC, 2003), 10–11. See Exodus 7–13.

in Anatolia.²⁴ Then there seems to have been a series of epidemics at the turn of the twelfth century, perhaps something on the order of a pandemic. Homer's *Iliad* described a devastating disease sweeping through Greeks besieging Troy (1250 BC?), Ramses V seems to have died of smallpox in 1157 BC, and, according to the biblical book of Samuel, the Philistines were struck by a plague at Ashdod after they defeated the Israelites (1140 BC?) and carried off the Ark of the Covenant.²⁵ These are of course ancient tales (and one pharaonic mummy), but they do suggest a link between war and disease in the Late Bronze Age.

If these ancient stories do tell us something of the conditions around 1200 BC, they hint at the scale of *the third general crisis that brought an end to the Bronze Age world, what I am calling the Preclassical global crisis.* Disease must have brewed in larger cities and then moved with the expansion of Late Bronze trade and with the increasingly extensive warfare that accompanied that trade, and that followed its collapse. Something dramatic clearly happened in the late thirteenth and the twelfth centuries. Quite suddenly, over perhaps a half century, the Bronze Age palace polities that surrounded the Mediterranean collapsed, and never recovered their ancient form. While the details have long been in debate, the Bronze Age collapse clearly involved the movement of peoples down from the northern Balkans, from Sardinia and Sicily in the west, and from semiarid regions east of the Jordan.

Some of these were piecemeal migrations, others violent raids. Mycenae declined from 1250 and the palace system collapsed around 1190, the people taking refuge in hilltop forts on the mainland, on Crete, and in the Greek islands. Some of the Mycenaeans seem to have moved south to Cyprus and the Levant coast, perhaps in alliance with roving "Sea Peoples" from the west. Starting in 1208 BC, Egypt began an epic series of frontier struggles against invading Libyans and Sea Peoples. While managing to defend the Nile Delta, Egypt had been essentially pushed out of the Levant by 1150 BC, where people resisting the extractions of the palace economies occupied the hills and forged the first proto-Israelite communities. To the north in Anatolia, the now venerable empire of the Hittites collapsed around 1200 BC, swept into oblivion by Sea Peoples, famine, or rebellion. In Mesopotamia, central state power in Assyria and Babylon waned, as they lost control of a

---

²⁴ Panagiotakopulu; "Pharaonic Egypt and the Origins of Plague," 273; Snodgrass, *World Epidemics*, 11.

²⁵ Snodgrass, *World Epidemics*, 12; George Childs Kohn, *Encyclopedia of Plague and Pestilence: From Ancient Times to the Present* (New York, 2001), 266–7, 407; Lawrence I. Conrad, "The Biblical Tradition for the Plague of the Philistines," *Journal of the American Oriental Society* 104 (1984), 281–7; see I Samuel 5–6. Tom Slattery, *The Tragic End of the Bronze Age: A Virus Makes History* (San Jose, CA, 2000) surveys the evidence for smallpox in a monocausal argument for the end of the Bronze Age.

countryside increasingly occupied by nomadic pastoralists, many coming from the mountains to the east and beyond. Between 1100 BC and 900 BC, the ancient traditions collapsed to the extent that very few texts survive. By all accounts, the firm impression is that settlements contracted and populations collapsed.[26]

* * *

The Preclassical Crisis and the Age of Iron, 1200–300 BC

The Bronze Age in western Asia and the eastern Mediterranean thus came to an end in a perfect storm of tribulations. But war, disease, and wandering peoples were the symptoms rather than the initial cause. While it is agreed that the rigidity and oppressive extraction of the Late Bronze Age palace system contributed to the collapse, this was not simply a class struggle. Nor was it a Malthusian crisis of overpopulation. Rather, earth system forces had a foundational role in the Bronze Age collapse. A convincing case has been made that an "earthquake storm" running from 1225–1175 BC toppled cities throughout the eastern Mediterranean.[27] And climate change also played a key role in the longer and wider crisis that brought the Bronze Age to an end.

[26] Van de Mieroop, *A History of the Ancient Near East*, 178–94; Issar and Zohar, *Climate Change*, 163–88; William W. Hallo, "From Bronze Age to Iron Age in Western Asia: Defining the Problem," J. D. Muhly, "The Crisis Years in the Mediterranean World: Transition or Cultural Disintegration?" Jeremy Rutter, "Cultural Novelties in the Palatial Aegean World: Indices of Vitality or Decline?" Vassos Karageorghis, "The Crisis Years: Cyprus," Trude Dothan, "Social Dislocation and Cultural Change in the 12th Century B.C.," William G. Dever, "The Late Bronze Early Iron I Horizon in Syria-Palestine: Egyptians, Canaanites, 'Sea Peoples,' and Proto-Israelites," Patricia Maynor Bikai, "The Phoenicians," and James Weinstein, "The Collapse of the Egyptian Empire in the Southern Levant," all in William A. Ward and Martha Sharp Joukowsky, eds., *The Crisis Years: The 12th Century B.C.: From beyond the Danube to the Tigris* (Dubuque, IA, 1992), 1–26, 61–86, 99–130, 142–50; Robert Drews, *The End of the Bronze Age: Change in Warfare and the Catastrophe ca 1200 B.C.* (Princeton, NJ, 1993), 48–72, 209–25. For detailed recent analysis, see Assaf Yasur Landau, *The Philistines and Aegean Migration at the End of the Late Bronze Age* (New York, 2010); the articles in Eliezer D. Oren, ed., *The Sea Peoples and Their World: A Reassessment* (Philadelphia, PA, 2000), and in Seymour Gitin et al., eds., *Mediterranean Peoples in Transition: Thirteenth to Early Tenth Centuries, BCE* (Jerusalem, 1998). For accessible syntheses, see Manuel Robins, *Collapse of the Bronze Age: The Story of Greece, Troy, Israel, Egypt, and the Peoples of the Sea* (San Jose, CA, 2001) and N. K. Sandars, *The Sea Peoples: Warriors of the Ancient Mediterranean*, rev. ed. (London, 1985).

[27] Amos Nur, "Poseidon's Horses: Plate Tectonics and Earthquake Storms in the Late Bronze Age Aegean and Eastern Mediterranean," *JArchS* 27 (2000), 43–63; Amos Nur, with Dawn Burgess, *Apocalypse: Earthquakes, Archaeology, and the Wrath of God* (Princeton, NJ, 2008), 224–45.

The last Hallstatt grand solar minimum had ended around 3000 BC, and with it the millennial Siberian High that had made the Mid-Holocene fourth millennium so climatically stressful. (See Figure III.3 and a global model in Figure II.5c.) In the middle of the second millennium, the Hallstatt solar minimum returned, a "Preclassical Crisis" that echoed the fourth millennium Mid-Holocene Crisis and the seventh millennium Late Neolithic Crisis. It was primarily shaped by a long epoch of lower solar input running from the fifteenth century BC to the eighth century BC, with deep minima at 1450 BC, 1000 BC, and 800 BC. These solar minima seem to have pushed south both the Intertropical Convergence Zone (measured in the Cariaco sediments) and the edge of the northern sea ice, manifested in a double-headed cycle of ice rafting in the North Atlantic running from 1400 BC to 650 BC and peaking around 1300 BC and 900 BC. The El Niño pattern seems to have strengthened considerably around 1500 BC. These forces were compounded by a strong Siberian High, with initial symptoms at and after 1500 BC and strong from 1150 BC to 850 BC, which for centuries controlled northern and probably global climates, sending outbursts of cold winter weather felt as far south as the Aegean Sea and the Red Sea. As a final blow, just at the end of this Hallstatt cycle, solar insolation reached a minimum (the "Homeric") at 800 BC not seen since 2900 BC, followed by another slightly shallower minimum at 400 BC.[28]

In the Mediterranean and into Asia, the effects of this prolonged crisis seem to have brought another strange NAO couplet, such as had happened in the Mid-Holocene Crisis: two periods of the negative mode of the North Atlantic Oscillation separated by severe drought. The NAO, as we have seen, comes in two flavors: in a warm world, the NAO has a generally "positive mode," with warm winter westerlies flowing to northern Europe; in a colder world, the NAO in its negative mode follows the ITCZ south, sending reduced winter westerlies through southern Europe and the eastern Mediterranean into Asia. Such a classic negative pattern seems to have pertained in about half of the Preclassical Crisis. The ice-rafting cycle running from 1400 BC to 650 BC was matched at each end by periods of high lake levels in the Mediterranean and central Europe, suggesting strong southern precipitation, and thus the negative mode of the NAO. Then, when the Siberian High intensified at 1150 BC, these high lake levels were interrupted, and evidence mounts for severe dry conditions in Southwest

[28] F. Steinhilber et al., "Interplanetary Magnetic Field during the Past 9300 Years Inferred from Cosmogenic Radionuclides," *JGR* 115 (2010), A01104; Gerard Bond, "Persistent Solar Influence on North Atlantic Climate during the Holocene," *Science* 294 (2001), 2131; Eelco J. Rohling et al., "Holocene Atmosphere-Ocean Interactions: Records from Greenland and the Aegean Sea," *ClimDyn* 18 (2002), 587–93; Heiko Lars Legge and Jörg Mutterlose, "Climatic Changes in the Northern Red Sea during the Last 22,000 Years as Recorded by Calcareous Nannofossils," *Paleoceanography* 21 (2006), PA 1003, 4, 13; Rodbell et al., "An ~15,000-Year Record of El Niño-Driven Alluviation in Southwestern Ecuador."

Asia. Conversely, after both of the last of the major solar minima ended and the Siberian High faded around 750 BC, the high Mediterranean lake levels returned and glaciers advanced in the Alps, both markers of a negative NAO. It would appear that the longer crisis was manifested in western Eurasia as a long period of a predominant negative NAO, as winter westerlies moved south from northern to southern Europe following the Intertropical Convergence Zone, and then were interrupted by the blast of the Siberian High.[29]

The first effects were felt in the north as early as the 1390s, when cooling in southern England began to undermine Bronze Age settlements on Dartmoor, leading to its permanent abandonment. Precipitation at Lake Van in Turkey, a good measure of stream flow in the Tigris-Euphrates system, began to drop to new lows after 1300 BC, and did not recover until roughly 200 BC; east of Lake Van, Lake Tecer dried out for the third time in 2,000 years. Water levels in the Dead Sea plummeted to levels well below those of the 3200 BC and 2200 BC crisis levels. Around the Indian Ocean, precipitation on the Oman coast and at Mount Kilimanjaro was at highs around 1300–1200 BC but then fell together, recovering around 900–800 BC; there appears to have been a corresponding drop in the precipitation in the Ethiopian Highlands and a Nile drought around 1200 BC. Just to compound the situation, the mid-twelfth-century eruption of Hekla on Iceland (possibly connected to the "earthquake storm" in the Mediterranean) probably caused a severe setback in the North Atlantic, visible in Irish oak tree rings around 1159 BC. As we shall see, the Preclassical Crisis also had formative impacts in China and the Americas.[30]

---

[29] Giraudi et al., "The Holocene Climatic Evolution of Mediterranean Italy"; Magny, "Holocene Climate Variability as Reflected by Mid-European Lake-Level Fluctuations; Hanspeter Holzhauser et al., "Glacier and Lake-Level Variations in West-Central Europe over the Last 3500 Years," *Holocene* 15 (2009), 789–801; Celia Martin-Puerta et al., "Regional Atmospheric Circulation Shifts Induced by a Grand Solar Minimum," *NatGeosc* (May 6, 2012) (DOI:10.1038/NGEO1460).

[30] Eelco J. Rohling et al., "Holocene Climate Variability in the Eastern Mediterranean and the End of the Bronze Age," in C. Bachhuber and R. B. Roberts, eds., *Forces of Transformation: The End of the Bronze Age in the Mediterranean* (Oxford, 2009), 2–5; Bernhard Weninger et al., "The Impact of Rapid Climate Change on Prehistoric Societies during the Holocene in the Eastern Mediterranean," *Documenta Praehistorica* 36 (2009), 7–59, at 44–8; Lemcke and Sturm, "δ¹⁸o and Trace Element Measurements as Proxy for the Reconstruction of Climate Changes at Lake Van," 662–70; Migowski, "Holocene Climate Variability … from the Dead Sea Sedimentary Record," 427; Fleitmann et al., "Holocene ITCZ and Indian Monsoon Dynamics"; Thompson et al., "Kilimanjaro Ice Core Records"; Stanley, "Nile Flow Failure," 399; Butzer, "Environmental Change in the Near East," 133; Matthew J. Amesbury et al., "Bronze Age Upland Settlement Decline in Southwest England: Testing the Climate Change Hypothesis," *JArchS* 35 (2008), 87–98; Kuzucuoğlu et al., "Mid- to Late-Holocene Climate Change in Central Turkey," 182, 185; G. A. Zielinski et al., "Record of Volcanism since 7000 B.C. from the Gisp2 Greenland Ice Core and Implications for the Volcano-Climate System," *Science* 264 (1994), 948–52; M. G. L. Baillie, "Extreme Environmental Events and

The advance of this cold, dry climate has to be a fundamental explanation of the demise of the Bronze Age of the greater Mediterranean. While around 1210 BC Egypt had been able to send grain to the Hittites, who were already overcome by drought, within forty years a combination of warfare-driven inflation and drought led to food shortages that around 1075 BC fatally undermined the New Kingdom. Colder climate would certainly explain the debated role of migratory peoples from the north – the Dorians – in the demise of Mycenae and perhaps even Troy. Droughts presumably drove the Libyans to attack the Nile Delta, and cold weather and droughts may well have played a role in setting in motion the Sea People raiders, apparently coming from Sardinia and Sicily, the forbears of pirate communities who would ravage the Mediterranean for centuries to come.[31]

Recently discovered DNA evidence supports one ancient tale of drought and migration. According to Herodotus, the Etruscans of northern Italy had their origins in the province of Lydia on the east coast of Turkey, where, after an eighteen-year drought some time during the twelfth century, half the population emigrated by ship to Tuscany. Recent analysis of DNA from the modern inhabitants of an isolated village in Tuscany and from Tuscan cattle breeds suggests a unique pattern of Near Eastern origins for both people and cattle.[32] These Tuscan cattle breeds are marked by an even more distant prior migration. Following each of the great climate reversals of the Bronze Age is more evidence of the arrival and dispersal of drought-resistant Indian

the Linking of Tree-Ring and Ice-Core Events," in Jeffrey S. Dean et al., eds., *Tree Rings, Environment, and Humanity: Proceedings of the International Conference, Tucson, Arizona, 17–21 May 1994* (Tucson, AZ, 1996), 703–11; Françoise Chalié and Françoise Gasse, "Late-Glacial-Holocene Diatom Record of Water Chemistry and Lake Level Change from the Tropical East African Rift Lake Abiyata (Ethiopia)," *PPP* 187 (2002), 259–83. The Nile drought and a wider east African drought may have been simply a result of the wider deterioration, but, like the 3200 drought, correlate with a two-century retreat in North Atlantic ice rafting, implying that a warming northern summer (in the context of continuing cold winter Siberian High conditions) contributed to stalled rainfall in East Africa. A somewhat similar situation seems to have shaped the Nile drought at the beginning of the Medieval Climate Anomaly. See Chapter 9.

[31] Karl W. Butzer, "Long-Term Nile Flood Variation and Political Discontinuities in Pharaonic Egypt," in J. Desmond Clark and Steven A. Brandt, eds., *From Hunters to Farmers: The Causes and Consequences of Food Production in Africa* (Berkeley, CA, 1984), 102–12; Butzer, "Collapse, Environment, and Society," 3634–5; Dafna Langgut et al., "Climate and the Late Bronze Age Collapse: New Evidence from the Southern Levant," *Tel Aviv* 40 (2013), 149–75; D. Kaniewski et al., "Late Second–Early First Millennium BC Abrupt Climate Changes in Coastal Syria and Their Possible Significance for the History of the Eastern Mediterranean," *Quaternary Research* 74 (2010), 207–15; Bernhardt et al., "Nile Delta Vegetation Response"; Thucydides, *History of the Peloponnesian War*, Rex Warner, trans. (London, 1954, rev. ed., 1972), 37–9.

[32] Alessandro Achilli et al., "Mitochondrial DNA Variation of Modern Tuscans Supports the Near Eastern Origin of Etruscans," *AJHG* 80 (2007), 759–68. For a critical review of the Lydia drought story, see Robert Drews, "Herodotus 1.94, the Drought ca. 1200 B.C., and the Origin of the Etruscans," *Historia* 41 (1992), 14–39.

Zebu cattle in Southwest Asia. First arriving in the Mesopotamian lowlands after 3000 BC, they had spread to Syria and the Levant by the time of the crisis of the thirteenth century to the twelfth century; the Tuscan cattle bear the genetic mark of this Zebu migration. As they adopted drought-resistant cattle, eastern Mediterranean people also adapted their architecture; a study of domestic structures on Crete suggests a shift from well-ventilated houses with outdoor hearths – appropriate for year-round, humid, warm-to-hot climates – to poorly ventilated houses with indoor hearths, suitable for drier, colder winters.[33]

On the Russian and Central Asian steppes, there appear to have been two strategies in the face of the advancing millennial Siberian High. To the north and east, agricultural villages were abandoned for nomadism, while to the south irrigation systems were begun in what would become the great oasis centers of the Silk Road. Within several hundred years, the northern nomads had developed into tribes of warriors, among them the Cimmerians and the Scythians, mounted on horseback and armed with powerful compound bows, who began to harass the Eurasian and East Asian frontiers around 800 BC. Further south, the decline of Assyria and Babylon was somewhat delayed relative to the north, perhaps not commencing until 1150 BC, but the migration of nomadic peoples driven out of the north clearly played a role in their collapse, followed by the drought and famine attested in detail in surviving texts. Steppe warriors would shape Eurasian history for the next 2,500 years, pressing on and compromising the primary Bronze Age states exposed to incursion from Inner Asia.[34]

Out of this crisis Iron Age societies and eventually classical civilizations would emerge. The rise of iron was a direct result of the collapse of the palace systems. The royal households had continued to monopolize international trade, and with it the long-distance flow of tin and copper ores worked into bronze in centralized royal foundries. As the twelve-century crisis brought this ritualized royal gift trade to an end, the production of metal was severely threatened. Bronze became scarce, and iron began to emerge as an alternative. Some scholars currently argue that serious iron-working had its origins on Cyprus around 1200 BC, following a wave of

---

[33] R. Negrini et al., "Differentiation of European Cattle by AFLP Fingerprinting," *Animal Genetics* 38 (2007), 60–6; Roger Matthews, "Zebu: Harbingers of Doom in Bronze Age Western Asia?" *Antiquity* 76 (2002), 438–46; Jennifer Moody, "Changes in Vernacular Architecture and Climate at the End of the Aegean Bronze Age," in Bachhuber and Roberts, eds., *Forces of Transformation*, 6–19.

[34] Issar and Zohar, *Climate Change*, 163; Thomas J. Barfield, *The Perilous Frontier: Nomadic Empires and China* (Cambridge, MA, 1989), 28–9; J. Neumann and S. Parpola, "Climate Change and the Eleventh-Tenth Century Eclipse of Assyria and Babylonia," *Journal of Near Eastern Studies* 46 (1987), 161–82; Victor Lieberman, *Strange Parallels: Southeast Asia in Global Context, c. 800–1830. Vol. II: Mainland Mirrors: Europe, Japan, China, South Asia and the Islands* (New York, 2009), 85–7, 92–114.

turmoil, perhaps the arrival of shiploads of Mycenaeans or Sea People.[35] Wider prospecting for tin and copper may have located iron deposits; the search for iron may also have found more tin and copper. But the future lay with iron. More difficult to work, iron deposits were nonetheless rich and well distributed, unlike tin and copper. As ironworking skills emerged, it increasingly became the metal of choice. Widely distributed, it was more difficult to control from a central place, resulting in a wide dispersion of iron production systems. Used occasionally during the Bronze Age for ornament, iron became the utilitarian metal, used for knives, hoes, picks, shovels, and plowshares, while swords and especially ornaments continued to be crafted from bronze. Techniques of hardening iron and converting iron into steel evolved slowly. It would be hundreds of years, perhaps not until 700 BC, before iron was in wide use, and in the interval flint remained in wide use as a cheap and accessible means to a cutting edge, particularly in sickles.[36] But starting as an unsatisfactory replacement for the grand metal of the former age, iron and steel with their ubiquity and increasing strength and edge would radically advance humans' abilities to manipulate the natural world around them.

Iron was only the most obvious part of a wider complex of new elements to emerge in the wake of the final Bronze Age crisis, with the collapse of the palace systems. Merchants were freed from royal control, and became for the first time relatively free entrepreneurs; in a certain sense the opening of the Iron Age saw the rise of capitalism in its earliest form. Decentralized metal production and autonomous merchants were both symptomatic of the collapse of centralized authority and of the rise of a proliferation of small polities. In this context, as the ancient Bronze Age centers were collapsing, smaller polities emerged in the relative power vacuum, smaller polities with oligarchic aristocracies rather than divine kings. Some of these would evolve into variations on the Greek polis, with their great men and

---

[35] James D. Muhly, "The Bronze Age Setting," Jane C. Waldbaum, "The First Archaeological Appearance of Iron and the Transition to the Iron Age," Anthony M. Snodgrass, "Iron and Early Metallurgy in the Mediterranean," in Theodore A. Wertime and James D. Muhly, eds., *The Coming of the Age of Iron* (New Haven, CT, 1980), 25–98, 335–74; Vincent C. Pigott, "Introductory Comments," James D. Muhly, "Copper and Bronze in Cyprus and the Eastern Mediterranean," Jane C. Waldbaum, "The Coming of Iron in the Eastern Mediterranean: Thirty Years of Archaeological and Technological Research," in Vincent C. Pigott, ed., *The Archaeometallurgy of the Asian Old World* (Philadelphia, PA, 1999), 1–58; Drews, *The End of the Bronze Age*, 73–6.

[36] For the survival of stone tools through the Bronze Age and into the Iron Age, see Steven A. Rosen, *Lithics after the Stone Age*; Curtis N. Runnels, "Flaked-Stone Artifacts in Greece during the Historical Period," *JFdArch* 9 (1982), 364–73; and Akkermans and Schwartz, *The Archaeology of Syria*, 353. On the slow spread of iron, especially in the Aegean, see Peter Haarer, "Problematizing the Transition from Bronze to Iron," in Andrew J. Shortland, ed., *The Social Context of Technological Changes: Egypt and the Near East, 1650–1550 BC* (Oxford, 2001), 255–71.

plebian households prosperous enough to mobilize sons and servants in mass levee, as iron-clad infantry ready to defend the city-state. With the collapse of the palaces went the scribes and their ancient pictographic writing systems, gradually replaced by new alphabetical writing systems more accessible to ordinary people, those of the greater Mediterranean world and southwest Asia erupting out of Phoenician origins. Religious historians argue that these centuries, an "Axial Age" spanning Eurasia, saw the emergence of monotheistic world religious traditions framed by ethical and philosophical traditions developed by cadres of clerics and scholars.[37] And on the northern frontier, European societies rapidly developed, first in the vacuum left by the collapse of the Near Eastern world and then in the thickening of trade, increasingly weaving them into – and actually shaping – the economic fabric being reconfigured by the smaller, more dynamic societies of the recovering Mediterranean into a new Iron Age world system of competing imperiums.[38]

* * *

A Global View on Optimum and Crisis

This discussion has focused on Southwest Asia and the eastern Mediterranean, where at roughly 500 BC the Iron Age transition was poised at the edge of classical antiquity. We need to – unfortunately only briefly – consider the rest of the world, especially the growing populations of China, India,

---

[37] Karen Armstrong, *Great Transformation: The Beginning of our Religious Traditions* (New York, 2006); Shmuel N. Eisenstadt, ed., *The Origins and Diversity of Axial Age Civilizations* (Albany, NY, 1986); Johann P. Arnason et al., eds., *Axial Civilization and World History* (Leiden, 2005).

[38] Jorgen C. Meyer, "Trade in the Bronze Age and Iron Age Empires: A Comparison," in Peter F. Bang et al., eds., *Ancient Economies, Modern Methodologies: Archaeology, Comparative History, Models and Institutions* (Bari, 2006), 89–106; Liverani, "The Collapse of the Near Eastern Regional System," 70–3; Hallo, "From Bronze Age to Iron Age," 3; Muhly, "The Crisis Years in the Mediterranean World," 11, 19, 20; Sherratt, "What Would a Bronze-Age World System Look Like?" 33–47; Susan Sherratt and Andrew Sherratt, "The Growth of the Mediterranean Economy in the Early First Millennium BC," *WdArch* 24 (1993), 361–78; Andrew Sherratt, "Europe Prehistory," in R. A. Butlin and R. A. Dodgshon, eds., *An Historical Geography of Europe* (Oxford, 1998), esp. 15–23; Andrew Sherratt and Susan Sherratt, "Technological Change in the East Mediterranean Bronze Age: Capital, Resources, and Marketing," in Shortland, *The Social Context of Technological Change*, 15–38; Michael Rowlands, "From 'the Gift' to Market Economies: The Ideology and Politics of European Iron Age Studies," and Kristian Kristiansen, "The Emergence of the European World System in the Bronze Age: Divergence, Convergence and Social Evolution during the First and Second Millennia BC in Europe," in Kristian Kristiansen and Jorgen Jenson, eds., *Europe in the First Millennium B.C.* (Sheffield, 1994), 1–31; Drews, *The End of the Bronze Age*, 224–5; I. J. Gelb, *A Study of Writing*, rev. ed. (Chicago, IL, 1963), 166–205; I. J. Gelb, *The Origins of the Alphabet* (Amherst, NY, 2002).

tropical West Africa, and the emerging high cultures of Mesoamerica. Here the story is united by the wider tropical climate system spanning the Pacific, the Caribbean, and the Central Atlantic. While all of the connections are not entirely clear, it would appear that trans-Pacific fluctuations in the Intertropical Convergence Zone, combined with the rising pulse of ENSO variation in the Late Holocene, gave all three of these regions a common rhythm. Redeveloping after the Mid-Holocene transition, the ENSO system dominated the basic conditions of life for the peoples of the wider Indo-Pacific region and the Atlantic tropics. While conditions were not precisely coterminous, as climate teleconnections and local conditions determined the timing of regional climate change, the pulse of climate around the Pacific Rim seems to provide the basic chronological framework for the fortunes of these societies and civilizations. While the evidence is still somewhat sparse, a strong case can be made that the global tropics felt the impact of the Hallstatt solar cycle and the Preclassical Crisis, with a cold north aligned with droughts across southern Asia, and extremes of El Niño and La Niña assaulting the west coast of the Americas.

According to all of the proxies, the El Niño/Southern Oscillation reemerged in the centuries after 3000 BC.[39] (Figure II.1 illustrates only one of several similar estimates.) It may be that the 2200 BC crisis was caused by El Niño: the 2200 BC event was manifested around the Indo-Pacific in different ways, all suggestive of the rising influence and volatility of the El Niño pattern.[40] In South Asia, the result was continuing declines in the volume and duration of the summer monsoon, and by 1900 BC the Harappan cities of the Indus Valley had faded away in the face of intensifying droughts. In northern China, this crisis registered in the beginning of the massive flooding (and cold winter monsoons) that launched the career of the perhaps mythical "Yu the Great" and opened the path to Chinese state formation. It was in this context that bronze arrived in China, moving down into the Central Plain from metal-using cultures on the eastern Eurasian steppe.[41] (See Figures III.3, III.4.)

---

[39] It may well be that the variation in the Cariaco Basin titanium sediments, a measure of the north–south variation of the ITCZ, is the best measure of ENSO available. See Athanasios Koutavas et al., "Mid-Holocene El Niño-Southern Oscillation (ENSO) Attenuation Revealed by Individual Foraminifera in Eastern Tropical Pacific Sediments," *Geology* 34 (2006), 993–6.

[40] Hong et al., "Inverse Phase Oscillations"; Barbara A. Maher and Mengyu Hu, "A High-Resolution Record of Holocene Rainfall Variations from the Western Chinese Loess Plateau: Antiphase Behaviour of the African/Indian and East Asian Summer Monsoons," *Holocene* 16 (2006), 309–16.

[41] Katheryn M. Linduff and Jiajun Mei, "Metallurgy in Ancient East Asia: Retrospect and Prospects," *JWP* 22 (2009), 265–81; Katheryn M. Linduff, "Introduction," in Katheryn M. Linduff et al., eds., *The Beginnings of Metallurgy in China* (Lewiston, NY, 2000), 1–28, and the essays in this volume. See also Andrew Sherratt, "The Trans-Eurasian Exchange:

The first reemergence of El Niño conditions at roughly 3000 BC had brought a bounty of cold waters and maritime resources to the north coast of Peru, allowing the emergence of the cotton pre-ceramic societies, which grew to considerable size without benefit of the New World staple, maize. Then after 1800 BC, rising El Niño precipitation and later La Niña droughts (marked by a great spike in the Cariaco records suggesting a sharp southward movement of the ITCZ) seem to have pushed these societies to change. In a transition into what is known as the *Initial Period*, societies on the northern Peruvian coast and to the south adopted maize, ceramics, and irrigated cultivation. The great pre-ceramic sites were abandoned, and smaller settlements were established away from the coast in inland river valleys.[42] Across the Pacific to the west, Polynesian migration from China and Southeast Asia into the central and eastern Pacific might well have been driven episodically by the westerly winds during El Niño-dominated epochs, the first coming with the rising El Niño winds after 3000 BC, and the second with the rising El Niño of the Preclassical Crisis, roughly 1100 BC.[43]

In China, the early Xia/Erlitou polity lasted roughly 300 years, from 1900–1600 BC, when it was superseded by one of its many rising competitors, the Shang, generally seen as the first major state in China. The fading of Xia/Erlitou established an enduring pattern: here and for the next 3,000 years dynastic changes would coincide with epochs of failed summer monsoons (which should bring rainfall) and intense, cold, dry winter monsoons[44] (see Figures III.4, III.5c). Climatically, these monsoon failures varied with the ebb and flow of the ITCZ as measured across the Pacific at the Cariaco basin in Venezuela, suggesting a wider systemic connection. Epochs of monsoon failure weakened the power and legitimacy of the Chinese polity, not unlike the way periods of low Nile (also possibly ENSO driven in part) undermined the Egyptian polity. Tax receipts fell, poverty

---

The Prehistory of Chinese Relations with the West," in Victor H. Mair, ed., *Contact and Exchange in the Ancient World* (Honolulu, HI, 2006), 30–61.

[42] Jonathan Haas et al., "Dating the Late Archaic Occupation of the North Chico Region in Peru," *Nature* 432 (204), 1020–3, at 1022; Michael E. Moseley, *The Incas and Their Ancestors: The Archaeology of Peru*, rev. ed. (London, 2001), 131–58; Richard L. Burger, *Chavin and the Origins of Andean Civilization* (London, 1992), 57–103.

[43] Atholl Anderson et al., "Prehistoric Maritime Migration in the Pacific Islands: An Hypothesis of ENSO Forcing," *Holocene* 16 (2006), 1–6.

[44] Yancheva, "Influence of the Intertropical Convergence Zone on the East Asian Monsoon" demonstrates the general relationship between weak summer monsoons and strong winter monsoons, and the striking chronology of winter monsoons in the Lake Huang Maar sediments (south China coast), the ITCZ proxy at Cariaco, and the traditional sequence of Chinese history. See her reply in a critical exchange in *Nature* 450 (2007), E8–9; and Timothy Brook, *The Troubled Empire: China in the Yuan and Ming Dynasties* (Cambridge, MA, 2010). Here I use the modern dating for the rise of the Shang; see Chun-shu Chang, *The Rise of the Chinese Empire: Nation, State, and Imperialism in Early China, ca. 1600 B.C.–A.D. 8* (Ann Arbor, MI, 2007), 14.

and famine spread, rebellions broke out, and rising smaller states saw the opportunity to strike against the hegemonic imperial state. Cold climate would also bring incursions of northern nomads into the Chinese heartland. Conversely, good monsoon conditions allowed the Chinese state to prosper and for rice and millet agricultures to spread to the north and the south.[45] The Shang dynasty enjoyed 500 years of success until the onset of the Preclassical Crisis, when an epoch of strong winter monsoons starting around 1150 BC apparently contributed to its gradual weakening before its final conquest by the Western Zhou in 1050 BC. Carrying this analysis forward, the Zhou was the preeminent power in central China for nearly 600 years of reasonably good monsoon conditions until 475 BC, when the beginning of two centuries of intense winter monsoons launched the period of Warring States. With the improvement of monsoon conditions two and a half centuries later, first the short but pivotal Qin dynasty (221–207 BC) and then the long-enduring Han began to unify China. The Han dynasty lasted until the next major failure of the monsoons around AD 220, with a brief interval of crisis (the Wang Mang interregnum) at AD 9–24, exactly at a brief burst of cold winter monsoons. The pattern would recur throughout Chinese history until the fall of the Ming dynasty in 1644.[46]

Along the South American coasts, and increasingly into the interior valleys, the peoples of the Andean "Initial Period" were similarly stressed by the Hallstatt-driven Preclassical Crisis, here manifested in a rising intensity of El Niño/La Niña variation (see Figures II.1, II.5c, III.3, III.5d). These impacts seem to have peaked between 1000 BC and 700 BC, when massive beach ridges were formed by mega El Niños – compounded by highland reglaciation and even a tsunami – shattering the remaining coastal settlement and driving a general depopulation. Andean recovery came in what is known as the *Early Horizon* of 800 BC to 200 BC, with growing populations now protected by large fortifications. In this Early Horizon context of competing chiefdom societies, a wider integration was forged in the great ritual sphere of the Chavin, circling a cult of a supernatural jaguar. In a manner broadly analogous to that of the Chalcolithic interaction spheres of fifth- and fourth-millennium Mesopotamia, these societies managed complex irrigation systems in an arid climate, moved goods on herds of pack animals – llamas rather than donkeys – and crafted an elaborate ornamental metallurgy from copper, silver, and gold. It might well be appropriate to compare the Chavin to the Axial Age world religions that were emerging in the Old World Iron Age societies. The Chavin sphere reached its peak of influence in a period of intense drought between 400 BC and 200 BC,

[45] Mark Elvin, *The Retreat of the Elephants: An Environmental History of China* (New Haven, CT, 2004), 9–85. For the same argument for China, and the world as a whole, for AD 1000 to the present, see the studies coauthored by David D. Zhang, cited in Chapter 6, note 12.

[46] Chang, *The Rise of the Chinese Empire*, 14–64.

providing as did later Andean empires a system of geographical connection across regions beset by unpredictable droughts and floods. As the droughts faded, new local powers emerged. As was happening at precisely the same time with the Han in China and the Romans in the Mediterranean, centralized, militarized states of the Peruvian "Early Intermediate" period – Moche, Nasca, and Tiwanaku – developed around 200 BC.[47]

In Mesoamerica, a mild version of the global Preclassical Crisis had important impacts, and the sequence of cultures was again strikingly similar. The rising Preclassical pattern of ENSO activity seems to have reached the region around 1500 BC, bringing shifting patterns of rainfall and benefiting a few important regions[48] (see Figure II.1). The effective exploitation of maize began during the Early Formative around 1500 BC, with growing villages and populations, especially in the central highlands and on the gulf coast. By 1200 BC, in a rough parallel to the Chavin, the great Olmec pilgrimage sites on the gulf coast began to provide a religious integration of large reaches of Mesoamerica. Olmec civilization went into decline by 600 BC and, as in the Andes, China, and Rome, emerging militarized city states – most importantly in the valley of Teotihuacan – emerged to dominate Mexico by 300 BC.[49] In North America, the impacts of the Preclassical Hallstatt and Siberian High were more obvious, with the decline of the relatively sizeable Late Archaic societies between 1200 BC and 800 BC. When the Early Woodland stabilized, it too developed an extremely wide-ranging interaction sphere, first in the Adena and then the Hopewell cultures, which managed burial cults and a widespread trade throughout eastern North America.[50]

If the rise and collapse of centers and polities in China and the Americas seem to have been shaped by the Pacific-wide pulsing of ENSO, circumstances in India and West Africa comprise a second remarkably similar pairing, in which the impact of the global Preclassical Hallstatt Crisis of around 1300–700 BC can be detected. In both India and West Africa, iron-using agricultural peoples advanced east and south into rainforest regions, pushed

[47] Moseley, *The Incas and Their Ancestors*, 163–222; Burger, *Chavin and the Origins of Andean Civilization*, 128–90, 210, 222, 224–9; Karen Olsen Bruhns, *Ancient South America* (Cambridge, 1994), 174–84, 126–39; James B. Richardson, *People of the Andes* (Washington DC, 1994), 87–90; Daniel H. Sandweiss et al., "Variation in Holocene El Niño Frequencies: Climate Records and Cultural Consequences in Ancient Peru," *Geology* 29 (2001), 603–6.

[48] Lewis C. Messenger, Jr., "Ancient Winds of Change: Climatic Settings and Prehistoric Social Complexity," *Ancient Mesoamerica* 1 (1990), 21–40, esp. 27.

[49] Susan Toby Evans, *Ancient Mexico and Central America: Archaeology and Culture History* (New York, 2008), 137–234, esp. 123, 133, 150, 158, 168; Christopher A. Pool, *Olmec Archaeology and Early Mesoamerica* (New York, 2007).

[50] Brian M. Fagan, *Ancient North America: The Archaeology of a Continent* (New York, 2005), 421–56; Samuel E. Munoz et al., "Synchronous Environmental and Cultural Change in the Prehistory of Northeastern United States," *PNAS* 107 (2010), 22008–13.

by increasingly dry conditions to the north. These were literally legendary migrations.

In India, the migrating peoples are known as the makers of the "Painted Gray Ware"; they developed ironworking shortly after 1000 BC (see Figure III.3). The authors of the Vedic texts, these peoples have long been reputed to have been Indo-European speakers, possibly the outcome of a fusion of Harappans with horse-using warriors from northern Iran (possibly kin to the Mitani-Hurrians who started migrating toward Mesopotamia and Syria around 2500 BC). The origins of these peoples are a matter of intense debate, but these origins are not really critical here. Most important, tribes and clans of these ironworking, agricultural peoples gradually settled the Ganges Valley from the northwest, led by priests who developed the outlines of Brahmin Hinduism in worship of fire, setting off enormous conflagrations to destroy the jungle. Starting their movement around 1200 BC in the midst of the general waning of the Indian summer monsoon, a waning perhaps intensified by cold snow-covered land surfaces in Tibet, these peoples occupied the entire Ganges Valley by 400 BC.[51]

West Africa suffered a similar desiccation between roughly 2000 BC and 500 BC, driven for the most part by cycles of ice rafting that cooled the Atlantic from 2700–1900 BC and then the Preclassical Siberian High of 1200–700 BC[52] (see Figure II.2). As the Sahel shifted further south, Sahelian herding peoples began to work the edge of the rainforest more intensively, adopting and fully domesticating plants cultivated and harvested by forest peoples, most importantly yams, groundnuts, and oil palms. Copper and then ironworking spread through the region after 800 BC, and together the yam and iron tools – and bananas that recently had spread from East Africa – powered a southward migration into the forested regions of what is

---

[51] Romila Thapar, *Early India: From the Origins to AD 1300* (London, 2002), 98–136; Madhav Gadgil and Ramachandra Gupta, *This Fissured Land: An Ecological History of India* (Oxford, 1992), 78–81. On the controversial question of language groups in India, see Peter Bellwood, *First Farmers: The Origins of Agricultural Societies* (Malden, MA, 2005), 210–17; and Edwin F. Bryant and Laurie L. Patton, eds. *The Indo-Aryan Controversy: Evidence and Inference in Indian History* (London, 2005). New evidence may push the earliest working of iron in India back to around 1800–1500 BC: Rakesh Tewari, "The Origins of Iron Working in India: New Evidence from the Central Ganga Plain and the Eastern Vindhyas," *Antiquity* 77 (2003), 536–44. For monsoon climate, see the citations in Chapter 4, note 25, and Michael Staubwasser, "An Overview of Holocene South Asian Monsoon Records – Monsoon Domains and Regional Contrasts," *Journal Geological Society of India* 68 (2006), 433–46; Netajirao R. Phadtare, "Sharp Decrease in Summer Monsoon Strength 4000–3500 cal yr B. P. in the Central Higher Himalaya of India Based in Pollen Evidence from Alpine Peat," *QuatRes* 53 (2000), 122–9.

[52] Syree Weldeab et al., "Holocene African Droughts Relate to Eastern Equatorial Atlantic Cooling," *Geology* 33 (2005), 981–4; J. M. Russell et al., "725 yr Cycle in the Climate of Central Africa during the Late Holocene," *Geology* 31 (2003), 677–80; F. A. Street-Perrott et al., "Drought and Dust Deposition in the West African Sahel: A 5500-Year Record from Kajemarum Oasis, Northeastern Nigeria," *Holocene* 10 (2000), 293–302.

now Cameroon. Out of this complex emerged the Bantu-speaking peoples, who moved south and east through central Africa, adopted cattle rearing, and after roughly AD 200 spread rapidly south through eastern Africa to KwaZulu-Natal.[53]

* * *

Human Health in the Bronze Age Optimum and the Iron Age/Preclassical Crisis

At this juncture it may be wise to review what little we know of human health between the first rise of the state and the close of the Preclassical Crisis. Here we will concentrate on Southwest Asia and the eastern Mediterranean. Paleobiologists are closely examining skeletal evidence from the Bronze and Iron Ages, and if we have no grand synthesis, general patterns are emerging. It is clear that four broad parameters shaped health across the 2,500 years of the Bronze and Iron Ages. First, dependence on agriculture in increasingly crowded circumstances was a pervasive reality. Second, these were steeply stratified societies, in which access to resources and nutrition must have varied drastically by class and caste. Third, as we have seen, there are sketchy and scrappy suggestions that epidemic disease expanded considerably with commerce and warfare during the Late Bronze Age and the Crisis centuries, with the rising circulation of peoples and commodities. Finally, there is the climate, which can be summarized baldly as a mild Bronze Age Optimum deeply fissured by three reversals, the final one of which led into the Preclassical 800-year epoch of colder, drier climates.

The evidence on population density and agricultural dependence is somewhat ambiguous. Bronze Age skeletons from the greater Mediterranean suggest an improvement of general conditions as the Neolithic gave way to the Early Bronze Age (see Figure III.6). In Egypt, in western Iran, and in Greece and western Turkey, men and usually women increased in stature from the Neolithic into the Bronze Age. Similarly in Egypt dental markers of nutrition stress were relatively high in the Late Neolithic Predynastic, but fell in samples from the early Bronze Age and the Middle Kingdom.[54] Further out

---

[53] Susan Keech McIntosh, "The Holocene Prehistory of West Africa, 10,000–1000BP," and James L. A. Webb, "Ecology & Culture in West Africa," in Emmanuel Kwaku Akyeampong, ed., *Themes in West African History* (Athens, OH, 2006), 20–8, 40–2; David W. Philipson, *African Archaeology*, third edition (Cambridge, 2005), 195–203, 234–69; Bellwood, *First Farmers*, 218–22; Kairn A. Klieman, *"The Pygmies Were Our Compass": Bantu and Batwa in the History of West Central Africa, Early Times to c. 1900 C.E.* (Portsmouth, NH, 2003), 95–132.

[54] Ted A. Rathbun, "Skeletal Pathology from the Paleolithic through the Metal Ages in Iran and Iraq," and J. Lawrence Angel, "Health as a Crucial Factor in the Changes from Hunting to Developed Farming in the Eastern Mediterranean," in Mark N. Cohen and George J.

on the Eurasian Bronze Age periphery, peoples in Britain, Denmark, and on the Latvian plains stood between 171 cm and 172 cm in height, while men in Egypt and the eastern Mediterranean hovered in the high 160s. Dental health declined considerably, strikingly in Britain, where heights increased from the Neolithic.[55] Samples from early dynastic Shang, Zhou, and Han in China, with tooth loss and shrinking stature, suggest declining health. In Vietnam, the transition from Neolithic to "Metal Age" cultures saw a sharp increase in evidence for infectious disease. Conditions in Harappa appear to have been considerably better than the conditions in either China or Vietnam.[56] Some of the increase in dental caries can be attributed paradoxically to improved cooking methods and new foods (like dates) that left corrosive sugars on people's teeth.[57] Increasing numbers of Harris lines might suggest increasing childhood malnutrition, but the considered opinion is that it reflects the increased likelihood that children were surviving weaning and then seasons of food scarcity and borderline starvation. In Egypt, male and female stature declined from a peak in the Early Dynastic through the Old Kingdom and the Middle Kingdom, suggesting that rising stratification increasingly limited nutrition available to ordinary people[58]

Armelagos, eds., *Paleopathology at the Origins of Agriculture* (New York, 1984), 51–73, 137–67; Sonia R. Zakrzewski, "Variations in Ancient Egyptian Stature and Body Proportions," *AJPA* 121 (2003), 219–29; Anne P. Starling and Jay T. Stock, "Dental Indicators of Health and Stress in Early Egyptian and Nubian Agriculturalists, A Difficult Transition and Gradual Recovery," *AJPA* 134 (2007), 520–8.

[55] Pia Bennike, *Paleopathology of Danish Skeletons: A Comparative Study of Demography, Disease and Injury* (Copenhagen, 1985), 50–1; Guntis Gerhards, "Secular Variations in the Body Stature of the Inhabitants of Latvia (7th millennium BC–20th c. AD)," *Acta Medica Lituanica* 12 (2005), 33–9; John Robb et al., "Social 'Status' and Biological 'Status': A Comparison of Grave Goods and Skeletal Indicators from Pontecagnano," *AJPA* 115 (2001), 213–22; Charlotte Roberts and Margaret Cox, "The Impact of Economic Intensification and Social Complexity on Human Health in Britain from 6000 BP (Neolithic) and the Introduction of Farming to the Mid-Nineteenth Century AD," in Mark Nathan Cohen and Gillian M. M. Crane-Kramer, eds., *Ancient Health: Skeletal Indicators of Agricultural and Economic Intensification* (Gainesville, FL, 2007), 149–63.

[56] Ekaterina A. Pechenkina et al., "Diet and Health in the Neolithic of the Wei and Middle Yellow River Basins, Northern China," in Cohen and Crane-Kramer, eds., *Ancient Health*, 264, 266–7, 269; Marc F. Oxenham, "Skeletal Evidence for the Emergence of Infectious Disease in Bronze and Iron Age North Vietnam," *AJPA* 126 (2004), 359–76; Nancy C. Lovell, "Anaemia in the Ancient Indus Valley," *International Journal of Osteoarchaeology* 7 (1997), 115–23. There appears to have been no fundamental change at Ban Chiang in Thailand: Michael Pietrusewsky and Michele Toomay Douglas, "Intensification of Agriculture in Ban Chiang: Is There Evidence from the Skeletons?" *Asian Perspectives* 40 (2002), 157–78.

[57] John R. Lukacs, "Dental Paleopathology and Agricultural Intensification in South Asia: New Evidence from Bronze Age Harappa," *AJPA* 87 (1992), 133–50, esp. 147–8; Greg C. Nelson et al., "Dates, Caries and Tooth Loss during the Iron Age of Oman," *AJPA* 108 (1999), 333–43.

[58] Zakrzewski, "Variations in Ancient Egyptian Stature," 223–8. A study of linear hypoplasia (Harris lines) in the prehistoric Nile basin suggests a slightly different pattern: Harris lines

(see Figure III.6). In one Mediterranean-Middle Eastern sample, elite men were larger (as determined by skull measurements) than commoners; at Mycenae, men and women buried in the royal tombs were taller than those buried in more ordinary burials.[59] Thus it would appear that these populations weathered the transition into the early state with varying results, living increasingly physiologically stressed lives, in patterns that suggest that food was not shared equally in these stratified societies.

As for epidemics, the archaeological record is opaque. There appear to have been no mass burials of plague victims recovered archaeologically, such as are found in medieval Europe during the Black Death. A distinct drop in signs of skeletal infection between the Neolithic and Bronze Ages in Iran (30 percent to 3 percent) may represent the impact of quick and sudden death from new diseases during epidemics, which would not have allowed time for lesions to develop on bones. Iranian Bronze and Iron Age skulls show a high level of bony damage to the inner ear, perhaps evidence of severe infections from measles or the common cold.[60] But if the ancient texts – and common logic – suggest that epidemics may have been on the rise in the Late Bronze Age and into the Crisis, archaeological confirmation is apparently lacking.

If we do take these texts somewhat seriously, however, it is interesting that a cluster of reports of epidemics during the twelfth-century crisis is followed by a long silence until the eighth century, when Plutarch reported an epidemic striking central Italy. The one exception to this gap in epidemic reports comes in 1019 BC, when the Israelites were struck by an epidemic.[61] This epidemiological gap certainly can be explained by a literacy gap: the primitive Early Iron Age was not a time when very much of anything was written down. It could also be the case that the reduced commerce – and reduced long-range warfare – of the Early Iron Age gave the peoples of the greater Mediterranean a respite from the onslaught of disease. If so, this does not mean that their health circumstances were particularly good. Throughout western Eurasia during the Iron Age, the skeletons suggest that populations were somewhat shorter and less healthy than their Bronze Age forebears. From Britain to Iran, virtually no sample of Iron Age men reached a height of 170 cm. In northeast Hungary, where Bronze Age and Iron Age samples have been carefully compared, male height rose slightly from

increase sharply between the Upper Paleolithic and the Late Neolithic and then improve through the Middle Kingdom, where the stature study shows a decline in height: Starling and Stock, "Dental Indicators of Health and Stress."

[59] Rathbun, "Skeletal Pathology ... in Iran and Iraq," 147; citing D. J. Finkel, "Sexual Dimorphism and Settlement Pattern in Middle Eastern Skeletal Populations," in R. L. Hall, ed., *Sexual Dimorphism in Homo Sapiens: A Question of Size* (New York, 1982), 165–85, at 182; Angel, "Health ... in the Eastern Mediterranean," 66.

[60] Rathbun, "Skeletal Pathology ... in Iran and Iraq," 155.

[61] Snodgrass, *World Epidemics*, 11–14.

168 cm to 169 cm, while female height fell from 157 cm to 154 cm, and there is "substantial" evidence of an increase of signs of poor health, including Harris lines, caries, tooth loss, and various signs of anemia.[62] In Greece, levels of strontium and zinc in bones dropped between the Late Bronze and the Early Iron Age, suggesting that traditions of coastal fishing were abandoned as pirates and raiders made venturing on the sea too dangerous.[63] On the other hand, in at least one well-studied context, the transition to the smaller societies of the Iron Age, health clearly improved. In Britain, if individuals were somewhat shorter, they had strikingly lower rates of poor dental health, anemia, and Harris lines than did either the preceding Bronze Age or the succeeding Roman occupation.[64]

Thus if indicators of health continued to be poor, they did not completely plummet with the transition from the Bronze Age to the Iron Age. It might be suggested that various influences were working against each other as the powerful Bronze Age polities collapsed. On one hand, the Bronze Age polities may have provided a certain level of food security and physical safety; on the other, their rising tide of commerce and warfare carried with it the threat of epidemic. The small, isolated communities of the Early Iron Age were exposed to constant local raiding and the impossibility of resupply in the case of crop failure; they were also probably less exposed to exotic disease, and in more equalitarian societies there may have been fewer stresses of stratification. Then, of course, there is the issue of climate. During the course of the Bronze Age, the crises at 2200 BC and 1600 BC certainly must have caused centuries of health trauma and depopulation. There are hints in the skeletal data that the long epoch of cold, dry, and erratic climate had a particular impact on health. Here the evidence of closed, poorly ventilated Iron Age domestic structures on Crete seems particularly clear.[65] Cold weather by itself was not necessarily the health hazard, so much as the specific living condition during such weather. Airless houses, crowded with people and their animals and their various wastes, with fires constantly filling rooms with smoke, would have degraded severely the health of their occupants. Such conditions would have been set in a pattern of crowded walled villages, fortified against the rising tide of Iron Age raiding and piracy to which Thucydides bore testimony. If the collapse of long-range trade and war might have relieved the threat of devastating virgin soil epidemics, these winter conditions would have intensified the effects of low-grade infectious disease and tuberculosis, compounded by poor nutrition. Conversely, the

[62] Douglas U. Ubelaker and Ildikó Pap, "Skeletal Evidence for Health and Disease in the Iron Age of Northeastern Hungary," *International Journal of Osteoarchaeology* 8 (1998), 231–51, esp. 248–9.

[63] Angel, "Health … in the Eastern Mediterranean," 65.

[64] Roberts and Cox, "The Impact of Economic Intensification," 154–7.

[65] Moody, "Changes in Vernacular Architecture and Climate at the End of the Aegean Bronze Age."

combination of warming climate and greater trade circulation (and colonizing warfare), as the Preclassical Hallstatt waned after 700 BC, brought the
spread of epidemic malaria from North Africa into Sicily and then southern
Italy.[66]

When the Preclassical Halstatt/Siberian High waned, imperial systems
began to reemerge and to attain a scale and durability not seen since or
even during the Bronze Age, starting with the Neo-Assyrian conquest of
Babylon and then Egypt in the seventh century. The two millennia that followed would be shaped throughout the Old World, and also in the New,
by such massive imperial hegemonies: the Medes, the Persians, the Seleucid
dynasty, Parthia, Bactria, Maurya, the Han dynasty, the Roman empire, the
Moche, the Nasca, Teotihuacan, the Maya. This would also be an epoch
united by climate, and the imperial systems of the ancient world crashed in
spectacular ruin between AD 200 and AD 500, when rising ENSO intensity,
Asian drought, and an inter-Hallstatt ice-rafting cold cycle interrupted the
broader Ancient-Medieval Optimum. But in the longer scheme of things the
relatively good weather persisted until around 1280, and the next millennial Siberian High launched the Little Ice Age decisively at 1400. Outside
parts of the medieval tropics, the two millennia of the ancient and medieval
worlds would not see the truly devastating climatic shifts that had marked
the two millennia of the Bronze Age.

But in the Old World, this long optimum would be an epoch of devastating pandemic. Twice during this millennium the Old World suffered great
punctuations of culture and population, punctuation driven not primarily
by climate but by epidemic disease. And each time these assaults struck relatively stable, reasonably sustainable societies advancing moderately within
the limits of the organic economy. These epidemic assaults, I argue, were as
systemically exogenous as were the great climate crises that periodically had
brought down Bronze Age civilizations. Like the final Bronze Age crisis, the
final medieval crisis brought a creative destruction to human cultural, social,
and economic systems, opening the door to new directions. And throughout,
human health and well-being was shaped in complex ways by the hierarchies of imperial and regional economy as well as by regimes of climate and
disease.

---

[66] Robert Sallares et al., "The Spread of Malaria to Southern Europe in Antiquity: New
Approaches to Old Problems," *Medical History* 48 (2004), 311–28.

8

A Global Antiquity, 500 BC–AD 542

The Problem of Growth in Antiquity

Throughout global prehistory during the last four millennia BC, the trajectory and pulse of climate change provided one of the fundamental variables in the human condition, establishing the boundaries within which life was conducted. Under these conditions, it is safe to say, population growth rarely came near to overwhelming local resources. In general, however, populations did grow, particularly in the Old World centers running from the eastern Mediterranean to China. Here obviously the slow, incremental advance of techno-agrarian adjustment of the inheritance of the Late Neolithic "secondary products revolution" played a fundamental role, as slight improvements in material culture allowed populations to expand slowly but inexorably, the trajectory of their increase regularly set back by natural disasters of various scales. The net result seems to fit the economist's model of the Malthusian stalemate: by this account, as populations rose or as climates shifted slightly, people either moved or gradually adopted new crops and new techniques in Boserupian intensifications that may have temporarily improved conditions until the slow rise in numbers or another refraction in climate washed out the improved effect.[1]

Such is the classic account. But the world historians see another dynamic at work, an incremental, cyclical ratcheting of culture and technology, best expressed in Jack Goldstone's framework of efflorescences, or Eric Jones's "growth recurring."[2] These pulses in the human condition can be dated from earliest agricultural origins, but start more markedly with the Late Neolithic

---

[1] James W. Wood, "A Theory of Preindustrial Population Dynamics: Demography, Economy, and Well-Being in Malthusian Systems," *CA* 39 (1998), 99–216 probably captures the process.

[2] Jack A. Goldstone, "Efflorescences and Economic Growth in World History: Rethinking the 'Rise of the West' and the Industrial Revolution," *JWH* 13 (2002), 323–90; Eric L. Jones, *Growth Recurring: Economic Change in World History* (Ann Arbor, MI, 2000 [1988]).

intensification of agrarian practice and mastery of ceramics. Out of the kiln and glazing would evolve the knowledge of metals that has underwritten all subsequent economies, and at the time shaped the accumulation of political power that would be structured by and perpetuate the material memory systems of writing and monumental art. Whether the complex of bronze metals and the palace economy brought much to the well-being of the agrarian village is subject to real debate, but it is incontestable that it was associated with a significant rise in human population. Across the Old World, ordinary people in the semiarid monsoonal belt may not have been better off, but there were more of them. It is not unreasonable, as Goldstone argues, to say that these Bronze Age expansions thus had some of the qualities of Smithian growth, as growing populations, larger domains, and economic specialization expanded upon the rudiments of market exchange established during the Late Neolithic. We certainly need to be very cautious here in talking about markets in the wider sense, because palace systems controlled so much of the Bronze Age economy, and there are real questions about how much benefit of rising wealth in these ancient empires trickled down into ordinary households, to say nothing of the imperial expropriation of land and labor. But if we stretch our categories somewhat, it is tempting to see Schumpeterian dimensions to the rise of new sociologies and technologies in the Iron Age. Joseph Schumpeter assigned the role of creative destruction in the modern economy to economic depressions, undermining entrenched institutions and technologies, and paving the way for new. In the ancient and medieval worlds, severe exogenous impacts from nature can be described as having the force of Schumpeterian creative destruction, most apparently during the final stages of the Mid-Holocene Crisis (~3200–3000 BC), China's first state transition (~2200–1900 BC), and the Preclassical Crisis (~1200–900 BC).

Out of technological and institutional consequences of the Bronze Age crisis, I argue in this and the following chapter, two long cycles of slow growth structured the history of the Old World, global epochs of classical antiquity and the Middle Ages, running from the fifth century BC to the fifteenth century AD. And in the Old World and the New, exogenous natural forces – both climatic and epidemic – not necessarily Malthusian overpopulation, framed the material boundaries of human existence.

* * *

China, Iron, and Rotary Power

We can begin this examination of classical antiquity and the medieval world by examining the spread of iron in China. Just as the Bronze Age proper came late to China, so did the Iron Age. Rather than a slow development after 1200 BC as in the Mediterranean, iron came to China in a rush during the era of the Warring States, roughly 475–220 BC. Here the parallel circumstances shaping these creative destructions are intriguing: just as the millennial Siberian High accompanied the collapse of the Mediterranean Bronze Age palace polities, opening the way for the rise of iron, rising challenges to the decaying Zhou polity in the monsoon crisis starting around 500 BC set the stage for the rapid development of iron technology in China. Bronze smelting and casting had been a palace monopoly in China as in the Mediterranean world, and here the collapse of central control was the critical factor. It may be that the idea of ironworking spread to China from the Mediterranean or from India, probably via Central Asia. But the rapidity of its adoption, and the way uniquely Chinese bronze casting techniques were applied to ironwork, indicate that Chinese skills were particularly important. But this transition occurred not in the context of the Zhou or Han dynasties, but in the peripheral and "barbarian" state of Wu, in the southern Yangzi valley during the waning decades of the Zhou, the so-called Spring and Autumn period, from the 580s to the 460s BC. Wu, described as a more "democratic" polity, was one of the few localities where agricultural tools were made of bronze, and a sophisticated bronze metallurgy thrived outside of an authoritarian palace control. It was here that ironworking first developed in China and then spread to other regions during the interstate rivalries of the ensuing Warring States period.[3]

Strikingly, once it had achieved considerable stability, the Han polity returned to the Bronze Age system and established a royal monopoly over the iron industry in 120 BC.[4] Nonetheless, the Han period (206 BC–AD 220) is notable for a series of innovations that radically increased agricultural productivity. Settled rather than slash-and-burn agriculture had been established after 600 BC, and fallowing and manuring patterns developed over the next several hundred years. The Han developed the curved, cast-iron moldboard plowshare (cast in new state-controlled foundries) and the horse-drawn seed drill, which were put to a new rationalized plowing and planting regime on the royal lands in the dry farming north, and spread from there to the large-landed ruling classes. A rotary winnowing fan, a hand-cranked machine separating grain from chaff, was invented in the wheat/millet region of the north around the same time and later spread to the rice-growing south. And new and more efficient breast-band and collar harnesses allowed for more horse traction to be converted into useful energy.[5]

---

[3] Donald B. Wagner, *Iron and Steel in Ancient China* (Leiden, 1993), 97–146; Bennet Bronson, "The Transition to Iron in Ancient China," in Vincent C. Pigott, ed., *The Archaeometallurgy of the Asian Old World* (Philadelphia, PA, 1999), 177–98; Luthar von Falkenhausen, "The Waning of the Bronze Age: Material Culture and Social Developments, 770–481 B. C.," in Michael Loewe and Edward L. Shaughnessy, eds., *The Cambridge History of Ancient China: From the Origins of Civilization to 221 B.C.* (New York, 1999), 525–39.

[4] Donald B. Wagner, *The State and the Iron Industry in Han China* (Copenhagen, 2001).

[5] Mark Elvin, *The Pattern of the Chinese Past* (Stanford, CA, 1973), 23–4; Nishimjima Sadao, "The Economic and Social History of the Former Han," in Denis Twitchett and Michael

The invention of the rotary winnowing fan in China opens up the question of mechanics and energy efficiency, as well as the chronology of these advances. As long as the human or animal muscles were providing the direct striking action – cutting, chopping, threshing, pulling – that mediated between nature and nutrition, there were real and absolute limits to the improvement of the human material condition. Metal – bronze and iron – improved the efficiency of muscle action in these direct striking actions. But the mechanics of rotary action – first applied to traction – further multiplies the efficiency of direct muscle action.

Thus the rotary fan was significant. But it also appears that the rotary fan had a spotty history in ancient China: invented in the wheat/millet north during the second century BC, it spread eventually to the south, but was forgotten in the north, where farmers reverted to traditional threshing, tossing, and sifting to extract chaff from the grain.[6] Current research places the earliest continuous development of rotary power in the eastern Mediterranean, rather than China, as a late Iron Age innovation. Before it can be baked into bread, grain must be ground into flour, and since the Neolithic this had involved grinding grain between two stones, the upper stone pushed by hand. Starting in the fifth century BC, various rotary mills were developed across the Mediterranean for grinding grain and crushing olives; some were small, hand-turned devices – rotary querns – and some were larger ones operating like a capstan, with grindstones in a tight box attached to a spoked capstan, which could be turned by one or more men, or even a donkey. This rotary mill was gradually converted into a water-powered grinding mill via the development of geared irrigation devices (the *saqiya*) around 240 BC by the Hellenistic intellectuals at work in Alexandria. Before the first century BC, the vertical water mill was commonplace in western Anatolia, and from there it spread around the Roman world over the next several centuries. The city of Rome would have massive grinding mills operating by the third century AD.[7] Similarly an argument has been developed

---

Loewe, eds., *The Cambridge History of China, Vol. 1: The Ch'in and Han Empires, 221 BC–AD 220* (New York, 1986), 561–6; Robert Temple, *The Genius of China* (New York, 1986), 15–27.

[6] Temple, *The Genius of China*, 24.

[7] Örjan Wikander, "Water-Mills in Ancient Rome," *Opuscula Romana* 12 (1979), 13–36; M. J. T. Lewis, *Millstone and Hammer: The Origins of Water-Power* (Hull, 1998), 13–73; Örjan Wikander, "The Water Mill," in Örjan Wikander, *Handbook of Ancient Water Technology* (Leiden, 2000), 394–8; Andrew Wilson, "Machines, Power, and the Ancient Economy," *JRS* 92 (2002), 9–17; Lucio Russo, *The Forgotten Revolution: How Science Was Born in 300BC and Why It Had to Be Reborn*, Silvio Levy, trans. (Berlin, 2004 [Milan, 1996]), 124–5; Helmuth Schneider, "Technology," in Walter Scheidel et al., eds., *The Cambridge Economic History of the Greco-Roman World* (New York, 2007), 144–71. On Bronze Age connections between China, Siberia, and points west, see Andrew Sherratt, "The Trans-Eurasian Exchange: The Prehistory of Chinese Relations with the West," in Victor H. Mair, ed., *Contact and Exchange in the Ancient World* (Honolulu, HI, 2006), 30–61.

that water-powered trip-hammers were used by the beginning of the first millennium AD to support Roman mining in Spain. The trip-hammer was an invention loosely rooted in foot-powered tilt hammers for grinding grain and the Greek invention of the reciprocating cam. By contrast, it would appear that water-powered mills did not develop in China until the fifth century AD, possibly through exposure to the Mediterranean mill at the Hellenistic Central Asian empire of Bactria.[8]

This new interpretation challenges Joseph Needham's long-established claim that mills did not develop in Europe until the Middle Ages, thus giving a priority to Chinese invention – and to medieval technological innovation. But a rising body of scholarship posits that the classical societies of the Mediterranean were far more technologically sophisticated than historians have assumed. In this understanding, the Middle Ages in Europe may only barely have recovered the advances of the ancient world, lost during the so-called Dark Ages.[9] And one of this interpretation's central advocates, archeologist Kevin Greene, argues that these advances of Mediterranean antiquity need to "be seen as the maturing of the European iron age, when the use of iron first proliferated in all spheres of use." Greene suggests an analogy between the Iron Age-classical sequence and that running from the Early Neolithic domestications to the "secondary products revolution." Writing about the Roman empire, Greene similarly argues that the imperial "economy does not show signs of advance or evolution, simply an intensification of everything that already existed in Greek and Roman republican times."[10]

Such an understanding suggests that the Iron Age itself – in some measure shaped by climate reversal – was a fundamental technological revolution, elaborated and "intensified" in the ages of classical empires. The revolution involved increased capacities for cutting, pounding, and grinding. Thus widespread iron tools would allow more people to cut more wood, soil, or leather in less time; grinding innovations would allow more grain to be converted to flour in less time. Both fundamentally reduced, if they did not eliminate, the muscle power required for daily labor. In the Mediterranean, this was an earlier and longer revolution, and one gradually incorporated into

---

[8] Lewis, *Millstone and Hammer*, 62–5, 76–121; Wikander, "The Water Mill," 394, n 96; Wikander, "Industrial Applications of Water Power," and "The Roman Empire," in Wikander, ed., *Handbook*, 400–10, 651–2.

[9] See note 8, and Bert Hall, "Lynn White's *Medieval Technology and Social Change* after Thirty Years," in Robert Fox, ed., *Technological Change: Methods and Themes in the History of Technology* (London, 1996), 85–101; Kevin Greene, "Technology and Innovation in Context: The Roman Background to Mediaeval and Later Developments," *JRA* 7 (1994), 22–33.

[10] Kevin Greene, "Technological Innovation and Economic Progress in the Ancient World: M. I. Finley Reconsidered," *EconHistR* 53 (2000), 55; Kevin Greene, *The Archaeology of the Roman Economy* (London, 1986), 170.

the economies of major imperial systems; in China, it was a later revolution, more quickly incorporated into empire. Either case raises the question of whether these innovations, and the systemic changes in which they were embedded, contributed in fact to an improvement in human well-being, or whether these improvements were overwhelmed by population growth. Was there an enduring Malthusian stalemate, or was there at least a moment, perhaps of several centuries duration, of economic growth and general human improvement during classical antiquity? The following pages consider this question, its implications, its critics, and its climatic and epidemiological contexts.

Global Antiquity: Numbers and Climate

We need to situate the question of economic growth in the ancient empires in two conditioning contexts, population growth and climate change, or the lack thereof. Any increase in an economic surplus would have to be distributed to a growing population. Our measures of population are entirely too primitive, but such as they are, they are worth reviewing.

Population growth is a simple measure of success, though its measurement is not so simple. Here issues of imperial scale are a fundamental part of the story. In the Old World, as the Iron Age matured, the scale of political domains suddenly expanded to typically five times the size of the largest Late Bronze Age polities.[11] Following the brief resurgence of the Assyrian empire and its conquest of Egypt, the Iranian Medes built an empire during the seventh and sixth centuries that stretched from the Black Sea to Afghanistan, in turn swallowed up by the Persian Achaimenids, who between 550 BC and 330 BC ruled a huge swath of territory reaching from Central Asia to Egypt and the Balkans. The Persians were stopped in 480 BC from flowing over the Mediterranean by a league of Greek city-states, small by comparison, but with colonial outposts scattered far and wide. Alexander the Great's vast but ephemeral conquests around 330 BC spawned a necklace of Hellenistic empires and kingdoms running from Greece to India, among them long-lasting sizable polities such as Bactria, Parthia, and the Seleucid domain. Then, after 200 BC, Rome emerged to dominate the entire Mediterranean world and the Han all of China.

The estimates in McEvedy and Jones are suggestive.[12] They estimate that the populations of the Mediterranean, India, and China already composed roughly 75 percent of global population at 400 BC, a proportion that would remain stable for centuries to come, perhaps the product of growth during

[11] Rein Taagepera, "Size and Duration of Empires Systematics of Size"; –, "Size and Duration of Empires: Growth-Decline Curves, 3000 to 600BC," *Social Science Research* 7 (1978), 108–27, 180–96.

[12] Colin McEvedy and Richard Jones, *Atlas of World Population History* (New York, 1978).

the Iron Age.[13] Between 400 BC and AD 200, the combined populations of China, India, the Mediterranean, and Europe grew by 74 percent, while population throughout the rest of the world grew by 30 percent.[14] Then, during the two centuries after AD 200 – as empires collapsed – the populations of the three Old World imperial regions declined by 7 percent, while the population throughout the rest of the world increased by 28 percent.

The reconstruction by Jean Noël Biraben suggests a roughly analogous pattern. (Figure III.2 presents Biraben's estimates.) His figures show the combined populations of North Africa, Southwest Asia, China, India, and Europe, roughly the world of the plough, comprising roughly 80 percent of global population between 400 BC and AD 200, growing by 75 percent while populations throughout the rest of the world grew by only 39 percent. Then, between AD 200 and AD 400, the populations of the Old World plough cultures and empires declined by 30 percent, while populations throughout the rest of the world increased by 32 percent.[15] By either measure the fortunes of empire were reflected in population growth, and that population growth was indeed substantial, potentially erasing the benefits of technological, social, and political innovations. Perhaps the great empires were simply treading water, desperately meeting the demands of growing populations, but not much else.

The fortunes of classical empires in the Old World core and beyond were shaped by a remarkably beneficent climate, the Classical Optimum running between a Hallstatt Solar minimum – the Preclassical Crisis – and a cold episode defined by ice rafting in the North Atlantic – the Dark Ages. These in turn would be followed by another northern "optimum" and then another

[13] It may be significant, or it may be a function of false assumptions, but it is interesting that, according to McEvedy and Jones's 1978 estimates, global population grew at a faster rate between 1000 BC and 500 BC, the era of the Mediterranean Iron Age, than it did during classical antiquity. It is possible that smaller Iron Age states generated fewer large-scale epidemics.

[14] For a comparable use of these figures, see Walter Scheidel, "Demography," in Scheidel et al., eds., *The Cambridge Economic History of the Greco-Roman World*, 42–4.

[15] Jean Noël Biraben, "Essai sur L'Évolution di Nombre des Hommes," *Population* 34 (1979), 13–24, at p. 16. See also David Christian, *Maps of Time: An Introduction to Big History* (Berkeley, CA, 2004), 344–5. The only virtue of these figures is that they give a rough sense of scale and claim global coverage. But they require interpretive choices that sometimes have been challenged by regional studies, which as yet have not integrated into a global picture. For Italy, for example, McEvedy and Jones follow a minimalist view, which posits an increase from 5 million to 7 million between 200 BC and AD 0; a case can be made that the non-slave population of Italy grew from roughly 5 million to at least 12 million. Among Roman specialists even the advocates of more minimal Italian figures see the population of the entire Roman empire rising from perhaps 45 million to 70 million between the turn of the millennium and AD 165, far larger than estimates that can be generated from McEvedy and Jones. Neville Morley, "The Transformation of Italy, 225–28 B. C.," *JRS* 91 (2001), 50–62; Walter Scheidel, "Human Mobility in Roman Italy, I: The Free Population," *JRS* 94 (2004), 2–3.

Hallstatt solar grand minimum – the Little Ice Age. This simple wave of two optima divided by a cool epoch, and bracketed by severe climate crises, defines the fundamental pulse of 2,000 years of human history. In essence, this 2,000-year interval was divided into two optimums and an intervening cold spell: the Classical Optimum, the Dark Ages, and the Medieval Warm Period, now known as the Medieval Climate Anomaly. This sequence shaped the broad outlines of continuing "strange parallels" in global circumstances[16] (see Figures III.5a–d).

As the Preclassical Hallstatt-Siberian High faded there were two deep solar minima centering at ~750 BC and 325 BC. Each of these solar minima matches with evidence for serious droughts and famines in Greece, but these events must have been sharp oscillations in the enduring influence of stronger winter westerly precipitation across the Mediterranean and into Asia that were shaped by the final stage of the negative North Atlantic Oscillation in the Preclassical Crisis. Glaciers advanced in the Alps, European rivers had disastrous floods, and lakes across the Mediterranean and into Anatolia were at high stands, as was the Caspian Sea, all markers of the south-flowing winter westerlies of a negative NAO.[17] The Homeric minima of roughly 750 BC seem to have contributed to the rise and dispersal of the nomadic Scythian warriors, as a pocket of the steppes received increased rainfall in that century, feeding grassland grazing for vast herds of horses.[18]

---

[16] Victor Lieberman, *Strange Parallels: Southeast Asia in Global Context, c. 800–1830. Vol. II: Mainland Mirrors: Europe, Japan, China, South Asia and the Islands* (New York, 2009).

[17] John M. Camp, "Drought and Famine in the 4th Century B.C.," *Hesperia Supplements* 20 (1982), 9–17; –, "A Drought in the Late 8th Century B.C.," *Hesperia* 48 (1979), 397–411. Critiques of Camp's Greek drought thesis are cited in Walter Scheidel, "The Greek Demographic Expansion: Models and Comparisons," *Journal of Hellenic Studies* 123 (2003), 130, n 57. For the NAO precipitation evidence, see Celia Martin-Puetra, "Arid and Humid Phases in Southern Spain during the Last 4000 Years: The Zoñar Lake Record, Córdoba," *Holocene* 18 (2008), 907–21; C. Giraudi et al., "The Holocene Climatic Evolution of Mediterranean Italy: A Review of the Continental Geological Data," *Holocene* 21 (2011), 105–15; Michel Magny et al., "Late-Holocene Climatic Variability South of the Alps as Recorded by Lake-Level Fluctuations at Lake Ledro, Trentino, Italy," *Holocene* 19 (2009), 575–89; Hanspeter Holzhauser et al., "Glacier and Lake-Level Variations in West-Central Europe over the Last 3500 Years," *Holocene* 15 (2009), 789–801; M. G. Macklin, "Past Hydrological Events Reflected in the Holocene Fluvial Record of Europe," *Catena* 66 (2006), 145–54; Catherine Kuzucuoğlu et al., "Mid- to Late-Holocene Climate Change in Central Turkey: The Tecer Lake Record," *Holocene* 21 (2011), 183; S. B. Kroonenberg et al., "Solar-Forced 2600 BP and Little Ice Age Highstands of the Caspian Sea," *QuatInt* 173–4 (2007), 137–43. The Tecer lake records of 850–70 BC is of a humid period, interrupted by three sharp droughts at 677–630 BC, 450 BC, and 300 BC, which seems to support the Greek drought thesis.

[18] B. van Geel, "Climate Change and the Expansion of the Scythian Culture after 850 BC: A Hypothesis," *JArchS* 31 (2004), 1735–42; Frank Schlütz and Frank Lehmkuhl, "Climatic Change in the Russian Altai, Southern Siberia, Based on Palynological and Geomorphological Results, with Implications for Climatic Teleconnections and Human History since the Middle Holocene," *VHAb* 16 (2007), 101–18; V. G. Dirksen et al., "Chronology of Holocene

But after the fourth century minima the Mediterranean world and Europe experienced a remarkable stretch of stable warm climate for the next 600 to 800 years, the Classical Optimum. Dominated by a positive NAO mode, with warm winter westerlies running north toward Scandinavia, glaciers in the Alps retreated, Mediterranean lake levels fell, and an enduring pattern of dry summers with moderate winter precipitation took hold from the Mediterranean into Anatolia. In pre-Roman Italy, archaeological surveys have demonstrated the impact of the Classical Optimum. Bronze Age settlements had been widely distributed, but around 1100 BC, during the preclassical Halstatt crisis in what is called the *proto-Villanovan*, wide areas were abandoned and settlements were centralized around defensible hill forts. This pattern persisted through the Iron Age, until in the fifth and fourth centuries isolated farms were settled in secure areas around powerful city-states. Then, "fairly suddenly" from the fourth to the third centuries, as summarized by Nicola Terrenato, "vast regions" of Italy and regions of the central Mediterranean were settled "on an absolutely massive scale," driving "what is in most cases the deepest landscape transformation of antiquity."[19]

The demographic expansion behind these thousands of new farms was based, then, on a benevolent climate and the rise of political security. These climate conditions would reverse during the fourth century AD, with significantly cooler temperatures in northern Europe between 300 and 350 driven by the onset of the next cycle of ice rafting in the North Atlantic, followed after 500 by the return of a strong negative NAO mode, shifting the winter westerlies south into the Mediterranean. The definitive, global break toward the Dark Ages would come with a deep cold temperature spike after AD 536, something to which we shall return.[20]

This Classical Optimum was global in scope, if not in all details. What then of populations, empires, and human well-being during this long Classical Optimum? The warm, dry temperatures of the Classical Optimum literally may have opened the way for the Roman empire in western Europe, as it favored the grain and wine economy of the Mediterranean over the

Climate and Vegetation Changes and Their Connection to Cultural Dynamics in Southern Siberia," *Radiocarbon* 49 (2007), 1103–21.

[19] Nicola Terrenato, "The Essential Countryside of the Roman World," in Susan E. Alcock and Robin Osborne, eds., *Classical Archaeology* (Malden, MA, 2007), 139–61, esp. 140–3.

[20] For the temperature data mentioned here, see Ulf Buntgen et al., "2500 Years of European Climate Variability and Human Susceptibility," *Science* 331 (2011), 578–82; Frederik C. Ljungqvist, "A New Reconstruction of Temperature Variability in the Extra-Tropical Northern Hemisphere during the Last Two Millennia," *Geografiska Annaler: Series A* 92 (2010), 339–51; and the data developed by Keith Briffa and Timothy Osborn for figure 6.10 (B2000) in the *Climate Change 2007 – The Physical Science Basis* available at http://www.cru. uea.ac.uk/~timo/datapages/ipccar4.htm accessed August 8, 2012. For the NAO discussion, see the citations in notes 17–18, and Mia Tiljander et al., "A 3000-Year Palaeoenvironmental Record from Annually Laminated Sediment of Lake Korttajärvi, Central Finland," *Boreas* 32 (2003), 566–77.

cold-adapted cattle-based Celtic Iron Age economies; conversely, the climatic reversal that set in around AD 300, bringing cold, wet weather south through Europe, undermined the imperial agro-economy.[21] In China, as we have already seen, the progress of the Han dynasty was precisely bracketed by two massive crises of the monsoon regime (see Figures III.4, III.5c). The Qin state founded the first united Chinese dynastic empire in 221 BC, after the fading of the cold winter monsoons that underlay the era of the Warring States. Roughly parallel with the expansion of the Roman republic, the Qin extended their power from their original territory on the upper Yellow River deep into southern China and consolidated various regional barriers against northern nomads into the Great Wall. The Han – taking power in 206 BC – launched a long series of expansionary wars of conquest starting in 138 BC that absorbed the rest of southern China and extended into Vietnam, Korea, and far to the west into Central Asia. Succumbing to the cost of imperial overreach, Yellow River flooding, and a short, sharp monsoon failure, the Han dynasty was interrupted briefly by the short interregnum of the Wang-Mang emperor (AD 6–23). The Wang-Mang in turn had a similar series of tribulations. Flooding, harvest failures, and the Red Eyebrow peasant rebellion effectively led to the restoration of the Han to power by AD 25. The second Han dynasty lasted another two centuries, reigning in an era during which poverty and the pressures of border nomads drove a massive internal migration from north China to the south, setting off further struggles with indigenous peoples. The later Han attempted to manage these forces but were undermined by a century-long monsoon failure beginning around AD 170 and peaking at roughly 210, which contributed both to northern nomadic incursions and to the rise of the Yellow Turban peasant rebels in 184. Eventually the last emperor of the declining Han was overthrown in 220 by warlord generals who had fought to suppress the Yellow Turbans.[22]

Fundamental changes came to Japan as well during this period, but set against a longer chronology. The indigenous preagricultural Jomon had flourished in the third millennium, in the Middle Jomon period, which seems to have seen a broad surge of population during an epoch of moderate winter monsoons. But, where the intensifying winter monsoons had

[21] Carole L. Crumley, "The Ecology of Conquest: Contrasting Agropastoral and Agricultural Societies' Adaptation to Climatic Change," in Carole L. Crumley, ed., *Historical Ecology: Cultural Knowledge and Changing Landscapes* (Santa Fe, NM, 1994), 183–201; Brian Fagan, *The Long Summer: How Climate Changed Civilization* (New York, 2004), 189–212.

[22] Chun-shu Chang, *The Rise of the Chinese Empire: Nation, State, and Imperialism in Early China, ca. 1600 B.C.–A.D. 8* (Ann Arbor, MI, 2007); Albert M. Craig, *The Heritage of Chinese Civilization*, second edition (Upper Saddle River, NJ, 2007), 32–41. Derk Bodde, "The State and Empire of the Ch'in," Michael Loewe, "The Former Han Dynasty," Hans Bielenstein, "Wang Mang, the Restoration of the Han Dynasty, and Later Han," B. J. Mansvelt Beck, "The Fall of Han," and Patricia Ebrey, "The Economic and Social History of the Later Han," in Twitchett and Loewe, eds., *The Cambridge History of China*, 38–52, 81–90, 205–7, 237–56, 264–74, 334–76, 621–2.

pushed Late Neolithic Chinese societies toward the state, they had led to a general decline in Jomon Japan, where a colder, wetter climate seems to have reduced population. The fundamental shift in Japan came as the optimum set in, after the peak of cold winter monsoons that had shaped China's Warring States period. Around 300 BC, the Yayio culture arrived in Japan from Korea, bringing with it both paddy rice cultivation and the roots of the modern Japanese language. As the Yayoi/Japanese expanded, they pushed the Jomon descendants north, where they ultimately became known as the Ainu. Around AD 300, as estimates of northern hemisphere temperature suggest a sharp cooling, the first proto-states emerged in both Japan and Korea, manifested in mound-built tombs that had been the markers of the early state in China. Populations in Japan surged to 5 million by AD 600.[23]

The Americas saw a general pattern not unlike that of the Mediterranean and China (see Figures III.3, III.5b, III.5d). In the Andes, the Early Intermediate societies had emerged around 200 BC, most important the Nasca and Moche states that controlled large stretches of territory along the coast and the valley interior. These true states endured between peaks of ENSO flooding and drought impacts, between roughly 200 BC and AD 600. Similarly, Mesoamerica was dominated by large ritual states of the Late Formative and Early Classic, between roughly 300 BC and AD 600. The great interior city-state at Teotihuacan, with a population of more than 100,000, put serious stress on highland resources, and seems to have survived unrest and factional struggles during the late fourth century. In the sixth century AD it would be toppled from within during a period of droughts. In the Yucatan lowlands, the Maya emerged as a series of great ritual states somewhat later, around AD 250, based on local kingships dating back several hundred years. Embroiled in Teotihuacan's struggles during the late fourth century, Tikal nonetheless rose to become the primate Early Classic Maya center, until here too drought during the sixth century contributed to a period of unrest and decline.[24]

* * *

[23] Gina L. Barnes, *The Rise of Civilization in East Asia: The Archaeology of China, Korea, and Japan* (London, 1999), 168–91, 222–45; the estimates of Japanese population are suggested in William Wayne Farris, *Daily Life and Demographics in Ancient Japan* (Ann Arbor, MI, 2009), 9, 102–3; and –, *Japan's Medieval Population: Famine, Fertility, and Warfare in a Transformative Age* (Honolulu, HI, 2006), 26, 100, 170, 262; Sean Lee and Toshikazu Hasegawa, "Bayesian Phylogenetic Analysis Supports Agricultural Origins of Japonic Languages," *Proceedings of the Royal Society B*, published online before print May 4, 2011, doi:10.1098/rspb.2011.0518; Gergana Yancheva et al., "Influence of the Intertropical Convergence Zone on the East Asian Monsoon," *Nature* 445 (2007), 74–7.

[24] James B. Richardson, *People of the Andes* (Washington, DC, 1994), 101–21; Susan Toby Evans, *Ancient Mexico and Central America: Archaeology and Culture History* (New York, 2008), 253–81, 291–314; David Hodell et al., "Terminal Classic Drought in the Northern Maya Lowlands Inferred from Multiple Sediment Cores in Lake Chichancanab (Mexico)," *QSR* 24 (2005), 1413–27; Gerald Haug et al., "Climate and the Collapse of

The Rise of Rome

The geographic reach and relative longevity of these vast empires shaped a series of common characteristics. They were forged upon a common set of political, organizational, and technological capabilities that allowed them to project their power and authority over subject peoples, and both these subjects and the requirements of their control contributed to the flow of wealth to the imperial center. In exchange for political and economic submission, subject peoples were incorporated into a common legal and market system that built conditions of relative peace and stability internal to imperial borders. The communications that ran within and between these empires moved not only soldiers and commodities, but diseases.

Thus there were benefits – and perils – to life in the ancient classical empires. The benefits derived from the general condition of legal and economic stability, establishing a general condition of protection from extreme uncertainty, and the opportunity for the circulation of commodities and technology within the *pax imperium*. However, these empires were built upon extractive violence: the destruction and literal massacre and enslavement of peripheral peoples fed the prosperity – and the numbers – of the peoples within the empire. Within the borders of empire populations grew and significant groups seemed to prosper. But this dynamic of conquest both fed and fed upon a culture of elite privilege running up to a cult of the emperor, a culture that depended on the ever-more efficient extraction of a surplus from the producer classes. Thus, while there may well have been economic growth in these ancient empires, its benefits seem to have accrued disproportionately to imperial elites, in a process of reward for service that comprised the central dynamic of imperial politics. But enough of the benefit appears to have trickled down to the ordinary household to drive population growth – populations constantly exposed to the scouring and abrasion of endemic, endogenous disease circulating within the empire, and occasionally shattered by epidemic, exogenous disease that burst across imperial boundaries into virgin soil.

In any event, it is clear that populations grew out of the benefits of imperial expansion. In the case of Rome, historian Nathan Rosenstein argues that the foundations for the Roman population growth lay in the very process of imperial expansion: the recruitment of young men into the republican legions to fight the three Punic Wars against Carthage between 264 BC and 146 BC fed a flow of income into the Roman countryside and thus an increase in fertility that fed the war machine. In turn, when the wars wound

Maya Civilization," *Science* 299 (2003), 1731–5; Peter B. deMenocal, "Cultural Responses to Climate Change during the Late Holocene," *Science* 292 (2001)," 670–1; David Hodell et al., "Solar Forcing of Drought Frequency in the Maya Lowlands," *Science* 292 (2001), 1367–70.

down, this expansion set the stage for a crisis of overpopulation that eventually contributed to the transition from republic to empire, including massive colonization of Romans in the western provinces.[25] Ancient Mesopotamia presents a generally similar picture to that of republican Rome. By one estimate Mesopotamia grew suddenly: a stable population of roughly a third of a million suddenly increasing to almost half a million around 200 BC, and reaching a million and a half by AD 500. This growth matches the establishment of Hellenistic and then Parthian and Seleucid polities that aggressively developed irrigated agriculture in the Tigris-Euphrates, establishing a prosperity that fed the new armored cavalry that defended these empires.[26] The general picture seems clear: empires grew in population not just from additions by conquest but from their internal dynamics.

The question of whether these internal dynamics included markets – and shaped economic growth – has been the subject of an extended debate among ancient historians for decades, following Moses Finley's pronouncement that commercial interest had no place in ancient societies defined by status and honor. In recent years, the battle between status and interest has subsided with the development of several models that stress the operation of markets in the ancient world, but also the constraints of imperial purposes, uncertain information, and an ever-present threat of arbitrary power to the enforcement of contract. Peter Bang has suggested that the best comparison for the ancient economy is neither modern nor quasi-tribal, but that of the bazaar of the early modern Moghul or Ottoman empires.[27] Primitive

---

[25] Nathan Rosenstein, *Rome at War: Farms, Families and Death in the Middle Republic* (Chapel Hill, NC, 2004); Scheidel, "Human Mobility," 10–13, 19–21; Keith Hopkins, *Conquerors and Slaves* (Cambridge, 1978), 1–115.

[26] Thomas M. Whitmore et al., "Long Term Population Change," in B. L. Turner et al., *The Earth as Transformed by Human Action: Global and Regional Changes in the Biosphere over the Past 300 Years* (Cambridge, 1990), 27–30; Robert McC. Adams, *Land behind Baghdad: A History of Settlement of the Dyala Plains* (Chicago, IL, 1965), 61–83; Peter Christensen, *The Decline of Iranshahr: Irrigation and Environments in the History of the Middle East, 500 B.C. to A.D. 1500* (Copenhagen, 1993), 49–72; John R. McNeill and William H. McNeill, *The Human Web: A Bird's Eye View of World History* (New York, 2003), 85–6.

[27] The debate began with Moses I. Finley, "Technical Progress and Economic Growth in the Ancient World," *EconHistR* 2nd ser., 18 (1965), 29–45; and Moses I. Finley, *The Ancient Economy* (London, 1973); challenged by M. W. Frederikssen, "Theory, Evidence and the Ancient Economy," *JRS* 65 (1975), 164–71. Jones, *Growth Recurring*, 48–72; Jean Andreau, "Twenty Years after Moses I. Finley's *The Ancient Economy*," and Richard Saller, "Framing the Debate over the Ancient Economy," in Walter Scheidel and Sitta von Reden, eds., *The Ancient Economy* (New York, 2002), 33–49, 251–69; and Paul Millet, "Productive to Some Purpose? The Problem of Ancient Economic Growth," in David J. Mattingly and John Salmon, eds., *Economies beyond Agriculture in the Classical World* (London, 2001), 17–48 provide particularly good reviews of the debate. On the recently emerging new perspectives, see Peter F. Bang, *The Imperial Bazaar: A Comparative Study of Trade and Market in a Tributary Empire* (Cambridge, 2008); Peter F. Bang et al., "Introduction," and Elio Lo

perhaps, the meager protections that imperial law allowed to a flow of commodities provided a buffer against extreme adversity that smaller polities might lack. Such is one explanation for the decline of Athens, the great power of the Mediterranean during the fourth century BC, but unable to make the leap from city-state to empire, and thus protect its seaborne food supply in time of war.[28] Conversely, the work of Peter Garnsey has established that the flow of commodities around the Mediterranean under Roman law ensured that if food shortages were common in the Roman world, full-scale famine was rare to nonexistent. The supply of food to the city of Rome was solved by conquest and the diversion of wheat to Rome, first in Italy itself, then Sicily and North Africa, and finally when Mark Antony and then Octavian Augustus secured Egypt as a Roman province: the Nile became the most regular and predictable breadbasket for the great cities of the empire. Merchant syndicates, not the state, funded the great ships that supplied Rome with Egyptian wheat, supported by a system of banking and capitalization that looked a lot like the system that would finance trade in the early modern world 1,500 years later.

In the final analysis, however, the empire existed for empire, not commerce. If goods flowed around the Mediterranean, it was at the command and to the benefit of an imperial hierarchy centered on Rome and Italy, which functioned free of taxation in a system of provincial tribute that drove hard currency to the center. Commerce operated under the wings of this tributary empire, supplying the needs of a center that over time lost much of its productive capacity, while subordinated to fundamentally political priorities. Thus much of the distribution that kept ordinary Romans in grain was mandated by empire – if mobilized by private merchants.[29]

Leading the response to Moses Finley in the 1980s, Keith Hopkins argued that growth did occur within the bounds of the Roman empire:

[T]he size of the surplus produced in the Mediterranean basin during the last millennium BC and the first two centuries AD gradually increased. The upward trend was

Cascio, "The Role of the State in the Roman Economy: Making Use of the New Institutional Economics," in Peter F. Bang et al., *Ancient Economies, Modern Methodologies: Archaeology, Comparative History, Models and Institutions* (Bari, 2006), 16–21, 215–34; and the debate among R. Bruce Hitchner, Richard Saller, and Avner Greif in J. G. Manning and Ian Morris, eds., *The Ancient Economy: Evidence and Models* (Stanford, CA, 2005), 207–42.

[28] Peter Garnsey, *Famine and Food Supply in the Graeco-Roman World* (Cambridge, 1988), 150–64; –, *Cities, Peasants, and Food in Classical Antiquity: Essays in Social and Economic History* (Cambridge, 1998), 183–200; Michael Jameson, "Famine in the Greek World," and "Peter Garnsey, "Famine in Rome," in Peter Garnsey and C. R. Whitaker, eds., *Trade and Famine in Classical Antiquity* (Cambridge, 1983), 6–16, 56–65.

[29] Garnsey, *Famine and Food Supply*, 167–277; Peter Temin, "A Market Economy in the Early Roman Empire," *JRS* 91 (2001), 169–81; Peter Temin, "Financial Intermediation in the Early Roman Empire," *JEconH* 64 (2004), 705–33; David Kessler and Peter Temin, "The Organization of the Grain Trade in the Early Roman Empire," *EconHistR* 60 (2007), 313–32.

gradual, not very large but significant, and with many oscillations either way. The growth in the surplus produced and extracted was largely the result of two factors, political change and the spread of technical and social innovations.[30]

The evidence for this economic prosperity has been seen in a long arc of expansion and contraction measured in a wide variety of material sources, rising in the second century BC under the late Roman republic, peaking in the early empire, and falling during and after the second century AD (see Figure III.8). Such is the curve of the number of recovered shipwrecks in the Mediterranean, apparently reflecting a surge of shipping during these four centuries; similar curves of rise and fall emerge from careful surveys of the archaeological remains of Roman farms and manors, and of monument building.[31] Another marker can be found in the dendrochronological records from the northern edge of the empire: the archaeologically recovered numbers of trees felled for construction across northern Europe rose and fell with the same arc as shipwrecks.[32] The distribution of Roman and provincial pottery around the empire provides a complex view of ebb and flow of the imperial economy, with distantly traded pottery disappearing in the outer provinces as the empire retreated, and wheel-made pottery giving way to more primitive hand-thrown pots. In Italy itself the same collapse of ceramics trade has been demonstrated for the mid-to-late sixth century, as rural areas lost connections with urban centers, including in the Tiber region around the city of Rome itself.[33] Chemical markers in Greenland ice and European peat sediments for pollution from Roman silver, lead, and

---

[30] Keith Hopkins, "Introduction," in Peter Garnsey et al., eds., *Trade in the Ancient Economy* (London, 1983), xiv.

[31] For an overview, see Willem Jongman, "The Rise and Fall of the Roman Economy: Population, Rents and Entitlement," in Bang et al., *Ancient Economies*, 237–54. On shipping, see Keith Hopkins, "Rome, Taxes, Rents, and Trade," in Scheidel and Von Reden, eds., *The Ancient Economy*, 211–12, n 48, citing A. J. Parker, *Ancient Shipwrecks of the Mediterranean and the Roman Provinces* (London, 1992), 10ff. See also Keith Hopkins, "Models, Ships, and Trade," in Garnsey and Whittaker, eds., *Trade and Famine in Classical Antiquity*, 84–109. On farms and manors: Mamoru Ikeguchi, "A Method for Interpreting and Comparing Field Survey Data," in Bang et al., eds., *Ancient Economies*, 137–58.

[32] Ulf Buntgen, "2500 Years of European Climate Variability and Human Susceptibility," figure 2c.

[33] Bryan Ward-Perkins, *The Fall of Rome and the End of Civilization* (New York, 2005), 87–120, esp. 100–4; D. P. S. Peacock and D. F. Williams, *Amphorae and the Roman Economy: An Introductory Guide* (London, 1986), 54–66; C. J. Going, "Economic 'Long Waves' in the Roman Period? A Reconnaissance of the Romano-British Evidence," *Oxford Journal of Archaeology* 11 (1992), 93–117; Helen Patterson and Alessia Rovelli, "Ceramics and Cons in the Middle Tiber Valley from the Fifth to the Tenth Centuries AD," in Helen Patterson, ed., *Bridging the Tiber: Approaches to Regional Archaeology in the Middle Tiber Valley* (Rome, 2004), 269–84; Paul Arthur and Helen Patterson, "Ceramics and Early Medieval Central and Southern Italy: 'A Potted History,'" in Riccardo Francovich and Ghislaine Noyé, eds., *La Storia dell'Alto Medioevo italiano (VI-X secolo) alla luce dell'archeologia* (Firenze, 1994), 409–42.

copper production in Spain and the Balkans rise slowly from 500 BC and then peak in the first century AD, and then fall away, never to be matched until the expansion of mining and smelting in early modern Europe.[34] The late second-century decline in silver production had an inevitable result on the debasement of the silver content of coin, which fell from 40 percent in AD 250 to less than 4 percent by AD 270.[35] In a direct measure of household well-being, the consumption of animals – pigs, cattle, sheep – throughout the empire rose a little later, during the first century BC, peaked during the second century AD, and collapsed during the fifth and sixth centuries.[36] It was in this arc of economic expansion – marked by rising urbanization, improved roads and shipping, a unified coinage, and intensified agriculture – that water-powered technologies for grinding grain and stamping metal ores, as well as industrial-scale potteries and olive-pressing operations, made their way around the Mediterranean.[37]

There is no consensus among Roman historians, however, that this constituted true economic growth. All would agree that any growth of the Roman economy looks paltry when compared with the explosive changes of the past two centuries. But in its own framework, set against the Iron Age background and allowing for population growth, one school – perhaps dominant in recent years – follows Hopkins in arguing for Smithian growth in the Roman empire, in which large populations in large polities create a broad economic expansion. In particular the early empire forged by Augustus after the Civil Wars, across the century and a half of reasonably good government and civil stability beginning at AD 14, was a period of general prosperity. In Paul Millett's opinion it was one of "modest but more or less sustained

---

[34] Wilson, "Machines, Power and the Ancient Economy," 26–8; Jerome O Nriagu, "Tales Told in Lead," *Science* 281 (1998), 1622–3; Kevin J. R. Rosman et al., "Lead from Carthaginian and Roman Spanish Mines Isotopically Identified in Greenland Ice Dated from 600 B.C. to 300 A.D.," *EnvSciTech* 31 (1997), 3413–16; Sungmin Hong et al., "History of Copper Smelting Pollution during Roman and Medieval Times Recorded in Greenland Ice," *Science* 272 (1996), 246–9; Sungmin Hong et al., "Greenland Ice Evidence of Hemispheric Lead Pollution Two Millennia Ago by Greek and Roman Civilizations," *Science* 265 (1994), 1841–3.

[35] Keith Hopkins, "Taxes and Trade in the Roman Empire, (200 B.C.–A.D. 400)," *JRS* 70 (1980), 101–25 at 123; Greene, *The Archaeology of the Roman Economy*, 60–1.

[36] Jongman, "The Rise and Fall of the Roman Economy: Population, Rents and Entitlement," 245; Anthony King, "Diet in the Roman World: A Regional Inter-Site Comparison of the Mammal Bones," *JRA* 12 (1999), 168–202. See also Michael MacKinnon, *Production and Consumption of Animals in Roman Italy* (Portsmouth, RI, 2004), esp. 189–240.

[37] Wilson, "Machines, Power, and the Ancient Economy," 5–34; David J. Mattingly, "First Fruit? The Olive in the Roman World," in Graham Shipley and John Salmon, eds., *Human Landscapes in Classical Antiquity: Environment and Culture* (London, 1996), 213–54; Robert Bruce Hitchner, "Olive Production and the Roman Economy: The Case for Intensive Growth in the Roman Economy," in Scheidel and Von Reden, eds., *The Ancient Economy*, 71–83; Patricia L. Fall et al., "Agricultural Intensification and the Secondary Products Revolution along the Jordan Rift," *HumEcol* 30 (2002), esp. 466–73.

and generalized growth"; Richard Saller's educated guess is that per capita productivity rose by about 25 percent over roughly three centuries. Willem Jongman describes an "advanced organic economy" in which – during its first centuries – the benefits were "enjoyed by relatively large segments of the population." He with others stresses the importance of olive oil, wine, and pork as accessible luxuries in the diet of ordinary Romans during this earlier period, which can be compared to that of southern Europe during the early modern era.[38]

But another school is not so certain, and the data behind the model of an arc of growth has come under increasing scrutiny. First and foremost, these measures in broad outline roughly track the growth and decline of estimated population in the Mediterranean and Europe, which would not imply fundamental per capita improvement in well-being. Walter Scheidel has argued that the critical issue is the rate of growth, not its simple scale, proposing that growth rates – based on the shipping data – surged in the war-torn decades of the Late Republic, in the second century BC, followed by a long, slow decline in growth rates into the Early Imperial centuries. He has also argued that there was a small but significant stratum of middling prosperity in the Roman world, but that in general, the aggregate calculus of Roman wealth suggests that the majority of the imperial population could not have been living much more than a subsistence existence. Andrew Wilson has responded with a countervailing argument that the shipwreck data has serious flaws and biases, because it depends on spotting mounds of amphorae on the sea bottom: most of this work has been done along the southern European coast, and may miss a large volume of shipping along the African coast. More important, a shift from amphorae to wooden barrels and larger ships taking open water routes may mean that these measures need to be fundamentally reconsidered. He proposes that a rising capacity of fish salting vats and frequency of African red-slipped pottery – the signature ceramic of the imperial export trade – through AD 200 provide a better proxy of the

---

[38] Millet, "Productive to Some Purpose?" 35; Saller, "Framing the Debate over Growth in the Ancient Economy," 259–60; Willem M. Jongman, "The Early Roman Empire: Consumption," in Scheidel et al., eds., *The Cambridge Economic History of the Greco-Roman World*, 592–618, quotes from 596–7; Robert C. Allen, "How Prosperous Were the Romans? Evidence from Diocletian's Price Edict (301 AD)," in Alan Bowman and Andrew Wilson, eds., *Quantifying the Roman Economy* (New York, 2009), 327–45. A new effort to excavate the poor, the Roman Peasant Project, has begun to produce results that may suggest a similar picture: at a small and remote fourth- to fifth-century farming household in north central Italy, evidence for market integration (coins and ceramics), landscape mobility (building stone), and consumption of older, working cattle hints that the Roman peasant family may not have been totally impoverished. Mariaelena Ghisleni et al., "Excavating the Roman Peasant I: Excavations at Pievina (GR)," *PBSRom* 79 (2011), 95–145. Willem Jongman presents a detailed assessment of the Roman economy that broadly concurs with my analysis in "Re-constructing the Roman economy," in Larry Neil and Jeffrey Williamson, eds., *The Cambridge History of Capitalism*, vol. 1 (New York, 2014), 75–100.

imperial economy. But even Wilson leaves open as an unanswered question whether these centuries saw intensive Smithian growth, Boserupian running in place, or its imperial corollary: simple growth by conquest extraction.[39]

Throughout, it would appear, the imperatives of the center drove this economic expansion. Rome itself, with a population of a million and the focus of the imperial elite, with perhaps a few other magnate cities, was an engine of consumption. Producing relatively little itself, the great city provided a market for provincial production throughout the empire. The coin that paid for this production was not free, however, and was generated in "tribute": taxes and rents that similarly flowed from provinces to the center. In this circulation of value, a certain prosperity flowed into the hands of those who produced the goods for these markets. The army itself was also an agent of economic growth, particularly on the peripheries of the empire where the legions were garrisoned, fed, and supplied by local peoples who were paid in coin (once they had survived the violent incorporation into empire).[40]

So, the Roman empire at its height might have been beginning to "get ahead," or it might have been simply just "running in place." Even if economic productivity drifted above the rate of population growth, it was not by much, and over time the benefits were increasingly concentrated in the hands of the few. Just as there is a consensus on slow per capita growth, there is a consensus on a massively stratified society, in which a tiny aristocratic fraction of the population garnered a wildly disproportionate share of the wealth of the empire. The Roman elites measured their wealth primarily in land, and managed to accumulate most of the productive soils of Italy and the provinces.[41] And the Roman rich kept getting richer: Keith Hopkins argues the wealth of the Roman elites more than doubled during the first century AD, and then increased five to eight times over the next three

---

[39] Walter Scheidel, "In Search of Roman Economic Growth," *JRA* 22 (2009), 46–70; Walter Scheidel and Steven J. Friesen, "The Size of the Economy and the Distribution of Income in the Roman Empire," *JRS* 99 (2009), 61–91; Walter Scheidel, "Stratification, Deprivation and Quality of Life," in Margaret Atkins and Robin Osborne, eds., *Poverty in the Roman World* (New York, 2006), 40–59; William V. Harris, *Rome's Imperial Economy: Twelve Essays* (New York, 2011), 27–54, 257–87; Andrew Wilson, "Indicators for Roman Economic Growth: A Response to Walter Scheidel," *JRA* 22 (2009), 71–82; Andrew Wilson, "Approaches to Quantifying Roman Trade," in Bowman and Wilson, eds., *Quantifying the Roman Economy*, 213–49.

[40] Hopkins, "Taxes and Trade in the Roman Empire"; Hopkins, "Rome, Taxes, Rent, and Trade," 223–30; Neville Morley, *Metropolis and Hinterland: The City of Rome and the Italian Economy* (London, 1996); David Mattingly et al., "Leptiminus (Tunisia): A 'Producer City'?" in Mattingly and Salmon, eds., *Economies beyond Agriculture in the Classical World*, 66–89; Paul Middleton, "The Roman Army and Long-Distance Trade," in Garnsey and Whittaker, eds., *Trade and Famine*, 75–83.

[41] Jongman, "The Rise and Fall of the Roman Economy," 248–9; Hopkins, "Rome, Taxes, Rents, and Trade," 204–8; Mary T. Boatwright et al., *The Romans: From Village to Empire* (New York, 2004), 144–6.

centuries.[42] They accumulated this wealth through their privileged relationship with the Roman state, through the rents extracted from lands acquired for public service. Certainly there was a middling class of merchants, shopkeepers, and artisans, even small farmers, who would have had a share of the rewards of the imperial economy, as would legionnaire colonists granted lands in occupied provinces. But generally, for the majority of the population and especially the poor free families of Rome and the slave population, the major material benefit deriving from the empire was the moderate food stability shaped by the imperial marketplace. Inside the buffer of empire they might be guaranteed a subsistence, if however minimal.

A similar argument for the negative impact of stratification has been made for imperial Han China in exactly the same period, with regard to the impact of iron technology on agriculture during the Han. Whether these innovations translated into a period of prosperity and well-being for ordinary peasant families is in considerable doubt. By one estimate the population of China grew from 40 million to 60 million during the era of the Han (206 BC–AD 220), and perhaps this growth consumed the energy and productivity gains of Han innovation. More important, these innovations seem to have contributed to increasing stratification in Chinese society, particularly during the later Han period, with smallholders unable to invest in the new heavy equipment and falling into debt and tenancy, while powerful landowning families prospered.[43]

Human skeletons provide some evidence for the health and well-being of the peoples of the age of classical empires (see Figure III.6). As yet, most of this evidence is only available for regions in western Eurasia, so that is where this discussion will focus. Here we need to sort out the competing roles of climate, disease, stratification, and imperial geography. A number of indications suggest that the waning of the cold millennial Siberian High and the arrival of the warm Classical Optimum may have contributed to increased human health. Lawrence Angel recorded a dramatic increase in adult stature for both men and women around 650 BC, at the transition from the Iron Age to classical and Hellenistic societies in the eastern Mediterranean; he was struck by the evidence for an "immense total health advance [in] Classical times."[44] In Denmark, a people tall in the Bronze Age

---

[42] Hopkins, "Rome, Taxes, Rents, and Trade," 207. For the archaeology of increasing stratification, see Neil Christie, *From Constantine to Charlemagne: An Archaeology of Italy, AD 300–800* (Aldershot, 2006), 428–37; Ken Dark, "The Late Antique Landscape of Britain, AD 300–700," in Neil Christie, ed., *Landscapes of Change: Rural Evolution in Late Antiquity and the Early Middle Ages* (Aldershot, 2004), 279–300.

[43] Sadao, "The Economic and Social History of the Former Han"; Ebrey, "The Economic and Social History of the Later Han," in Twitchett and Loewe, eds., *The Ch'in and Han Empires,* 363, 616–26.

[44] J. Lawrence Angel, "Health as a Crucial Factor in the Changes from Hunting to Developed Farming in the Eastern Mediterranean," in Mark N. Cohen and George J. Armelagos, eds.,

got even taller in the first centuries AD, after an interval of skeletal evidence lost to Iron Age cremations.[45] But the evidence for Britain, in roughly the same climate zone, but conquered by the Romans in AD 43, is not so positive. Where Danish men averaged 177 cm, British men from the same period stood at 169 cm, a minute gain since the Iron Age, and across a series of health indicators – tooth loss, enamel hypoplasia (Harris lines), dental caries – Roman Age British skeletons suggest worse health than do their Iron Age forbears.[46] Similarly, at the center of the empire, a careful new study of skeletons in central Italy indicates that Italians were a centimeter or two shorter during the imperial centuries than they had been during the Iron Age or would be during the Middle Ages: Roman men averaging 164–165 cm and women 152–153 cm. This matches an army regulation from the late fourth century AD, stipulating that Italian recruits be at least 165 cm (5'5"), a suggestion that this stood in the middle-to-upper end of heights among men in rural Italy.[47]

These regional and imperial differences have been confirmed in a massive study of almost 10,000 individuals across Europe from the year 0 to 1800[48] (see Figures III.7, III.8). Very broadly, European heights were lower during the age of empire, grew as the empire fell apart, and then declined during the Dark Ages. Looking at regional variation during the first three centuries AD, male heights in the Mediterranean were the shortest (~168 cm), those in northern and eastern Europe – beyond the reach of the empire – the tallest (~171 cm), and those in Austria, the Rhine, and Britain falling somewhere

---

Paleopathology at the Origins of Agriculture (New York, 1984), 65. Ian Morris argues for a rising standard of living in Greece during these centuries in "Archaeology, Standards of Living, and Greek Economic History," in Manning and Morris, eds., *The Ancient Economy*, 91–126.

[45] Pia Bennike, *Paleopathology of Danish Skeletons: A Comparative Study of Demography, Disease and Injury* (Copenhagen, 1985), 51.

[46] Charlotte Roberts and Margaret Cox, "The Impact of Economic Intensification and Social Complexity on Human Health in Britain from 6000 BP (Neolithic) and the Introduction of Farming to the Mid-Nineteenth Century AD," in Mark Nathan Cohen and Gillian M. M. Crane-Kramer, eds., *Ancient Health: Skeletal Indicators of Agricultural and Economic Intensification* (Gainesville, FL, 2007), 149–63; Charlotte Roberts and Margaret Cox, *Health and Disease in Britain from Prehistory to the Present Day* (Thrupp, Glouc., 2003), 101–3, 131–2, 135–6, 140–1, 396.

[47] Monica Giannecchini and Jacopo Moggi-Cecchi, "Stature in Archeological Samples from Central Italy: Methodological Issues and Diachronic Changes," *AJPA* 135 (2008), 284–92; Peter Garnsey, *Food and Society in Classical Antiquity* (Cambridge, 1999), 57–9. See also Sara C. Bisel and Jane F. Bisel, "Health and Nutrition at Herculaneum," in Wilhelmina F. Jashemski and Frederick G. Meyer, eds., *The Natural History of Pompeii* (Cambridge, 2002), 451–75.

[48] Nikola Koepke and Joerg Baten, "The Biological Standard of Living in Europe during the Last Two Millennia," *EREconH* 9 (2005), 61–95, at 76, 77. See also the closing comments in Klavs Randsborg, "Barbarians, Classical Antiquity and the Rise of Western Europe: An Archaeological Essay," *P&P* 137 (1992), 8–24.

in between (~169 cm). During the fifth and sixth centuries, when the empire had decisively broken up, heights in all regions rose together. Thus we can construct a general picture of heights and well-being during the ten centuries between the waning of the Preclassical Crisis (1200–700 BC) (with its Hallstatt solar grand minimum and strong Siberian High) and the final fall of Rome in the sixth century AD. As we have seen, the Iron Age peoples living during the colder climates of the Preclassical Crisis had been relatively short. During the subsequent centuries of the Classical Optimum, the peoples of societies beyond the reach of the Roman empire grew in stature – and apparently in well-being. Those within the bounds of the empire may have done somewhat better than did their Iron Age forebears, but not to the extent of the free peoples beyond the empire.

What can explain this pattern? In brief, disease, childhood stress, nutrition, and work. The market – both imperial and local – moved commodities, including food, across considerable distances, but it also moved diseases. There is a strong consensus that the empire established a vast pool of routine disease exchange that had paradoxical effects. Diseases once restricted to certain localities spread widely, some possibly moving from the general population to affect mostly children. Ancient historians see a series of waterborne diseases –typhoid, dysentery, probably cholera – as endemic, along with tuberculosis and pneumonia. Malaria was deeply entrenched in the vast Italian marchlands. The disease burden would have impacted individuals disproportionately during their growing years, thus contributing to the restricted heights of adults inside the empire. Certainly this disease burden would have been much heavier in the great cities of the empire, but also in the densely populated towns that comprised the secondary and tertiary hubs of the imperial economy.[49]

Another source of short stature in the Roman empire may have been a general cultural neglect of small children. Scholars have long surmised that children in the Roman world were subtly neglected, and skeletal evidence is beginning to bear this out. Evidence suggests infants were kept swaddled and out of the sunlight, underfed, and then weaned earlier than they were in European societies beyond the empire. The result was much higher levels of cribia orbitalia, scurvy, and rib fractures, and a failure to thrive: children at Herculaneum were decidedly shorter than they could have been.[50]

[49] Robert Sallares, *Malaria and Rome: A History of Malaria in Ancient Italy* (Oxford, 2002); Robert Woods, "Ancient and Early Modern Mortality: Experience and Understanding," *EconHistR* (2007), 373–99; Morley, *Metropolis and Hinterland*, 39–54; Alex Scobie, "Slums, Sanitation, and Mortality in the Roman World," *Klio* 68 (1986) 399–422; Garnsey, *Food and Society in Classical Antiquity*, 43–51.

[50] Garnsey, *Food and Society in Classical Antiquity*, 50–61, 106–12; Mary E. Lewis, "Life and Death in a Civitas Capital: Metabolic Disease and Trauma in the Children from Late Dorset Dorchester, Dorset," *AJPA* 142 (2010), 405–16; Tracy L. Prowse et al., "Isotopic and Dental Evidence for Infant and Young Child Feeding Practices in an Imperial Roman

Then there is milk and red meat, a quick and easy source of protein for growth. If the consumption of meat grew during the high empire, the strong consensus is that only elite and middling households – and the men in the legions – had regular access to meat in their diets. Meat consumption in the empire had a three-point regional pattern: northern Europe (Gaul) tended strongly toward cattle, the Near East toward sheep, and the densely occupied Italian heartland toward pigs, which could be raised on limited grounds. Beyond the empire, in northern Europe, the frequency of cattle bones in archaeological sites seems to explain the taller stature of adult men and women. In Italy, the rise and fall of an imperial population is bracketed by the rise and fall of the pig, as measured from the evidence from sites around the Bay of Naples. Around 200 BC, with rising population densities, cattle bones fell sharply and pig bones rose even more; during the fifth and sixth centuries AD, pig bones wobbled and fell, replaced by sheep and goats, the traditional meat of the Mediterranean diet ever since. The classical image of the suckling pig at the Roman feast thus has strong archaeological support, but increasingly these were feasts for the fortunate few. The majority of the working and destitute poor would get by on grain and vegetables, with the occasional sausage, or fish if they lived on the coast, or – among the peasant majority – perhaps an old ox or milk cow past its working life. Thus, despite the maritime movement of grain that evened out the worst possibilities of famine, shortages of food must have contributed to the short stature of the peoples of the empire.[51]

Finally there is work. Most of the data for mediocre stature in the empire is for men, and it may be that labor routines within the empire, sweeping up teenaged boys into more arduous routine tasks, may have contributed to short adult stature.[52] But one anomalous figure in the height data suggests an alternative trajectory for women. In Lawrence Angel's figures for the eastern Mediterranean (Greece and Anatolia), women suddenly grew taller during Roman times, reaching heights not attained since the Mesolithic (158 cm).[53] This could be ascribed to a sampling error, but there is a possibility that it reflects reality, driven by technological change. According to the most recent

Skeletal Sample," *AJPA* 137 (2008), 294–308; Tracy L. Prowse et al., "Isotopic Evidence for Age-Related Variation in Diet from Isola Sacra, Italy," *AJPA* 128 (2000), 2–13; Bisel and Bisel, "Health and Nutrition at Herculaneum," 456–8.

[51] Nikola Koepke and Joerg Baten, "Agricultural Specialization and Height in Ancient and Medieval Europe," *ExpEconH* 45 (2008), 127–46; King, "Diet in the Roman World," 172; Garnsey, *Cities, Peasants, and Food*, 226–52; Garnsey, *Food and Society in Classical Antiquity*, 51–61; MacKinnon, *Production and Consumption of Animals*, 209–10; Oliver E. Craig et al., "Stable Isotopic Evidence for Diet at the Imperial Coastal Site of Velia (1st and 2nd Centuries AD) in Southern Italy," *AJPA* 139 (2009), 572–83.

[52] Richard H. Steckel, "Nutritional Status in the Colonial Economy," *WMQ*, 3d ser., 56 (1999), 34; –, "Stature and the Standard of Living," *JEconL* 33 (1995), 1908–40.

[53] Angel, "Health ... in the Eastern Mediterranean," 55.

reconstruction, by M. J. T. Lewis, the water mill was first widely used on the coastal streams of Asia Minor some time during the last centuries BC. Lewis quotes the poet Antipater of Thessalonica, who wrote in the last years BC of the virtues of water-powered mills over the hand-turned rotary quern.

Hold back you hand from the mill, you grinding girls, even if the cock-crow heralds the dawn, sleep on. For Demeter has imposed the labours of your hands on the nymphs who leaping down upon the topmost part of the wheel, rotate its axle; and with encircling cogs it turns the hollow weight of the Nisyrian millstones. If we learn to feast toil-free on the fruits of the earth, we taste again the golden age.[54]

The "grinding girls" slept late and, freed from excessive toil at the grind-stone, may well have enjoyed a growth spurt. It is entirely possible that, relieved by the water mill from the labor of grinding grain, a female occu-pation since the Neolithic, the young women in the eastern Mediterranean grew to adult heights unseen since the Mesolithic, if not exactly "the golden age."

* * *

The Fall of Rome?

So what of the storied decline and fall of the Roman empire? In recent decades, the very framework of a Roman collapse has been in doubt, replaced by a model of a gradual transition running seamlessly from late antiquity into the early Middle Ages.[55] Most recently, however, a revived catastrophism has challenged this gradualist model: the empire fell because it could not withstand the assaults of wave upon wave of barbarian warriors.[56] Here the question revolves around the shifting strengths of the empire and its barbar-ian opponents. Edward Gibbon, writing a moral tale in the mid-eighteenth century, focused on the softening of martial values and valor and the dys-functionality and failure of Roman imperial governance. Some have blamed the literally stupefying effects of metallic lead in the pottery, glass, and wine that graced the tables of the Roman elite.[57] Not convinced by evidence for

---

[54] Lewis, *Millstone and Hammer*, vii, 66–9.

[55] This perspective was launched by Peter R. L. Brown, *The World of Late Antiquity: From Marcus Aurelius to Muhammed* (London, 1971). See also –, "The World of Late Antiquity Revisited," *Symbolae Osloenses* 72 (1997), 5–30.

[56] Ward-Perkins, *The Fall of Rome*; Peter Heather, *The Fall of the Roman Empire: A New History of Rome and the Barbarians* (Oxford, 2006); Bryan Ward-Perkins, "Continuitists, Catastrophists, and the Towns of Post-Roman Northern Italy," *PBSRom* 67 (1997), 157–76.

[57] For a variety of opinions, see H. A. Waldron, "Lead Poisoning in the Ancient World," *Medical History* 17 (1973), 391–9; J. O. Nriagu, *Lead and Lead Poisoning in Antiquity* (New York, 1983); and John Scarborough, "The Myth of Lead Poisoning among the Romans: A Review Essay," *Journal of the History of Medicine and Allied Sciences* 39 (1984), 469–75.

structural decline, Peter Heather and Bryan Ward-Perkins focus on the contingencies of military struggle with the barbarian Germans. Ward-Perkins sees a sudden crisis at the beginning of the fifth century; Heather concurs, but also stresses the growing sophistication and unity of those barbarians, gradually learning by association with the empire, and relentlessly pressed from the eastern steppes by the advancing Hun.[58] Other recent scholarship argues that a decline had set in within the empire itself, shaped by the shrinking economy and falling populations described previously.[59]

Economists, demographers, and traditional environmental historians would be certainly disappointed with political explanations, and might instinctively turn to a Malthusian model, in which overpopulation led to "inevitable" stresses that doomed the empire to collapse. Such is the direction to which critics of the Roman growth model incline. Certainly the local ecologies of some locations, especially isolated mining and smelting regions, were indeed devastated by the heavy metal sediments deposited in Roman times.[60] The agricultural needs of rising populations did indeed transform lowland ecologies. But most recent paleoecological studies see little sign of a fundamental crisis of soils and forests in the late Roman Mediterranean.[61]

[58] Ward-Perkins, *The Fall of Rome*, 42–9; Heather, *The Fall of the Roman Empire*, 450–9.

[59] Here see Richard Duncan-Jones, "Economic Change and the Transition to Late Antiquity," in Simon Swain and Mark Edward, eds., *Approaching Late Antiquity: The Transformation from Early to Late Empire* (Oxford, 2004), 20–52, and the archaeological landscape literature cited elsewhere in this chapter. Ward-Perkins feels that while the "jury should remain out" regarding economic decline in the West, "any decline was not overwhelming" (see *The Fall of Rome*, 42).

[60] Graeme Barker, "A Tale of Two Deserts: Contrasting Desertification Histories on Rome's Desert Frontiers," *WdArch* 33 (2002), 488–507, esp. 496–504.

[61] Such is the conclusion of Peregrine Horden and Nicholas Purcell, *The Corrupting Sea: A Study of Mediterranean History* (Malden, MA, 2000), 298–341; A. T. Grove and Oliver Rackham, *The Nature of Mediterranean Europe: An Ecological History* (New Haven, CT, 2001), esp. 288–311. See also John R. McNeill, *The Mountains of the Mediterranean World: An Environmental History* (New York, 1992), 72–84. For studies that stress natural versus human impacts, see J. R. M. Allen et al., "Holocene Environmental Variability – the Record from Lago Grande di Monticchio, Italy," *QuatInt* 88 (2002), 69–80; Lothar Schulte, "Climatic and Human Influence on River Systems and Glacial Fluctuations in Southeast Spain since the Late Glacial Maximum," *QuatInt* 93–4 (2002), 85–100; Michael Magny et al., "Assessment of the Impact of Climate and Anthropogenic Factors on Holocene Mediterranean Vegetation in Europe on the basis of Palaeohydrological Records," *PPP* 186 (2002), 47–59; Laura Sadori and Biancamaria Narcisi, "The Postglacial Record of Environmental History from Lago di Pergusa, Sicily," *The Holocene* 11 (2001), 655–701; Guy Jalut et al., "Holocene Climatic Changes in the Western Mediterranean, from South-East France to South-East Spain," *PPP* 160 (2000), 255–90. For two recent studies stressing human impacts, see F. Oldfield et al., "A High Resolution Late Holocene Palaeo Environmental Record from the Central Adriatic Sea," *QSR* 22 (2003), 319–42; and David K. Chester and Peter A. James, "Late Pleistocene and Holocene Landscape Development in the Algarve Region, Southern Portugal," *Journal of Mediterranean Archaeology* 12 (1999), 169–96. Oldfield and colleagues stress the apparent impact of human land clearance during the Late Bronze Age and the Middle Ages, but on the former they admit the "real possibility that the record is also influenced by climate

However, they also find in a number of locations, most clearly in the northern Levant, that late Roman times saw a massive volume of soil erosion. In the Levant, this soil loss permanently ruined regions that had supported agriculture for millennia. Clearly, Roman pressures of population and empire put significant stress on Mediterranean landscapes, beyond the signals of human presence and alteration that since the Late Neolithic appear in many Old World ecological studies. But this impact was not, apparently, continuous, but sudden, late in the Roman period. The author of the best study of this late Roman erosion sees a "high likelihood" that climate – specifically a shift toward intense seasonal rains at the transition to the Dark Ages – played a role in this degradation (see Figure III.8). There is now reasonably definitive evidence for this "likelihood": new studies show conclusively that, following the onset of North Atlantic ice rafting around AD 350, the North Atlantic Oscillation shifted from a more positive to a more negative mode, pushing the winter westerlies south into the Mediterranean, bringing a surge of winter and spring precipitation, after hundreds of years of moderately dry climate. Flooding recorded in the sediments along the Arno River – including entire ships buried in flood deposits – suggests that episodes of extreme rain might have begun around 300 BC in central Italy. Fredric Cheyette sees these advancing rains as fundamentally undermining the grain-based economy of Italy and southern France. In south central Anatolia, a century-long drought broke sharply around AD 540, followed by several hundred years of humidity, suggesting enhanced rainfall. In northern Europe, precipitation dropped significantly between AD 200 and AD 350, recovered, and then fell again to millennial lows around AD 450, as the NAO negative mode set in for the Dark Ages. Thus these paleoecological studies strongly suggest that the massive soil degradation associated with the Roman empire was driven by both population pressure and climatic contingency, though – as we shall see – the sequencing was not precisely what one might expect. They also broadly concur with political historians' recent view that the empire was in relatively good order into the fourth century.[62]

change, especially a trend toward desiccation" (334), desiccation that corresponded to the crises of the late second millennium BC. They conclude that "one notable feature common to both" the marine and lake sediments that they studied in the Italian Adriatic "is the absence of any strong indication of human impact on vegetation during the Roman period" (335). Sadori and Narcisi, analyzing data from central Sicily, find that human impact "did not produce devastating impacts on the already open landscape" after the aridification of the Mid-Holocene (670). Barker, "A Tale of Two Deserts" (496), concludes that Roman frontier farmers in Libya used soil-conserving practices. J. Donald Hughes continues to argue for a degradation in recent work, including "Environmental Impacts of the Roman Economy and Social Structure: Augustus to Diocletian," in Alf Hornberg et al., *Rethinking Environmental History: World-System History and GEC* (Lanham, MD, 2007), 27–40; *The Mediterranean: An Environmental History* (Santa Barbara, CA, 2005), esp. 197–8.

[62] Jesse Casana, "Mediterranean Valleys Revisited: Linking Soil Erosion, Land Use and Climate Variability in the Northern Levant," *Geomorphology* 101 (2008), 429–42, quote from

What was the longer-range dynamic of climate, here suggested as a critical trigger of soil erosion in the late Roman Mediterranean? The global Classical Optimum would indeed come to an end between AD 300 and AD 600, with its influence felt around the world.[63] The Chinese Han dynasty was – it appears – extremely sensitive to sudden collapse in the monsoon regime, as evidenced by the dynastical crises at AD 9 and AD 220. If the Roman world began to decline starting in the late second century AD, however, no major climate signal at all suggests any causal argument (see Figures II.1, III.5a, III.8). Relative to the grand minima of 700 BC and 300 BC, of AD 600, and of the era of the Little Ice Age, solar activity was stable between AD 100 and AD 500. While there were minor fluctuations toward the Siberian High between AD 75 and AD 125, these were nothing compared to the Halstatt solar minimum–driven surges of 1200 BC and AD 1400. Ice rafting in the North Atlantic tipped past its minimum in AD 200, but could not have been a major force until AD 350, though its first stages must have been associated with the declining precipitation in northern Europe, and the first bursts of extremes rains in the Mediterranean after AD 300. The new temperature estimates for northern Europe indicate a distinct cooling setting in around AD 250, and there would be an intense cold spike around AD 536. But it does not seem likely that fundamental climate change drove a decay of the Roman economy before AD 200.[64]

---

p. 438; Christoph Zielhofer, "Sedimentation and Soil Formation Phases in the Ghardimaou Basin (Northern Tunisia) during the Holocene," *QuatInt* 93–4 (2002), 109–25, esp. 122, sees a similar late Roman crisis in Tunisia. See also M. Benvenuti et al., "Late-Holocene Catastrophic Floods in the Terminal Arno River (Pisa, Central Italy) from the Story of a Roman Riverine Harbor," *Holocene* 16 (2006), 863–76; and C. Viti-Finzi, "Fluvial Solar Signals," in K. Gallagher et al., eds., *Landscape Evolution: Denudation, Climate and Tectonic of Different Times and Space Scales* (London, 2008), 106–15. On the environmental impact of depopulation from warfare and disease in Roman times, see also McNeill, *Mountains of the Mediterranean World*, 78–81, 84–6. For the negative NAO precipitation shift from north to south, see the sources cited in notes 17–19 and Fredric L. Cheyette, "The Disappearance of the Ancient Landscape and the Climatic Anomaly of the Early Middle Ages: A Question to be Pursued," *Early Medieval Europe* 16 (2008), 127–65, esp. 157–64; and Jessie Woodbridge and Neil Roberts, "Late Holocene Climate of the Eastern Mediterranean Inferred from Diatom Analysis of Annually-Laminated Lake Deposits," *QSR* 30 (2011), 3381–92.

[63] See Chapter 9.

[64] See notes 17–19. As this volume was going to press, two state of the art analyses of climate in the Roman world were published: Michael McCormick et al., "Climate Change during and after the Roman Empire: Reconstructing the Past from Scientific and Historical Evidence," *JInterdH* 43 (2012), 169–220; Sturt Manning, "The Roman World and Climate: Context, Relevance of Climate Change, and Some Issues," in W. V. Harris, ed., *The Ancient Mediterranean Environment between Science and History* (Leiden: E.J. Brill 2013), 103–70. The McCormick team sees the beginnings of climate instability around AD 200, followed by a recovery, and then a sharp deterioration setting in around AD 400. The team stresses, however, that the Nile flood was particularly favorable for agriculture through AD 155, after which it became increasingly erratic (see pp. 189–90). Manning sees warm optimum conditions through AD 200, followed by a regionally variable epoch of 500, when marked deterioration prevailed.

The answer here seems quite simple and well-known: devastating epidemic disease. A central structural dynamic in the decline of Rome, particularly its western domain, has to lie in a spiraling population decline, which undermined military recruitment, economic demand, and even political skill. The most obvious explanation for this relentless but mosaic pattern of demographic decline lies in the series of epidemics that swept along Mediterranean trade routes and lines of march starting in the late second century. William McNeill, in his classic *Plagues and Peoples*, explains the epidemics of late antiquity in terms of the confluence of civilizational disease pools, and suggests that growing population and growing trade along the Old World core running from China through India to the Mediterranean was a powerful conduit for new diseases. The fact that epidemics struck China soon after they hit the Mediterranean suggests the possibility that India may have been the source of some of these devastating plagues. Alternatively, the common source of the plague probably lay in the tangle of central Asian trade routes: one team of geneticists argues that its ultimate genetic root lies in the Tibetan plateau.[65]

While epidemic disease was a constant in the Roman world, three epidemics stand out as particularly intense, with impacts perhaps rivaling that of the Black Death of the 1350s. The first of these, the Antonine Plague, carried back to Rome by legions returned from Babylon and an assault on the Parthian Empire, struck a reasonably stable empire in AD 165. Generally thought to have been smallpox, the Antonine Plague lasted for fifteen years, and ended after it may have killed Marcus Aurelius, the last of a line of five so-called Good Emperors who had ruled since AD 96. Epidemics then struck various parts of the empire every twenty-five to thirty years: in Nubia in 200; in the armies on the Euphrates in 232; and then another fifteen-year-long epidemic, Cyprian's Plague, perhaps smallpox, perhaps measles, apparently emerged from Ethiopia in AD 251. Localized epidemics are recorded over the fourth and fifth centuries, often associated with warfare, but in AD 542 a deadly epidemic known as Justinian's Plague spread north from Egypt; now genetically identified as bubonic plague, this epidemic flared, ebbed, and flared again for centuries, before it finally faded in the 800s[66] (see Figure III.8).

---

[65] William H. McNeill, *Plagues and Peoples* (New York, 1977), 97–128; Michael McCormack, "Toward a Molecular History of the Justinianic Plague," in Lester K. Little, ed., *Plague and the End of Antiquity: The Pandemic of 541–750* (New York, 2007), 302–4; Yujun Cui et al., "Historical Variations in Mutation Rate in an Epidemic Pathogen, *Yersinia pestis*," *PNAS* 110 (2013), 577–82, at 579; Jongman, "Re-constructing the Roman economy."

[66] R. P. Duncan-Jones, "The Impact of the Antonine Plague," *JRA* 6 (1996), 108–36; Mary Ellen Snodgrass, ed., *World Epidemics: A Cultural History of Disease from Prehistory to the Era of SARS* (Jefferson, NC, 2003), 19–26; Dionysios Ch. Stathakopoulos, *Famine and Pestilence in the Late Roman and Early Byzantine Empire: A Systematic Survey of Subsistence Crises and Epidemics* (Aldershot, 2004); Peregrine Horden, "Mediterranean Plague in the Age of Justinian," in Michael Maas, ed., *The Cambridge Companion to the Age of Justinian* (New

The impact of these plagues was catastrophic, but apparently selective. Willem Jongman paints a powerful picture: the Antonine Plague of AD 165 that set off these waves of epidemics was an exogenous event, not "a classic Malthusian check: it came on the crest of a wave of rising prosperity rather than as the apex of growing misery." In sum, he argues, "it is our best bet to explain why over such a wide range, things suddenly began to go wrong in the second century AD."[67] Annual lists of taxpayers in rural Egypt suggest certain districts lost as much as 70–90 percent of their population between the late 150s and the late 160s. Series of dated documents and artifacts indicate a steep if temporary decline in Roman economic activity, building construction, marble production, and even coinage in the late 160s and 170s; the impact of Cyprian's Plague may have been worse.[68] Roman silver mining in Spain collapsed during these years, though raids by North African warriors apparently played a role as well.[69] The numbers of animal bones in Roman sites dropped precipitously, suggesting a poorer diet, and the number of recovered wrecks fell, suggesting a slowing of trade. Various sources, including archaeological surveys, suggest that population began to decline in Italy, Spain, and France from peaks in the late second century, never really recovering until medieval times. A recent synthesis of the distribution of African Red Slip Ware, the diagnostic imperial export ceramic, suggests a massive collapse in production at 250, the beginning of Cyprian's Plague and a long "third-century crisis." McEvedy and Jones's estimates suggest that population around the Mediterranean might have fallen by a third between AD 165 and AD 400. Greece and the Near East may have been

---

York, 2005), 134–60. For the genetic isolation of the DNA of the plague bacillus in skeletons dating from the epoch of the Justinian Plague, see Michael Harbeck et al., "Yersinia Pestis DNA from Skeletal Remains from the 6th Century AD Reveals Insights into Justinianic Plague," *PLOS Pathogens* 9 (2013), e1003349; Michel Drancourt et al., "*Yersinia Pestis* Orientalis in Remains of Ancient Plague Patients," *EmInfDis* 13 (2007), 332–3; Ingrid Wiechman and Gisela Grupe, "Detection of *Yersinia Pestis* DNA in Two Early Medieval Skeletal Finds from Aschheim (Upper Bavaria, 6th Century A.D.)," *AJPA* 126 (2005), 48–55; Michel Drancourt et al., "Genotyping, Orientalis-like *Yersinia Pestis*, and Plague-like Pandemics," *EmInfDis* 10 (2004), 1585–92.

[67] Willem Jongman, "Roman Economic Change and the Antonine Plague: Endogenous, Exogenous, or What?" in E. Lo Cascio, ed., *L'impatto della "peste antonina"* (Bari, 2012), 253–63; Jongman, "The Rise and Fall of the Roman Economy," 243.

[68] Duncan-Jones, "The Impact of the Antonine Plague," 120–34. Genetic analysis now suggests that the bubonic plague first emerged in China or Central Asia (former Soviet Union) sometime before 600 BC. If so, the eruption of bubonic plague in the Mediterranean world from roughly AD 540 would have been the result of re-eruption of dormant reservoirs in the peripheries of the region, or re-transmission from China/Central Asia. The weight of the historical evidence suggests the former explanation. On genetic origins, see Giovanna Morelli, "*Yersinia Pestis* Genome Sequencing Identifies Patterns of Global Phylogenetic Diversity," *NatGen* 42 (2010), 1140–3.

[69] Wilson, "Machines, Power, and the Ancient Economy," 28; Duncan-Jones, "Economic Change," 37, 47, 50.

hit by the earlier plagues, but they recovered, going through a resurgence of population and prosperity before they were devastated by the Justinian Plague that started during the 540s. Here, depopulation by epidemic would have coincided with the intensification of severe rainfall that paleoecological studies suggest for the Mediterranean. If this is the case, the soil erosion would have had yet another specific cause. The hillside terracing that allowed the spread of agriculture into marginal areas required considerable labor to maintain. The loss of population would have undermined any efforts to repair the agricultural improvements built up over the previous several hundred years of Roman-era expansion. Thus epidemic depopulation must join severe rainfall as part of the explanation for the massive erosion that occurred in late Roman times.[70]

What of the survivors of the plague? Might they not have done better, as is the case for Europe after the Black Death, when a sudden fall in numbers led to several centuries of improved standards of living? The consensus is reasonably clear: things got worse in the wake of the ancient plagues for the ordinary peoples of the Roman world. Rather than having more to go around, the survivors had to carry a heavier burden. The Roman elites demanded the same payments in rent and taxes as before, and spiraling concentration of wealth was the result. With nothing of real value in which to invest, they invested in land, with the result that they simply grew richer while the people grew poorer and poorer, descending toward serfdom if not outright slavery.[71]

Thus it would appear that the plagues of the late second and third centuries made a major contribution to the decline of the western Mediterranean, but may not have impacted the reemergence of the east, as manifested in the eastern empire and then the Byzantine empire. The classic understandings of

---

[70] Bryan Ward-Perkins, "Land, Labor, and Settlement," in Averil Cameron et al., *The Cambridge Ancient History, Vol. XIV: Late Antiquity: Empire and Successors, A.D. 425–600* (Cambridge, 2000), 320–7; Greene, *The Archaeology of the Roman Economy*, 98–141; Tamara Lewit, *Agricultural Production in the Roman Economy, A.D. 200–400* (Oxford, 1990), 27–55; Neil Christie, "Barren Fields? Landscapes and Settlements in Late Roman and Post-Roman Italy," in Graham and Shipley, eds., *Human Landscapes in Classical Antiquity*, 254–83; H. Vanhaverbeke et al., "Late Antiquity in the Territory of Sagalassos," and Fabio Saggioro, "Late Antique Settlement on the Plain of Verona," in William Bowden et al., *Recent Research on the Late Antique Countryside* (Leiden, 2004), 247–81, 505–34; Wilson, "Approaches to Quantifying Roman Trade"; Elizabeth Fentress et al., "Accounting for ARS: Finewares and Sites in Sicily and Africa," in Susan E. Alcock and John F. Cherry, eds., *Side-by-Side Survey: Comparative Regional Studies in the Mediterranean World* (Oxford, 2004), 147–62, esp. 148–9. For a congruent older synthesis, see A. H. M. Jones, *The Later Roman Empire, 284–602: A Social, Economic, and Administrative Survey* (Norman, OK, 1964), 812–23, 1040–5. On depopulation and erosion, see Chapter 6, notes 22–3.

[71] Willem Jongman, "The Early Roman Empire: Consumption," Elio Lo Cascio, "The Early Roman Empire: The State and the Economy," Andrea Giardina, "The Transition to Antiquity," in Scheidel et al., eds., *The Cambridge Economic History of the Greco-Roman World*, esp. 612, 616–17, 646–7, 757–63.

the decline of the western empire involve endless warfare and civil strife, the withering of long-distance trade, barbarians on and over the frontier, and the rise of Christianity. Each of these can be connected relatively directly to a plague-driven depopulation.

From the beginning of the third century, Rome was wracked by challenges from beyond its borders, and wars constantly fed both famines and epidemics. The Antonine Plague of 165–80 was introduced by warfare in the east, and Cyprian's Plague of 251–66 was embedded in a long series of wars to defend the frontiers running from 234–84, at the end of which the empire was effectively divided in half. Epidemics accompanied war in 310–13, 359–63, 378–9, 406–10, and from the 440s to the 470s. The Justinian Plague arrived in Italy in 542, during the Gothic-Byzantine Wars; the combination of war, famine, and epidemic brought utter and final devastation to the ancient center of empire. As local trade collapsed, rural Italians abandoned the lowlands and huddled in rough new mountain villages, as they had in the last crisis, at the close of the Bronze Age.[72]

Thus a dynamic of first war and epidemic, and then a triad of climate, war, and epidemic, has to lie at the center of an explanation of the long decline and final collapse of the empire. The steady erosion of population left fewer people to serve in the army, to tend the fields, to labor in urban workshops, and to man the ships in a foreign trade perhaps now somewhat suspect in an age of rampant disease. Skills grew scarce; public works were not maintained. The result must have left less circulating wealth for the old elite to glean from rents and taxes, while deaths in their ranks left room for rising men. In addition to invasion from without, the empire was wracked by civil war, and a string of short-lived emperors, many originally foreign mercenaries, who tried and failed to grab the reins and rewards of power. This instability was not dissimilar from the instability that would ruin France and England in the Hundred Years' War and the War of the Roses, following the Black Death. The overall effect was the militarization of a collapsing society, as magnates raised armies to capture more of the shrinking surplus. Some of these new men were "barbarians," Germans and others from across the frontier, who were first invited as mercenaries to build up the ranks of the waning Roman army, and then made their move to grab power.[73] Finally, there is the slow but inexorable rise of a new world religion. Sociologist Rodney Stark has developed an argument that the numerical rise of Christianity, first in Asia Minor and then in the West, was driven by a differential mortality

---

[72] Boatwright et al., *The Romans*, 432–8; Snodgrass, *World Epidemics*, 19–21; Stathakopoulos, *Famine and Pestilence*, 46–8, 180–1, 189–97, 205, 220–6, 232–9, 243–4, 270–8; Heather, *The Fall of the Roman Empire*; Ward-Perkins, *The Fall of Rome*; Christie, "Barren Fields?"; Riccardo Francovich and Richard Hodge, *Villa to Village: The Transformation of the Roman Countryside in Italy, c. 400–1000* (London, 2003), 61–74; Terrenato, "The Essential Countryside of the Roman World," 140.

[73] Boatwright et al., *The Romans*, 398–416, 432–8; Jones, *The Later Roman Empire*, 1035–8.

between pagans and Christians, who offered their believers close communities of care giving.[74] Whatever the causal connection, the new religion spread following the devastations of disease, was officially granted toleration in 313, and was declared the state religion in AD 380.

In 378, two years before the establishment of Christianity, a barbarian horde destroyed the Roman army at the battle of Adrianople; by 410 these Visigoths had sacked Rome and moved on to Gaul in search of land. By this point, climate change seems to have once again entered the picture. The Goths were one of a variety of groups pressing in upon the Roman frontiers, attracted by an increasingly poorly defended frontier, but also entering into complex trade relations across this boundary.[75] Increasingly they were harried from the steppe by a new group, the Huns, who had emerged recently from the Central Asian steppes. If the empire itself was not affected initially by climate change, tree ring evidence from the edge of the steppes suggests that after ~AD 200 – and more decisively after ~AD 350 – an increasing frequency of drought put Germans, Goths, and Huns on the move and into Europe.[76] Climate change may have contributed to agrarian disruption on and beyond the frontiers: pressed by the Huns, the Visigoths were in a desperate search for food and supply when they demanded entry into the empire, leading to the battle of Adrianople.[77] Such droughts seem to have been a manifestation of the onset of cooler climate across the northern hemisphere, marked by ice rafting off Greenland, though not by any serious advance of the Siberian High. If conditions certainly did not reach the scale of the final Bronze Age crisis or the Little Ice Age that would arrive a millennium later, it is clear that the Classical Optimum was over, and for the duration of the ice-rafting episode, roughly running from AD 375 to AD 800, climate conditions in northwest Eurasia were colder and more variable than those during the Classical Optimum or the ensuing Medieval Optimum, so-called.[78] Very roughly, these were the textbook Dark Ages.

---

[74] Rodney Stark, *The Rise of Christianity* (Princeton, NJ, 1997), 73–94, 113–16.

[75] C. R. Whitaker, "Trade and Frontiers of the Roman Empire," in Garnsey and Whitaker, *Trade and Famine*, 110–27; Boatwright et al., *The Romans*, 434.

[76] McCormick et al., "Climate Change," stress the impact of Central Asian drought on these "barbarian" invasions: 189–92, 199. See also David H. Holt, "Did Extreme Climate Conditions Stimulate the Migrations of the Germanic Tribes in the 3rd and 4th Centuries AD? An Examination of Historical Data, Climate Proxy Data, and Migration Events," PhD thesis, Fulbright College of Arts and Sciences, Environmental Dynamics, The University of Arkansas at Fayetteville (2002); Schlütz and Lehmkuhl, "Climate Change in the Russian Altai, 101–18, esp. 114; on the Huns, see Heather, *The Fall of the Roman Empire*, 146–58.

[77] Heather, *The Fall of the Roman Empire*, 158–81; Whitaker, "Trade and Frontiers of the Roman Empire," 110, 118–21. For an archaeological perspective on the impact of the Gothic invasion, see Andrew Poulter, "Cataclysm on the Lower Danube: The Destruction of a Complex Roman Landscape," in Christie, *Landscapes of Change*, 223–53.

[78] The Medieval Optimum is something of a misnomer from a global perspective. See Chapter 9 on the Medieval Climate Anomaly.

A fascinating argument links an episode of catastrophic climate change and the onset of Justinian's Plague, and indeed the end of the classical age around the Old World. The IPCC study of northern hemispheric temperature based on tree rings indicates a short but vicious spike of cold temperatures around AD 540 (see Figure III.5a). David Keys has compiled the evidence to support the argument that a massive volcanic eruption occurred in AD 536, blanketing the earth in a sulphur haze. Keys placed this eruption in Indonesia or Papua New Guinea, but recent work suggests that the location was the volcano Ilopango in El Salvador. Cutting solar input for as much as a decade, this volcanic haze was recorded in texts from Britain to Korea, describing dark days, a dim sun, and mid-summer frosts; in south China it rained yellow dust that could be "scooped up in handfuls."[79] Keys argues that this brief disruption had a series of profound effects. Droughts across the Asian grasslands sent a final wave of nomads against the frontiers of the eastern empire, further eroding a Roman legacy finally lost when the Turks – set in motion in the 540s by droughts in Mongolia – destroyed the last vestiges of Byzantium in the mid-fifteenth century. In Yemen, Keys argues that massive floods following the 536 event from the 540s to the 590s destroyed the massive Marib Dam – which had regulated the flow of irrigation waters for the ancient Arabian kingdom of Saba. This crisis, combined with the plague, destroyed the population and political power of Yemen, allowing the balance in Arabia to shift to Medina. Here the prophet Mohammed emerged to found Islam, a world religion that – with Christianity – would redefine the cultural geography of the shattered pieces of the ancient Mediterranean and southwest Asian empires. The plague itself was a product of the 536 event, Keys also argues. He proposes that the rains that followed a decade of post-eruption drought set off a burst of reproduction among mice in East Africa, mice carrying fleas that are hosts to the bubonic plague. He argues that with this explosion of the mouse population, fleas carrying the plague bacillus were transferred to black rats living in the shipping involved in transporting elephant ivory north through the Red Sea to the Mediterranean. This sequence, he suggests, was the origin of the Justinian Plague that hit the Mediterranean in 542 and then flared for centuries.[80]

---

[79] Figure 6.10 in *Climate Change 2007*. David Keys, *Catastrophe: An Investigation into the Origins of the Modern World* (New York, 1999), quote from 149–50; Robert Dull et al., "Evidence for the Ilopango TBJ Eruption as the Trigger of the AD 536 Event," Association of American Geographers Meeting, New York, February 24, 2012. See also the essays in Joel Gunn, ed., *The Years without Summer: Tracing A.D. 536 and Its Aftermath* (Oxford, 2000); and Ionnis Antoniou and Anastasios K. Sinakos, "The Sixth-Century Plague, Its Repeated Appearance until 746AD and the Explosion of the Rabaul Volcano," *Byzantinische Zeitschrift* 98 (2005), 1–4.

[80] David Key, *Catastrophe*; Robert Sallares, "Ecology, Evolution, and Epidemiology of Plague," in Little, ed., *Plague and the End of Antiquity*, 284–5; R. B. Stothers, "Volcanic Dry Fogs, Climate Cooling, and Plague Pandemics in Europe and the Middle East," *ClimCh* 42 (1999),

Keys traces his thesis to the four corners of the earth, from Indonesia, to Britain, to south China, to Mexico. It would appear that the 536 event was a wildcard punctuation exacerbating but causally unrelated to the climatic decline that had set in during the third century. He may well be right that this "catastrophe" sharply marked the close of the ancient world and the beginning of something new, if not quite what he calls "the modern world." But if many of the structures of the ancient world collapsed in the middle of the sixth century, and new structures began to emerge, the emergence of a coherent medieval world would take some time to coalesce. Natural forces operating around the globe played an important part in shaping this slow development. The Justinian Plague and its continuations ravaged the Near East and the eastern Mediterranean for more than 200 years, reversing its recent regrowth of population, while it had less of an ongoing impact on western and northern Europe because post-Roman society was insulated from long-distance trade by its very poverty. McNeill speculates that the "swarming" of both Viking Norse and Islamic Arab warriors may have reflected the growth of populations somewhat isolated from the later stages of the Justinian Plague. The plague may have erupted in China during the seventh century.[81]

In sum, it would not appear that Malthusian overpopulation fundamentally drove the collapse of Old World antiquity. While they may – or may not – have been caught in a tightening Malthusian trap, there is no reason to believe that these were societies on the knife edge of collapse. Absent the primary impact of exogenous epidemic disease and the secondary impact of abrupt climate change, there is no reason to think that they might not have continued on trajectories that were already longer than the entire history of the modern economy. Perhaps they were not poised to launch that economic modernity, but they were not necessarily preordained to collapse either. Certainly political structures imposed profound limits on the viability of ancient policy and decision making, but it is difficult not to see wider and more profound limits imposed by natural forces.

713–23; and Fagan, *The Long Summer*, 208–10. There is a sixty-year gap in the GISP2 data between AD 540 and AD 600 that may have destroyed a significant volcanic signature in the Greenland ice. The impact of the 536 event can be seen in Figure 8.2.b, illustrating animal bones in the archaeological sites around Naples. Here the dominance of pig bones in the archaeological record – and presumably the middling and elite diet – was twice briefly disrupted, first at the beginning of the first century AD, apparently a reflection of economic crisis following the eruption of Vesuvius in AD 79, and second in the middle of the sixth century, at the time of the 536 event.

[81] McNeill, *Plagues and Peoples*, 113–15.

9

The Global Dark and Middle Ages, AD 542–1350

The millennium from AD 500 to AD 1500 is suffering from an identity crisis. The convenient labels of *Dark Ages* and *Middle Ages* have come under
attack from historians seeking to unsettle our standard narrative chronology, and to get at the qualities of lived experience during these centuries.
Peter Brown led the way, smoothing out the discontinuities between an Age
of Rome and the Middle Ages with the construct of a "Late Antiquity" running from roughly AD 400 to AD 900, condemning the Dark Ages to outer
darkness. At the other end of the spectrum, the terms *late medieval* and
early modern, covering the period from 1350 to 1815, are equally problematic because the people of the period had no sense of themselves as ending
the Middle Ages or launching "modernity," at least before 1700. In general,
historians are questioning the cultural periodization of the entire domain
before 1700, proposing that it all should simply be seen as premodern. Then
of course there is the question of whether modernity is a universal, or a term
fundamentally a feature of North Atlantic societies from some time in the
eighteenth century.[1]

When I wear my hat as a cultural historian, I am happy to engage in these
debates, but the older terms make some sense from an earth systems perspective. Here we enter directly into Victor Lieberman's world of "strange
parallels."[2] Just as they uncannily support traditional understandings of the
chronology of a longer antiquity running between 3000 BC and the "fall of
Rome," the boundaries and constraints imposed by the action of climate and

---

[1] Peter Brown, *The World of Late Antiquity: From Marcus Aurelius to Muhammed* (London,
1971); Bryan Ward-Perkins, "Continuitists, Catastrophists, and the Towns of Post-Roman
Northern Italy," *PBSRom* 67 (1997), 157–76; Howard Kaminsky, "From Lateness to Waning
to Crisis: The Burden of the Later Middle Ages," *Journal of Early Modern Europe* 4 (2000),
85–125; Carol Symes, "When We Talk about Modernity," *AHR* 116 (2011), 715–26.
[2] Victor Lieberman, *Strange Parallels: Southeast Asia in Global Context, c. 800–1830. Vol.
II: Mainland Mirrors: Europe, Japan, China, South Asia and the Islands* (New York, 2009),
79–84.

disease broadly reinforce the traditional historical chronology for the next millennium. Climate and disease made Brown's Late Antiquity a tough time in both hemispheres, perhaps a "Dark Age." The climatic Middle Ages also have some global coherence, with an early Middle Age running from 900–1275 seeing an optimum in some places, in others quite the reverse, followed by a late Middle Age running to 1550 and encompassing the entering phases of the Little Ice Age. The epoch running from the fourteenth century to the seventeenth century does broadly make sense as a hinge toward modernity, for reasons spelled out in the next chapter. While I try to be respectful of historians' interpretive concerns, I must also respect the chronology imposed by natural history and the needs of nonspecialists for familiar signposts. So I will use old labels here, in telling a story in this chapter that echoes that of the last two chapters, and anticipates the next two. The five-millennium sequence running from the first origins of the state to our contemporary world can be seen as a series of surges and setbacks, Lieberman's "strange parallels." Very broadly, the surges were the Bronze Age, the longer-lasting ancient-medieval world, and our contemporary modernity; the setbacks were shaped by the Mid-Holocene, Preclassical, and Little Ice Age Hallstatt solar minima that preceded and intervened, at 4000–3000 BC, 1200–600 BC, and AD 1300–1700. But just as the Bronze Age epoch was segmented in China, India, the Americas, and the greater Mediterranean by various local earth systems events, more recent premodern history has its boundaries too: the irregular onset of the Dark Ages, the medieval climate regime, the Black Death, and the calamitous sixteenth-to-seventeenth century crises that encompassed both hemispheres in different but reinforcing ways. And just as we ask questions about Smithian growth in a global antiquity, so too we must ask the same question of the Middle Ages and the early modern period.

* * *

Climate Reversals in the Tropics and the North

The Dark Ages, AD 400–900

Very broadly and diffusely, the end of a global classical antiquity was shaped in some measure by a *climatic global Dark Age* running from roughly AD 400 to AD 900. This reversal was coherent in many parts of the world, but it did not have the reach and consequences of the two Hallstatt minimum/Siberian High epochs that bracketed both classical antiquity and the Middle Ages. Rather than a strong Siberian High at work, these climatic Dark Ages were marked in a cold northern hemisphere by a round of North Atlantic ice rafting, and by ENSO variation in the Pacific tilting toward the El Niño mode, with erratic floods and droughts along the Andean coast. The

Asian monsoon regimes during the Dark Ages seem to have been somewhat detached from these forces, perhaps because the ENSO pattern was somewhat more sporadic than it had been before 400 or would be after 900. This quasi-global Dark Age was followed by a strong reversal – the epoch of a *Medieval Climate Anomaly* – that brought drought to some of the tropics and two centuries of warm stable climate to most of the north (see Figures III.5a–d).

There are hints of the beginnings of this shift by the third century AD, when the Intertropical Convergence Zone (ITCZ) shifted south, matching a sharp drop in northern temperatures. By AD 350 to AD 400, when these conditions were reversed temporarily, the critical forces shaping Dark Age climate were in place, perhaps linked with a solar minimum that peaked at 400. In the North Atlantic and the southwest Pacific, there were sharp and simultaneous shifts toward both ice rafting and a cooling of the Pacific Warm Pool: the reversal of the minimal North Atlantic ice and warm waters in the Pacific Warm Pool that had been critical features of the Classical Optimum. Ice rafting in the North Atlantic would bracket the entire Dark Ages in a double-headed surge running through the ninth century AD. The water temperature in the southwest Pacific would oscillate in six sub-century swings between AD 400 and about AD 1000, apparently shaping a series of oscillations between predominantly El Niño and La Niña modes, contrasting with both the Classical Optimum and the medieval regime, when the west Pacific waters were generally warm, and ENSO in a La Niña mode. The ITCZ as measured in the Caribbean slowly slid south after 400, reaching an extreme between 750 and 850, another marker of a cold north regime. In China, the summer monsoon seems to have weakened from 300 to 600, and the winter monsoon intensified between 450 and 600. These conditions clearly intensified between 500 and 600, with the onset of the Vandal Solar Minimum, which would peak around 690, and the powerful impact of the AD 536 volcanic mega-eruption. These forces brought the climatic Dark Ages decisively to Europe, with the winter westerlies shifting south (with a negative mode of NAO) and sharply increasing in the Mediterranean into Anatolia, Southwest Asia, and probably Central Asia. Conversely, generally declining summer monsoons in South Asia through 900 were shaped by a strong El Niño pattern of the ENSO. An unnamed solar minimum at AD 900 (coinciding with a century or more of significant volcanic eruptions) intensified these conditions, with shattering impacts on societies throughout the world. But after AD 900, most of these conditions reversed: ice rafting receding from the North Atlantic, ENSO shifting toward a La Niña mode, northern hemisphere temperatures rising, the NAO shifting back to positive mode and drying the Mediterranean and Southwest Asia. With the La Niña pattern, South Asian and Chinese summer monsoons both strengthened, if not without some reversals. But the trajectory was established, and the unique arc of early medieval climate had begun, running from AD 900 to AD 1300.[3]

Leaving the causal forces to the climate scientists, we can map the impacts of climate stress in the post-ancient Dark Ages, between ~AD 400 and AD 900. Population stagnated in Europe and China, which barely managed by AD 1000 to restore their population levels of AD 200, 800 years earlier. Similar forces may have shaped the rough contours of Indian history (see Figures III.5b, III.9). Measures of the South Asian monsoon suggest increasingly drier conditions during the Dark Ages, consonant with a colder north, a cooler West Pacific Warm Pool, and the El Niño ENSO mode. The classical Gupta empire emerged in the Ganges Valley around 315, was at its peak between 375 and 415, and completely gone by 550. The Gupta seem to have emerged after harsh droughts at the turn of the fourth century and collapsed after similar droughts at the end of the fifth century. The arrival of a branch of the Huns from Central Asia at around 500 contributed to the final collapse of the Gupta into various warring kingdoms. Islamic Arabs began to conquer the western approaches to the subcontinent in the eighth century, when two estimates show South Asia in the midst of a long advance toward drought conditions running from roughly AD 600 to AD 900.[4]

The first several centuries of the Dark Age climate pattern were the background context for the rise and spread of Islam in Arabia and across the arid zone from India to Spain. It seems likely that the catastrophic flooding of the early Dark Ages, with the ongoing impacts of the Justinian Plague, shaped the march of early Islam. On the positive side, however, the Mediterranean and Southwest Asia continued to have relatively high precipitation throughout the negative NAO Dark Ages.[5] Such might well have provided the material

[3] Gerald Haug et al., "Southward Migration of the Intertropical Convergence Zone through the Holocene," *Science* 293 (2001), 1304–8; Christopher M. Moy, "Variability of El Niño/ Southern Oscillation Activity at Millennial Timescales during the Holocene Epoch," *Nature* 420 (2002), 162–5; Donald Rodbell et al., "An ~15,000-Year Record of El Niño-Driven Alluviation in Southwestern Ecuador," *Science* 283 (1999), 516–20; Ashish Sinha et al., "The Leading Mode of Indian Summer Monsoon Precipitation Variability during the Last Millennium," *GRL* 38 (2011), L15703; L. Tan et al., "Climate Patterns in North Central China during the Last 1800 yr and the Possible Driving Force," *Climates of the Past* 7 (2011), 685–92. For the Indus Valley, see U. von Rad et al., "A 5000-Yr Record of Climate Change in Varved Sediments from the Oxygen Minimum Zone off Pakistan, Northeastern Arabian Sea," *QuatRes* 51 (1999), 39–53; Michael McCormick et al., "Climate Change during and after the Roman Empire: Reconstructing the Past from Scientific and Historical Evidence," *JInterdH* 43 (2012), 169–220, esp. 191–202.

[4] Romila Thapar, *Early India: From the Origins to AD 1300* (London, 2002), 280–9, 332–4; Judith E. Walsh, *A Brief History of India* (New York, 2006), 47–50, 57–62.

[5] D. Kaniewski et al., "The Medieval Climate Anomaly and the Little Ice Age in Coastal Syria Inferred from Pollen-Derived Palaeoclimatic Patterns," *GPC* 78 (2011), 178–87; Jessie Woodbridge and Neil Roberts, "Late Holocene Climate of the Eastern Mediterranean Inferred from Diatom Analysis of Annually-Laminated Lake Sediments," *QSR* 30 (2011), 3381–92;

underpinnings of the strength of the Islamic Golden Age, and an agriculture that supported the rise of cities across the Arab-Islamic domain. Here opinion is divided, with one camp describing an Islamic Green Revolution of new species and new agricultural techniques, while another sees more continuities with classical times and only minimal population growth across the Islamic world; as is usually the case, the resolution may lie somewhere in the middle, but it may well turn out that Islamic achievements were based in some small measure in the stronger southerly flow of the Atlantic winter westerlies.[6]

All of the various estimates for ENSO on the Andean coasts suggest a sequence of wild extremes of precipitation between AD 400 and AD 1000 (see Figure III.5d). The onset of Dark Age ENSO climatic whiplash conditions shaped the collapse of two Early Intermediate Peruvian cultures, the Moche and the Nasca, which emerged around 200 BC and collapsed in a burst of mega-El Niño flooding and a severe drought in the late 500s AD; at roughly the same time the great city-state of Teotihuacan collapsed, as droughts hit the Mexican highlands. As the Moche and Nasca faded, new cultures of the "Middle Horizon" emerged, deploying new strategies of settlement and subsistence to withstand the challenges of an epoch of erratic El Niño impacts. The Huari, in the southern highlands, invested in extensive irrigation systems that drew from high-altitude water sources; the Tiwanaku, around high-altitude Lake Titicaca, grew crops on unique raised beds in the lake. Both lasted several hundred years as coherent urban-centered empires: the Huari splintered after 800, and the Tiwanaku around 1100, under the impact of the droughts shaped by the Pacific medieval La Niña regime.[7]

Catherine Kuzucuoğlu et al., "Mid- to Late-Holocene Climate Change in Central Turkey: The Tecer Lake Record," *Holocene* 21 (2011), 183; Michael Netser, "Population Growth and Decline in the Northern Part of Eretz-Israel during the Historical Periods as Related to Climatic Changes," Mira Bar-Matthews et al., "Middle to Late Holocene (6,500 Yr. Period) Paleoclimate in the Eastern Mediterranean Region from Stable Isotopic Composition of Spelothems from Soreq Cave, Israel," in Arie S. Issar and Neville Brown, eds., *Water, Environment and Society in Times of Change* (Dordrecht, 1998), 127–45, 203–14.

[6] For work supporting the argument for an Islamic Green Revolution, see Andrew M. Watson, *Agricultural Innovation in the Early Islamic World: The Diffusion of Crops and Farming Techniques, 700–1100* (Cambridge, 1983); Robert McC. Adams, *Land behind Baghdad: A History of Settlement of the Dyala Plains* (Chicago, IL, 1965), 97–102; Richard Bulliet, *Cotton, Climate, and Camels in Early Islamic Iran: A Moment in World History* (New York, 2009). For the critique, see Peter Christensen, *The Decline of Iranshahr: Irrigation and Environments in the History of the Middle East, 500 B.C. to A.D. 1500* (Copenhagen, 1993); and Michael Decker, "Plants and Progress: Rethinking the Islamic Agricultural Revolution," *JWH* 20 (2009), 187–206.

[7] Michael E. Moseley, *The Incas and Their Ancestors: The Archaeology of Peru*, rev. ed. (London, 2001), 223–43; James B. Richardson, *People of the Andes* (Washington, DC, 1994), 101–21, 129–30, 133, 135; L. G. Thompson et al., "Glacial Records of Global Climate: A 1500-Year Tropical Ice Core Record of Climate," *HumEcol* 22 (1994), 83–95; Izumi Shimada et al., "Cultural Impacts of Severe Droughts in the Prehistoric Andes: Application

A similar climatic sequence shaped the history of the tropical Maya. Until recently, the collapse of the Mayan civilization in the Yucatan interior has been seen as a classic case of an endogenously driven collapse, in which population growth on fragile tropical soils undermined the environmental sustainability of the culture.[8] Such may have been at work, to some measure. But it has been demonstrated decisively that the course of Mayan history was also shaped by a series of droughts.

Where Andean cultures were subject to the volatile Pacific regime, with some moderating influences running from the South American monsoon driven by easterly trade winds from the South Atlantic, the Yucatan and Mesoamerica generally are watered by a summer rainy season, when a north-riding ITCZ brings precipitation off the Caribbean via easterly trade winds. The southward shift of the ITCZ, common during El Niño years when easterlies are interrupted, brings summer drought to Mesoamerica. Preclassical Mayan culture developed during the relatively stable conditions of the Classical Optimum over several centuries leading up to AD 200, when a series of sharp droughts, measured in sediments at Cariaco and from two lakes in the Yucatan, coincide with a period of abandonment (see Figure III.5d). Classical Mayan culture developed for more than 300 years before another abandonment during the 580s known as the *Mayan hiatus*, coinciding with the droughts that undermined Teotihuacan in Mexico and the Moche and the Nasca in Peru. Reestablished in the 600s, the Mayan hierarchy contended with dry Dark Age conditions by constructing its primate temple cities as elaborate water-management systems, building temples on high points, and collecting rainy season runoff in adjacent quarries and lagoons. While Mayan agricultural practice and population growth might well have

of a 1,500-Year Ice Core Precipitation Record," *WdArch* 22 (1991), 247–70. David Keys (*Catastrophe*, 189–91) associated the pivotal drought with the 536 event, but he appears to misdate the Quelccaya drought, which is well dated by the Thompson team at AD 562–94. Michael W. Binford, "Climate Variation and the Rise and Fall of an Andean Civilization," *QuatRes* 47 (1997), 235–48; Patrick Ryan Williams, "Rethinking Disaster-Induced Collapse in the Demise of the Andean Highland States: Wari and Tiwanaku," *WdArch* 33 (2002), 361–74; Tom D. Dillehay and Alan L. Klata, "Long-Term Human Response to Uncertain Environmental Conditions in the Andes," *PNAS* 101 (2004), 4325–50; Peter B. deMenocal, "Cultural Responses to Climate Change during the Holocene," *Science* 292 (2001), 667–73, esp. 671–2; Tom Dillehay et al., "Pre-Industrial Human and Environmental Interactions in Northern Peru during the Late Holocene," *Holocene* 14 (2004), 272–81; R. B. Manners et al., "Floodplain Development, El Niño, and Cultural Consequences in a Hyperarid Andean Environment," *Annals of Association of American Geographers* 97 (2007), 229–49; Allison C. Paulson, "Environment and Empire: Climatic Factors in Prehistoric Andean Culture Change," *WdArch* 8 (1976), 121–32.

[8] Clive Ponting, *A Green History of the World: The Environment and the Collapse of Great Civilizations* (New York, 1991), 78–83; Charles L. Redman, *Human Impact on Ancient Environments* (Tucson, AZ, 1999), 139–46; Jared Diamond, *Collapse: How Societies Choose to Fail or Succeed* (New York, 2005), 157–77.

been unsustainable in the long run, when crisis came it was driven by exogenous climatic conditions. After a recovery and 200 years of further expansion, the great Mayan cities began to decline during the late 700s, and soon after 900 had utterly collapsed. The evidence from the Cariaco basin, from the Yucatan lakes, and from the Quelccaya ice cap all show a series of sharp droughts occurring within a drier period beginning at 760. This advancing drought was a dimension of the final stages of the Dark Age climate regime, shaped by an increasingly southern position of the ITCZ, coherent with a rising volatility of El Niño flooding and droughts in the Andes. The Maya may not have collapsed, precisely, so much as they shifted, from agrarian societies around the great temple cities of the interior to a more trade-oriented economy on coastal regions in the northern Yucatan. Population pressure and environmental degradation probably put Mayan society under stress but – as one careful summary has put it – it "is probably not coincidental" that a dramatic cultural transformation coincided with a powerful climatic impact.[9]

The final transformation of the Maya around AD 900 was one symptom of a wider global climatic event that intensified the closing century of the Dark Age climatic system. A minor solar minimum and coincident volcanic eruptions seem to have driven a simultaneous drop in northern hemisphere temperatures, the advance of the Chinese cold winter monsoon, and the retreat of the Asian summer monsoon. In particular, the fate of societies in the Americas and in China are curiously linked, and suggests that a wider Pacific influence was at work.

---

[9] R. B. Gill, *The Great Maya Drought: Water, Life, and Death* (Albuquerque, NM, 2000); Susan Toby Evans, *Ancient Mexico and Central America: Archaeology and Culture History* (New York, 2008), 317–48; Gergena Yancheva et al., "Influence of the Intertropical Convergence Zone on the East Asian Monsoon," *Nature* 445 (2007), 74–7; David Hodell et al., "Terminal Classic Drought in the Northern Maya Lowlands Inferred from Multiple Sediment Cores in Lake Chichancanab (Mexico)," *QSR* 24 (2005), 1413–27; Gerald Haug et al., "Climate and the Collapse of Maya Civilization," *Science* 299 (2003), 1731–5; deMenocal, "Cultural Responses," 670–1; David Hodell et al., "Solar Forcing of Drought Frequency in the Maya Lowlands," *Science* 292 (2001), 1367–70; Nicholas P. Dunning et al., "Kax and Kol: Collapse and Resilience in Lowland Maya Civilization," *PNAS* 109 (2012), 3652–7; Patricia A. McAnamy and Tomas Gallareta Negron, "Bellicose Rulers and Climatological Peril? Retrofitting Twenty-First Century Woes on Eighth-Century Mayan Society," in Patricia A. McAnamy and Norman Yoffee, eds., *Questioning Collapse: Human Resilience, Ecological Vulnerability and the Aftermath of Empire* (New York, 2010), 142–75, esp. 159–63; Jason Yeager and David A. Hodell, "The Collapse of Mayan Civilizations: Assessing the Interaction of Culture, Climate, and Environment," in Daniel H. Sandweiss and Jeffrey Quilter, eds., *El Niño, Catastrophism, and Cultural Change in Ancient America* (Washington, DC, 2008), 187–242; David A. Hodell, "Climate and Cultural History of the Northwestern Yucatan Peninsula, Quintana Roo, Mexico," *ClimCh* 83 (2007), 215–70, quote from 238. Another line of analysis suggests that droughts launched epidemics of hemorrhagic fever, leading to massive mortality: Rodolfo Acuna-Soto et al., "Drought, Epidemic Disease, and the Fall of Classical Period Cultures in Mesoamerica (AD 750–950): Hemorrhagic Fevers as a Cause of Massive Population Loss," *MedHyp* 65 (2005), 405–9.

The records from the Huguang Maar lake sediments – which measure the strength of the cold, dry winter monsoon in southern China – matches the California drought estimates and the Cariaco titanium record remarkably well, suggesting trans-Pacific connections running along the Intertropical Convergence Zone. The Huguang Maar record of winter monsoon intensity also, as we have seen, tracks the rise and fall of Chinese polities with remarkable precision through the first millennium AD (see Figure III.5c). In the wake of the Han dynasty, which collapsed in 220 during a period of strong, dry, cold winter monsoons, the Jin polity roughly matched the closing chronology of the Peruvian Moche and Nasca cultures, and the Mayan Pre-Classic, running from 265–420, collapsing at the onset of another spike of winter monsoon intensity.

The Jin had not unified China but competed with other parallel dynastical polities during a cold and unstable era of "Disunity" from 220 to 589, when China was finally reunited under the Sui and then the Tang dynasty in 618. The role of natural forces in the post-Disunity centuries is clear and obvious, and can be tracked not only by the winter monsoon, but in a growing list of increasingly refined indexes of the summer monsoon, including a long stalagmite record from the eastern edge of the Tibetan plateau and a synthesis of North China records – both going back 1,800 years, and tree ring annual temperature estimates for China and Mongolia that date back to AD 800.[10] Epidemic disease also played a fundamental role.

The summer monsoon records suggest that the entire period of Disunity was one of moderate summer monsoons, but increasing around 550. The brief but significant span of the Sui dynasty from 589 to 617, which reunified China for the first time since the Han, coincided with the end of this period of strong monsoons, and its final years saw a series of floods that set off the rebellions that brought down the dynasty.[11] The Tang dynasty – from 617 to 907 – had virtually the exact dates of the Late Classic Maya, and coincided with the height of Huari and Tiwanaku Peru. Successfully ruling a united and expanding China during its first century, early in the eighth century, the Tang regime was stressed by recurring onslaughts of flood, drought, and locusts from around 710 to 730 and simultaneously became embroiled with frontier struggles in the west, during which a severe "pestilence" broke out among the steppe tribes. These frontier wars set off

---

[10] Pingzhong Zhang et al., "A Test of Climate, Sun, and Culture Relationships from a 1810-Year Chinese Cave Record," *Science* 322 (2008), 940–2; Tan et al., "Climate Patterns in North Central China during the Last 1800 yr." The tree ring data is published in Timothy A. Osborn and Keith R. Briffa, "The Special Extent of 20th-Century Warmth in the Context of the Past 1200 Years," *Science* 311 (2006), 841–4, and Box 6.4, chapter 6, "Paleoclimate," in *Climate Change 2007 – The Physical Science Basis*.

[11] Arthur F. Wright, "The Sui Dynasty (581–617)," in Denis Twitchett, ed., *The Cambridge History of China, Vol. 3: Sui and T'ang China, 589–906, Part I* (Cambridge, 1979), 144–60.

the punishing An Lu-Shan Rebellion of 755–63 that sapped the resources and legitimacy of the Tang. In its closing years, bubonic plague – possibly introduced from the nomad steppe via the rebel armies – devastated broad regions of coastal southern China, cutting Chinese populations drastically. Weakened by rebellion, the collapse of central authority, and the impact of plague, the Tang court struggled on for another century or so, before finally it collapsed in 907, as the droughts, floods, locusts, and famine caused by fifty years of harsh winter monsoons and weak summer monsoons, and thirty years of plunging summer temperatures, launched waves of brigand-age and rebellion.[12]

These events unfolded exactly at the same time as the Mayan crisis and broadly with the collapse of Andean Middle Horizon cultures, and comprised some of the final acts of the global Dark Ages. There are thus remarkable parallels in the fate of societies around the circum-Pacific during this millennium, shaped, it would appear, by a trans-Pacific pattern of climatic change linked along the ITCZ, and by its southward shift during the 800s and 900s.[13] Intense drought in the Yucatan and El Niño flooding followed by drought along the Andean coast matched intense winter cold in northeast Asia. On both sides of the ocean, long-established societies collapsed as productive systems failed, people starved, and rebellions and wars destroyed ancient patterns of authority. And these late Dark Age Pacific events had their Atlantic analogs as well, during several centuries of recorded severe winters between 750 and 950, across Europe to the Black Sea, which match up with indications of volcanic eruptions in the Greenland ice records. Broadly coinciding with the Carolingian empire launched by Charlemagne, this sequence of cold winter climates stressed, if it did not impede, the rise of western Europe at the close of the first millennium.[14]

The Medieval Climate Anomaly, AD 900–1275

The South American La Niña droughts following AD 900 marked the beginning of a fundamental shift to very different global climate patterns: the *Medieval Climate Anomaly* (MCA), an enduring climatic pattern that as much as anything else gives the Middle Ages a global coherence. It was shaped fundamentally by a lower rate of volcanic action between about 960 and 1150, and a "grand solar maximum" running from the eleventh to

[12] See Denis Twitchett, "Hsuan-Tsung (Reign 712–56)," 355–7, 419, 435–63; C. A. Peterson, "Court and Province in Mid- and Late T'ang," 464–83; and Robert M. Somers, "The End of the T'ang," 682, 696, 720–1, 728, all in Twitchett, ed., *The Cambridge History of China*, Vol. 3. William H. McNeill, *Plagues and Peoples* (New York, 1976), 147–9.

[13] Yancheva et al., "Influence of the Intertropical Convergence Zone," 76–7; Nicholas E. Graham et al., "Tropical Pacific – Mid-Latitude Teleconnections in Medieval Times," *ClimCh* 83 (2007), 241–85, esp. 276–7.

[14] Michael McCormick et al., "Volcanoes and the Climate Forcing of Carolingian Europe, A.D. 750–950," *Speculum* 82 (2007), 865–95.

the thirteenth century. The two great global oceanic pumps responded: the thermohaline pump off Greenland intensified and the West Pacific Warm Pool piled up with warmer waters. The result was a warm north, a monsoon surge in Asia, and severe droughts in parts of the equatorial tropics.

Seen from Europe, the Mediterranean circuit, southern Asia, and eastern North America, this was a Medieval Optimum, echoing the Classical Optimum, with warm stable climates developing after 900 and dominating between 950 and 1150. Here the receding ice rafting off Greenland signaled the strengthening of thermohaline circulation, drawing equatorial heat up into the North Atlantic. As the icebergs in the North Atlantic melted away, the ITCZ shifted north and a warm and vigorous Gulf Stream warmed the North Atlantic and northwest Europe. Simultaneously, the North Atlantic Oscillations shifted to its positive mode, drawing winter precipitation away from the Mediterranean to the north. Temperatures in the northern hemisphere were extremely warm and stable, warmer than they would be until the opening of the twentieth century. As a measure of this warmth, it was during the opening of this warm sequence, between the 860s and 1000, that the Norse Vikings settled first Iceland and then Greenland.[15]

The Medieval Climate Anomaly, however, had complex and contrary impacts across many other parts of the world. The ITCZ, as measured at Cariaco, shifted north decisively between 900 and 1075. The strong thermohaline pump off Greenland pulled warm South Atlantic waters north, and a warmer North Atlantic enhanced the easterly trade winds flowing to the west over South America and the Pacific. The easterly trade winds would have strengthened the Walker Circulation and pushed warm Pacific waters to the West Pacific Warm Pool, which was particularly warm – with high sea levels – between 1000 and about 1260. The ENSO variation declined and a deep and sustained La Niña episode began.[16] The Medieval Climate

[15] The Medieval Climate Anomaly was originally described in H. H. Lamb, *Climate, History, and the Modern World*, second edition (New York, 1995), 172–82. Various teams have developed annual temperature estimates for the northern hemisphere. In various figures I use the data developed by Frederik C. Ljungqvist for "A New Reconstruction of Temperature Variability in the Extra-Tropical Northern Hemisphere during the Last Two Millennia," *Geografiska Annaler: Series A* 92 (2010), 339–51; and by Keith Briffa and Timothy Osborn for figure 6.10 (B2000) in *Climate Change 2007 – The Physical Science Basis*. Important recent syntheses include Michael E. Mann et al., "Global Signature and Dynamical Origins of the Little Ice Age and Medieval Climate Anomaly," *Science* 326 (2009), 1256–60; Graham et al., "Tropical Pacific." On the NAO, see Valérie Trouet et al., "Persistent Positive North Atlantic Oscillation Mode Dominated the Medieval Climate Anomaly," *Science* 324 (2009), 78–80; and –, "North Atlantic Storminess and Atlantic Meridional Overturning Circulation during the Last Millennium: Reconciling Contradictory Proxy Records of NAO Variability," *GPC* 84–5 (2012), 48–55. For a popular rendition, see Brian Fagan, *The Great Warming: Climate Change and the Rise and Fall of Civilizations* (New York, 2008); for the Norse, see 87–105.

[16] Marie-Alexandrine Sicre et al., "A 4500-Year Reconstruction of Sea Surface Temperature Variability at Decadal Time-Scales off North Iceland," *QSR* 27 (2008), 2041–7; Broxton W.

Anomaly brought drought and crisis to much of the tropics, but it brought regular monsoons to southern Asia and mild warm climates to much of the temperate north mid-latitudes, especially those facing the Atlantic, where it was experienced as the "Medieval Optimum" or Medieval Warm Period," replicating some of the features of the Ancient Optimum. It came to an end as a great burst of El Niños struck the Pacific American coasts around 1260; the southern Asia monsoons began to fail and the North Atlantic climate began to turn colder and more erratic. The opening stages of the Little Ice Age proper would follow.

* * *

Population and Health in the Old World Dark and Middle Ages

How did people of the Old World fare during the Dark Age interval between antiquity and the Middle Ages? These were the centuries of plague, climate downturn, and imperial collapse. They brought a serious decline in population: if Jean Biraben's numbers are even roughly correct, the populations of the Old World core regions declined by a quarter between AD 200 and AD 400, and barely recovered by 1000. Clearly the bubonic plague that struck China in 762, and perhaps the steppe forty-five years earlier, was in some way connected to the Justinian Plague and its aftershocks that continued to surge through the wider Mediterranean world into the ninth century. These impacts reached as far as Japan, which had until the sixth century been insulated from continental disease regimes. But Buddhist missionaries introduced smallpox to Japan in 552, and starting in the eighth century recurring incursions of smallpox and measles – separated enough to negate earlier immunities – worked to stabilize and even suppress population growth. By 806, the plague also reached Japan, which did not see significant population growth until the thirteenth century.[17]

But smaller populations meant more resources for fewer people, and the collapse of imperial trade minimized the circulation of the diseases that had killed so many. If adult stature is any measure, depopulation was reasonably good for routine health. We do not have global data, but the European evidence for stature is quite striking. Those people who survived the onslaught

---

Bird et al., "A 2,300-Year-Long Annually Revolved Record of the South American Summer Monsoon from the Peruvian Andes," *PNAS* 108 (2011), 8583–8; Mann et al., "Global Signature and Dynamical Origins"; Graham et al., "Tropical Pacific."

[17] McNeill, *Plagues and Peoples*, 124–7; William Wayne Farris, *Population, Disease, and Land in Early Japan, 645–900* (Cambridge, MA, 1985), 50–73; –, *Japan's Medieval Population: Famine, Fertility, and Warfare in a Transformative Age* (Honolulu, HI, 2006), 12–66; –, *Daily Life and Demographics in Ancient Japan* (Ann Arbor, MI, 2009), 1–37; Ann B. Jannetta, *Epidemics and Mortality in Early Modern Japan* (Princeton, NJ, 1987), 16–32, 65–70, 114–17, 147–50, 191–200.

of plague, and made the adjustment to both the advance of colder climates and the erosion of imperial structures, were larger than their forbears. The results of a variety of studies suggest that Europeans living in the sixth century were roughly 2–2.5 cm taller than those living in the age of empire (see Figure III.7). While these heights declined somewhat during the next few centuries, they remained taller than the Roman-era average, and generally climbed in the first two centuries of the Medieval Optimum, the eleventh and twelfth centuries. British skeletons indicate that post-Roman peoples were not only taller but moderately healthier, as measured by tooth loss, Harris lines, and caries (dental decay). Strikingly, stature declined in Viking Denmark, where population growth, internal stratification, and long-range raiding and trade may have taken a toll.[18] But the prevailing story is plain: once freed of the density, inequality, exposure to disease, and detrimental childrearing of imperial times, European health improved.

Health improved in much smaller populations, and in societies that were beginning to be fundamentally reordered. With the end of the coercive structures of the empire and the rise of Christianity, a new religion centered on the nuclear family, ancient patterns of elite polygamy and commoner slavery gave way to a classic household structure centered on the monogamous family.[19] (The exception to this rule of nuclear families, of course, was the rise of celibate religious orders.) Peasant households may have owed vertical obligations to overlords, but they were relatively free to manage their day-to-day affairs. For at least several centuries they did so in an almost wild, relatively abandoned landscape of temperate forests and wetlands, in which wild food was reasonably plentiful, as was land for agriculture.[20] Of course the lower heights in the eighth to tenth centuries might suggest that the advancing cool wet climates of the Dark Ages almost offset the advantages of surviving the end of empire, as must have the gradual recovery of

---

[18] Charlotte Roberts and Margaret Cox, "The Impact of Economic Intensification and Social Complexity on Human Health in Britain from 6000 BP (Neolithic) and the Introduction of Farming to the Mid-Nineteenth Century AD," in Mark Nathan Cohen and Gillian M. M. Crane-Kramer, eds., *Ancient Health: Skeletal Indicators of Agricultural and Economic Intensification* (Gainesville, FL, 2007), 149–63; Charlotte Roberts and Margaret Cox, *Health and Disease in Britain from Prehistory to the Present Day* (Thrupp, Glouc., 2003), 164–286, 396; Pia Bennike, *Paleopathology of Danish Skeletons: A Comparative Study of Demography, Disease, and Injury* (Copenhagen, 1985), 50–3.

[19] Jack Goody, *The Development of the Family and Marriage in Europe* (Cambridge, 1983).

[20] Michael Williams, *Deforesting the Earth: From Prehistory to Global Crisis* (Chicago, IL, 2003), 102–36; Richard C. Hoffman, "Economic Development and Aquatic Ecosystems in Medieval Europe," *AHR* 101 (1996), 631–69, esp. 632–4; Klavs Randsborg, *The First Millennium in Europe and the Mediterranean: An Archaeological Essay* (Cambridge, 1991), 29–31; Marc Bloch, *French Rural History: An Essay on Its Basic Characteristics*, Janet Sondheimer, trans. (1931; Berkeley, CA, 1966), 5–7. For an argument for post-plague recovery, see Walter Scheidel, "A Model of Demographic and Economic Change in Roman Egypt after the Antonine Plague," *JRA* 15 (2002), 97–114.

population: heights peaked at the trough of population, and then declined as numbers grew.[21]

But there is also another context for the post-Roman surge in European heights, with some sinister implications. Michael McCormick has concluded in a massive study that "the origins of the European economy" lay in a restoration of trade between Europe north of the Alps and the Mediterranean beginning in 750, a pattern that echoes the center-periphery routes that had structured this relationship in the Bronze and Iron Ages. Here disease played a central role. The collapse of trade with the collapse of empire had meant that an autarchic trans-Alpine Europe was relatively free of the recurring bouts of plagues that continued to strike the Mediterranean and the Near East. However, one of the final plagues devastated the local supply of labor in the emerging Islamic world, and McCormick argues that the renewal of ties between north and south between 750 and 900 was in fact driven by a slave trade, as men and women captured in war and raiding across Europe were sold south into the Islamic Mediterranean world.[22]

Significant as this slave trade may have been, it had no discernable impact on the course of European demographic history, for after the tenth century Europe began a rise to unprecedented levels of population, as did the world at large, in what is called the medieval cycle of population growth. Global population may have quadrupled between 1000 BC and the ancient peak of population in AD 200; between 600 and 1300 it almost doubled, most of that increase coming after 1000. Europe, India, and China grew particularly rapidly; comprising about half of the world population in 1000, they made up more than 60 percent of the world total by 1250.

* * *

Growth and Crisis in the Medieval World, 1000–1350

For 200 to 300 years, medieval peoples of much of Europe and Asia basked in the warm, mild climates brought by the Medieval Climate Anomaly, and

---

[21] For a rather pessimistic view, see Kathy L. Pearson, "Nutrition and the Early Medieval Diet," *Speculum* 72 (1997), 1–32. For an argument that the climate deterioration would have had minimal impact on small early medieval populations, see Richard Hodges, *Dark Age Economics: The Origins of Towns and Trade, A. D. 600–1000* (London, 1982), 139.

[22] Michael McCormack, *The Origins of the European Economy: Communications and Commerce, AD 300–900* (New York, 2001), esp. 733–77; –, "New Light on the 'Dark Ages': How the Slave Trade Fuelled the Carolingian Economy," *P&P* 197 (2002), 17–54; see also David Keys, *Catastrophe: An Investigation into the Origins of the Modern World* (New York, 1999), 15; Mary Ellen Snodgrass, ed., *World Epidemics: A Cultural History of Disease from Prehistory to the Era of SARS* (Jefferson, NC, 2003), 25. For the further history of the slave trade from Europe into the Islamic world, see Robert C. Davis, *Christian Slaves, Muslim Masters: White Slavery in the Mediterranean, the Barbary Coast, and Italy, 1500–1800* (New York, 2003).

increased their numbers. Did their economies keep up with these numbers? Even get ahead a bit, through a cycle of Smithian growth? The fortunes of these growing medieval populations is the subject of a long and hard-fought debate. Was there "economic growth" during the Middle Ages? Or were the Old World centers facing a Malthusian crisis when the Black Death rode in from the steppes of Asia in the middle of the fourteenth century?

Southern Asia

The medieval La Niña drove different outcomes, some positive, some negative. Across southern Asia from south China to India, after an epoch of drought, summer monsoons returned for roughly 500 years. In India, the enhanced monsoons underwrote the increased longevity of the Hindu and Buddhist kingdoms of the classical age, particularly across south India, where stronger monsoons supported an expansion of agriculture in the dry interior. By AD 1000, merchants in these South India kingdoms were engaged in a vigorous trade with newly emerged complex societies across the Bay of Bengal. Here in Southeast Asia the strong medieval monsoons shaped a parallel florescence, contributing to the rise of the Pagan Kingdom in Burma, the Khymer in Cambodia, the Champa on the central coast of Vietnam, and the Ly and Than dynasties in the Red River valley in northern Vietnam[23] (see Figures III.5b, III.9).

Thus across South Asia to Southeast Asia, as in northern Europe, the La Niña of the Medieval Climate Anomaly brought favorable climates, while it lasted, until the end of the thirteenth century. But other regions did not do quite so well in these medieval La Niña centuries. As the positive NAO carried summer warmth and winter precipitation into northern Europe, drought struck across the Mediterranean, into Southwest Asia as far as Iran, and into Central Asia.[24] From the Atlantic to the Indian Ocean, equatorial Africa saw harsh drought conditions between 1000 and 1250.[25] The flow

[23] Sinha et al., "The Leading Mode of Indian Summer Monsoon"; Yanni Gunnell et al., "Response of the South Asian Runoff-Harvesting Civilization to Northeast Rainfall Variability during the Last 2000 Years: Instrumental Records and Indirect Evidence," *The Holocene* 17 (2007), 207–15; Thapar, *Early India*, 321–42, 363–86; Lieberman, *Strange Parallels*, 101–12, 224–6, 363–4.

[24] Guy Jalut, "Holocene Climatic Changes in the Western Mediterranean, from South-East France to South-East Spain," *PPP* 160 (2000), 255–90; Celia Martín-Puerta, "Arid and Humid Phases in Southern Spain during the Last 4000 Years: The Zoñar Lake Record, Córdoba," *Holocene* 18 (2008), 907–21; Trouet, "Persistent Positive North Atlantic Oscillation Mode"; Fa-Hu Chen et al., "Moisture Changes over the Last Millennium in Arid Central Asia: A Review, Synthesis and Comparison with Monsoon Region," *QSR* 29 (2010), 1044–68; Ian Boomer et al., "Advances in Understanding the Late Holocene History of the Aral Sea Region," *QuatInt* 194 (2009), 79–90; Philippe Sorrel, "Climate Variability in the Aral Sea Basin (Central Asia) during the Late Holocene Based on Vegetation Changes," *QuatRes* 67 (2007), 357–70.

[25] Dirk Verschuren, "Decadal and Century-Scale Climate Variability in Tropical Africa during the Past 2000 Years," in R. W. Batterbee et al., eds., *Past Climate Variability in Europe and*

of water in the Nile River dropped drastically between 930 and 1350, interrupted after 1070 by a century of extremely high flooding[26] (see Figures III.5a, III.10).

Shaped by different forces acting within the wider global warming of the Medieval Climate Anomaly, the suppression of the Nile flow and the northward shift of the winter westerlies brought devastation to societies around the eastern Mediterranean and to the east. Ronnie Ellenblum has synthesized the effects of these droughts, and sees them starting around 950 but particularly focused between 1020 and 1070, precisely the period when Europe was emerging from the Dark Ages (see Figure III.5b). Harvest failures in Egypt were followed by cold droughts from southern Italy to Iraq, and then by agricultural and political collapses in Iran and Baghdad, the weakening of cities, the abandonment of lands, and the rise of nomadic incursions on all sides. During the droughts, Egypt suffered catastrophic famines, often compounded by earthquakes and plague, in the 960s, the 1020s, and around 1200; while Europe doubled its population from 36 million to 79 million between 1000 and 1300, Egypt stagnated at 5 million. In a fascinating if perhaps controversial argument, Ellenblum claims that the three great early medieval droughts undermined surviving Christian cultures throughout the region south of Byzantium, and drove a surge of Islamization.[27]

North America
Matching the weakened Atlantic monsoons in West Africa, the South American monsoon, which flows from the South Atlantic to water the Amazon region up to the height of the eastern Andes, reached its worst

---

Africa (Dordrecht, 2004), 139–58; T. M. Shanahan et al., "Atlantic Forcing of Persistent Drought in West Africa," *Science* 324 (2009), 377–80; J. M. Russell and T. C. Johnson, "Little Ice Age Drought in Equatorial Africa: Intertropical Convergence Zone Migrations and El Niño-Southern Oscillation Variability," *Geology* 35 (2007), 21–4.

[26] Nicholas Graham argues that the East African and Nile droughts were shaped by a heated Indian Ocean blocking the northward run of the ITCZ and the summer rains into Ethiopia; Fekri Hassan suggests a pattern in which the initial phases of a northern warming – in this case 910 to 1070 – were associated with Nile droughts. Similar conditions of a Nile drought during a sudden warming of the North Atlantic occurred at 3200 BC and 1200 BC. See Figure III.3. Nicholas Graham et al., "Support for Global Climate Reorganization during the 'Medieval Climate Anomaly,'" *ClimDyn* 37 (2011), 1217–45; Fekri A. Hassan, "Extreme Nile Floods and Famines in Medieval Egypt (A.D. 930–1500) and Their Climatic Implications," *QuatInt* 173–4 (2007), 101–12.

[27] Ronnie Ellenblum, *The Collapse of the Eastern Mediterranean: Climate Change and the Decline of the East, 950–1072* (Cambridge, 2012); Carl F. Petry, ed., *The Cambridge History of Egypt, Vol. I: Islamic Egypt, 640–1517* (Cambridge, 1998), 116, 152, 208, 221, 228. Richard Bulliet, in *Cotton, Climate, and Camels in Early Islamic Iran*, attributes this climate shift to an expansion of the Siberian High, but it was particularly moderate during the Medieval Climate Anomaly. It is more likely that droughts caused by north-shifted winter westerlies were involved.

recorded drought conditions during the tenth and eleventh centuries.[28] On the Pacific side, La Niña droughts in Peru and in western North America – sometimes termed *megadroughts* – put stress, at times catastrophic stress, on American populations. In North America, the warmth of the Medieval Climate Anomaly brought an ambiguous benefit. The Mesoamerican food complex centered on maize/corn was by its nature tropical, and cooler climates to the north had blocked its adoption north of the Southwest, where a variety called Maiz de Ocho developed after the arrival of Mesoamerican progenitors around 1000 BC. After roughly AD 700, this Maiz de Ocho variety began to spread into the Mississippi valley; by AD 1000, significantly warmer temperatures and longer growing seasons made it a staple of growing and concentrating populations. By the fourteenth century, malnutrition derived from a corn-dependent diet was clearly evident in these populations.[29] But the warm temperatures of the Medieval Climate Anomaly also brought severe drought to the California coast, in the desert Southwest, and into the Plains. Along the southern California coast, the medieval La Niña megadroughts diminished resources after AD 800, driving rising violence, nutritional stress, and social hierarchy and complexity. In the American desert Southwest, facing the earliest La Niña conditions, the ancient Pueblo peoples developed increasingly dense and sedentary village systems based on intensified corn agriculture, in a pattern reminiscent of Harappan urbanization as the South Asian monsoons began to fade around 2600 BC.[30]

Another drought-launched trajectory toward complex society developed in the central Mississippi valley, which may have comprised something of a refuge for peoples affected by drought on the upper Missouri River east to northern Illinois, perhaps something like events in Mesopotamia in the

[28] Broxton W. Bird et al., "Holocene Tropical South American Hydroclimate Revealed from a Decadally Resolved Lake Sediment δ18O Record," *EPSL* 310 (2011), 192–202; Bird et al., "2300-Year-Long Annually Resolved Record ... ".

[29] Steadman Upham et al., "Evidence Concerning the Origin of Maiz de Ocho," *AmAnth* 89 (1987), 410–19; D. C. Hyland et al., "Corn, Cucurbits, Cordage, and Colonization: An Absolute Chronology for the Appearance of Mesoamerican Domesticates in the Jordana Basin, New Mexico," *North American Archaeologist* 26 (2005), 147–64; Daniel Richter, *Before the Revolution: America's Ancient Pasts* (Cambridge, 2011), 12–15; Brian M. Fagan, *Ancient North America: The Archaeology of a Continent,* fourth edition (London, 2005), 464–7. Malnutrition among dense North American populations is discussed in Chapter 10.

[30] Edward R. Cook et al., "Megadroughts in North America: Placing IPCC Projections of Hydroclimatic Change in a Long-Term Palaeoclimate Context," *JQS* 25 (2010), 48–61, figure 7; Douglas J. Kennett and James P. Kennett, "Competitive and Cooperative Responses to Climatic Instability in Coastal Southern California," *AmAntiq* 65 (2000), 379–95; L. Mark Raab and Daniel O. Larson, "Medieval Climate Anomaly and Punctuated Cultural Evolution in Coastal Southern California," *AmAntiq* 62 (1997), 319–36; Philip L. Walker, "Cranial Injuries as Evidence of Violence in Prehistoric Southern California," *AJPA* 80 (1989), 313–23; –, "Porotic Hyperstosis in a Marine-Dependent California Indian Population," *AJPA* 69 (1986), 345–54.

fourth millennium BC. The middle of North America seems to have been affected by both the Pacific La Niña pattern and the growing humidifying strength of the North Atlantic oceanic warming, which would not peak until roughly 1200. Thus, while there was an intense drought in the mid-Mississippi region around 940–85, the next century was relatively humid, with rising water tables. Corn agriculture was well established by AD 900, and its intensification during the humid eleventh century provided the base for a growing population building a massive proto-urban temple complex at Cahokia, at the fork of the Ohio and Mississippi, starting around AD 1050[31] (see Figure III.5b).

The final centuries of the Medieval Climate Anomaly had devastating impacts in North America, in the form of a wave of megadroughts on a scale not since recorded. The ITCZ had moved sharply south between 1050 and 1100, but was moving north between 1100 and 1300, continuing the static La Niña-like ENSO pattern that dominated the MCA. The North Atlantic waters were at their warmest at 1200, as measured by IRD ice rafting, though northern hemisphere temperature was already declining. A volatile transition between the last manifestations of the Medieval Climate Anomaly and the opening of the Little Ice Age was taking shape. In the plateau regions of the Southwest and in the middle reaches of the Mississippi valley, extensive village-based populations had emerged with the onset of the warm, dry conditions of the MCA at AD 900. These societies, and the Late Woodland peoples to the east were now fed by corn agriculture. Powerful, coercive social hierarchies rapidly emerged in what is known as the Mississippian culture. Chaco Canyon, in the Southwest, and the city-state of Cahokia, at the confluence of the Ohio and the Mississippi, were important centers of population, ritual, and presumably forms of governance across large areas. Both regions and their respective centers prospered during the El Niño interval in the eleventh century, but went into significant decline at the middle of the thirteenth century, during the peak of the medieval La Niña. In the Southwest, a first phase of megadrought between 1120 and 1150 forced the abandonment of the ritual center at Chaco; under continuing impact of drought the ancient Pueblo around 1250 congregated at Mesa Verde in great cliff towns built for defense, before suddenly abandoning the plateau for the Rio Grande Valley around 1300. In the Mississippi valley, the droughts hit in a series of progressively deep swings between 1100 and 1245, driving a decline in the the population of Cahokia from a peak at 1075–1100. The first truly severe drought struck around 1140, forcing the abandonment of prairie farming communities in Illinois that had supported the Cahokia

---

[31] Cook et al., "Megadroughts in North America," figures 7, 8; Song Feng, "Atlantic and Pacific SST Influences in Medieval Drought in North America Simulated by the Community Atmospheric Model," *JGR* 113 (2008); Larry V. Benson et al., "Cahokia's Boom and Bust in the Context of Climate Change," *AmAntiq* 74 (2009), 467–83.

population. The 1140–55 drought and three successive droughts through 1245 each coincided exactly with four constructions of palisade fortifications; by 1350 Cahokia was essentially abandoned.[32] Similarly, drought seems to have played a role in the various abandonments of the second-order Mississippian sites to the south at Etowah, Georgia and Moundville, Alabama, between 1250 and 1375.[33]

China and Mongolia

While the fortunes and fates of all of these societies can be framed in the model of additive growth suggested by Adam Smith, the debate over a medieval Smithian growth has centered on the rise of population and the performance of economy in Song China and the European High Middle Ages. Song China, from AD 960 to AD 1279, was the more dramatic story. Both Europe and China grew, but Song grew – and crashed – much more spectacularly. Between 1000 and 1200, Chinese populations more than doubled from 56 million to 128 million. Urban populations reached into the millions. Behind this explosive growth lay a century of warm temperatures and strong summer monsoons – and short-lived economic revolution. Song rulers established a context in which innovation and commercialization were supported. Rice paddy agriculture was transformed into an advanced cycle of two and three crops per year with new tools and methods, new seeds, and massive investments in irrigation. The government opened seven new ports to trade with Japan and Southeast Asia, and massively expanded its coinage to support commerce. Iron production for commerce and war was revolutionized, increasing twelvefold. The expansion of iron production contributed to a wood supply crisis in North China; coal had been in use in small quantities since the fourth century, but between 1050 and 1126 it became the primary source of domestic and industrial fuel in North China. Key

---

[32] Robert Oglesby et al., "The Role of the Atlantic Multidecadal Oscillation on Medieval Drought in North America: Synthesizing Results from Proxy Data and Climate Models," *GPC* 84–5 (2012), 56–65; Cook et al., "Megadroughts in North America"; Benson et al., "Cahokia's Boom and Bust"; Larry Benson et al., "Anasazi (Pre-Columbian Native-American) Migrations during the Middle-12th and Late 13th Centuries – Were They Drought Induced?" *ClimCh* 83 (2007), 187–213; –, "Possible Impacts of Early-11th, Middle-12th-, and Late-13th Century Droughts on Western Native Americans and the Mississippian Cahokians," *QSR* 26 (2007), 336–50; and Terry L. Jones et al., "Environmental Imperatives Reconsidered: Demographic Crises in Western North America during the Medieval Climate Anomaly," *CA* 40 (1999), 137–56; Tim Folger, "Ancient America's Culture of War," *Discover* (2003), 65–9; Brian R. Billman et al., "Cannibalism, Warfare, and Drought in the Mesa Verde Region during the Twelfth Century, A.D.," *AmAntiq* 65 (2000), 145–78.

[33] Here I compare the Etowah and Moundville histories, summarized in John H. Blitz, "New Perspectives in Mississippian Archaeology," *JArchRes* 18 (2010), 1–39, with the regional reconstructed drought patterns in the North American Drought Atlas, available at http://iridl.ldeo.columbia.edu/SOURCES/.LDEO/.TRL/.NADA2004/.pdsi-atlas.html (accessed August 8, 2012).

innovations elsewhere in the Song economy included papermaking, print-
ing, gunpowder, and the first mechanical processing of textiles.[34] Sending
shipping out into the China Sea – and trading caravans overland – the Song
dominated an emerging medieval world system running east through Central
Asia and India. William McNeill has argued that China's economic revolution during the Song "tipped a critical balance in world history" toward the
rise of the modern market economy and its power and reach.[35]

China's explosive economic and population growth – and pressure on
resources in the north – may well have anticipated the rise of the modern
world, but we can only hope that its quick demise is not also an anticipa-
tion of things to come. China's population fell from a peak of 128 million
in 1200 back to 70 million in 1400. This was not, however, an endogenous
crisis of sustainability, even though the sudden expansion of population in
the north contributed to an early shift to fossil fuel. This population growth
coincided with a seemingly countervailing seventy-year-long sequence of
exceptionally cold, dry winter monsoons – which itself must have contributed to the fuel crisis impelling the conversion to coal.[36] Chinese climate
by itself cannot explain China's terrible population crash; Chinese society
and economy made great strides in the face of adverse conditions. But if cli-

[34] Mark Elvin, *The Pattern of China's Past* (Stanford, CA, 1973), 113–99; Yoshinoba Shiba,
Commerce and Society in Sung China (Ann Arbor, MI, 1970), esp. 45–50, 103–40, 202–
13; David Christian, *Maps of Time: An Introduction to Big History* (Berkeley, CA, 2004),
274–8; William H. McNeill, *The Pursuit of Power: Technology, Society, and Armed Force
since A. D. 1000* (Chicago, IL, 1982), 24–57; Robert Hartwell, "A Revolution in the Chinese
Iron and Coal Industries during the Northern Sung, 960–1126 A.D.," *Journal of Asian
Studies* 21 (1962), 153–62; –, "Markets, Technology, and the Structure of Enterprise in the
Development of the Eleventh-Century Iron and Steel Industry," *JEconH* 26 (1966), 29–58;
–, "The Evolution of the Early Northern Sung Monetary System, A. D. 950–1025," *Journal
of the American Oriental Society* 87 (1967), 28–89. On Song imperial order and intellectual
life, see F. W. Mote, *Imperial China, 900–1800* (Cambridge, MA, 1999), 92–168.

[35] Janet L. Abu-Lughod, *Before European Hegemony: The World System, A. D. 1250–1350*
(New York, 1989); McNeill, *The Pursuit of Power*, 25; see also George Modelski and William
R. Thompson, *Leading Sectors and World Powers: The Coevolution of Global Politics and
Economics* (Columbia, SC, 1996), 142–76.

[36] Here it must be mentioned that there are several different measures of Chinese climate in
the Middle Ages, and they do not precisely match up (see Figure III.5c). The Osborn-Briffa/
IPCC Box 6.4 East Asian tree ring summer temperature estimates show a cold spike slightly
after AD 900, matching the Huang Maar terminal-Tang dynasty cold spike. Then the two
records diverge. The Huang Maar record shows another period of cold, dry winters between
1050 and 1100, and then a long amelioration until about 1550, followed by a two-century
cold period centering around 1640: the infamous seventeenth-century crisis. The Osborn-
Briffa/IPCC record indicates a continuous jagged decline until 1640, when it "rejoins" the
Huang Maar record. A record from the ShiHua Cave near Beijing has decidedly cold periods at 800–50 and 1460–1590. T.-L. Ku and H.-C. Li, "Speleothems as High-Resolution
Paleoenvironment Archives: Records from Northeastern China," *Proc. Indian Acad. Sci.
(Earth Planet. Sci.)* 107 (1998), 321–30.

mate does not necessarily and directly explain China's loss of population, it played a contributing role with the key players of conquest and disease.

China's medieval crisis came in three stages. First, the northern Song domains fell to the Manchurian Jurchen tribal nomads in a sudden onslaught in the late 1120s. Almost a century later, in 1214–15, the Mongols led by Chinggis Khan conquered north China; then, after continuing economic development, the southern Song regions were conquered by the Mongols in 1279. Climate played a triggering role in these events (see Figure III.5c).

Looking at the various detailed estimates of the summer monsoon and summer temperatures, a very precise story emerges. When the Tang collapsed in 907, China was suffering the combined effects of a strong winter monsoon, a weak summer monsoon, and cold summer temperatures. The Northern Song never faced quite this combination of climatic stress, and its economic strength – and perhaps its more compact geography – may have been a shield against collapse, protecting it against a severe cold snap around 1000.[37] But temperature shifts do seem to have played a powerful role.

Very broadly, China and Central Asia fared quite differently during the Medieval Climate Anomaly and the subsequent Little Ice Age (see Figures III.5c, III.10). China seems to have had reasonably strong monsoon precipitation, though segmented by sharp reversals, until the fourteenth century. Conversely, an analysis of arid Central Asia since AD 1000 finds drought conditions until a sharp rise in humidity at 1350, followed by peak humidity between about 1550 and 1750, shaped by the north-to-south shift of the Atlantic westerlies at the onset of the Little Ice Age. Pollen evidence from the Altai Mountains indicates dry colder conditions from 1000 to 1380, with severe cold between 1208 and 1307. Assuming that Manchuria and Mongolia shared this MCA aridity, then the entire rise and expansion of the Manchurian Jurchens and then the Mongols under Genghis Khan and his successors from the early twelfth century into the thirteenth century unfolded during dry conditions in the Asian interior. It would appear that spikes of cold summer temperature in China – combined with rewarming in Mongolia – set the stage for dynastic collapse and invasion. When the Jurchen invasion (from Manchuria) came in 1127 it was in the context of a warm rebound from twenty years of cold in Mongolia, but a cold spike in China. Similarly, the Mongol invasion of North China in 1214 followed thirty years of cold summer conditions in both regions, but was launched as Mongolia was warming and China was suffering the most intense summer cold since the Tang crisis ~AD 900. The Mongol conquest of the southern

---

[37] While at its peak the Tang covered more than 2 million square miles (5.2 megameters²), the Northern Sung was about two-thirds that size, at around 1.15 million square miles (3 megameters²). Data from Rein Taagepera, "Size and Duration of Empires: Systematics of Size," *Social Science Research* 7 (1978), 117. Thanks to Philip Brown for pointing out this key distinction.

Song domains in 1279 again came at a time of Mongolian warming and Chinese cold, again roughly as cold as the terminal Tang period. The same pattern would be repeated in the 1640s, when the Ming fell to the Manchu. Climate clearly played a decisive role in these events, though the survival of the Northern Song indicates that it was not sufficient in and of itself.[38]

Violent conquest in a time of cold brought mass death. The Mongol conquest of North China was insanely destructive: peasants were massacred or forced into human wave attacks, food production was disrupted, and presumably epidemics broke out, though other than one among the Mongol army itself they seem to have been unrecorded. Population in the north dropped from 50 million in 1195 to 8.5 million in 1235. The Mongol conquest of the Song south under Kublai Khan in 1279 was far less destructive, as the increasingly civilized Mongols sought to preserve the productive power of this society. But sixty years later, in 1331, epidemics began to sweep across China, slaughtering untold thousands, and the total failure of the summer monsoon marked the first stages of the Little Ice Age in East Asia. In these conditions, the country rose in rebellion against the Mongol Yuan dynasty, replacing it with the Ming in 1368.[39]

Was China's massive population in the early thirteenth century unsustainable? Certainly there were resource issues in the dry north. But again, like in the Roman empire, this was not a "Malthusian crisis," or at least it never got to that stage. Just as North China's resource crisis must have been shaped by an episode of harsh dry climate, China's population crash was driven by exogenous forces: violent despoliation by steppe nomads and then massive mortality from the plague, compounded by civil war and the change of regimes.

Into the Little Ice Age

As they had around AD 900, with the simultaneous crises in the Mayan Yucatan and Tang China, the trans-Pacific forces of the Medieval Climate Anomaly seem to have shaped parallel events from the mid-thirteenth century in East Asia and North America. Across the Pacific, the East Asian summer temperatures and records of megadroughts in Central and North America during the Medieval Climate Anomaly swung in a strikingly

[38] Chen et al., "Moisture Changes over the Last Millennium in Arid Central Asia"; Frank Schlütz and Frank Lehmkuhl, "Climate Change in the Russian Altai, Southern Siberia, Based on Palynological and Geomorphological Results, with Implications for Climate Teleconnections and Human History since the Middle Holocene," *VHAb* 16 (2007), 101–18, at 114–15; Tan et al., "Climate Patterns in North Central China during the Last 1800 yr"; Mote, *Imperial China*, 193–248. Temperature proxies from Osborn-Briffa/IPCC Box 6.4. The peaks of these cold summer periods in China were 907–10, 996–1001, 1097–1100, 1137–41, 1216–20, 1276–81, and 1357–60.

[39] Thomas J. Barfield, *The Perilous Frontier: Nomadic Empires and China* (Cambridge, MA, 1989), 203–6; McNeill, *Plagues and Peoples*, 142–4, 263.

similar pattern. These waves of crisis in thirteenth-century China and North America were shaped broadly by the suppression of ENSO variation during the last centuries of the Medieval Climate Anomaly.

By the second half of the thirteenth century, there were strong signs that the MCA was coming to an end. It is tempting to see a critical role for the massive volcanic eruption in 1258 (El Chichon?), triggering an enormous El Niño surge, which produced the massive "Miraflores" flooding in Peru, and perhaps shaping a wave of climate changes from the Pacific ITCZ to the North Atlantic.[40] The last decades of the century would also see the onset of the Wolf solar minimum, the first of three solar minima that would play a key role in the Little Ice Age. But the most important force at work was the dynamic between a cooling north and the restarting of the ENSO variation, bringing stronger El Niño/La Niña cycles to the Americas, and an end to the strong South Asian monsoon that had distantly influenced climates from the Eastern Mediterranean to China since around AD 950 (see Figure III.5d).

In North America, the reemergence of El Niño brought an end to the great MCA megadroughts, and Mississippian centers reemerged in the southeast, though not at Cahokia. Elsewhere, the end of the Medieval Climate Anomaly brought powerful stresses to the societies around the Pacific rim. In the western Pacific, the sudden reassertion of strong El Niños, pulling warm waters to the east, drove a sudden fall in sea level and temperature, leading to endemic violence, settlement retreat, and the end of the great age of Polynesian migrations. Along the Peruvian coast in the now warm and stormy eastern Pacific, the Chimu empire, which first began to develop between 1000 and 1100, built an elaborate seagoing chain of coastal commerce during this epoch, deploying great sailing rafts built of balsa wood and reeds.[41]

Far to the west, southern Asia suddenly saw a reversal of the strong monsoon conditions – shaped by the static medieval ENSO – that had underwritten the region's medieval efflorescence. As the monsoons weakened after 1250 – and completely failed in the "Khmer drought" of the 1350s and 1360s – the long-established South Indian Hindu kingdoms, the Pagan kingdom in Burma, Angkor Wat in Cambodia, and the Dai Viet polity, all fell to rising challenges during the thirteenth and fourteenth centuries, in India manifested in Mongol raiders and in the Islamic Delhi Sultanate, founded

[40] These events are comparable to the dramatic events around 3100 BC that brought the Mid-Holocene transition to an end. See Richard B. Stothers, "Climatic and Demographic Consequences of the Massive Volcanic Eruption of 1258," *ClimCh* 43 (2000), 361–74; Julien Emile-Geay et al., "Volcanoes and ENSO over the Past Millennium," *JClim* 21 (2008), 3134–48; Gifford H. Miller et al., "Abrupt Onset of the Little Ice Age Triggered by Volcanism and Sustained by Sea-Ice/Ocean Feedbacks," *GRL* 39 (2012), L02708.

[41] Patrick D. Nunn, "Environmental Catastrophe in the Pacific Islands around A. D. 1300," *Geoarchaeology* 15 (2000), 715–40; Richardson, *People of the Andes*, 139–46.

in 1206.[42] And in the Mediterranean and Europe the shift of the North Atlantic Oscillation from a positive (warm north) to a negative (cold north) mode reconfigured the pattern of drought and precipitation. This global shift marked the beginning of the Little Ice Age.

Europe

The Little Ice Age would be part of the wider complex that brought the Middle Ages to an end in Europe, a process that stands as one of the great questions in historical writing. Here there is a long-standing debate about the nature of the medieval economy, its ability to support the growing European population, the nature of the crisis of the fourteenth century, and its role in the longer transition to modernity.[43] European populations more than doubled in the Middle Ages, from about 30 million in 1000 to a peak of 70 million in 1300. Were these peoples getting ahead or simply barely running in place? Starting with the early work of French historian Henri Pirenne, the "commercialization" argument sees a European economy developing long-distance trade and regional specialization as it entered the High Middle Ages, supporting its growing population. Here – as with the Song – the theoretical framework might be minimally "Boserupian," arguing that relative peace and mild climate allowed the growth of population, while development in the economy simply offset this growth. Or it might be "Smithian," in which the dynamic of economic growth began to surpass population growth. Another corollary to the commercialization thesis would be that European population growth was reasonably sustainable, or at least would correct itself with enough time: thus the adherents of commercialization would see the crisis of the fourteenth century as fundamentally caused by exogenous forces beyond the ken and control of

---

[42] Thapar, *Early India*, 425–41; Victor Lieberman, "Charter State Collapse in Southeast Asia, ca. 1250–1400, as a Problem in Regional and World History," *AHR* 116 (2011), 937–63; Lieberman, *Strange Parallels*, I: 119–23, 236–42, 370–1, II: 83–4; Edward R. Cook et al., "Asian Monsoon Failure and Megadrought during the Last Millennium," *Science* 328 (2010), 486–9; Delia W. Oppo et al., "2,000-Year-Long Temperature and Hydrology Reconstruction from the Indo-Pacific Warm Pool," *Nature* 460 (2009), 1113–16; Gunnell et al., "Response of the South Indian Runoff Harvesting Civilization"; Anil K. Gupta et al., "Abrupt Changes in the Asian Southwest Monsoon during the Holocene and Their Links to the North Atlantic Ocean," *Nature* 421 (2003), 354–7; David M. Anderson, "Increase in the Asian Southwest Monsoon during the Past Four Centuries," *Science* 297 (2002), 596–9; Brendan M. Buckley et al., "Climate as a Contributing Factor in the Demise of Angkor, Cambodia," *PNAS* 107 (2010), 6748–52.

[43] Here I am indebted to the historiographical reviews in John Hatcher and Mark Bailey, *Modeling the Middle Ages: The History and Theory of England's Economic Development* (Oxford, 2001); Barbara F. Harvey, "Introduction: The 'Crisis' of the Early Fourteenth Century," in Bruce M. S. Campbell, ed., *Before the Black Death: Studies in the "Crisis" of the Early Fourteenth Century* (Manchester, 1991), 1–24; and Nils Hybel, *Crisis or Change: The Concept of Crisis in the Light of Agrarian Structural Reorganization in Late Medieval England* (Aarhus, 1988).

medieval peoples. Two other contending arguments see the crisis as fundamentally endogenous. One, the Brenner thesis, is fundamentally focused on the longer-range transition toward capitalist class relations beginning in the fourteenth and continuing into the seventeenth century.[44] The Malthusian position argues that Europe's population by the early fourteenth century, almost double the Roman peak at AD 200, was fundamentally unsustainable, and that the Black Death was simply the agent of an "inevitable" crisis of human numbers.

Let us focus on the spectrum from happy growth to utter misery that runs between the commercializing and Malthusian positions. These have tumbled in a classic historiographical brawl for almost a century. The earliest orthodoxy lay with the commercialization model, consolidated by Henri Pirenne's thesis – published in 1925 – that the rise of Europe began with the revival of trade in the eleventh century, and the establishment of medieval towns and cities and a merchant class operating from within their walls. Pirenne was followed in 1931 by Marc Bloch's great work on the expansion of medieval European agriculture; here he described the movement from the dry uplands into the rich wet river valley soils, impenetrable to the light scratch plow but which could be turned with the heavy wheeled mold-board plow, drawn by teams of oxen and then horses.[45] The rise of towns and cities involved in long-distance trade then provided markets for agricultural production, which spread into new lands and gradually improved through time. In the early 1960s, a set of short, powerful essays by Lynn White provided the technological underpinnings to the commercial thesis. White emphasized the role of iron and the horse in the medieval economies, both in arming and mounting hosts of warrior knights, but also in constructing and drawing the new heavy plow. He argued in particular that a yoke harness, first developed in China, allowed horses much greater efficiency over the ancient and Roman breast-band harness, which choked the horse as it leaned into the load. Most important, however, he argued for a revolution in water-powered machinery, claiming that medieval technology made significant energy advances over what he took to be backward Romans.[46]

---

[44] T. H. Ashton and C. H. E. Philpin, eds., *The Brenner Debate: Agrarian Class Structure and Economic Development in Pre-Industrial Europe* (Cambridge, 1985); Hatcher and Bailey, *Modeling the Middle Ages*, 66–120.

[45] Henri Pirenne, *Medieval Cities: Their Origins and the Revival of Trade*, Frank D. Halsey, trans. (1925; Princeton, NJ, 1952); Marc Bloch, *French Rural Society: An Essay on its Basic Characteristics*, Janet Sondheimer, trans. (1931; Berkeley, CA, 1966), 5–20, 48–56. For England, see Richard H. Brintnell, *The Commercialization of English Society, 1000–1500*, second edition (Manchester, 1996).

[46] Lynn White, Jr., *Medieval Technology and Social Change* (New York, 1962); White's celebration of medieval technology has been amplified by several scholars into a central theme in the history of technology: Jean Gimpel, *The Medieval Machine: The Industrial Revolution of the Middle Ages* (New York, 1976); Frances Gies and Joseph Gies, *Cathedral, Forge, and Waterwheel: Technology and Invention in the Middle Ages* (New York, 1994).

The commercialization thesis was advanced in the work of economists Graeme Snooks, Eric Jones, Douglass North, and Robert Paul Thomas, who see the origins of "the rise of the West" in the economic and ecological advantages launched in the High Middle Ages. Snooks has attempted to quantify curves of long-range English economic growth starting in the eleventh century. Jones stresses the ecological advantages of a temperate climate, with young, glacially turned soils, well watered by multiple rivers and ample seasonal rainfall, arguing that these ecological benefits began to make a difference as European societies north of the Alps emerged from the postimperial ruin. North and Thomas stress the institutional and legal structures that organized capital and protected individual property ownership and exchange with the development of European production, markets, and trade.[47]

A countervailing Malthusian thesis developed between the late 1940s and 1950s, shaped in some measure by a growing realization of the massively expanding global populations in the postwar era. Most powerfully articulated by Michael M. Postan, the Malthusian position has been that the economic expansion celebrated by the commerce thesis was simply driven by the growth of population, which in 300 years across Europe grew from 30 million to 70–80 million and in England alone tripled from about 2 million to almost 6 million. In this interpretation, whatever technological and agricultural improvements occurred were utterly swamped by population growth, and Europe as of 1300 stood on the edge of an endogenously driven Malthusian crisis, where population numbers far exceeded the capacity of an organic economy to sustain them. A growing population forced the commitment of an increasing acreage to growing cereal crops, which deplete the soil, rather than animal grazing, the manure from which improves the soil. The Malthusian position is buttressed by new examinations of medieval technology, which have debunked Lynn White. Their most fundamental critique is supported by the historians studying the ancient worlds, arguing that Lynn White had simply been in error in stating that milling technology first developed in Europe in the Middle Ages: medieval people did not invent new technologies but simply continued systems developed in antiquity.[48] A

---

[47] Graeme Donald Snooks, *Economics without Time: A Science Blind to the Forces of Historical Change* (Ann Arbor, MI, 1993), 240–69; Eric Jones, *The European Miracle: Environments, Economies and Geopolitics in the History of Europe and Asia*, second edition (New York, 1987); Douglass C. North and Robert Paul Thomas, *The Rise of the Western World: A New Economic History* (Cambridge, 1973). See also David S. Landes, *The Wealth and Poverty of Nations: Why Some Are So Rich and Some So Poor* (New York, 1998), 3–28.

[48] Bert Hall, "Lynn White's *Medieval Technology and Social Change* after Thirty Years," and Richard Holt, "Medieval Technology and the Historians: The Evidence for the Mill," in Robert Fox, ed., *Technological Change: Methods and Themes in the History of Technology* (Amsterdam, 1996), 85–122; Kevin Greene, "Technology and Innovation in Context: The Roman Background to Medieval and Later Developments," *JRA* 7 (1994), 22–33.

central pillar of the Malthusian argument as advanced by Postan rests on an argument for economic and nutritional stress from the close of the thirteenth century, stress that turned into population decline after 1300. Thus, in the Malthusian argument, the weakened and impoverished medieval poor stood on the edge of inevitable disaster, coming first in a Great Famine in northern Europe between 1315 and 1322 that perhaps killed 10 percent of the population. These early fourteenth-century famines were followed by the Black Death, which killed roughly a half of the remaining population.[49]

Economists working on long-term demographic and economic change reject the commercialization thesis, subscribing implicitly or explicitly to Postan's Malthusianism. To them the record seems plain: whatever economic expansion that occurred during the High Middle Ages was swamped by population growth, and then undermined with the great slaughter of the Black Death. David Findley and Mats Lundhal argue that "a Malthusian crisis of major proportions was clearly looming." John Komlos and Sergey Nefedon are particularly explicit: they see the causes of the Black Death mortality as fundamentally "endogenous," not the product of "exogenous" natural forces. "[T]he crisis can be conceptualized as being an inherent part of the European demographic system," they argue, "the European population had reached a Malthusian ceiling by 1300 so that a prolonged downturn would have occurred in any event. To be sure, the Black Death exacerbated the process and was even its proximate cause but not, it seems to us, its fundamental determinant."[50]

Where the most enthusiastic of the commercialization scholars see Europeans getting ahead in the High Middle Ages, the Malthusians see them as falling behind. In between lies the modern consensus, which can be called either a Boserupian "running in place" or a Malthusian trap. Here the economists seem out of step with the dominant consensus among medieval economic historians, which is that the outer (perhaps Malthusian) limits of an advanced organic economy might have been reached, but a crisis on the scale of what occurred in the fourteenth century was by no means inevitable. Populations grew first in response to the spread of market opportunities in a newly stable High Middle Ages, but then production increased with

[49] M. M. Postan, "Some Economic Evidence of Declining Population in the Later Middle Ages," *Economic Historical Review* 2 (1949–50), 221–46; M. M. Postan and John Hatcher, "Population and Class Relation in Feudal Society," in Aston and Philpin, eds., *The Brenner Debate*, 64–78; Emmanuel Le Roy Ladurie, *The Peasants of Languedoc*, John Day, trans. (Urbana, IL, 1974); see the summary discussions in Hybel, *Crisis or Change*, 138–45, 178–97; and Hatcher and Bailey, *Modeling the Middle Ages*, 21–65.

[50] Ronald Findlay and Mats Lundhal, "Demographic Shocks and the Factor Proportion Model: From the Plague of Justinian to the Black Death," in Ronald Findlay et al., eds., *Eli Heckscher, International Trade, and Economic History* (Cambridge, MA, 2006), 157–96, quote at 190; John Komlos and Sergey Nefedon, "A Compact Macromodel of Pre-Industrial Population Growth," *Historical Methods* 35 (2002), 93.

the growth of population: the classic Boserupian intensification model.[51] By all recent accounts, medieval agricultural systems were doing a reasonably good job of feeding the growing numbers of Europeans, given a predictable environment. But the Medieval Optimum – and then the respite from serious epidemics – came to an end between the 1270s and 1350. The ensuing crisis, the modern consensus holds, was indeed fundamentally shaped by exogenous climatic and biological forces. In their absence, European population would have stabilized through the operation of Malthusian preventive checks, and the continuing slow accumulation of Boserupian innovations. Their understanding is best summarized by great medievalist David Herlihy:

> European populations had grown to extraordinary levels during the central Middle Ages, but the result was not a Malthusian reckoning or crisis but a deadlock. In spite of frequent famine and widespread hunger, the community in ca. 1300 was successfully holding its numbers. It is likely that this equilibrium could have been maintained for the indefinite future.... That did not happen; an exogenous factor, the Black Death, broke the Malthusian deadlock. And in doing so it gave to Europeans the chance to rebuild their society along much different lines.[52]

The critique of Postan's Malthusianism began in the mid-1960s. The argument for an agrarian crisis was based on early and selective work in the particularly good English archives, but new and ongoing research has demonstrated that no such crisis was brewing. Regions where peasants had particularly small land tenures did not show signs of economic stress, because they were generally places with a lot of accessible wild land – "waste." There is no evidence for soil exhaustion in crop yields and no wave of desertion of the land. Along the south coast of England, advanced farming techniques were allowing continuous cropping; elsewhere if yields were low they were not declining. Throughout this new literature is strong evidence for improving agricultural methods offsetting the impact of rising population.[53] A sequence of recent work has demonstrated quantitatively that agricultural

---

[51] The strongest advocate here is Karl Gunnar Persson, *Pre-Industrial Economic Growth: Social Organization and Technological Progress in Europe* (Oxford, 1988), esp. 63–88.

[52] David Herlihy, *The Black Death and the Transformation of the West*, Samuel K. Cohn, Jr., ed. (Cambridge, MA, 1997), 38–9. See pp. 31–8 for a general critique of the Malthusian crisis position. See also Kaminsky, "The Lateness to Waning to Crisis" for a thorough critique of the Marxist and Malthusian crisis interpretations.

[53] This literature is analyzed in detail in Hybel, *Crisis or Change*; and Hatcher and Bailey, *Modeling the Middle Ages*. See also the formative discussions in Barbara F. Harvey, "The Population Trend in England between 1300 and 1348," *Transactions of the Royal Historical Society* 5th ser., 16 (1966), 23–42; H. E. Hallam, *Rural England, 1066–1348* (Sussex, 1981), 10–16, 245–64; Harvey, "Introduction"; Bruce M. S. Campbell, "Ecology vs. Economics in Late Thirteenth- and Early Fourteenth-Century English Agriculture," in Del Sweeney, ed., *Agriculture in the Middle Ages: Technology, Practice, and Representation* (Philadelphia, PA, 1995), 21–40; Edward Miller and John Hatcher, *Medieval England: Towns, Commerce, and Crafts, 1086–1348* (London, 1995), 393–429; and Bruce M. S. Campbell, *English Seignorial Agriculture, 1250–1450* (Cambridge, 2000), 386–430.

productivity was extremely high in the century before the Black Death, but then fell as population fell and there were fewer mouths to feed. Bruce Campbell and Mark Overton summarize the findings of their monumental analysis of six centuries of farming in the county of Norfolk, in eastern England, as follows:

> Until the early eighteenth century the trends suggest a Boserupian rather than a Malthusian response to the stimulus of population increase, in so far as population growth, accompanied by falling real wages and rising grain prices, was associated with rising not falling yields. Conversely, yields fell when, after 1350, and again after 1650, population growth eased, wage rates rose and grain prices fell.

A series of parallel studies similarly found that European agriculture was producing at levels significantly below its technological limit, and that productivity often rose in a gradual process of intensifying innovation.[54]

Gregory Clark concurs on medieval productivity, arguing that "the growth of population in the thirteenth century may in part be a result of gains in the efficiency of agriculture." Clark finds a high but stable productivity in English agriculture, driven by population and demand, shaping a Malthusian relationship between land and population. But his interpretation is one of stasis rather than crisis, a rather mild Malthusianism: "The Malthusian world was not necessarily one where people were pressed to the limits of physical subsistence."[55] Another recent study argues that not only was land productivity high but also labor productivity itself was high. Medieval agriculture was meeting the demands of an ever larger market. The rising number of horses employed in agriculture apparently did not contribute directly to productivity in the field, but the relative speed of the horse cart over the slow-moving oxcart helped integrate the peasant farmer into the market. Rather than resignation in the face of Malthusian decline, these historians and others see rational management and intensive efforts to maintain soil fertility to support these results. A similar rational response was manifested in the grinding of grain: when water mills reached the limits of local capacity, major investments were made in windmills and tidemills. If these were inventions of the ancient world, they were aggressively deployed to meet the needs of growing medieval populations.[56]

---

[54] Bruce M. S. Campbell and Mark Overton, "A New Perspective on Medieval and Early Modern Agriculture: Six Centuries of Norfolk Farming c 1250–c. 1850," *Past and Present* 141 (1993), 38–105, quote from 96. See also the summary of literature in S. R. Epstein, *Freedom and Growth: The Rise of States and Markets in Europe, 1300–1750* (London, 2000), 45–6.

[55] Gregory Clark, "The Long March of History: Farm Wages, Population, and Economic Growth, England 1209–1869," *EconHistR* 60 (2007), 97–135, quote from 125.

[56] Eona Karakacili, "English Agrarian Labor Productivity Rates before the Black Death: A Case Study," *JEcH* 64 (2004), 24–60; John Langdon, *Horse, Oxen, and Technological Innovation: The Use of Draught Animals in English Farming from 1056 to 1500* (Cambridge, 1986),

The corollary to this picture of Boserupian efforts to confront Malthusian limits in economy might have been a similar effort in demographic. If Europe was not facing an "inevitable crisis," then it certainly was approaching over-population, and Malthus proposed the preventive check of marital restraint to forestall the positive check of crisis mortality. John Hatcher and Mark Bailey suggest that "prudential" marriage patterns limiting fertility might well have come into play in England if the plague had not arrived. One careful study shows that the people of Lincolnshire, at least, practiced a quite restrained marriage pattern before the Black Death, with women marrying at twenty-four and men at almost thirty-two.[57]

Whether or not the high productivity of medieval agriculture translated into higher nutrition for ordinary people is very much an open question. Diets in the century before the Black Death among the laboring poor were heavily weighted toward the consumption of grains, suggesting a very limited protein intake. Christopher Dyer's work on this question focuses on the impact of class stratification on medieval peasant impoverishment. Despite his critique of the Postan thesis, his analysis suggests that conditions were indeed extremely difficult for the peasantry.[58]

But just as the economic historians are finding a surprisingly strong agrarian economy before 1350, so too the physical anthropologists have been finding surprisingly large people in the Middle Ages. The best study available to date, by Koepke and Baten, is very suggestive, though certainly not the last word. Their aggregate numbers for the eleventh and twelfth centuries suggest dramatic news for the advocates of economic growth; it suggests that Europeans grew by 2 cm during a time when population numbers grew by a third, from 36 million to 58 million (see Figure III.7). But their data for this period is mostly from thinly populated eastern Europe and Scandinavia, with the Mediterranean, France, Germany, and Britain barely represented at all. Other studies similarly find medieval adult males in Scandinavia and Britain achieving a height of 171–172 cm on average,

---

264–72; David Stone, "Medieval Farm Management and Technological Mentalities: Hinderclay before the Black Death," *EconHistR* 4 (2001), 612–38; –, *Decision-Making in Medieval Agriculture* (Oxford, 2005); Holt, "Medieval Historians and Technology: The Evidence of the Mill," 112–13. See also John Langdon, *Mills in the Medieval Economy: England, 1300–1540* (Oxford, 2004), 8–64.

[57] Hatcher and Bailey, *Modeling the Middle Ages*, 56–7; H. E. Hallam, "Age at First Marriage and Age at Death in the Lincolnshire Fenland, 1252–1478," *PopSt* 39 (1985), 55–69, at 60; see also Hallam, *Rural England*, 245–64. Hallam's data is somewhat different than the conclusions drawn by David Herlihy, who generalized from relatively elite and anecdotal contexts that women married in their late teens in the central Middle Ages: *Medieval Households* (Cambridge, MA, 1985), 103–10. For a dubious assessment, see Harvey, "Introduction."

[58] Christopher Dyer, *Standards of Living in the Later Middle Ages: Social Change in England, c. 1200–1520* (Cambridge, 1989), 6–7, 109–89, esp. 151–60, and –, "Changes in Nutrition and Standard of Living in England, 1200–1500," in Robert W. Fogel, ed., *Long-Term Changes in Nutrition and the Standard of Living* (Berne, 1986), 35–44.

significantly taller than their counterparts in the Roman empire.[59] Here the evidence from cemeteries in London may indicate that the most vulnerable population, the poor in the medieval cities, did suffer from the impact of the hard times of the early fourteenth century. The East Smithfield Plague cemetery, containing almost 100 measurable adult skeletons of individuals dying between 1348 and 1350, provides a tightly dated sample of such a population, and can be compared with cemeteries dating from 1200–1320 and from 1350–1540. The plague victims in the mass burials in East Smithfield, adult men and women, were generally two centimeters or more shorter than the adults in the earlier and later cemeteries.[60] Further work, with similarly closely dated samples, will be required to see if there was indeed a general downward trend in stature in the decades before 1350, both in England and on the continent. William Jordan, the expert on the famines of 1315–22, while skeptical of the Malthusian Postan thesis and seeing the restoration of good diets after 1322, argues that the famines potentially weakened a

[59] Nikola Koepke and Joerg Baten, "The Biological Standard of Living in Europe during the Last Two Millennia," *EREconH* 9 (2005), 61–95; Richard H. Steckel, "New Light on the 'Dark Ages': The Remarkably Tall Stature of European Men during the Medieval Era," *Social Science History* 28 (2004), 211–29; –, "Health and Nutrition in the Pre-Industrial Era: Insights from a Millennium of Average Heights in Northern Europe," in Robert C. Allen, et al., eds., *Living Standards in the Past: New Perspectives on Well-Being in Asia and Europe* (New York, 2008), 227–54, esp. 240–3; Roberts and Cox, *Health and Disease in Britain*, 163, 195, 396. In contrast to the typically dire picture of the medieval diet before the Black Death, Vern Bullough and Cameron Campbell, "Female Longevity and Diet in the Middle Ages," *Speculum* 55 (1980), 317–25 argue that serious iron deficiencies in Roman and early medieval diets led to extreme female anemia and very high female mortality, but that this was mitigated by the thirteenth century with improved diet (meat, beans, greens) as well as the use of iron cooking pots.

[60] Heights estimated from femoral length, three London cemeteries, 1200–1540, compared with larger English medieval samples:

	Heights		Individuals	
	Male	Female	Male	Female
Spital Square (Priory and Hospital) ~1200–~1320:	169.5	161.1	20	10
East Smithfield Black Death cemetery mass graves, 1348–50:	167.6	160.6	61	30
St Mary Graces (burial ground at Cisterian Abbey) 1350–1540:	170.1	163.9	28	14
England: Early Medieval ~410–1050:	172	161	996	751
England: Late Medieval ~1050–1550:	171	159	8,494	7,929

The cemetery data is posted on the Museum of London Center for Bioarchaeology Web site: http://www.museumoflondon.org.uk/Collections-Research/LAARC/Centre-for-Human-Bioarchaeology/Database/Medieval+cemeteries/ (accessed August 8, 2012). English medieval data from Roberts and Cox, "The Impact of Economic Intensification and Social Complexity on Human Health in Britain," 154.

generation of Europeans coming of age in the decades prior to the onslaught of the Black Death.[61]

But such a nutritional deficit – I argue – was the result of the onset of weather unseen for 400 years, not necessarily overpopulation and soil exhaustion. And so too, the Black Death was an assault from the natural world. The scholars who have settled on a moderate Malthusian-Boserupian "running-in-place" understanding of the High Middle Ages are unanimous that the fundamental forces at work in the fourteenth century crisis were exogenous to the socioeconomic system, Postan and modern economists notwithstanding. There was nothing necessarily inevitable about the scale of the mortality that the Black Death unleashed. As had happened before to relatively stable organic economies occupying reasonably good regional ecologies, the crisis was the result of severe natural disasters, not the inner dynamics of demographic and economic systems.[62] This is not to say, however, that the continuing shocks to these systems did not have long-term consequences; these will be the subject of the next chapter.

* * *

The Little Ice Age and the Black Death

Both the wave of epidemics commencing with the Black Death and the climatic impact of the Little Ice Age were exogenous assaults by nature upon medieval societies. Each would have dramatic early manifestations in the fourteenth century – what Bruce Campbell has called "an act of Schumpterian creative destruction" – and then settle into an enduring pattern that would not break until the beginning of the eighteenth century.[63] Together, epidemics and abrupt climate change set off a dynamic of exogenous shocks that must be seen as foundational to the emergence of the modern world, just as the climate shocks of 4000–3000 BC and 1200–600 BC contributed first to

---

[61] William Chester Jordan, *The Great Famine: Northern Europe in the Early Fourteenth Century* (Princeton, NJ, 1996), 185–7.

[62] See in particular, Hatcher and Bailey, *Modeling the Middle Ages*, 18–20, 159–60; Harvey, "Introduction," 2–3, 19–24; Mark Bailey, "*Per impetum maris*: Natural Disaster and Economic Decline in Eastern England, 1275–1300," in Campbell, ed., *Before the Black Death*, 184–208; Miller and Hatcher, *Medieval England: Towns, Commerce, and Crafts*, 426–9; Persson, *Pre-Industrial Economic Growth*, 86–8; Michael Morineau, "Malthus: There and Back from the Period Preceding the Black Death to the 'Industrial Revolution,'" *JEEconH* 27 (1998), 137–202, esp. 143–5; and most recently John Langdon and James Masschaele, "Commercial Activity and Population Growth in Medieval England," *P&P* 190 (2006), 35–81; and Bruce M. S. Campbell, "England, Wales, Scotland, and Ireland, 1290–377: The Anatomy of a Crisis," paper presented at the Ninth Anglo-American Seminar on the Medieval Economy and Society, Lincoln, July 6–9, 2007.

[63] Bruce M. S. Campbell, "Nature as Historical Protagonist: Environment and Society in Pre-Industrial England, *EconHistR* 63 (2010), 284.

the rise of the earliest states, and then launched the Bronze Age crisis and transition to the Iron Age and classical antiquity.

Thus the Little Ice Age can be set in the perhaps cyclical series of four "millennial Siberian High Epochs" that have marked the Holocene roughly every 2,500 years. But the opening moves of the Little Ice Age were quite protracted, running from the close of the Medieval Warm Period – or Climate Anomaly – in the thirteenth century to the sixteenth century, when the Little Ice Age proper began around 1560 (see Figures III.5a, IV.2). Because its earliest beginnings were already being felt when the Black Death arrived in the Mediterranean in 1347, we need to attend to the beginnings of this sequence here, and return to it in more detail in the following chapter.

The Little Ice Age had its origins in the interaction of solar variability, volcanic eruptions, and oceanic and atmospheric circulation, forcings and interactions about which climate scientists are in hot debate. A cluster of solar minima unseen for thousands of years certainly must have played a central role. There had been a moderate solar minimum in the late seventh century (the Vandal minimum) and again in the middle of the eleventh century (the Oort minimum), but from roughly 1075 to 1275 there were two uninterrupted warm centuries of a solar "grand maximum." Temperature estimates for the northern hemisphere indicate that the eleventh century was the warmest until the onset of modern industrial warming less than a century ago, so the Oort minimum does not appear to have cooled the global system immediately. Volcanic eruptions played a considerable role in shaping medieval weather: the warm eleventh century coincided with a century and a half when there was a minimum of volcanic activity, bracketed by periods between roughly 650–950 and 1150–1350 when significant volcanic eruptions paralleled jagged cooler spells across the northern hemisphere.[64] In general, there was a clear linkage between brief global coolings set off by serious volcanic eruptions – in which veils of sulphur obscured the sun for several years in a row – and harvest disruptions that brought dearth and famine (see Figure III.5a). Such would have been an enduring pattern since the rise of agriculture, but it can only be measured somewhat in the relatively recent past.[65] Volcanic eruptions increased from roughly

---

[64] Briffa-Osborne/IPCC Figure 6.10 Holocene temperature data; Gregory A. Zielinski, "Record of Volcanism since 7000 B.C. from the GISP2 Greenland Ice Core and Implications for the Volcano-Climate System," *Science* 264 (1994), 948–52; McCormick et al., "Volcanoes and the Climate Forcing of Carolingian Europe"; Paul A. Mayewski et al., "Holocene Climate Variability," *QuatRes* 62 (2004), 243–55, esp. 250–2; Stothers, "Climatic and Demographic Consequences of the Massive Eruption of 1258"; Richard B. Stothers, "Far Reach of the Tenth-Century Eldgjá Eruption, Iceland," *ClimCh* 39 (1998), 715–26.

[65] McCormick et al., "Volcanoes and the Climate Forcing of Carolingian Europe"; William S. Atwell, "Volcanism and Short-Term Climatic Change in East Asian and World History, c. 1200–1699," *JWH* 12 (2001), 29–98; Richard B. Stothers, "Volcanic Dry Fogs, Climate Cooling, and Plague Pandemics in Europe and the Middle East," *ClimCh* 42 (1999), 713–23.

AD 1100, and they overlapped with the next solar minimum – the Wolf minimum – which ran from about 1270 to 1370, and then was followed by two more even stronger minima – the Spörer and the Maunder – which ran from 1400 to 1550 and 1640 to 1725 respectively. Together the Wolf, Spörer, and Maunder minima constituted a Hallstatt Grand Minimum, on the 2,300-year cycle driving the Siberian Millennial High that reached back to the Bronze Age Crisis of 1200–700 BC and the Mid-Holocene Crisis of 4000–3000 BC. At the same time, the volcanic eruptions were of equal significance: the 1258 eruption –possibly El Chichon in Mexico – left the largest sulphur signature of any eruption in the Holocene, exactly coinciding with a sudden southward spike in the ITCZ, as measured at both Cariaco and southern China (Dongge Cave) and probably a massive El Niño (see Figure III.5d).

Exactly how these solar and volcanic forcings combined with oceanic and atmospheric circulation to launch the Little Ice Age is a matter of considerable debate, but it is safe to suggest that the solar forces were fundamental and the mega-eruption a possible trigger.[66] What is clear is that a series of stages led up to the extreme Little Ice Age conditions of the seventeenth century. One center of the debate over Little Ice Age origins involved the North Atlantic thermohaline pump, in which the sinking of saline-dense waters off the coast of Greenland drives the circulation of warm tropical waters north from the Caribbean, as well as driving the entire oceanic circulation system.[67] There is growing evidence that the thermohaline circulation (THC) pump did slow during the Little Ice Age, as measured by various measures of salinity, silt size, and water transportation. Several of these records suggest that the THC slowed, recovered, and slowed again, the two slowdowns coming around 1400 and after 1600, perhaps corresponding to the Spörer and Maunder minima.[68] If warm summers in the far north are any indication of a vigorous and warm Gulf Stream, however, the persistence of

---

[66] Thomas J. Crowley, "Causes of Climate Change over the Past 1000 Years," *Science* 289 (2000), 270–7; F. Jansen et al., "Paleoclimate," in *Climate Change 2007: The Physical Science Basis*, 433–97; Gifford H. Miller et al., "Abrupt Onset of the Little Ice Age Triggered by Volcanism and Sustained by Sea-Ice/Ocean Feedbacks."

[67] See George H. Denton and Wallace S. Broecker, "Wobbly Ocean Conveyer Circulation during the Holocene?" *QSR* 27 (2008), 1939–50; Wallace S. Broecker, "Was a Change in Thermohaline Circulation Responsible for the Little Ice Age?" *PNAS* 97 (2000), 1339–42.

[68] David C. Lund et al., "Gulf Stream Density Structure and Transport during the Past Millennium," *Nature* 444 (2006), 601–4, figure 3; Johan Nyberg et al., "A Centennial-Scale Variability of Tropical North Atlantic Surface Hydrology during the Late Holocene," *PPP* 183 (2002), 25–41, figures 7d, e; David E. Black et al., "Eight Centuries of North Atlantic Ocean Atmosphere Variability," *Science* 286 (19990, 1709-13; Giancarlo G. Bianchu and I. icholas McCave, "Holocene Periodicity in North Atlantic Climate and Deep-Water Flow South of Iceland," *Nature* 397), 515-17. See also Marie-Alexandrine Sicre, "Decadal Variability of Sea Surface Temperatures off North Iceland over the Last 2000 Years," *Early and Planetary Science Letters* 268 (2008), 137–42.

reasonably warm summer temperatures in northern Sweden – and in aggregate throughout the northern hemisphere – may suggest that the THC pump did not definitively weaken until after 1550. But between 1550 and 1725 the ice core records and tree ring estimates all suggest that both winters and summers were extremely cold. These records suggest that the period from the close of the Medieval Climatic Anomaly (MCA) and the worst of the Little Ice Age (LIA) can be divided into at least three discrete periods: a MCA-LIA transition between 1150 and 1400, an LIA I of cold winters from 1400 to 1550, and an LIA II of cold summers and winters from 1550 to 1725.[69] Let us look the beginning of this epic cold period in some detail.

The first formal phase of the Little Ice Age, 1400–1550, was characterized by cold, stormy winters and warm summers; LIA II, from 1550–1700/25, by cold winters and summers. What of the MCA/LIA transition from 1150 to 1400? This period needs to be divided at roughly 1275, approximately the beginning of the Wolf minimum. The volcanically active period of 1150–1275 saw slightly cooler northern summers, but at roughly 1275 a pattern of warm but extremely erratic and stormy summer weather settled into the North Atlantic until 1400. One recent analysis suggests that this stormy summer pattern was shaped by a combination of low winter storminess, weakened onshore summer winds, and thus cold incursions coming off Greenland to hit warm Gulf Stream waters. This period still had moderate winters and warm summers, but the new pattern of summer storms brought driving rains to northern Europe.[70] One has to wonder whether this pattern was shaped in some way by the massive volcanic eruption of 1258 and the simultaneous explosion of El Niños measured off the coast of Peru and in the Quelccaya Ice Cap. Following the Wolf and coinciding with the Spörer minimum and the beginning of the last major advance of ice rafting in the North Atlantic, the beginning of Little Ice Age I in 1400 must have been shaped by the decline of solar warmth in the northern hemisphere, combined in some way with the 1258 eruption and the massive expansion of El Niños that lasted well into the fifteenth century.[71]

[69] Loren D. Meeker and Paul A. Mayewski, "A 1400-Year High-Resolution Record of Atmospheric Circulation over the North Atlantic and Asia," *Holocene* 12 (2002), 257–66.

[70] A. Dawson et al., "Greenland (GISP2) Ice Core and Historical Indicators of Complex North Atlantic Climate Changes during the Fourteenth Century," *Holocene* 17 (2007), 427–34.

[71] Bert Rein et al., "A Major Holocene ENSO Anomaly during the Medieval Period," *GRL* 31 (2004); Lonnie G. Thompson et al., "Annually Resolved Ice Core Records of Tropical Climate Variability over the Past ~1800 Years," *Sciencexpress* April 4, 2013; Davide Zanchettin et al., "On ENSO Impacts on European Wintertime Rainfalls and the Modulation by the NAO and the Pacific Multi-Decadal Variability Described through the PDO Index," *IJC* 28 (2008), 995–1006; Vladimir N. Kryjov and Chung-Kyu Park, "Solar Modulation of the El-Niño/Southern Oscillation Impact on the Northern Hemisphere Annual Mode," *GRL* 34 (2007), L10701 (arguing for increased ENSO influence on the northern hemisphere during solar minima); Julien Emile-Geay et al., "Volcanoes and ENSO of the Past Millennium," *JClim* 21 (2008), 3134–48; Michael Mann et al., "Volcanic and Solar Forcing of the Tropical

The stormy summers of the early transition into the Little Ice Age had significant impacts across the European domain. Viking Norse – marauding along European coasts and rivers since the eight century – had settled Iceland and then Greenland between AD 860 and AD 1000. The erratic climate of the later thirteenth century began to undermine the Greenland settlements: the western Norse settlement collapsed by 1340, and soon thereafter contacts with Europe became extremely erratic. The eastern Norse settlement hung on until almost 1500, when Europeans abandoned Greenland to the Arctic ancestors of the Inuit, the expanding peoples of the Thule culture.[72] Along the coast of England and northern Europe, increased storminess brought flooding, inundating towns and consuming farmland. Then, as Bruce Campbell has powerfully explained, between 1315 and 1322, seasons of continuous rainfall destroyed the crops in the ground for several years running, bringing the Great Famine that may have killed a tenth of the total population of northern Europe. Misery affected both beast and man: during the cold, wet summer of 1316, when crops failed throughout northern Europe, a rinderpest-like disease began to spread from central Europe, reaching Ireland in 1321, probably killing half of Europe's cattle.[73]

By the time the "Little Ice Age I" began in 1400, the Black Death had already struck, sweeping through western Asia, the Mediterranean, up into northern Europe, and even south across the desert trade routes into West Africa, killing as much as half the populations in its path between 1346 and 1353. Since the turn of the twentieth century it has been generally agreed that the Black Death was the bubonic plague. The plague bacillus, *Yersinia pestis*, diverged from the less virulent soil-dwelling bacillus *Yersinia pseudotuberculosis* sometime within the past 20,000 years. It is harbored in

Pacific over the Past 1000 Years," *JClim* 18 (2005), 447–56; Drew T. Shindell and Gavin A. Schmidt, "Dynamic Winter Climate Responses to Large Tropical Eruptions since 1600," *JGR* 109 (2004), D05104.

[72] Diamond, *Collapse*, 178–276; Brian Fagan, *The Little Ice Age: How Climate Made History, 1300–1850* (New York, 2000), 66–9; Andrew W. Dugmore et al., "Cultural Adaptation, Compounding Vulnerabilities and Conjunctures in Norse Greenland," *PNAS* 109 (2012), 3658–63; Robert McGhee, "Contact between Native North Americans and the Mediaeval Norse: A Review of the Evidence," *AmAntiq* 49 (1984), 4–26. Lamb, *Climate, History, and the Modern World*, 173–7, 187–9.

[73] Campbell, "Nature as Historical Protagonist," 289, 299–305; Bruce M. S. Campbell, "Physical Shocks, Biological Hazards, and Human Impacts: The Crisis of the Fourteenth Century Revisited," in Simonetta Cavaciocchi, ed., *Le interazioni fra economia e ambiente biologico nell'Europe preindustriale. Secc. XIII-XVIII (Economic and biological interactions in pre-industrial Europe from the 13th to the 18th centuries)* (Prato, 2010), 13–32; –, "Panzootics, Pandemics, and Climatic Anomalies in the Fourteenth Century," paper in preparation for publication; Bailey, "*Per impetum maris,*" in Campbell, ed., *Before the Black Death*, 184–208; Jordan, *The Great Famine*; James A. Galloway and Jonathan S. Potts, "Marine Flooding in the Thames Estuary and Tidal River c. 1250–1450: Impact and Response," *Area* 39 (2007), 37079; Fagan, *The Little Ice Age*, 28–44. Lamb, *Climate, History, and the Modern World*, 190–9.

fleas that infest a variety of burrowing rodents, and from these reservoirs it can erupt into human populations in its bubonic, pneumonic, or septisemic forms. The bubonic plague is spread by flea bites (and perhaps body lice), pneumonic from the coughing of infected persons, and septisemic from infected blood.[74] There has been – it should be said – a dissenting body of opinion that the Black Death was simply not the plague at all. This account has been the subject of raging criticism in the past twenty years. A number of scholars dispute the diagnosis of the plague; one camp argues that it was an Ebola-like virus called hemorrhagic fever,[75] and another camp that it was an as yet unknown disease.[76] It may yet emerge that plague was a major element of a complex of diseases that assaulted the Old World in the middle of the fourteenth century.[77] In some measure, it does not really matter what the actual disease was, only that enormous numbers died from very rapidly dispersing infection.

Nonetheless, recent advances in genetic testing have found undisputed genetic markers of *Yersinia pestis* (YP) in the teeth of fourteenth-century plague victims, in France, Germany, the Netherlands, and Britain. Most diagnostically, YP DNA has been isolated in teeth and bones from the East Smithfield plague pit in London, dug specifically for the victim of the first assault of the Black Death in 1348–50, but not in a control sample from another London cemetery closed before 1348.[78] Clearly the bubonic plague

[74] Mark Achtman et al., "*Yersinia Pestis*, the Cause of the Plague, is a Recently Emerged Clone of *Yersinia Pseudotuberculosis*," *PNAS* 96 (1999), 14043–8; –, "Microevolution and History of the Plague Bacillus, *Yersinia Pestis*," *PNAS* 101 (2004), 17837–42; Xiao-Zhe Huang et al., "Current Trends in Plague Research: From Genomics to Virulence," *Clinical Medicine & Research* 4 (2006), 189–99; Saravanan Ayyadurai et al., "Body Lice, *Yersinia Pestis* Orientalis, and Black Death," *EmInfDis* 16 (2010), 892–3. On the plague in West Africa, see Gérard L. Chouin and Christopher R. Decorse, "Prelude to the Atlantic Trade: New Perspectives on Southern Ghana's Preatlantic History (800–1500)," *Journal of African History* 51 (2010), 123–45, at 143–4.

[75] Susan Scott and Christopher J. Duncan, *The Biology of Plagues: Evidence from Historical Populations* (New York, 2001); –, *Return of the Black Death: The World's Greatest Serial Killer* (Chichester, 2004).

[76] Samuel K. Cohn, Jr., *The Black Death Transformed: Disease and Culture in Early Renaissance Europe* (London, 2002); James W. Wood et al., "The Temporal Dynamics of the Fourteenth-Century Black Death: New Evidence from English Ecclesiastical Records," *Human Biology* 75 (2003), 427–48; M. Thomas et al., "Absence of *Yersinia Pestis*-Specific DNA in Human Teeth from Five European Excavations of Putative Plague Victims," *Microbiology* 150 (2004), 341–54; George Christakos and Ricardo Olea, "New Space-Time Perspectives on the Propagation Characteristics of the Black Death Epidemic and Its Relation to Bubonic Plague," *Stochastic Environmental Research and Risk Assessment* 19 (2005), 307–14; Samuel K. Cohn, Jr. and Guido Alfani, "Households and Plague in Early Modern Italy," *JInterdH* 38 (2007), 177–205.

[77] John Thielman and Francis Cate, "A Plague of Plagues: The Problem of Plague Diagnosis in Medieval England," *JInterdH* 37 (2007), 371–93.

[78] Didier Raoult et al., "Molecular Identification of 'Suicide PCR' of *Yersinia Pestis* as the Agent of Medieval Black Death," *PNAS* 97 (2000), 12800–3; Ingrid Wiechman and Gisela

in its roughly modern genetic form was at work during the Black Death. But many questions remain. Was it working synergistically with other diseases? Typhus and pneumonia come to mind. And what was its history, and the trajectory of its geographic spread?

The history of the plague bacillus is a matter of great debate. Until very recently it has been assumed that three different modern varieties of the plague – *y.p antique*, *medievalis*, and *orientalis* – defined by their capacities to ferment various sugars, caused the Justinian Plagues, the Black Death, and the wave of plague that spread from China to the western United States and elsewhere at the turn of the twentieth century. DNA tests reported in 2004 and 2007 might have collapsed this distinction, arguing that the Justinian Plague, and possibly also the Black Death, were of the *y.p. orientalis* strain.[79] On the other hand, a phylogenetic analysis of modern-occurring YP published in 2010 argued that the plague is structured by the tri-part model, with three branches running back to a common origin at least 2,600 years ago in China, diverging about 700 years ago. A part of one branch, surviving in China and Kurdistan, is seen as the bacillus involved in the Justinian Plague and the Black Death; another with a more global distribution is seen as variously potentially spread by Admiral Zheng He's fleet to East Africa, and as the source of the early twentieth century spread.[80] But in 2011, in a detailed genomic reconstruction of YP DNA from East Smithfield, another team of researchers working with new-generation DNA sequencers sharply contradicted this model. This study finds a common ancestor of all modern plague in the Black Death period (AD 1282–1343, 95 percent probability). Thus there may be no ancient root of the modern bubonic plague directly connected back to the era of the Justinian and other ancient plagues. Rather, all of the modern plague varieties emerged suddenly from a common root sometime at the turn of the fourteenth century, and they all have a very close relationship to the plague bacillus DNA found in a modern Chinese marmot population.[81]

Grupe, "Detection of *Yesrsinia Pestis* DNA in Two Early Medieval Skeletal Finds from Aschheim (Upper Bavaria, 6th Century A.D.)," *AJPA* 126 (2005), 48–55; Stephanie Haensch et al., "Distinct Clones of *Yersinia Pestis* Caused the Black Death," *PLoS Pathogens* 6 (2010), e1001134; Verena J. Schuenemann et al., "Targeted Enrichment of Ancient Pathogens Yielding the pPCP1 Plasmid of *Yestinia Pestis* from Victims of the Black Death," *PNAS* 108 (2011), E746–E552. For a useful overview of this literature, see Lester K. Little, "Plague Historians in Lab Coats," *P&P* 213 (2011), 267–90.

[79] Michel Drancourt et al., "Genotyping, Orientalis-like *Yersinia Pestis*, and Plague Epidemics," *EmInfDis* 10 (2004), 1585–92; –, "*Yersinia Pestis* Orientalis in Remains of Ancient Plague Patients," *EmInfDis* 13 (2007), 332–3.

[80] Giovanna Morelli et al., "*Yersinia Pestis* Genome Sequencing Identifies Patterns of Global Phylogentica Diversity," *Nature Genetic* 42 (2010), 1140–3.

[81] Kirsten Bos et al., "A Draft Genome of *Yersina Pestis* from Victims of the Black Death," *Nature* 478 (2011), 506–10.

This battle among the geneticists is not over, because the most recent study is being bitterly contested.[82] But a few possible scenarios of a "final" model might be suggested. First, the standard "single disease" model might be upheld with further work, especially when DNA studies can be conducted on victims of ancient epidemics. Alternatively, the new model of a sudden medieval eruption might prevail. Exactly what this model means for a disease history is still up for grabs; it simply establishes that the YP DNA from East Smithfield, a Chinese marmot, and the modern plague bacillus are very closely related. It does not exclude the possibility that the plagues of the ancient world were extinct versions of something quite similar, and it does not necessarily require that that the plague erupted first in East Asia. This and other studies are suggesting, very importantly, that the plague had a complex, contorted history, with many different eruptions, die-backs, and extinctions.[83] It may well turn out that the plague – or something like it – has emerged from the natural background of soil bacteria several times in global history, but this is simply speculation.

This struggle over plague genetics wildly complicates a long-standing debate about the geographic history of the plague. The long-established story has the Black Death emerging as bubonic plague somewhere in East Asia, and traveling east with the Silk Route caravans to the Black Sea, from where at the siege of the Genoese trading port of Kaffa by the Mongol Golden Horde it was injected into the European system in 1347.[84] The most recent survey of the spread and impact of the Black Death, by Ole Benedictow, challenges this traditional account of origins and diffusion. Advancing one side of a debate that runs back to the 1970s, he disputes the model of a sudden transfer of the plague all the way across Asia. He argues from newly considered Russian sources that – contrary to the traditional account – the plague had its origins in rodent colonies in the region somewhere between the Caspian Sea and the Crimea and infested the 1346 Mongol siege lines, first infecting the besiegers and then the besieged, whose flight across the Black Sea carried the plague into Europe. Critics of the classic Silk Route model of diffusion argue that its origins lie in unexamined prejudices about a "filthy East," and see no obvious human mechanism that would allow the plague to move quickly between the widely separated trading cities in Central Asia.[85] Combined with the

---

[82] Yujun Cui et al., "Historical Variations in Mutation Rate in an Epidemic Pathogen, *Yersinia Pestis,*" *PNAS* 110 (2013), 577–82; Ewan Callaway, "The Black Death Decoded," *Nature* 478 (2011), 444–6; Nicholas Wade, "Scientists Solve Puzzle of Black Death's DNA," *NYT* October 12, 2011.

[83] Bos et al., "A Draft Genome"; Haensch, "Distinct Clones."

[84] McNeill, *Plagues and Peoples*, 141–9.

[85] Ole J. Benedictow, *The Black Death, 1346–1353: The Complete History* (Woodbridge, Eng., 2004), 48–54. See also Timothy May, *The Mongols in World History* (London, 2012), 199–210. For earlier arguments, see John Norris, "East or West? The Geographic Origin

recent genetic arguments for a sudden medieval eruption, his arguments have some interesting implications. The Chinese marmot is not definitive proof for an East Asian origin, and a strong case has been made for the origins of the medieval plague from natural sources in the region running from Kurdistan and Azerbaijan north toward the southern Russian steppe and the Crimea, where the first outbreak occurs. It is not impossible that the medieval plague erupted out of a natural host as the troops of the Golden Horde were excavating their siege lines around Kaffa. If the plague had its origins in western Asia, it was not – Benedictow argues – the source of the epidemics that hit China in 1331. And, if the plague spread from the Caspian-Crimean region during a Mongol siege – rather than traversing the Silk Road – it was the result of a contingent combination of accidents, and not a great confluence of diseases across the length of Eurasia, as William McNeill classically argued.[86]

The climate context of the Black Death may add another element of contingency, a point stressed in the recent genomic reconstruction of medieval YP.[87] Bruce Campbell sees this climate-disease connection beginning with wet and miserable European cattle: during the cold wet summer of 1316, when crops failed throughout northern Europe, a rinderpest-like disease began to spread from central Europe, reaching Ireland in 1321, probably killing half of Europe's cattle. He further argues that a series of harsh years between 1348 and 1353 set the stage for the advance of the plague in western Eurasia. This cold snap appears slightly earlier in the tree ring record, between 1343 and 1349.[88] But this mid-century cooling certainly set the stage for the reception of the plague across Europe, disrupting harvests and

of the Black Death," *Bulletin of the History of Medicine* 51 (1977), 1–24. This article was followed by a brief and unconvincing critique by Michael Dols, and a long response by Norris. See *Bulletin of the History of Medicine* 52 (1978), 112–20. See also Uli Schamilglou, "Preliminary Remarks on the Role of Disease in the History of the Golden Horde," *Central Asian Survey* 12 (1993), 447–57; and Andrew Noymer, "Contesting the Cause and Severity of the Black Death: A Review Essay," *PopDevR* 33 (2007), 616–27. For further critique of the rapid spread model, see Timothy Brook, *The Troubled Empire: China in the Yuan and Ming Dynasties* (Cambridge, MA, 2010), 64–7. On the problems of the geographic representation of the spread of the Black Death, see David C. Mengel, "A Plague on Bohemia? Mapping the Black Death," *P&P* 211 (2011), 3–34.

[86] Benedictow, *The Black Death*, 31–4, 44–54; McNeill, *Plagues and Peoples*, 134, and passim. For a description of the modern distribution of natural plague vectors and reservoirs in Asia, see David T. Dennis et al., *Plague Manual: Epidemiology, Distribution, Surveillance, and Control* (Geneva: Word Health Organization, 1999), 72–9. Charles Creighton's detailed discussion of the evidence on famine and pestilence in fourteenth century China argues that the first outbreak of the plague in China was in 1352, not 1331. Charles Creighton, *A History of Epidemics in Britain from A.D. 664 to the Extinction of the Plague* (Cambridge, 1901), 152–4.

[87] Bos et al., "A Draft Genome."

[88] Campbell, "Nature as Historical Protagonist," 289, 299–305; Campbell, "Physical Shocks"; Campbell, "Panzootics, Pandemics, and Climatic Anomalies in the Fourteenth Century."

food supplies and thus further compromising the nutritional status of the European poor.

If Campbell's argument suggests a climatic context for the arrival of the Black Death, Central Asian climatic patterns suggest that something similar might explain its origins, if we assume that it came out of the west Asian steppe, and not China (see Figure III.10). The same southward shift in the Atlantic westerlies that brought famine and rinderpest to Europe during the 1320s hit arid Central Asia during the 1330s and 1340s, and may have altered the local ecologies supporting marmots, which act as key wild hosts to the plague. A long-established view is that the first manifestation of the Black Death was in a pestilence that hit the town of Issyk-Kul in Kyrgyzstan in 1338–9.[89] Though low-resolution data from Issyk-Kul does not show high humidity until the seventeenth century, it lies in the path of the westerlies, and high-resolution sites to the east and west show strong indications of wet conditions starting in the 1330–40s.[90] Thus it is possible that the sudden onset of wet conditions drove a spike in native YP-bearing rodents, launching the Black Death.

In any event, virtually any combination of explanations – plague or non-plague, trans-Asiatic or Caspian, climate driven or not – the Black Death seems to have been a fundamentally exogenous event. It came from outside the routine structures and trajectories of the sociodemographic-economic systems to devastate the peoples of greater Eurasia. Density of population may not have been a factor either, if Benedictow is right and the plague was more devastating in the countryside, or if he was wrong, and it spread along the oases of the Silk Route. Perhaps the nutritional status of its victims was significant, but perhaps not.

Here Benedictow's massive analysis of Black Death mortality has something suggestive to say, and it is supported by detailed analysis of the plague burials in London and Denmark. Throughout his analysis, Benedictow has attempted to calculate the relative mortality rates of the propertied and unpropertied across the medieval Mediterranean and northern Europe.

[89] R. Pollitzer, *Plague* (Geneva, 1954), 13–14; Philip Zeigler, *The Black Death* (New York, 1969), 25–6.

[90] Chen et al., "Moisture Changes over the Last Millennium in Arid Central Asia." Chen's evidence for south-shifting westerlies in the early Little Ice Age puts in doubt arguments that suggest that a waning East Asian monsoon was a climate trigger for the Black Death: see Kyrre Linné Kausrad et al., "Modeling the Epidemiological History of Plague in Central Asia: Palaeoclimatic Forcing of a Disease System over the Past Millennium," *BMC Biology* 8 (2010), and Campbell, "Panzootics, Pandemics," 22–3. There is also a possible volcanic connection. In a Greenland ice layer dated to 1344 there is a significant mark of volcanic sulphur (46ppb), the largest between the enormous marker at 1258 (323ppb), and another at 1459 (56ppb). Zielinski, "Record of Volcanism since 7000B.C." Keys, *Catastrophe*, and Sallares, "Ecology, Evolution, and Epidemiology of Plague," in Little, ed., *Plague and the End of Antiquity*, offer different models for the 536 eruption and 541 commencement of the Justinian Plague.

Overall, in a series of comparable records, he finds that the poor suffered a supermortality of roughly 5–10 percent over their propertied and even elite neighbors, neighbors who lived in well-built stone structures, were better fed and clothed, and had larger households that increased the odds of adult survival, shaping the fate of small children, who died of starvation if left alone.[91] Given that the wealth differential was far greater than 5–10 percent, it seems clear that the poor did not suffer proportionate to their poverty – and that wealth did not protect disproportionately the more sufficient. Similarly, an analysis of a sample of London plague victims – compared with a slightly earlier sample of routine attritional mortality from urban Denmark – suggests that the plague did not simply strike down the weak and disabled. Looking at the presence of various bone lesions that indicate frailty from long-term ill health or bouts of malnutrition, Sharon DeWitte and James Woods find that – while the plague victims were somewhat selective for indications of frailty – they were significantly less so than their Danish counterparts dying in routine, nonepidemic circumstances. This is very close to a smoking gun demonstrating that the Black Death was an exogenous event, not primarily shaped by Malthusian forces.[92]

Thus these very different approaches and evidence suggest that the Black Death sliced through populations virtually indiscriminately, with no overwhelming bias toward the poor and malnourished. Yet another telling sign of the survival of the poor is the rapid filling of the emptied farm tenancies by lucky survivors: the catastrophe of the epidemics was followed by a rapid reshuffling, in which people of little property took up inheritances from their unlucky but propertied relations, or moved some considerable distances to find favorable lands to rent. The Black Death opened the way for the poor to rise, much to the detriment of the old order.[93]

* * *

Their fortunes, and those of all of the survivors of the wider global crises that cracked the epoch of the Middle Ages, is the opening problem for the next chapter, as peoples around the world adjusted to centuries of the worst climatic conditions since the Younger Dryas. At this point we should briefly review what we have learned about the human condition over the forty-four centuries between the first emergence of the state and the Black Death.

---

[91] Benedictow, *The Black Death*, 263; Morineau, "Malthus: There and Back," 143–4.

[92] Sharon N. DeWitte and James W. Wood, "Selectivity of Black Death Mortality with Respect to Preexisting Health," *PNAS* 105 (2008), 1436–41; see also Beverley J. Margerison and Christopher J. Knusel, "Paleodemographic Comparison of a Catastrophic and an Attritional Death Assemblage," *AJPA* 119 (2002), 134–43.

[93] Benedictow, *The Black Death*, 262–3; John Hatcher, "England in the Aftermath of the Black Death," *P&P* 144 (1994), 3–35; Barbara A. Hanawalt, *The Ties That Bound: Peasant Families in Medieval England* (New York, 1986), 124–40.

What of Thomas Malthus's understandings, which would appear to have taken quite a beating in these pages? I would suggest that Malthus was indeed right, but in ways he might not have been able to imagine. Fundamentally, Malthus argued that – absent significant technological achievement – population would eventually be checked, either through the preventive checks of human intervention or the positive checks of human misery. What I have been suggesting here is that – over the *long durée* of Late Holocene history – both positive checks and technological achievements operated far beyond the range that he and most subsequent investigators have imagined or proposed. Rather than the hair-trigger balance between population growth and imminent misery that is so central to contemporary Malthusian analyses, the evidence that I have explored here suggests a more "punctuated" model – in exactly the sense established for the paleo-world by Niles Eldridge and Stephen Gould. Outside of small societies in marginally ecological circumstances, the great preponderance of the human condition since 3000 BC has been an experience of relative continuities interrupted by overwhelming impacts erupting from natural sources. Rather than endogenous pressures, exogenous forces time and again explain the great "collapses" of the ancient and medieval worlds.

Here I should be as clear as possible: I am not claiming that ancient and medieval peoples achieved dramatic technological breakthroughs that radically altered their relationship with the natural worlds. There certainly were fundamental, if gradual breakthroughs, most important the emergence and spread of iron metallurgy and rotary power, which allowed societies to grow to unprecedented sizes, when natural conditions permitted. A gradual maturing of agrarian systems, shaped by a constant, slow Boserupian innovation driven by and driving population growth, occasionally brought conditions of actual "economic growth" to discrete populations who mobilized and benefited from state power. Their lives were relatively uncomfortable and perhaps unpleasant; their societies and economies were relatively sustainable – and resilient. But – as in the paleo-world – these conditions of demographic and occasional economic growth fundamentally required favorable natural conditions. While a new historical ecology is suggesting that ancient and medieval peoples did not degrade their environments quite as much we have thought, the new climate science has allowed us to precisely measure the impact of the abrupt climate reversals that destroyed these favorable conditions. As important, the new climate science has destroyed the refuge of skeptical historians, who traditionally discount the impact of natural forces because they presumably operated as an unknowable constant. These natural forces are now "knowable," and they were not "constant." Finally, I have sketched some of the highlights of a parallel reassessment of the scale and penetration of epidemic disease, and the renewed appreciation for its importance as a similarly exogenous force in human history. What I may not have conveyed quite sufficiently is the degree to which the exogenous natural forces of climate and epidemic were mediated by the eminently endogenous human capacity for warfare. As an increasing number of scholars are arguing, climatic reversal, epidemic disease, and war have long been an unholy trinity: climate reversal brought violent struggles over resources, and the march of armies moved and transmuted exotic biota into epidemic disaster. But the operation of these apocalyptic horsemen across these millennia was not random but patterned, and patterned fundamentally by the pulse of the natural world.[94]

Within a century of the first hints of the Little Ice Age – bringing Asian drought and American El Niño – and the onslaught of the Black Death, the first elements of a very new departure were taking shape. The beginnings of the transition to modernity – with its global integration and revolutionary transformations of technology and energy – are the subject of the next chapter.

---

[94] See the studies coauthored by David D. Zhang, cited in Chapter 6, note 12; and Thomas F. Homer-Dixon, *Environment, Scarcity, and Violence* (Princeton, NJ, 1999).

PART IV

INTO THE MODERN CONDITION

List of Figures and Tables for Part IV: Into the Modern Condition

Figures

Tables

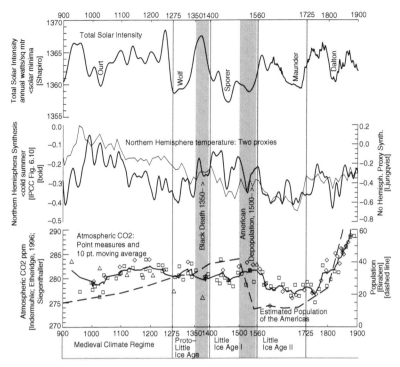

Figure IV.1. The Little Ice Age, disease, and New World depopulation, 900–1900.

Against the backdrop of the solar forcings and temperature readings of the Little Ice Age, the drop in atmospheric CO$_2$ from ~280 pp to ~275 ppm might well be attributable to oceanic feedbacks driven by climate change. But the collapse of native population in the Americas after 1500, William Ruddiman suggests, might have itself caused this CO$_2$ decline, given the regrowth of forests, especially in tropical regions. This raises the question of whether population, collapse, forest regrowth, and CO$_2$ drawdown might have intensified the Little Ice Age around 1560. Note the relatively minor drop in CO$_2$ after the Black Death.

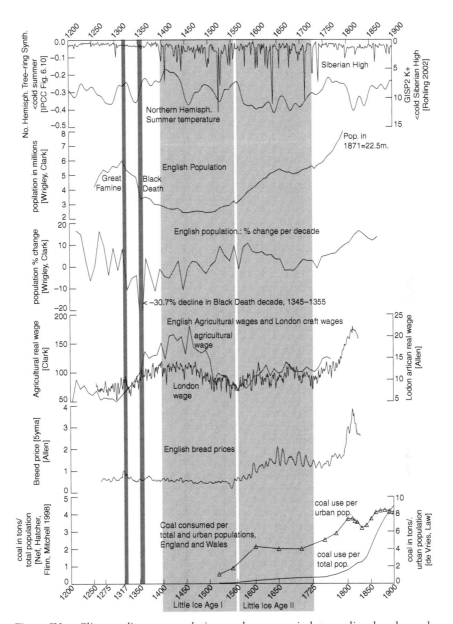

Figure IV.2. Climate, disease, population, and economy in late medieval-early modern England, 1200–1900.

After the Black Death and the onset of the early stages of Little Ice Age English population and wages varied inversely. Then in the Little Ice proper, after 1560, population and bread prices rose sharply for a century, while the consumption of coal relative to urban population shot up.

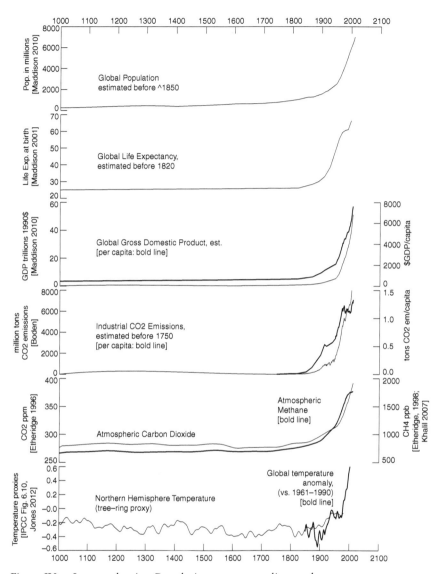

Figure IV.3. Into modernity: Population, economy, climate change, 1000–present.

All the indicators of modernity – population, life expectancy, industrial economies, atmospheric CO2, and global temperatures – all moved up suddenly and virtually simultaneously – in the "j-curve" postulated by climate scientist Michael Mann.

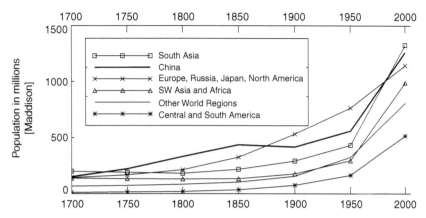

Figure IV.4. Estimated global populations by world regions, 1700–present.

World populations have grown in two phases since 1700. In the first phase, China and the North Atlantic region, grew from 1700, though China's growth stalled in the middle of the nineteenth century. In the second phase, since 1950, population growth slowed somewhat the developed regions of North Atlantic and Japan, while the developing world, including China, surged.

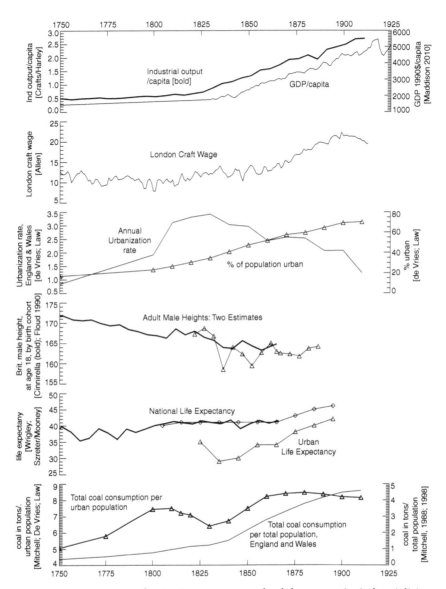

Figure IV.5. Economy, urbanization, energy, and adult stature in industrializing England, 1750–1925.

While English cities grew dramatically from 1800 to the 1850s, the industrial economy began to grow significantly only after 1825, and wages lagged and living conditions worsened. The heights of men at age eighteen fell through the first half of the nineteenth century, and urban life expectancy dropped dramatically from the 1820s to the 1840s. Strikingly during these decades national coal consumption relative per urban population dropped by a third.

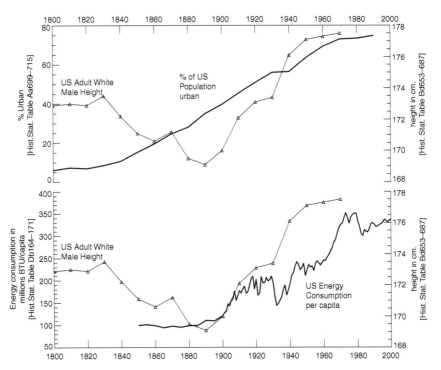

Figure IV.6. Urbanization, energy, and adult stature in the United States, 1800–2000.

Not unlike in Britain, adult male height in the United States dropped dramatically through the nineteenth century with urbanization. Strikingly, its recovery after the 1880s tracked the rising national consumption of fossil energy.

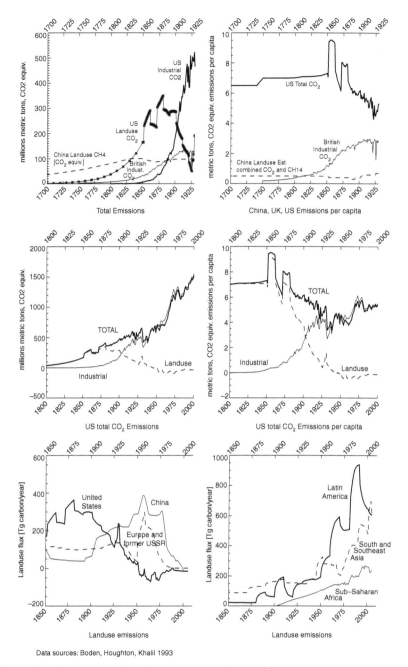

Data sources: Boden, Houghton, Khalil 1993

Figure IV.7. Industrial and land-use emissions by world regions, 1750–present.

In the mid-to-late nineteenth century, landuse in the United States were the single most important source of greenhouse gas emissions in the world, surpassing estimated emissions from Chinese agriculture in the 1830s, and surpassed by industrial emissions around 1900. Strikingly, the mid-nineteenth century was "dirtiest" period in U.S. emissions per capita. Landuse emissions spiked after World War II in Europe, Soviet Union, and China, but generally the developed world has seen a steady decline, by comparison with Latin America, Su-Saharan Africa, and Southern Asia.

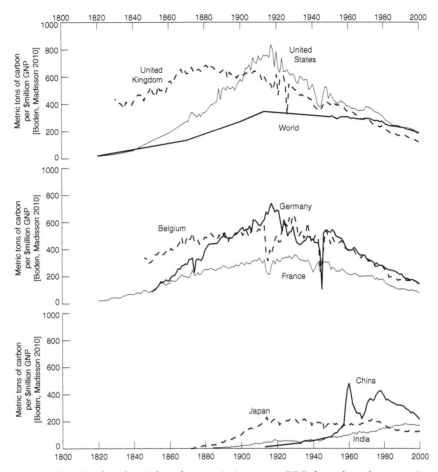

Figure IV.8. Total industrial carbon emissions per GDP by selected economies, 1800–2000.

The emission of CO$_2$ from fossil fuels per GDP reached different peaks in the economic history of different global regions: around the 1880s in the United Kingdom, 1920 in the United States France, Germany, and Japan, and double peak in the late 1950s and the late 1970s in China.

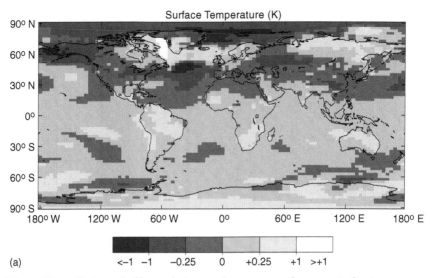

Figure IV.9a. Estimated effects of nineteenth-century anthropogenic forcings.

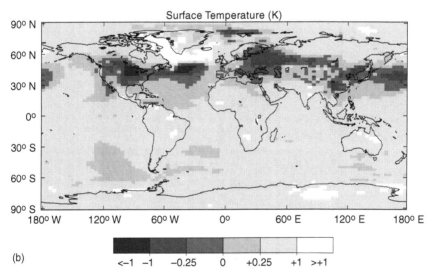

Figure IV.9b. Estimated effects of twentieth-century anthropogenic forcings.

The best estimate of anthropogenic warming by Simon Tett and his team suggests that by 1900 the equatorial regions had begun to warm (lighter shades), but the Arctic and the industrial north mid-latitudes were somewhat cooler (darker shades) than they had been in 1800. By 2000 the entire earth was showing signed of warming except the industrial belt running from North America to China, apparently protected by a local haze of sulfate aerosols.

Figures redrawn by James DeGrand from Tett, pp. 25, 27, with the permission of the Metoffice.

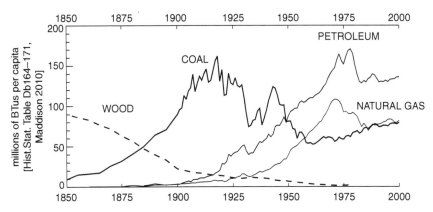

Figure IV.10. U.S. energy consumption per capita, by fuel, 1850–2000.

After a decisive energy transition from wood to coal around 1880, and what appeared to be a transition around 1950 from coal to petroleum and natural gas, coal consumption began to grow again in the 1960s, filling an enormous demand for electrical generation.

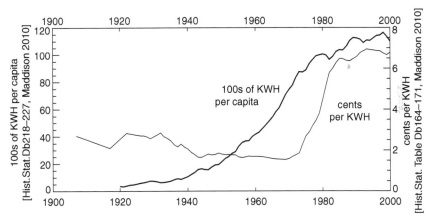

Figure IV.11. U.S. electrical consumption and cost, 1900–2000.

From the 1930s to the 1970s, electrical generation per capita in the United States rose dramatically, while costs per kilowatt hour fell. Then in the 1970s improvements in generator efficiency stalled, costs rose dramatically, and generation per capita slowed.

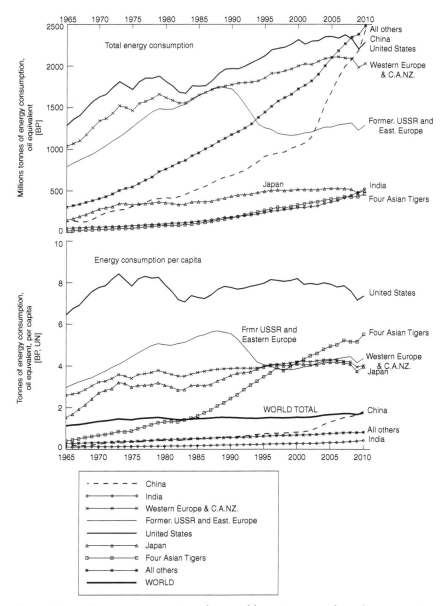

Figure IV.12. Energy consumption by world regions, total and per capita, 1965–2010.

The United States led the world in total consumption of energy until roughly 2008, when it was surpassed by China and a large group of developing countries. The United States still leads in consumption per capita, but is down somewhat from a peak in the early 1970s. The collapse of the Soviet Union is registered here in a massive cut in energy consumption. The surge in total consumption by "all others," in the context of zero growth per capita, indicates that energy use in these countries is simply driven by population growth.

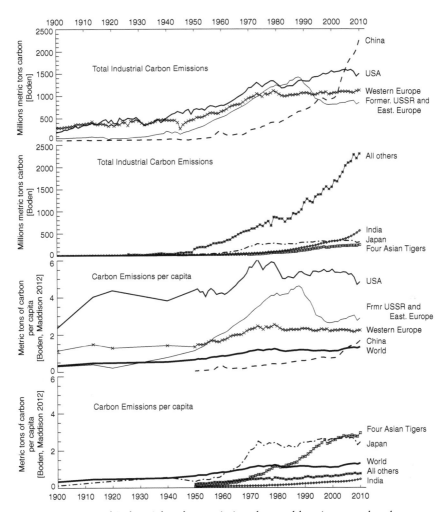

Figure IV.13. Total industrial carbon emissions by world regions, total and per capita, 1900–2000.

Industrial carbon emissions roughly track energy consumption, but can be tracked back to 1900. Here the contrast between total emissions, and emissions per capita is immediately apparent.

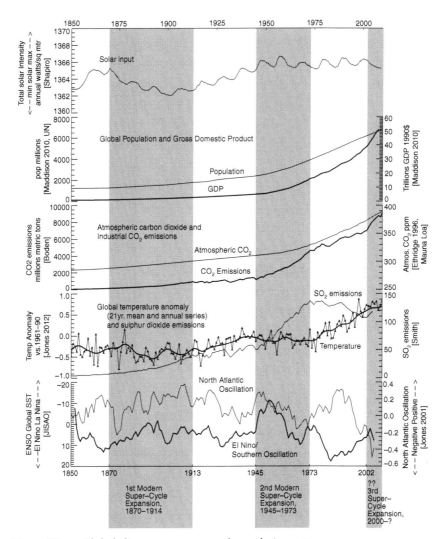

Figure IV.14. Global climate, economy, and population, 1850–2010.

Looking back to 1850, it is apparent that there have been two phases to recent global warming: 1915 to 1945, and 1975 to present, with a reasonably stable period in between Solar warming – and stalling of sulfate emissions both seem to account for the first period of warming, during the world wars and the Depression. During the post-war supercycle expansion down to 1973 solar influence was stable, but both CO$_2$ and sulfates rose sharply, producing no net gain in warming. Since 1973 solar influence has been stable, CO$_2$ rising irregularly, but sulfates have been falling, due to both regulation and the collapse of the Soviet Union. The result has been a sharp three-decade increase in global temperatures. One of the results may be a disruption of the typical relationship between the North Atlantic Oscillation and the ENSO systems.

TABLE IV.1. Coal consumption by sector, United Kingdom, 1816–1913

	Coal consumption per population, United Kingdom, in tons, by sector			Annual percent increase of coal consumption per population, United Kingdom, in tons		
	Domestic household use	General manufacture	Iron and steel	Domestic household use (%)	General manufacture (%)	Iron and steel (%)
1816	0.48	0.25	0.10			
1830	0.45	0.29	0.15	−0.4	1.2	4.0
1840	0.43	0.37	0.27	−0.3	2.4	7.7
1855	0.54	0.65	0.56	1.6	5.1	7.2
1869	0.63	0.97	0.86	1.2	3.5	3.8
1887	0.77	1.26	0.74	1.2	1.7	−0.8
1903	0.76	1.47	0.66	−0.1	1.0	−0.6
1913	0.77	1.49	0.81	0.1	0.2	2.2

Note: Coal consumption in the United Kingdom shifted from urban domestic heating to manufacturing by the mid-nineteenth century, surging in iron and steel production in the 1830s and, with the introduction of high-pressure steam engines, in the 1840s and 1850s.
Sources: Coal consumption: Mitchell, (1988); Population: Mitchell, (1998).

TABLE IV.2. Industrial horsepower and railroad miles, United Kingdom/Great Britain, 1824–1900

	1000 horsepower in textile factories United Kingdom		Horsepower in textile factories per 100,000 population, United Kingdom		Miles of Railroads in Great Britain,	Miles of railroads in Great Britain per million population, England, Wales, Scotland
	Water power	Steam power	Water power	Steam power		
1824/25		40		1.8	27	1.8
1838	27	72	1.0	2.8	742	41.6
1850	25	108	0.9	3.9	6,084	294.3
1856	23	136	0.8	4.9	7,650	347.1
1861	28	372	1.0	12.7	9,446	400.4
1867	30	323	1.0	10.6	12,319	494.5
1870	26	462	0.8	14.8	13,500	522.4
1900					18,680	509.1

Note: Railroads expanded dramatically in Britain in the 1840s, steam-driven horsepower in textile mills in the later 1850s.
Sources: Horsepower, 1825:Musson; Horsepower, 1838–1870: Mitchell, (1988); Railroad miles: Mitchell, with Deane, (1971), 225–6. Population: Mitchell, (1998).

TABLE IV.3. The epidemiological transition, environmental impacts and hazards, and the industrial revolutions/modern super-cycles

	Stages of the Epidemiological Transition	Environmental Hazards/Impacts							Industrial Revolutions and Modern Super-Cycles
Agrarian Holocene		Traditional Local Hazards: sanitation, biomass smoke							
1450	1. First efforts to control crisis pandemics		North Atlantic Mortality Decline		North Atlantic Local Hazards				
1720	2. Control of endemic smallpox								Household/shop proto-industrialization
1760									1st Industrial Revolution: [low to high pressure steam]
1820	3. Control of Childhood Diseases	North Atlantic Urbanization Regional Industrial Impacts		North Atlantic Fertility Decline					
1870	Onset of Control of Tropical Diseases					North Atlantic Regional Hazards		Developing World Local Hazards	1st Modern Super-Cycle: 2nd Industrial Revolution (steel, electrical, chemical)
1914									1st Great Interruption
1945		Global Atmospheric-Biospheric Impacts	Developing World Mortality Decline						2nd Modern Super-Cycle: The postwar recovery and boom
1960	4. Advanced Medical Science: Increased Longevity			Developing World Fertility Decline			Global Impacts		
1973–2000								Developing World Regional Hazards	2nd Great Interruption
Early 21st century									3rd Industrial Revolution: Electronic, Biotech
									3rd Modern Super-Cycle?

TABLE IV.4. Economy, demography, and emissions: Europe and the United States, 1850–1925

Country	Percent Urban [cities of 10,000+] 1890	Per Capita GDP (1990 International Geary-Khamis dollars)				Infant Mortality (deaths under the age of one year, per 1,000 live births)				Crude Birth Rates (births per 1,000 women)				CO_2 emissions in metric tons/capita			Electrical generation in Kilowatt hrs/capita 1925
		1850	1875	1900	1925	1850	1875	1900	1925	1850	1875	1900	1925	1875	1900	1925	
United States	27.6%	$1,806	$2,599	$4,091	$6,282			149	71		30.7	32.3	24.3	0.82	2.37	4.01	528
Switzerland	16.0%	$1,488	$2,645	$3,833	$5,388		193	139	60		36.5	28.2	18.5	0.13	0.47	0.53	1020
United Kingdom	55.0%	$2,330	$3,434	$4,492	$5,144	158	149	147	72		36.2	29.1	18.7	2.26	2.78	2.80	269
Netherlands	33.4%	$2,371	$2,880	$3,424	$5,031	190	203	144	59	36.8	33.0	32.0	24.5	0.39	0.78	1.24	181
Belgium	34.8%	$1,847	$2,861	$3,731	$4,666	151	153	153	97	33.0	32.3	28.5	18.4	1.39	2.02	2.74	282
Denmark	23.6%	$1,767	$2,112	$3,017	$4,378	141	138	126	82	29.3	31.4	29.7	20.8	0.21	0.56	0.93	111
France	25.9%	$1,597	$2,219	$2,876	$4,166	164	172	148	92	26.7	25.4	21.7	18.8	0.47	0.87	1.44	274
Germany	28.2%	$1,428	$2,112	$2,985	$3,532	294	261	208	109	35.6	39.1	35.5	20.3	0.68	1.64	1.99	322
Austria	15.8%	$1,650	$2,112	$2,882	$3,367	251	256	221	128	37.5	39.0	36.5	19.8	0.45	1.26	0.79	325
Sweden	13.7%	$1,289	$1,973	$2,561	$3,233	151	130	95	59	31.3	30.5	26.7	17.5	0.14	0.49	0.58	607
Italy	21.2%	$1,350	$1,835	$1,785	$2,921		215	168	118	31.3	36.9	33.5	28.1	0.03	0.11	0.22	165
Norway	16.7%	$956	$1,550	$1,877	$2,863	109	104	88	51	31.5	31.0	29.6	20.1	0.16	0.51	0.75	2548
Czechoslovakia	~16%	$1,079	$1,551	$1,729	$2,606	254	260	233	146	40.0	39.8	35.2	25.2		1.00	0.96	145
Ireland	18.0%				$2,573		97	102	70		30.2	23.2	20.8	0.02		0.55	
Spain	26.8%	$1,079	$1,496	$1,786	$2,451		195	175	138		35.8	34.8	29.2	0.05	0.16	0.23	69
Finland		$911	$1,211	$1,668	$2,328		167	135	92	35.8	37.0	32.9	23.6	0.01	0.06	0.14	163
Hungary	17.6%			$1,682	$2,279	252		215	180		43.5	38.9	27.7		0.37	0.33	53
Poland	14.6%			$1,536					163				33.5		0.70	0.50	63
Romania	14.3%			$1,415			298	199	197			40.2	36.5		0.03	0.19	18
Greece	14.0%	$816		$1,351	$2,140				92	35.0		25.7		0.01	0.02	0.09	22
Portugal	12.7%	$923	$959	$1,302	$1,446				146	33.5		30.9	32.0	0.07	0.12	0.13	24
USSR	9.3%		$943	$1,237	$1,370		266	260	178		50.4	49.1	42.7	0.02	0.16	0.09	18
Yugoslavia	~4%			$902	$1,198			154	144				34.6		0.02	0.15	0
Bulgaria	11.2%			$1,223	$922						40.5	40.1	36.0		0.02	0.09	5
Albania				$685								40.8	36.0				
Means of European data	20%	$1,430	$1,985	$2,051	$2,947		192	156	106		33	29	24	0.38	0.64	0.75	304

The demographic transition – declining infant mortality and declining birth rates – in late-nineteenth and early-twentieth century Europe and the United States was tied directly economic growth, electrical consumption, and CO_2 emissions.
Sources: Urban population: Weber; GDP and Population: Madisson; Infant Mortality and Crude Birth Rate: Chesnais; CO_2 emissions: Boden, et al., Electrical generation: Mitchell (1998).

10

Climate, Demography, Economy, and Polity in the Late Medieval–Early Modern World, 1350–1700

The epoch between the Black Death and the onset of the Industrial Revolution was the fundamental hinge of human history. During the three and a half centuries between 1350 and 1700, the path of the human condition was shaped by a final florescence of the patterns that had consolidated after the last Hallstatt solar crisis and the Old World Iron Age and by a profound deflection toward the explosive expansions, capacities, and perils of our modern condition.

Perhaps because of this epoch's fundamentally contradictory, transitional nature, again we have a problem with labels and definitions. Traditionally, in chronologies defined by European history, this era consists of the Late Middle Ages, from 1350 to 1500, and the early modern period, from 1500 to 1815. Obviously, no one at the time would have recognized their respective "lateness" or "earliness," though they might well have sensed enduring continuity and new departures. But in hindsight we can see broad parallel shifts in societies around the globe, in a wave front of advance that looks more like that of the ancient world than it does that of the Middle Ages. These three centuries saw not just a recovery from the Black Death in Eurasia and the medieval megadroughts in parts of the tropics, but a long surge of population growth, trade, Smithian economic growth, and the consolidation of the authority and reach of state governance. Perhaps the entire period from the recovery from the Black Death to the first launch of the steam engine could be called "late archaic," or better yet, "late organic," because from 1700 forward we can see the beginnings of the mineral energy economy.

But this "late organic era" also saw a profoundly new geopolitical – indeed global ecological – reality. For the first time in world history since the Paleolithic dispersals, the peoples and ecologies of the world united into a global commercial and political economy, driven by the inhabitants of a peripheral yet geographically favored corner of Eurasia. Rising populations and cultural energies would shape the critical synergy of urbanization and global trade and empire building. These would be the first critical steps beyond the Smithian "efflorescences" of limited and episodic economic growth that had characterized the human condition in the ancient and medieval worlds.[1] In Europe, but particularly in England, a perfect storm of demographic, ecological, political, and cultural factors drove a world-historical divergence, in which a small people suddenly mobilized energy from far beyond the local limits of sun, soil, and annual biomass. Such would be the roots of a global divergence that would have devastating impacts in the New World and that would powerfully shape our modern condition. And both the "late organic" consolidation and the early modern rupture would unfold in the context of the most recent Hallstatt solar minimum, the Little Ice Age, posing enormous challenges for states and economies. The results would profoundly shape our current condition.

* * *

Population in and beyond the Third Age of Epidemics, 1300–1800

We should begin this examination of the early modern transition with a review of the estimated growth of global populations, from the efforts of French demographer Jean-Nöel Biraben and others.[2] Here I adopt the fiction that there have been three "ages of epidemics," though there probably have been more. The first, described in Chapter 7, marked the end of the Near Eastern/Mediterranean Bronze Age civilizations; the second and third, described in Chapters 8 and 9, marked the crises of the ancient and medieval worlds. Just as the ancient plagues lingered on for centuries, so too the Black Death had aftershocks of plague and other maladies that continued to ravage Old World populations until the end of the seventeenth century. Nonetheless, global populations again rose to unprecedented numbers. Where population may have doubled to ~440 million during the seven and a half centuries from the Dark Ages to the eve of the Black Death, it tripled to almost a billion between the late fourteenth century and 1800. Since 1800, the modern growth of population has taken us to our current condition, at more than 7 billion people around the world. If the trajectory of human populations is shaped like a hockey stick, the long, slow climb from the Paleolithic being the metaphorical stick handle and the short, sudden expansion of the modern age the jutting blade, the epoch between the Black

---

[1] Jack A. Goldstone, "Efflorescences and Economic Growth in World History: Rethinking the 'Rise of the West' and the Industrial Revolution," *JWH* 13 (2002), 323–90; Eric L. Jones, *Growth Recurring: Economic Change in World History* (Ann Arbor, MI, 2000 [1988]).

[2] These comments are based on the figures developed by Jean-Noël Biraben, "Essai sur l-Évolution du Nombre des Hommes," *Population* 34 (1979), 13–24, as extended to 2000 in David Christian, *Maps of Time: An Introduction to Big History* (Berkeley, CA, 2004), 344–5; with some numbers interpolated, and the data for China from 1400 to 1700 substituted from Colin McEvedy and Richard Jones, *Atlas of World Population History* (New York, 1979), 171.

Death and the onset of the Industrial Revolution is the heel, where everything suddenly changed.

If the aggregate is one of a collective expansion, the details tell a different story. Populations in different global regions had sharply divergent trajectories over these four centuries, reflecting fundamental reshaping of the global political economy, in what was the first age of globalization (see Figure III.2). The Old World core regions of China, India, Southwest Asia, and Europe maintained and widened their lead on the rest of the world, though not without certain stresses. China and India grew the most rapidly after the crises of the thirteenth and fourteenth centuries, China suffering a serious crisis in the seventeenth century, but massively expanding in the eighteenth; India apparently surviving the seventeenth century to stagnate in the eighteenth. Slowly recovering from the Black Death, Europe expanded, if not on quite the trajectory of China, staggering in the seventeenth century, recovering and expanding in the eighteenth. Certain other Asian regions – specifically Japan and Southeast Asia – expanded as well. Across the Eurasian continent, then, the early modern period through 1700 followed a roughly common trajectory of a general rise in population and economic dynamism until a seventeenth-century crisis. But if they suffered during the seventeenth century, most Old World polities survived intact: social and political formations were much more adaptive and resilient in the face of the Little Ice Age than had been the Bronze Age palace states that collapsed with the last Hallstatt minimum of 1200–700 BC.

There were, however, losers in the population race, reflecting the new balance of power in the early modern world. While we have to assume that populations grew in the Americas following the waning of the medieval megadroughts, the sudden reconnection of the Old and New Worlds after 1492 brought population collapse in the Americas under an assault of war, enslavement, disease, and ecological disruption. Similarly, population in sub-Saharan Africa was advancing on a trajectory roughly coequal with that of the population in Europe, but by the seventeenth century, populations in parts of the sub-Saharan region began to decline with the onslaught of the slave trade. And, as dramatically and importantly, the populations of Southwest Asia and North Africa, now unified under various Islamic regimes, stagnated after AD 1000, oscillating between 30 million and 40 million from the end of the ancient world into the nineteenth century. Once the center of global population concentrations in antiquity, this greater "Middle East" running from Morocco to Istanbul to Afghanistan was surpassed by China around AD 560, by India around 1000, by Europe in the eleventh century, by sub-Saharan Africa in the twelfth, and by New World populations in the thirteenth.

By themselves, the new and unprecedented heights of population across Eurasia might well have produced a "Malthusian" crisis, endogenously, just by simple overpopulation. Certainly, a case can be made for a Malthusian crisis in the seventeenth century.[3] But again, the situation was not so simply endogenous. The growth of these populations occurred in the teeth of a second fundamental circumstance, a period of abrupt climate deterioration traditionally known as the *Little Ice Age*. The Little Ice Age was driven by another of the 2,300-year cycle Hallstatt super minima – I refer to it as the *Fourth Millennial Siberian High* to align it with the global cold epochs of ~7000–6000 BC, ~4000–3000 BC, and 1200–600 BC, each of which marked key moments in the Holocene history of humanity: the "secondary products revolution," the rise of states, and the Bronze Age–Iron Age transition. It may be, however, that the Little Ice Age opened more abruptly and reached a greater intensity than any Holocene climate shift since the glacial Younger Dryas. In any event, a combination of population and climate forces intersected in the early modern period, most emphatically in the seventeenth century, clearly a century of crisis, manifested most powerfully in the collapse of Chinese populations and the notching of European peoples, but also in a wave of political upheaval and revolutions across the Old World.

But as much as "crisis," this was an epoch of response and "agency"; here cause and effect are woven into a tangle of threads. This early modern age saw the forging of global empires and the growth of large and prospering European populations; the two seem to have been mutually reinforcing. In bringing epidemic disease under control, European societies began to damp down the crisis mortality that had been the overarching constraint in the human condition since the earliest times. This was, I argue, the beginning of a staged "epidemiological transition" that eventually led to our current condition of extremely high life expectancies in virtually the entire world.[4] Then certain societies, most strategically the English, benefited from new sources of energy derived from both annual and paleo-biomass. Annual biomass energy flows from agriculture and the primary extraction of fish, fur, and timber; empires allowed the expropriation of biomass amounting to millions of free or "ghost" acres, effectively expanding the ecological footprint of the imperial power. At the same time, agricultural innovation produced greater efficiencies in the organic economy of that home country, independently injecting more caloric energy into that society. If ancient biomass energy in the form of centuries-old peat already was being dug to burn for fuel, the long seventeenth century saw the exponential increase in the mining and burning of coal in England, setting the stage for the role of fossil fuel in industrial production. The launching of these new energy systems, imperial,

---

[3] For a Malthusian interpretation, see Jack A. Goldstone, *Revolution and Rebellion in the Early Modern World* (Berkeley, CA, 1991); on crisis, see Geoffrey Parker and Leslie M. Smith, eds., *The General Crisis of the Seventeenth Century*, second edition (London, 1997).

[4] For an overview of the thesis of the epidemiological transition, see James C. Riley, *Rising Life Expectancy: A Global History* (New York, 2001), 6–31.

domestic organic, and domestic mineral, all required concerted action and an enhanced "regime capacity" – the ability of a society and polity to initiate and follow through on complex collective projects. The dynamics of regime capacity, population, and energy emerge in this chapter, and dominate the next, which provides an account of the accelerating pace of transformation of our modern condition. These questions emerge immediately, when we begin to consider regional trajectories out of the era of the Black Death and through the Little Ice Age.

* * *

The Question of Growth and Divergence

The early modern era, particularly in a broad Eurasian context, presents interpretive challenges. Clearly, with the growth of populations across Eurasia there was a broad and general advance of social and economic circumstances. Strong and convincing arguments can be made that Asian economies were as prosperous and dynamic as European economies well into the eighteenth century. In the hot debate over whether the decisive break between Europe and Asia came in the Middle Ages, around 1500, or around 1800, I am reasonably comfortable with the later date.[5] But regional trajectories along these roughly parallel tracks also began to build toward decisively different outcomes that would unfold in the centuries to come, and to shape the way humanity entered the modern world.

It is increasingly clear that economies expanded with and beyond their populations as the postmedieval centuries unfolded. This was a strong, pervasive cycle of Smithian growth, in which rising populations drove a division and specialization of labor. Here the key term is *industrious* rather than *industrial*. Akira Hayami first coined the term the *industrious revolution* to describe the intensification of labor in Tokagawa Japan, and Jan de Vries has appropriated the term – with due credit – to describe the wider early modern acceleration of Smithian economic growth in Europe and across the

[5] Here I follow in general outline the arc of argument in Fernand Braudel, *Civilization and Capitalism: 15th to 18th Century*, 3 vols., Siân Reynolds, trans. (New York, 1979); Joseph Fletcher, "Integrative History: Parallels and Interconnections in the Early Modern Period, 1500–1800," *Journal of Turkish Studies* 9 (1985), 37–57; C. A. Bayley, *Imperial Meridian: The British Empire and the World, 1780–1830* (London, 1989), 16–34; John F. Richards, "Early Modern India and World History," *JWH* 8 (1997), 197–209; the essays in Victor Lieberman, ed., *Beyond Binary Histories: Re-Imagining Eurasia to c. 1830* (Ann Arbor, MI, 1999); Philippe Beaujard, "The Indian Ocean in Eurasian and African World-Systems before the Sixteenth Century," *JWH* 16 (2005), 41–465; John F. Richards, *The Unending Frontier: An Environmental History of the Early Modern World* (Berkeley, CA, 2003); and Victor Lieberman, *Strange Parallels: Southeast Asia in Global Context, c. 800–1300. Vol. I: Integration on the Mainland and Vol. II: Mainland Mirrors: Europe, Japan, China, South Asia and the Islands* (New York, 2003, 2009), esp. II: 1–122.

Old World.[6] Kenneth Pomeranz and R. Bin Wong have launched a literature that has established that European and Chinese standards of living were broadly equivalent through the eighteenth century. Reconstructing the real wages earned by urban artisans and laborers in China, Japan, India, Turkey, and Europe, economic historians are coming up with complex results, but the general pattern suggests a general similarity – with different patterns of wages and prices – across many parts of Asia and Europe during the longer early modern period.[7]

These broad parallel advances in economy were matched by the consolidation of increasingly effective militarized states, imperial and proto-national, with widely similar impulses toward ideologies of universal empire and millennialism. Here it might be suggested that the effectiveness of the early modern empires stands in significant contrast to relatively weak medieval polities, which Stephen Epstein sees as suffering from legal integration problems stifling the growth of markets, governance bottlenecks overcome during the fifteenth and sixteenth centuries.[8] In China, the Ming dynasty replaced the Mongol Yuan in 1368, after three decades of epidemic and summer monsoon failure. The Ming ruled for almost 300 years, rebuilding the Grand Canal and an imperial city at Beijing, building the Great Wall, raising vast armies and fleets, and managing a revitalization of agriculture that supported flourishing urban commerce and a doubling of population between 1350 and 1600.[9] If the Mongol tradition was ejected from China, it lived on among ambitious descendants. The first of these was Timur or

---

[6] Jan de Vries, *The Industrious Revolution: Consumer Behavior and the Household Economy, 1650 to the Present* (New York, 2008), 78–87; –, "The Industrial Revolution and the Industrious Revolution," *JEconH* 54 (1994), 249–70; –, "Economic Growth before and after the Industrial Revolution: A Modest Proposal," in Maarten Prak, ed., *Early Modern Capitalism: Economic and Social Change in Europe, 1400–1800* (New York, 2001), 177–94.

[7] The key works that have established the early modern economic commonalities are Kenneth Pomeranz, *The Great Divergence: China, Europe, and the Making of the Modern World Economy* (Princeton, NJ, 2000); and R. Bin Wong, *China Transformed* (Ithaca, NY, 1997). This literature is summarized in Gale Stokes, "The Fate of Human Societies: A Review of Recent Macrohistories," *AHR* 106 (2001), 508–25; Tommy Bengtsson et al., *Life under Pressure: Mortality and Living Standards in Europe and Asia, 1700–1900* (Cambridge, MA, 2004), 38–42. Important recent analyses include Robert C. Allen, "India in the Great Divergence," in Timothy J. Hatten et al., eds., *The New Comparative History: Essays in Honor of Jeffrey G. Williamson* (Cambridge, MA, 2007), 9–32; and the essays by Kenneth Pomeranz, Prasannan Parthasarathi, and Robert C. Allen in Robert C. Allen et al., eds., *Living Standards in the Past: New Perspectives on Well-Being in Asia and Europe* (New York, 2008), 23–76, 99–130. See also Süleyman Özmucur and Şevket Pamuk, "Real Wages and Standards of Living in the Ottoman Empire, 1489–1914," *JEconH* 62 (2002), 293–321.

[8] S. R. Epstein, *Freedom and Growth: The Rise of States and Markets in Europe, 1300–1750* (London, 2000).

[9] F. W. Mote, *Imperial China: 900–1800* (Cambridge, MA, 1999), 598–621, 646–53, 685–722, 747–69.

Tamerlane, who between the 1360s and 1398 forged a vast domain extending from the Black Sea to Delhi, and who eventually died in 1405 in a failed attempt to retake Ming China. A century later his mantle was taken up by Babur and then Akbar, who in the sixteenth century conquered all of India for the Mughal empire.[10] In Anatolia, the conquest of Constantinople in 1453 marked the transition of the Ottomans from local emirate to territorial empire, which within a century had spread far along the North African coast and was knocking on the gates of Vienna.[11] A parallel process unfolded in Europe with the rise of the Spanish-Austrian Habsburg alliance, eventually foiled by resistance from the French, the Dutch, and the English. Thus historians see societies across the entire Old World as roughly equivalent in standard of living and governmental heft. Something of almost the same order can be said for the state polities of the New World. In the Andes and in Mexico, the recovery from crises of the Medieval Climate Anomaly set the stage for Inca and Aztec polities, which can be compared in scale, reach, and effective governance to the great contemporary Eurasian empires.[12]

This eminently was an era when great land-based empires – broadly symmetrical in their power – dominated the global state. As Victor Lieberman has stressed, much of the parallel developments during this age rested in the simultaneous power and reach of Inner Asian warrior rulers, conquering and governing the Old World civilizational core regions: India, China, Southwest Asia.[13] But size was not everything. One of the fundamental questions about the early modern period is why a small, marginal region that had never particularly distinguished itself on the world stage – England – should move in four short centuries from the utter devastation of the Black Death to dominate the world and to launch ecological changes that define the central features of modernity. One explanation of this divergence has emphasized cultural and political attributes, and I take culture and politics into account. But – as I have suggested throughout this book – culture is framed and constrained by context, and it is with those material contexts that I begin.

Global geography played a certain role in the emergence of Western Europe from its less than central past. Like Mesopotamia and the Mediterranean circuit, it was favored by a diversity of seas and coasts, from the shallow Baltic and North Seas that reach into the boreal interior to the deepwater

[10] Beatrice F. Manz, *The Rise and Rule of Tamerlane* (New York, 1999), 90–106; John F. Richards, *The Mughal Empire, Vol. I.5, The New Cambridge History of India* (New Delhi, 1993), 6–57.

[11] Carter V. Findley, *The Turks in World History* (New York, 2005), 93–132; Alan Mikhail, *Nature and Empire in Ottoman Egypt: An Environmental History* (New York, 2011).

[12] James B. Richardson, *People of the Andes* (Washington, DC, 1994), 146–64; Susan Toby Evans, *Ancient Mexico and Central America: Archaeology and Culture History* (New York, 2008), 447–511.

[13] Lieberman, *Strange Parallels*, II: 92–122.

Atlantic that in turn connects with the Mediterranean and led out into the western and southern unknown. The demands of navigating these different waters fueled the development of new and evolving maritime skills. The land itself was complex, with multiple river systems and mountain barriers that, with the adjacent oceans, shaped a flow of weather that typically guarantees Western Europe moderate and predictable precipitation. If not as fertile as the alluvially recharged soils of the Nile valley and central China, European soils were relatively young, recently mechanically rejuvenated by glacial action, and capable of supporting stable hardwood forests. And if Europe was not a hearth of domestication, its temperate climate and soils were well suited for the diffusion and elaboration of the southwestern Asia food package of grains and animals. This agrarian ecology, evolving out of ancient Mediterranean forms in the Middle Ages to increased productivity through the more frequent use of animal plows and heavy wooden and iron implements, could support growing populations, and still had room for improvement. And tectonics helped as well: there have been no active volcanoes between Iceland and central Italy, and few damaging earthquakes north of the Mediterranean. For millennia Western Europeans could be reasonably sure that nature would not deliver deadly, costly, and unpredictable devastation.[14]

This geography had a strategic element as well. Europe's mountain barriers and multiple river systems, as well as its generalized access to the sea, provided an impediment to empire: after the Romans, no single imperial polity ever managed to dominate the entire subcontinent. The result was a relatively stable system of multiple states, bounded by rivers and ranges, in which states might struggle for advantage, but rarely gain decisive and enduring preeminence. Except perhaps the Austrian Habsburgs who stood against the Ottomans, Europe was also a protected periphery, insulated from the Inner Asian steppe warrior conquest that cost the Byzantines, the Islamic world, India, and China so dearly, either in direct and devastating conquest or in the blood and treasure of defense. Rather than defending against eastern threats, Western Europe could venture to the west, where in the late fifteenth century it became apparent lay vast New World continents brimming with fish, fur, timber, soil, and even treasure.[15]

These apparent advantages have encouraged one school of historians to see Europe's divergence from Asia starting deep in the medieval past. Graeme Snooks has modeled a long-run estimate of European economic growth beginning at roughly AD 1000, when Angus Maddison's estimates

---

[14] Eric L. Jones, *The European Miracle: Environments, Economies and Geopolitics in the History of Europe and Asia*, second edition (New York, 1987), 3–28.

[15] Ibid., 34–7, 104–8; Barry Cunliffe, *Facing the Ocean: The Atlantic and Its Peoples, 8000 BC–AD 1500* (Oxford, 2001), 517–53; Lieberman, *Strange Parallels*, II: 92–114; William H. McNeill, *Europe's Steppe Frontier, 1500–1800* (Chicago, IL, 1964), 16–123.

of GNP have the Islamic regions, India, and China all ahead of Europe. Maddison charts a course of divergence in GNP that begins somewhere between 1000 and 1500, when Europe in his calculations had surpassed all of these ancient centers of civilization.[16]

Arguments for Europe's economic divergence from the major Old World centers, particularly China and India, before 1800 are hotly disputed by a competing school, led first by Andre G. Frank and now Pomeranz and Wong. Contesting any long-run European advantage, these historians argue that the "rise of the West" was a matter of empire building and armed coercion rather than internal economic development, and that a resulting "divergence" began to be apparent only after 1800. Pomeranz, in particular, has presented a case that China was on a par with Europe, and the Yangtze Valley with England, through the end of the eighteenth century, when England gained ground through a windfall of biomass in the form of "ghost acres" in a tropical empire and underground in the form of vast accessible coal deposits.[17]

If there were broad parallels across the Old World, there clearly were strategic shifts that would be of great consequence. Within the European economy, between 1500 and 1800, the center of gravity shifted from the Mediterranean south to northern Europe, particularly to the Netherlands and England. More precisely, Italy led the European economy from the Middle Ages into the Renaissance, and in 1500 was the most prosperous region in Europe, followed by Belgium. In both regions, dynamic relationships between growing cities and rural labor fed advanced textile industries, while Italy prospered as the entrepôt between Christian Europe and the Islamic Mediterranean. By 1600, the Netherlands had overtaken Italy and Belgium, and England was close behind; by 1700, the Netherlands and England were in the lead.[18]

What happened to southern Europe, particularly Italy, is a matter of considerable debate. Clearly, the more than half century of destructive war in

---

[16] Graeme D. Snooks, *Economics without Time: A Science Blind to the Forces of Historical Change* (Ann Arbor, MI, 1993), 246–69; Angus Maddison, *Contours of the World Economy, 1–2030 AD* (New York, 2007), 70–1, data available at http://www.ggdc.net/MADDISON/oriindex.htm (accessed August 8, 2012). See also David Levine, *At the Dawn of Modernity: Biology, Culture, and Material Life in Europe after the Year 1000* (Berkeley, CA, 2000).

[17] Andre Gunder Frank, *ReOrient: Global Economy in the Asian Age* (Berkeley, CA, 1998); –, *World Accumulation, 1492–1789* (New York, 1978); Pomeranz, *The Great Divergence*. Pomeranz's findings are challenged by Mark Elvin, an environmental historian of China, who sees a classic Malthusian crisis brewing in Chinese population growth and progressive environmental degradation: see *The Retreat of the Elephants: An Environmental History of China* (New Haven, CT, 2004), 454–71.

[18] Robert C. Allen, "The Great Divergence in European Wages and Prices from the Middle Ages to the First World War," *ExpEconH* 38 (2001), 411–47; Jan Luitten van Zanden, "Early Modern Economic Growth: A Survey of the European Economy, 1500–1800," in Prak, ed., *Early Modern Capitalism*, 69–87; Şevket Pamuk, "The Black Death and the Origins of the 'Great Divergence' across Europe, 1300–1600," *EREconH* 1 (2007), 289–317.

Italy between 1494 and 1559 took its toll. So too, as Robert C. Davis has recently demonstrated, the rising toll of slave raiding from the Barbary states on the shipping and coastlines of Mediterranean Europe, taking at least a million Europeans into slavery in North Africa by the end of the seventeenth century, must have had a devastating effect on Mediterranean economies. A more long-term ecological argument suggests that the colder and moister north generated more exploitable biomass – particularly timber – to support a rising population in an organic economy.[19] Each of these factors would have shaped how north and south were positioned to participate in an emerging era of intercontinental trade. All of these considerations are enmeshed in a tangle of issues involving the ways Europe and its constituent parts emerged from the trauma of the Black Death.

Thus it is clear that certain strategic factors increasingly began to favor Europe, particularly northwest Europe, building over the course of the early modern epoch but becoming evident particularly at the end of the seventeenth century. Recovering, if not immediately, from the trauma of the Black Death and the ensuing age of warfare, Europeans launched voyages of exploration that quickly evolved into programs of empire building that devastated the peoples of the New World and sub-Saharan Africa.

We can conveniently divide this story of European empire building into four "interpretive centuries." First, in a long fifteenth century from 1350 to 1492, the collapse of populations brought a struggle for resources both internal and external, as European states emerged in an era of competitive warfare that graded into a maritime search for new global trade routes. The next several centuries saw the elaboration of a system of competitive empires, focusing on Asian spices and American silver in the sixteenth century, then on American sugar produced by African slaves in the seventeenth and eighteenth centuries. In sequence, the Portuguese launched the age of exploration in the fifteenth century and with the Spanish led the sixteenth century, the Dutch led an overlapping seventeenth century from the 1560s to the 1660s, and the English led a long eighteenth century running into the nineteenth, as the early Industrial Revolution began to share the stage with global empires.[20]

* * *

[19] Robert C. Davis, *Christian Slaves, Muslim Masters: White Slavery in the Mediterranean, the Barbary Coast, and Italy, 1500–1800* (New York, 2003), 23–48, 139–74; Paolo Malanima, "The Energy Basis for Early Modern Growth, 1650–1820," in Prak, ed., *Early Modern Capitalism*, 51–69.

[20] Ronald Findlay and Kevin H. O'Rourke, *Power and Plenty: Trade, War, and the World Economy in the Second Millennium* (Princeton, NJ, 2007); George Modelski and William R. Thompson, *Leading Sectors and World Powers: The Coevolution of Global Politics and Economics* (Columbia, SC, 1996); Peter J. Hugill, *World Trade since 1431: Geography, Technology, and Capitalism* (Baltimore, MD, 1993), 9–15.

The Aftermath of the Third Age of Epidemics

An account of Europe's conquest of the early modern world and its trajectory toward industrial modernity has to be grounded in the trauma of the exogenous demographic shock of the Black Death. The term *shock* comes from economic theory, positing that a functioning economic system will be "shocked" onto a different path of development by an external force, here mass death by epidemic disease. As the famous French historian Marc Bloch wrote, modernity was forged in a "crisis of seigneurial revenues."[21] Most fundamentally, if the survivors of the Black Death were traumatized, they generally did better than they had in the past. The flow of money upward from peasant to lord that drove the medieval economy was disrupted, with huge effects at many levels.

Such had not been the case 800 years before – at least in the West – after pandemic and war assaulted the ancient world, and the difference lies in political structures. The ancient plagues had hollowed out the western Roman empire, which eventually collapsed. But in the era of the Black Death there was no grand empire to undermine, only small states to clash with each other. The Hundred Years' War, central to these contests, began in 1337 as a dynastic struggle over territory between the French House of Valois and the Anglo-Norman House of Plantagenet/Anjou. Launched in the wake of the Great Famine and just before the impact of the Black Death, the Hundred Years' War can be seen as a resource war, not entirely different from the frontier and dynastic wars that shattered the empire after AD 200. As kingdom turned on kingdom, nobility and gentry found in service to the monarch a hope of recovering by territorial acquisition and plunder what they had lost in peasant death, and in peasant demands for release from lordly obligations. Mobilization, taxation, grinding campaigns and sieges, and marauding freebooters and highwaymen wore down French peasant and artisan populations already diminished by climate change, famine, and plague in what has been termed the *crisis of feudalism*. Lasting until 1453, and spawning or coinciding with wars in Iberia and Brittany, the Hundred Years' War – with recurring rounds of epidemic – certainly slowed the recovery of population in France. Escaping the worst of the Hundred Years' War, the English immediately plunged into the equally devastating Wars of the Roses, the struggle between the royal houses of York and Lancaster for the English crown that broke out immediately following English defeat in France. English population did not begin to recover its numbers until after

---

[21] Marc Bloch, *French Rural History: An Essay on Its Basic Characteristics*, Janet Sondheimer, trans. (Berkeley, CA, 1966), 102; David Herlihy, *The Black Death and the Transformation of the West* (Cambridge, MA, 1997); Ronald Findlay, "Globalization and the European Economy: Medieval Origins to the Industrial Revolution," in Henryk Kierzkowski, ed., *Europe and Globalization* (New York, 2002), 32–63.

the Tudors ended the war in 1487 and reestablished political and social stability.[22]

Immanuel Wallerstein's analysis of the fifteenth century hinges on the role of these wars in reshaping European polities and economies in the wake of the demographic destruction wrought by the Black Death. Effectively, an era of war had to be brought to an end and order restored, and the agent of that order was a new kind of monarch. These Renaissance monarchs –Louis XI, Henry VII, and Ferdinand and Isabella – mobilized their societies in war to form the first effective European states. Victory required money to pay for the new troops and equipment to fight these wars: masses of lightly armored pike-bearing infantry and archers, followed by the first artillery, massive siege guns. Medieval courtly warfare of heavily armored nobles and knights quickly became a thing of the past, as the new monarchs invested in new armies composed of hired mercenaries, armed with expensive gunpowder weaponry, and funded by new taxes managed by an emerging corps of royal bureaucrats. In an escalation of military investment, the new fourteenth-century infantry and artillery were followed between the 1490s and the 1550s by massive fortifications, arquebuses and muskets, and the artillery armament of naval vessels. These costly advances in military technology, a rolling "military revolution" intended to bring preeminence of nation over nation, led over the long run to stalemate in Europe. But – as Geoffrey Parker has written – this internal struggle "paid handsome dividends," as during the sixteenth century European powers turned their attention out onto the world, to forge "the first global hegemony in history."[23]

If new, more effective, political institutions were killing people in wars to restore order in late medieval Europe, they were also saving lives, if slowly and gradually, in the first tentative steps in the epidemiological transition that would establish the fundamental ground of modernity. As the plague struck Italian cities in 1348, public health officers were immediately commissioned to stem the tide of epidemic; the first quarantine for ships was imposed at the Italian port of Ragusa in 1377. By the end of the century, Italian cities

[22] Guy Bois, *The Crisis of Feudalism: Economy and Society in Eastern Normandy, c. 1300–1550* (Cambridge, 1984), 263–368; Desmond Seward, *The Hundred Years War: The English in France, 1337–1453* (London, 1978), 73–5, 193–5, 263–5; Christopher Allmand, *The Hundred Years War: England and France at War, c. 1300–1450* (Cambridge, 1988), 120–35; Margaret L. Kekewich and Susan Rose, *Britain, France, and the Empire, 1350–1500* (Houndmills, 2005), 3–11, 72–84, 135–63.

[23] Immanuel Wallerstein, *The Modern World System, Vol. I: Capitalist Agriculture and the Origins of the European World Economy in the Sixteenth Century* (New York, 1974), 21–33; Geoffrey Parker, *The Military Revolution: Military Innovation and the Rise of the West, 1500–1800*, second edition (New York, 1996), 6–18, 24–8, 89–92, quote from 154; Clifford J. Rogers, "The Military Revolutions of the Hundred Years War," in Clifford J. Rogers, ed., *The Military Revolution Debate: Readings on the Military Transformation of Early Modern Europe* (Boulder, CO, 1995), 55–94.

and provinces were authorizing permanent boards of health, and by the 1460s, systems for quarantining ships were routine in ports with frequent trade to the eastern Mediterranean. If plague outbreaks continued sporadically through the seventeenth century, step by step European cities, nations, and physicians learned how to contain the plague through concerted government action, isolating the potentially infectious and the infected, and indeed caring for the sick. Samuel Cohn has recently argued that in the struggle with the plague European physicians threw aside ancient practice and began to treat the sick based on their cumulative observations of case histories; indeed he claims that the self-confident, triumphant humanism of the Renaissance – "a new culture of secularism, state-building, and 'fame and glory'" – was the result of these successful efforts to stem the tide of disease. If the rough estimates that we have are even vaguely correct, populations in most of Europe had by 1500 almost regained from the losses of the Black Death.[24]

The bubonic plague had not run its course in the east, however, and expanded its reach in the emerging Ottoman empire from a natural reservoir in Kurdistan. The plague erupted into Europe in 1665, when it reached London; in a series of epidemics in eastern Europe between 1703 and 1716; and when it devastated Marseilles in 1721. But the network of maritime quarantines and plague hospitals, augmented by a cordon sanitaire established on the Austrian-Ottoman frontiers after 1710 (and abandoned only in 1871), worked to stamp out the plague in Western Europe. In this effort began the process of stemming the crisis mortality that had constrained human populations for eons.[25] Similarly, if throughout the early modern period harvest failure led to dearth and even famine, increasingly effective local and national governments began to direct the shipment of grain and keep famine mortality to a minimum.[26]

[24] Samuel K. Cohn, Jr., "The Black Death: End of a Paradigm," *AHR* 107 (2002), 703–38, esp. 707–9, 737–8; Samuel K. Cohn, Jr., *The Black Death Transformed: Disease and Culture in Early Renaissance Europe* (London, 2002), 48–9, 223–52. See also Jean-Noël Biraben, *Les hommes et la peste en France at dans les pays européens et méditerranéens* (Mouton, 1975–6), 1: 118–30, 2: 85–181; Carlo M. Cipolla, *Public Health and the Medical Profession in the Renaissance* (New York, 1976), 11–66; William McNeill, *Plagues and Peoples* (New York, 1976), 150–1, 162–5; Michael W. Flinn, *The European Demographic System, 1500–1800* (Baltimore, MD, 1981), 58–61; Sheldon Watts, *Epidemics and History: Disease, Power, and Imperialism* (New Haven, CT, 1997), 15–25.

[25] Daniel Panzac, *La Peste dans L'Empire Ottoman, 1700–1850* (Leuven, 1985), 105–8; Daniel Panzac, *Quarantaines at Lazarets: L'Europe and la Peste d'Orient (XVIIe-XXe siècles)* (Aix-en-Provence, 1986), 31–61, 67–93; Gunther E. Rothenberg, "The Austrian Sanitary Cordon and the Control of the Bubonic Plague: 1710–1871," *Journal of the History of Medicine* 28 (1973), 15–23; Watts, *Epidemics and History*, 24–5; Katerina Konstantinidou et al., "Venetian Rule and Control of Plague Epidemics on the Ionian Islands during 17th and 18th Centuries," *EmInfDis* 15 (2009), 39–43.

[26] For two key overview essays that conclude that governmental action was fundamental to suppressing crisis mortality, see John D. Post, "Famine, Mortality, and Epidemic Disease

The theory of the epidemiological transition posits a series of four stages in which mortality declined and life expectancy increased: a waning of pandemics, the decline of communicable childhood diseases, the decline of respiratory disease and infant mortality, and the medical containment of degenerative diseases.[27] The efforts to control the plague starting in the fifteenth century should be seen as the opening of the first stage. During the eighteenth century, these "macro" efforts at public health and crisis mitigation of the first transition stage would be augmented by "micro" efforts, with the first inoculations for smallpox, in the onset of the second stage. Though other elements were at work, which we consider in the pages to follow, there is a broad consensus that improvements in governance and medical-scientific practice, if far from perfect, helped to stem the tide of crisis mortality and to shape early modern Europe's population expansion from the fifteenth century. But if Europe clearly began to bring the epidemics and ensuing crisis mortality under control, this was not the case in Islamic Southwest Asia and North Africa, where populations did not recover their numbers until the nineteenth century. Here religious understandings of the plague seem to have played an important role, in combination with the legal structure of landholding.

European medical efforts against epidemic were one dimension of a wider Christian response to the plague. The sudden appearance of the Black Death launched a wave of millenarian anxieties through European societies. The plague was seen by many as a harbinger of the Apocalypse, and inspired in 1348–50 a series of extremist movements, including flagellants abusing themselves to expiate the sins that had brought the plague and mobs who massacred Europe's Jews and remaining Muslims for bringing the plague to Europe. The apocalyptic response to the plague was carried forward in the coming centuries by the millenarianism of Joachim of Fiore, whose writings contributed equally to mystical Catholicism and the beginnings of the Protestant Reformation, less than a century and a half after the onset of the Black Death. Such visions of the Christian millennium would also con-

in the Process of Modernization," *EconHistR*, 2d ser., 29 (1976), 14–37; and Andrew B. Appleby, "Epidemics and Famine in the Little Ice Age," *JInterdH* 10 (1980), 643–63; see also Flinn, *The European Demographic System*, 97–8; Steven L. Kaplan, *Bread, Politics and Political Economy in the Reign of Louis XV* (Hague, 1976), 19–96; and Marc Raeff, "The Well-Ordered Police State and the Development of Modernity in Seventeenth- and Eighteenth-Century Europe: An Attempt at a Comparative Approach," *AHR* 80 (1975), 1221–43.

[27] Here I follow Riley, *Rising Life Expectancy*, 19–23. The concept of the epidemiological transition was proposed in Abdel R. Omran, "The Epidemiological Transition: A Theory of Population Change," *The Milbank Memorial Fund Quarterly* 49 (1971), 509–38; and extended in S. Jay Olshansky and A. Brian Ault, "The Fourth Stage of the Epidemiologic Transition: The Age of Delayed Degenerative Diseases," *The Milbank Quarterly* 64 (1986), 355–91.

tribute to both Spanish and English justifications for empire in the coming centuries.[28]

These millenarian impulses centered on an understanding of the plague as divine judgment for human sins, sins demanding expiation by atonement and improvement. The first onslaught of the Black Death – if Ole Benedictow is right – may have struck rich and poor in roughly equal terms; during ensuing bouts of the plague, those with the resources to escape to the country or to protect themselves from contact with the contagious did so. The effectiveness of this isolation, and enduring assumptions that sin and disease were disproportionately associated with outsiders and the poor, must have contributed to the impulse to erect the crude regulations and barriers that made up the early quarantines – public health was part and parcel of an effort to improve and regulate society for the greater glory of God, and the survival, and perhaps the profit, of the propertied.[29] Something broadly similar, demographically speaking, seems to have unfolded in Japan. Increasing contacts with the Asian mainland during the Middle Ages brought waves of epidemics that limited Japanese population growth through the thirteenth century. But particularly in the seventeenth century, when the Tokagawa shogunate drastically reduced and channeled the flow of commerce, Japan avoided the impact of certain devastating diseases. Behind the isolation of this political quarantine, Japanese population benefited from the "first epidemiological transition," doubling to 31 million in a single century.[30]

---

[28] Norman Cohn, *The Pursuit of the Millennium: Revolutionary Millenarians and Mystical Anarchists of the Middle Ages*, rev. ed. (New York, 1970), 131–47; Herlihy, *The Black Death*, 59–69; Marjorie Reeves, *The Influence of Prophecy in the Late Middle Ages: A Study in Joachimism* (Oxford, 1969), 295–305, 359–60; Pauline Moffitt Watts, "Prophecy and Discovery: On the Spiritual Origins of Christopher Columbus's 'Enterprise to the Indies,'" *AHR* 90 (1985), 73–102; Leonard I. Sweet, "Christopher Columbus and the Millennial Vision of the New World," *Catholic Historical Review* 72 (1986), 369–82; John L. Phelan, *The Millennial Kingdom of the Franciscans in the New World*, second edition (Berkeley, CA, 1970), 5–38, 69–77, 118–25; David Armitage, *The Ideological Origins of the British Empire* (New York, 2000), 61–70, 82–99; Peter French, *John Dee: The World of an Elizabethan Magus* (New York, 1972), 177–98; Nicholas H. Clulee, *John Dee's Natural Philosophy: Between Science and Religion* (London, 1988), 180–9, 220–30; and Arthur H. Williamson, "An Empire to End Empires: The Dynamic of Early Modern British Expansion," *Huntington Library Quarterly* 68 (2005), 227–56.

[29] Ole J. Benedictow, *The Black Death, 1346–1353: The Complete History* (Woodbridge, UK, 2004), 381–2 and passim.

[30] McNeill, *Plagues and Peoples*, 124–7; William Wayne Farris, *Population, Disease, and Land in Early Japan, 645–900* (Cambridge, MA, 1985), 50–73; –, *Japan's Medieval Population: Famine, Fertility, and Warfare in a Transformative Age* (Honolulu, HI, 2006), 12–66; –, *Daily Life and Demographics in Ancient Japan* (Ann Arbor, MI, 2009), 10; –, "Famine, Climate, and Farming in Japan, 670–1100," in Mikael Adolphson et al., *Heian Japan, Centers and Peripheries* (Honolulu, HI, 2007), 275–304; Ann B. Jannetta, *Epidemics and Mortality in Early Modern Japan* (Princeton, NJ, 1987), 16–32, 65–70, 114–17, 147–50, 191–200.

The Islamic world had suffered plagues intermittently since the after-shocks of the Justinian Plague, which lingered in the eastern Mediterranean for hundreds of years. The Islamic injunctions regarding the plague were perhaps more humanitarian than those of the Christian Europeans: flight from the plague was discouraged because it meant abandoning one's com-munity and perhaps spreading the epidemic. Plague was a judgment on the infidel, but a blessing on the Muslim: a "good death" by the plague was the equivalent of martyrdom in *jihad*. Though Islamic physicians were not unanimous on this point, it was widely assumed that the plague was not caused by a contagion, but by *jinn* demons acting out the will of God.[31] Though often quietly ignored by those seeking protection in flight, these religious teachings had to have contributed to the failure of the Middle East to recover from the Black Death.

Other forces were at work in Egypt, the most productive agricultural region in the Islamic world. Here landownership and its income were assigned to Mamluk warrior-slaves who served the sultan, but who could not pass their properties to ensuing generations. Living in barracks in Cairo and engaging in a complex factional politics, the Mamluks thus had no inter-est in the long-term development of their holdings. When the Black Death struck, they continued their demands for income from a peasantry dying in huge numbers. The result was that Egyptian agriculture – especially the irrigation systems that required collective labor – quickly deteriorated, and did not recover for centuries. Recent careful research in Ottoman archives suggests that the plague might have waned somewhat in the century follow-ing the Black Death. But first with the Ottoman conquest of Constantinople in 1453 and the aggressive expansion of the empire during the sixteenth century, the plague became endemic, circulated by the commerce and troop movements around the Ottoman Mediterranean. In addition, it seems that in large parts of the Middle East, the widespread practice of birth control – a reaction to "bad times" – played an important role in the ongoing limiting of population growth.[32]

Such was not the case in Europe. While Egyptian landlords maintained tight control over rural labor, European landlords failed.[33] Manorial

---

[31] Michael W. Dobbs, *The Black Death in the Middle East* (Princeton, NJ, 1977), 109–21, 285–98; McNeill, *Plagues and Peoples*, 165–8.

[32] Stuart W. Borsch, *The Black Death in Egypt and England: A Comparative Study* (Austin, TX, 2005), 245–55; Findlay and O'Rourke, *Power and Plenty*, 127–31; Watts, *Epidemics and History*, 25–39; Mikhail, *Nature and Empire in Ottoman Egypt*, 201–41. On the plague in the Ottoman empire, see Nükhet Varlik, "Conquest, Urbanization and Plague Networks in the Ottoman Empire, 1453–1600," in Christine Woodhead, ed., *The Ottoman World* (London, 2011), 251–63. Sam White, "Rethinking Disease in Ottoman History," *International Journal of Middle Eastern Studies* 42 (2010), 549–67 emphasizes the impact of the second phase of the Little Ice Age. On family limitation, see Basim Musallam, *Sex and Society in Islam: Birth Control before the Nineteenth Century* (New York, 1983), 105–21.

[33] Borsch, *The Black Death in Egypt and England*, 113–17.

systems were already in some disarray before the Black Death, and where landholders attempted to maintain the shreds of feudal control, they were confronted with peasant rebellions, such as Watt Tyler's Revolt in England in 1381.[34] Throughout Europe, the exogenous shock of the Black Death, sweeping away a third to a half of the population, made life easier for the survivors at the broad producing base of the social pyramid. While elites scrambled to replace "seigniorial revenues," the working people of Europe enjoyed a bonanza for about two centuries, until roughly the middle of the sixteenth century: fewer hands meant higher wages; fewer mouths meant lower prices. Labor was in demand and could set the terms of its employment. Marginal lands farmed in the twelfth and thirteenth centuries were abandoned to sheep and cattle, and the terms of tenure of productive arable land shifted toward simple tenancy or even yeoman ownership. Despite the continuing risks of epidemic, an increasingly mobile people contributed to growing numbers in towns and cities. Expanding silver mining in Central Europe provided the raw material for the money that drove this late medieval economy. If the post-plague economies were not as productive as they had been before the Black Death, there was more to go around, and more to be spent on goods manufactured by neighbors – and on luxuries imported from the fabled East.[35]

* * *

Emerging European Empires, New World Depopulation

There was good money to be made in the ancient trade with the East. Even though the Black Death had raged along the Central Asian trade routes, and the collapse of Mongol power had disturbed it somewhat, trade still moved across the overland route, even if Europeans were not as closely involved as before the Black Death, when the Genoese were based at Kaffa on the Black Sea. Nonetheless, silk from China and spices from Southeast Asia flowed to Europe through Islamic middlemen, and they could be moved to Europe for greater profit if a direct trade could be developed. Portuguese sailors, closely followed by the Spanish and then the Dutch and the English, made the opening explorations around Africa and into the Indian Ocean at the end of the fifteenth century. Here the flush wages of prosperous European workers combined with the armaments of the military revolution and the

[34] Wallerstein, *The Modern World System*, I: 23–4.
[35] Findlay and O'Rourke, *Power and Plenty*, 111–20; Ronald Findlay and Mats Lundahl, "Toward a Factor Proportion Approach to Economic History: Population, Precious Metals, and Prices from the Black Death to the Price Revolution," in Ronald Findlay et al., eds., *Bertil Ohlin: A Centennial Celebration, 1899–1999* (Cambridge, MA, 2002), 495–528; Herlihy, *The Black Death*, 40–51.

millenarian impulses of European Christianity to forge the opening of the
age of global empire.

European empire building spread in two directions virtually simultaneously. Soon after the Portuguese cleared the Cape of Good Hope in 1488,
opening a new passage free of Islamic control to the Indian coasts, Ceylon,
and the spice islands of Indonesia, the Spanish sent a Genoese captain –
Christopher Columbus – on a suicidal mission to find a western route to the
Indies. By the 1530s, the basic structures of sixteenth-century ocean-borne
empire were in place: the Portuguese launching an ambitious venture to
control the trade of the Indian Ocean as well as establishing outposts on the
coast of Brazil, and the Spanish acting on the claims of Columbus and then
Ferdinand Magellan to conquer from Mexico and Peru to the Philippines.
Harassed by French and English raiders from the 1560s, the Iberian powers
were from the 1590s displaced by the armed trading company of the Dutch
republic in the Indian Ocean and the coast of China, and challenged by
Dutch power along the Brazilian and Surinam coasts. Finally, the English
would enter the struggle in earnest in the first decades of the seventeenth
century, settling scattered foothold colonies along the temperate North
American coast and at Barbados and the Leeward Islands, followed by trading forts in India.

The sixteenth- and seventeenth-century European empires thus reached
into many corners of the world, particularly the tropics. There was a fundamental ecological logic to these first global empires: the search for complementary biomes. Living in the temperate zone, Europeans sought out
different biomes that produced commodities not available at home. Thus
parallel imperial trajectories were launched into the boreal forests of Russia
and North America in search of a harvest of furs, the American trade linked
to the fishing fleets that were probably on the Grand Banks decades before
Columbus sailed. But the tropics were where the real wealth lay, literally,
because the late medieval "science" of alchemy posited that metals were
volatile and boiled to the surface under the heat of the tropical sun. Thus
the initial and continuing impetus for empire was to gain control of the
exotic products of the east: pepper, cloves, nutmeg, the fine spices from
Southeast Asia, tea from China and Ceylon. Silver would pay for spices:
Cortes and Pizarro first looted gold and silver from their Aztec and Incan
conquest, and soon thereafter silver mining became the central feature of the
Spanish empire, and an increasing stream of silver bullion flowed into Spain,
the European economy, and then east to India, Southeast Asia, and China.
Later features of these emerging empires developed out of an older agriculture. Sugar had been grown on intensive plantations with coerced labor in
the eastern Mediterranean since Roman times, moving progressively west
during the Middle Ages, to Cyprus, Crete, Sicily, the North African coast,
and then into newly discovered Atlantic islands: Madeira, Cape Verde, the
Azores, and the Canaries. Soil depletion and the destruction of the enslaved

populations of these islands contributed to the Portuguese ventures along the African coast, where they began the African slave trade to support the production of sugar. From the Atlantic islands it was only a relatively short hop to Brazil, where native Brazilian peoples were enslaved from the 1530s to work in the cane fields and mills. Over the second half of the century, as they died out, the Portuguese switched to African labor, and the Atlantic slave trade was born.[36]

Four key points need to be established at the outset regarding the reconfiguration of power, population, and well-being around the globe in the early modern era. *First,* there were obvious losers. Since the rise of the state, the focus of population and political and cultural power had run in a band around the southern mid-latitudes where the earliest complex societies and subsequent empires had formed, from the Mediterranean through South and Southwest Asia to China and then the great Mesoamerican formations. During the Middle Ages, the Old World civilizations had been linked in a balanced series of regional economies from east to west, and from their release from the droughts of the Medieval Climate Anomaly New World civilizations had been accelerating in their scale and complexity.[37] Now, specific dynamics of epidemic shock, dynastic millenarian impulse, and the technological spiral of the military revolution suddenly put a distant corner of Eurasia in a position of world domination.

Second, the crisis mortality of the Black Death was matched and rematched by the assault of a host of Old World diseases on New World societies. Here mass death came through the combination of "virgin soil" contact with Old World disease and the disruption and degradation of population ecologies through violent dispossession and then enslavement.[38]

[36] Wallerstein, *The Modern World System,* I: 43–4, 88–90; Findlay and O'Rourke, *Power and Plenty,* 158–75, 212–26; A. J. Russell-Wood, *A World on the Move: The Portuguese in Africa, Asia, and America, 1415–1808* (New York, 1992), 8–26; Philip D. Curtin, *The Rise and Fall of the Plantation Complex: Essays in Atlantic History* (New York, 1990), 17–57; J. H. Elliott, *Empires of the Atlantic World: Britain and Spain in America, 1492–1830* (New Haven, CT, 2006), 88–114; Stuart B. Schwartz, *Sugar Plantations in the Formation of Brazilian Society: Bahia, 1550–1835* (New York, 1985), 3–72; C. R. Boxer, *The Dutch Seaborne Empire, 1600–1800* (Harmondsworth, 1973), 187–214.

[37] Janet L. Abu-Lughod, *Before European Hegemony: The World System, A.D. 1250–1350* (New York, 1989); Linda Shaffer, "Southernization," *JWH* 5 (1994), 1–21; Findlay and O'Rourke, *Power and Plenty,* 120–42; Brian S. Bauer, *Ancient Cuzco: Heartland of the Inca* (Austin, TX, 2004), 71–138; William T. Sanders et al., *The Basin of Mexico: Ecological Processes in the Evolution of a Civilization* (New York, 1979), 1: 183–219; Fletcher, "Integrative History"; Beaujard, "The Indian Ocean."

[38] The modern literature on the Amerindian epidemics was launched in the mid-1970s with a series of formative works: Alfred W. Crosby, "Virgin Soil Epidemics as a Factor in the Aboriginal Depopulation in America," *WMQ,* 3d ser., 33 (1976), 289–99; Alfred W. Crosby, *The Columbian Exchange: Biological and Cultural Consequences of 1492* (Westport, CT, 1972), 35–63, 122–64; McNeill, *Plagues and Peoples,* 176–207. Noble D. Cook, *Born to Die: Disease and New World Conquest, 1492–1650* (New York, 1998) provides the

Spanish soldier-settlers in the Caribbean quickly decimated local populations before moving on to the Mexican coast, where a smallpox epidemic
opened their way into the valley of the Aztecs, as it would a few years later
in Incan Peru. A host of diseases from both temperate and tropical Old
World locales – smallpox, influenza, measles, mumps, typhus, malaria, yellow fever, dengue fever, even the plague – swept through Mexico, Peru, and
coastal Brazil. It may be that epidemics struck in hemispheric waves that
reflected European epidemiology: measles in the 1530s, typhus or plague
in the 1540s, influenza in the late 1550s, measles in the 1590s. In Peru, the
death toll was greater in the tropical lowlands, where populations dropped
from 7.5 million to less than 130,000 between 1525 and 1571; in highland
Peru, the death toll was still fearsome, but not quite as devastating, dropping
the population from 4.6 million to 1.3 million. In Brazil, the first truly catastrophic epidemics came during the 1550s, apparently part of an Atlantic-
wide contagion of influenza.[39] Genetic research indicates that Amerindian
depopulation caused a serious bottleneck, suggesting a roughly 50 percent
decline in the sixteenth century.[40]

Recent research on Mexico argues that these epidemics had both Old
World and New World origins. Smallpox killed roughly 8 million people
during the 1519–21 conquest. But it was followed by a series of even more
devastating epidemics of local origin, hemorrhagic fevers known as *cocoliztli* apparently erupting from rodent populations. The first of these broke out
in 1545, and killed as many as 15 million Mexicans, perhaps 80 percent of
the total native peoples; a second in 1576 cut the surviving population in
half, to 1.5–2 million total. Spaniards were unaffected, and the consensus
is that these epidemics fed on the crowded and degraded conditions of the
native population, reduced to servitude on semifeudal *encomiendas*.[41]

In North America, isolation helped buffer the first shocks of the European
encounter. But Spanish incursions – de Soto's expedition followed by a mission system on the Florida coast – cut the Indian population of the southeast
by 1600. Then the establishment of small settlements of English and Dutch,

most authoritative region-by-region overview focusing on Mexico and Central and South
America. John D. Daniels, "The Indian Population of North America in 1492," *WMQ*, 3d
ser., 49 (1992), 298–320 and David S. Jones, "Virgin Soils Revisited," *WMQ* 3d ser., 49
(2003), 703–42 provide recent overviews of the debates about North America.

[39] Cook, *Born to Die*, 95–133; C. T. Smith, "Depopulation of the Central Andes in the 16th
Century," *CA* 11 (1970), 453–64, at 459.

[40] Brendan O'Fallon and Lars Fehren-Schmitz, "Native Americans Experienced a Strong
Population Bottleneck Coincident with European Contact," *PNAS* 108 (2011), 20444–8.

[41] Rodolfo Acuna-Soto et al., "When Half the Population Died: The Epidemic of Hemorrhagic
Fevers of 1576 in Mexico," *FEMS Microbiology Letters* 240 (2004), 1–5; Rodolfo Acuna-
Soto et al., "Megadrought and Megadeath in 16th Century Mexico," *EmInfDis* 8 (2002),
360–2. These diseases may have been or related to the hanta virus that erupted in the
American southwest in 1993. Cook's 1998 synthesis in *Born to Die*, 137–40, cites typhus
outbreaks in 1545–6 and 1576, and cocoliztli in 1566 and 1587–8.

particularly when they brought children from the disease environments of European coastal cities and towns, sent waves of epidemic disease into the northeast interior. A recent study argues that the worst of the epidemic mortality struck in the American southeast with the expansion of English slaving networks after 1670. By 1700, North American Indian populations had dropped by almost 500,000, mostly east of the Mississippi and among Pueblo peoples subjugated by Spanish outposts on the Rio Grande. By 1800, after massive smallpox epidemics set off by the American Revolutionary War had spread far into the continental interior, North American Indian peoples at best numbered only one million people.[42]

Recent detailed studies have suggested a series of important new perspectives on the mass epidemics in the post-Columbian New World. Paleopathologists working in the middle Mississippi and Ohio Valley conclude unequivocally that "compromised health status among late prehistoric peoples is a significant factor in understanding post-Columbian depopulation," and that "lessened dietary variation, nutritional imbalances, and deficiencies were likely and would have led to reduced levels of immunocompetence."[43] The evidence points to a complex mosaic of disease impacts, with variable exposures and chronologies of infection unfolding over centuries. The picture is of significant sixteenth-century and early seventeenth-century "first-contact" epidemics compounded by ongoing episodes of disease, as regions came into direct and ongoing relations between natives and settlers. Disease movement came in "spurts and bursts," as it ripped through dense settlements and then slowed at "buffer zones" until spreading to other population centers. Henry Dobyns has argued that native trading centers throughout the sixteenth and seventeenth centuries were particularly vulnerable. Among the missionized peoples of the southeast, the work of Clark Larsen, David Jones, and others stresses the wider "suite" of post-contact conditions including malnutrition, overwork, and the disruption of delicate subsistence systems compounding disease to shape the ongoing decline.[44]

---

[42] Daniels, "The Indian Population of North America"; Douglas Ubelaker, "North American Indian Population Size: Changing Perspectives," Dean R. Snow, "Disease and Population Decline in the Northeast," Russell Thornton et al., "Depopulation in the Southeast after 1492," in John W. Verano and Douglas H. Ubelaker, eds., *Disease and Demography in the Americas* (Washington, DC, 1993), 169–96; Elizabeth A. Fenn, *Pox Americana: The Great Smallpox Epidemic of 1775–1782* (New York, 2001); Alan Gallay, *The Indian Slave Trade: The Rise of the English Empire in the American South, 1670–1717* (New Haven, CT, 2002); Paul Kelton, *Epidemics and Enslavement: Biological Catastrophe in the Native Southeast, 1492–1715* (Lincoln, NE, 2007).

[43] Jane E. Buikstra, "Diet and Disease in Late Prehistory," in Verano and Ubelaker, eds., *Disease and Demography*, 87–102, quote at 98; Anthony J. Perzigian et al., "Prehistoric Health in the Ohio River Valley," in Mark Nathan Cohen and George Armelagos, eds., *Paleopathology at the Origins of Agriculture* (New York, 1984), 347–66, quote at 361.

[44] Clark Larsen et al., "Population Decline and Extinction in La Florida," Thompson et al., "Depopulation in the Southeast," and Henry F. Dobyns, "Native American Trade Centers

The Old World contribution of disease in this Colombian Exchange may have been balanced by a New World "return" in the form of syphilis, though the debate on this point continues.[45] But the relative lack of diseases originating in the New World flowing to the Old leads us to a complex of issues involving mortality, nutrition, and Malthus. Complex societies north of Peru were relatively recently established in the New World, and especially so in North America, where food sufficient to support large, dense populations – corn/maize – was introduced only between AD 500 and AD 1000. Lacking the disease vectors of domesticated animals and isolated from the Old World imperial circulation of diseases, New World populations had not been subjected to the waves of crisis mortality from epidemic disease that had long afflicted the Old World. The price of this innocence, even prior to European incursion, may have been a significant level of malnutrition, if the osteological analyses are correct. The corn-beans complex may have supported rapidly growing populations, but it seems possible that these dense American populations were getting too large, and were nutritionally compromised.[46] Without crisis mortality-driven population reductions, even if a Columbian impact had been delayed for several centuries Amerindian populations might well have reached their own endogenous Malthusian limits. But Amerindians did not reach such an endogenous outcome because an exogenous event intervened.

as Contagious Disease Foci," in Verano and Ubelaker, *Disease and Demography*, 25–40, 177–96 (quote from 193), 215–22; Clark Larsen and Christopher B. Ruff, "The Stresses of Conquest in Spanish Florida: Structural Adaptation and Change before and after Contact," Brenda J. Baker, "Pilgrim's Progress and Praying Indians: The Biocultural Consequences of Contact in Southern New England," and Ann M. Palkovich, "Historic Epidemics among the Pueblos," in Clark Spencer Larsen and George R. Milner, eds., *In the Wake of Contact: Biological Responses to Conquest* (New York, 1994), 21–46, 87–96; Marvin T. Smith, "Aboriginal Depopulation in the Postcontact Southeast," in Charles Hudson and Carmen Chaves Tesser, eds., *The Forgotten Centuries: Indians and Europeans in the American South, 1521–1704* (Athens, GA, 1994), 257–75; Jones, "Virgin Soils Revisited."

[45] The pendulum in the syphilis debate is swinging decidedly toward New World origins. See Kristin Harper et al., "On the Origin of the Treponematoses: A Phylogenetic Approach," *PLOS Neglected Tropical Diseases* 2 (2008), e148; Connie J. Muiigan, "Molecular Studies in *Treponema Pallidum* Evolution," *PLOS Neglected Tropical Diseases* 2 (2008), e184; and Bruce M. Rothschild et al., "First European Exposure to Syphilis: The Dominican Republic at the Time of European Contact," *Clinical Infectious Diseases* 31 (2000), 936–41. Compare with Crosby, *The Columbian Exchange*, 122–64 and McNeill, *Plagues and Peoples*, 193–4.

[46] On late prehistoric North America, see note 42, and Mary Lucas Powell, "Health and Disease in the Late Prehistoric Southeast," in Verano and Ubelaker, eds., *Disease and Demography*, 41–54; Susan Pfeiffer and Scott I. Fairgrieve, "Evidence from the Ossuaries: The Effect of Contact on the Health of Iroquoians," in Larsen and Milner, eds., *In the Wake of Contact*, 47–62; and Jerome C. Rose et al., "Paleopathology and the Origins of Maize Agriculture in the Lower Mississippi Valley and Caddoan Culture Areas," in Cohen and Armelagos, eds., *Paleopathology*, 393–424, at 424. For an interpretation quite similar to that advanced here, see Alfred W. Crosby, "Infectious Diseases and the Demography of the Atlantic Peoples," *JWH* 2 (1991), 119–33, at 120. See also Marvin Harris's controversial argument regarding protein deficiencies in Aztec Mexico: *Cannibals and Kings* (New York, 1977), 147–66.

Food globalization was the *third* key outcome of early modern empire. If it is possible that New World foods in and of themselves might not have supported New World populations for too much longer, it is clear that, in combination with the Old World food packages, they have been feeding humanity ever since. This globalization of food is the third key outcome of the encounter of Old and New Worlds. The Columbian Exchange involved an exchange of DNA, *both* pathogenic and nutritional. New World foods, most importantly corn/maize, potatoes, and eventually cassava/manioc, moved east and powerfully shaped the early modern rise of population in the Old World.

Columbus brought a flint variety of corn/maize back from the Caribbean to Seville in the 1490s, and its earliest extensive Old World cultivation seems to have followed the course of empire; farmers were growing it in the Cape Verde Islands and along the West African coast by the 1540s. By the late sixteenth century, flint corn was grown in northern Italy and in the Middle East, where it was known as Turkish wheat. It spread more universally across southern Europe at the end of the seventeenth century, as it did in China and India. Throughout Eurasia, corn filled the ecological gaps in the Old World food system, growing in dry upland soils that would produce neither wheat nor rice, and supported the considerable eighteenth-century population increases, which in China involved the colonization of hilly and mountainous territory well beyond the domain of wet rice cultivation. If corn became the new food of the warmer, drier Old World "south," potatoes became that of the colder, damper Old World "north" and of mountainous regions. Despised as a dirty food, the antithesis of the "noble grain," the potato took longer to be adopted. But over the seventeenth century, the potato was widely adopted first as a famine recovery food in the Netherlands after the Thirty Years' War, then by poor cottagers in English-occupied Ireland. During the eighteenth century, it took hold in Germany, eastern Europe, Russia, and the highlands of China and the Mediterranean, again as both agroecological extender and a famine crop for the poor. Manioc spread later, during the nineteenth century, into the tropical Old World, as corn and potatoes and a host of supporting New World species – beans, peanuts, tomatoes, chilies – were entrenched into Old World foodways.[47]

The result was an energy revolution for Old World peoples. The sheer volume of calories added to the Old World diet on an annual basis can only be guessed at, but it must be seen as an enormous addition to the energy available to support Old World societies. But it is clear that American foods

[47] Kenneth F. Kiple, *A Moveable Feast: Ten Millennia of Food Globalization* (New York, 2007), 135–49; Crosby, *The Columbian Exchange*, 165–202; John R. McNeill, *The Mountains of the Mediterranean World: An Environmental History* (New York, 1992), 89–91; James C. McCann, *Maize and Grace: Africa's Encounter with a New World Crop, 1500–2000* (Cambridge, MA, 2005), 23–7, 40–2, 63–77; Richards, *The Unending Frontier*, 81, 114–15, 124, 130–3; Richards, *The Mughal Empire*, 190.

helped to support the dramatic surge of population in the Old World, especially in China, where population more than doubled between 1650 and 1800, and in Europe, where populations grew by at least 60 percent. Land was used more effectively and consistently, and simply was able to produce more digestible biomass with the inclusion of New World crops in the agricultural mix. Some of this New World-derived production, particularly corn, was used for animal feed, but as such certainly added to the caloric/biomass total available to Old World peoples. We typically think of energy as something burned in a hearth or an engine, but food calories are certainly burned in the metabolic engines of living bodies. These added food calories worked in combination with institutional action to stem the tide of epidemics, and thus to stem the tide of crisis mortality in the Old World. Whether this added nutrition did much more for human well-being in aggregate other than to stabilize the extremes of mortality is an open question, however.[48]

Exotic crops entered the European food chain by trade as well. Such of course was the original purpose of the armed expansion of early modern European commerce. In chronological priority this meant the spices and teas of Southeast Asia and China; to these we can add the sugar moving into the Atlantic circuit, and coffee, originally from Yemen. The New World added two more: tobacco, particularly the sweet varieties from the Orinoco, and cacao, the base ingredient of chocolate. Of these, sugar and tobacco, with coffee and cacao, would become central to the plantation agriculture established in the Americas from Brazil through the West Indies and north to the Chesapeake. Along with tea, all are mildly addictive pharmacopic stimulants, and their impact was exactly that on early modern European society, which was at the same time experimenting with a range of new distilled alcohol products. As gin, rum, whiskey, and tobacco displaced beer, ale, and wine in the taverns, coffee and chocolate became the preferred

---

[48] Crosby, *The Colombian Exchange*, 165–70; Malanima, "The Energy Basis for Early Modern Growth"; John Komlos, "The New World's Contribution to Food Consumption during the Industrial Revolution," *JEEconH* 27 (1998), 67–84; Findlay and O'Rourke, *Power and Plenty*, 160–1; Flinn, *The European Demographic System*, 96; Thomas McKeown, *The Modern Rise of Population* (London, 1976), 131–2; William L. Langer, "American Foods and Europe's Population Growth, 1750–1850," *Journal of Social History* 8 (1975), 51–66. Here it might be noted that I am straddling a great debate involving disease and nutrition in the early modern population expansions. On one hand, a public health camp currently led by James Riley in *Rising Life Expectancy* argues that the containment of disease in the "epidemiological transition" was fundamental to the rise of population since 1500; on the other hand, a nutrition school launched by Thomas McKeown and recently synthesized by Robert Fogel in *The Escape from Hunger and Premature Death, 1700–2100: Europe, America, and the Third World* (New York, 2004) argues that rising incomes, a rising standard of living, and improving nutrition was critical. I see both at work, nutrition more important in China, and public health more important in a better-fed Europe, particularly northwest Europe. For a useful discussion, see Simon Szreter, "Industrialization and Health," *British Medical Bulletin* 69 (2004), 75–86.

drinks of merchants congregating at urban coffeehouses to learn the latest commercial news. Tea – drunk with copious amounts of sugar – became the focal point of a new female-controlled area of respectability and sociability; if sugar eroded teeth, the tea may have had certain medicinal benefits. In short the "new groceries" brought to Europe by an imperial commerce would reconfigure the shape and quality of everyday life, and they would unleash new demands for households goods that would be met by expanding manufacturing enterprises.[49]

The trade in "new groceries" brings us back to winners and losers in the early modern world, and a *fourth* central outcome of early modern imperial globalization. Over the long run, the outcome of the early modern period into the nineteenth century would be the rising dominance not just of Europe, but of northwest Europe, most especially Britain. Over the past several decades, among the various debates surrounding Britain's rise to commercial and industrial dominance, there has been something of a struggle between those who argue that Britain's rise can be explained as an autonomous phenomenon, ending at the water's edge of an island nation, and those who see the rise of Britain, and the rise of Europe more broadly, as grounded in intercontinental trade and empire building.[50] Certainly, there are particular features unique to Britain – a relatively open society, constitutional protections of rights and capital, and useful endowment of paleo-energy in the form of coal – that go a long way toward explaining its sudden emergence at the end of the seventeenth century.[51] But an emerging literature has established quite decisively that access to the Atlantic and direct participation in

---

[49] In a large literature, see Neil McKendrick et al., *The Birth of a Consumer Society: The Commercialization of Eighteenth-Century England* (Bloomington, IN, 1982); Sidney W. Mintz, *Sweetness and Power: The Place of Sugar in Modern History* (New York, 1985); the many essays in John Brewer and Roy Porter, eds., *Consumption and the World of Goods* (New York, 1993); Woodruff D. Smith, *Consumption and the Making of Respectability, 1600–1800* (New York, 2002); Alan McFarlane, *The Savage Wars of Peace: England, Japan, and the Malthusian Trap* (Houndmills, 2003), 124–53; Brian Cowan, *The Social Life of Coffee: The Emergence of the British Coffeehouse* (New Haven, CT, 2005); Marcy Norton, *Sacred Gifts, Profane Pleasures: A History of Tobacco and Chocolate in the Atlantic World* (Ithaca, NY, 2008); and Paul Freedman, *Out of the East: Spices and the Medieval Imagination* (New Haven, CT, 2008).

[50] Among those advocating a "water's edge" approach to Europe and Britain, see most importantly Patrick O'Brien, "European Economic Development: The Contribution of the Periphery," *EconHistR* 35 (1982), 1–18. E. A. Wrigley, another proponent of autonomous development, has hinted that there might be some grounds for a wider, global approach: see *Poverty, Progress, and Population* (New York, 2004), 45 n 4, 219.

[51] David S. Landes, *The Wealth and Poverty of Nations: Why Some are so Rich and Some are so Poor* (New York, 1998); Douglas North and Robert Paul Thomas, *The Rise of the Western World: A New Economic History* (New York, 1973), 146–58; Joel Mokyr, *The Enlightened Economy: An Economic History of Britain, 1700–1850* (New Haven, CT, 2009); E. A. Wrigley, *Continuity, Chance, and Change: The Character of the Industrial Revolution in England* (New York, 1988).

empire building were fundamental to economic growth and development in the early modern era. As measured by urbanization and by rough estimates of GNP, the Atlantic trading and empire-building nations – Portugal, Spain, France, the Netherlands, and Britain – grew more rapidly as a group than other European countries. Italy's fall from late medieval dominance is particularly notable; having thrived as the intermediary entrepôt in the eastern trade through Islamic lands, the north Italian commercial cities were cut off from the new Atlantic trade by Spain's control of the Strait of Gibraltar. And if Portugal and Spain led early modern empire building, success in war also mattered. Their leading position was quickly surpassed after defeat by the Dutch, who in turn gave way to the English.[52]

* * *

The Little Ice Age, New World Depopulation, and the Origins of the African Slave Trade

This entire sweep of global transformation unfolded in the context of climate conditions not seen since the end of the Bronze Age, and that may have been the most severe since the Younger Dryas. The Little Ice Age certainly did not cause the rise of the early modern empires, but it certainly shaped and channeled the course of events in these centuries. Before we examine its impact, we need briefly to chart its course.

As we have seen in the previous chapter, the roots of the Little Ice Age and the dynamics of its course lie in a complex interaction of declines in solar output, sequences of volcanic eruptions, and atmospheric and oceanic circulation. The erratically warm and rainy summers of the fourteenth-century North Atlantic (a "proto-LIA"), shaped both the European Great Famine and the spread of the bubonic plague, which requires warmth for its propagation. On the other side of the world, the fading of the medieval La Niña and the reassertion of a highly variable ENSO regime in the Pacific shaped declining summer monsoons in Asia, peaking first in the "Khmer" drought of roughly 1350–70 that undermined medieval kingdoms in South and Southeast Asia.

---

[52] On empire, trade, and growth, see Daron Acemoglu et al., "The Rise of Europe: Atlantic Trade, Institutional Change, and Economic Growth," *AER* 95 (2005), 54–579; Robert C. Allen, "Progress and Poverty in Early Modern Europe," *EconHistR* 56 (2003), 403–43; Pomeranz, *The Great Divergence*; Findlay and O'Rourke, *Power and Plenty*; and Joseph E. Inikori, *Africans and the Industrial Revolution in England: A Study in International Trade and Economic Development* (New York, 2002). Ultimately, this approach has its roots in the arguments first proposed in Eric Williams, *Capitalism and Slavery* (Chapel Hill, NC, 1944). For urbanization, see Jan de Vries, *European Urbanization, 1500–1800* (Cambridge, MA, 1984) and Jan de Vries and Ad van der Woude, *The First Modern Economy: Success, Failure, and Perseverance of the Dutch Economy, 1500–1815* (Cambridge, UK, 1997), 57–78, 507–21.

The first phase of the Little Ice Age proper, what I will call "LIA I," started abruptly at 1400, with the storms shifting from summer to winter, marked by the sea salt and potassium in the Greenland ice cores (indicators of the fourth Holocene millennial Siberian High), evidence of ice rafting and of the weakening of the thermohaline pump (see Figures III.4a, III.7).

After the Pacific ENSO shifted toward a stronger El Niño state, for reasons as yet unexplained, the South Asian summer monsoon seems to have improved during the fifteenth and sixteenth centuries, if not without certain setbacks. It is possible that this relief was shaped by the moderation of the Sporer solar minimum, which peaked around 1470 and then moderated to 1600. However, around 1560, global conditions seem to have turned sharply worse through 1700, and can be called "LIA II." The Siberian High, strong since 1400, remained strong until a few final winter blasts in the early eighteenth century, while northern summer temperatures dropped decisively around 1560. Around the Indo-Pacific regions, the ENSO system held to a strong El Niño state during the seventeenth century, while winter and summer monsoons in China and India deteriorated to their worst readings in what is called the "Ming drought" of the 1630s and 1640s. These decades saw particularly strong volcanic eruptions followed by the advancing Maunder solar minimum, the most intense since the final years of the preclassical Hallstatt, which peaked during the 1690s. This sharp "ice age" cooling drove the Intertropical Convergence Zone to the furthest southern position that it had taken since the Younger Dryas. It was in this context that atmospheric CO_2 dropped from about 282 ppm to about 278 ppm: not much it might seem, but striking in light of its long and very slow rise over the Holocene, and its explosive rise since 1750.

Little Ice Age climates shaped the conditions in which the indigenous peoples of the New World first encountered European explorers and settlers, and raise complicated questions about reciprocal effects and causes. Megadroughts continued to afflict North America and Mexico, peaking in the Mississippi Valley from the 1350s to the 1380s, the 1450s, and 1560s, the worst of which were far more extreme than any in recent centuries (see Figure III.5b). These Little Ice Age droughts, in which crops suffered and food was scarce, clearly put New World peoples at a disadvantage when they first encountered European explorers. Twenty years of drought in the Valley of Mexico in the mid-1400s seriously affected the Aztecs, and northern Mexico was suffering another twenty-year drought when Cortes arrived in 1519. Similarly, the first Spanish and English incursions along the James River in Virginia in 1570, 1585, and 1607 took place during three serious droughts in the Tidewater region, accelerating the trajectory toward conflict and violence.[53] Recently the epidemic mass death of the

[53] Edward R. Cook et al., "Megadroughts in North America: Placing IPCC Projections of Hydroclimatic Change in a Long-Term Palaeoclimate Context," *JQS* 25 (2010), 48–61;

native peoples of Mexico has been attributed in part to the effects of the sixteenth-century American megadrought: the hemorrhagic *cocoliztli* fevers that killed as many as 15 million Mexicans between 1545 and the 1570s, it is argued, had their origins in a rodent virus that intensified during drought years and spread with multiplying rodents in years of increased rainfall. The same mechanism, this team proposes, explains a possible massive decline of Mayan and Mexican populations at the end of the classic period between 800 and 950, when Mexico and Central America were struck by a previous massive drought.[54]

If the Little Ice Age may have contributed to the mass death of native Americans, these mass deaths may in turn have contributed to the intensity of the Little Ice Age. Such is the argument advanced by William Ruddiman. Piqued by a student's question about the little ripples in atmospheric CO_2 between roughly AD 300 and AD 1800, Ruddiman boldly proposed in 2003 that they were the result of mass death by epidemic disease. The argument hinges on carbon drawdown: as epidemics killed huge populations, he argues, the regrown forest cover absorbed enough CO_2 to have an effect on its level in the atmosphere, and in fact on global climate. Thus he proposed that three massive die-offs – the results of the ancient plagues, the Black Death, and the New World epidemics – had respectively caused the Dark Ages and the Little Ice Age. The primary evidence for this pandemic-driven cooling argument lies in CO_2 measurements from Antarctic ice cores, which wobble between ~282 ppm and ~275 ppm between AD 200 and AD 1800. Many climate scientists see these CO_2 declines as oceanic responses driven by natural forcings of solar minima and global temperature.[55]

There is no definitive resolution to this debate yet: Ruddiman has defended his arguments, and a number of younger scientists are testing his models.

David W. Stahle et al., "Tree-Ring Reconstructed Megadroughts over North America since A.D. 1300," *ClimCh* 83 (2007), 133–49; Jose Villanueva-Diaz et al., "Winter-Spring Precipitation Reconstructions from Tree Rings for Northeast Mexico," *ClimCh* 83 (2007), 117–31; Matthew D. Therrell et al., "Aztec Drought and the 'Curse of One Rabbit,'" *Bulletin of the American Meteorological Society* 85 (2004), 1263–72; David W. Stahle et al., "The Lost Colony and Jamestown Droughts," *Science* 280 (1998), 564–7; David G. Anderson et al., "Paleoclimate and the Potential Food Reserves of Mississippian Societies: A Case Study from the Savannah River Valley," *AmAntiq* 60 (1995), 258–86; B. G. Hunt and T. I. Elliott, "Mexican Megadrought," *ClimDyn* 20 (2002), 1–12.

[54] Rodolfo Acuna-Soto et al., "Drought, Epidemic Disease, and the Fall of Classical Period Cultures in Mesoamerica (AD 750–950): Hemorrhagic Fevers as a Cause of Massive Population Loss," *MedHyp* 65 (2005), 405–9; Acuna-Soto et al., "Megadrought and Megadeath"; Acuna-Soto et al., "When Half the Population Died."

[55] Ruddiman's original argument was made in William F. Ruddiman, "The Anthropogenic Greenhouse Era began Thousands of Years Ago," *ClimCh* 61 (2003), 261–93, at 279–85; and Ruddiman, *Plows, Plagues, and Petroleum: How Humans took Control of Climate* (Princeton, NJ, 2005), 119–46; the subsequent debate can be followed in *Plows, Plagues, and Petroleum*, 211–14, and in his most recent response in "The Early Anthropogenic Hypothesis: Challenges and Responses," *Reviews of Geophysics* 45 (2007), RG4001.

The state of the debate varies with each of the three pandemic epochs. The argument for the ancient world is the most tenuous, hanging on the evidence of six questionably dated CO_2 readings stretching across 600 years. It also seems problematic given that so many of these epidemic deaths took place in the semiarid Mediterranean circuit and Southwest Asia, where reforestation sufficient to draw down carbon in sufficient volume to affect global balances is questionable. More and better-dated ice core CO_2 readings are available for the era of the Black Death, but when they are averaged the medieval CO_2 decline is long and moderate, and seems to start around 1200, not 1350 (see Figure IV.1). Possibly, as Ruddiman has argued, the thirteenth-century CO_2 decline might have been a result of the disastrous depopulation of China with the Mongol invasions. Again, there are questions of whether enough agricultural land was abandoned and sufficiently reforested after the Black Death to achieve a significant carbon drawdown. In Europe, much of the depopulated lands were kept deforested by the expansion of grazing of cattle and especially sheep; a significant post-Mongol reforestation of dry north China seems equally unlikely.[56]

But the evidence for the CO_2 impact of the New World epidemics is much stronger. The combined CO_2 data shows a sharp drop between 1550 and 1650, exactly when the New World death tolls were at their highest (see Figure IV.1). Here the Mexican *cocoliztli* epidemics, which took place in the more arid highlands, were probably less important than the mass death in the lowland regions stretching from southern Mexico to Columbia Peru, and the Amazon basin, where modern deforestation is uncovering the remains of unknown complex societies. Sixteenth-century forest regrowth potentially would have consumed an enormous volume of carbon; a recent and very convincing analysis compares new archaeological evidence for a sharp reduction in biomass burning in the tropical Americas with the volume of reforested temperate and tropical forest that would have been produced by tens of millions of deaths. It finds that Ruddiman's thesis has considerable merit.[57] This will be a hot debate in the coming years, but the weight of

[56] Here see Thomas B. van Hoof et al., "A Role for Atmospheric CO_2 in Preindustrial Climate Forcing," *PNAS* 105 (2008), 15815–18; Thomas B. van Hoof et al., "Forest Re-Growth on Medieval Farmland after the Black Death Pandemic – Implications for Atmospheric CO_2 Levels," *PPP* 237 (2006), 396–411; Dan Yeloff and Bas van Gel, "Abandonment of Farmland and Vegetation Succession following the Eurasian Plague Pandemic of AD 1347–52," *Journal of Biogeography* 34 (2007), 575–82.

[57] Richard J. Nevle and Dennis K. Bird, "Effects of Syn-Pandemic Fire Reduction and Reforestation in the Tropical America on Atmospheric CO_2 during European Conquest," *PPP* 264 (2008), 25–38; see also Franz X. Faust et al., "Evidence for the Postconquest Demographic Collapse of the Americas in Historical CO_2 Levels," *Earth Interactions* 10/11 (2006), 1–14; D. F. Ferretti et al., "Unexpected Changes to the Global Methane Budget over the Past 2000 Years," *Science* 309 (2005), 1714–17. On the Amazon, see Martti Pärssinen et al., "Pre-Columbian Geometric Earthworks in the Upper Purús: A Complex Society in Western Amazonia," *Antiquity* 83 (2010), 1084–95; Michael J. Hechenberger et al.,

the evidence at present suggests that the sudden disappearance of at least three-quarters of the native peoples of the Americas during the sixteenth and seventeenth centuries made a significant contribution to the intensity of the second stage of the Little Ice Age.

The Little Ice Age played an equally harrowing role in the advance of the slave trade in western Africa, and the onset of a slow decline of population in the general sub-Saharan region. Since the Mid-Holocene transition, African climates had been dry and variable, governed in western Africa by advances of cold temperatures in the North Atlantic and the associated ebb and flow of the Intertropical Convergence Zone. Historical and paleoecological studies concur that the climate of the Sahel and savannah region running from the Niger to the Atlantic was generally quite dry during and following the Medieval Climate Anomaly.[58] The effect was to shift the boundaries between desert, Sahel, and woodland-forest regions to the south, and to push the range of the livestock-killing tsetse fly to the south as well. Nomadic peoples, dependent on camels, horses, and Zebu cattle, spread through this expanded Sahel territory, and by the thirteenth century had founded Islamic empires controlling the trade in gold and slaves across the Sahara with large forces of mounted warriors. In one influential reconstruction, the interior Mali and Songhay empires flourished until wet-dry oscillations in the sixteenth century moved the tsetse fly boundary north, and opened new routes through the Sahara, along which a Moroccan army marched in 1590–1 to sack Timbuktu. From at least the 1630s, if not before,

---

"Pre-Columbian Urbanism, Anthropogenic Landscapes, and the Future of the Amazon," *Science* 321 (2008), 1214–17; Eduardo Góes Neves, "Ecology, Ceramic Chronology and Distribution, Long-Term History, and Political Change in the Amazonian Floodplain, in Helaine Silverman and William H. Isbell, eds. *Handbook of South American Archaeology* (New York, 2008), 359–79.

[58] George E. Brooks, *Landlords and Strangers: Ecology, Society, and Trade in Western Africa, 1000–1630* (Boulder, CO, 1993), 7–25; T. M. Shanahan et al., "Atlantic Forcing of Persistent Drought in West Africa," *Science* 324 (2009), 377–80; F. A. Street-Perrott et al., "Drought and Dust Deposition in the West African Sahel: A 5500-Year Record from Kajemarum Oasis, Northeastern Nigeria," *Holocene* 10 (2000), 293–302. Two central African sites in the eastern Congo and Malawi reveal climate patterns similar to these West African sites: J. M. Russell and T. C. Johnson, "Little Ice Age Drought in Equatorial Africa: Intertropical Convergence Zone Migrations and El-Niño-Southern Oscillation Variability," *Geology* 35 (2007), 21–4; Erik T. Brown and Thomas C. Johnson, "Coherence between Tropical East African and South American Records of the Little Ice Age," *Geochemistry, Geophysics, Geosystems* 6 (2005), Q12005. These studies conflict with the assessment of Sharon E. Nicholson, "The Methodology of Historical Climate Reconstruction and Its Application to Africa," *JAfrH* 20 (1979), 31–49, who sees relatively wet climates prevailing except from 1300 to 1450 and from the end of the eighteenth century into the nineteenth. See the useful syntheses of this debate in James L. A. Webb, *Desert Frontier: Ecological and Economic Change along the Western Sahel, 1600–1850* (Madison, WI, 1995), 4–5 and James C. McCann, *Green Land, Brown Land, Black Land: An Environmental History of Africa, 1800–1991* (Portsmouth, NH, 1999), 23–31.

West Africa was subjected to increasingly dry conditions, a manifestation of the second stage of the Little Ice Age, bringing severe droughts and famines during the 1640s and 1680s.[59] To the south, in west central Africa (Angola), droughts have been documented from the late sixteenth century forward. Here droughts drove a movement in and out of enslavement, with the failure of the rains forcing people in marginal areas to accept subordination to better-endowed lineages in temporary slavery; their descendants would establish their own villages when conditions improved.[60]

A series of forces coalesced in the sixteenth to seventeenth centuries: the variability of Little Ice Age climates helped to splinter the great West African states and to drive larger numbers in growing populations into slavery, exactly at the moment that Europeans, led by the Portuguese, arrived on West African coasts. From the 1510s, African peoples were siphoned off into the Atlantic labor system, first to Atlantic islands and then to Brazil, the Caribbean, and eventually North America. The slave trade grew to monstrous proportions, and swept up as many as 28 million people, who were transported to the Americas, the Islamic world, and regional African destinations, or who died in these forced migrations.[61] Between 1519 and 1650, characterized as a wetter period in the West African Sahel but dry in Angola, about 3,500 slaves were transported per year, two-thirds from Angola. But after 1650, when the full drought impacts of the Little Ice Age struck the Sahel, the slave trade expanded enormously, tripling by 1675 and doubling again by 1700.[62] Certainly climate did not drive the rise of the slave trade, but it set the conditions, encouraging the rise of small warring states and increasing the general stress on the population with crop failure and famine. After growing until roughly 1600 at a rate comparable to the population of Europe, sub-Saharan population began a long decline that was not reversed

---

[59] See Brooks, *Landlords and Strangers*, 169–74, 319; the paleoclimate studies cited in note 58, which show dry climates through the seventeenth century; Webb, *Desert Frontier*, esp. 3–26; and Curtin, *The Rise and Fall of the Plantation Complex*, 120–2. Quite differently, east Fircan climate operated in reverse to that of these West African regions, and saw higher rainfall during the Little Ice Age. Dirk Verschuren et al., "Rainfall and Drought in Equatorial East Africa during the Past 1,100 Years," *Nature* 403 (2001), 410–14.

[60] Joseph C. Miller, "The Significance of Drought, Disease, and Famine in the Agriculturally Marginal Zones of West-Central Africa," *JAfrH* 23 (1982), 17–61; –, "Lineages, Ideology, and the History of Slavery in Western Central Africa," in Paul E. Lovejoy, ed., *The Ideology of Slavery in Africa* (London, 1981), 40–71; –, "The Paradoxes of Impoverishment in the Atlantic Zone," in David Birmingham and Phyllis M. Martin, eds., *History of Central Africa, Vol. One* (London, 1983), 118–59.

[61] Patrick Manning, "The Slave Trade: The Formal Demography," in Joseph E. Inikora and Stanley L. Engerman, eds., *The Atlantic Slave Trade: Effects on Economies, Societies, and Peoples* (Durham, NC, 1992), 119–20.

[62] David Eltis, "The Volume and Structure of the Transatlantic Slave Trade: A Reassessment," *WMQ*, 3d ser., 58 (2001), 44.

until after the end of the slave trade in the nineteenth century. No one has attempted to calculate the CO_2 impact of this decline.

* * *

The Little Ice Age and Early Modern Eurasia

The Little Ice Age, as our most recent Hallstatt millennial solar minimum, is a fundamental dimension of the complex final passage of the early modern era, as we are defining it here as spanning from 1350 to 1700. From the 1560s to 1700, global climate was shaped by a sequence of cold summer and winters, and Old World populations suffered severely, if nothing like Adam Smith's "dreadful misfortunes" that had been falling upon New World peoples since the turn of the sixteenth century. The Old World seventeenth-century crisis, however, is best compared to the pervasive crises that assailed Late Bronze Age societies around 1200 BC, or Late Neolithic/Chalcolithic societies during the fourth millennium BC. The consequences of climatic stress were powerfully manifested across Eurasia.[63]

Early Little Ice Age climates may have been background contexts for the launching of early modern explorations and empires, but they certainly shaped the sudden retrenchment of one great global effort. Dynastic ambition, religious conviction, and calculations of geopolitical and economic advantage mobilized the European voyages that set out to discover and control new routes to the Indies. But when the Portuguese arrived on the Malabar Coast of India in 1498, they had entered an oceanic arena into which China had ventured first, almost a century previously, during an interval of imperial expansion briefly permitted by the ebb and flow of the East Asian monsoon systems.

From the time of the Bronze Age, as we have seen, Chinese regimes were subject to the relatively regular oscillation of the summer and winter monsoons. Most recently, droughts and famine in the 1350s had contributed to the Red Turban Rebellions that had undermined the Mongol Yuan dynasty and ushered in the Ming. Serious droughts caused by the failure of the summer monsoon in the advancing Little Ice Age – Timothy Brook has labeled them China's "Nine Sloughs" – would intensify until the mid-seventeenth

---

[63] The debates over the seventeenth-century crisis running back to seminal essays by Eric Hobsbawm and Hugh Trevor-Roper have been reviewed in Jonathan Dewald, "Crisis, Chronology, and the Shape of European Social History," *AHR* 113 (2008), 1031–52; J. H. Elliott, "The General Crisis in Retrospect: A Debate without End," in Philip Benedict and Myron P. Guttmann, eds., *Early Modern Europe: From Crisis to Stability* (Newark, DE, 2005), 31–51; and Geoffrey Parker and Leslie M. Smith, "Introduction," and Niels Steensgaard, "The Seventeenth-Century Crisis," in Parker and Smith, eds., *The General Crisis of the Seventeenth Century*, 1–86; Lieberman, *Strange Parallels*, II: 79–84; Findley, *The Turks in World History*, 127–8.

century, when the Ming itself collapsed, and was in turn replaced by the Manchu Qing.[64] But the Ming persevered and endured for almost three centuries, and their success was manifested in both the mobilization and abandonment of great voyages of exploration in the early fifteenth century.

Throughout the Middle Ages, a vast trade diaspora of Chinese merchants in Southeast Asia and India linked the Chinese economy to the West, and in the early fifteenth century, the Ming emperor sent huge naval squadrons out into the Indian Ocean. These were the seven voyages of Admiral Zheng He, which took fleets of dozens of Chinese naval vessels in vast circuits of the Indian Ocean as far as east Africa and Aden, including extensive trade and tributary missions in Southeast Asia and India. The first six of these voyages took place between 1405 and 1422, and the final voyage, which reached the Red Sea and the East African Coast, lasted from 1430 to 1433. These expeditions were driven by the vision of Ming Emperor Yung-Lo, as part of a policy of expansion and conquest that spread Chinese power into Mongolia, Central Asia, and Vietnam. The opening of Yung-Lo's reign in 1402, however, started just as a thirty-five-year period of bountiful summer monsoons was coming to an end, and the first stage of the Little Ice Age was beginning, with the onset of the millennial Siberian High. By the time of his death in 1424, the consequences were beginning to be felt in the beginnings of thirty years of drought across China, with even more severe conditions in Mongolia (see Figure III.5c). The result would be several decades of regional famines, rebellions, and Mongol incursions. In the face of these conditions, Yung-Lo's successors were more concerned with stabilizing their domain. Court politics drove the end of the voyages, as priorities turned to famine relief and defending against raiding Mongols, who in 1449 defeated a Chinese army and nearly plundered the new capital at Beijing. The Ming turned their attention to defending the realm: building the Great Wall would take priority over state-directed contact and trade with the outside world.[65]

[64] Frederick W. Mote, "The Rise of the Ming Dynasty, 1330–1367," in Frederick W. Mote and Denis Twitchett, eds., *The Cambridge History of China, Vol. 7: The Ming Dynasty, 1368–1644, Part I* (Cambridge, 1988), 29–42; Edward L. Dreyer, "Military Origins of Ming China," in Mote and Twitchett, eds., *The Cambridge History of China*, 7: 59–60; Timothy Brook, *The Troubled Empire: China in the Yuan and Ming Dynasties* (Cambridge, MA, 2010).

[65] Hok-Lam Chan, "The Chien-wen, Yung-lo, and Hung-his, and Hsüan-te Reigns, 1399–1435," in Mote and Twitchett, eds., *The Cambridge History of China*, 7: 220–41, 256–76; Denis Twitchett and Tilemann Grime, "The Sheng-t'ung, Ching-t'ai, and T'ien-shun Reigns, 1436–1464," in Mote and Twitchett, eds., *The Cambridge History of China*, 7: 319–31; Edward L. Dreyer, *Zheng He: China and the Oceans in the Early Ming Dynasty, 1405–1433* (New York, 2007), 60–1, 166–73; Louise Levathes, *When China Ruled the Seas: The Treasure Fleet of the Dragon Throne 1405–1433* (New York, 1993), 173–80, 185; Arthur Waldron, *The Great Wall of China: From History to Myth* (New York, 1990), 72–107.

The fact that the Ming regime survived between 1440 and 1520, the worst climate conditions in four centuries, was, in part, testimony to the internal divisions among the Mongols, who might well have toppled a weaker dynasty. But it was also a testimony to genuine efforts the Ming emperors made to attend to the welfare of the people, whether by rain-making rituals – apparently effective in 1370 – or aggressive policies of frontier settlement and famine relief.[66] Rebuilding the Grand Canal eased the shipment of grain between north and south; its opening in 1415 undermined the need for a naval force in the South China Sea, sporadically beset by pirate fleets. The result of the Ming administration was massive population growth, which might have reached 200 million by 1600.[67] But by 1600, these efforts were failing because of factional court politics, in the face of a combined failure of the summer monsoons and an advance of the dry winter monsoon unseen for more than 600 years. This was the East Asian manifestation of the cold winters and summers of the Little Ice Age's second stage: as they both peaked during the 1630s and the 1640s, after decades of drought, famine, epidemic, and rebellion, the Ming collapsed, and the Manchu – Manchurian inheritors of the wider steppe tradition – swept to power. The succeeding Manchu-Qing dynasty immediately launched programs to stabilize and improve conditions around the country, and was able to generate famine relief on a sufficient scale to the end of the next century.[68]

Such was China's experience of a wider seventeenth-century crisis. Ironically, its close neighbor, Japan, managed to avoid the calamity that struck the length of Eurasia. Trade with China had been one of the factors behind Japan's slow population growth until the early modern period. Rather than taking hold permanently and building routine immunities, disease flowed into Japan sporadically, hitting non-immune populations. But after centuries of stagnation and slow growth Japanese population shot up during the seventeenth century, and Tokagawa trade restrictions are seen as playing a key role. But if political isolation helped Japan's population grow, the cooler temperatures of the Little Ice Age may have played a role as well.

[66] John D. Langlois, "The Hung-wi Reign, 1368–1398," in Mote and Twitchett, eds., *The Cambridge History of China*, 7: 122, 281, 298; Chan, "The Chien-wen … Reigns," 334–5; Timothy Brook, "Communications and Commerce," in Frederick W. Mote and Denis Twitchett, eds., *The Cambridge History of China, Vol. 8: The Ming Dynasty, 1368–1644, Part II* (Cambridge, 1998), 606–7; Richards, *The Unending Frontier*, 118; Elvin, *The Retreat of the Elephants*, 192–5.

[67] Dreyer, *Zheng He*, 168–70; Willard J. Peterson, "New Order for the Old Order," in Willard J. Peterson, ed., *The Cambridge History of China, Vol. 9: Part One: The Ch'ing Empire to 1800* (Cambridge, 2002), 5.

[68] Ramon H. Myers and Yeh-Chien Wang, "Economic Developments, 1644–1800," in Peterson, ed., *The Cambridge History of China*, 9: 585–604, 621–3, 631; Michael Marmé, "Locating Linkages and Painting Bull's Eyes around Bullet-Holes? An East Asian Perspective on the Seventeenth-Century Crisis," *AHR* 13 (2008), 1080–9; Goldstone, *Revolution and Rebellion in the Early Modern World*, 349–415.

Asamu Saito has extended the count of famines in Japan back to the seventh century, and finds that famines declined slowly from the thirteenth century, perhaps shaping the slow growth of population that followed. But there was a sharp reduction in famines from the middle of the sixteenth century forward, and here climate may have played a key role. Rice crops require a wet spring, and spring droughts contribute decisively to their failure. Thus the relatively warm temperatures – and dry springs – running back to the ninth century and the Medieval Climate Anomaly probably explain the regular famines of Heian and medieval Japan. The cooling of the Little Ice Age and a declining number of summer droughts – reducing crop failure and famine – may have worked in combination with Tokugawa state policy to drive up Japanese numbers in the seventeenth century.[69]

If Japan avoided a seventeenth-century crisis, the rest of Eurasia – led by Ming China – did not. European historians have debated the idea of a seventeenth-century crisis for fifty years and, if some are inclined toward skepticism, the evidence is more than clear.[70] Between the 1550s and roughly 1700, the length of Eurasia was wracked by war, rebellion, revolution, famine, and epidemic, and it is increasingly clear that the 2,300-year Hallstatt-cycle millennial Siberian High – the most recent in a series running deep into prehistory – was a critical force in a century or more of misery. This cycle had advanced since the turn of the fourteenth century, when the seesaw of the Indo-Pacific system had tilted toward stronger El Niño variation and declining Asian summer monsoons. Recent measurements suggest that the trajectory of monsoon failure was remarkably similar in northern China and eastern India, and India's course through the Little Ice Age bears some careful comparison to that of China (see Figures III.5c, III.3–III.7).

The withdrawal of the Chinese from the Indian Ocean in the 1430s left open a domain of unarmed and relatively peaceful commerce that the Portuguese assaulted in the early sixteenth century. But even if control of the seas was lost to armed European commerce, the circumstances of the Indian subcontinent were not immediately adversely affected. Europeans wanted Indian spices and textiles, and they were happy to pay for them with American silver and gold. The result was a boom of prosperity that explains the high wages of North Indian artisans in the seventeenth century, as they sold their goods into a chain running back to Lisbon and London. This trade-based prosperity was a broad background to violent empire building and sporadic famine crisis.

---

[69] Osamu Saito, "Climate and Famine in Historic Japan: A Very Long-Term Perspective," paper presented at the conference on "Environment and Society in the Japanese Islands: From Prehistory to the Present," Tokai University Pacific Center, Honolulu, Hawaii, March 28–9, 2011.

[70] See note 63.

While the Portuguese were well established in the southwest coast of India by 1510, the Mughal descendants of Timur and distantly the Mongols were approaching from the northwest, out of the passes from Afghanistan. Babur's decisive victories at Panipat and Kanua in 1526 and 1527 establishing Mughal power at Agra and Delhi were fought at the onset of a sharp summer monsoon failure (perhaps driven by a sharp spike in the Siberian High). Famines reported for this decade may have both military and climatic causes.[71] Where Chinese population fell during the collapse of the Ming in the early seventeenth century, India's population may have grown slowly during the seventeenth century.[72] Timurid Mughal conquest established something of a "Pax Islamica" across northern India, but their wars of conquest continued for decades and, with massive building projects like the Taj Mahal, were funded through a very effective system of taxation that may have extracted the entire surplus from the peasantry. At the same time, droughts and famines struck with varying severity in the seventeenth century, most intensely with serious monsoon failures in the dry Gujarat and the Deccan at the onset of the "Ming drought" between 1629 and 1632 and in 1702 to 1704, when millions died and cannibalism was reported; there were minor but notable drought-driven famines during the 1650s and 1680s.[73] In all likelihood, prosperity and crisis were a mosaic patchwork in seventeenth-century India. When the Mughal empire began to come under strain during the early eighteenth century, it was not the result of the monsoon, which generally remained strong until the 1760s, but of military overreach, Hindu resistance, and the growing power of the British East India Company[74] (see Figure III.9).

[71] Richard, *The Mughal Empire*, 5–9; William A. Dando, *The Geography of Famine* (London, 1980), 128, 134; A. Lovejoy, *The History and Economics of Indian Famines* (London, 1914), 136–7; Charles W. McCinn, *Famine Truths, Half Truths, Untruths* (Calcutta, 1902), 29–32.

[72] Myers and Wang, "Economic Developments"; Irfan Habib, "Population," in Tapen Raychaudhuri and Irfan Habib, eds., *The Cambridge Economic History of India* (Cambridge, 1982), I: 167 concludes that Indian population grew from ~150 million in 1600 to ~200 million in 1800. McEvedy and Jones, *Atlas of World Population History*, 183, show an even rise from 130 million in 1600 to 170 million in 1800; Biraben proposes 145 million in 1600, a drop in population from 175 million at 1700 to 165 million at 1750, and then a rise to 180 million in 1800, without explanation. Ajit Das Gupta, "Study of the Historical Demography of India," in D. V. Glass and Roger Revelle, eds., *Population and Social Change* (London, 1972), 426, 430, 435, arrives at 135 million in 1600 and 154 million in 1800.

[73] For droughts and famines, see note 71 and Irfan Habib, "Mughal India," and H. Fukazawa, "Maharashtra and Deccan," in Raychaudhuri and Habib, eds., *The Cambridge Economic History of India*, I: 224–5, 476–7.

[74] John F. Richards, "The Seventeenth-Century Crisis in South Asia," *Modern Asian Studies* 24 (1990), 625–38, esp. 629–30; Richards, *The Mughal Empire*, 236–7, 253–97; David Clingingsmith and Jeffrey G. Williamson, "Deindustrialization in 18th and 19th Century India: Mughal Decline, Climate Shocks, and British Industrial Ascent," *ExpEconH* 45 (2008), 209–34.

The Little Ice Age struck the Ottoman empire sharply and catastrophically during the 1590s. As in previous cold epochs, the cooling of the Little Ice Age drove a shift in the North Atlantic Oscillation from positive to negative mode, bringing increasing precipitation south into the Mediterranean and as far east as Central Asia[75] (see Figure III.10). But during the 1590s, a combination of forces shaped a particularly intense drought in southern Anatolia and into the Levant. In a strange couplet that echoed the previous two Siberian Highs, the NAO negative precipitation seems to have been blocked by a strong high over the Baltic – a western manifestation of the Siberian High – driving cold winds south and west. In addition, a sulphur veil from strong volcanic eruptions in the early 1590s would have affected temperatures around the world. The resulting drought, cold, and famine drove a fifteen-year rebellion, and permanently undermined the strength of the Ottoman empire.[76]

Crisis should undermine routine health, and in Europe, at least, we have something of the evidence necessary for a history of routine health in the early modern era. Skeletal evidence and military records indicate that Western European adult stature fell by several centimeters during the stressful sixteenth and seventeenth centuries (see Figure III.7). More dramatically, particularly in Germany and Central Europe, the crisis was manifested in the destruction and severe mortality of the Thirty Years' War of 1618–48, which was embedded in a longer struggle between the Protestant peoples of the Netherlands against the Catholic Spanish Hapsburgs that took place from 1568 to 1648.[77] The long-run outcome of the crisis in Europe was to end definitively the leading position of the south and to launch northwest

---

[75] Fa-Hu Chen et al., "Moisture Changes over the Last Millennium in Arid Central Asia: A Review, Synthesis and Comparison with Monsoon Region," *QSR* 29 (2010), 1044–68; Catherine Kuzucuoğlu et al., "Mid- to Late-Holocene Climate Change in Central Turkey: The Tecer Lake Record," *Holocene* 21 (2011), 183–6; Valérie Trouet et al., "Persistent Positive North Atlantic Oscillation Mode Dominated the Medieval Climate Anomaly," *Science* 324 (2009), 78–80.

[76] Sam White, *The Climate of Rebellion in the Early Modern Ottoman Empire* (New York, 2011); A. Nicault et al., "Mediterranean Drought Fluctuation during the Last 500 Years Based on Tree-Ring Data," *ClimDyn* 31 (2008), 227–45; William S. Atwell, "Volcanism and Short-Term Climatic Change in East Asia and World History, c. 1200–1699," *JWH* 12 (2001), 29–96.

[77] On heights, see Richard H. Steckel, "Health and Nutrition in the Pre-Industrial Era: Insights from a Millennium of Average Heights in Northern Europe," in Allen et al., eds., *Living Standards in the Past*, 227–54, esp. 241–7; Nikola Koepke and Joerg Baten, "The Biological Standard of Living in Europe during the Last Two Millennia," *EREconH* 9 (2005), 61–95, at 76, 77; John Komlos, with M. Hau and N. Bournguinat, "The Anthropometric History of Early-Modern France," *EREconH* 7 (2003), 159–89. For perceptions of mortality during this era of crisis, see Andrew Cunningham and Ole Peter Grell, *The Four Horsemen of the Apocalypse: Religion, War, Famine, and Death in Reformation Europe* (Cambridge, 2000).

Europe – especially the Netherlands and England – to preeminence.[78] In this process, the English Revolution, unfolding in stages during the 1640s and the late 1680s, played a central role, ultimately establishing the institutional framework for the First Industrial Revolution. But at its onset it was merely part of a wider array of violent political crises that encompassed Ming China, Russia, Ottoman Turkey, Central Europe, Italy, France, and the Netherlands, as well as all of the British Isles and the new English colonies on the North American coast.

Jack Goldstone and Geoffrey Parker have developed interpretations of the seventeenth-century crisis solidly grounded in ecological circumstances. Focusing on state crises in China, Turkey, and England, Goldstone put population at the center of his interpretation. After a slow recovery from the Black Death through 1500, societies across Eurasia experienced dramatic population growth during the sixteenth century reaching and exceeding late medieval highs, driving a great inflation of prices, contributing to a failure of state revenues, competition among elites, and the eruption of popular ideologies and movements that led to revolution, or at least insurgency.[79]

To this point, I have resisted population-driven Malthusian arguments as a necessary cause of crises, positing that the growth of populations was typically accommodated by "Boserupian" adjustments. Goldstone has advanced a straightforward Malthusian argument for a bottleneck of population and resources, because population rose so fast that relatively rigid state institutions were simply overwhelmed. On the other hand, Parker has decisively altered the equation with the first definitive analysis of the impact of the Little Ice Age on seventeenth-century histories.[80] While he might disagree, nothing in his interpretation precludes elements of Goldstone's analysis.

[78] For part of a large literature on the economic impact of the seventeenth-century crisis, see Jan de Vries, *The Economy of Europe in an Age of Crisis, 1600–1750* (New York, 1976); Theodore K. Rabb, "The Effect of the Thirty Years War on the German Economy," *Journal of Modern History* 34 (1962), 40–51; Henry Kamen, "The Economic and Social Consequences of the Thirty Years War," *P&P* 39 (1968), 44–61; Immanuel Wallerstein, *The Modern World System II: Mercantilism and the Consolidation of the European World Economy, 1600–1750* (New York, 1980), 12–35.

[79] Goldstone, *Revolution and Rebellion in the Early Modern World*; Jack A. Goldstone, "East and West in the Seventeenth Century: Political Crises in Stuart England, Ottoman Turkey, and Ming China," *Comparative Study of History and Society* 30 (1988), 103–42.

[80] Geoffrey Parker, *The Global Crisis: War, Climate and Catastrophe in the Seventeenth-Century World* (New Haven, CT, 2013); –, "Crisis and Catastrophe: The Global Crisis of the Seventeenth Century," *AHR* 113 (2008), 1053–1879. Emmanuel le Roy, Ladurie's *Histoire humaine et comparée du climat: Tome 1, Canicules et glaciers XIIIe-XVIIIe siècles* (Fayard, 2004), 183–530 discusses "le hyper petit âge glaciaire" only as it affected Europe. For formative earlier arguments for the impact of the second stage of the Little Ice Age, see Gustaf Utterström, "Climatic Fluctuations and Population Problems in Early Modern History," *Scandinavian EconHistR* 3 (1955), 3–47; Hubert H. Lamb, *Climate, History and the Modern World*, second edition (London, 1995), 211–41; Christian Pfister and Rudolph Brázdil, "Climatic Variability in Sixteenth-Century Europe and Its Social Dimension: A Synthesis," *ClimCh* 43 (1999), 5–53.

But Parker has established the range and specificity of Little Ice Age climate impact that makes clear that a simple endogenous Malthusian argument cannot be advanced to explain a civilizational crisis.[81] Certainly populations were growing, but from the 1550s they were growing in the face of the cold winters *and* summers of the second stage of the Little Ice Age. Most important, Parker documents the role of two clusters of volcanic eruptions in the 1630s and early 1640s, intensifying the adverse conditions of the early Maunder Minimum across the northern hemisphere that shaped the timing of political upheaval as well as severe droughts and famines throughout the northern hemisphere.[82] Emerging literatures are demonstrating that not only grain prices fluctuated with climate, leading to subsistence crises, but that early modern Europeans found a scapegoat for their troubles in the form of the "weather-making witch": the great witch hunts of the early modern period exactly bracket the second stage of the Little Ice Age.[83] An interpretation of the impact of abrupt climate change in the previous three epochs of the Millennial Siberian High – buried in prehistory thousands of years ago – must be highly conjectural. But given the wealth of detail available for the seventeenth century, Parker and Goldstone have given us a detailed view into the social and political dynamics of the most recent of these crises.

This was a global, rather than a Eurasian crisis, however. It had many dimensions, but in the wider context of industrious Smithian expansions, the setbacks of the Little Ice Age have to be set in dynamic relation to the devastation of the impacts of Old World diseases on the New World. And while the great land-based empires suffered, new seaborne empires were being built. One of these, the newest, would simultaneously – if briefly – come to dominate the world in both imperial reach and a new mineral-based economy. The remainder of this chapter and much of the next examine this pivotal society.

* * *

Early Modern England in the Age of Empire, the Little Ice Age, and the Seventeenth-Century Crisis

Two countries in northern Europe were particularly successful in riding out the traumas of the Little Ice Age and the seventeenth-century crisis, and

---

[81] Jack Goldstone has told me that if the climate data now developed had been available in the late 1980s, his interpretation of the seventeenth century would have been somewhat differently argued.

[82] Parker, "Crisis and Catastrophe," 1070–2. On volcanic impacts on climate, see Atwell, "Volcanism and Short-Term Climatic Change."

[83] Walter Bauernfeind and Ulrich Woitek, "The Influence of Climatic Change on Price Fluctuations during the 16th Century Price Revolution," *ClimCh* 43 (1999), 303–21; Emily Oster, "Witchcraft, Weather, and Economic Growth in Renaissance Europe," *JEconP* 18 (2004), 215–28; Wolfgang Behringer, "Climatic Change and Witch-Hunting: The Impact of the Little Ice Age on Mentalities," *ClimCh* 43 (1999), 335–51.

one would emerge to dominate the global economy until the end of the nineteenth century. The Netherlands and England were clearly the seventeenth-century leaders in the European economy, by virtue of their aggressive pursuit of trade and empire. England was gaining on the Netherlands by the close of the century, and within another century developed into the first industrial nation. The result of England's rise would be an accelerating, mutating modernity, called Schumpeterian growth, that would transform the European and North American economies by 1900, and transform the entire world during the next century, driven by and driving a colossal expansion of global populations. In an instant of geological time, perhaps ten to fifteen generations in human time, humanity would erupt suddenly as an independent force in the earth system of biosphere, geosphere, and atmosphere, perilously undermining the conditions of its own existence. This is the topic of my final chapters, but here we need to look relatively carefully at England's trajectory from the late Middle Ages through the early modern epoch.

The uniqueness of this trajectory was certainly not apparent at the time, and it has become less so to recent historians. Prevailing over both a traditional view of dramatic economic growth in an early industrial revolution and a newer view that sees the path toward modernity set in England from the Middle Ages, a revisionist economic history launched by Nicholas Crafts and Knick Harley in the 1980s has mapped a new understanding with some familiar features. This synthesis explains the shape of change as a slow-building "efflorescence" of an advanced organic economy arcing into the early nineteenth century, building upon Boserupian or Smithian processes common to advanced state-based economies around the early modern world. But it also explains this change in terms of the consequences of England's sudden achievement of a series of entrepreneurial, intellectual, and political breakouts, launching a Schumpeterian fossil-fueled machine revolution and a new and enduring re-constitution of political economy.[84] These events, unfolding in a short decade between 1688 and 1698, were shaped but not determined by England's success in evading the worst of the seventeenth-century crisis. Their impact was also facilitated by England's sudden success

---

[84] For the traditional view, see Walter W. Rostow, *The Stages of Economic Growth* (New York, 1960); Phyllis Deane and W. A. Cole, *British Economic Growth, 1688–1959* (Cambridge, 1962); David S. Landes, *The Prometheus Unbound: Technological Change and Industrial Development in Western Europe from 1750 to the Present* (Cambridge, 1969); for the long-run view, see Snooks, *Economics without Time*; Maddison, *Contours of the World Economy*; Levine, *At the Dawn of Modernity*; for the revisionist view, see N. F. S. Crafts, *British Economic Growth during the Industrial Revolution* (Oxford, 1985); N. F. S. Crafts and C. R. Harley, "Output Growth and the British Industrial Revolution: A Restatement of the Crafts-Harley View," *EconHistR* 45 (1992), 703–30; De Vries, "The Industrious Revolution and the Industrial Revolution"; De Vries, "Economic Growth before and after the Industrial Revolution"; Goldstone, "Efflorescences and Economic Growth"; Wrigley, *Poverty, Progress, and Population*, 17–43.

in controlling the worst impacts of crisis mortality. An ongoing debate contests whether – fundamentally – England's breakout depended on unique qualities of its political and intellectual culture or its demographic system, or the relatively external contributions of coal deposits and empire. Clearly all of these forces were at work and it is not my inclination or purpose to decide this debate. I am more comfortable with a synthesis – a "perfect storm" interpretation – that sees a unique set of conditions coming together to launch the modern world in early modern England.[85]

England's passage through the century or so following the Black Death was not a particularly auspicious launch to modernity. Not only was English population decimated by the plague itself during the 1350s, but it continued to fall for another 100 years, and never began to recover until after 1500, when most of continental Europe already had turned the corner. If the most recent calculation is right, English population peaked at 5.98 million in 1315, fell to about 5 million after the Great Famine, and then again to 3.4 million after the Plague, before reaching a floor of roughly 2.4 million during the 1440s, where it stayed until the beginning of a population boom at the beginning of the sixteenth century[86] (see Figure IV.2).

Why population continued to fall and then stayed so low so long, and how the late medieval economy shaped this conjuncture, is a matter of some debate. One influential argument is that the English people shifted to a "low-pressure" demographic system following the Black Death, featuring low mortality balanced by low fertility. The relatively high wages that the plague survivors could command, this model contends, contributed to a higher standard of living that encouraged the restraints of the preventive check, low fertility. A higher per capita wealth led to higher demands for a range of domestic products and services, leading to women being drawn into the workforce as artisans and servants, thus contributing to the decline in fertility.[87] The data on the export of raw wool and cloth from the 1340s suggests the shape of this economy. Cloth exports were low relative to raw wool in the mid-fourteenth century, but the ratio reversed by 1400, if not

[85] At the moment, the poles of this debate are represented by Pomeranz, *The Great Divergence* and Wong, *China Transformed* versus Landes, *The Wealth and Poverty of Nations* and Mokyr, *The Enlightened Economy*. For an important statement of a perfect storm synthesis, see Robert C. Allen, *The British Industrial Revolution in Global Perspective* (Cambridge, 2009), 106–55.

[86] Gregory Clark, "The Long March of History: Farm Wages, Population, and Economic Growth, England 1209–1869," *EconHistR* 60 (2007), 120; see also the estimates in John Langdon and James Masschaele, "Commercial Activity and Population Growth in Medieval England," *P&P* 190 (2006), 65.

[87] E. A. Wrigley and R. S. Schofield, *The Population History of England, 1451–1871: A Reconstruction* (London, 1981), 450–3; Herlihy, *The Black Death*, 51–7; Mark Bailey, "Demographic Decline in Late Medieval England: Some Thoughts on Recent Research," *EconHistR* 49 (1996), 3–7; P. J. P. Goldberg, *Women, Work, and Life Cycle in a Medieval Economy: Women in York and Yorkshire c.1300–1520* (Oxford, 1992), 345–61.

before, with cloth exports in 1400 perhaps ten times their level in 1350. The late fourteenth-century expansion collapsed during the fifteenth century, as the wool trade paced a wider rise and then the stagnation of the post-Plague economy. Part of this economic collapse is attributed to the lack of a supply of silver money, which had by 1400 severely diminished as it was spent in the East in a surge of demand for spices and silks, and as European mining declined. These money supply issues would be addressed when European mining was recommenced on a grand scale in the 1460s, soon to be augmented by the flow of silver from the New World.[88]

As much as the money supply was a factor in this economic stagnation, however, so too was ongoing mortality. Apparently, continental Europe in aggregate recovered its population loss by 1500. But epidemics struck England recurrently after 1350: in 1379–83, 1389–93, 1405–7, 1433–9, and the 1450s through the 1470s, followed by a final sixteenth-century crisis in 1556–7. If wages were high in post-Plague England, a shrinking population clearly undermined the economic expansion. Depopulation spurred the enclosure movement, in which farmland was consolidated into pasturage for the sheep that provided the wool for the textile trades.[89] These epidemics were of such a scale and frequency that it seems impossible that they could have been accompanied by low fertility: thus it appears more likely that a high-pressure system pertained throughout the post-Plague period, high mortality presumably matched by high fertility, a fertility perhaps constrained by the sporadically hard times during the fifteenth century. It seems entirely likely that epidemics were followed by surges in marriages and births, as David Herlihy found to be the case in post-Plague Tuscany.[90]

---

[88] John Hatcher, "The Great Slump of the Mid-Fifteenth Century," in Richard Brintnell and John Hatcher, *Progress and Problems in Medieval England* (Cambridge, 1996), 237–72; B. R. Mitchell, *British Historical Statistics* (Cambridge, 1988), 358–9; Findlay and O'Rourke, *Power and Plenty*, 116–18.

[89] Ian Blanchard, "Population Change, Enclosure, and the Early Tudor Economy," *EconHistR*, 2d ser., 23 (1970), 427–45.

[90] Pamela Nightingale, "Some New Evidence of Crises and Trends of Mortality in Late Medieval England," *P&P* 187 (2005), 33–68; John Hatcher, "Understanding the Population History of England, 1450–1750," *P&P* 180 (2003), 83–130, esp. 95–101; Bailey, "Demographic Decline," 2–3, 9–17; John Hatcher, "Mortality in the Fifteenth Century: Some New Evidence," *EconHistR* 2d ser., 39 (1986), 19–38; –, *Plague Population and the English Economy, 1348–1530* (London, 1977), 55–62; Barbara Harvey, *Living and Dying in England, 1100–1540: The Monastic Evidence* (Oxford, 1993), 142–6; Langdon and Masschaele, "Commercial Activity," 78–9; Barbara Hanawalt, *The Ties that Bound: Peasant Families in Medieval England* (New York, 1986), 90–104; David Herlihy and Christiane Klapisch-Zuber, *Tuscans and their Families: A Study of the Florentine Catasto of 1427* (New Haven, CT, 1985), 81–90. Hatcher, "Understanding the Population History," 100–2, notes that The Cambridge School Project data shows very high marriage rates at the beginning of its run, from 1540 to 1561, which look suspiciously like the end of a high late medieval marriage rate. E. A. Wrigley et al., *English Population History from Family Reconstitution, 1580–1837* (Cambridge, 1997), 614.

As important, these ongoing epidemics were closely associated with the Hundred Years' War and the War of the Roses, expensive foreign and civil wars that extracted men and taxes and spread disease.

The situation changed quite rapidly during the early sixteenth century, in both population and economy. From its fifteenth century floor of 2.4 million, population grew to 3 million by 1550, to more than 4 million by 1600, and to 5.3 million by 1650. The textile export trade boomed through the 1550s, when it staggered and then struggled to recover for the rest of the century, as export merchants displaced the Italian merchants in markets in Turkey and beyond, and Protestant refugees from France introduced a range of new technologies. Iron production, as measured by the number of blast furnaces, exploded during the sixteenth century, rising from a handful of sites to more than eighty.[91] On the other hand, the sixteenth-century growth of population was matched by an inexorable slide in wages, as a rising tide of laboring hands undermined the bargaining position of labor (see Figure IV.2). By the end of the century, concerns had risen about the numbers of the "wandering poor."[92]

Why did population begin to rise so rapidly? The estimates of birth and marriage rates that begin in the 1540s suggest that both were falling from earlier higher rates, but they remained quite high. What seems to have changed, fundamentally, was the death rate, although it can be measured only indirectly. Gregory Clark's half-decade estimates of population running back to 1250 suggest that English population was in decline until roughly 1450 and did not begin to rise until the first decades of the sixteenth century, under the impact of severe ongoing epidemics. Even if English population began to rise around 1500, it was struck by continuing crisis mortality through the years of the influenza epidemic of 1555–7, a volatility that some argue is obscured in the sample from which the Wrigley-Schofield data is based.[93] But it is clear that from the 1560s, if not before, English population

---

[91] Robert Brenner, *Merchants and Revolution: Commercial Change, Political Conflict, and London's Overseas Traders, 1550–1653* (Princeton, NJ, 1963), 3–23; J. F. Fisher, "Commercial Trends and Policy in Sixteenth-Century England," *EconHistR* 10 (1940), 95–117; G. Hammersley, "The Charcoal Iron Industry and Its Fuel, 1540–1750," *EconHistR* 2d ser., 26 (1973), 595–6; Allen, "Progress and Poverty in Early Modern Europe."

[92] Clark, "The Long March," 99–100 (table 1, purchasing power, day wages of agricultural workers); Robert C. Allen, London Building Crafts Wages/Silver Price (Feinstein), from data set constructed by Robert C. Allen, University of Oxford, "Prices and Wages in London & Southern England, 1259–1914," *Consumer Price Indices, Nominal / Real Wages and Welfare Ratios of Building Craftsmen and Labourers, 1260–1913, International Institute of Social History data files available at* http://www.iisg.nl/hpw/data.php#europe, accessed August 8, 2012.

[93] Clark, "The Long March," 120. Paul Slack, *The Impact of the Plague in Tudor and Stuart England* (London, 1985), 57–8, 61–2 provides data on the frequency of epidemics in English towns from the 1480s to the 1660s, which can be compared with Nightingale's mortality evidence for 1300 to 1500 in "Some New Evidence of Crises and Trends of Mortality."

growth was freed of the threat of countrywide epidemics, declining only in several decades during the late seventeenth century and in a final year of crisis mortality in 1729. If crisis mortality did not totally disappear, it clearly stopped determining English demography sometime during the sixteenth century. If English population was slow to recover after the Black Death, lagging by a century or more, it grew at twice the pace of continental Europe during the sixteenth century.[94]

This mid-sixteenth-century decline in crisis mortality marks the onset of the first stage of the epidemiological transition in England, the "waning of pandemics."[95] As such it also marks the beginning of the long-range modern demographic revolution, in which continuing high fertility in a context of falling mortality drives a massive population expansion before a fall in fertility slows this growth, establishing the modern ideal of a "low-pressure" demographic system. It seems reasonably clear that the worst epidemics tapered off at the end of the fifteenth century, allowing a surge of fertility-driven population growth in sixteenth-century England. Here we should propose some distinctions, however, in scales of mortality. What I have been discussing would be called first-order crisis mortality – in which epidemics spread wide and deep in the affected population, and had discernible effects on total numbers. An enduring second-order crisis mortality would have been more local in its impact, driving deaths higher than births in discrete towns and villages for a year or two, but having no fundamental effect on national numbers. If we accept the Wrigley-Schofield numbers, and my extrapolation of Clark's population figures to percent gain or loss, first-order mortality prevailed from 1350 to the end of the fifteenth century, and cropped up again in 1555–7. Over the following century, second-order mortality crises certainly occurred, but after the Great London Plague of 1665 they would become a thing of the past. The advance of medical knowledge and public health in the second and third stages of the epidemiological

---

[94] Population estimates from Clark, "The Long March," 120, and Wrigley et al., *English Population History*, 614. On mortality decline, see Nightingale, "Some New Evidence of Crises and Trends of Mortality," 66–8; Bailey, "Demographic Decline," 16–17; David Loschky and Ben D. Childers, "Early English Mortality," *JInterdH* 24 (1993), 85–97; D. M. Palliser, "Tawney's Century: Brave New World of Malthusian Trap?" *EconHistR* 2d ser., 35 (1982), 344–7. Hatcher, in "Understanding the Population History," 102–4, challenges the basis of the mortality calculations generated by Wrigley and Schofield between 1541 and the 1560s, arguing that epidemic mortality remained "extremely volatile," and that the earliest that England could have shifted to a low-pressure system was the 1580s. See also Ronald Lee, "Population Homeostasis and English Demographic History," *JInterdH* 25 (1985), 635–66; Ronald Lee and Michael Anderson, "Malthus in State Space: Macro Economic-Demographic Relations in English History, 1540–1870," *Journal of Population Economics* 15 (2002), 195–220; and John S. Moore, "Jack Fisher's 'Flu': A Visitation Revisited," *EconHistR* 46 (1993), 280–307. The mid-seventeenth-century declines were driven by fertility decline.

[95] Riley, *Rising Life Expectancy*, 21.

transition would suppress an ongoing background mortality gradually during the eighteenth and nineteenth centuries. Malthus's positive checks were disappearing in England in the seventeenth century.[96]

If it is not particularly clear why the first-order epidemics stopped around 1500, there are a number of good reasons why this happened sometime during the sixteenth century. First, the English state finally began to intervene to ameliorate what were, relatively speaking, very backward conditions of public health. Where Italians had quarantine measures in place from the 1370s, the first English mandates for public health came only in 1518, as part of an effort by Henry VIII to emulate continental Renaissance states. These were followed from 1578 by the "Plague Orders," which came as English counties and towns began to establish procedures to feed – and restrict the movement of – the poor that would result in the Poor Law of 1601. Food shortage was closely linked with increased disease mortality, because the lack of food not only weakened the poor, but set them in motion, bringing them into contact with urban disease pools. Draconian as they were, the Poor Laws contributed to a rising body of governmental regulation and action that slowly restricted the reach of epidemic disease and the impact of famine.[97]

In synergy with the rise of an effective state in England there were natural forces at work, most important the climatic stages of the Little Ice Age (see Figure IV.2). If we compare the estimates of the percent change of English population with those for northern hemisphere summer temperatures, a distinct – if seemingly paradoxical – relationship emerges. Relative to the cold summers of the second stage of the Little Ice Age, summer temperatures before 1500 were quite warm, if erratic. Particularly striking is that, in the centuries between the 1350s and the 1750s, warm summer temperatures correlate with dramatically *declining* population growth, and colder summer temperatures often correlate with *rising* population. The Black Death seems to have struck at the onset of a century of warm summer conditions, and the combination of warm summers – actually warm autumns – and the lingering plague contributed to the stagnation of population. This was followed by a seesaw of cold summers/population growth and warm summers/population declines through the 1550s, followed by the cold summer temperatures of Little Ice

---

[96] Here see Mary J. Dobson, *Contours of Death and Disease in Early Modern England* (Cambridge, 1997); and Esteban A. Nicolini, "Was Malthus Right? A VAR Analysis of Economic and Demographic Interactions in Pre-Industrial England," *EREconH* 11 (2007), 99–121.

[97] Keith Wrightson, *English Society, 1580–1680* (New Brunswick, NJ, 1982), 121–82; Slack, *The Impact of the Plague*, 199–341; Paul Slack, *Poverty and Policy in Tudor and Stuart England* (London, 1988), 113–87; Paul Slack, *From Reformation to Improvement: Public Welfare in Early Modern England* (Oxford, 1998); Michael Braddick, *State Formation in Early Modern England, c.1550–1700* (Cambridge, 2000), 103–35; Steve Hindle, *The State and Social Change in Early Modern England, 1550–1640* (New York, 2002), 1–36, 94–115, 171–230.

Age II, and generally growing populations. From the 1540s to the 1660s, crude death rates and temperatures varied *inversely*: in a very clear pattern, death rates rose with warm temperatures and fell with colder temperatures. Such a pattern would fly in the face of the understandable assumption that cold summers increased the possibility of harvest failure and food shortage, and thus potentially mortality. Presumably, more detailed records will show small mortality spikes with very cold summers, but smaller than warm summers, during which the plague returned. But the big killer in this "third great age of epidemics" was the plague, which brewed during hot summers as rats and fleas multiplied, and then struck in the autumn months. Conversely, cold summers would have suppressed the plague.[98] Thus it would appear that the cooler summers of the late Little Ice Age helped to mitigate the worst of late medieval crisis mortality in England.

The serious impact of cold summers on crops and food production during the Little Ice Age is thus hidden behind these aggregate numbers. Bruce Campbell has established the clear impact of climatic conditions on agricultural conditions during the century and a half following the Black Death. Just as the Great Famine of 1315–22 was driven by increasingly wet and cold summers, so too crop yields throughout the fourteenth and fifteenth centuries followed the path of the advancing Little Ice Age. Conditions were poor during the immediate Black Death years, and for a quarter century following, ameliorating during a "Chaucerian anomaly" for twenty years after 1375, and then deteriorating after 1400, with particularly bad conditions during the 1430s–40s and 1470s–80s. Paradoxically, perhaps, these were not years of rising mortality, because after its initial onslaught in 1348–50, the plague spiked with warmer summers and receded with colder ones. The improved agriculture of the warm Chaucerian anomaly was no match for an endemic bubonic plague.[99]

Thus epidemic and not famine was the great killer. It is apparent that famine was restricted to particular contexts, and disappeared earlier in England than it did on the continent, where, by the measure of adult stature, standards of living were severely impacted during the era of the Thirty Years' War and the Little Ice Age.[100] There was a distinct geography of famine in sixteenth- and seventeenth-century England, focusing on regions and districts that did not grow their own grains, and thus were dependent on food imports. Famines

[98] On the seasonality of the plague, see Benedictow, *The Black Death*, 132, 135–9, 233–5; and Cohn, *The Black Death Transformed*, 140–87.

[99] Bruce M. S. Campbell, "Grain Yields on English Demesnes after the Black Death," in Mark Bailey and Stephen Rigby, eds., *Town and Countryside in the Age of the Black Death* (Turnout, 2012), 121–74, esp. 142–62; Mark Bailey and Stephen Rigby, eds., "Agriculture in Kent in the High Middle Ages," in Sheila Sweetinburgh, ed., *Later Medieval Kent, 1220–1540* Woodbridge, UK, (2010), 25–50, esp. 42–50; see also Peter G. Beidler, "The Plague and Chaucer's Pardoner," *The Chaucer Review* 16 (1982), 257–69.

[100] See note 77.

struck in the upland areas in the north of England, and more generally in areas that had specialized in sheep raising, small-scale industry, or mining. When shortages struck these import-dependent regions, food prices rose, and the poorest of the population suffered, especially if the Poor Law provisions were badly administered, or if dearth-weakened people moved into urban areas and died of disease. But elsewhere in England famines were a thing of the past. In aggregate, a rise in bread prices is only associated with significant mortality during the Great Famine period of the 1320s, and the inflation of prices during the latter half of the sixteenth century, stressful as it was, did not set off mass starvation (see Figure IV.2). The last suggestions of English famine – in the northern county of Cumberland – came in 1649, while famine remained a serious threat on the Continent for another century.[101]

Thus, if the cold summers and winters of the second stage of the Little Ice Age shaped a wider "seventeenth-century crisis" across much of the Old World, England escaped the worst of its material effects. Clearly the structural situation was particularly perilous – indeed Malthusian – for England at the opening of the seventeenth century. A rising population occupied a small and circumscribed territory, and was contending with much colder climatic conditions, a dynamic of territorial and climatic circumscription that bears comparison with the Mesopotamian Lowlands in the fourth millennium BC. Such should have led to disaster, but self-conscious and effective efforts changed the energy equation. If the Industrial Revolution proper would not be launched until the eighteenth century and begin to be measurable in terms of growth until the early nineteenth century, early modern English society engineered a multifaceted "energy revolution" that left it teetering on the boundary between an advanced organic economy and a modern mineral-based, fossil-fueled economy.[102]

* * *

The Seventeenth-Century English Energy Revolution

An account of an energy revolution in early modern England might well begin with the microclimates of household and person. The typical medieval

---

[101] Post, "Famine, Mortality, and Epidemic Disease in the Process of Modernization"; Andrew B. Appleby, *Famine in Tudor and Stuart England* (Palo Alto, CA, 1978); Appleby, "Epidemics and Famine in the Little Ice Age"; P. R. Galloway, "Annual Variations in Deaths by Age, Deaths by Cause, Prices, and Weather in London, 1670–1830," *PopSt* 39 (1985), 487–505; John Walter and Walter Schofield, "Famine, Disease, and Crisis Mortality in Early Modern Europe," in John Walter and Walter Schofield, eds., *Famine, Disease, and the Social Order in Early Modern Society* (Cambridge, 1989), 1–74.

[102] Here I am obliged to the formative insights in Richard G. Wilkinson, *Poverty and Progress: An Ecological Perspective on Economic Development* (New York, 1973), 112–37; and Wrigley, *Continuity, Chance, and Change*.

house had been an impermanent structure, a timber frame finished with thatch roofing and wattle and daub (stick and mud) walls. By the fifteenth century, middling families were beginning to replace these houses with more permanent construction of stone and even brick, and a "great rebuilding" began during the late sixteenth century, stretching into the eighteenth century.[103] It is tempting to see these stronger, warmer structures as a response to the winter cold of the Little Ice Age, as it is to see the growing demand for woolen cloth as a similar response. As obviously, but with perhaps more portent, the rise of coal as a domestic fuel was a central part of this Little Ice Age energy revolution.

Though it has been a matter of some debate, it is clear that by the middle of the sixteenth century England was suffering a fuel shortage. Wood was in growing demand for construction, for ship building, and to supply the charcoal for the burgeoning numbers of blast furnaces, glassworks, and other hearth-dependent industries. But the particular pressure – as revealed in price – was on the "underwood" used to heat domestic houses, which jumped ahead of the general background of rising prices during the 1540s.[104] The price of fuel wood was a particular problem in the cities, especially London, which grew from a tiny 55,000 in 1520 to 200,000 in 1600, and more than half a million by 1700, the largest city in Europe.[105] The only thing that allowed such growth in the context of the Little Ice Age was coal, mined on the northeast English coast and shipped by barge via the North Sea and the Thames River up to London. Coal production and consumption rose from modest beginnings in the early sixteenth century to a million tons in 1600 and almost 4 million tons by 1700. Compared to total population, the growth of coal production appears to be a slow and steady rise until the end of the nineteenth century (see Figure IV.2). But another picture emerges if we compare it to the population of the cities, where it was primarily burned for household heat (and where it probably drove the production of the large proportion of the output of industrial hearths), and to Angus Maddison's estimates of GNP. Rather than a slow and steady rise, coal use per urban

[103] W. G. Hoskins, "The Rebuilding of Rural England, 1570–1640," *P&P* 4 (1953), 44–59; R. Machin, "The Great Rebuilding: A Reassessment," *P&P* 77 (1977), 33–56.

[104] Oliver Rackham, *Ancient Woodland: Its History, Vegetation, and Uses in England* (London, 1980), 161–8; Oliver Rackham, *Trees and Woodland in the British Landscape* (London, 1976), 84–93; Hammersley, "The Charcoal Iron Industry and Its Fuel"; Michael W. Flinn, "Timber and the Advance of Technology: A Reconsideration," *Annals of Science* 15 (1959), 109–20; Hugill, *World Trade since 1431*, 65–72; Rolf Peter Sieferle, *The Subterranean Forest: Energy Systems and the Industrial Revolution* (Cambridge, 2001), 78–137; Sieferle discusses the subsequent wood crisis in eighteenth-century Germany on pp. 138–80. On the continuing pressure on charcoal for iron making, see Brinley Thomas, *The Industrial Revolution and the Atlantic Economy: Selected Essays* (London, 1993), 1–34.

[105] E. A. Wrigley, "Urban Growth and Agricultural Change: England and the Continent in the Early Modern Period," *JInterdH* 15 (1985), 683–728.

population and GNP jumps first between 1550 to 1600 and then begins to climb again in the middle to the end of the eighteenth century.[106]

Energy from coal made a fundamental difference in the rise of England's economy. The Netherlands had an arguably more advanced economy at the turn of the seventeenth century, but it had only peat beds as a source of non-wood fuel, which produces less than half the heat of coal, and it was producing less than half the raw tonnage of the English coal works. The result was a fundamental limitation in scale and productivity that as measured by the size and density of cities; if the Netherlands was the most urbanized country in Europe, England was closing fast, and by 1750 London was three times the size of Amsterdam. On a per capita basis, England and the Netherlands in 1700 may have been producing an equivalent amount of heat from coal and peat respectively, but England had far greater reserves of paleo-heat. Because London and the satellite provincial cities powered the English economy during the seventeenth and eighteenth centuries, warming the cities was literally driving the economy, and this heat was derived from energy that was a "free" addition to the organic production of the land surface that had previously been the fundamental limitation to growth.[107]

Such organic limitations have been considerably overstated. Increasingly historians are arguing that the limits of an organic economy had rarely been reached, and such was certainly the case in seventeenth-century England. The Little Ice Age "energy revolution" had an organic as well as a mineral component. While there is considerable debate over the timing of an English agricultural revolution, it seems clear that between the late sixteenth and early nineteenth centuries, agricultural practice and productivity improved in a series of stages, in response to market demands generated by trade and urbanization and driven by the capitalist consolidation of holdings in the enclosure movement. These efforts involved an ongoing campaign to drain the wet swampy fens of eastern England, the use of increasing amounts of

---

[106] Coal data in figure 4.2 from Joseph U. Nef, *The Rise of the British Coal Industry* (London, 1932), 1: 19–20; John Hatcher, *The History of the British Coal Industry, Vol. I, Before 1700: Towards the Age of Coal* (Oxford, 1993), 68; Michael W. Flinn, *History of the British Coal Industry, Vol. 2, 1700–1830: The Industrial Revolution* (Oxford, 1984), 26; B. R. Mitchell, *International Historical Statistics: Europe, 1750–1993*, fourth edition (New York, 1998), 426, 428, 431, 477, 480; and population data (urban = places of 10,000 or more) from De Vries, *European Urbanization*, 30; and C. M. Law, "The Growth of Population in England and Wales, 1801–1911," *Transactions of the Institute of British Geographers* 41 (1967), 142. My argument here assumes that urban populations were more modern and required the output industrial production more than rural populations.

[107] Wrigley, *Continuity, Chance, and Change*, 34–67; De Vries and Van der Woude, *The First Modern Economy*, 37–40, 709–10, 719–20; J. W. de Zeeuw, "Peat and the Dutch Golden Age: The Historical Meaning of Energy-Attainability," *A.A.G.Bijdragen* 21 (1978), 3–32; Richards, *The Unending Frontier*, 221–33; Malanima, "The Energy Basis for Early Modern Growth," 57–8, 64–5. Populations from Wrigley, "Urban Growth," 688; Mitchell, *International Historical Statistics*, 74–6.

mineral fertilizers, the adoption of turnips and clover as fodder crops (the latter also having the virtue of fixing nitrogen in the soil), a gradual improvement of animal breeds, and experimentation with new systems of crop rotation. An increasing diversification of crops, and growing of more oats, had a huge impact on the sheer volume of animal power the English could bring to bear in their economy, especially for transportation. This crop diversification, especially the increasing mix of spring with fall-maturing crops, is credited with playing a central role in minimizing the impact of famine in England after the early seventeenth century, by contrast with France, where famines persisted for another century. The most recent quantitative analyses find a distinct break toward higher English agricultural productivity after 1600, in a pattern similar to Holland, but in sharp contrast to the rest of Europe. It may even be that by the end of the seventeenth century rising life expectancies contributed to rising productivity, as farmers with a longer horizon of return could make long-term investments in new, more efficient practices. These improvements would accelerate again at the end of the eighteenth century, and they involved the destruction of the customary rights of rural communities by the rise of new classes of yeoman and gentry farmers. But it would appear that these improvements helped to preserve and expand the food supply in the face of the cold of Little Ice Age II as well as the rising populations of the late sixteenth and then the eighteenth centuries, and were a key dimension of England's broader early modern "energy revolution."[108]

If English agriculture was becoming more productive during the seventeenth century, it was feeding – for the moment – a more slowly growing population. This slowing growth was not so much caused by climate change

---

[108] The following argue for a sixteenth-seventeenth-century agricultural revolution: Eric Kerridge, *The Agricultural Revolution* (London, 1967); E. L. Jones, *Agriculture and the Industrial Revolution* (New York, 1974), 41–85; Robert C. Allen, "Tracking the Agricultural Revolution in England," *EconHistR* 53 (1999), 209–35; Simon J. M. Davis and John V. Beckett, "Animal Husbandry and Agricultural Improvement: The Archaeological Evidence from Animal Teeth and Bones," *Rural History* 10 (1999), 1–17; and E. A. Wrigley, "The Transition to an Advanced Organic Economy: Half a Millennium of English Agriculture," *EconHistR* 59 (2006), 435–80. Wrigley's perspective is more gradual than that of Clark, who, in "The Long March," finds relatively productive agriculture from the High Middle Ages, with a distinct increase after 1640, or that of Robert C. Allen, who find a sharp increase in English and Dutch productivity after 1600. See Allen, "Progress and Poverty in Early Modern Europe," and "Economic Structure and Agricultural Productivity in Europe, 1300–1800," *EREconH* 3 (2000), 1–26. Mark Overton, *Agricultural Revolution in England: The Transformation of the Agrarian Economy 1500–1850* (Cambridge, 1996) argues for an eighteenth-century breakout. On the spring crops and the end of English famines, see Andrew Appleby, "Grain Prices and Subsistence Crises in England and France, 1590–1740," *JEconH* 39 (1979), 865–87. On the energy implications, see Richards, *The Unending Frontier*, 205–21; Malanima, "The Energy Basis for Early Modern growth," 63–6; and Wrigley, "The Transition," 356–461, on oats and animal power. On life expectancy, see Estaban A. Nicolini, "Mortality, Interest Rates, Investment, and Agricultural Production in 18th Century England," *ExpEconH* 41 (2002), 130–55.

and crisis as it was a response; in Malthusian terms it was a preventive rather than a positive check. As populations rose during the sixteenth century, contemporary observers were alarmed at the rising numbers of wandering poor. A solution was soon found in territorial expansion and the transfer of excess population. In the 1580s, Richard Hakluyt Sr. and Jr., advisors to Queen Elizabeth, memorialized the crown on the benefits of planting the "frey" of England's poor on the shores of North America. There they would found a new people with the aboriginal inhabitants, establish a bulwark against the Spanish, and become productive citizens of a prospective empire, showering wealth upon the realm. This emigration had already started in the 1560s, as Elizabeth authorized expeditions to conquer and colonize Ireland. English and Scottish colonization in Ireland was closely followed by a flood of emigration to the West Indies and the North American coasts, starting with Virginia and Massachusetts, where vast stretches of temperate biome faced them across the Atlantic, an ecological coincidence that has no parallel elsewhere in the world. The seventeenth-century emigrations from England to Ireland and the New World set off a vast expropriation of American biomes, not for the temporary purposes of simple resource extraction, but for the transfer and propagation of entire populations.

These out-migrations – totaling as many as half a million people – contributed to the stagnating of English population growth in the mid-to-late seventeenth century. Roughly 400,000 crossed to the New World; others went to Ireland or into military or naval service. Two hundred twenty thousand were shipped to the West Indies where they died in great numbers; roughly 175,000 landed on the North American mainland.[109] With the exception of the family migration to New England, the majority of these migrants were young men, and their departure left thousands of young women without marital prospects. The result was a rising age at marriage and a declining likelihood of marriage for young women in England; by the late seventeenth century, roughly a quarter of English women were not marrying. The result was the decisive onset of a moderate pressure demographic system, in which a lower mortality was matched by a controlled fertility, driving down gross reproductive rates. The result was an "overshoot" – English

---

[109] English emigration to the New World is detailed in Henry A. Gemery, "Emigration from the British Isles to the New World, 1630–1700," in Paul Uselding, ed., *Research in Economic History* 5 (1980), 179–231; and reviewed in Russell R. Menard, "Migration, Ethnicity, and the Rise of an Atlantic Economy: The Re-Peopling of British America, 1600–1790," in Rudolph J. Vecoli and Suzanne M. Sinke, eds., *A Century of European Migrations, 1830–1903* (Urbana, IL, 1991), 58–77; –, "Whatever Happened to Early American Population History?" *WMQ*, 3rd ser., 50 (1993), 356–66; and Nicholas Canny, "English Migration into and across the Atlantic during the Seventeenth and Eighteenth Centuries," in Nicholas Canny, ed., *Europeans on the Move: Studies on European Migration, 1500–1800* (Oxford, 1994), 39–75. For a longer discussion, see John L. Brooke, "Ecology," in Daniel Vickers, ed., *A Companion to Colonial America* (Malden, MA, 2003), 44–75.

population growth stalled and indeed reversed for several decades.[110] But in relieving population pressures, seventeenth-century emigration released England from the circumscribed conditions of island geography, rising population, and deteriorating climate that marked an especially severe bottleneck during the wider seventeenth-century crisis.

An organic and mineral energy revolution and an emigration-driven release from population growth differentiated English circumstances from the rest of Europe, including Holland. If societies across Eurasia were all experiencing a general rise in population, complexity, and Smithian economic growth, England stood in a particularly favored position, with new and expanding markets developing from both of its special departures in energy and empire. Some of these markets were internal, certainly, but without the added accelerant of international trade and extractive empire, internal "water's edge" markets would not have been able to move the English economy ahead of those of the rest of Europe. As Kenneth Pomeranz has argued, the combination of coal and colonies gave England a decided advantage.[111]

But the colonies were not simply "ghost acres," expanding the simple biomass available to the English population. The commodities that came out of these colonies, and from the wider tropical trade, exerted a force of their own, on Europe at large, but particularly England. Obviously, England benefited from the profits made from reexporting sugar, tea, coffee, and tobacco to European markets that had no access to the Atlantic trade. But, as important, these commodities – as powerful psycho-stimulants – acted to reshape the cultural and social milieus in which they were consumed. Coffee, chocolate, and tobacco all figured in new forms of male sociability, in which the new institution of the coffeehouse rapidly emerged during the late seventeenth century, as a place of commercial information and exchange. Tea drinking, with liberal applications of sugar, was a central part of a wider complex of consumption that drove a reconfiguration of social space in respectable middling households, opening the way to new forms of female-dominated sociability that required new investments in domestic goods. Another imperial drink, rum, displaced ale as the center of another form of sociability. All of these tropical stimulants could not, by themselves, by weight as bulk commodities, have done that much to reshape European economies. But as stimulants – drugs – they had powerful effects, driving a reshaping of the definitions of social life that in turn drove mounting demand

[110] Wrigley and Schofield, *The Population History*, 201, 219–33, 421–30, 469–71, 528–9. On how emigration reduces rates of natural reproduction in a source society, see Jean-Claude Chesnais, *The Demographic Transition: Stages, Patterns, and Economic Implications: A Longitudinal Study of Sixty-Seven Countries Covering the Period 1720–1984* (Oxford, 1992), 153–86.

[111] Pomeranz, *The Great Divergence*.

for new things. This tropical influence extended to the new cotton textiles coming from Indian looms, textiles that added new expectations for clothing – including for the first time underwear – that both drove demand and had a positive effect on cleanliness and health. These demands for a rising tide of fashionable new things were just beginning to be manifested at the end of the seventeenth century, and they would drive the English economy during the coming century. And the rapidly growing numbers of people, free and slave, inhabiting the imperial domain would for a time make their own significant contribution to this Smithian growth, in their rising demand for production by English manufacturing.[112]

This dynamic would require a consolidation of national governance and imperial authority, such as was under way at the end of the seventeenth century. The ten years between 1688 and 1698 brought a critical transition for the English – soon to be British – polity that established a constitutional platform upon which the First Industrial Revolution would be built. Overreaching with a demand for a Catholic succession to the English throne, the Stuart monarch James II was overthrown in the Glorious Revolution in 1688. The Dutch Protestant prince William of Orange was granted a constitutional monarchy in exchange for recognizing the supremacy of Parliament. With the monarch limited and an elected government in unambiguous control for the first time in English history, the way was clear to establish powerful institutions that would be insulated from royal manipulation. The Bank of England, established in 1694, rapidly became the most effective system of public credit in Europe, funding the government and the mobilization of the naval and military forces that ensured British prosperity into the early twentieth century, and managing the flow of capital formation that would eventually fund the First Industrial Revolution. The Board of Trade emerged as the key governing body for all foreign commerce and for the colonies, until the American Revolution.[113]

These agencies of empire and the fiscal-military state were matched by a wider culture of applied science that was moving toward a breakthrough to mineral-fueled mechanical power. With its founding by Charles II in 1661,

---

[112] W. D. Smith, *Consumption and the Making of Respectability*, 152–62; Cowan, *The Social Life of Coffee*; David Ormrod, *The Rise of Commercial Empires: England and the Netherlands in the Age of Mercantilism, 1650–1770* (New York, 2003); Nuala Zahediah, *The Capital and the Colonies: London and the Atlantic Economy 1660–1700* (Cambridge, 2010), 2–5, 238–92; Inkori, *Africans and the Industrial Revolution in England*, 405–72.

[113] Douglass C. North and Barry R. Weingast, "Constitutions and Commitment: The Evolution of Institutions Governing Public Choice in Seventeenth-Century England," *JEconH* 49 (1989), 803–32; Joel Mokyr, "The Intellectual Origins of Modern Economic Growth," *JEconH* 65 (2005), 285–351; David Stasavage, *Public Debt and the Birth of the Democratic State: France and Great Britain, 1688–1789* (Cambridge, 2003); Jack Goldstone, "The Rise of the West – or Not? A Revision to Socio-Economic History," *Sociological Theory* 18 (2000), 175–94.

the Royal Society emerged as focal point of a wider experimental science in the seventeenth century, in which gentlemen speculators, craftsmen, and entrepreneurial metallurgists combined to advance a collective knowledge of physical principles and machinery. Science – and politics – led back to coal. Stuart tax policy had placed the burden of taxation on "hearths" – sites of industrial production burning wood and coal – rather than land – the income stream of the landed aristocracy and gentry. One of the first measures that the new parliament voted in 1689 was to reverse this tax policy, shifting the weight of taxation from hearths to land. National fiscal policy tilted away from an organic, agricultural past toward a mineral-based, industrial future.[114]

Then, as all-out war with the French drove unprecedented demands for production – exactly in the decade of the coldest climate of the Maunder Minimum and the entire Little Ice Age – the English economy placed new pressures on the coalfields. These had once been open-pit operations, but increasingly the search for coal required deep mining, and the mines were beginning to reach the water table and to flood. In addition, heavy loads had to be lifted out of the depths. Experiments with vacuum pumps had been carried out since the Renaissance, but in the circle of the Royal Society, the efforts of Robert Boyle and Robert Hooke, followed by French exile Denis Papin, were carried to commercial success by Thomas Savery, who patented his steam engine in 1698, and publicized it in a tract called *The Miner's Friend*.[115]

Savery's engine, belching smoke at the mine heads, was a primitive monster, pumping water in a simple reciprocating action. New and more efficient engines would be developed by Thomas Newcomen and James Watt in the coming century. But Savery's engine marked a key moment in England's energy revolution, the point at which fossil-fueled mechanical action became a reality. The course was set for a fossil-fueled modernity, in which vast energy sources drawn from geological time would hyper-accelerate human economies and inexorably alter global ecologies.

[114] Steven Pincus, *1688: The First Modern Revolution* (New Haven, CT, 2009), 382–93.
[115] Richard Leslie Hills, *Power from Steam: A History of the Stationary Steam Engine* (New York, 1989), 13–20.

Global Transformations: Atlantic Origins, 1700–1870

During the three centuries since Thomas Savery launched his first steam engine, the forces of modernity have spread around the world with increasing power and complexity. Like the ripples in a pond spreading from a thrown rock, these forces have brought linked constellations of change to peoples across the entire planet, constellations with interlocking economic, demographic, and technological dimensions. The fundamental drivers of this process rest in the trajectory that European societies took during the early modern era: the rise of new dynamics of trade, state power, and empire building; the shift toward a lower-mortality demographic regime; and the consequences of the energy revolution that began at the end of the seventeenth century. The result was a transition from a world lightly populated by humanity and subject to essentially natural forces to a thickly populated world in which those human numbers and their economies now are playing an inexorable role in reshaping nature itself.

This history took an instant in geological time, but it has unfolded in a sequence of discrete processes and events that first unfolded relatively slowly, and then with an increasing and frightening acceleration, in which we can measure demographic doublings and atmospheric surges in the course of an incomplete lifetime. Thus in the 260 years between the announcement of Savery's engine in 1698 and the first regular CO_2 readings on Mauna Loa, Hawaii in 1958, when I was five years old, global population advanced from 680 million to 2.9 billion people, and CO_2 in the atmosphere grew from a Little Ice Age low of roughly 278 ppm to 315 ppm. In 1974, when I traveled across Europe and much of Asia, these figures stood at 4 billion people and 330 ppm; now, in late 2013, they stand at 7.2 billion people and brushing up against 400 ppm. The methane readings are equally stunning and following the exact same trajectory (see Figure IV.3). The last time that CO_2 stood at the present level in earth history was approximately 15 million years ago during the middle of the Miocene epoch, 10 million years before proto-humans began to diverge from the higher primates. Modernity has shaped an entirely new world, the Anthropocene epoch.

Mediating between the sheer numbers of humanity and its "exhaust" of greenhouse gases, ozone, and toxic pollution stands the global economy, and it is economic history that gives shape and direction to the transition of Holocene to Anthropocene. In this chapter, I propose a sketch of this history as a series of powerful waves, as economic mobilization raced to keep up with – and also contributed to – the inexorable demands of population growth, and gradually began to impose accelerating impacts on the natural sources and sinks of the dynamic earth system. These waves of economic transformation are set in their wider ecological context, in the context of both the stages of the epidemiological transition that progressively reduced regional and then global mortality, and the local, regional, and now global environmental hazards and impacts generated by those growing populations. To open this account, we need to set the stage by looking at the circumstances of global climate as the worst of the Little Ice Age tapered off, by sketching the basic outlines of population growth, and by framing an essential hypothesis for this chapter: that suddenly Malthus does begin to really matter, as we move across the boundary from premodernity to modernity. Once this model is established, we will work through the steps that took us to our contemporary situation, in this chapter following the First Industrial Revolution and its context and consequences through the 1860s, then in the next two working through the Second Industrial Revolution to the present.

* * *

The End of the Little Ice Age and the Beginning of Modern Population Growth, 1700–1860s

The opening of our modern era saw a rapid release from the most intense conditions of the second stage of the Little Ice Age. As an increasingly active sun dissipated the Maunder Minimum, the cold winter conditions of the last Siberian High epoch drew to an end, closing with three deep cold winters around 1709, 1728, and 1740, each of which brought crisis conditions to continental northern Europe[1] (see Figure III.5a). But then the cold lifted entirely, and the northern hemisphere experienced a stretch of warm summers and moderate winters unseen since before 1400. These temperatures would fall again somewhat in the final decades of the century, as a last and

---

[1] Andrew Appleby, "Grain Prices and Subsistence Crises in England and France, 1590–1740," *JEconH* 39 (1979), 865–87; Emmanuel le Roy Ladurie, *Histoire humaine et comparée du climate I: Canicules et glaciers XIIIe–XVIIIe siècles* (Fayard, 2004), 509–12, 573–612; Emmanuel le Roy Ladurie, *Histoire humaine et comparée du climate II: Disettes et Revolutions, 1740–1860* (Fayard, 2006), 541–7.

lesser solar minimum – the Dalton Minimum – brought a final cooling of the longer Little Ice Age that lasted into the 1840s, reflected in a final surge of ice rafting in the North Atlantic. Northern temperatures recovered to almost the eighteenth-century levels for the next seventy-five years. If we ignore the Dalton Minimum, we might be tempted to call the entire period from the 1730s to the 1920s the "Modern Optimum." But generally, climate scientists see the Little Ice Age continuing in formal terms into the early twentieth century, and one marker was continuing turbulence to the ENSO-monsoon belt from the Indian Ocean to the Andean Pacific coasts. Receding sharply at the close of the Maunder Minimum, El Niño variation rose to a late eighteenth-century peak, weakened at the opening of the Dalton, oscillated in strength across the nineteenth century, and then rose sharply in the twentieth[2] (see Figure III.7).

Combined with the rising temperature in the northern hemispheres since the 1920s, the rising intensities of El Niño in the last century lead us into the evidence for the Anthropocene, our current condition where global climates have been fundamentally altered by human numbers and economic activity. Here the record of the two key greenhouse gases, CO_2 and methane, becomes a critical marker (see Figure IV.3). Reflecting the slow reaction of oceanic-atmospheric linkages as well as advancing deforestation, CO_2 began to recover from its Little Ice Age/New World epidemic-driven decline after 1750, stabilized around 1815 at levels slightly higher than its peak in the Medieval Warm Period, and then began a sharp climb around 1850 into territory unseen since the late Pliocene if not before. Methane followed a similar if slightly more volatile course, recovering from a Little Ice Age decline by 1750, but then began a relentless increase that – like CO_2 – would accelerate sharply during the twentieth century. This dramatic rise in greenhouse gases is only one dimension of the patterns of human-induced climate change that began to build in the early modern period and – according to one recent analysis – to have a "significant impact by the early nineteenth century."[3]

The modern rise of global population tracks the ascent of atmospheric CO_2 and methane almost perfectly. This chapter and the next are devoted to exploring the origins and development of the intimate relationship between recent climate change and modern population growth. But human population did not rise inexorably throughout the world in one broad advance. Rather, it came in two distinct waves, marking our modern distinction between developed and developing regions (see Figure IV.4).

---

[2] See Figure 9.4 and Joëlle L. Gergis and Anthony M. Fowler, "A History of ENSO Events since A.D. 1525: Implications for Future Climate Change," *ClimCh* 92 (2009), 343–87.

[3] Quote from Simon F. Tett et al., "The Impact of Natural and Anthropogenic Forcings on Climate and Hydrology since 1550," *ClimDyn* 28 (2007), 29.

With the beginning of the eighteenth century, the consequences of the seventeenth-century crisis were rapidly mitigated, but the generality of the rise of early modern populations was somewhat more focused than it had been between 1400 and 1600. As of 1700, China and the north latitude societies comprised roughly 40 percent of global population, only slightly more than their traditional share. But by the mid-to-late nineteenth century this ancient pattern was broken, and these populations surged to comprise roughly 60 percent of the global total. China's population as much as tripled between 1700 and 1820, plateauing at 412 million in the 1840s. The combined populations of Europe, Russia, Japan, and North America almost quadrupled between 1700 and 1900, reaching the half billion mark in the decade before 1900, and comprising about a third of world population. But China fell into stasis and crisis in the mid-nineteenth century, and South Asia, all of Africa, and Southwest Asia lost ground, dropping from about 45 percent to 38 percent of the global total. Then, during the twentieth century, and especially after 1950, all of the broadly mid-latitude and tropical societies that prior to 1900 had declined relative to a temperate north expanded enormously, restoring the general proportions of premodern global population distributions, but at ten times the total numbers on earth in 1700.

This northern and tropical sequencing of modern population growth reflects the step-wise unfolding of the "demographic revolution" of the past 300 years, as declining mortality and then fertility drove the ballooning of populations around the world. Traditionally we consider the dynamics of this demographic revolution in relation to the industrial revolution that began to unfold first in England in the century following Thomas Savery's invention of a practical steam engine. But the onset of the industrial revolution itself was surprisingly halting and delayed, and was for the most part detached from the eighteenth-century advance of population in China and the global north. These parallel but mostly decoupled circumstances require a consideration of the effects of globalization and empire building on the beginning of both population growth and human-induced climate change.

In some measure, of course, there was an ongoing relationship between the fortunes of population and apparently natural climate change. The release from the worst of the Little Ice Age after 1700 certainly contributed to the surge of northern populations. China benefited in particular from a stretch of improving and stable warm summer temperatures not seen since before 1400. Population growth in Europe and the new North American settler societies similarly benefited from the relative freedom from crop failure during this eighteenth-century temperature optimum. Occasionally, as in the hard winters of the final Siberian High in 1709, 1728, and 1740 and the northern coolings set off by the eruption of the Laki Craters in Iceland in 1783 and Tambora in 1815, northern populations suffered effects that might have reminded them of the harsher world of the Little Ice Age.

In the summer of 1788, cold-induced crop failures may have contributed to the intensity of the "Great Fear" that mobilized popular sentiment at the outset of the French Revolution in 1789. The frosts and snows of the cold summer of 1816, following the Tambora explosion, brought hardship throughout the northern hemisphere. Commenting on both the severity of the Dalton Minimum and the post-Tambora summer, a minister in mountainous western Massachusetts wrote in 1829 that "the succession of cold summers and unfruitful seasons, ending with 1816, frightened many, who fled to the west, dreaming of perpetual sunshine and unfailing plenty."[4] But these were traumatic exceptions to a generally benevolent northern climate. The Dalton Minimum brought the eighteenth-century optimum to an end, and may have played a role in stalling Napoleon's armies before Moscow in 1812 (just as an intensely cold winter stalled Hitler in 1942). But the Dalton was mild relative to the Maunder Minimum of more than a century before. Even if it played a role in world events, climate did not fundamentally constrain the human condition in the northern latitudes during the eighteenth and nineteenth centuries.

Conversely, however, the tropical south may have suffered while the temperate north prospered. If the worst of the Little Ice Age climate ended in the northern hemisphere, the ENSO variability remained strong if erratic. A series of devastating droughts set off severe famines in India, beginning in the late 1760s and running through 1825, most notably the 1788–93 Bengal famine. A second series of El Niño-driven droughts spanned the late nineteenth century. Both periods saw the accelerating expansion of European empires in the tropics. In India, the eighteenth-century droughts followed the gradual collapse of the Mughal empire, but contributed to destabilizing cycles of warfare and population movement, and compounded an agrarian disruption that was already undermining the competitive advantage of Indian textiles by driving up the price of grain. The devastating famines in Bengal accelerated the extension of the British East India Company's reach and the incorporation of India into a British imperial economy[5] (see Figure III.9).

---

[4] Ladurie, *Disettes et Revolutions*, 112–22, 143–80; Richard B. Stothers, "The Great Dry Fog of 1783," *ClimCh* 32 (1996), 79–89; C. S. Witham and C. Oppenheimer, "Mortality in England during the 1783–4 Laki Craters Eruption," *Bulletin of Vulcanology* 67 (2005), 15–26; Alan Taylor, "'The Hungry Year': 1789 on the Northern Border of Revolutionary America," in Alessa Johns, ed., *Dreadful Visitations: Confronting Natural Catastrophe in the Age of the Enlightenment* (New York, 1999), 145–81; John D. Post, *The Last Great Subsistence Crisis in the Western World* (Baltimore, MD, 1977); Chester Dewey, in *A History of the County of Berkshire, Massachusetts, in Two Parts …, by Gentlemen of the County …* (Pittsfield, 1829), 11.

[5] David Arnold, "Hunger in the Garden of Plenty: The Bengal Famine of 1770," in Johns, "The Bengal Famine of 1770," in Johns, ed., *Dreadful Visitations*, 81–111; Rajat Datta, "Crises and Survival: Ecology, Subsistence and Coping in Eighteenth Century Bengal," *Calcutta Historical Journal* 18 (1996), 1–34; Urmita Roy, "Famine and Dearth in Late Eighteenth-Century Bengal," *Bengal, Past and Present* 112 (1993), 57–67; David Clingingsmith and

Mike Davis has argued that the late nineteenth-century El Niño-driven droughts and famines brought a further extension of imperial control to India, shaped the expansion of European empire in Africa, and contributed to the sequence of crises that devastated nineteenth-century China.[6] But in China there is solid ground for invoking Malthus.

China prospered perhaps too much during the eighteenth century, benefiting from the capable governance of the early Qing regime, the climatic optimum, and new American crops. Despite a marital system that limited fertility by both social injunction and infanticide, population grew at a pace far beyond historical experience.[7] Populations in the rice-growing regions grew beyond capacity and responded both intensively and extensively. As Chinese society had done since antiquity, a rising population adapted by intensifying production in a Boserupian or Smithian mode, in a version of the "industrious revolution" of increased household specialization and effort that was occurring in contemporary Europe.[8] The population also responded by expanding into frontier regions and Central Asia, conquering Tibet, Mongolia, and much of Turkestan by the 1750s and 1760s, in an expansive response not unlike the internal frontier expansion of medieval Europe, Russia into Siberia, or early modern England into Ireland and North America. Han migrants moved from the rice-growing lowlands into the lightly populated hill and mountain regions, supporting their expansion by growing New World crops of potatoes and corn. This expansion set off the first rebellions of the next century, as the indigenous Miao of the mountains southwest of Hunan rose in 1795 against the "guest peoples" settling among them. Over the next sixty years, these frontier stresses, overpopulation, growing poverty, hostility to the alien Qing Manchus, and disruptions launched by the penetration of European commerce all fueled rebellion, exterminating warfare, and epidemic disease. In Yunnan, ethnic confrontations at mountain mines set off the Muslim Rebellion in 1856, which combined with eruption of bubonic plague out of natural rodent reservoirs; eventually this eruption would build and spread to become the source of the global plague epidemic of the late 1890s. The Muslim Rebellion was

Jeffrey G. Williamson, "Deindustrialization in 18th and 19th Century India: Mughal Decline, Climate Shocks and British Industrial Ascent," *ExpEconH* 45 (2008), 209–34; Christopher A. Bayly, "South Asia and the 'Great Divergence,'" *Itinerario* 24 (2000), 89–103.

[6] Mike Davis, *Late Victorian Holocausts: El Niño Famines and the Making of the Third World* (London, 2001).

[7] Kenneth Pomeranz, *The Great Divergence: China, Europe, and the Making of the Modern World Economy* (Princeton, NJ, 2000); 4–41; R. Bin Wong, *China Transformed: Historical Change and the Limits of European Experience* (Ithaca, NY, 1997), 22–5; James Z. Lee and Wang Feng, *One Quarter of Humanity: Malthusian Mythology and Chinese Realities, 1700–2000* (Cambridge, MA, 1999), 63–99; James Z. Lee and Cameron D. Campbell, *Fate and Fortune in Rural China: Social Organization and Population Behavior in Liaoning, 1774–1873* (Cambridge, MA, 1997), 55–102.

[8] Pomeranz, *The Great Divergence*, 91–8; Wong, *China Transformed*, 14–22.

part of a wider series of upheavals – the White Lotus, Nein, and the Taiping Rebellions of the 1850s and 1860s – that should have brought down the Qing dynasty. But – with some foreign intervention – these rebellions were suppressed with incredible violence, and by 1870 China's population had dropped from more than 400 million to roughly 360 million. Forty-one years later, the Qing Manchu fell and the republic was formed, ending millennia of dynastic rule.[9]

Here, for what seems to have been the first time in human history, it is clear that nature – in the form of abrupt climate change or virgin soil epidemics – played only a very minor role in a great civilizational crisis. There may have been climate impacts in nineteenth-century China from either the Dalton Minimum or ENSO, but they were relatively mild compared to the utterly unprecedented press of human numbers. The key factor in China's nineteenth-century crisis was a massive rise in population to levels triple the highest medieval number, and clearly beyond the carrying capacity of even an advanced multi-cropping but essentially organic agricultural economy. It is here that it seems appropriate to invoke a traditional model of Malthusian overpopulation. Thus we may posit that the launch toward modernity drove *the transition from essentially exogenously driven to endogenously driven crises*[10] (see Figure III.5c).

Behind China's eighteenth-century population increase was a buffering of mortality encouraged by an effective imperial rule, the moderation of climate, and particularly the adoption of New World crops. In a metaphor, perhaps, for our modern condition, a destabilizing globalization permitted China's eighteenth-century release from population constraints and set the stage for a classically Malthusian crisis. Previously, throughout the ancient and medieval worlds, the sustainability of a local population was grounded – for better or worse – in a local agro-ecology.[11] The constraints of

---

[9] John F. Richards, *The Unending Frontier: An Environmental History of the Early Modern World* (Berkeley, CA, 2003), 112–47; Susan Mann Jones, "Dynastic Decline and the Roots of Rebellion," and Philip A. Kuhn, "The Taiping Rebellion," in John K. Fairbank, ed., *The Cambridge History of China, Vol. 10: Late Qing, 1800–1911, Part I,* (Cambridge, 1978), 108–13, 132, 144, 264–317; Ping-ti Ho, *Studies on the Population of China, 1368–1953* (Cambridge, MA, 1959), 236–48; Carol Benedict, *Bubonic Plague in Nineteenth-Century China* (Stanford, CA, 1996), 17–99; Jonathan D. Spence, *God's Chinese Son: The Taiping Heavenly Kingdom of Hong Xiuquan* (New York, 1996), 79–95; Stephen R. Platt, *Autumn in the Heavenly Kingdom: China, the West, and the Epic Story of the Taiping Civil War* (New York, 2012), 270–303.

[10] Very specifically see Peter C. Perdue's assessment in *China Marches West: The Qing Conquest of Central Eurasia* (Cambridge, MA, 2005), 237–52. Though he does not precisely invoke Malthus, John R. McNeill sees population growth starting in the sixteenth century driving an ecological overshoot in the Mediterranean highlands after 1800. See *The Mountains of the Mediterranean World: An Environmental History* (New York, 1992), 2–11, 272–358.

[11] An exception to this rule was the various spreading patterns of Neolithic crops in prehistory. It is unlikely that any of these took effect as quickly as the adoption of New World crops in

this local organic system were slowly and incrementally advanced through Boserupian innovations and corresponding social and cultural constraints. New World foods comprised an energy shock to Chinese society that was sufficient to break down constraints on population expansion – yet insufficient to support that growing population in the long run. New World foods were also – it might be added – an exogenous shock, so this was not a purely endogenous crisis. But on the other hand it seems that – for the first time in human history – this was a crisis for which natural forces of abrupt climate change or virgin soil epidemic – exogenous to human economies – cannot be invoked as significant actors.

If China failed to match population growth with intensified Smithian growth, running up against real Malthusian limits, neighboring Japan just barely squeezed through a similar crisis. Japanese population plateaued at 31 million in the early eighteenth century, at very high levels, three to four times the numbers in Great Britain. With these numbers piled up behind the ocean barrier, without the ghost-acreage/ghost energy of either empire or coal deposits (or even peat), Japan had no choice but to make the best possible use of limited natural resources in an organic economy. Thus there certainly were Malthusian pressures in eighteenth-century Japan, pressures partially resolved through interrupted, delayed, or deferred marriage, and infanticide, which drastically slowed population growth. A certain limited expropriation did occur, a harbinger of twentieth-century projections: Japanese foresters, traders, fishermen, and settlers moved north into the Ainu lands on Hokkaido and the Sakhalin Islands, in a colonization not unlike that of Russians in Siberia and French, Dutch, and English in North America. Then there was amazingly hard work: the term *industrious revolution* was coined to describe the intensification of labor in Tokugawa Japan. Organic resources were conserved and put to new efficient uses, such as the herring ground up for fertilizer; meat protein was replaced with soy, forests were carefully conserved, fuel was sparingly burned. New World species began to contribute to the food supply. As the Japanese intensified their efforts to make a living in a small place, they even managed to raise their GDP, if we are to trust Angus Maddison's quantification.[12]

---

eighteenth-century China. For Malthusian arguments regarding nineteenth-century China, see Mark Elvin, *The Retreat of the Elephants: An Environmental History of China* (New Haven, CT, 2004), 454–71; Mark Elvin, *The Pattern of the Chinese Past* (Stanford, CA, 1973), 298–316; Ho, *Studies on the Population of China*, 169–226, 266–78; and Victor Lieberman, *Strange Parallels: Southeast Asia in Global Context, c. 800–1300. Vol. 2: Mainland Mirrors: Europe, Japan, China, South Asia and the Islands* (New York, 2009), 573–4.

[12] Conrad Totman, *Early Modern Japan* (Berkeley, CA, 1993), 233–79; Robert Y. Eng and Thomas C. Smith, "Peasant Families and Population Control in Eighteenth-Century Japan," *JIH* 6 (1976), 417–45; Richards, *The Unending Frontier*, 148–92; Lieberman, *Strange Parallels*, 448–69; Jan de Vries, *The Industrious Revolution: Consumer Behavior and the Household Economy, 1650 to the Present* (New York, 2008), 78–87; Angus Maddison, *Contours of the World Economy, 1–2030 AD* (Oxford, 2007), 382.

Thus, during the eighteenth century, both China and Japan suddenly reached human numbers beyond or barely within the limits sustainable by organic economies. Such is the fundamental paradox of modernity: an initial escape from the limits imposed by an organic nature produces human numbers on such a scale that second, and third, and fourth steps are required, launching an autocatalytic spiral of technology, mineral energy economies, scientific progress, and human well-being and Promethean or Schumpeterian growth. The resulting modernity is both an absolute break from the premodern past, and an accelerating engine of planetary change.

Population growth was and is a fundamental force in the modern world, in ways it was not before, when natural forces clearly had the upper hand. Qing China was not the only society growing extremely rapidly from 1700 to the mid-nineteenth century. China's growth rate was probably double that of both antiquity and the Middle Ages, and it exceeded growth in Europe. But China's growth was exceeded slightly by that of Great Britain until 1850, and by that of England and Wales during an uninterrupted ascent from the 1730s to the 1820s (see Table III.1b). If England's rate of growth was far surpassed by that of the American colonies/United States between 1700 and 1850, it – like China's – was probably double that of the High Middle Ages, and far exceeded that of the rest of Europe.[13] Again, while to this point I have avoided Malthusian arguments of overpopulation, there are as good grounds for invoking them for late eighteenth-century England as for China and Japan. If this was a Malthusian situation, England responded in a new way, though at a slow first-adopter pace as we shall see, moving away from the intensive Smithian growth of the organic-based industrious revolution (enhanced by imperial reach) to the sustained Schumpeterian growth of the mineral-based industrial revolution. England had its own safety valve in the American colonies, which started from microscopic settler populations to grow by massive frontier expansion, wresting an entire continent from American Indian occupants for an explosively expanding advanced organic agriculture. The twenty-year doubling of American populations inspired Benjamin Franklin in 1750 to write a tract on population and the Atlantic trade that was a precursor to Thomas Malthus's *Essay on the Principles of Population*. By the 1750s, Americans in older and relatively crowded sections of the northeast coast were shifting toward the intensification of the industrious revolution, and by the 1830s they started toward what the English had launched during the 1550s: the nonrenewable, fossil fuel, mineral-based economy.[14]

---

[13] On the implications of England's eighteenth-century growth, see Esteban A. Nicolini, "Was Malthus Right? A VAR Analysis of Economic and Demographic Interactions in Pre-Industrial England," *EREconH* 11 (2007), 99–121.

[14] On the eighteenth-century American industrious revolution, see Daniel Vickers, *Farmers and Fishermen: Two Centuries of Work in Essex County, Massachusetts, 1630–1850* (Chapel

Thus we may argue that mortality decline and population growth during the eighteenth century launched the modern world, and *caused rather than was caused by* the industrial revolution.[15] It was a globalization of food resources and an expansion of global agriculture that launched modernity. These processes also saw the origins of an issue particularly salient to our modern condition: the processes by which human action has shaped climate change and global warming.

* * *

The Beginnings of the Modern Anthropocene

The human role in forcing climate change was first proposed as far back as 1896, but only since the late 1980s has its significance been widely appreciated.[16] In part this was because its most obvious manifestation – a global rise in temperature beyond the norms of the Holocene – was only then becoming measurable, and it has only become undeniable by the general public within the past half decade. But the origins of climate change and global warming in its modern manifestation – building on the wisps of anthropogenic gas emissions that William Ruddiman has proposed began in

Hill, NC, 1994); John L. Brooke, "Ecology," in Daniel Vickers, ed., *A Companion to Colonial America* (Malden, MA, 2003), 63–7.

[15] On mortality decline and population growth as a driver for the English economy, see Gregory Clark, "What Made Britannia Great? How Much of the Rise of Britain to World Dominance by 1850 Does the Industrial Revolution Explain?" in Timothy J. Hatton et al., eds., *The New Comparative Economic History: Essays in Honor of Jeffrey G. Williamson* (Cambridge, MA, 2007), 33–57; John Komlos, "The Industrial Revolution as an Escape from the Malthusian Trap," Discussion Paper 2003–13, Dept. of Economics, University of Munich; Joel Mokyr, "Technological Progress and the Decline of European Mortality," *AER* 83 (1993), 324–30; Brinley Thomas, "Escaping from Constraints: The Industrial Revolution in a Malthusian Context," *JInterdH* 15 (1985), 729–53; Richard G. Wilkinson, *Poverty and Progress: An Ecological Perspective on Economic Development* (New York, 1973), 112–37. For wider arguments and perspectives on interdependence of population growth and technological change, see Michael Kremer, "Population Growth and Technological Change, One Million B.C. to 1990," *Quarterly Journal of Economics* 108 (1993), 681–716; Oded Galor and David N. Weil, "Population, Technology, and Growth: From Malthusian Stagnation to the Demographic Transition and Beyond," *AER* 90 (2000), 806–28; Charles I. Jones, "Was an Industrial Revolution Inevitable? Economic Growth in the Very Long Term," *Advances in Macroeconomics* 1/2/article 1 (2001), 1–43; Ronald D. Lee, "Malthus and Boserup: A Dynamic Synthesis," in David Coleman and Roger S. Schofield, eds., *The State of Population Theory: Forward from Malthus* (Oxford, 1986), 96–103; James W. Wood, "A Theory of Preindustrial Population Dynamics: Demography, Economy, and Well-Being in Malthusian Systems," *CA* 39 (1998), 99–135; and Stephen Shennan, "Demography and Cultural Innovation: A Model and Its Implications for the Emergence of Modern Culture," *CArchJ* 11 (2001), 5–16.

[16] For the intellectual history of climate change since 1896, see Spencer R. Weart, *The Discovery of Global Warming* (Cambridge, MA, 2003).

the Early Bronze Age – lie in the expansions of global populations and agriculture that began in the eighteenth century.

The analysis of these anthropogenic influences on the atmosphere are best considered in a framework of climate change rather than simply global warming, because human action both warms and cools the earth. The calculation of modern climate change involves the balance of positive warming influences and negative cooling influences, both natural and human caused. The natural causes are the solar and volcanic forcings that we have considered throughout this book: across most of the past three centuries, the warming influence of solar forcing has been offset or negated by the cooling from volcanic sulfate aerosols. On the human side, the changing surface albedo of lands cleared of forests for lumber and agriculture – especially in the snow-covered northern hemisphere – have had a small cooling influence, as have the sulfate aerosols emitted from fossil fuel burning. But these cooling influences of human action are more than offset by warming; measured in watts of heat per square meter of the earth's surface, human action now imposes about a watt and a half of cooling versus about 3.2 watts of warming, for a net warming influence of ~1.5 watts per square meter. The burning of biomass and fossil fuels puts huge amounts of CO_2, some methane, and black carbon in the atmosphere, all of which have powerful warming properties by enhancing the greenhouse effect, by which an increasing amount of solar heat is retained within the chemical envelope of the atmosphere. Modern chemical industry also has put halocarbons and ozone into the atmosphere, with a warming effect. But agriculture and land clearance have played a major warming role. Land that is cleared of forest, often through burning, emits huge amounts of CO_2, as does the annual plowing and harrowing of soil. But agriculture also contributes huge amounts of methane to the atmosphere, either from cattle digestive systems or emissions from rice paddies, essentially artificial wetlands, which are also a source of natural methane emissions.[17]

Of these greenhouse gases, CO_2 and methane hit long-term lows during the era of the Little Ice Age. Methane levels in the atmosphere began to climb in the 1730s, and in the 1770s tipped over the highest previous level at about 725 ppb (see Figure IV.3). Presently, after 130 years of unprecedented increase, atmospheric methane now stands at more than 1,700 ppb, higher than it has been for millions of years. CO_2 began its climb out of the LIA minimums in the 1750s, regained a typical Holocene level of 284 ppm just before 1800, and then in the 1840s began its sharp climb toward its contemporary level of 395 + ppm. For most of the nineteenth century, the effects of human-produced greenhouse gases on global temperature was small enough to be offset by the net cooling contributed by volcanic eruptions. But in

---

[17] *Climate Change 2007: The Physical Science Basis*, 210–15; James Hansen et al., "The Efficacy of Climate Forcings," *JGR* 10 (2005), D18104.

sum it would appear that human activity by 1900 might have contributed the warming equivalent of one or two tenths of a degree centigrade to the global temperature balance. Global temperature has increased .8°C since 1900, and .6°C since the 1970s, of which at least three-quarters is caused by human action. The most recent comprehensive analysis argues that from the early nineteenth century "the entire instrumental record [of climate] may be 'contaminated' by anthropogenic influences."[18]

Of course William Ruddiman would argue that this contamination began 5,000 years ago, and it is in this spirit that we need to consider the first modern human influences on climate. These would come from two sources, the burning of fossil fuels and land clearance and farming. As we have seen, England had been burning coal for domestic and industrial heat in significant volumes since the late sixteenth century. Certainly there were already some serious local impacts; as early as the late thirteenth century London was renowned as a dirty city because of heating with sulphurous coal.[19]

But England's CO_2 emissions might have made up a thousandth of the total human-derived emissions around the world. The vast majority of human greenhouse emissions was coming from agriculture, either from CO_2 or from methane, which has a significantly higher warming potential. As early as 1700, British CO_2 emissions from coal burning totaled slightly less than the CO_2 derived from forest clearance and agriculture in the American colonies, and until 1900, American agricultural land use emissions dwarfed British coal emissions (see Figure IV.7). Before roughly the 1830s, the largest single source of greenhouse emissions was methane rising from Chinese rice paddies. This invisible plume rising and mixing into the global troposphere since the Bronze Age, Ruddiman argues, moderated the longer cooling tendencies of the mid-to-late Holocene. Chinese methane emissions were superseded in the 1830 by the accelerating impact of North American land clearance, which produced the largest global volume of greenhouse emissions until the end of the nineteenth century.[20]

[18] Thomas J. Crowley, "Causes of Climate Change over the Past 1000 Years," *Science* 289 (2000), 270–7; James Hansen et al., "Global Temperature Change," *PNAS* 103 (2006), 14288–93; Tett et al., "The Impact of Natural and Anthropogenic Forcings," 3, 29.

[19] William Te Brake, "Air Pollution and Fuel Crises in Preindustrial London, 1250–1650," *Technology and Culture* 16 (1975), 337–59.

[20] See William F. Ruddiman et al., "Early Rice Farming and Anomalous Methane Trends," *QSR* 27 (2008), 1291–5. The data discussed here and presented in Figure IV.7 is from R. A. Houghton, "Carbon Flux to the Atmosphere from Land-Use Changes: 1850–2005," (2008), in *TRENDS: A Compendium of Data on Global Change* (Carbon Dioxide Information Analysis Center, Oak Ridge National Laboratory, http://cdiac.ornl.gov/trends/landuse/houghton/houghton.html, accessed August 8, 2012); Tom Boden et al., "Global CO_2 Emissions from Fossil-Fuel Burning, Cement Manufacture, and Gas Flaring: 1751–2008" (June 10, 2011), (Carbon Dioxide Information Analysis Center, Oak Ridge National Laboratory, Oak Ridge, Tennessee 37831–6290, data file at http://cdiac.ornl.gov/ftp/ndp030/global.1751_2008.ems, accessed August 8, 2012); and M. A. K. Khalil et al., "Methane Sources in China: Historical

Whether or not methane has been quite as potent a contributor to global warming as this analysis might suggest, two points stand out. First, the origins of modern climate change were laid down in the expansion of population and agriculture during the eighteenth and nineteenth centuries. Agricultural sources, whether in North America or China, were far and away the most potent sources of greenhouse gas emissions until the very end of the nineteenth century, during what is known as the *Second Industrial Revolution,* as the massive urbanization of the United States and Europe drove the opening of the era of advanced technologies in which we live.

Second, the origins of the industrial revolution in the eighteenth and early nineteenth century, the subject of one of the most complex literatures in the historical discipline, was by these quantitative measures not an extremely significant source of greenhouse emissions until the 1870s and 1880s. Interestingly, this assessment comports with that of historians measuring economic growth and transformation through the first half of the nineteenth century. This is not to say that the First Industrial Revolution that began to unfold in England in the eighteenth century was inconsequential. But like the Neolithic agricultural revolution, the industrial revolution had a long, slow start in a very small place, and its global impact took time to develop.

* * *

Industrial Revolutions

If the Industrial Revolution was slow to manifest itself in either CO_2 emissions or Gross National Product, it was under way. Explaining the transition to sustained modern economic growth based on accelerating technological

Current Emissions," *Chemosphere* 26 (1993), 127–42, at 142. See also David I. Stern and Robert K. Kaufmann, "Annual Estimates of Global Anthropogenic Methane Emissions: 1860–1994," Center for Energy and Environmental Studies, Boston University, http://cdiac. esd.ornl.gov/trends/meth/ch4.htm, accessed August 8, 2012. My analysis hinges on the estimate by the team led by James Hansen that in total, the cumulative forcing of climate from anthropogenic CO_2 is the modern equivalent of 1.55 watts/meter^2, and that of anthropogenic methane is .55. Moving from this ratio, it would appear that the most appropriate multiplier to convert methane emissions into the "CO_2 equivalent" is 5.5. This is near but not the same as the 500-year "CO_2 equivalent" global warming potential of 7.6 proposed for methane in the 2007 IPCC Report. Hansen et al., "Efficacy," 40; IPCC, *Climate Change 2007*, 212. For the scale of North American deforestation, see Michael Williams, *Americans and Their Forests: A Historical Geography* (New York, 1989); Gordon G. Whitney, *From Coastal Wilderness to Fruited Plain: A History of Environmental Change in Temperate North America from 1500 to the Present* (New York, 1994), 121–226. The *TRENDS* land use CO_2 data is discussed in R. A. Houghton, "The Annual Net Flux of Carbon to the Atmosphere from Changes in Land Use 1850–1990," *Tellus* 51B (1999), 298–313 and R. A. Houghton et al., "Changes in Terrestrial Carbon Storage in the United States. I: The Role of Agriculture and Forestry," *Global Ecology & Biogeography* 9 (2000), 125–44.

innovation – what is known as *Schumpeterian growth* – is probably the central question in modern economic history. The most satisfactory interpretations cast a wide net, balancing the long-term developments of European science and economic development with the accelerating dynamic of the military revolution and the rise of competing global empires. I have suggested that the cold temperatures of the Little Ice Age played something of a minor background role, shaping European demands for the domestic goods that the early Industrial Revolution would produce. Much more important, the waning of crisis mortality and the unprecedented rise of population around the North Atlantic, literally fed in some degree by New World foods, set in place a driver of demand. But this demand had to be met with a supply, a supply that broke out from the limits of the traditional organic economy. A failure of this supply of manufactured commodities, wages, and, in general, economic growth would indeed have led to Malthusian consequences, as occurred in nineteenth-century China. Indeed even in much of Europe such Malthusian pressures were in play through most of the nineteenth century, as rising populations pushed up against very slow economic change, forcing a stagnation in the standard of living. Thus the first phases of the Industrial Revolution were geographically extremely specific, and can only be explained in terms of a perfect storm of flexible culture, protective institutions, geographic circumscription, available paleo-fuels, and a thrust to empire. And even England, where this First Industrial Revolution was launched, failed to maintain enough momentum to lead the Second Industrial Revolution that closely followed, and in which we are still very much enmeshed.

Such considerations require that we address issues of chronology and space. The Industrial Revolution began in England in the late eighteenth century and then developed in continental Europe, the United States, and East Asia. During this process, economic leadership shifted from England to Germany and the United States, and then toward Japan, and now includes China and India. Since the late nineteenth century, economic growth has been directly linked to institutionalized centers of research and innovation and to governmental action, both of which have also been instrumental in the advances in public health and medicine that have driven the sudden and massive decline in mortality that has quadrupled world population during the past century. The result has been an uneven global development that is now compounded by an emerging understanding of the uneven impacts of the global warming ensuing from this economic and demographic growth: more severe in the tropical regions that have seen sharp recent population growth but little per capita economic growth. Thus an interpretation of the past several centuries must juggle an incomplete spiraling of economic and demographic expansion, spreading from a fading center, leaving vast regional inequalities while it destabilizes the earth system that has sustained humanity for millions of years.

How exactly should we describe – and explain – this burst of economic transformation? Description requires a chronology, and the simplest and most authoritative chronology is well established.[21] Rather than one industrial revolution, there have been at least two, and possibly three. The First Industrial Revolution began in the eighteenth century in England, building on the foundation of Savery's steam engine. This was the era of accelerating innovation in the mechanization of textile spinning and weaving, driven by water and then steam power, of key innovations in wrought iron production, and the deployment of the early railroad. Over time it was powered increasingly by the coal-powered steam engine, subject to a constant stream of innovation that after 1800 led to the increasing efficiencies of the high-pressure engine. The key players in this First Industrial Revolution were an array of gentlemen of science, entrepreneurs, and gifted mechanics, first and foremost English, but also French and American. With the rise of the Prussian state in the mid-nineteenth century, a new sociology of technological change emerged: the scientific laboratory established by a triad of nations, corporations, and universities to accelerate industrial development through applied science. Thus was launched the Second Industrial Revolution, in which rapid development and deployment of advances in steel and chemicals were fundamental to the construction of a new urban infrastructure powered in complex new ways by electricity, oil, and the internal combustion engine, and to rapid improvements in medical science that led to dramatic reductions in mortality and extensions of life expectancy. Finally, the explosive invention, deployment, and improvement of microchip electronics and biotechnology since World War II may comprise a Third Industrial Revolution.

This industrial revolutions approach benefits from its chronological simplicity, but it suffers somewhat from being perhaps overly focused on technology and the inventor as the drivers of economic growth. In essence, it is a technology-driven, supply-side model. Thus I also will draw somewhat eclectically from two other models, developed respectively by capitalist and communist economists. Both incorporate the demands of growing populations in shaping economic change.

Walter Rostow's classic analysis focused on the sequence of demands of consuming households and national economies in stressing that the Industrial Revolution began by supplying the growing demand for cheap household goods in a "Take-off," shifted toward the construction of infrastructure with the nineteenth-century construction of cities and railroads in a "Drive to Maturity," and back to supplying households with increasingly sophisticated consumer durables in an almost utopian "Age of

[21] Joel Mokyr, *The Gifts of Athena: Historical Origins of the Knowledge Economy* (Princeton, NJ, 2002), 78–118; –, *The Lever of Riches: Technological Creativity and Economic Progress* (New York, 1990), 81–148.

High-Mass-Consumption."[22] An even more ambitious approach to describing this accelerating history was broached in the 1920s by Soviet Russian economist Nikolai Kondratiev to predict the collapse of capitalism. Its key features were taken up by a decidedly conservative Joseph Schumpeter in the 1930s, and since elaborated into a model of "long waves" of economic upswings and downswings, each driven by the growth of population and demand and shaped by a key technology.[23] Kondratiev and Schumpeter modeled four industrial long waves: a first from the 1760s to the 1820s centering on the first stationary steam engines, a second from the 1820s to the 1870s focusing on the railroad, a third opening in the 1870s driven by revolutions in steel and electricity, and a fourth beginning in the 1920s marked by the internal combustion engine. During the past several decades, speculation has arisen about a fifth wave centering on the microchip and computers. In their most chronologically ambitious form, long waves have been traced back to Sung China in the tenth century; to Italy in the High Middle Ages; to early modern long waves dominated by Portuguese, Dutch, and English empire building; and finally to the industrial long waves.[24] All of the long waves share a model in which a sudden augmentation of resources, either through commercial advantage, imperial expropriation, or technological extension, drives a period of economic expansion that tapers off – after about sixty years – as diminishing returns set in, and the economic expansion falters and turns into a contraction. In particular, the model of the industrial long wave incorporates a logic of rising demand pitted against the plateaus of energy efficiency that each key invention can achieve, diminishing returns that are met by clusters of technical innovations produced during the depths of the depressions that mark the end of each wave. Vaclav Smil, in his noted synthesis of global energy history, focuses on the "prime movers" that produce the exponentially growing volume of energy resources required in post-agrarian societies: stationary and mobile steam engines, steam turbines, internal combustion engines, and gas turbines.[25] A more recent literature defines prime

[22] W. W. Rostow, *The Stages of Economic Growth: A Non-Communist Manifesto* (New York, 1960).

[23] For recent important statements of the Kondratiev-Schumpeter approach, see Carlota Perez, *Technological Revolutions and Financial Capital: The Dynamics of Bubbles and Golden Ages* (Cheltenham, 2002); Chris Freeman and Francisco Louçã, *As Time Goes By: From the Industrial Revolutions to the Information Revolution* (Oxford, 2001); Roger Lloyd-Jones and M. J. Lewis, "The Long Wave and Turning Points in British Industrial Capitalism: A Neo-Schumpeterian Approach," *JEEconH* 29 (2000), 359–401; George Modelski and William R. Thompson, *Leading Sectors and World Powers: The Coevolution of Global Politics and Economics* (Columbia, SC, 1996); Andrew Tylecote, *The Long Wave in the World Economy: The Present Crisis in Historical Perspective* (London, 1992); Joshua S. Goldstein, *Long Cycles: Prosperity and War in the Modern Age* (New Haven, CT, 1998).

[24] Modelski and Thompson, *Leading Sectors and World Powers*, 70–104, 142–208; Peter J. Hugill, *World Trade since 1431: Geography, Technology, and Capitalism* (Baltimore, MD, 1993), 9–41.

[25] Vaclav Smil, *Energy in World History* (Boulder, CO, 1994), 223–47.

movers and innovations that increase the "flow-through" speed of material processing as "general purpose technologies." Indeed, we might well extend the model of the general purpose technology back through time to include the control of fire, the three stages of stone tool technology, the pottery kiln, writing, bronze, iron, and the rotary principle discovered with the wheel and the hand quern, which led to the basic principles of simple mechanics, the waterwheel, and the windmill.[26]

Clearly, the inexorable growth of population and demand, particularly as urbanization multiplies that demand for "things" and energy, is fundamental to the assumptions of the long wave models. However, while the long wave approach is promising, and provides a useful structure of description, it has proved difficult to pin down its cycles and turning points with great precision.[27] Thus it is simpler to follow Joel Mokyr's two-stage account of a First Industrial Revolution driven by steam and coal beginning in the eighteenth century and running to the 1870s, followed by a Second Industrial Revolution driven by steel, oil, turbine-generated electricity, and interlocking complexes of corporate, university, and national institutions. But along the way in the following discussion I will draw on Rostow, Kondratiev, and Schumpeter to propose how growing, increasingly urban populations put rising pressures on the capacities and efficiencies of technological systems. Necessarily I will map this sketch against the outlines of the global demographic revolution and the sudden burst of industrial greenhouse gases that has so altered our relationship with the earth system.

* * *

The First Industrial Revolution

The traditional story of the origins of the Industrial Revolution begins in England in the middle of the eighteenth century with "a wave of gadgets" suddenly launching a wave of prosperity and growth. These inventions began with Thomas Newcomen's redesign of the Savery steam engine in 1712 and John Kay's flying shuttle, which sped up the handloom, in 1733. After Abraham Darby's successful reduction of coal into slow, even-burning

---

[26] Richard G. Lipsey et al., *Economic Transformations: General Purpose Technologies and Long-Term Economic Growth* (Oxford, 2006); Elhanan Helpman, ed., *General Purpose Technologies and Economic Growth* (Cambridge, MA, 1998); Timothy F. Bresnahan and M. Trajtenberg, "General Purpose Technologies: 'Engines of Growth'?" *Journal of Econometrics* 65 (1995), 83–108.

[27] For critiques of the Kondratiev long wave model, see Solomos Solomou, *Phases of Economic Growth: 1850–1973: Kondratieff Waves and Kuznets Swings* (Cambridge, 1988); Nathan Rosenberg and Claudio R. Frischtak, "Technological Innovation and Long Waves," *Cambridge Journal of Economics* 8 (1984), 7–24. See the very useful discussion in David H. Fischer, *The Great Wave: Price Revolutions and the Rhythms of History* (Oxford, 1996), 273–7.

coke, a series of technical adjustments led to a dramatic rise in the volume of coal used in various hearth-based industries. A wave of canal building across England provided the cheap transportation necessary to carry the heavy loads of raw materials and finished products flowing through these expanding iron furnaces, potteries, and glassworks. The classic period of inventions came during the 1750s to the 1780s, with Richard Arkwright's "water frame" and James Hargreaves's jenny, combined in Samuel Compton's "mule" to establish the foundation of all mechanically spun yarn, followed by Henry Cort's 1784 invention of the puddler roller, which would fundamentally expand the production of wrought iron, a requirement for machine and engine building. The most important of these engines was transformed by James Watts's condenser (1769) and double-acting engine (1782, 1784), which reduced the consumption of coal, and his sun-and-planet gearing, which achieved steam-powered rotary action – rather than a reciprocating action – for the first time. Here fossil fuel technology was applied to the same rotary problem that Iron Age stoneworkers had achieved in replacing the pestle grinder with the hand quern sometime around 600 BC, and Greek mechanics had transferred to the waterwheel 300 years later.[28]

An older, celebratory history has long hailed these "macroinventions" as delivering a shock to the English economy, jolting it out of slow, cumulative Smithian growth into sustained and rapid Schumpeterian growth.[29] But the immediate impact was not quite so dramatic, despite its clear long-range significance. A series of measures suggests that economic growth in eighteenth-century England was actually relatively slow and gradual (see Figure IV.5). Nicholas Crafts and Knick Harley have persistently and persuasively argued that industrial output grew at a very modest pace between 1700 and the 1820s, when it began to climb substantially. Similarly, Angus Maddison's estimate of gross domestic product suggests a very moderate increase during the eighteenth century, with growth coming in the 1830s. Coal use per capita did not increase dramatically until the 1820s and 1830s as well, indicating that England was still operating as an advanced organic economy, if mineral enhanced. And, most important, English wages were flat until the end of the Napoleonic Wars in 1815, when they began to rise modestly,

[28] T. S. Ashton, *The Industrial Revolution, 1760–1830* (Oxford, 1997 [1948]), 48–75; David S. Landes, *The Unbound Prometheus: Technological Change and Industrial Development in Western Europe from 1750 to the Present* (New York, 1969), 41–114; Mokyr, *The Lever of Riches*, 81–113; Rick Szostak, *The Role of Transportation in the Industrial Revolution: A Comparison of England and France* (Montreal, 1991); Rolf Peter Sieferle, *The Subterranean Forest: Energy Systems and the Industrial Revolution* (Cambridge, 2001), 110–37.

[29] See note 27 and Phyllis Deane and W. A. Cole, *British Economic Growth, 1688–1959* (Cambridge, 1962). The most recent synthesis, Robert C. Allen, *The British Industrial Revolution in Global Perspective* (New York, 2009), stresses high wages in Britain relative to the Continent (discussed in Chapter 9), cheap energy, and the impact of technological invention.

and then more sharply after 1870. Thus if the mechanical inventions of the British Industrial Revolution were launched in the 1760s, there was at least a fifty-year delay before the benefits began to be manifested in the general economy.[30]

There were a few mitigating factors, most important population growth. The beginning of this First Industrial Revolution was launched in the context of – and clearly in response to – an extremely rapid increase in population. After roughly eighty years of relative stability, the population of England and Wales in the 1730s began a course of ninety years of uninterrupted growth, rising at an increasing rate from 5.5 million to 12.3 million.[31] Here it was clear that the grip of crisis mortality had been broken. In previous centuries, rising temperatures – paradoxically – had led to higher death rates and falling population, but from the 1730s forward, English population moved completely independently of any climate-disease vector (see Figure IV.2). The suppression of plague and famine was matched by the success of inoculation and vaccination for smallpox, which reduced smallpox deaths sharply over the course of the mid-to-late eighteenth century in the British Isles and the American colonies. The variety and quality of food eaten by English working people during the eighteenth century also seems to have improved somewhat. So too a general improvement of conditions of simple drainage, public health, and medicine – manifestations of a stable government and society – contributed to the growth of population. It is worth noting that this was the second of four stages of the epidemiological transition that would add up to the "modern decline in mortality." The first had occurred around 1480–1500, the second here in the eighteenth century, and the third and fourth would follow in the late nineteenth and twentieth centuries, as modern science radically extended life expectancy.[32]

[30] N. F. R. Crafts, *British Economic Growth during the Industrial Revolution* (Oxford, 1985); N. F. R. Crafts and C. K. Harley, "Output Growth and the British Industrial Revolution: A Restatement of the Crafts-Harley View," *EconHistR* 45 (1992), 703–30. GDP data from Angus Maddison, "Historical Statistics of the World Economy: 1–2006 AD"; coal production from B. R. Mitchell, *International Historical Statistics: Europe, 1750–1993*, fourth edition (London, 1998) (*I.H.S:E.*) 426, 428, 431–2, 477, 480, 482, 484; wages from Robert C. Allen, "The Great Divergence in European Wages and Prices from the Middle Ages to the First World War," *ExpEconH* 38 (2001), 411–47, and –, "Wages and Prices in London and Southern England, 1259–1914" (http://www.nuff.ox.ac.uk/users/allen/studer/london. xls, accessed August 8, 2012). See also Gregory Clark, "The Condition of the Working Class in England, 1209–2004," *Journal of Political Economy* 113 (2005), 1307–40; Luis Angeles, "GDP Per Capita or Real Wages? Making Sense of Conflicting Views on Pre-Industrial Europe," *ExpEconH* 45 (2008), 147–63. On the tension between the Crafts-Harley thesis and the long wave perspective, see Freeman and Louçã, *As Time Goes By*, 22–31.

[31] E. A. Wrigley et al., *English Population History from Family Reconstitution, 1580–1837* (Cambridge, 1997), 614.

[32] Gareth Williams, *The Angel of Death: The Story of Smallpox* (Houndmills, 2010); Peter Razzell, *The Conquest of Smallpox: The Impact of Inoculation on Smallpox Mortality in Eighteenth Century Britain* (Sussex, 1997); Mary J. Dobson, *Contours of Death and Disease*

This inexorable, unstoppable rise in numbers helps explain the paradox of slow growth in an age of industrial miracles. If English wages did not rise, neither did they fall. Such a fall was the fate of most of Europe, whose recovery from the seventeenth-century crisis looks a little like that after the Black Death, when rising populations led to falling wages. In effect, England in the first fifty years of the First Industrial Revolution was running in place, struggling to meet the economic demands of a burgeoning population, and further burdened with a sequence of wars in North America and then against Napoleon that required virtually continual national mobilization. Between 1800 and 1820, the wars with Napoleon, the constraints of the Corn Laws, and the Dalton Minimum all contributed to an enormous spike in the price of bread (see Figure IV.2). The impact of all this on the English worker was not inconsequential: annual hours of work increased significantly after 1750. But day wages did not fall, something that is seen as a triumph in what was still really only a mineral-enhanced organic economy facing a series of countervailing pressures. Paradoxically, England was industrializing without growing.[33]

England's eighteenth-century population growth began in the contexts of early proto-manufacturing and a growing empire. Population expansion had its origins in the 1730s, twenty years before the "age of industrial gadgets." E. A. Wrigley and the Cambridge School have well established that this growth stemmed as much from the advance of fertility as from a decline of mortality. And fertility was rising in particular sorts of places. Villages and districts where the putting-out system of cottage production took hold offered the prospect of household independence to young men and women without having to wait for parents to die to inherit rights to a farm. Thus young married people flocked to these early centers of household manufacture, took up work, and began to produce larger families than they would have if they had delayed marriage.[34] If English wages were higher than wages were on the Continent, manufacturing spread in regions where

in Early Modern England (Cambridge, 1997); Carole Shammas, "Food Expenditures and Economic Well-Being in Early Modern England," *JEconH* 43 (1983), 89–100; Elizabeth A. Fenn, *Pox Americana: The Great Smallpox Epidemic of 1775–1782* (New York, 2001); David Loschky and Ben D. Childers, "Early English Mortality," *JInterdH* 24 (1993), 85–97; James C. Riley, *Rising Life Expectancy: A Global History* (New York, 2001), 15–25; and Massimo Livi-Bacci, *A Concise History of World Population*, third edition (Malden and Oxford, 2001), 58–62, 95–100.

[33] Angeles, "GDP Per Capita or Real Wages?" 158; Allen, "The Great Divergence in European Wages"; Nicholas Crafts, "The First Industrial Revolution: Resolving the Slow Growth/ Rapid Industrialization Paradox," *Journal of the European Economic Association* 3 (2005), 525–34; Wilkinson, *Poverty and Progress*, 112–37; Linda Colley, *Britons: Forging the Nation, 1707–1837* (New Haven, CT, 1992).

[34] David Levine, *Family Formation in an Age of Nascent Capitalism* (New York, 1977), 58–87; David Levine, *Reproducing Families: The Political Economy of English Population History* (New York, 1987), 94–159; Wrigley et al., *English Population History*, 186–93, 427–9.

wages were relatively low and agriculture had long been more precarious – the northern hill country, particularly Lancashire and Yorkshire. The output – and population growth – of the upland districts was tied to that of a wider world through the city of Birmingham. It is now well established that the export trade to Europe, and importantly to the Americas and Africa, took up a critical portion of this early manufacturing. Textiles and metal wares made their way to the settler societies on the American mainland as well as to the slave plantation regions of the West Indies and to the slave trade on the African coast. Throughout England, and Europe to a lesser degree, the impact of empire on the economy was felt in the new demands for household goods generated by the addictive properties of colonial sugar, tea, coffee, and tobacco. But a critical part of this demand was generated in the empire itself, to the extent – as Joseph Inikori has firmly established – that the demand for certain varieties of checked cotton cloth for the African slave trade stimulated the transition to the water-powered mechanization of spinning launched by Arkwright and Hargreaves in the 1750s and 1760s.[35]

There was thus a direct link between empire and the rise of manufacturing, broadly as Eric Williams proposed seventy years ago in *Capitalism and Slavery*.[36] We might also point to wider global questions involving empire, manufacturing, and the natural world. If we consider elements of the global carbon balance, we see a reflection of how the fortunes of the Anglo-Atlantic peoples were coming at the considerable expense of others. In North America, land clearance for agriculture produced CO_2 emissions

---

[35] On empire, export markets, and industrial development, see in particular Joseph E. Inikori, *Africans and the Industrial Revolution in England: A Study in International Trade and Economic Development* (New York, 2002), 91–123; 405–72; and P. K. O'Brien and S. L. Engerman, "Exports and the Growth of the British Economy from the Glorious Revolution to the Peace of Amiens," in Barbara L. Solow, ed., *Slavery and the Rise of the Atlantic System* (New York, 1991), 177–209; Joel Mokyr, "Introduction," in Joel Mokyr, ed., *The British Industrial Revolution: An Economic Perspective* (Boulder, CO, 1993), 68–78; Nuala Zahediah, "London and the Colonial Consumer in the Late Seventeenth Century," *EconHistR* 47 (1994), 239–61; Woodruff D. Smith, *Consumption and the Making of Respectability, 1600–1800* (London, 2002); Robert C. Allen, "Progress and Poverty in Early Modern Europe," *EconHistR* 56 (2003), 403–43; David Ormrod, *The Rise of Commercial Empires: England and the Netherlands in the Age of Mercantilism, 1650–1770* (New York, 2003); Daron Acemoglu et al., "The Rise of Europe: Atlantic Trade, Institutional Change, and Economic Growth," *AER* 95 (2005), 546–79; Ronald Findlay and Kevin H. O'Rourke, *Power and Plenty: Trade, War, and the World Economy in the Second Millennium* (Princeton, NJ, 2007); 311–64. See Inikori, *Africans and the Industrial Revolution*, 484 n 10, for a pointed critique of Pomeranz's neglect of the role of global markets in *The Great Divergence*.

[36] Eric Williams, *Capitalism and Slavery* (London, 1964). For discussions of the historiography of the Williams thesis, see William A. Green, "Race and Slavery: Considerations on the Williams Thesis," in Barbara Solow and Stanley Engerman, eds., *British Capitalism and Caribbean Slavery: The Legacy of Eric Williams* (New York, 1987), 25–49 and Inikori, *Africans and the Industrial Revolution*, 1–7, 136–8.

that quickly surpassed those of early English industrialization. Conversely, tropical Africa, where mechanized checked cotton textiles bought many of the people who labored to clear these American forests, was probably a net carbon sink. Estimates of land use emissions from tropical Africa between 1850 and 1900, when population was rising slightly, suggest that on balance it was drawing down carbon, by a very slight ratio. Sub-Saharan African populations had been falling since 1600 under the impact of the slave trade, and it would seem likely that forests and woodlands had been regrowing during this period of population decline, steadily absorbing rather than emitting carbon.[37] In North America and Mexico, the impact of epidemic disease continued unabated, accelerating during the American Revolution, when smallpox spread during the war, leaving inoculated armies and civilians protected, but devastating native peoples at the furthest reaches of the continent.[38] And on the other side of the world, the effects of El Niño drove droughts in Bengal that contributed to the demise of the Indian handloom textile industry and the rise of the British mechanized textile industry.[39]

A formative condition in these global processes clearly was the explosive rate of population growth in England starting in the 1730s, a rate of growth that shaped an endogenous Malthusian crisis comparable to that in contemporary China. England would not suffer a crash, but it would suffer as it desperately ran in place, searching for solutions to shortfalls and bottlenecks. There are good reasons to see the spread of the new textile machinery from the 1760s in the classic understanding as a solution to a technological bottleneck, what Thomas Hughes calls a "salient," which was limiting the flow of production. The entire history of incremental "micro-invention" that followed is a tale of inventors and mechanics seeking to solve particular technical problems – innumerable frictions – to increase the speed and lower the cost of production and distribution of goods. The initial textile inventions stood, however, as "macroinventions" that broke from previous paradigms to solve the pressures of increasing demand.[40] But if the application of these initial technologies was making a difference from the 1760s it was too limited to break through to be visible in any per capita measures. In fact, while investments in canals show no sign of decline, there was a sharp drop in manufacturing investments during the 1770s, driven by what Brinley Thomas calls a "crucial bottleneck": Abraham Darby's coke could be used to produce pig iron, but not wrought iron. The real breakout would not come until after a series of inventions made their way into the

---

[37] Houghton, "Carbon Flux to the Atmosphere from Land-Use Changes: 1850–2005."

[38] Fenn, *Pox Americana*.

[39] Clingingsmith and Williamson, "Deindustrialization in 18th and 19th Century India."

[40] Thomas P. Hughes, "The Dynamics of Technological Change: Salients, Critical Problems, and Industrial Revolutions," in Giovanni Dosi et al., eds., *Technology and Enterprise in Historical Perspective* (Oxford, 1992), 97–118; for micro- and macroinventions, see Mokyr, *Lever of Riches*, 12–13, and Allen, *The British Industrial Revolution*, 135–271.

ironworks – first the Wood brothers' crucible system, and then Henry Cort's puddling and rolling system, patented in 1784, which utilized coke burning and resulted in a faster process and a cheaper product. This wrought iron, now cheaply available in rolled sheets, could be used to construct steam engine boilers, but the forged iron components of the piston engine itself would require precision metal grinding, cutting, lathing, and screw making, another bottleneck salient that was broken around 1800 in the Maudslay machine shop. Much of the Cort wrought iron was consumed in the military and naval mobilization against Napoleon.[41]

Another bottleneck involved food. Despite the continuing productivity improvement in English agriculture, it was not sufficient to feed the growing population, and from the 1760s grain, butter, meat, and livestock began to be imported in rising volumes from Ireland, which increasingly began to function as England's breadbasket. The restrictive British Corn Laws were abolished in 1846, but it took until the 1850s for steamship transport from North America and Australia to move huge amounts of grain, fundamentally lowering the cost of food in Britain, and in Europe in general.[42] But during the first decades of the nineteenth century, the poor in England's growing population faced something approaching a subsistence crisis.

This crisis was manifested in a spectrum of domains that all bear on energy. Food costs spiked from the late 1790s to 1820, and did not taper off to eighteenth-century norms until the late nineteenth century. In this context, during wartime and Dalton Solar Minimum conditions, England's rate of urbanization climbed to its highest levels since the late sixteenth century, in a bubble of rural-to-urban migration that peaked between 1800 and 1830. During this burst of urbanization, in 1810 and 1820, British cities actually suffered an "energy deficit": the volume of total coal consumption relative to *urban* population actually declined before rising steadily until the end of the century (see Figure IV.2). Conditions of housing declined on a national average, most notoriously in the new crowded industrial districts. Across the Irish Sea, the impact of the extraction of food from a literally

---

[41] Thomas, "Escaping from Constraints," 732–9; Brinley Thomas, *The Industrial Revolution and the Atlantic Economy: Selected Essays* (London, 1993), 100–20; Mokyr, *Lever of Riches*, 93–5, 103–5.

[42] Mark Overton, *Agricultural Revolution in England: The Transformation of the Agrarian Economy 1500–1850* (Cambridge, 1996) argues for a sharp increase in agricultural productivity during the eighteenth and early nineteenth centuries. Brinley Thomas and others claim that English agriculture by itself was insufficient to support the population, which increasingly required Irish imports, and after the repeal of the Corn Laws, imports from Europe and North America. Thomas, "Escaping from Constraints," 739–53; Thomas, *The Industrial Revolution and the Atlantic Economy*, 81–100; Lloyd-Jones and Lewis, "The Long Wave and Turning Points in British Industrial Capitalism," 365–72; Hugill, *World Trade*, 75–6; E. J. T. Collins, "Food Supplies and Food Policy," in E. J. T. Collins, ed., *The Agrarian History of England and Wales: Volume VII, 1850–1914 (Part I)* (Cambridge, 2000), 33–9; Ralph Davis, *The Industrial Revolution and British Overseas Trade* (Leicester, 1979), 122, 124.

colonial economy was particularly severe, leading to the hyper-dependence of Irish cottagers on a very few varieties of New World potato. The resulting Irish Potato Famine was set off by a blight of fungus that struck across Europe, but devastated the Irish crop three times between 1845 and 1848. Coinciding with wheat and rye failures across Europe and a general financial crisis, the Irish famine and subsequent mass emigration cut Ireland's population by a quarter in less than a decade, in a subsistence crisis not seen in Europe since the seventeenth century.[43]

The full benefits of the late eighteenth-century technological synthesis would only reach the general economy after 1820, when the Crafts-Harley estimates of industrial output and other measures of industrial investment suddenly surged in a burst of growth[44] (see Figure IV.5). But this post-Napoleonic surge in the economy notwithstanding, the bottlenecks of population and resources that shaped this entire period can be conceived as an *energy deficit* that bore particularly hard on the poorest half of the population. This "deficit" has been the subject of the "standard of living debate" since contemporaries including Karl Marx and Frederick Engels took up the pen in protest.[45]

By a host of measures the living conditions of British laboring peoples at best stalled during these opening decades of the First Industrial Revolution. Real wages did not rise until 1820, then increased only very slightly, and did not grow consistently until the 1870s.[46] These wages were inadequate to support high-fertility families, leading to serious increases of infant mortality in British cities during the 1830s and 1840s, reflected in higher mortality rates in the cities than in the country as a whole[47] (see Figure IV.5). The

---

[43] Gregory Clark, "Shelter from the Storm: Housing and the Industrial Revolution, 1550–1909," *JEconH* 62 (2002), 489–511; Cormac Ó Gráda et al., eds., *When the Potato Failed: Causes and Effects of the "Last" European Subsistence Crisis, 1845–1850* (Turnhout, 2007).

[44] See index of industrial production, Crafts and Harley, "Output Growth and the British Industrial Revolution," 725–7 ("revised best guess"); and figures for investment in industrial machinery and equipment, in Thomas, "Escaping from Constraints," 735.

[45] For an overview of the origins of the debate, see the "Editor's Introduction," in Arthur J. Taylor, ed., *The Standard of Living in Britain in the Industrial Revolution* (London, 1975), xi–lv.

[46] Charles Feinstein, "Pessimism Perpetuated: Real Wages and the Standard of Living in Britain during and after the Industrial Revolution," *JEconH* 58 (1998), 625–58; Gregory Clark, "Farm Wages and Living Standards in the Industrial Revolution: England, 1670–1869," *EconHistR* 54 (2001), 477–505 (data at http://gpih.ucdavis.edu/files/England_1209-1914_(Clark).xls accessed August 8, 2012); Allen, "The Great Divergence in European Wages"; Allen, "Wages and Prices in London and Southern England, 1259–1914." These data series challenge the more optimistic interpretations presented in Peter H. Lindert and Jeffrey G. Williamson, "English Workers' Standard of Living during the Industrial Revolution: A New Look," *EconHistR* 36 (1983), 1–25.

[47] Paul Huck, "Infant Mortality and Living Standards of English Workers during the Industrial Revolution," *JEconH* 5 (1995), 528–50; Simon Szreter and Graham Mooney, "Urbanization,

paltry wage increase in the 1820s was more than offset by increased hours at work and the loss of leisure time; and women and children were drawn into industrial work to scrabble together the difference.[48]

Adult stature – a direct consequence of general health and nutrition – followed a similar trajectory (see Figures III.7, IV.5). Typically in the premodern past, the urban-born were shorter than their rural counterparts, and the rising urbanization mapped a concurrent shortening of stature. Reflecting the fact that England was the richest country in eighteenth-century Europe, English adults were taller than their continental contemporaries, but their stature trended lower through time, with shorter heights spreading north from London and southeast England by 1800. Progressively shorter adult heights were recorded through the first half of the nineteenth century, reaching lows in the cohorts born during the 1830s and the "hungry '40s." The entire period between 1820 and 1865 is seen as an epoch when English working families were unable to "maintain an adequate nutritional status." An increasing proportion of the food calories consumed during these decades – particularly by women and children – came from sugar, which substituted quick energy for sustained nutrition. Equally significant, working people were unable to maintain adequate sanitation in early nineteenth-century industrial cities. Crowded into ramshackle districts without safe water sources or sewage disposal, or even light or air, England's early industrial workers suffered from rising rates of tuberculosis and periodic onslaughts of cholera.[49]

Mortality, and the Standard of Living Debate: New Estimates of the Expectation of Life at Birth in Nineteenth-Century British Cities," *EconHistR* 51 (1998), 84–112; Simon Szreter, *Health and Wealth: Studies in History and Policy* (Rochester, NY, 2005), 146–61; Wrigley et al., *English Population History*, 272–6.

[48] Hans-Joachim Voth, "The Longest Years: New Estimates of Labor Inputs in England, 1760–1830," *JEconH* 61 (2001), 1065–82; –, *Time and Work in Industrial England, 1750–1830* (Oxford, 2003), 234–41; Sara Horrell and Jane Humphries, "'The Exploitation of Little Children': Child Labor and Family Economy in the Industrial Revolution," *ExpEconH* 32 (1995), 485–516.

[49] Roderick Floud et al., *The Changing Body: Health, Nutrition, and Human Development in the Western World since 1700* (Cambridge, 2011), 134–69; Francesco Cinnirella, "Optimists or Pessimists? A Reconsideration of Nutritional Status in Britain, 1740–1865," *EREconH* 12 (2008), 351; John Komlos, "An Anthropometric History of Early-Modern France," *EREconH* 7 (2003), 159–89; –, "Shrinking in a Growing Economy: The Mystery of Physical Stature during the Industrial Revolution," *JEconH* 58 (1998), 779–802; – "The Secular Trend in the Biological Standard of Living in the United Kingdom, 1730–1860," *EconHistR* 46 (1993), 115–44; Stephen Nicholas and Richard H. Steckel, "Heights and Living Standards of English Workers during the Early Years of Industrialization, 1770–1815," *JEconH* 51 (1991), 937–57; Paul Johnson and Stephen Nicholas, "Health and Welfare of Women in the United Kingdom, 1785–1920," in Richard H. Steckel and Roderick Floud, eds., *Health and Welfare during Industrialization* (Chicago, IL, 1997), 210–49. For more "optimistic" interpretations, see Roderick Floud et al., *Height, Health and History: Nutritional Status in the United Kingdom, 1750–1880* (Cambridge, 1990), 287–306; and Roderick Floud and Bernard Harris, "Health, Height, and Welfare: Britain, 1700–1980," in Steckel and Floud,

Lurking behind this "penalty" or "insult" to the health of the British working class during the First Industrial Revolution was the "urban energy deficit": the fact that steam and coal did not begin to assume a significant working burden until the middle of the nineteenth century. If a burst of urbanization began after the turn of the century and a notable increase of industrial production began after 1820, the effective application of coal and steam power to industrial work was apparent only from the mid-1850s (see Figure IV.5; Tables IV.1, IV.2). The limited role of coal in British industrial production was particularly evident during the peak of urban growth and declining health and nutrition between the 1820s and the 1840s, when a disproportionate amount of industrial work still required severe physical exertion, notoriously in the manual return action required for spinning mules and in the proliferation of child labor. Coal consumption certainly accelerated in iron and steel production during the 1830s, reflecting British investments in railroads. A similar acceleration was not seen in "general manufactures" until the early 1850s and 1860s, when a new generation of steam engine technology took hold. Despite their acclaim, James Watts's engines were not all that numerous, and of very low horsepower: by 1800, there were about 490 total, each of about twenty-five horsepower. Most of the engines built by Watts and the weaker atmospheric engines built by his competitors were still put to work in mining; mechanized textile spinning was often driven by horsepower until the 1790s, when the price of feed for horses increased dramatically with the onset of the Dalton Minimum, bringing an increasing use of waterpower and the first experiments with steam-driven spinning. Once James Watts's patent expired in 1800, innovation began quickly to move the steam engine from a low-horsepower, low-pressure engine to a high-horsepower, high-pressure engine. The work of Richard Trevithick and Arthur Woolf provided the basis for the first railroad and steamboat engines. However, while steam power advanced in cotton textile manufacturing after 1820, it was of the older, low-pressure technology. As late as 1838, watermills still provided 20 percent of the power in English cotton mills, and almost 40 percent in woolen mills, and the high-pressure engines were only introduced in the 1840s and 1850s. The horsepower of steam engines in textile work expanded dramatically from the 1850s to the 1860s, with the sudden spread of the high-pressure engines, producing a comparable burst in coal consumption per industrial production. By one estimate, water power and steam provided the equivalent of eight horsepower per person in 1800, fewer than fourteen in 1830, but more than seventy in 1870; steam advanced from a quarter of the capacity of water power in 1800 to equivalent in 1830 to almost ten times more in 1870.[50]

eds., *Health and Welfare during Industrialization*, 91–127; on sugar, see Sidney W. Mintz, *Sweetness and Power: The Place of Sugar in Modern History* (New York, 1986), 108–34.

[50] G. N. von Tunzelmann, *Steam Power and British Industrialization to 1860* (Oxford, 1978), 26–30, 79–91, 117–21, 219–25, 234–6; Richard L. Hills, *Power from Steam: A History of*

Despite this clear mid-century steam revolution, large sectors of the British economy remained unmechanized until the end of the century, meaning that the "motive power" in these trades was still provided by human muscles, if now organized for mass production.[51]

The steam engine may have been an emerging technology, but quite clearly it is difficult to see it as a prime mover driving the British economy until the 1850s. Certainly coal was a very significant fuel for domestic heating and industrial hearths as it had been for more than 200 years. But there was obviously a serious lag between the invention of the steam engine and its mass application to rotary action. If industrial production grew from 1820, it did not have the benefit of an efficient prime mover for another twenty to thirty years, and in the meantime, the economy continued to involve significant "organic" inputs by the working poor, moving in increasing numbers into English cities since 1800.[52]

the Stationary Steam Engine (Cambridge, 1989), 141–61; William S. Humphrey and Joe Stanislaw, "Economic Growth and Energy Consumption in the UK, 1700–1975," *Energy Policy* 7 (1979), 29–42; data from Mitchell, *British Historical Statistics*, 258, 370, 373, 375; Mitchell, *I.H.S:E*, 79–87; B. R. Mitchell with Phyllis Deane, *Abstract of British Historical Statistics* (Cambridge, 1971), 225–6; Crafts and Harley, "Output Growth and the British Industrial Revolution," 725–7 ("revised best guess"); see also John Kanefsky, "The Diffusion of Power Technology in British Industry, 1760–1870," PhD Thesis, Exeter University, 1979, 338, reproduced in Hills, *Power from Steam*, 235.

[51] A. E. Musson, "Industrial Motive Power in the United Kingdom, 1800–70," *EconHistR* NS 29 (1976), 415–39; Raphael Samuel, "The Workshop of the World: Steam Power and Hand Technology in Mid-Victorian Britain," *History Workshop* 3 (1977), 6–72; Dolores Greenberg, "Reassessing the Power Patterns of the Industrial Revolution: An Anglo-America Comparison," *AHR* 87 (1982), 1237–61; see also John W. Kanefsky, "Motive Power in British Industry and the Accuracy of the 1870 Factory Return," *EconHistR* 32 (1979), 360–75 for higher estimates in 1870.

[52] While I have been stressing the endogenous role of population growth as the fundamental driver in pushing England into early industrialization, in a Boserupian intensification in which technology would eventually provide the push to sustained Schumpeterian growth, it is worth considering the role of exogenous climate conditions in this early nineteenth-century burst of English urbanization. Food prices had been rising over the last half of the eighteenth century, but they spiked up between 1800 and 1820 (see Figure IV.2). Rising food prices encouraged a wave of enclosures in southern England authorized by Parliament, which reduced the land available to the rural poor for subsistence production. Some of this price rise must have been driven by population growth, but its worst increase – driving a small downturn in real wages – came during the years of the simultaneous onset of the cold Dalton Minimum and the sudden acceleration of urbanization. All of these would seem to be linked, with the result that English cities were swollen suddenly with the rural poor after 1800, driving the 1810–20 urban coal deficit. Urban data (cities of population greater than 10,000) from Jan de Vries, *European Urbanization, 1500–1800* (Cambridge, MA, 1984), 30; C. M. Law, "The Growth of Urban Population in England and Wales, 1801–1911," *Trans. of the Institute of British Geographers* 41 (1967), 142; coal data from B. R. Mitchell, *British Historical Statistics* (Cambridge, 1988), 247–8. Law and de Vries arrive at different figures for 1800/1: 2,132,000 and 1,870. I use an average of 2 million. Food price data from Allen, "Wages and Prices in London and Southern England, 1259–1914"; Clark, "Farm Wages and Living Standards in the Industrial Revolution," 502–4; Gregory Clark, "The Long March of

The history of the early industrial revolution is thus not one of easy triumph of steam and coal, of mechanized, mineral-powered machinery replacing organic and natural power. If it marked the key turning point from Smithian to Schumpeterian economic growth, this transition came at a considerable cost to the well-being of English working peoples. The industrial transformation was also, it would appear, driven fundamentally by the new trajectory of population growth that had accompanied the imperial globalization that had begun to unfold after 1492. Clearly, the long, slow transition to a high-efficiency steam engine shaped a stressful bottleneck for the growing English population; if it did not cause a crisis, this technological lag certainly left its mark. If the forced transition to urban manufacturing in England was driven by a trajectory of population expansion, its mid-century stresses had striking parallels in the Irish Potato Famine, the 1857 war against British rule in India, the Chinese Taiping Rebellion, and the American Civil War, traumatic upheavals shaped by the effects of a century of globalization-driven population growth and the imperial movement of commodities.[53]

Looking beyond England, it is notable that the industrial revolution moved much more slowly on the Continent, where population growth had been much more limited as yet. As of 1851, as Britain celebrated its new economy at the Crystal Palace Exhibition in London, the total steam power at work in Britain was probably greater than that in all of continental Europe. Reflecting both an ancient connection between England and the Low Countries and the strategic location of coal and iron ore, Belgium was the first to develop steam-powered industry, and maintained an industrial economic edge per capita until the First World War. France came next, following a unique path to industrialization, given the resistance of French peasants to moving off the land, and its lack of coal resources. Germany was the fourth of the Continent's early industrializers, delayed by its complex political unification and by the enduring impact of seventeenth- and eighteenth-century warfare. As of 1850, France and Germany had strong economies, as measured by GDP, but had barely begun to industrialize, as measured by CO_2 emissions, and continued to lag as of 1870, when they fought the first of three wars for preeminence on the Continent and in the wider global arena. By 1913, Germany had surpassed France in developing a modern industrial infrastructure, and had surpassed it in population. If anything, development in Germany and France was led by railroad building,

History: Farm Wages, Population, and Economic Growth, England 1209–1869," *EconHistR* 60 (2007), 108–9 (data at http://gpih.ucdavis.edu/files/England_1209–1914_(Clark).xls accessed August 8, 2012). For a recent discussion of the enclosures and rural conditions, see Cinnirella, "Optimists or Pessimists?" 347–9.

[53] Here see Douglas R. Egerton, "Rethinking Atlantic Historiography in a Postcolonial Era: The Civil War in a Global Perspective," *Journal of the Civil War Era* 1 (2011), 79–95; Platt, *Autumn in the Heavenly Kingdom*.

which was well developed by 1870. Of course the future of industrial growth and industrial emissions lay with the United States, which as of the mid-nineteenth century ranked somewhere between Belgium and Germany, but would shoot to the lead during the final decades of the century.[54]

* * *

Emissions and Atmosphere, 1800–1880

This mid-century context of rapidly expanding coal consumption prompted an English economist, William Stanley Jevons, to worry about Britain's long-term supply of coal, in *The Coal Question*, published in 1865. If he was not the first to have these concerns, Jevons's analysis was the formative statement of a theory of resource depletion – complete with nervous references to Malthusian predictions. He wrote only three decades before Svante Arrhenius, a scientist in a relatively pristine Sweden (where CO_2 emissions were at a level last seen in England around 1720), published his first concerns in 1896 about the role of emissions from coal burning in driving a future greenhouse thickening of the atmosphere and global warming.[55] But as of the 1890s – if they were advancing rapidly – industrial emissions were still producing less CO_2 than was the reduction of natural landscapes to agriculture. Natural landscapes retain vast quantities of carbon in soils and vegetation that are released into the atmosphere through burning, decay, and soil respiration when it is cleared and plowed for farming. Land use emissions of CO_2 remained higher than industrial emissions until around 1910, and with the emissions from methane added to the agricultural CO_2 emissions, the greenhouse loading of the atmosphere by agriculture alone would almost double, and exceeded industrial CO_2 emissions until around 1960.

But if we look closely at the nineteenth century, three sources of land use emissions are obvious (see Figure IV.7). *First*, the methane emissions from rice production for the enormous and growing Chinese market were the most significant single source of greenhouse gases until roughly the 1830s. Then they were superseded around 1830 by the *second* emission source: the enormous eruption of CO_2 emanating from the clearing of the forests, prairies, and plains in the United States. And *third*, the late nineteenth century saw a sudden acceleration of agricultural emissions in the tropics,

[54] Rondo Cameron and Larry Neal, *A Concise Economic History of the World*, fourth edition (New York, 2003), 227–43; Peter N. Stearns, *The Industrial Revolution in World History* (Boulder, CO, 1993), 41–8; railroad mileage from Mitchell, *I.H.S.:E.*, 673–7.

[55] William Stanley Jevons, *The Coal Question: An Inquiry Concerning the Progress of the Nation, and the Probable Exhaustion of Our Coal-Mines* (London, 1865); Sieferle, *The Subterranean Forest*, 184–202; Weart, *The Discovery of Global Warming*, 5–8.

from Central and South America to Southeast Asia and India to subtropical Africa, which continued until 1910.

Thus, where China had been the long-established source of the bulk of agricultural greenhouse emissions, settler-imperial expansions into the temperate and tropical biospheres were powerful new sources of greenhouse emissions over the nineteenth century. For a half century, from roughly 1835 to 1885, U.S. land use CO_2 emissions alone were the single most important source of greenhouse forcing produced in the global economy, peaking around 1880 at 350 million metric tons of CO_2 per year. It exceeded the combined industrial emissions of the four European industrial leaders until about 1902, and the total industrial CO_2 emissions of the United States until a few years later. Stunningly, the greenhouse impacts of deforesting the continental United States exceeded *on a per capita basis* the greenhouse impacts of the enormous twentieth-century industrial emissions. Except for a brief interlude when cotton production was disrupted during the Civil War, agricultural emissions from 1700 to the 1880s averaged about six and a half to seven metric tons of carbon per person; during the twentieth century, industrial CO_2 emissions ranged between four and five and a half metric tons of carbon per person, with the exception of the Depression decade of the 1930s.[56]

Tropical emissions expanded in two phases, driven by empire and global markets; the first and longer expansion between 1870 and 1900 started in South and Southeast Asia, doubling the annual carbon flux from ~100 million to ~225 million metric tons; a second short burst focused on the tropical Americas, almost doubling again to 400 million metric tons (see Figure IV.7). Similarly, after a long nineteenth-century crisis marked by rebellions and foreign intervention, China began to recover after 1900, in a burst of agricultural expansion that may have doubled its CO_2 emissions in little more than five years. In sum, the tropical emissions offset the declining American emissions after 1880, but the final burst to 1910 put the tropical peak at about 550 million metric tons of carbon. This burst of tropical CO_2 was now overshadowed by the enormous level of global industrial CO_2 emissions, which hit 950 million metric tons just before the First World War.[57]

[56] The data discussed here and presented in Figure IV.7 is from Houghton, "Carbon Flux to the Atmosphere from Land-Use Changes: 1850–2005"; Boden et al., "Global CO_2 Emissions from Fossil-Fuel Burning, Cement Manufacture, and Gas Flaring: 1751–2008"; and Khalil et al., "Methane Sources in China: Historical Current Emissions," 142. For the history of land expropriation in North America and the wider domain of the "Neo-Europes," see John C. Weaver, *The Great Land Rush and the Making of the Modern World, 1650–1900* (Montreal, 2003).

[57] See cites in notes 20 and 56, and also Kees Klein Goldewijk, "Estimating Global Land Use Change over the Past 300 Years: The Hyde Database," *GBC* 15 (2001), 417–33, esp. data on 426–8; and Navan Ramankutty and Jonathan A. Foley, "Characterizing Patterns of Global

With the exception of China, the driving force behind the bulk of these rising agricultural emissions lay in expanding global markets. Two processes were at work in the United States. In the north from central New York and Pennsylvania through the Midwest to the trans-Mississippi plains, vast stretches were cleared for grain agriculture, producing crops of corn and wheat that fed growing cities in the east and in Europe, while enormous regions were lumbered for urban and railroad construction. To the south, from the Carolina low country to the plains of east Texas, equally vast stretches of land were cleared for cotton agriculture. This crop was cultivated by an enslaved people bound in a servitude revitalized by the connection of cotton and the new textile mills in the north of England and New England; this uncompensated labor was yet another devastating casualty of the Schumpeterian transition. Because they burned huge quantities of wood, the railroads and steamboats that carried both of these crops across the continent added to the biomass-derived greenhouse burden of CO_2 and black soot.[58] The expansion in the tropics from the 1870s was driven by the final phase of European empire building, as Britain, France, Germany, Belgium, and Portugal divided the world among them, conquered huge new territories in Africa and Southeast Asia, and then pressed the monocrop production of cotton, rubber, teas, coffee, cocoa, and bananas, and the timbering of valuable tropical hardwoods. A similar and more dramatic expansion took place in Latin America during the first decade of the twentieth century, particularly in Brazil where the Atlantic Coastal Forest was finally destroyed in the rapid development of coffee agriculture, driven by American and European investment. These agricultural expansions resulted not only in massive greenhouse emissions, but in the loss of huge quantities of glacial-temperate soils and tropical lateritic soils.[59]

Land Use: An Analysis of Global Croplands Data," *GBC* 12 (1998), 667–85. While agricultural expansions in nineteenth-century Russia are often compared with those in North America, they had far less greenhouse impact, hovering at about 50 million metric tons per year from 1850 to 1900. Given that forest clearance was comparable, and that land expansion in the nineteenth-century United States and Russia were 133 million and 83 million hectares respectively, the reasons for the difference in estimated CO_2 emissions probably lies in the different carbon content of temperate and semiarid soils. See Michael Williams, *Deforesting the Earth: From Prehistory to Global Crisis* (Chicago, IL, 2003), 285–91, 301–24 and J. M. Melillo et al., "Land-Use Change in the Soviet Union between 1850 and 1980: Causes of a Net Release of CO_2 to the Atmosphere," *Tellus* 40B (1988), 116–28.

[58] Williams, *Americans and Their Forests*, 111–390, esp. 118–20, 354–61; Jeremy Atack and Peter Passell, *A New Economic View of American History from Colonial Times to 1940*, second edition (New York, 1994), 274–97, 299–304, 403–6, 414–19.

[59] The tropical land boom is described in Richard P. Tucker, *Insatiable Appetite: The United States and the Ecological Degradation of the Tropical World* (Berkeley, CA, 2000); Williams, *Deforesting the Earth*, 354–79; Warren Dean, *With Broadax and Firebrand: The Destruction of the Brazilian Atlantic Forest* (Berkeley, CA, 1995), 168–220; Timothy C. Weiskel, "Toward an Archaeology of Colonialism: Elements in the Ecological Transformation of the Ivory

By 1900, the sum of nineteenth-century agricultural and industrial emissions was beginning to have a slight but discernible impact on atmospheric greenhouse gases, tracking the curve of global population increase (see Figure IV.9a). Atmospheric methane concentrations had risen steadily since the close of Little Ice Age conditions in 1730, and by 1900 had reached about 865 ppm, almost 20 percent higher than the Holocene norm of ~725 ppm. Following LIA lows, atmospheric CO_2 had risen to Holocene norms of about 285 ppm by 1810, and after 1850 began a sharp ascent that put it at ~297 ppm in 1900. According to the most recent modeling analysis, these slight changes were forcing alterations in global climate. Sorting out the natural forcings from the anthropogenic forcings, this team finds evidence for significant temperature and precipitation changes. In the northern hemisphere, the effect was one of cooling, particularly in the northeast and Midwestern United States and in a band running from Russia into Siberia, locally enhanced by the decrease in surface albedo and "roughness" caused by deforestation. A more northern band from Greenland to Britain and Scandinavia was significantly warmer. Around the equatorial tropics, the effect was one of a unified warming, with increased precipitation in the ENSO band across the central Pacific, and drought in the Caribbean, India, and the Arabian peninsula.[60] Thus it would appear at least likely that the sum of the increased emissions over the nineteenth century played at least a small role in enhancing the El Niño patterns that developed during the later nineteenth century, and that are seen as causing drought and mass famine in India, northern China, and parts of sub-Saharan Africa in the late 1870s and the 1890s. These El Niño droughts, Mike Davis has argued, combined with European imperial trajectories to set the stage for the forging of the modern "Third World."[61]

How far, then, had a global transformation come by 1870? Very clearly this was just the beginning. On the surface, the changes appear slight. In particular, the impact of the industrial revolution was deceptively meager. The emissions from both coal-driven manufacturing and transport were certainly having severe local pollution impacts, but their impact on a global atmospheric budget is as difficult to detect as was their contribution to the well-being of British, European, and American populations, in broad aggregate.

Coast," in Donald Worster, ed., *The Ends of the Earth: Perspectives on Modern Environmental History* (New York, 1988), 141–71; Boris G. Rozanov et al., "Soils," Ian Douglas, "Sediment Transfer and Siltation," in B. L. Turner et al., *The Earth as Transformed by Human Action: Global and Regional Changes in the Biosphere over the Past 300 Years* (New York, 1990), 203–34; John R. McNeill, *Something New under the Sun: An Environmental History of the Twentieth-Century World* (New York, 2000), 38–43.

[60] Tett et al., "The Impact of Natural and Anthropogenic Forcings," 24–7.

[61] Davis, *Late Victorian Holocausts*; Richard H. Grove and John Chappell, "El Niño Chronology and the History of Global Crises during the Little Ice Age," in Grove and Chappell, eds., *El Niño – History and Crisis: Studies from the Asia-Pacific Region* (Cambridge, 2000), 5–34.

Until the 1830s, the most profound source of greenhouse gases was the most ancient: methane emissions from rice agriculture. Here, however, lies the driver of the origins of our modern condition: rice methane emissions were caused by an unprecedented growth in population, one that marked China, Britain, and the United States. Here, I would suggest, Malthus actually had it right: there was indeed an alarming increase in population relative to resources in the eighteenth and nineteenth centuries. China grew exponentially and suffered a true endogenous Malthusian crisis. Britain used empire, ingenuity, human toil, and finally a "free" paleo-solar energy to tread water until the end of the great eighteenth-century struggle in 1815, and then to begin increase in output and productivity that by the 1860s was beginning to improve the general well-being of its people. The most dramatic story was that of the North American colonies that became the United States in 1776. Here a vast expanse of open land, dispossessed from its native occupants, was the means by which Americans escaped Malthus and multiplied in great number. The literal opening of that land, the destruction of ancient forests and forest soils, invisibly released gushers of carbon into the atmosphere. If a new warmer global atmospheric pattern was emerging by the end of the nineteenth century, the carbon released across North America was the single most significant source of the greenhouse gases driving this transition. Americans would continue to play a central role in this transformation during the coming century.[62]

---

[62] Here the classic arguments in David M. Potter, *People of Plenty: Economic Abundance and the American Character* (Chicago, IL, 1954) are still very persuasive.

12

Launching Modern Growth: 1870 to 1945

Urbanization, a New Political Economy, and the Second Industrial Revolution

The environmental history of the modern world has been shaped by a complex balancing of massively expanding populations, wildly divergent rates of economic growth, and their impacts on the natural world. During these decades, we moved from what the environmental economists call an "empty earth" to a "full earth," from an earth in which the planetary systems of sources and sinks could manage the somewhat destructive behavior of one of its more successful species, to an earth where this behavior has begun to threaten the sustainability of that species in the earth system.[1]

For our purposes here it is useful to divide the economic history of the modern world into a series of great expansions and interruptions. There have been at least two great expansions, as measured by gross national product, which are – in an unconscious echo of geological terminology – labeled *super-cycles* (see Table IV.3 and Figures IV.3 and IV.14). The first modern expansion or super-cycle was driven by a "Second Industrial Revolution" in nations around the North Atlantic, and took place from the 1870s to the First World War; the second expansion or super-cycle began after World War II and ended in the 1970s. These great super-cycle expansions were stalled by two "great interruptions," the era of the world wars and depression of 1914 to 1945, and the era of the great oil and financial crises of 1973 and 1979 through the 1980s, slowing global growth episodically. Despite the recession of 2008, economists are arguing that since roughly the year 2000 we have been at the beginning of a new, third super-cycle driven by

---

[1] Herman E. Daly, "From Empty-World Economics to Full-World Economics: Recognizing an Historical Turning Point in Economic Development," in R. Goodland et al., eds., *Population, Technology, and Lifestyle: The Transition to Sustainability* (Washington, DC, 1992), 23–38; A. J. McMichael, *Planetary Overload: GEC and the Health of the Human Species* (Cambridge, 1993).

the explosive emergence of the Chinese and Indian economies and by complex new trading relationships.[2] With each turn of the cycles, the reach of the modern economy became more powerfully global in its influence. If we think of these expansions and contractions since 1870 in terms of the long waves or long cycles Nicholai Kondratiev and François Simiand proposed, they fall into two and a half waves, three expansionary "A" periods interrupted by two declining "B" periods.

Along with GNP, the anthropogenic emissions of greenhouse gases that comprise the exhaust of industrial society have surged and subsided since 1870 with the expansions and interruptions of the global economy. Thus the ebb and flow of the global economic engine had profound ecological consequences. In the very long-term view of a geological or evolutionary timescale, of course, these impacts on nature itself may be minimal. If humanity were suddenly taken out of the picture, the natural systems of the earth might recover quite quickly and persist until the end of the life of the sun, assuming of course that the earth could absorb the toxic impact of the breakdown of modern technology. But clearly our behavior has a primary impact on our own well-being, on our place in nature, on the quality, sustainability, and very viability of our continuation as an earth-bound species. Environmental impacts on nature result in environmental hazards to human life.

Thinking historically, environmental impacts and their resulting hazards fall in three broad chronological sequences, those of traditional agrarian societies, of industrializing, urbanizing societies, and of high-intensity modern societies; in recent discussions these are referred to as *brown, gray,* and *green hazards* (see Table IV.3). The first began with the first sedentary villages during the Mesolithic, such as in the Natufian settlements where archaeologists find the accumulated discarded remains of a very messy people.[3] Quite simply, mess breeds hazard, and messy people in higher densities can brew hazards of their own making. Thus since the first sedentary settlements of the post-Pleistocene world, human societies have been living in villages,

---

[2] For the term *super-cycle*, see Gerard Lyons (Standard Chartered Bank), *The Super-Cycle Report* (London, 2010), 17–19 (available at http://www.standardchartered.com/id/_documents/press-releases/en/The%20Super-cycle%20Report-12112010-final.pdf, accessed August 8, 2012).

[3] On environmental health hazards, see Kirk R. Smith and Majid Ezzati, "How Environmental Health Risks Change with Development: The Epidemiologic and Environmental Risk Transitions Revisited," *Annual Review of Environment and Resources* 30 (2005), 291–333; Gordon McGranahan, *The Citizens at Risk: From Urban Sanitation to Sustainable Cities* (London, 2001), 4–6; A. J. McMichael, *Human Frontiers, Environments, and Disease: Past Patterns, Uncertain Futures* (Cambridge, 2001), 151–4, 283–386; John R. McNeill, *Something New under the Sun: An Environmental History of the Twentieth-Century World* (New York, 2000), 55–117. On the Natufian, see Tania Hardy-Smith and Philip C. Edwards, "The Garbage Crisis in Prehistory: Artifact Discard Patterns at the Early Natufian Site of Wadi Hammeh 27 and the Origin of Household Refuse Disposal Strategies," *JAnthArch* 23 (2004), 253–89.

towns, and cities choking with wood and coal smoke, littered with trash, and reeking of sewage. These endogenous conditions, as well as the density-driven forces of soil degradation and deforestation – if they rarely led to an absolute Malthusian collapse – shaped a general background of poor health, endemic disease, and susceptibility to major exogenous shocks of virgin soil epidemic and abrupt climate change.

Paradoxically, the onset of economic modernity both brought solutions to these enduring hazards of the preindustrial human condition, and launched successive waves of environmental impacts, which have shaped the environmental hazards of industrial society. The first surge of environmental impact was driven by technologies degrading local and regional ecosystems in moments of unprecedented urban and industrial transformation, led by the first great super-cycle expansion in the North Atlantic of the 1870s to 1914: these first impacts are discussed in the following pages in the framework of an urban environmental crisis. The second wave of impacts and hazards is the closing focus of this chapter: the impact of large and rapidly growing agricultural and industrial economies on global systems of the atmosphere and biological life itself. If this atmospheric story has occupied an important place in this book, it will take central stage as we consider the dynamics of expansion and interruption during the past six decades.

I would propose that the demands of growing urbanized populations around the North Atlantic, drawing resources from formal and informal empires, and driving a rising tide of trade and production, have been the central dynamic forces for the global transformation of the past century and a half. But their simple growth comprised a crisis in itself. The ways the growing, industrializing city confronted the traditional hazards of health and welfare is an appropriate place to start a consideration of our modern world. Population growth, economic demand, the perils and pleasures of human density, and an advancing command of science and technology all shaped the Second Industrial Revolution that formatively defined the modern world. We are still working out the consequences, as we struggle into a Third Industrial Revolution.

* * *

Atlantic Cities and the First Wave: Environmental Crisis and Social Reform

During the eighteenth century, in what is called the second stage of the epidemiological transition, the rising empire-based prosperity in northwest Europe, coupled with the first results of the early scientific revolution, began to push back some of the worst local environmental hazards of poor sanitation and bad water quality. These efforts, we shall see, were pushed forward during the coming century in efforts to suppress smallpox and childhood diseases. But by the middle of the nineteenth century, new threats to human welfare sprang up, driven in part by these very successes at preserving population.

Since the rise of the state 5,000 years ago, urban populations have been markers and drivers of economic health and change. Detached from direct production on the land, the scale of cities has been a function of the productivity of the countryside. Urban populations need to be fed, clothed, housed, and entertained, framing a massive demand for the social and economic organization of resources. They also provided the concentrated mental and labor power that made large political and economic systems flourish. But cities also are a general burden: human density is obviously an active agent in the local, regional, and global ecosystems. We can conceive of sustainability as a balancing between the "economic services" that human societies generate and the "natural services" of the ecosystem in which they are situated, made of the interacting dimensions of the geo-, bio-, hydro-, and atmospheres.[4] Cities as large concentrations of humanity have always threatened to overwhelm the natural services of their localities. Removed from the land, city people required the delivery of sanitary water and safe food in supplies sufficient to ensure reasonable conditions. In the premodern past, cities were demographically unsustainable; urban disease environments, brewing contagion that killed the majority of wave after wave of rural in-migrants, played a central role in limiting the scale of population growth over time. Cities essentially functioned as permanent sites of crisis mortality.[5] Degradation of natural services has always been a feature of human existence, and is fundamentally density dependent, and thus – in the terms that I have used in this book – endogenous to human action.

I have argued to this point that these endogenous degradations, while probably serious, were *never by themselves sufficient* to trigger the collapse of significant civilizations. But over the course of the nineteenth century, as the scale of urban population in Europe and then the United States began to reach levels never before seen, the pressures of resource demand and

---

[4] On natural or ecosystem services, see Robert Costanza et al., "The Value of the World's Ecosystem Services and Natural Capital," *Nature* 387 (1997), 253–60; Gretchen C. Daily, ed., *Nature's Services: Societal Dependence on Natural Ecosystems* (Washington, DC, 1997); Martin V. Melosi, *The Sanitary City: Urban Infrastructure in America from Colonial Times to the Present* (Baltimore, MD, 2000), 2–6; Joel Tarr, *The Search for the Ultimate Sink: Urban Pollution in Historical Perspective* (Akron, OH, 1996), 7–35, 385–411, and the special issues of *EcolEcom* 25/1 (1998) and 41/3 (2002).

[5] Here see Tarr, *The Search for the Ultimate Sink*; Vaclav Smil, *Energy in Nature and Society: General Energetics of Complex Systems* (Cambridge, MA, 2008), 308–15; Martin V. Melosi, *Garbage in the Cities: Refuse, Reform and the Environment*, rev. ed. (Pittsburgh, PA, 2005), 1–6; McMichael, *Human Frontiers, Environments and Disease*, 250–82; Laurie Garrett, *The Coming Plague: Newly Emerging Diseases in a World out of Balance* (New York, 1994), 234–59; and William H. McNeill, *Plagues and Peoples* (New York, 1977), 55–9.

local environmental hazard to public health reached what has rightly been termed a "general environmental crisis."[6] Where typical urban populations in the Atlantic world comprised 5 percent or less of national totals in 1800, by the end of the century they comprised 15 percent to 25 percent or more. With their numbers driving the demand for global commodities and North Atlantic industrial production, cities were beginning to have a systemic impact on the world at large, but they also were spawning conditions that threatened the future of their own societies. The mid-to-late nineteenth century saw the opening of broad-based efforts to address these issues on a host of fronts, efforts to protect the quality of life for national and then global populations that would during the twentieth century become the overriding priority of governments and of civil society at large.[7]

Industrialization, rising national wealth, and urbanization all rose together in the late nineteenth century. As of 1890, the United Kingdom, the industrial leader, led the world in this transition, with 55 percent of its population living in cities of 10,000 or more. It was followed by Belgium, the first continental industrial nation, at 35 percent, and the Netherlands, the early modern economic leader, at 33 percent. France and Germany, the other two continental leaders, ranked close to the United States at 26–28 percent. Italy and Spain, with long histories of urbanization, had about a fifth of their populations living in cities of 10,000 or more, but with generally low levels of industrialization and GDP (see Table IV.4).

In the United States, the rate of increase in coal production closely followed the rate of urban growth; thus Americans did not suffer the "energy deficit" of the English in the first decades of the century. A significant proportion of that coal production was devoted to domestic heat, because American railroads were wood-powered far into the century and water power remained very significant for manufacturing; steam power from coal did not exceed power from water and wood until the 1880s.[8] But railroads

---

[6] Christine M. Rosen, *The Limits of Power: Great Fires and the Process of City Growth in America* (New York, 1986), 4. Michael Haines's analysis in "Malthus and North America: Was the United States Subject to Economic-Demographic Crises," in T. Bengtsson and O. Saito, eds., *Population and Economy: From Hunger to Modern Economic Growth* (Oxford, 2000), 165–82 suggests that we might see these as Malthusian crises.

[7] For the scale of nineteenth-century urbanization, see Jan de Vries, *European Urbanization, 1500–1800* (Cambridge, MA, 1984), 30, 45–8; Adna F. Weber, *The Growth of Cities in the Nineteenth Century: A Study in Statistics* (New York, 1899), 20–154; McNeill, *Something New under the Sun*, 269–95; Brian J. L. Berry, "Urbanization," in B. L. Turner et al., *The Earth as Transformed by Human Action: Global and Regional Changes in the Biosphere over the Past 300 Years* (New York, 1990), 103–20.

[8] Jeremy Atack et al., "The Regional Diffusion and Adoption of the Steam Engine in American Manufacturing," *JEconH* 40 (1980), 281–308; Dolores Greenberg, "Energy Flow in a Changing Economy, 1815–1880," in Joseph R. Frese and Jacob Judd, eds., *An Emerging Independent American Economy, 1815–1875* (Sleepy Hollow, NY, 1980), 29–59; Louis C. Hunter, *A History of Industrial Power in the United States, 1780–1930. Vol. II: Steam*

and cities were clearly linked in a dynamic feedback, as the pace of urbanization and railroad construction surged during the 1840s and 1850s, across the northern United States in particular. If slave-grown cotton had funded the American balance of international payments until the 1860s, grain from northern farms became a very significant export as European cities grew, the British Parliament repealed the exclusionary Corn Laws in the 1840s, and Ukrainian sources were disrupted by war in the 1850s. The labor systems in grain agriculture, requiring workers only for short periods at planting and harvesting, fed a dynamic of the mechanization of northern agriculture that in turn contributed to a demand for manufacturing, which was also encouraged by the demands of the railroads and shipping carrying the grain to American and European markets. As William Cronon has described mid-nineteenth-century Chicago, the emerging American cities became huge milling machines, processing the natural resources of the great American interior. Into this northern dynamic of grain agriculture, railroads, and urban manufacturing flowed a rising tide of immigrants, first from Ireland, Germany, and China, later from Scandinavia, Italy, Poland, and Russia, building the railroads, settling the prairies, and driving the rising tide of urban manufacturing after the Civil War.[9]

By the 1870s, the United States stood between Belgium and France in the key markers of economic modernization: GDP per capita and CO_2 emissions (see Table IV.4). It also suffered its own version of the urbanization bottleneck that had begun to operate in England at the beginning of the century, measured most directly in the stature of American males over the nineteenth century. American slaves in the cotton South, certainly, bore the brunt of this and an earlier crunch. Conditions had been particularly bad for the slave generation born during the deprivations of the American Revolution, but slaves born in the 1830s averaged about 5'7", about the same as English industrial workers, but less than American white males.[10]

Power (Charlottesville, NC, 1985), esp. 90–117; Nathan Rosenberg and Manuel Trajtenberg, "A General Purpose Technology at Work: The Corliss Steam Engine in the Late Nineteenth-Century United States," *JEconH* 64 (2004), 61–99; Sean P. Adams, *Old Dominion, Industrial Commonwealth: Coal, Politics and Economy in Antebellum America* (Baltimore, MD, 2004).

9 Jeremy Atack and Peter Passell, *A New Economic View of American History from Colonial Times to 1940*, second edition (New York, 1994), 274–95, 402–6; Carville Earle and Ronald Hoffman, "The Foundation of the Modern Economy: Agriculture and the Costs of Labor in the United States and England, 1800–1860," *AHR* 85 (1980), 1055–94; William Cronon, *Nature's Metropolis: Chicago and the Great West* (New York, 1991); David Ward, *Cities and Immigrants: A Geography of Change in Nineteenth Century America* (New York, 1972), 11–84, 105–24.

10 Richard H. Steckel, "A Peculiar Population: The Nutrition, Health, and Mortality of Slaves from Childhood to Maturity," *JEconH* 46 (1986), 721–41; Ted A. Rathbun and Richard H. Steckel, "The Health of Slaves and Free Blacks in the East," in Richard H. Steckel and Jerome C. Rose, eds., *The Backbone of History: Health and Nutrition in the Western Hemisphere* (New York, 2002), 208–25.

During the eighteenth century there had been a slight difference among whites in the North and the South; northerners were more likely to begin work at an earlier age and were thus shorter, but generally whites averaged 5'8" (see Figures III.7, IV.6). But starting with the cohort of northern native white men born in the 1830s, adult heights began to fall quite sharply from this 5'8" (173 cm) plateau to a minimum of 5'6.5" (170 cm), for the cohort born in the 1880s. A similar fall in life expectancy tracked this fall in adult height. Quite simply, these measures chart the impact on health of the early urban-industrial transformation in the United States. Life in the cities separated Americans from the farms that produced safe food, often involved arduous work at young ages, and exposed them to diseases and other dangers that they would not have encountered in rural America.[11]

As much as English workers, Americans living in explosively growing mid-nineteenth-century cities were exposed to a host of perils, the conditions of the "general environmental crisis." Cities built as small commercial centers were overwhelmed at mid-century, as railroads brought massive but haphazard concentrations of industries and working people needing shelter and sustenance. Riot and mass violence seemed to threaten the maintenance of public order. Garbage and sewage was removed only by payment to private collectors, and its disposal was weakly regulated. Malaria was endemic as far north as coastal Massachusetts and interior Ohio until the end of the nineteenth century. Cholera followed international shipping from Asia to Europe to American seaport cities; there were cholera epidemics in 1832, 1849, and 1867. The threat of mass fire was another critical danger: between the 1830s and 1906 devastating fires struck Boston, New York, Pittsburgh, St. Louis, Chicago, Charleston, Baltimore, San Francisco, and a host of smaller cities. Given the wealth of timber in North America, most of the structures in the sprawling new cities were wood frame construction uniquely susceptible to fire, and nineteenth-century cities were notoriously unplanned, subject to the competing priorities of a host of private interests. Addressing the threat of contagious disease required massive investments in water and sewage systems, and building fireproof cities required massive investments in new materials, as well as safely distributed lighting and heating systems that did not require open flames. And generally, building a

[11] Roderick Floud et al., *The Changing Body: Health, Nutrition, and Human Development in the Western World since 1700* (Cambridge, 2011), 296–350; Dora L. Costa and Richard H. Steckel, "Long-Term Trends in U.S. Health, Welfare, and Economic Growth," in Richard H. Steckel and Roderick Floud, eds., *Health and Welfare during Industrialization* (Chicago, IL, 1997), 47–90; Robert W. Fogel, "Nutrition and the Decline in Mortality since 1700: Some Preliminary Findings," in S. L. Engerman and R. E. Gallman, eds., *Long-Term Factors in American Economic Growth* (Chicago, IL, 1986), 439–555, esp. 464–7, 511. See also Robert W. Fogel, *Without Consent or Contract: The Rise and Fall of American Slavery* (New York, 1989), 354–69, on the impact of the depression and immigration in American cities between 1837 and the 1850s, and Floud et al., *The Changing Body*, 296–361.

safe city required a strong web of urban government and regulation, and asserting direct public control of services provided haphazardly by private companies jealously guarding the profits. Fighting fires; delivering water, gas, and electricity; and removing sewage and garbage all would have to be brought under the control of city and state governments.[12]

Retooling for a safe, healthy, fireproof city was a central part of a wider late nineteenth-century Atlantic movement for reform. These efforts had to overcome the stiff ideological resistance of those committed to the dogmas of the classical liberal marketplace. The mercantilist policies of early modern monarchs and parliaments had channeled the workings of the market for the benefit of the nation, but the opening of the nineteenth century had seen the rejection of these policies for the framework of *laissez faire* announced in Adam Smith's *Wealth of Nations*. The seminal moment in this market-driven politics was Britain's simultaneous repeal of the Corn Laws and dramatic rollback of the Poor Laws in reaction to the rural Swing Riots against mechanized harvesting. But a countervailing rejection of the commodification of all elements of human behavior was equally powerful, and the market, revolution, and reform would struggle for preeminence far into the twentieth century. The most powerful critique was that of Robert Owen, Karl Marx, and Friedrich Engels, whose reaction to the iniquities of industrial labor and capital during the 1820s and through the 1840s would fuel the communist vision of a world without markets. Evangelical visions of a perfect world drove the antislavery cause and the wider movement for the reform of prisons, education, and public health. This Anglo-American axis of reform had its origins in an Atlantic evangelicalism that dated back to the eighteenth century, and stressed the role of voluntary associations. But the experiences of the depression of the 1840s, the American Civil War, the rise of the Prussian state, a rising fear of socialist revolution, and indeed a pervasive anxiety about social "degeneracy" all contributed to a harder, more state-oriented approach, eventually manifested in the wider efforts of governments around the North Atlantic to address the issues of public

---

[12] Zane L. Miller and Patricia M. Melvin, *The Urbanization of Modern America: A Brief History*, second edition (New York, 1987), 31–124; Charles E. Rosenberg, *Cholera Years: The United States in 1832, 1849, and 1866* (Chicago, IL, 1962); Martin V. Melosi, *Effluent America: Cities, Industry, Energy, and Environment* (Pittsburgh, PA, 2001), 17–67; Melosi, *Garbage in the Cities*, 17–41; Cronon, *Nature's Metropolis*, 169–80; Rosen, *The Limits of Power*; Karen Sawislak, *A Smoldering City: Chicagoans and the Great Fire, 1871–1874* (Chicago, IL, 1995); Sara E. Wermeil, *The Fireproof Building: Technology and Public Safety in the Nineteenth-Century American City* (Baltimore, MD, 2000), 73–185; Mark Tebeau, *Eating Smoke: Fire in Urban America, 1800–1950* (Baltimore, MD, 2003), 89–284; Peter C. Hoffer, *Seven Fires: The Urban Infernos that Reshaped America* (New York, 2006), 64–203; Mark H. Rose, *Cities of Light and Heat: Domesticating Gas and Electricity in Urban America* (University Park, MD, 1995); Harold Platt, *Shock Cities: The Environmental Transformation and Reform of Manchester and Chicago* (Chicago, IL, 2005).

safety and health that advancing economic transformation had turned into a "general crisis."[13]

Bridging this transition was the emerging public movement that recognized the devastation of the natural environment as an unacceptable cost of economic modernization, both in the moral threat of destroying natural worlds and the more practical threat of destroying natural services to human sustainability. Henry David Thoreau and John Muir, the prophets of American environmental protection, grounded this moral vision in Transcendentalist perfectionism; Stanley Jevons saw Malthusian threats in resource dependence and degradation. Theodore Roosevelt brought the power of the national state to bear for conservation on both of these grounds. Very broadly, alarming conditions in the late nineteenth century mobilized people across a wide Progressive front in self-conscious responses to threats of social, environmental, and Malthusian degradation. Acting in concert in associations and through government, they saw their efforts as standing between the unsustainable threats of the unregulated market and violent revolution.[14]

* * *

[13] Simon Szreter, *Health and Wealth: Studies in History and Policy* (Rochester, NY, 2005), esp. 23–45, 98–145, 203–41; Peter Baldwin, *Contagion and the State in Europe, 1830–1930* (Cambridge, 1999); Anne Hardy, *The Epidemic Streets: Infectious Disease and the Rise of Preventive Medicine, 1856–1900* (Oxford, 1993); John Opie, *Nature's Nation: An Environmental History of the United States* (Fort Worth, TX, 1998), 242–343; Nancy Tomes, *The Gospel of Germs: Men, Women, and the Microbe in American Life* (Cambridge, MA, 1998); Melosi, *The Sanitary City*, 58–204; Platt, *Shock Cities*; David J. Rothman, *The Discovery of the Asylum: Social Order and Disorder in the New Republic* (Boston, MA, 1971); Charles E. Rosenberg, *No Other Gods: On Science and American Social Thought* (Baltimore, MD, 1976), 109–40; Thomas L. Haskell, *The Emergence of Professional Social Science: The American Social Science Association and the Nineteenth-Century Crisis of Authority* (Chicago, IL, 1977), 48–100; James Kloppenberg, *Uncertain Victory: Social Democracy and Progressivism in European and American Thought, 1870–1920* (New York, 1986); Daniel T. Rodgers, *Atlantic Crossings: Social Politics in a Progressive Age* (Cambridge, MA, 1998); Daniel Pick, *Faces of Degeneration: A European Disorder, c.1848–c.1918* (New York, 1989). If I see a role for nutrition in early modern population growth (see Chapter 9), it should be apparent that I am in full agreement with the argument that public health – rather than simply nutrition as a function of economic growth (the McKeown thesis) – drove the nineteenth-century phase of the mortality transition. See in particular Szreter, *Health and Wealth*, 146–61. But see Jean-Claude Chesnais's comments on the "false dichotomy between public health and economic development in the mortality decline," *The Demographic Transition: Stages, Patterns, and Economic Implications* (Oxford, 1992), 78–85; and James Colgrove, "The McKeown Thesis: A Historical Controversy and Its Enduring Influences," *American Journal of Public Health* 92 (2002), 725–9.

[14] Roderick Nash, *Wilderness and the American Mind*, rev. ed. (New Haven, CT, 1973), 84–140; Opie, *Nature's Nation*, 186–214, 370–403; Donald Worster, *Nature's Economy: A History of Ecological Ideas*, second edition (New York, 1994), 59–111; –, *A Passion for Nature: The Life of John Muir* (New York, 2008); Gabriel Kolko, *The Triumph of American*

The Second Industrial Revolution

The Progressive reformers' construction of the safe and healthy city was fundamentally bound up in the Second Industrial Revolution, the leap to technology-capital-driven Schumpeterian growth that spanned Walt Rostow's "drive to maturity" and the opening of his "age of high mass-consumption," and Nicholai Kondratiev's third and fourth long waves, between roughly 1870 and 1920. Forging an entirely new paradigm of energy and the application of power, the Second Industrial Revolution was the first great expansion of the modern economy, what is now called the *first super-cycle* (see Table IV.3, Figure IV.14). Energy historian Vaclav Smil argues without exaggeration that these few decades launched "the fundamental means to realize nearly all of the 20th-century accomplishments" in energy and technology, and constitutes human "history's most remarkable discontinuity"; the Second Industrial Revolution, Smil argues, was analogous to evolutionary punctuation as modeled by Stephen J. Gould and Nils Eldridge.[15] In great measure, I would like to argue, the fundamental impetus behind the Schumpeterian Second Industrial Revolution was the pressing need to address the mid-century crisis of massively expanded, newly urbanized North Atlantic populations faced with the traditional hazards of health and welfare. And while the Second Industrial Revolution helped to solve these local hazards, it would quickly spawn new regional hazards and eventually the global impacts that we face today.

The Second Industrial Revolution began in 1873 with Andrew Carnegie's construction of steel works on the Bessemer system at Braddock's Field in Pittsburgh. The new Bessemer furnaces radically reduced the cost of steel production, while they consumed enormous tonnages of coke. This was the first of a continuing series of new technologies based on advanced scientific knowledge: the Bessemer converter was rapidly replaced by the even more productive open hearth furnace. The new steel built the railroads, factories, and cities of a new economy that was driven by inventions and applications developed in research and development (R & D) laboratories funded by corporations and nation-states from Berlin to Chicago. Innovation would no longer be an informal hit-or-miss process guided by rule-of-thumb experience, but would emerge out of an interlocking complex of universities, corporations, and national laboratories. Following the advent of cheap steel, the second pillar of the new technology was the steam turbine, developed by

---

Conservatism: A Reinterpretation of American History, 1900–1916 (New York, 1963); Samuel P. Hays, *Conservation and the Gospel of Efficiency: The Progressive Conservation Movement, 1890–1920* (Cambridge, MA, 1957); Samuel P. Hays, *The Response to Industrialism: 1885–1914* (Chicago, IL, 1957); Robert H. Wiebe, *The Search for Order, 1877–1920* (New York, 1967).

[15] Vaclav Smil, *Creating the Twentieth Century: Technical Innovations of 1867–1914 and Their Lasting Impact* (New York, 2005), 5–7.

British and Swedish engineers in the 1880s out of ancient ideas and French experience with the water turbine, and first applied in shipping and then in electrical generation. The high-pressure turbine was and is to this day fundamental to the most obvious marker of the Second Industrial Revolution, electricity. Again, the key breakthroughs came in Europe, with generators, dynamos, and alternating current experimental in the 1870s and practical in the 1880s. Incandescent electric lighting was also practical by the late 1870s, and within a decade coal-powered steam turbines' spinning dynamos were providing electricity for street lighting, streetcars, and households. The first modern use of electricity had been in the telegraph in the 1840s, and by the 1890s another electrical form of communication, the telephone, was practical and beginning to go into commercial use.[16]

The same decades saw a revolution in chemicals, driven in great part by Germany's geographic isolation from global resources, a geo-strategic situation that would have enormous consequences in the first half of the twentieth century. German scientists concentrated first on developing synthetic dyes, and then on the chemistry of ammonia and nitrates that allowed the synthesis of nitrogen fertilizer through the famous Haber-Bosch process, which usefully also could be switched to the production of explosives. Americans and Belgians worked along another path that led from vulcanized rubber to plastics. With simultaneous leaps in medical knowledge of germs, infection, and consciousness, the expanding command of chemistry led to the production of an array of medicines, from anesthetics and antiseptics to aspirin. On another front, starting with the first Pennsylvania oil strikes in 1859 and then in the Caspian Sea in 1873, a new fossil fuel – petroleum – began to augment coal. Oil's first use as kerosene displaced whale oil for lighting, as did – locally – its geological cousin, natural gas. But oil's future lay centrally as a powerful propulsion fuel, as both diesel and gasoline. Steel, electricity, chemicals, and the beginning of the oil industry all played a role in the development and refinement of the internal combustion engine and the early automobile, made practical and commercial after its first demonstration in Germany in 1885. By the 1890s, the first research was under way that would lead to diesel engines and gas turbines, which in the coming century would literally be the prime movers of global commerce, by truck, ship, and jet airplane.[17]

[16] Chris Otter, *The Victorian Eye: A Political History of Light and Vision in Britain, 1800–1910* (Chicago, IL, 2008); Louis C. Hunter and Lynwood Bryant, *A History of Industrial Power in the United States, 1780–1930. Vol. III: The Transmission of Power* (Cambridge, MA, 1991), 185–352; Robert Friedel and Paul Israel, *Edison's Electric Light: Biography of an Invention* (New Brunswick, NJ, 1986).

[17] David C. Mowery and Nathan Rosenberg, *Paths of Innovation: Technological Change in 20th-Century America* (New York, 1998), 11–46; Smil, *Creating the Twentieth Century*, 33–257; Joel Mokyr, *The Lever of Riches: Technological Creativity and Economic Progress* (New York, 1990), 113–38; Joel Mokyr, *The Gifts of Athena: Historical Origins of the*

All of these developments moved rapidly; clearly, as American and north-ern European populations grew at increasing rates, the race for significant technological and economic breakthroughs was intensifying. Despite rising populations, GDP per capita also rose in Europe's core industrial coun-tries. While Britain retained its overall advantage, Germany in particular was closing the gap: the British/German GDP ratio moved from 175/100 in 1850 to 135/100 in 1914, while the British/Belgian and British/French ratios remained roughly stable at around 125/100 and 150/100 respectively. More important, the United States surged ahead, first catching up with Belgium and then surpassing Britain by 1905 in a long advance starting in the late 1870s.[18]

Here Britain encountered the paradox of the first adopter. Having made a huge cumulative investment in steam, most importantly in high-pressure steam engines in the 1850s and 1860s, it remained locked into a First Industrial Revolution paradigm, losing its leading technological position to Germany and the United States that, as catch-up adopters, were better able to make investments in the new technology.[19] Britain's loss of leading posi-tion is perhaps best illustrated in its electrical generation capacity on the eve of the First World War, when it was per capita less than half that of Germany or the United States, and only slightly larger than that of France.[20] But it was the United States, not the scientific powerhouse that Germany had become, that reaped the rewards. American innovators and inventors like Thomas Edison and Henry Ford were particularly adept at commercializing the primary advances in technology emerging from European universities and laboratories, by 1914 launching the beginnings of Walt Rostow's "age of mass-consumption." Here the American corporation, forged in unique colo-nial circumstances and transformed by the growth of the railroad, emerged as the central economic institution of the Second Industrial Revolution.[21]

Knowledge Economy (Princeton, NJ, 2002), 85–104; Thomas J. Misa, *A Nation of Steel: The Making of Modern America, 1865–1925* (Baltimore, MD, 1995), 45–89; Vaclav Smil, "The Two Prime Movers of Globalization: History and Impact of Diesel Engines and Gas Turbines," *Journal of Global History* 2 (2007), 373–94.

18 Analysis of GDP data from Angus Maddison, "Historical Statistics of the World Economy: 1–2006 AD," http://www.ggdc.net/maddison/ accessed August 2, 2012.

19 Alfred D. Chandler, *Scale and Scope: The Dynamics of Industrial Capitalism* (Cambridge, MA, 1990), 274–86.

20 Analysis of population data from Maddison, "Historical Statistics"; and electrical produc-tion data from B. R. Mitchell, *International Historical Statistics: Europe, 1750–1993*, fourth edition (London, 1998) (*I.H.S.E.*), 562–3; and Bernard C. Beaudreau, *Energy and the Rise and Fall of Political Economy* (Westport, CT, 1999), 95; 1912 gigawatt hours/1910 popula-tion: France .035; United Kingdom .053; Germany .117; United States .118. The U.S. data apparently does not include hydroelectricity, which might have made up 15–20 percent of American electrical generation, perhaps more.

21 Mowery and Rosenberg, *Paths of Innovation*, 6; Alfred Chandler, *The Visible Hand: The Managerial Revolution in American Business* (Cambridge, MA, 1977), 81–121; Chandler, *Scale and Scope*, 496–502.

This transition to massive and rapid production would require enormous amounts of energy. Initially, this energy would come from coal, but, by the 1920s, the consumption of petroleum would begin its long rise.

Most fundamentally, in terms of energy, the Second Industrial Revolution introduced a new flexibility and intensity of power consumption.[22] First, electric motors allowed a radical restructuring of work. Where with steam a single engine was linked to machines with drive shafts, gears, and loops of leather belting, electric motors of many sizes could be arranged throughout a workplace and along a line of work flow, and finely calibrated to the application. Electrification drove a relentless "deepening" of energy intensity of the economy – the mechanizing of a host of complex operations formerly done by hand – and it allowed the specialization of tasks along a power-driven assembly line, first designed and implemented by Henry Ford (see Figure IV.11). The result fundamentally undermined the ancient position of skilled labor, while driving a vast increase in productivity. Second, the internal combustion engine brought inanimate power to transportation to a range of scales, from motorcycles and cars to buses and heavy trucks, and then with the Wright Brothers to the air itself. Again, the escape from the massive immobility of the steam engine allowed for a finely tuned application of power to a host of specific transportation tasks, multiplying the range of economic activity.[23] But this new age depended most importantly on moving beyond the infrastructural investments of the opening of the Second Industrial Revolution toward the marketing of consumer durables to individual households. These include a range of household gadgets, lights, stoves, refrigerators, vacuum cleaners, and, most important, the automobile. And to fully depend on the household for economic growth required steady employment and rising wages, qualities that would require a new framework and role for public policy and governance.

Both tensions and compatibilities existed between the explosively transformative new economy of the Second Industrial Revolution and the agendas

[22] On energy intensity, see Beaudreau, *Energy and the Rise and Fall*, 91–132; Bernard C. Beaudreau, *Energy and Organization: Growth and Distribution Reexamined* (Westport, CT, 1998), 35–48; John R. Moroney, "Energy, Capital, and Technological Change," *Resources and Energy* 14 (1992), 368–80; and the literature reviewed in David I. Stern, "Progress on the Environmental Kuznets Curve?" *Environment and Development Economics* 3 (1998), 173–98; Magnus Lindmark, "Patterns of Historical CO_2 Intensity Transitions among High and Low-Income Countries," *ExpEconH* 41 (2004), 426–47; and Fabien Prieur, "The Environmental Kuznets Curve in a World of Irreversibility," *Economic Theory* 40 (2009), 57–90.

[23] Thomas P. Hughes, *Networks of Power: Electrification in Western Society, 1880–1930* (Baltimore, MD, 1983); David A. Hounshell, *From the American System to Mass Production, 1800–1932: The Development of Manufacturing Technology in the United States* (Baltimore, MD, 1984), 217–330; Smil, *Creating the Twentieth Century*, 33–153; David E. Nye, *Consuming Power: A Social History of American Energies* (Cambridge, MA, 1998), 133–54.

of the Atlantic reformers. The new industries were driven by the priorities and values of market capitalism, which stood in tension with the reformers' wider social vision. The pace of technological and scientific change fueled the anxieties of the middle class around the Atlantic, which was both excited and unnerved by electricity, germ theory, the telephone, and the car.[24] But the new technologies achieved many of the reformers' material goals. The products of the Second Industrial Revolution – electric lighting, mass production of pumping and sewer lines, streetcars and subways, automobiles, new medicines – all contributed to the rebuilding of the urban landscape in ways that the reformers advocated and actively shaped. The internal combustion engine, for example, can be seen as solving the biotic crisis of feeding and cleaning up after "animal traction": energy inputs were shifted from oats to oil. Suggestively, adult white male heights recovered from the "insult" of early urbanization precisely with the massive expansion of energy consumption in the 1890s, different measures of the wider transformation (see Figure IV.6). The result still involved a tension between commercial priorities of profit and the reformers' vision of a healthier, safer social environment, but at the time it seemed to capitalists and reformers that a mutually satisfactory new paradigm was emerging, with gradually improving conditions for urban working peoples, and new suburban utopias emerging for the car-driving middle class.[25] As the twentieth century opened, the scientific, medical, and productive advances launched by the Second Industrial Revolution were beginning to mitigate some of the worst of the "insults," the "general environmental crisis," of the First Industrial Revolution, while it was sowing the seeds for new and much graver insults and crises in the decades and centuries to come.

* * *

The Demographic Revolution, 1800–1945

If the reformers saw improvements in the lives of the people of the North Atlantic during the first decades of the twentieth century, much of their effort revolved around the parameters of what we now know as the *Demographic Revolution*. The conditions of fertility, mortality, and general

---

[24] T. J. Jackson Lears, *No Place of Grace: Antimodernism and the Transformation of American Culture, 1880–1920* (New York, 1981); Neil Harris, "Utopian Literature and Its Discontents," in Richard Bushman et al., *Uprooted Americans: Essays to Honor Oscar Handlin* (Boston, MA, 1979), 211–44.

[25] Nye, *Consuming Power*, 157–85; Rose, *Cities of Light and Heat*; Sam Bass Warner, *Streetcar Suburbs: The Process of Growth in Boston, 1870–1900* (Cambridge, MA, 1978); on consumption, see the most recent review in David Steigerwald, "All Hail the Republic of Choice: Consumer History as Contemporary Thought," *JAmH* 93 (2006), 385–413.

population growth were fundamental to the new world that the reformers and industrialists were creating.

Population growth is a function of levels of births and deaths: when births exceed deaths, population grows; when deaths exceed births, population falls, rapidly. Looking back very briefly to the origins of human population growth, it bears remembering that during the Late Neolithic the balance of fertility and mortality had to have shifted enough to allow the first significant population expansions. This did not occur with early domestication, but with the innovations of the Late Neolithic secondary products revolution, which established the beginnings of real agrarian households and villages, and a sufficient surplus to drive a burst of fertility – before a subsequent rise in epidemic mortality fueled by early urban concentrations. The result was the high-pressure demographic system of high fertility and high mortality, which oscillated with varying conditions (exogenous and endogenous) until the modern demographic revolution. Since the eighteenth century, a reverse sequence has been unfolding: first mortality fell while fertility remained high, and then fertility fell, leaving a society in a low-pressure demographic system in which its members enjoy good general health and long life expectancy.[26] Broadly speaking, this is what has happened, first in northwest Europe and its settler colonies, then in southern and eastern Europe, and then in various trajectories of completion to Asia and finally Africa. This is a process that has at its center the epidemiological transition that has been developing in stages since the recovery from the Black Death, and that has spread in a very loose and somewhat controversial relationship with the wider process of global economic growth.

The demographic transition is described typically as a broad social process that unfolded without conscious plan. But there is good reason to see the hands of "reformers" at work, indeed from the first quarantines imposed in post-Black Death Italy, in driving the epidemiological transition that drove the very first steps of the wider demographic transition. Very broadly, the eighteenth-century stage of the mortality decline and the health transition depended fundamentally on the action and context of stable governments, and the action of circles of physicians, beginning to associate and communicate in medical societies. The suppression of the plague in late medieval Europe was a necessary beginning to the first stage of the epidemiological transition – the waning of pandemics – and the onset of the modern decline of mortality, and reached its most dramatic manifestations with the *cordon*

---

[26] The best recent analyses are Chesnais, *The Demographic Transition*; Massimo Livi-Bacci, *A Concise History of World Population*, third edition (Malden, MA, 2001); McMichael, *Human Frontiers, Environments and Disease*, 185–212; Ronald Lee, "The Demographic Transition: Three Centuries of Fundamental Change," *JEconP* 17 (2003), 167–90; and Paul Demeny and Geoffrey McNicoll, "World Population, 1950–2000: Perception and Response," *PopDevR* 32 (2006), 1–51.

sanitaire enforced by military action by the Hapsburgs on the Ottoman frontier, and the quarantine of plague-ridden Marseilles by the French government in 1721.

The second stage of the epidemiological transition was launched with the first promotion of inoculation for smallpox in England in the 1720s, a practice of infecting healthy persons with active disease serum commonly performed in Asia, and apparently as a folk medicine in Europe. Inoculation was only accepted widely after techniques were improved in the 1750s, and was superseded in the 1790s by vaccination, invented by Edward Jenner. As increasing numbers were inoculated for smallpox, a rapidly growing pool of smallpox survivors could provide close nursing care during an outbreak, and made smallpox increasingly a childhood disease. Epidemic disease was giving way to endemic disease as the focus of medical concern. Coming with a wider set of improvements associated with the early consumer revolution – mass-produced glass, ceramics, cotton underwear – the drastic reductions of death by smallpox in eighteenth-century England paralleled declines in a general syndrome of diarrhea and pneumonia that killed large numbers of children. Over the coming century – in the third stage of the epidemiological transition – scarlet fever, diphtheria, typhoid fever, and whooping cough would also become less fatal. By the end of the eighteenth century, both adult and infant-child mortality by disease across Great Britain and the American colonies were reduced to levels significantly below the norm on the European continent. As important, this decline in mortality, and population growth, was achieved *before* significant advances in per capita GDP, and it would appear that a stabilization of mortality was a prerequisite for economic growth, rather than the reverse.[27]

During the early nineteenth century, this suppression of childhood mortality spread into northern Europe, in Scandinavia, most strikingly in Norway, and in France and Belgium. Germany, central Europe, Russia, and southern Europe would not reduce infant mortality to these northern European levels until 1900 or later (see Table IV.4). As measured by general mortality rates, which were shaped most importantly by declining infant mortality, Norway kept its mortality rate below 20/1,000 reasonably consistently from 1815

[27] Richard A. Easterlin, *Growth Triumphant: The Twenty-First Century in Historical Perspective* (Ann Arbor, MI, 1996), 83–93; Stephen J. Kunitz, "Mortality since Malthus," in David Coleman and Roger Schofield, eds., *The State of Population Theory: Forward from Malthus* (Oxford, 1986), 279–302; James C. Riley, *Rising Life Expectancy: A Global History* (New York, 2001), 22; Peter Razzell, *The Conquest of Smallpox: The Impact of Inoculation on Smallpox Mortality in Eighteenth Century Britain* (Sussex, 1997); Stephen J. Kunitz, "Speculations on the European Mortality Decline," *EconHistR* 2nd ser., 36 (1983), 349–64; Michael W. Flinn, *The European Demographic System, 1500–1820* (Baltimore, MD, 1981), 92–5; Mary J. Dobson, *Contours of Death and Disease in Early Modern England* (Cambridge, 1997), 493–539; Estaban A. Nicolini, "Mortality, Interest Rates, Investment, and Agricultural Production in 18th Century England," *ExpEconH* 41 (2002), 130–55.

forward; as of 1850, it was well ahead of other European countries with infant mortality (to age one year) of 135 per 1,000 live births. Sweden's general mortality reached this threshold around 1845, the more industrialized Britain and Belgium during the 1880s and 1890s, and France and Germany around 1900. The understanding of microbial roots of infectious disease established by Louis Pasteur and Robert Koch had its most powerful immediate impacts, but a general attention to air, light, and cleanliness contributed to the decline of tuberculosis, the scourge of nineteenth-century industrial districts. Throughout, the decline in mortality across the nineteenth century was driven by advancing household cleanliness and public sanitation, powerfully shaped by the efforts of reformers, campaigns for literacy and primary education, and a "silent revolution" in government.[28]

In Britain, a persistently higher mortality in the industrializing cities was offset by a continuing high fertility rate, but in France, fertility was declining by the 1790s, resulting in a slowing of population growth that eventually began to concern French officials faced with the threat of a rising Germany. The differences between Britain and France were grounded in the different trajectories into the nineteenth century, Britain committed to a full-scale industrial strategy, and France dominated by farm households defending their claims and connections to the land and resisting urbanization.[29]

A similarly early fertility decline began among prosperous Americans in the eighteenth century, beginning with Quaker farming households in Pennsylvania in the 1750s, seeking to preserve a religiously sanctioned standard of living for their children. This early fertility transition among the Quakers was followed by an emerging ideology of female self-control among American middling and elite families after the revolution, and then by a more general decline in American fertility among native-born families, urban and rural, driven by the logic of providing more financial and emotional resources for children living their lives in an increasingly commercial, industrial, and urban society.[30] Offsetting the gradual decline in American

---

[28] General and infant mortality data from Mitchell, *I.H.S.:E.*, 93–109, 120–6. See Chesnais, *The Demographic Transition*, 58–9; Szreter, *Health and Wealth*, 146–61, 242–341; Tomes, *The Gospel of Germs*; Hardy, *The Epidemic Streets*; Melosi, *The Sanitary City*, 103–204; Mokyr, *The Gifts of Athena*, 163–217; Riley, *Rising Life Expectancy*, 64–74; Joseph P. Ferie and Werner Troesken, "Water and Chicago's Mortality Transition, 1850–1925," *ExpEconH* 45 (2008); 1–16.

[29] Chesnais, *The Demographic Transition*, 321–43.

[30] Barry Levy, *Quakers and the American Family: British Settlement in the Delaware Valley* (New York, 1988); Robert V. Wells, "Demographic Change and the Life Cycle of American Families," *JInterdH* 2 (1971), 273–82; Susan E. Klepp, *Revolutionary Conceptions: Women, Fertility and Family Limitation in America, 1760–1820* (Chapel Hill, NC, 2009); Richard A. Easterlin, "Factors in the Decline of Farm Family Fertility in the United States: Some Preliminary Research Results," *JAmH* 63 (1976), 600–14; Jenny Bourne Wohl, "New Results on the Decline in Household Fertility in the United States from 1750 to 1900," in Engerman and Gallman, eds., *Long-Term Factors in American Economic Growth*, 391–437; Chesnais, *The Demographic Transition*, 398–410.

fertility across the nineteenth century, immigration brought waves of young men and women to American cities and farms. These augmentations to the labor force improved the "dependency ratio" of workers to nonworkers (young and old), while it swelled the birth rate. This pattern was repeated in all of the "neo-Europes" that saw significant European immigration during the nineteenth century: the English-speaking United States, Canada, Australia, and New Zealand, and the new "southern cone" of Latin America, Argentina, Uruguay, and Chile. All of these developing settler countries had a similar demographic profile: large numbers of immigrants in their twenties and thirties having collectively large numbers of children, but at a declining rate over time per completed family. Conversely, the circumstances of countries of origin – especially Scandinavia, Spain, and Italy – had a different demographic structure, in which the emigration of young people drove down the birthrate, but also increased the dependency ratio, thus slowing economic development.[31]

Generally, however, the Demographic Revolution broke across Europe and its colonies of settlement from northwest to southeast, between the mid-eighteenth and early twentieth centuries. England, the first industrial adopter, was something of an oddity, in that lingering moderate mortality rates – increasing in the cities – were offset by a strong fertility; France was another oddity in its early fertility decline. But the general pattern was first a decline in mortality followed decades later by a decline in fertility. This stage of the transition was accompanied by a significant rise in life expectancy, on average across Europe from thirty-four to thirty-six years in the century between 1770 and 1870 to forty-three to forty-seven years by the decade before World War I. Over the intervening decades, population grew particularly rapidly, and either was drawn into new employment or siphoned off in emigration. Two types of demographic transitions began to be apparent: long and short. The first starters took more than a century to bring down first their death rates and then their birthrates; later starters could take far less time (see Table IV.4). Thus Sweden, and probably Norway, England, and Wales, had reached a minimal benchmark rate of 200 infant deaths per 1,000 live births around 1800, but did not bring their birthrates below 30 per 1,000 population until the 1880s and 1890s; Spain and Italy each took forty years to hit both of these goals, between around 1880 and around 1920; Hungary achieved both of these goals within three years, in 1920 and 1923.[32] This accelerating rate of demographic change reflected the accelerating cumulative knowledge in science, medicine, and technology that made up the second Scientific-Industrial Revolution unfolding from the 1870s to the outbreak of World War I. During the ensuing interwar decades, economic growth and the demographic transition began to unfold more widely,

---

[31] Chesnais, *The Demographic Transition*, 153–89.
[32] Mitchell, *I.H.S.:E.*, 93–126.

as the benefits of public health and primary medicine began to reduce mortality in Japan, Taiwan, Venezuela, Sri Lanka/Ceylon, and Mexico: smaller countries with increasingly effective governments.[33]

* * *

1914–1945: A World in Crisis, Growth on Hold

By the first decade of the twentieth century, the benefits of the wider transition of the Second Industrial Revolution and the construction of a healthier lived environment began to mitigate the "insults" to the health and welfare of working people in the expanding industrial core of the North Atlantic world. Adult height in England and the United States began to recover from the worse of its slump during the 1880s and 1890s. English working people had significantly more wage income, and were able to purchase a wider array of amenities than they could fifty years before.[34]

But the world stood on the edge of three decades of crisis, a First Great Interruption of the modern economy. Two world wars, worldwide epidemic, a long and shattering economic depression, and the rise of dictatorial-collectivist regimes stalled the seemingly inevitable trajectory of economic and social progress that had been accelerating since the 1870s. In a brutal irony, the entire sweep of world war, depression, and state-generated famine and genocide spanning from 1914 to the 1950s has to be seen as a unitary, interconnected crisis generated by the forces unleashed by the Second Industrial Revolution combined with the accelerating pace of late nineteenth-century imperialism.

World War I had its origins in the complex network of secret treaties that bound a coalition of European nations to mutual defense in response to the rise of Germany after its nation-building victories in 1866 and 1871, and in the explosion of industrial capacity after 1870 that drove the arms race that was solidifying the emergent "military-industrial complex." The war launched three decades of global mortality crisis that can only be called state-driven. Nineteen million men were killed between 1914 and 1918, and the war's immediate aftermath brought an epidemic that overshadowed even the slaughter of the war itself. The "Spanish influenza" epidemic of 1918–19 killed at least 50 million – and perhaps 100 million – people around the world, and a controversial argument suggests that it helped to

---

[33] Chesnais, *The Demographic Transition*, 57–78; James C. Riley, "Estimates of Regional and Global Life Expectancy, 1800–2001," *PopDevR* 31 (2005), 537–43.

[34] Floud et al., *The Changing Body*; Floud et al., *Height, Health and History*, 319–27; Costa and Steckel, "Long-Term Trends in U.S. Health, Welfare, and Economic Growth," 50–9; Carole Shammas, "Food Expenditures and Economic Well-Being in Early Modern England," *JEconH* 43 (1983), 89–100.

tip the balance for the Allies, striking earlier and harder in Germany and Austria.[35] Between 1917 and the 1930s, roughly 14 million died in civil war, famine, and state violence, as the Russian empire was transformed into the communist U.S.S.R. Then the rise of the Nazi regime in postwar Germany, and the expansion of Japan into China, Korea, and Southeast Asia, launched the world again into a total war that – with the genocide of the Holocaust – led to a total of 52 million dead between 1939 and 1945. In the next decade, between 14 million and 26 million died of famine in China, as Mao forced the collectivization of agriculture and industry.[36]

The origins and the course of both world wars were shaped by two vital commodities: food and oil. In great measure, the roots of both wars lay in Germany's sense that it had lost the race for nineteenth-century empire, and would have to carve one out on the Eurasian continent; Hitler visualized a German landed empire in the same terms as the United States' conquest of its west. Allied access to American food during World War I, and the Allies' blockade of Germany and Austria, was certainly a key determining factor in the eventual outcome of four years of bloody stalemate. Even before they were assailed by the "Spanish" flu, the Central Powers, military and civil alike, were being literally starved into submission. Food security was a fundamental part of Hitler's plan to conquer Eastern Europe and Russia: millions of Jews, Slavs, and Russians were to be starved to death, their lands all the way to the Urals to be settled by German farmers. The Holocaust against Europe's Jewry was only the first step. A similar anxiety about food drove Japanese expansion during the 1930s: the militarists feared that rural Japan was falling into a spiral of overpopulation and decline, and visualized Manchuria and China as a vast terrain for transplanted Japanese farming households. Again, secured by blockades and air and naval control, the agricultural productivity of the wider English-speaking imperial domain provided critical sustenance for victory, while Axis soldiers starved. But as wartime prices escalated, British bureaucrats in India utterly failed to stave off famine in Bengal, which killed 3 million people, half the death toll of Hitler's Holocaust.[37]

The course of World War I gradually focused attention on oil: it was the first major war fought on the back of the internal combustion engine. Paris was saved from German capture in September 1914 by a flotilla of taxis commandeered to move troops to the front; by 1916, the British government was worrying about a shortage of diesel and gasoline, and an expansion in

[35] Andrew Price-Smith, *Contagion and Chaos: Disease, Ecology, and National Security in the Era of Globalization* (Cambridge, MA, 2009), 57–82.
[36] Riley, *Rising Life Expectancy*, 40–4.
[37] Timothy Snyder, *Bloodlands: Europe between Hitler and Stalin* (New York, 2010), 21–58, 155–224; Lizzie Collingham, *The Taste of War: World War II and the Battle for Food* (New York, 2012), 18–74, 141–54, 180–247, 273–316; Cormac Ó'Gráda, *Famine: A Short History* (Princeton, NJ, 2009), 159–94.

American oil production eventually provided 80 percent of the oil the Allies needed. While the British set their sights on securing Arabian oil, Germany moved southeast, capturing the Rumanian oil fields; its failure to secure the rich Azerbaijan fields helped bring the war to an end. If the origins of World War II lay in national aspirations, these aspirations required oil as well. Germany's failure to gain control of oilfields in Russia, Azerbaijan, and Arabia sealed its fate, while Japan struck against the Americans, the British, and the Dutch in the Pacific in a decisive if ultimately unsuccessful effort to ensure oil production for a Japanese-Asiatic empire. American oil production was once again a decisive factor in the Allied victory in World War II.[38]

Allied victory in World War II more importantly involved a sweeping transformation in the role of government in the economy and society that had its roots in the reforming movements of the era of the launching of the Second Industrial Revolution. Very broadly, starting with the late nineteenth-century efforts to build healthier urban environments, governments in Germany, France, and Great Britain, and in the American states, if not yet the United States government, began to take an increasingly large role in shaping the welfare of their peoples. The French government was alarmed by the plummeting French fertility rate after its defeat by the Germans in 1871, and began to actively encourage larger families; British officials were equally alarmed at the turn of the century during the Boer War by the small size and ill health of urban recruits. The Bismarckian regime established paternalistic welfare and insurance systems that became the building blocks of central elements of the "national socialism" of the Nazis. In Russia, the communist dictatorship was grounded on the Marxist vision that capitalism inherently violated the welfare of the people, requiring total state control.[39]

The American version of this welfare state was in the end the more decisive. Building on the Progressive reforms in states and cities at the turn of the century, on the example of successful interventions after the San Francisco earthquake of 1906 and in war-ravaged France in 1918–20, and on the outrage that met the government's failure to act during the 1927 Mississippi floods, Americans were ready when Roosevelt launched the New Deal in 1933, after four years of the Great Depression.[40] The New Deal legislation

---

[38] Daniel Yergin, *The Prize: The Epic Quest for Oil, Money and Power* (New York, 1991), 167–83, 303–88.

[39] Rodgers, *Atlantic Crossings*, 267–408; George Steinmetz, *Regulating the Social: The Welfare State and Local Politics in Imperial Germany* (Princeton, NJ, 1993), 41–54, 219–20; Peter Baldwin, *The Politics of Social Solidarity: Class Bases of the European Welfare State, 1875–1975* (Cambridge, 1990), 1–53. David Hoffmann, *Cultivating the Masses: Soviet State Interventionism in Its International Context, 1914–1939* (Ithaca, NY, 2011) examines this question in a particularly well-developed comparative framework.

[40] Rodgers, *Atlantic Crossings*, 409–84; David M. Kennedy, *Freedom from Fear: The American People in Depression and War, 1929–1945* (New York, 1999), 32–3, 62–3, 89–90, 99–101,

of 1933–4 established a framework of a firm national regulation of the financial sector, and some limited efforts at direct relief. In 1935, under threat from a populist challenge, Roosevelt established the Social Security System. But he could not quite bring himself to abandon a firm tradition of balanced books in government, and thus resisted the advice of British economist John Maynard Keynes to adopt a "fiscal strategy" of spending government money heavily to offset the failure of private capital to invest. The country lurched into a second decline in 1937–8 before military spending had the Keynesian effect of jumpstarting the economy. (In Germany and Italy, military spending had this Keynesian effect from the mid-1930s.) This experience, and that of the massive governmental planning and action to win a two-front war, fundamentally inserted government into the structure of the economy. The United States government, which after World War II was the most powerful entity in the entire world, would have a fundamental role in driving new technologies that were vital to national defense. It would use the monetary power of the Federal Reserve to modulate the ebb and flow of the economy and to maintain the dynamic of economic growth that all saw as vital to prosperity and social peace. Given circumstance and mandate, the federal government stood capable of advancing social justice and exerting vast power in the marketplace. During the decades following World War II, the European and Japanese governments were even more committed to administering policies of economic recovery and social welfare as part of a wider postwar social contract. National governments, particularly the U.S. government, were now an inherent part of the global economy, and its relationship with the wider earth system.[41] And around the world, vast and growing populations during the postwar decades hoped to join in the prosperity that the U.S. government seemed to guarantee.

The interconnected crises of the first half of the twentieth century slowed – even stalled – the course of economic growth that should have spun off from the Second Industrial Revolution, even while important energy transitions unfolded. The reach of such growth would have inevitably been slow in developing from its origins in the 1870s, when a series of inventions – no matter how consequential – would have to replace the high-pressure steam engine regime that had just come on line in the 1850s and 1860s. Thus it

---

120–1, 147–9; Jeffrey A. Frieden, *Global Capitalism: Its Fall and Rise in the Twentieth Century* (New York 2006), 127–228; Barry Johnson, *Rising Tide: The Great Mississippi Flood of 1927 and How It Changed America* (New York, 1998), 369–77.

[41] Frieden, *Global Capitalism*, 229–300; Walter S. Salant, "The Spread of Keynesian Doctrines in the United States," in Peter A. Hall, ed., *The Political Power of Economic Ideas: Keynesianism across Nations* (Princeton, NJ, 1989), 27–52; Alan Brinkley, *The End of Reform: New Deal Liberalism in Recession and War* (New York, 1995), 128–35; Michael D. Bordo et al., "The Defining Moment Hypothesis: The Editors' Introduction," in Michael D. Bordo et al., eds., *The Defining Moment: The Great Depression and the American Economy in the Twentieth Century* (Chicago, IL, 1998), 1–20.

is not unreasonable to see the entire period between 1870 and 1945 as one of a long, arduous transition. Such is the case in the energy history of the United States, emerging as the most dynamic economy in the world. The Second Industrial Revolution overlapped in the United States with a preindustrial era: coal surpassed wood as a source of energy only in 1885, and reached 75 percent in 1901, when petroleum, natural gas, and hydroelectric power were collectively still smaller energy sources than wood (see Figure IV.10). Coal supplied 70 percent or more of the energy in the U.S. economy through 1920, when petroleum and natural gas began to grow in importance, reaching 50 percent of the energy supply in 1938, though coal use would expand during the war years.[42]

If electricity was repowering America, coal played an important but ultimately limited role. About a third of the electricity generated between 1920 and 1950 came from hydroelectric dams, but this proportion actually declined from 40 percent in 1920 to 28 percent in 1950. From 1930, about half of the total electricity generated in the United States came from burning coal; prior to that its proportion was much higher. But only about 10 percent of the coal consumption in the 1920s and 1930s was devoted to electricity: most (~75%) was in relatively old-fashioned uses in manufacturing, most of it for heat and energy.[43] Thus the nineteenth-century energy structure lingered well into the twentieth. As important as electricity was becoming in American manufacturing and household life, the full impact of the "electrical revolution" would only come after World War II. Before the war, electrical generation per capita was low by modern standards: during the early 1930s it was a fifth of what it would be in 1956, and a tenth of what it would be in 1970 (see Figure IV.11). Nonetheless, the structural transition was under way. Wiring of domestic houses and apartments advanced sharply, from about 10 percent in 1910 to just under 70 percent in 1930, stalled during the early years of the Depression, and then advanced again with Roosevelt's aggressive efforts to bring electricity to rural America. The purchasing of automobiles followed a similar trajectory, and also stalled during the Depression, at around 78 percent.[44] In Europe, there were far

---

[42] Table Db164–71 – Energy consumption, by energy source: 1850–2001, Susan B. Carter et al., eds., *Historical Statistics of the United States, Earliest Times to the Present: Millennial Edition* (New York, 2006).

[43] Calculated from Table Db218–27 – Electric utilities power generation and fossil fuel consumption, by energy source: 1920–2000, and Table Dd832–42 – Consumption of selected commodities in manufacturing coal, petroleum, and energy products: 1899–1981, Carter et al., eds., *Historical Statistics of the United States*.

[44] The difference between electrified dwellings (70 percent) and automobile registration per household (78 percent) may mark the frequency of two-car households, thus making household electrification the best marker of household "modernization" in the 1930s. Automobile registration in David C. Mowery and Nathan Rosenberg, "Twentieth-Century Technological Change," in Stanley L. Engerman and Robert E. Gallman, eds., *The Cambridge Economic History of the United States, Vol. III: The Twentieth Century* (New York, 2000), 832.

fewer cars and less electricity; only the small, mountainous countries of Switzerland, Norway, and Sweden, with great potential for hydroelectrical development, surpassed the United States in electrical generation per capita. In 1940, the United Kingdom, once the great industrial leader, had one car for every thirty-four people, versus one for every five people in the United States; it generated less than 600 kilowatt hours per person while the United States generated more than 1,000.[45]

Behind these figures lay a faltering world economy, devastated by the First World War and its aftermath, recovering to collapse into stagnation and autarky in the 1930s, and then devastated again by World War II. If the United States had advanced particularly sharply before World War I, and then again during the 1920s, its economy fell particularly hard during the 1930s, but then surged during the Second World War, as it became the industrial powerhouse for the Allied effort. Driving the great surge in U.S. productivity in the early 1940s lay the government's shift to a full Keynesian policy of massive deficit spending and macroeconomic management. One of the legacies would be a permanent link forged between government, technology, and economy that would lock in the United States as the world leader in the framework established in the 1870s at the launching of the Second Industrial Revolution, a link that may – or may not – have led to a "Third Industrial Revolution" beginning in the 1970s.[46] As important, these Keynesian policies put money in the pockets of ordinary Americans, who would start to spend wildly on energy-consuming household durable goods after the war. Indeed, the Depression was probably intensified and extended by the relative poverty of ordinary Americans in the 1920s. The late 1920s saw a peak of wealth and income inequality that had been rising sharply since at least the 1890s, and as of 1929, 71 percent of American households earned less than $2,500, at or below the poverty line. Forty percent or fewer owned their own houses.[47] As of 1929, Americans spent collectively $6.8 billion, 9 percent of their annual consumption, on durable household goods and cars. With the postwar boom, things began to change:

Household electrification from *Hist. Stat.*, Table Db234–41. Electrical energy retail prices, residential use, and service coverage: 1902–2000; Sue Bowden and Avner Offer, "Household Appliances and the Use of Time: The United States and Britain since the 1920s," *EconHistR* 47 (1994), 725–48; Martin V. Melosi, *Coping with Abundance: Energy and Environment in Industrial America* (Philadelphia, 1985), 135.

[45] European data from Mitchell., *I.H.S.:E.* 735–44, 562–8.

[46] Mowery and Rosenberg, *Paths of Innovation*, 123–66; Moses Abramovitz and Paul A. David, "American Macroeconomic Growth in the Era of Knowledge-Based Progress: The Long-Run Perspective," Mowery and Rosenberg, "Twentieth-Century Technological Change," in Engerman and Gallman, eds., *The Cambridge Economic History* III: 1–93; 860–5, 876–903; Mokyr, *The Gifts of Athena*, 105–18.

[47] William Leuchtenberg, *The Perils of Prosperity, 1914–1932* (Chicago, IL, 1958), 194; Ronald Tobey et al., "Moving Out and Settling In: Residential Mobility, Home Owning, and the Public Enframing of Citizenship, 1921–1950," *AHR* 95 (1990), 1395–1422, esp. 1401.

in 1950, this figure had risen to $26 billion, yet was only 14 percent of total consumption.[48]

Thus the "payoff" of the Second Industrial Revolution, the shift from Rostow's investment in infrastructure to the "Age of High Mass-Consumption," came in slow motion, delayed by the combinations of war, depression, and the failure of government to move soon enough to intervene in the capitalist market. If war and depression were aftershocks of the late nineteenth-century consolidation of global economic power, so too there was systemic crisis driven by failure to adjust wages to the logic of the new mass production economy, resulting in underemployment and underconsumption that contributed to the global slowdown.[49] And this was in the economy at the technological cutting edge of the Second Industrial Revolution; for all of its problems, the United States was more dynamic than post–World War I Europe, and a world away from Asia, Latin America, and Africa, which in several decades would be redefined from "colonial" to "Third World." The reach and depth of industrialization was still circumscribed, even faltering, during the first decades of the twentieth century.

* * *

Environmental Impacts, 1870–1945: The Second Wave

While the Second Industrial Revolution helped to mitigate the worst of the crisis of local hazards in the new urbanized society, it also launched new regional environmental impacts. Serious as they were, however, these impacts were still within a manageable range, relative to more recent history.

This second wave of human-created environmental hazards, most obviously industrial pollution of air and water, was first addressed in the wider framework of urban reform. The same broad stratum of reformers who were concerned about sanitation in the growing Euro-Atlantic cities were also concerned about the particulates and smogs brought by unrestrained coal burning. "Great smogs" could kill, as happened in Glasgow in 1909, in the Meuse Valley of Belgium in 1930, and in London in 1952. The manufacture of cars, engines, and weaponry produced rising emissions of toxic metals like cadmium, lead, nickel, and zinc. During the 1920s, with the rising numbers of cars and trucks, especially in the United States, the established smokestack source of emissions was augmented by a tailpipe source. Abatement of automobile pollution would not begin until the 1960s, but

---

[48] Table Be27–9: Distribution of income among taxpaying units – shares received by the top percentiles: 1913–1998; Table Be40: Distribution of household wealth: 1774–1998; Peter H. Lindert, "The Distribution of Income and Wealth," Ch. Be in Carter et al., eds., *Historical Statistics of the United States*.

[49] Beaudreau, *Energy and the Rise and Fall of Political Economy*, 108–9; Ronald Tobey et al., "Moving Out and Settling In."

efforts to control emissions of fly ash, containing various forms of heavy metals, began by 1915 in New York City, with the installation of various mechanical devices and filters to reduce the volume of soot, with limited success. Large coal-burning utilities replaced these devices in 1929 with electrostatic precipitators that were about 90 percent effective. Smaller industrial factories, as well as private houses and apartment buildings, continued to burn coal without fly ash controls into the 1950s, but by 1940 about 60 percent of the fly ash was being trapped.[50]

These were only the pollution effects that most obviously affected a particular locality, and that had the most obvious and immediate impacts on health. CO_2 would have a long-term global effect, but one that was invisible at the time. Another invisible effect was also at work, one that had a particularly regional or – rather – hemispheric impact. Burning fossil fuels emit sulfur dioxide, which oxidizes in the atmosphere into sulfuric acid, a key component of sulfate aerosols.

As do sulfate aerosols caused by volcanic eruptions, fossil-fuel-derived aerosols have a cooling effect, both by directly deflecting incoming solar energy, and by contributing to cloud buildup.[51] But building up in the troposphere rather than the stratosphere, aerosols have a regional rather than a global impact, and precipitate out of the atmosphere relatively quickly, requiring constant renewal. Such would have been provided by the North Atlantic economies of the Second Industrial Revolution, particularly in the constant expansion of emissions before the First World War.

The first indications of the industrial emission of sulfur dioxide and conversion to sulfate aerosols is apparent in the Greenland ice cores by the 1870s, and climbed dramatically around 1900, dipped with World War I and the Depression, and then climbed again during the 1940s. The fossil fuel–sulfate aerosol effect – and acid rain – would have had a strong effect downwind of the emissions, in plumes reaching eastward for hundreds of miles. Rising sulfate aerosol levels resulted in a regional cooling, counteracting the general global trajectory toward warming. These regional cooling effects exerted the strongest effects in eastern North America and the adjacent North Atlantic, and in northern Europe and the Eurasian regions to the east[52] (see Figure IV.9b and IV.14).

---

[50] McNeill, *Something New under the Sun*, 50–84; Joel A. Tarr and Robert U. Ayres, "The Hudson-Raritan Basin," in Turner et al., *The Earth as Transformed by Human Action*, 621–52, esp. 632–3; Peter Thorsheim, *Inventing Pollution: Coal, Smoke and Culture in Britain since 1800* (Athens, OH, 2006); B. Nemery et al., "The Meuse Valley Fog of 1930: An Air Pollution Disaster," *The Lancet* 357 (2001), 704–8.

[51] On sulfate aerosols, see the longer discussion at the end of this chapter.

[52] Simon F. Tett et al., "The Impact of Natural and Anthropogenic Forcings on Climate and Hydrology since 1550," *ClimDyn* 28 (2007), 3–34; Nicolas Paris, "First Sulfur Isotope Measurements in Central Greenland Ice Cores along the Preindustrial and Industrial Periods," *JGR* 107 (2002), ACH6; K. D. Williams et al., "The Response of the Climate System to the Indirect Effects of Anthropogenic Sulfate Aerosol," *ClimDyn* 17 (2001), 845–56;

By contrast to the short-lived sulfate aerosols, CO_2 persists for long periods of time in the atmosphere before the global carbon cycle washes it out. Thus, in an emerging irony, industrial emissions from northern economies were beginning to contribute to a long-term warming of the planet, with particularly strong effects at the tropics and the Arctic, but that warming was offset in the northern hemisphere with a regional layer of cooling and cloud-producing sulfate aerosols. Except for one prescient scientist in Sweden, Svante Arrhenius, who began to think about the possibility of global warming in the 1890s, these global effects were not noticeable to people who had more immediately pressing matters on their minds.

The emissions history of the period between 1870 and 1945 is marked by three patterns. First, industrial emissions followed an accelerating curve of growth from the 1870s that marked the staggering increase of coal consumption (and the bare beginnings of oil and natural gas consumption) that drove the advanced European and North American economies. But this smooth ascent came to an end in 1913–14, at the beginning of World War I. Having increased since 1870 by more than a factor of five in forty-five years, global emissions would increase by less than half during the next thirty-five years. If this sequence of growing and slowing of industrial emissions comprises the first two patterns, the third is a single arc of agricultural expansion in the tropics running continuously from 1870 to 1945, roughly tracking the rate of global population growth. These rising land use emissions were driven by agricultural expansion in the tropics and China, while the land use emissions in United States faded in importance.[53] Where industrial emissions surpassed land use CO_2 or methane emissions individually around 1910, in combination these two land use greenhouse gases still exceeded industrial totals through 1960 (see Figures IV.7, IV.14).

If the industrial emissions were still lower than land use emissions as of the 1890s, they were very significant. Virtually all of them were produced by the developed economies of the United States and Europe. European emissions led the United States through about 1905, and then leveled off for three decades starting with World War I; the U.S. emissions rate increased sharply from 1895 to 1929, collapsed with the Depression, and then surged upward with World War II and the postwar expansion.

There were two reasons for the decline in the rate of emissions in the 1920s, involving paradoxically both the stalling trajectory and the spreading impact of the Second Industrial Revolution. On one hand, the crises of war and depression reduced the pace of early twentieth-century economic

James E. Hansen, "Climate Forcings in the Industrial Era," *PNAS* 95 (1998), 12753–8; M. Legrand and Paul A. Mayewski, "Glaciochemistry of Polar Ice Cores: A Review," *JGR* 35 (1997), 219–43; Paul A. Mayewski et al., "An Ice-Core Record of Atmospheric Response to Anthropogenic Sulfate and Nitrate," *Nature* 346 (1990), 554–6.

[53] After 1960, the regrowth of forest cover in eastern North America would make the United States a net CO_2 sink for land use emissions.

growth, and with these wars and depressions industrial emissions declined. On the other hand, the direction of technological change inexorably shifted the North Atlantic economies away from coal and toward cleaner-burning petroleum and natural gas. Measured by metric tons of carbon emissions per gross domestic product, all of the early industrializers had peaks of "dirty" industrialization[54] (see Figure IV.8, IV.10). The United Kingdom had its dirtiest period per economic output between the 1850s and 1905, the era of the high-pressure steam engine, the United States and Germany from the 1890s to 1920. Belgium's emissions peaked during the recovery after World War I; Germany had a "dirty" recovery after World War II.

But from these early twentieth-century peaks of emissions/GNP, the trajectory in these Atlantic economies was toward lower emissions per GDP. This slowing of emissions was shaped by increased technological efficiencies and the transition from dirty coal to cleaner oil and gas. After World War II, such advancing efficiencies would be gobbled up in an expanding economy, and the rate of total emissions would explode, if not as fast as the increase in per capita GDP.[55] But in the context of the economic stagnation of the interwar period, the advancing efficiencies and the fuel transition meant that overall emissions rates were lower than they had been before 1914 and would be after 1945. Without the slowing of emissions starting with World War I, industrial emissions would have exceeded land use emissions around 1920, and the entire curve of emissions might have advanced as much as forty years earlier. Thus, for all of the miseries of the early twentieth century, depression and war delayed an impending climate crisis by many decades.

Whatever their sources, these emissions had their impact, though the ice core measures of atmospheric gases can only give us general trends, rather than accurate year-to-year or decade-to-decade oscillations (see Figure IV.14). Atmospheric CO_2, as measured in a smoothed sequence from the ice at Law Dome in Antarctica, began to rise during the 1840s and 1850s, moving from a near-Holocene-normal 285 ppm to a distinctly elevated 310 ppm in 1945. Sometime between 1875 and 1880, this measure slipped past the highest ice-recorded measurement in the past 800,000 years (298.2 ppm at 332,500 ybp in Marine Isotope Stage 9), about 50,000–75,000 years before the putative origins of Middle Paleolithic technology and modern human anatomy. Since the 1870s, the global atmospheric CO_2 levels began to reach levels not seen since the emergence of the genus *Homo* in the late Pliocene. Perhaps responding to the advancing pace of agricultural emissions in the

---

[54] On the implications of these dirty peaks, see the discussions of the environmental Kuznets curve cited in note 22. Ben Gales et al., "North vs. South: Energy Transition and Energy Intensity in Europe over 200 Years," *EREconH* 11 (2007) argues that the curve of energy transition is flattened if traditional fuels and their emissions are factored in.

[55] Robert U. Ayres et al., "Exergy, Power and Work in the US Economy, 1900–1998," *Energy* 28 (2003), 219–73, esp. 249–51; David L. Greene, "Vehicle Use and Fuel Economy: How Big is the 'Rebound' Effect?" *The Energy Journal* 13 (1992), 117–43.

tropics and China, atmospheric methane also increased, after a long rise from 1740, accelerating around 1900.[56]

Emissions and new concentrations of greenhouse gases had their first impacts on global temperature during these decades. Temperature estimates mark the early twentieth century as a period of significant warming (see Figure IV.14). The long-term tree ring measure suggests that temperatures on average in the northern hemisphere rose above the peak of the Medieval Warm Period, about AD 975, sometime between 1935 and 1940.[57] Some of this increase was due to increasing solar influence, recovering from a late nineteenth-century temperature decline and the slowing of volcanic activity in these years (which would have cooled the earth by putting solar-deflecting sulfate aerosols in the stratosphere). But it is also the consensus among climate scientists that greenhouse gases from human sources began to have a warming effect during these decades. Here there is something of a paradox, discussed in detail in the next chapter. Global temperatures rose during the First Great Interruption, during decades of depression and war, when the rate of warming CO_2 emissions slowed. But so did the rate of cooling sulfur dioxides. The result was that the great and persistent volumes of industrial and land use CO_2 discharged since the middle of the nineteenth century were at work in the warming of the Great Interruption of 1914–45. The persistent and now unmasked greenhouse gases, products of the nineteenth-century land boom and the Second Industrial Revolution, were the human contribution to measurable global climate change.[58]

The era of this First Great Interruption, from 1914 to 1945, was – oddly – the calm before the storm of global transformation. As traumatic and horrific as the course of human events was during these decades, the coming mid-twentieth-century decades of prosperity would have an even more profound impact on human history and the earth system. World populations would more than double, and a "second great super-cycle expansion" of the modern industrial economy would generate environmental impacts of global consequence.

[56] James Hansen et al., "Global Temperature Change," *PNAS* 103 (2006), 14288–93, at 14291, argues that current global temperatures are within one degree C of the highest temperatures since OIS 11, roughly 400,000 years ago. Given the current greenhouse gas buildup, we can expect to exceed that temperature level in the coming decades.

[57] I use the CRUTEM3 estimate because it extends back to 1850: see P. Brohan et al., "Uncertainty Estimates in Regional and Global Observed Temperature Changes: A New Data Set from 1850," *JGR* 111 (2006) D12106; it is similar to the NASA Land-Ocean Temperature Anomaly: Hansen et al., "Global Temperature Change"; see also Kevin E. Trenberth and Philip D. Jones, "Ch. 3: Observations: Surface and Atmospheric Climate Change," in *Climate Change 2007: The Physical Science Basis*, 241–53; and Timothy J. Osborn and Keith R. Briffa, "The Spacial Extent of 20th-Century Warmth in the Context of the Past 12000 Years," *Science* 311 (2006), 841–4.

[58] See Chapter 13, pages 421–31.

13

Growth beyond Limits: 1945 to Present

The arc of history since the end of the Second World War constitutes a fundamental new departure in the human condition. Building on the global reach of the war itself, the technologies of the Second Industrial Revolution suddenly penetrated every corner of the earth. The result was massive and virtually instantaneous. Populations mushroomed. And if economies have not been adequate to supply their aspirations, the energy mobilized to supply their needs is now literally transforming the earth system. The Anthropocene has arrived.

Underpopulation, not overpopulation, threatened ancient and medieval agrarian societies. When populations grew during climatic optimums, they generally managed to achieve incremental improvements to agricultural productivity. But life was not pleasant. A pervasive hierarchy – and poverty – shaped the human condition. A peasant family in the late Middle Ages, on average, had a standard of living not unlike that of a peasant family in the Bronze Age, and probably the late Neolithic. Average life expectancy at birth ranged from the low twenties to the mid-thirties at best.

But these societies were amazingly durable; they lasted for hundreds of years at a stretch, and then only collapsed when they were simply hammered by earth system forces – these crises were driven by exogenous factors of the natural environment, not endogenous pressures of overpopulation. And these societies did not severely degrade their environments: much of what earlier environmental historians have described as the negative environmental impacts of ancient societies is turning out to be driven by natural causes. This perspective allows us to reconsider the Malthusian calculus, broadly conceived. Ancient populations suffered poor individual life outcomes, with poor health and low life expectancy; conversely, they imposed relatively low environmental impact and enjoyed long-term societal sustainability. Whatever their flaws, and there were many, ancient societies should not be condemned for any major environmental failings. Modern populations, by contrast, enjoy excellent and improving high individual outcomes, with amazingly good health and high life expectancy, and are causing systemic changes on the entire global ecology. Whether they are sustainable is very much an open question.

In very recent memory, the double-edged sword of science and industry has carried humanity through a great and paradoxical transition to prosperity and peril. Throughout the world, people attuned to the perils upon us are sobered by how much it will cost and how long it will take to construct a new energy system to fill the place that fossil fuels now occupy in the delivery of essential services to massive new populations around the world. The transition from archaic to modern has taken several hundred years, but the fundamental departure has unfolded in the course of a single lifetime, since the end of World War II. The rapidity of this change is sobering, but its blinding speed may suggest that humanity can – and should – change course in yet another lifetime.

* * *

The Demographic Revolution, Part II: 1945 to Present

The critical calculus of global well-being shifted after 1945. Two broad conjunctures of geography, economy, and demography that departed from this historic relationship shaped the world during these decades. In the developed temperate North, the so-called First World of Europe, North America, Australia, New Zealand, and Japan experienced moderate population growth combined with an economic expansion never seen before in world history. In an underdeveloped tropical South, the so-called Third World, population exploded, while economic growth has come more slowly and fitfully. With this enormous expansion – if it may be abating – has come the problem of feeding and employing these unprecedented numbers.

The population numbers tell a fundamental part of the story. At the end of the "calamitous fourteenth century," world population stood at roughly 380 million; by sometime between 1700 and 1750, it had roughly doubled, hitting a level three times bigger than the peak of the ancient world. Crossing the one billion mark just after 1800, global population doubled its early eighteenth-century numbers around 1875, to roughly 1.4 billion. By the close of World War II, it stood at 2.5 billion, of which the largest single group, about 30 percent, consisted of the peoples of a developed temperate North extending from North America to Europe, the U.S.S.R., and Japan. Then, in the wake of the war, populations began to expand everywhere. The developed world had a post-Depression and postwar baby boom that temporarily reversed trajectories toward lower fertility, and lasted until 1960. Populations expanded massively in the tropical South, as the epidemiological transition spread definitively beyond the industrializing world. Between 1500 and 1900, the population of the global South reduced from 81 percent to 68 percent of the global total; by 2000, it rebounded to 81 percent, and will clearly increase in the next several decades.

Postwar population growth in the developing world had its roots in a combination of factors. The discovery of penicillin in the 1920s was important, as were advances in disease control and public health, stemming in some measure from Allied successes in keeping troops reasonably healthy in the tropics during World War II. Mosquito control programs, followed by DDT campaigns, radically reduced the scale of malaria in the tropics by 1970. In addition, simple improvements in waste disposal, involving careful placing and control of latrines rather than expensive sewage systems, had dramatic results in reducing mortality. Particularly important, education and literacy, especially among women, had a very important role in reducing infant and childhood mortality, as women could become part of a wider effort at improved sanitation and nutrition for their children. And quite strikingly, economic development per se, though not insignificant, had a somewhat muted role in increasing life expectancies. The United Nations demographic data divides the world into a more developed "north" (Europe including Russia, North America, Australia/New Zealand, and Japan), a less developed "south," and the forty-nine least developed countries, the large majority in sub-Saharan Africa and south central Asia. In the more developed world, where GDP/capita quadrupled, life expectancy grew from ~66 to ~76 between 1950 and 2005, while in the second-tier less developed world, where GDP per capita doubled, it grew from ~41 to ~67. Life expectancy in the third-tier least-developed nations – with GDP per capita barely moving forward from seventeenth-century European conditions – lagged behind but still advanced from ~36 to ~54.[1]

The other dimension of the demographic transition advanced as well, however. Despite the alarm sounded in the 1960s about the "population explosion," smaller countries with good educational systems managed to move through the fertility transition reasonably quickly, in some cases in a generation or so. The second-tier less developed countries cut their birthrates in half between 1970 and 2000, while the least developed countries saw a drop of about 25 percent. In Singapore, the crude birthrate dropped from 40 per 1,000 population in 1959 to less than 20 in 1974; this same drop occurred in Sri Lanka between 1943 and 1992, and in Taiwan between 1959 and 1984. Here again, rising rates of literacy and education have had a powerful role in reducing fertility, as women throughout the world gain

---

[1] United Nations, Department of Economic and Social Affairs, Population Division, World Population Prospects: The 2006 revision, Highlights, Working Paper No. ESA/P/WP.202 (2007), 18. James C. Riley, *Rising Life Expectancy: A Global History* (New York, 2001), 139, 74–7, 200–19; Jean-Claude Chesnais, *The Demographic Transition: Stages, Patterns, and Economic Implications* (Oxford, 1992), 57–86; Paul Demeny, "Population," in B. L. Turner et al., *The Earth as Transformed by Human Action: Global and Regional Changes in the Biosphere over the Past 300 Years* (New York, 1990), 41–54.

increasing knowledge of and control over their reproductive lives. China achieved a striking drop in births in the 1970s through the coercive one-child policy. Between 1950 and 2005, the second-tier developing countries cut their birthrates from ~43/1000 to ~20/1000, with an accelerated decrease from the 1970s to the 1990s, while the least developed countries cut their rate from ~48 to ~37, with significantly lower birthrates not projected until after 2020. The most significant exceptions lie in sub-Saharan Africa, where the birthrates are still generally in the forties per 1,000, and where AIDS has increased adult mortality at epidemic rates.[2]

Thus the demographic transition has spread and accelerated from its origins in northern Europe, where it took a century or more to complete. Demographers now see a "demographic convergence" in motion to be completed sometime during the next forty to fifty years, with rates of fertility and mortality relatively equalized throughout the world.[3] But in the course of this transition, populations have risen to Malthusian levels, more than fifteen times higher than the medieval level. One consequence of population growth – and expanded cash cropping for export – has been a massive clearance of land for agricultural uses and timbering, most dramatically in Latin America, but also in South and Southeast Asia. The results have been intense pressure on delicate tropical habitats, as well as global effects, including a surge of carbon and methane emissions, and the loss of tropical forest function in drawing down carbon. In some cases, lands cleared have been forest covered since the beginning of the Holocene or even before; in others we are seeing a reversal of the reforestation that followed the great Amerindian epidemics[4] (see Figure IV.1, IV.7). Even with these new tropical croplands, the pace of population growth outstripped the pace of food production, and starting in the 1940s in Mexico and then expanding through the 1960s, a concerted effort called the *Green Revolution* was launched to increase

[2] Population Division of the Department of Economic and Social Affairs of the United Nations Secretariat, World Population Prospects: The 2010 Revision (http://esa.un.org/unpd/wpp/Documentation/pdf/WPP2010_Volume-I_Comprehensive-Tables.pdf, accessed August 8, 2012); B. R. Mitchell, *International Historical Statistics: The Americas, 1750s–2005*, sixth edition (Basingstoke, 2007), 71–98; B. R. Mitchell, *International Historical Statistics: Africa, Asia, and Oceania, 1750–2005*, fifth edition (Basingstoke, 2007), 77–81; Jean-Pierre Guengant, "The Proximate Determinants during the Fertility Transition," United Nations Population publications (http://www.un.org/esa/population/publications/completingfertility/2RevisedGUENGANTpaper.PDF, accessed August 8, 2012).

[3] Chris Wilson, "On the Scale of Global Demographic Convergence 1950–2000," *PopDevR* 27 (2001), 155–71; but see the critique in Shawn F. Dorius, "Global Demographic Convergence? A Reconsideration of Changing Intercountry Inequality in Fertility," *PopDevR* 34 (2008), 519–37.

[4] Kees Klein Goldewijk, "Estimating Global Land Use Change over the Past 300 Years: The Hyde Database," *GBC* 15 (2001), 426; Michael Williams, *Deforesting the Earth: From Prehistory to Global Crisis* (Chicago, IL, 2003), 420–93.

food production in developing countries. New hybrid high-yield crops were developed, and massive amounts of synthetic nitrogen-based fertilizers and pesticides were deployed. The result was a huge increase in the food supply, but also a narrowing and "corporatizing" of the global seed stock, as well as massive impacts on both water systems and the atmosphere from the volumes of nitrogen applied. Because this modernized agriculture requires huge amounts of water, it is causing significant shortages – and tensions – in semiarid India, Pakistan, and the Middle East.[5] Increasingly, and particularly in Latin America, the trajectory of population growth and the corporatization of agriculture has led to a massive urbanization in the developing world. Currently, Latin America stands at about 65 percent urbanized, and Africa lags at less than 40 percent; sometime between 2020 and 2045, the developing world as a whole will reach 50 percent urbanized, a point that the developed world reached as a whole during the 1940s. The developing world is moving toward a three-tier social order. A small but growing middle class, sharing sprawling urban spaces with large numbers of people living in vast barrios and shantytown slums, displaced from rural societies that can only be described as imploding. The failure of these economies to support growing young populations is amply illustrated by the flood of economic migrants seeking employment in Western Europe and the United States during the past decades.[6]

* * *

[5] John R. McNeill, *Something New under the Sun: An Environmental History of the Twentieth-Century World* (New York, 2000), 219–26; Vaclav Smil, *Enriching the Earth: Fritz Haber, Carl Bosch, and the Transformation of World Food Production* (Cambridge, MA, 2001); John Perkins, *Geopolitics and the Green Revolution: Wheat, Genes, and the Cold War* (New York, 1997); Diane Raines Ward, *Water Wars: Drought, Flood, Folly, and the Politics of Thirst* (New York, 2002), 116–20.

[6] Population Division of the Department of Economic and Social Affairs of the United Nations Secretariat, World Urbanization Prospects: The 2011 Revision (http://esa.un.org/unpd/wup/index.htm accessed August 8, 2012). State of World Population 2007: Unleashing the Potential of Urban Growth (UNFPA, 2007); Allen C. Kelley and Jeffrey G. Williamson, *What Drives Third World City Growth?: A Dynamic General Equilibrium Approach* (Princeton, NJ, 1984); McNeill, *Something New under the Sun*, 283–95; A. J. McMichael, *Planetary Overload: GEC and the Health of the Human Species* (Cambridge, 1993), 259–83; Thomas F. Homer-Dixon, *Environment, Scarcity, and Violence* (Princeton, NJ, 1999), 155–66; Mike Davis, *Planet of Slums: Urban Involution and the Informal Working Class* (London, 2006), esp. 1–20, 151–73; Timothy J. Hatton and Jeffrey G. Williamson, "What Fundamentals Drive World Migration?" NBER Working Papers 9159, Sept. 2002; Stephen Castles and Mark J. Miller, *The Age of Migration (International Population Movements in the Modern World)*, third edition (New York, 2003), 78–93; U.N.H.C.R., 2009 Global Trends: Refugees, Asylum-Seekers, Returnees, Internally Displaced and Stateless Persons (Country Data Sheets, June 15, 2010) (http://www.unhcr.org/cgi-bin/texis/vtx/search?page=search&docid=4c11fobe9&query=2009%20Global%20Trends, accessed August 8, 2012).

The Age of High Growth and a Third Industrial Revolution?
The World Economy, 1945 to Present

The United States emerged from the Second World War as the sole surviving functional industrial power, and during the next several decades became the model for the successful mobilization of the Second Industrial Revolution into Rostow's "Age of High-Mass Consumption." The "American Century" (projected after a brief fear of a return to depression) was to be a utopian age of unlimited high economic growth. For two and a half decades, something like this vision came to pass, if entwined with the anxieties and distant wars of the Cold War struggle. With the United States leading the way, the world began an unprecedented advance of economic growth and demographic expansion. It also launched a startling assault on global ecosystems and the atmosphere itself.

This sixty-year period breaks into three phases: an American-led expansion to 1973, a global economic stagnation running into and through the 1980s, and then an epoch of global transfer of production in the context of an apparent shift into a "knowledge revolution," or "Third Industrial Revolution," that is defining the coming century. Together these trajectories comprise what can be called the *Second* and *Third Great Super-Cycle Expansions* of the modern economy.

The United States was the primary beneficiary and engine of the initial explosion of growth. From 1870 to 1929, U.S. gross domestic product grew at an annual rate of 1.9 percent; between 1934 and 2003, it grew at an annual rate of 2.75 percent; during the twelve particularly prosperous years between 1961 and 1973, it averaged 3.24 percent. As Europe and Japan recovered from the devastation of the war, they joined in this explosion of prosperity. The surge of the "northern economies" from 1945 to the early 1970s was firmly grounded in their head start since the late nineteenth century: the postwar boom was in great measure the ultimate realization of the potential of the technological system launched during the 1880s and stalled since 1914.

In particular, the 1960s were a notable period of interrupted growth driven by consumer durables. The 1920s to 1940s had seen the rapid spread of radios and slower spread of refrigerators and washing machines; the postwar decades saw the spread of more electricity-consuming household goods: TVs, stereos, VCRs, DVD players, personal computers, and now a vast array of personal electronics. Where before the war electrical household appliances had been particularly American, by the 1960s, a global consumption system was developing that included all of the more prosperous economies; by the 1970s, manufacturing for this global energy-consuming market had spread beyond the United States to the advanced European and Asian economies.

At the center of this expansion lay the key drivers of the Second Industrial Revolution: the combination of petroleum, the flexible distributed power of steam and jet turbines, electrical systems and variable-sized electric motors, and the internal combustion engine. As measured by electrical generation and the numbers of privately owned cars, the economies of Western Europe, the United States, Canada, Australia, and New Zealand were all broadly similar by 1960 and converged even more markedly over the next decade.[7] Energy supplies lay at the absolute center of this explosion of growth. Per capita electric generation was measured in the hundreds of kilowatt (KW) hours during the 1940s, and by the thousands during the 1980s. These were the drivers of the Second Great Super-Cycle Expansion.[8]

Throughout most of the developed world, the postwar years brought a relatively rapid transition from coal to oil and then increasingly to natural gas, which was more efficient and cleaner. Trains were converted to diesel, and then were displaced to a significant degree by jet airplanes, burning special grades of distilled-oil fuels. Electrical generation shifted toward oil and natural gas, though a few countries, France in particular, invested heavily in nuclear power. The United States stands out in reverting to coal. American coal use declined from wartime peaks through the mid-1950s, and then expanded to new highs, doubling between 1955 and 1995, virtually all of it burned to generate electricity. But oil was fundamental to the American economy, more than quadrupling per capita from the 1930s to the 1970s, and natural gas use expanded at an even greater rate[9] (see Figure IV.10).

Other world regions grew at a much lower rate, but they did prosper relative to the past for several decades following the war. Economic growth spread first and most obviously to parts of East Asia. Japanese recovery from the devastation of the war was gradual in the 1950s but accelerated in the 1960s, and by 1970 the Japanese matched their American and European counterparts in the consumption of cars and electricity. The postwar period saw – for a variety of reasons – the persistence of protectionist economic policies in Latin America, the communist "Second World," and in rapidly

---

[7] Vaclav Smil, *Transforming the Twentieth Century: Technical Innovations and the Consequences* (New York, 2006) offers an excellent overview of postwar consumer technologies. See also Sue Boyden and Avner Offer, "Household Appliances and the Use of Time: The United States and Britain since the 1920s," *EconHistR* 47 (1994), 715–48.

[8] Gerard Lyons (Standard Chartered Bank), *The Super-Cycle Report* (London, 2010), 17–19 (available at http://www.standardchartered.com/id/_documents/press-releases/en/The%20 Super-cycle%20Report-12112010-final.pdf, accessed August 8, 2012).

[9] Here see Robert W. Ayres et al., "Exergy, Power and Work in the US Economy, 1900–1998," *Energy* 23 (2003), 219–73; Benjamin Warr et al., "Long Term Trends in Resource Exergy Consumption and Useful Work Supplies in the UK, 1900 to 2000," *EcolEcom* 68 (2008), 126–40; Ben Gales et al., "North versus South: Energy Transition and Energy Intensity in Europe over 200 Years," *EREconH* 11 (2007), 219–53.

decolonizing Africa and Asia. These import-substituting industrial policies worked up to a point. Latin America, isolated from the world economy during World War II, pursued policies of protected industrialization in the postwar period, and was able to keep up with population growth and generate an expanding economy into the 1970s. After moderately rising incomes and growth rates in the 1950s and 1960s, especially in some parts of Latin America, these Second World countries were undermined by the energy shocks and debt crises of the 1970s and 1980s. The oil shocks of the 1970s, when first Arab and then Iranian oil was cut off following the 1973 Yom Kippur War and the 1979 Iranian Revolution, were a first blow. The embargoes doubled and tripled the price of oil and gas in a matter of weeks, exposing the central weakness of the global economy. These energy price shocks were entangled with a general global stagnation compounded by an enduring debt crisis for many energy-dependent developing countries that lasted through the 1980s and into the 1990s.[10] Behind the general stagnation lay and still lies the specter of systematic economic dysfunction, as enormous global populations may have overrun the limited capacity of the world economy to provide employment.

On the other hand, a number of national economies prospered during these decades, as well-educated but low-cost cohorts of labor were mobilized by determined political elites adopting the best industrial technology available, and generating huge quantities of cheap but sophisticated exports. Japan was the leader, surging in the 1960s on the basis of export manufacturing, though by the 1990s it began to suffer its own decline. Japan's neighbors rapidly emulated its example of growth through industrial exports. Starting in the 1960s, a set of small East Asian countries known as the "Four Asian Tigers" – South Korea, Hong Kong, Taiwan, and Singapore – joined this upward run. They have been followed by China and India. Here size helped: the emergence of strong export-based manufacturing in the small Asian Tigers has driven their GDP per capita up very quickly to levels comparable with Japan, Western Europe, and the United States.[11]

Elsewhere there was more of a mixed to poor record. A number of Second and Third World countries have significant oil resources, but oil revenues

---

[10] Jeffrey A. Frieden, *Global Capitalism: Its Fall and Rise in the Twentieth Century* (New York 2006), 363–91; Ronald Findlay and Kevin H. O'Rourke, *Power and Plenty: Trade, War, and the World Economy in the Second Millennium* (Princeton, NJ, 2007), 496–7; Daniel Yergin, *The Prize: The Epic Quest for Oil, Money and Power* (New York, 1991), 613–714; Paul Krugman, *The Return of Depression Economics and the Crisis of 2008* (New York, 2009), 30–138.

[11] Findlay and O'Rourke, *Power and Plenty*, 515–26. While most of the dramatic economic growth in the Asian economies is associated with production for export, there is still room to debate the relative roles of strong domestic governments in developing human capital through education and social planning versus export-based economics. The consensus may be that both are centrally involved in the Asian success story.

have been and continue to be the source of serious corruption and misappropriation.[12] Others, most importantly Brazil and Chile, have developed thriving agricultural export economies. The economies of the greater Soviet Bloc of Russia, Soviet Central Asia, and Eastern Europe managed to advance at about half the European rate through the 1970s, but faltered in the 1980s and suddenly collapsed with the fall of the Soviet Union. The new Russia, with the greater Middle East, is fundamentally dependent on the sale of oil and gas on the world market; the former Soviet Bloc, Russia with Eastern Europe, is projected to actually lose population in coming decades, in part a result of the collapse of the socialist health care system and a declining life expectancy for men.[13] Postcolonial Africa has done the worst of the global regions, barely maintaining a subsistence level per capita GDP, and it was further ravaged by AIDS, incapacitating and killing disproportionate numbers of young people of working age.[14]

The pressure of surging populations may well surpass the limits of technology, energy systems, and resources to provide the framework of well-being in a modern economy. Such limits involve two key areas: the supply of oil and the generation of electricity. Starting in the 1950s, geologist M. King Hubbert began to predict the life cycle of wells, fields, and regions of oil production with notable accuracy. Applied to world production, his model predicts that the production of oil will peak and begin to decline sometime between 2010 and 2020. During the past decade, however, new technologies for oil and natural gas survey and extraction have seemingly changed the calculus of predictions of peak oil.[15] Newly reported fields from around the world have suppressed much discussion of energy limits. Peak oil and natural gas will come, though it may not be upon us quite yet.

The second arena of energy constraint is less widely understood. Over the course of the first half of the twentieth century, incremental improvements in technology continuously improved the efficiency of electrical generation, by a factor of at least ten between 1907 and 1957. The result was greater amounts of electric power for progressively cheaper rates. Sometime

[12] "Oil, Politics, and Corruption," *The Economist*, Sept. 18, 2008.

[13] Riley, *Rising Life Expectancy*, 44–6.

[14] Findlay and O'Rourke, *Power and Plenty*, 517–18; Frieden, *Global Capitalism*, 369–76; UNAIDS, Report on the Global AIDS Epidemic 2008 (Geneva, 2008), 39–47; John Bongaarts et al., "Has the HIV Epidemic Peaked?" *PopDevR* 34 (2008), 199–224; Basia Zaba et al., "Demographic and Socioeconomic Impact of AIDS: Taking Stock of the Empirical Evidence," *AIDS: The Official Journal of the International AIDS Society* 18 (2004), S1–S7; Laurie Garrett, *The Coming Plague: Newly Emergent Diseases in a World out of Balance* (New York, 1994), 334–61.

[15] Yergin, *The Prize*, 715–68. Peak oil theory is described in Richard Hienberg, *The Party's Over: Oil, War and the Fate of Industrial Societies* (Gabriola Island, B.C., 2003), 81–122; and Kenneth S. Deffeyes, *Hubbert's Peak: The Impending World Oil Shortage* (Princeton, NJ, 2002). For a critique of peak oil theory, see Vaclav Smil, *Global Catastrophes and Trends: The Next Fifty Years* (Cambridge, MA, 2008), 77–91.

in the mid-1960s, these efficiency gains – measured in BTUs per kilowatt hour – leveled off after the failure of efforts to move to larger, more powerful "supercritical" boiler systems. The result was higher costs for electrical generation in the midst of the 1960s economic boom, and by the early 1970s contributed to the beginnings of increasing prices (see Figure IV.11). Significant efficiency improvements did not appear until 2006. Recently, attention has turned to the resistance to the flow of current in aging transmission lines. In both cases the friction of technology has quietly slowed the course of economic growth.[16]

It may well be that the energy and financial constrictions of the global economy in the 1970s and 1980s signaled that the technologies of the Second Industrial Revolution were reaching the point of diminishing returns, inadequate to manage the massive new populations in what can be called a Kondratiev wave "B" phase or even simply a Malthusian crisis. Certainly these pressures were generating the expected Boserupian response of incremental innovation, but not a massive public commitment.

There were signs by the 1970s that another revolution in applied science was under way. Perhaps it had been under way since the 1920s and 1930s, when advanced physicists hotly debated the principles of nuclear fission.[17] World War II ended with the explosion of two nuclear weapons over Japanese cities, and these conflagrations marked the beginning of what appears to be a "Third Industrial Revolution." The 1880s had seen the emergence of an industrial-academic-governmental complex to drive technological invention and innovation. Most fully developed in Germany, this government-driven research and development complex did not take hold in the United States in full form until the Second World War, where the Manhattan Project that developed the atomic bomb was the most obvious example. During the war, the U.S. government funded a wide range of applied science efforts, most importantly in nuclear science, synthetic rubber, penicillin, jet engines (gas

---

[16] David C. Mowery and Nathan Rosenberg, *Paths of Innovation: Technological Change in 20th-Century America* (New York, 1998), 118–20; Paul L. Joskow, "Productivity Growth and Technical Change in the Generation of Electricity," *The Energy Journal* 8 (1989), 17–38; Robert U. Ayres, "Resources, Scarcity, Technology, and Growth," in R. David Simpson et al., *Scarcity and Growth Revisited: Natural Resources and the Environment in the New Millennium* (Washington, DC, 2005), 142–55; Richard F. Hirsch, *Technology and Transformation in the American Electric Utility Industry* (New York, 1989); Jason Makensi, *Lights Out: The Electricity Crisis, The Global Economy, and What It Means to You* (Hoboken, NJ, 2007); Alexander Y. Vaninsky, "Environmental Efficiency of Electric Power Industry of the United States: A Data Envelopment Analysis Approach," *Proceedings of the World Academy of Science, Engineering, and Technology* 30 (2008), 584–90; TableDb218-27 – Electric utilities power generation and fossil fuel consumption, by energy source: 1920–2000 (Gavin Wright), in Susan B. Carter et al., eds., *Historical Statistics of the United States: Millennium Edition Online* (New York, 2012).

[17] Louisa Gilder, *The Age of Entanglement: When Quantum Physics Was Reborn* (New York, 2008).

turbines), radar, lasers, and the earliest electronic computers. At the end of the war, the U.S. government scooped up the best German government scientists and put them to work on developing the technology to put American astronauts and nuclear missiles into space. The massive scale of the wider postwar American military-industrial complex was light-years beyond any previous effort, and contributed in great measure to a series of interrelated breakthroughs sometimes described as a *Third Industrial Revolution*: most importantly in semiconductors and biotechnology. This transition is particularly obvious in medical science, optical fiber communications, and the rise of the personal computer and the Internet, symbolized by the first public demonstration in 1968 of the computer mouse by its inventor, Douglas Engelbart.[18]

This knowledge revolution is clearly the center of the trajectory into future economies, what has been called the *Third Great Super-Cycle Expansion*. But the question remains as to when such a future economy will bear fruit for the great majority of humanity. It requires a highly educated workforce who can handle information in a post–hard technology service sector. It has not been entirely clear, until recently, that the massive investment in high technology and computers was having any real effect on productivity.[19] And the advance of the knowledge industry and economic globalization from the 1990s has helped to reconfigure the global distribution of employment and production. As the United States and the United Kingdom in particular have pursued a knowledge-based economy during the past several decades, the transfer of manufacturing to East Asia has accelerated: the United States and Europe have ceded much of basic steel-and-electricity manufacturing on the model of the Second Industrial Revolution to the emerging Asian economies.

The results have been uneven and uncertain. The developed world saw high rates of growth in GDP/capita during the long decade of the 1960s, but it has not been able to match this pace since. In the United States, it is not entirely clear that the knowledge revolution can provide enough employment for the majority of Americans who have not had adequate education and training. The result has been the emergence of a two-tier economy as the American industrial base has been eroded by the rise of East

---

[18] Joel Mokyr, *The Gifts of Athena: Historical Origins of the Knowledge Economy* (Princeton, NJ, 2002), 106; David C. Mowery and Nathan Rosenberg, "Twentieth-Century Technological Change," in Stanley L. Engerman and Robert E. Gallman, eds., *The Cambridge Economic History of the United States, Vol. III: The Twentieth Century* (New York, 2000), 818–20, 842–3, 856–7, 861–2, 886–95.

[19] Stephen D. Oliner and Daniel E. Sichel, "The Resurgence of Growth in the Late 1990s: Is Information Technology the Story?" *JEconP* 14 (2000), 3–22; Tessaleno C. Devezas, "The Growth Dynamics of the Internet and the Long Wave Theory," and Robert U. Ayres, "Unconvinced about a 5th K-Wave: A Response to Devezas, et al.," *Technological Forecasting and Social Theory* 72 (2005), 913–37.

Asian competitors and then the national embrace of a globalized economy. Household wealth and income have become much more unequal, after a trend toward equality from the 1930s to the 1960s.

One of the results of this inequality, and the failure of the United States to develop a comprehensive health care system (until the Affordable Health Care Act of 2010), has been a reversal in the trajectory of American health over the past forty years. American adult stature on average has declined, while there has been a serious increase in rates of obesity and diabetes, which may have been shaped by federal policies to increase the volume of cheaper corn syrup calories in the American diet.[20]

As important, just as the world was getting more complicated, the developed world, led by the United States, abandoned the logic of a strong national presence in structuring the economy and more generally providing a collective regulation of national purposes. The wider "neoliberal" attack on the Keynesian tradition of government, led by Ronald Reagan and Margaret Thatcher, suddenly left humanity and nature to the whims of market decisions that might possibly work in small-scale societies, but are simply inadequate in a complex global world. The global economic crisis that began in 2008 has demonstrated that the financial arm of the wider "knowledge industries" has not been performing in ways that have advanced the general well-being, and requires serious governmental management.[21]

The benefits of late-adopting high-tech industrialization and globalization are very evident in the four small Asian Tigers, South Korea, Hong Kong, Taiwan, and Singapore, where starting in the mid-1960s per capita incomes have risen to almost match those of the developed world. The enormous economies of China and India are seen presently as looming giants, and China's GDP/capita has multiplied by a factor of six since the late 1970s, when it began its drive toward capitalism under one-party rule. But the sheer scale of their populations – and regional foci of economic development – has made the rapid economic progress in China and India look less impressive, though China is on the verge of becoming the second largest economy in

---

[20] Table Be27–9: Distribution of income among taxpaying units – shares received by the top percentiles: 1913–1998; Table Be40: Distribution of household wealth: 1774–1998; Peter H. Lindert, "The Distribution of Income and Wealth," Ch. Be in Carter et al., eds., *Historical Statistics of the United States*; John Komlos and E. Benjamin Lauderdale, "The Mysterious Trend in the American Heights in the 20th Century," *Annals of Human Biology* 34 (2007), 206–15; Greg Critser, *Fat Land: How Americans Became the Fattest People in the World* (Boston, MA, 2003), 7–19; Frank B. Hu, "Diet, Nutrition, and Obesity," in Frank B. Hu, ed., *Obesity Epidemiology* (New York, 2008), 275–300.

[21] David Harvey, *A Brief History of Neoliberalism* (New York, 2005); esp. 5–38, 186–8; Richard A. Posner, *A Failure of Capitalism: The Crisis of '08 and the Descent into Depression* (Cambridge, MA, 2009), 75–116, 148–219, 252–87; Krugman, *The Return of Depression Economics and the Crisis of 2008*, 139–91.

the world, tied directly to an American market.[22] Here too the rewards are unevenly distributed, and Chinese and Indian per capita incomes are still less than a quarter of those in Western Europe. The wider Second World of developing countries, across Latin America, Africa, and much of Asia, has only the smallest and most exploitative foothold in the manufacturing economies that the prosperous global North is ceding to East Asia, much less the knowledge industries of the Third Industrial Revolution.

The history of the global economy since the 1960s again can be tracked conveniently in the energy histories of the world's regions (see Figure IV.12). Global per capita consumption of energy was actually relatively stable after rising to a peak at 1.55 tons oil equivalent in 1979, declining in the poor economies of the early 1980s and early 1990s, reaching 1.55 again in 2003, and then suddenly rising to 1.65 by 2006. On a per capita basis, the United States and Europe have been relatively stable since 1980, while Japan rose markedly between the mid-1980s and mid-1990s.

Two trends canceled each other out in this decade: while the Asian Tigers' economic growth was matched by a quadrupling of energy consumption, the collapse of the Soviet Bloc led to a severe plunge in energy consumption. Then there is the very bottom of the per capita rankings, the wider developing and least developed world. Here it is China that stands out, with a slow, steady rise in total energy consumption since the early 1980s and then a rapid spurt since 2002, accounting for the largest single number in the recent global expansion. China's growing energy consumption surpassed that of Europe in 2004, and that of the United States in 2006. Here there is a clear pattern of global transfer: the sequence of expansion of energy consumption in Japan, the Tigers, and now China is matched by the stability of moderating increase in the United States and Europe; it is a result of the migration of industry from one part of the world to another. The rise of China since 2000 is a fundamental reality of a Third Great Super-Cycle Expansion.[23]

But it is the rest of the world, Africa, Latin America, the Middle East, Southeast Asia, and India, that is particularly surprising (see Figure IV.12). As a group, these regions barely register the slightest of increases in per capita energy consumption. But if we look at total consumption, the picture is rather different. Over the entire period since 1979, and as far back as 1965, total energy consumption has risen in these Third World regions more rapidly than anywhere else. In 1979, these regions consumed less than half that of the United States. In 1994, they surpassed the energy consumption of the United States, and have continued to rise in the years since, now taking over the dubious position of the leading consumer of energy in the world. But

---

[22] Michael Wines and Edward Wong, "China Takes Stage as World Economic Power, but Its Transformation Is Incomplete," *NYT*, April 2, 2009, A12.

[23] Lyons, *The Super-Cycle Report*.

neither the United States nor the Third World has seen any notable changes in per capita consumption in the past decade. While increasing energy consumption in East Asia has been driven by the transfer of industrial function from the United States and Europe, the rising energy consumption in the Third World has not resulted in a general rise in national incomes, but is driven by growing and increasingly urban populations, combined with the energy intensity of inefficient technologies.[24]

Overall, the basic story of the past sixty years is of significantly rising per capita wealth in the developed Western world, joined by the four Asian Tigers. The former Soviet Bloc countries did well into the mid-1970s and then crashed with the end of communist rule in 1989; the Second World rose gradually, with the least developed countries simply showing little or no signs of improving GNP/population. While summary statistics of the global economy suggest a global pattern of unprecedented growth, there is a very dark lining to this silver cloud.

First, this growth slowed during the 1970s and has not advanced at a comparable pace since. Second, the global statistics mask an accelerating divergence between haves and have-nots. There is clearly a severe economic divergence between a rich North and a poor South, if complicated by the rising manufacturing economies of China and India. New "Third Super-Cycle" technologies like microchips, optical fibers, photovoltaics, and bio-medicine, pointing toward a "space-age future," coexist in a global economy with near-barter-based systems rife with corruption. While the significant decline of mortality and the signs of a general controlling of fertility seem to point to a demographic convergence in the coming decades, the enormous demographic expansion has left large populations with very limited economic prospects.

The prospects for the coming century are grim, because these least developed countries will be the last to finish the demographic transition, and are projected to grow in population by more than 60 percent in the next two decades, compared with about 35 percent for the Second World, 11 percent for China, and about 7 percent for the developed world (including the four Asian Tigers), while the population of the former Soviet Bloc is expected to actually decline.[25] If convergences in demographic regime and scale of urbanization can be projected for the near future, such a convergence in economic well-being is far more problematic, particularly in the present climate of global depression launched by the 2008 financial crisis, in which rising food costs pushed an already growing number who eat a near

[24] Elizabeth Rosenthal, "In Poor Cities Buses May Aid Climate Battle," *NYT*, July 10, 2009, A1.

[25] Angus Maddison, "Historical Statistics of the World Economy: 1–2008 AD," March 2010 data file at http://www.ggdc.net/maddison/Maddison.htm, accessed August 8, 2012. UN categories revised.

starvation diet of fewer than 1,800 calories a day up to an estimated 1.02 billion, roughly 15 percent of the world's population.[26] Oil prices quadrupled from about $30 to $130 per barrel between 2002 and 2008, and then crashed with the 2008 economic downturn. But by early 2011 they were up to essentially their 2008 peak at $120 per barrel, and when the global economy expands again, the limitation on the supply of oil versus a massively expanding demand will again become obvious.

* * *

Environmental Impacts, 1945 to Present: Confronting the Third Wave

This, of course, is an account defined by gross national product of goods and services, and assumes some necessary relationship between that measure and the long-term well-being of a people. It has become increasingly apparent, however, that this assumption may not be sustainable. The technologies of the First and Second Industrial Revolutions were aimed in great measure at solving the problems of the hazards of public health of a traditional agrarian society becoming urban. But they launched second and third waves of environmental hazards, operating at the regional and global levels of the earth system, and – in some measure – at macroscopic and molecular pathways in the biosphere and atmosphere. Developed nations have by and large come to confront regional environmental impacts, if not without a political struggle, because mitigation of these impacts requires accounting for the cost of "free disposal" of wastes into the earth system. Coming to terms with the reality and potential consequences of the global impacts for which they are responsible has been an even more profound struggle, because the evidence is less immediately visible and the economic costs even higher. But while the developed world has had a century and half to mitigate the first two waves of human-created environmental hazard, all three patterns of environmental hazard – preindustrial, industrializing, and global – are hitting the peoples of the developing world simultaneously.

Environmental mitigation has its roots in the postwar years. The great London smog inversion of December 1952 set in motion serious legislation to restrict domestic and urban coal burning in Great Britain, shifting the burden of heating to natural gas-fired electricity, but marking an important step in the assertion of public, governmental authority over the most obvious, visible environmental impacts. In the United States, such efforts to control urban pollution had been under way for decades, but it would be the dramatic images of the Santa Barbara oil spills and the burning of the Cuyahoga River in Cleveland in 1969 that grabbed national attention and

---

[26] "UN: World Hunger Reaches 1 Billion Mark," Associated Press, June 19, 2009.

led to the first Earth Day and the establishing of the federal Environmental Protection Agency in 1970.[27]

In broad segments of the global public, anxieties about the threats posed by industrial technology had already taken new and more complex forms. The atomic destruction of Hiroshima and Nagasaki in the summer of 1945 became the catalyst for a new genre of popular culture, starting with the movie *Godzilla* in 1954, in which a monstrous dragon-dinosaur emerges from the sea floor, transformed by nuclear irradiation. American mothers had their own Godzilla moment in the late 1950s, when it became known that fallout from open-air nuclear testing was depositing radioactive strontium-90 into the food supply – and breast milk – all across North America. These fears deepened after the publication of Rachel Carson's 1962 *Silent Spring*, which dramatized the molecular biological impacts of DDT and other pesticides. The ensuing outrage launched political movements that led to national and international legislation, but also to a growing sensitivity to ways industrial waste of all kinds was entering hidden systemic pathways in the biosphere, and threatening the health of humanity. Lead poisoning in children had been a concern since the 1930s, but in the 1960s, attention turned to the lead additives in gasoline, which were strictly controlled in the United States starting with the 1970 Clean Air Act; Japan, suffering even worse conditions, followed suit.[28] During the 1970s, attention began to focus on acid rain, one of the by-products of the sulfur dioxide produced by coal combustion. Coal burning in the American Midwest, in northern Europe, and recently China, sends plumes of sulfur dioxide to the east, depositing acid in rainfall that corrodes buildings, kills mountain spruce forests, and destroys the delicate ecology of upland streams and lakes. Between the mid-1970s and the 1980s, national laws and international agreements began to reduce the level of sulfur emissions (as did the collapse of the environmentally dirty Soviet economy after 1989); by 2002, the global annual sulfur emission level had been cut by roughly 20 percent, with important unforeseen consequences[29] (see Figure IV.14).

[27] Peter Thorsheim, *Inventing Pollution: Coal, Smoke and Culture in Britain since 1800* (Athens, OH, 2006), 153–92; Joachim Radkau, *Nature and Power: A Global History of the Environment* (New York, 2008), 236–7; Joel A. Tarr and Robert U. Ayres, "The Hudson-Raritan Basin," in Turner et al., *The Earth as Transformed by Human Action*, 621–52.

[28] William M. Tsutsui, *Godzilla on My Mind: Fifty Years of the King of Monsters* (New York, 2003), 14–20; Terrence Rafferty, "The Monster that Morphed into a Metaphor," *NYT*, May 2, 2004; Adam Rome, "'Give Earth a Chance': The Environmental Movement and the Sixties," *AHR* 90 (2003), 525–54; Amy Swerdlow, *Women Strike for Peace: Traditional Motherhood and Radical Politics in the 1960s* (Chicago, IL, 1993), 80–7; Hal K. Rothman, *The Greening of a Nation? Environmentalism in the United States since 1945* (Fort Worth, TX, 1998), 83–134; Kirkpatrick Sale, *The Green Revolution: The American Environmental Movement, 1962–1992* (New York, 1993), 3–28; John Opie, *Nature's Nation: An Environmental History of the United States* (Fort Worth, TX, 1998), 404–63; McNeill, *Something New under the Sun*, 92–9.

[29] McNeill, *Something New under the Sun*, 99–102; S. J. Smith et al., "Anthropogenic Sulfur Dioxide Emissions: 1850–2005," *Atmospheric Chemistry and Physics* 11 (2011), 1101–16;

Thus, by the 1960s and 1970s, there was an emerging understanding that industrial economies were having not just local and regional impacts that were observable to the naked eye, but unseen impacts that were reaching into the very workings of the earth system. Some of these global systemic impacts were obvious and macroscopic, and a direct threat to human life. For centuries, an increasingly interconnected global economy had intentionally and unintentionally been moving biotic species between the continents, and during the last decades of the twentieth century, the threat of invasive species began to loom larger than just flocks of starlings and English sparrows. Invasive microbes and insects have destroyed the American chestnut and the American elm and threaten the ash and maple populations; zebra mussels coat shipping in the Great Lakes, while honeysuckle, purple loosestrife, and the kudzu vine clog woods, fields, and streams, overwhelming native species; other invasive species threaten the natural food chains throughout the world.[30] More important, rapid globalized human travel permitted by air transport has made every local outbreak of a new disease – typically crossing the animal-human boundary in a remote tropical location – a worldwide threat. Various influenzas erupt annually from the large pig and bird populations in south China to sweep the world. Some more serious emerging diseases – Ebola, SARs, West Nile Fever, and the H_1N_1 influenza virus – seem to have been contained. But HIV/AIDS has only been partially contained – in effect managed –and it has taken a massive toll on countries too poor to finance effective medical intervention. If it might have peaked, AIDS has devastated parts of southern and central Africa, and had the potential to have been the Black Death of the late twentieth century; wider catastrophic epidemics have been averted only by intense efforts of medical science.[31]

Other globalized threats are more subtle, but perhaps even more equally potent in the popular consciousness. Concerns about the threat of nuclear war and the safety of nuclear power plants and nuclear waste, both of which threatened to irradiate the planet for millennia to come, became the focus of worldwide protest even before the meltdowns at Three Mile Island and Chernobyl in 1979 and 1986 and President Reagan's decision to station tactical nuclear missiles in Europe in 1983. The costs of nuclear energy were already cooling investment. The result has been the stalling of new nuclear power generation in most countries for decades.[32] Similar major concerns emerged regarding the direct results of mid-century chemical innovations

---

D. I. Stern, "Global Sulfur Emissions from 1850 to 2000," *Chemosphere* 58 (2005), 163–75.

[30] See the National Invasive Species Information Center Web site, http://www.invasivespecies-info.gov/index.shtml (accessed August 8, 2012).

[31] UNAIDS, *Report on the Global AIDS Epidemic 2008*, 96–185; Bongaarts et al., "Has the HIV Epidemic Peaked?"

[32] McNeill, *Something New under the Sun*, 341–4; Sale, *The Green Revolution*, 57–60; Ramachandra Guha, *Environmentalism: A Global History* (New York, 2000), 90–1.

flowing out of the Second Industrial Revolution, specifically the impact of chlorofluorocarbons (CFCs) and polychlorinated biphenyls (PCBs), developed in the 1920s and 1930s as coolants in refrigerators, air conditioners, and transformers. First proposed in the 1970s, it was proved in 1985 that CFCs were eroding the stratospheric ozone layer, a protective shield that filters harmful ultraviolet solar radiation. Popular boycotts in the 1970s and the Montreal Protocol of 1987 first curtailed and then almost totally eliminated the emission of CFCs, in one of the most striking success stories of the modern environmental movement.[33]

By the time the Montreal Protocol was signed in 1987, the question of climate change and global warming induced by industrial emissions had been a serious subject of scientific debate and inquiry for fifteen years. With the heat wave of 1988 the question burst into public debate; by the time the public was beginning to be convinced by former Vice President Al Gore's 2006 movie *An Inconvenient Truth*, the reality that human economies were driving climate change was a solidly established consensus among scientists of a wide variety of specialties.[34]

Three sorts of evidence shape the argument for human impacts on global climate: measures of global temperature, measures of the quantities of atmospheric greenhouse gases, and measures of industrial emissions from countries and regions of the world, which must be balanced against the naturally occurring sources of greenhouse gases. All of these are approximations, but they have been subjected to critique, testing, and replication, and stand as a broad consensus and progressive refinement.

The first of these measures are those that estimate global and regional temperature over the long term. A number of related studies indicate that the twentieth century has seen warmer average temperature than any time in the past two millennia. Even more striking, a recent synthesis of evidence from around the Arctic Circle demonstrates that far northern temperatures had been cooling on a long, slow descent leading toward an eventual glaciation, only to be interrupted around 1870 in a warming that accelerated after 1900. It seems likely that this evidence can be squared with William Ruddiman's thesis: if whiffs of greenhouse gases emitted by emerging

---

[33] McNeill, *Something New under the Sun*, 111–15; Guus J. M. Velders et al., "The Importance of the Montreal Protocol in Protecting Climate," *PNAS* 104 (2007), 4814–19; Piers Forster and Venkatachalam Ramaswamy et al., "Chapter 2: Changes in Atmospheric Constituents and in Radiative Forcing," in Susan Solomon et al., eds., *Climate Change 2007: Contribution of Working Group I to the Fourth Assessment Report of the Intergovernmental Panel on Climate Change* (Cambridge, 2007), 145–62.

[34] Spencer R. Weart, *The Discovery of Global Warming* (Cambridge, MA, 2003), 142–92. Gore first put his concerns, developing since his undergraduate years in the 1960s, in print in *Earth in Balance: Ecology and the Human Spirit* (New York, 1993). On the wider political economy of climate change denial, see Weart, *The Discovery of Global Warming*, 166–7; George Monbiot, *Heat: How to Stop the Planet from Burning* (Cambridge, MA, 2007), 20–42.

agriculture since 3000 BC slowed a descent into a glaciation, this evidence strongly suggests that this slow descent was sharply reversed toward warming around 1870. Indeed, a careful review of temperature proxies running back to the beginning of the Holocene suggests that warming during the twentieth century has offset the total cooling that has occurred since the end of the Mid-Holocene Crisis, 5,000 years ago.[35]

Then there are the more direct estimates of temperature, records of instrumental reading. The oldest is the most limited in geographic scope: the series of instrumental temperature readings assembled for central England since 1659. For the twentieth century, these reading show a gradual climb from a late nineteenth-century cold spell from the 1890s to roughly 1940, then a stability and even cooling to the mid-1980s, followed by a sharp rise in temperature. Large-scale studies of global instrumental temperature readings covering the period since 1850 and 1880 show virtually the same pattern: two troughs of cool temperatures around 1890 and 1910, followed by a three-decade rise to 1940, then three and a half decades of stability and even slight cooling to roughly 1975, followed by distinct and continuous warming to the present.[36]

---

[35] Timothy J. Osborn and Keith R. Briffa, "The Spacial Extent of 20th-Century Warmth in the Context of the Past 12000 Years," *Science* 311 (2006), 841–4; Michael E. Mann et al., "Proxy-Based Reconstructions of Hemispheric and Global Surface Temperature Variations over the Past Two Millennia," *PNAS* 105 (2008), 13252–7; Darrell S. Kaufman et al., "Recent Warming Reverses Long-Term Arctic Cooling," *Science* 325 (2009), 1236–9. See also M. E. Mann et al., "Global-Scale Temperature Patterns and Climate Forcing over the Past Six Centuries," *Nature* 392 (1998), 779–87; Jan Esper et al., "Low-Frequency Signals in Long Tree-Ring Chronologies for Reconstructing Past Temperature Variability," *Science* 295 (2002), 2250–3; Anders Moberg et al., "Highly Variable Northern Hemisphere Temperature Reconstructed from Low- and High-Resolution Proxy Data," *Nature* 433 (2005), 613–17; Thomas M. Smith and Richard W. Reynolds, "A Global Merged Land-Air-Sea Surface Temperature Reconstruction Based in Historical Observations (1880–1997)," *JClim* 18 (2005), 2021–36; Eugene R. Wahl and Caspar M. Amman, "Robustness of the Mann, Bradley, and Hughes Reconstruction of Northern Hemisphere Surface Temperatures: Examination of Criticisms Based on the Nature and Processing of Proxy Climate Evidence," *Climate Change* 85 (2007) 33–69; E. Zorita et al., "How Unusual is the Recent Series of Warm Years?" *GRL* 35 (2008), L24706, 1–6; Shaun A. Marcott et al., "A Reconstruction of Regional and Global Temperature for the Past 11,300 Years," *Science* 339 (2013), 1198–1201. On the Ruddiman thesis, see Chapter 6, note 44.

[36] G. Manley, "Central England Temperature: Monthly Means 1659–1973," *Quarterly Journal of the Royal Meteorological Society* 100 (1974), 389–405; D. E. Parker et al., "A New Daily Central England Temperature Series," *IJC* 12 (1992), 317–42; David Parker and Briony Horton, "Uncertainties in Central England Temperature, 1878–2003 and some Improvements to the Maximum and Minimum Series," *IJC* 25 (2005), 1173–88; P. Brohan et al., "Uncertainty Estimates in Regional and Global Observed Temperature Changes: A New Dataset from 1850," *JGR* 111 (2006), D12106; James Hansen et al., "Global Temperature Change," *PNAS* 103 (2006), 14288–93. See also Kevin E. Trenberth and Philip D. Jones et al., "Chapter 3: Observations: Surface and Atmospheric Climate Change," in *Climate Change 2007: The Physical Science Basis*, 241–54, and figure 6.10, *Climate Change 2007:*

This twentieth-century rise in temperature has roughly tracked the dramatic rise in the volume of greenhouse gases (see Figure IV.3, IV.14). CO_2 had reached 295 ppm by the 1890s, only 10–15 ppm more than the preindustrial norm, and to 310 ppm as of World War II: since 1945, it has surged to 385 ppm, and shows no sign of slowing. Methane had reached 850 ppb as of 1900, about 150 ppb more than its Holocene norm; by World War II, it reached roughly 1125 ppm, and stands now at 1,750 ppm, though its rate of increase has slowed somewhat in the past twenty-five years. Nitrous oxide, a third major greenhouse gas associated with both agricultural and industrial activity, may actually have started its rise during the eighteenth century, accelerated after 1800, and then surged after 1945. CFCs, an important greenhouse gas, similarly grew steeply during the mid-twentieth century, but then tapered off after the boycotts and international agreement of 1974–87.

A general consensus exists that there has been a general cause-and-effect relationship between the rise in greenhouse gases and the rise in global temperature, both unprecedented in human history. But the story is more complex than a simple one-to-one relationship. For one thing, temperature does not follow directly the simple, practically exponential curve of rising greenhouse gases, but has increased in two periods, between 1910 and 1940, and since 1975. Explaining this step-wise increase in global temperature, and the wider dimensions of modern global climate change, requires consideration of all the factors involved: there are both positive (warming) and negative (cooling) forcings – forcings of both human and natural origin – and the various gases have different persistence rates in the atmosphere. Radiative forcing values – any solar or climatic influence that affects the warmth of the earth – are expressed in watts per square meter on the top of the earth's atmosphere. There are of course background forcing values that maintain the planet's "typical" Holocene temperature, solar radiation and the various

The Physical Science Basis. One small complication regarding the 1940s emerged recently, however. The global temperature data calculations suggested a peak of temperatures between 1940 and 1945, followed by a sharp drop, the largest in the record for the past century. Closer examination of the sources of data, however, suggests that the entire peak in the 1940s might have been a product of different measurement procedures. Before and after the war, Royal Navy vessels provided most of the sea surface temperatures from water retrieved from buckets; during the war, there was a surge of measurements taken by the U.S. Navy via engine intake valves. The U. S. engine room measurements seem to have been significantly warmer than the British bucket measurements, so a considerable portion of the bubble of higher global temperatures during the Second World War may be a statistical mirage. The data has been recalculated for these potential biases, and this new data is used here. See David W. J. Thompson et al., "A Large Discontinuity in the Mid-Twentieth Century in Observed Global-Mean Surface Temperature," *Nature* 453 (2008), 646–9, and the recalculations and discussion in J. J. Kennedy et al., "Reassessing Biases and other Uncertainties in Sea Surface Temperature Observations Measured In Situ since 1850: 1. Measurement and Sampling Uncertainties," and "2. Biases and Homogenization," *JGR* 116 (2011), D14103–4; and P. D. Jones et al., "Hemispheric and Large-Scale Land-Surface Air Temperature Variations: An Extensive Revision and an Update to 2010," *JGR* 117 (2012), D05127.

naturally occurring greenhouse gases such as CO_2 and methane. The analysis of modern climate change measures the forcings that make modern global temperatures deviate from this background norm, generally taken to be 1750, during the eighteenth-century optimum following the worst of the Little Ice Age.

The natural forcings have been discussed throughout this book: increases in solar activity are positive forcings (and decreases obviously negative); volcanic sulfur dioxide converted to sulfate aerosols is a negative forcing, because it blocks solar radiation, either directly as a component of the atmosphere or indirectly as it encourages cloud formation.[37] Volcanic cooling is transitory, because the eruption is generally a single event; when Mt. Pinatubo erupted in the Philippines in 1991, its cooling effect (- W/m²) lasted about two years. The human-derived positive forcings include carbon dioxide (CO_2), methane (CH_4), nitrous oxide (N_2O), chlorofluorocarbons (CFCs), and other chemicals. Other positive factors include increased ozone (O_3) generated by the chemical reaction of some of these compounds in the troposphere, and decreased ozone in the stratosphere – the "ozone hole" caused by CFCs and other manmade chemicals. In addition, climate scientists increasingly recognize that black soot particles from burning fossil fuels and biomass play an important role in positive forcing of the global climate. On the other hand, human inputs also include a very significant negative forcing, the sulfate aerosols that are another by-product of burning fossil fuels. In addition, the clearing of northern forests – reducing the albedo effect – has a cooling effect as well. NASA's leading atmospheric scientist, James Hansen, weighs the relative positive and negative forcings as follows:

	Watts/Square Meter		Persistence in the Atmosphere
	Positive	Negative	
CO_2	1.50		variable → centuries
CH_4	.55		10–100 years
CFCs	.37		10–100 years
N_2O	.15		10–100 years
Ozone	.40	-.06	weeks to years
Black Carbon Soot	.80		hours to days
Sulfate Aerosols		-2.1	hours to days
Land Use		-.15	
	--------	----------	
Anthropogenic Total:	+3.77	-2.31	= + 1.46
Solar	.3	Volcanic?	= < +.3

[37] This summary is informed by Forster and Ramaswamy et al., "Changes in Atmospheric Constituents and in Radiative Forcing," 131–234; James Hansen et al., "The Efficacy of Climate Forcings," *JGR* 110 (2005), D18104; A. Robertson et al., "Hypothesized Climate Forcing Time Series for the Last 500 Years," *JGR* 106 (2001), 14783–803.

The 2007 IPCC report comes to essentially the same conclusions about the sources of global warming over the past century: human influences have far outstripped natural forces.[38] Solar influence since roughly 1920 is stronger than it was during the Medieval Warm Period, but there have been far more volcanic events during the twentieth century than during the tenth and eleventh centuries, and the absence of eruptions may have been as important as solar irradiance in shaping the Medieval Warm Period. But natural forcings of solar warming and volcanic cooling may well have almost canceled each other out during the twentieth century, leaving human influences to explain the major part of the modern warming.[39]

Over the course of the twentieth century, CO_2 and methane emissions comprised the majority of human contributions to greenhouse warming. In the Second Great Super-Cycle Expansion that followed World War II, both land use and fossil fuel emissions surged upward. Land use emissions – amazingly enough – continued to exceed industrial emissions until roughly 1960; CO_2 from forest clearance and farming surged upward until about 1958; methane emissions rose sharply around 1945 and maintained a strong rate of increase. But the great transition came in energy consumption and fossil fuel emissions, which staggered irregularly upward during the depression and war years, but during the years of boom growth between 1945 and the 1970s shot upward, more than tripling, tracking energy consumption region by region, modulated by technological efficiency (see Figure IV.12, IV.13). The least efficient regions were the United States and the Third World, one because of its deep and dense commitment to high-energy intensity, the other because of its poverty. The most efficient region has been the most recently industrialized, the Asian Tiger countries. But the fundamental story of energy consumption in these boom years was the United States. The United States was the largest regional (and certainly national, by far) energy consumer during these decades, exceeding all of Europe in 1940, to be topped briefly by the Soviet Bloc in the 1980s, the non-Chinese developing world in the

---

[38] Hansen et al., "The Efficacy of Climate Forcings," 40; Forster and Ramaswamy et al., "Changes in Atmospheric Constituents and in Radiative Forcing," 136, 141, 200–9; atmospheric persistence from 203, 213–14, and most recently Re. Benestad and G. A. Schmidt, "Solar Trends and Global Warming," *JGR* 114 (2009), D14101.

[39] Here see Simon F. B. Tett et al., "Causes of Twentieth-Century Temperature Change near the Earth's Surface," *Nature* 399 (1999), 569–72; Thomas J. Crowley, "Causes of Climate Change over the Past 1000 Years," *Science* 289 (2000), 270–7, esp. figures 3a, 6; T. C. Johns, "Anthropogenic Climate Change from 1860 to 2100 Simulated with the HadCM3 Model under Updated Emissions Scenarios," *ClimDyn* 20 (2003), 583–612; Gabrielle C. Hegerle et al., "Detection of Human Influence on a New, Validated 1500-Year Temperature Reconstruction," *JClim* 20 (2007), 650–66; Smith and Reynolds, "A Global Merged Land Air and Sea Surface Temperature Reconstruction"; Hansen et al., "The Efficacy of Climate Forcings"; Hansen et al., "Global Temperature Change"; Simon F. Tett et al., "The Impact of Natural and Anthropogenic Forcings on Climate and Hydrology since 1550," *ClimDyn* 28 (2007); Zorita et al., "How Unusual is the Recent Series of Warm Years?"

1990s, and China itself in 2005. If on a per capita basis the United States may not have increased as dramatically as other regions, it maintained much of the enormous lead that it had established in the early twentieth century in energy and emissions. Thus in 2010 the average American emitted five times as much CO_2 as all other people combined, down from a peak ratio of seventeen to one in 1920 and more than eleven to one in 1950.[40]

The end result was a skyrocketing level of atmospheric CO_2 and methane. In 1945, atmospheric CO_2 plateaued at about 310 ppm, twenty-five points above the preindustrial norm, and by 1958, when the daily/monthly measurements started at Mauna Loa in Hawaii, it had climbed another five points. Fifty years later, it stands at 396, and is still climbing. Thus during the century after the introduction of the stationary high-pressure steam engine, CO_2 reading rose about twenty-five points; during the next half century it rose seventy points. Thus the pattern holds; expanding population, industrialization, and greenhouse emissions has in a single lifetime resulted in a totally transformed world.

But there is something of a paradox in these figures; the three postwar decades saw not only the massive expansion of greenhouse emissions and atmospheric gases, but a *stabilization* of global temperatures. This bears repeating: between 1945 and the 1970s, economic emissions and atmospheric greenhouse gases grew sharply, but temperature was stable. Equally paradoxically, temperature increased in the First Great Interruption between 1910 and 1940, when economies and emissions contracted or expanded only erratically, and then this pattern repeated itself during the 1980s and 1990s, when economies and emissions rates faltered, and temperature increased sharply. The answer to this paradox is *not* that there is no relationship between emissions and temperatures, but that this relationship is set in a more complex system, including natural forcings, *variable* persistence rates, and the *negative* forcing of industrial sulfur.

Solar influence was significant during the twentieth century, but ultimately the role of sulfate aerosols was probably more important. Sulfur dioxide, whether from volcanoes or smokestacks, is chemically converted in the troposphere to sulfate aerosols, which either reflect solar radiation directly, or by contributing to cloud formation. Either way, they serve as a potent negative forcing in the global greenhouse system. But they do not last long in the atmosphere, and thus need constant replenishment. Volcanic eruptions are ultimately limited in time and within months to years the cooling effects of even the biggest eruptions are washed out. Fossil fuel burning, most importantly in coal plants, over the past century has pushed a relatively constant and growing volume of sulfur dioxide into the atmosphere – like a series of constantly erupting volcanoes. The result has been a negative

---

[40] Michael R. Raupach et al., "Global and Regional Drivers of Accelerating CO_2 Emissions," *PNAS* 104 (2007), 10288–93.

forcing somewhat offsetting the positive forcing of CO_2, methane, and other anthropogenic greenhouse gases. By the end of the nineteenth century, this cooling was already apparent in a series of bands running east from the major industrial centers around the North Atlantic. Over the course of the twentieth century, this effect has become much stronger, forming a band of cooling that encompasses the entire northern hemisphere from the United States east across the North Atlantic through Eurasia and China to the northeast Pacific.[41]

This is the first of two key dimensions of variable sulfate distribution. The first is geographic and the second chronological (see Figures IV.9b, IV.14). Geographically, industrial sulfur dioxide emissions and resulting sulfate aerosols have *cooled the northern hemisphere*, the hemisphere that is responsible for the majority of the overall fossil emissions that are warming the earth; conversely, the nonindustrialized tropics are exposed to the brunt of the growing global warmth and little of the cooling influence of sulfate aerosols. But fossil fuel sulfur emissions have varied through time as well, mapping both the expansion and contraction of the global economy *and* the late twentieth-century efforts to control the worst of industrialized pollution. Here efforts to contain regional environmental impacts have released the underlying potential for serious global environmental impacts. It would appear that the two stages of rising temperatures in the twentieth century have involved different combinations of three basic conditions: increasing solar radiation, the expanding and persistent volume of greenhouse gases, and the intermittent expansion and contraction of more volatile sulfate aerosols. Quite simply, greenhouse gases have provided the consistent positive forcing, but they have been masked by the negative forcing of sulfate aerosols during periods of economic expansion. During periods of economic contraction, political collapse, and the onset of aggressive national and international efforts to clean up air pollution, the cooling mask slipped away slightly while greenhouse gases have continued to rise, and temperatures jumped dramatically.[42]

* * *

[41] Tett et al., "The Impact of Natural and Anthropogenic Forcings," 27.

[42] The role of sulfate aerosols in climate change has been under consideration since T. M. L. Wigley, "Could Reducing Fossil-Fuel Emissions Cause Global Warming?" *Nature* 349 (1991), 503–6, and Robert J. Charlson and Tom L. J. Wigley, "Sulfate Aerosol and Climatic Change," *SA* (Feb. 1994), 48–57. More recently, see J. F. B. Mitchell and T. C. Johns, "On Modification of Global Warming by Sulfate Aerosols," *JClim* 10 (1997), 245–67; K. D. Williams et al., "The Response of the Climate System to the Indirect Effects of Anthropogenic Sulfate Aerosol," *ClimDyn* 17 (2001), 845–56; Forster and Ramaswamy et al., "Changes in Atmospheric Constituents and in Radiative Forcing," 160–1; Tett et al., "The Impact of Natural and Anthropogenic Forcings," 22–9; and the extensive overview in Martin Wild, "Global Dimming and Brightening: A Review," *JGR* 114 (2009), D00D16, esp. 13–17.

The Modern Anthropocene

At this juncture it is worth reviewing the entire sweep of modern climate history in terms of seven phases, stretching perhaps from the Bronze Age – certainly the Little Ice Age – to the present. The first four have been discussed at length in the previous two chapters, the next three in this chapter (see Figure IV.14).

The first phase can be seen as the primal agrarian condition, as described by William Ruddiman, beginning at the opening of the Bronze Age and accelerating with the expansion of the Chinese population during the eighteenth century. Here the leading anthropogenic greenhouse gas was methane from rice agriculture. The second phase began during the 1840s and 1850s; if it saw faint whiffs of early industrial emissions, it was dominated by CO_2 emissions from the clearing of forested and prairie land across the North American continent, by David Potter's "people of plenty." In both of these periods, it is difficult to see the decadal trajectories in global climates as being affected more than minimally by these anthropogenic forcings; rather, the recovery from the Dalton Minimum and then the cold spells that marked the beginning and the end of the nineteenth century were clearly shaped by solar variation and volcanic activity.

In the third phase, between 1880 and 1910 – the First Great Super-Cycle Expansion (the Second Industrial Revolution) – the dramatic increase in greenhouse emissions was masked somewhat by solar decline and volcanic eruptions that were strong cooling influences, and by industrial sulfate emissions, which tracked and masked the rising CO_2 emissions of this period. The result here was a continuation of the late nineteenth-century cooling to around 1910, though it would appear that temperatures were higher than the estimated solar input might have predicted, compared to the previous century and a half. Thus there is the suggestion here that the expansion of greenhouse gases with the Second Industrial Revolution did begin to have a distinct stabilizing – if not quite warming – influence.

The fourth period, the First Great Interruption of 1910 to 1950, saw the reverse of most of these conditions, and the first of two significant warmings of global temperature. Solar irradiance increased significantly, and volcanic eruptions were minimal, but in addition industrial sulfates faltered, while CO_2 emissions were irregular, though there was a significant load established during the previous period. Careful studies suggest that the warming during the First Great Interruption was caused by a dynamic relationship between all of these factors with the natural positive forcings dominating: solar input must have been important, but reduced sulfate aerosols and the established if erratically growing greenhouse gases must have played a significant role.[43]

---

[43] T. M. L. Wigley, "The Observed Global Warming Record: What Does It Tell Us?" *PNAS* 94 (1997), 8314–20; P. A. Stott et al., "External Control of 20th Century Temperature by

The fifth phase was the Second Great Super-Cycle Expansion of the 1950s to the 1970s. Solar input was high, perhaps at a peak, and there were relatively few volcanic eruptions, so temperatures should have risen substantially. But they did not, but remained stable or declined slightly, the result – it is very clear – of the cross-pressures of positive and negative anthropogenic forcings. On one hand, greenhouse gases of all kinds – mostly from industrial sources in the United States, Europe, and the Soviet Bloc – surged into the atmosphere, again putting a positive pressure on global temperature. But these – and the positive forcing of an increased solar influence – were offset by the strong countervailing negative forcing of the great burst of sulfate aerosols that arose from the same industrial combustion. The result was a temperature impasse, and relatively stable-to-cooling temperatures through the early 1970s.

Then, over the next twenty-five years, in a sixth phase – the Second Great Interruption from the 1970s – conditions shifted again, with increasingly warmer global temperatures that have only intensified during the past decade. Solar influence was relatively high, but was stable and perhaps declining slightly. It was counterbalanced by the negative cooling effects of a series of strong volcanic eruptions like Mt. St. Helens and Mt. Pinatubo. Because of the series of economic recessions during these decades – and perhaps the beginning of significant energy efficiencies – global emissions of greenhouse gases rose considerably more slowly than they had during the postwar decades, which might have taken the pressure off the global system somewhat. But there was a huge volume of long-lived CO_2 in the atmosphere already. The key shift was the roughly 20 percent decline in the volume of sulfate emissions between 1979 and 2002, shaped by the collapse of the Soviet Bloc and the onset of serious air pollution controls in the United States, Europe, and Japan.[44] The drop in sulfate aerosols combined with the high standing volume of greenhouse gases can be the only explanation for the dramatic warming that has occurred since 1975, though the erosion of the stratospheric ozone layer by CFCs may also have contributed to the warming. On the other hand, there was some good news: the reduction in the rate of increase of CFCs by boycott and international treaty began to reduce the growth of some very potent greenhouse gases, as has the surprising slowing and stabilizing of methane emissions.[45]

Natural and Anthropogenic Forcings," *Science* 290 (2000), 2133–7; Gerald A. Meehl et al., "Solar and Greenhouse Gas Forcing and Climate Response in the Twentieth Century," *JClim* 16 (2003), 426–44; Thomas L. Delworth and Thomas R. Knutson, "Simulations of Early 20th Century Global Warming," *Science* 287 (2000), 2246–50; Tett et al., "Causes of Twentieth-Century Temperature Change."

[44] S. J. Smith et al., "Anthropogenic Sulfur Dioxide Emissions: 1850–2005," *Atmospheric Chemistry and Physics* 11 (2011), 1101–16; D. I. Stern, "Global Sulfur Emissions from 1850 to 2000," *Chemosphere* 58 (2005), 163–75. See discussion in Forster and Ramaswamy et al., "Changes in Atmospheric Constituents and in Radiative Forcing," 160–1.

[45] Velders et al., "The Importance of the Montreal Protocol"; M. Aslam Kahn Khalil et al., "Atmospheric Methane: Trends and Cycles of Sources and Sinks," *EnvSciTech* 41 (2007), 2131–7.

The seventh phase, the decade following the turn of the millennium, in what might be the beginning of the Third Great Super-Cycle Expansion, may replicate the pattern of the second super-cycle. (If so its energy/emissions history has already been notched by the impact of the worst of the 2008 recession (see Figures IV.12, IV.13). China has become a major source of emissions while the United States and Europe are stabilized, though at high levels. Both CO_2 and sulfur emissions are rising sharply again, and the effect of one may mask the other; once again: sulfur cooling seems to be cancelling out CO_2 warming, explaining why there has been an abatement in overall warming during the past decade.[46]

These phases of modern climate change obviously had their impacts on the wider global system, marked by a transition from natural to increasing anthropogenic influence. I have argued that, in the intervals between the great Millennial Siberian Highs, the Holocene global climate pattern centers on the oscillation of warming and cooling in the northern hemisphere, shaped by solar inputs, volcanic variation, and probably small shifts in thermohaline circulation in the North Atlantic. With a warm north, the Intertropical Convergence Zone has typically been pulled north, but a cooling north would allow the ITCZ to drift south, or may indeed push it south. Generally, with the ITCZ pulled toward a warm north, the Asian monsoon systems running west from the Western Pacific Warm Pool have been strong, while the El Niño phase of the Southern Oscillation has been weak. After the end of the Little Ice Age – the Fourth Siberian High – the El Niño systems followed the warming and cooling of the North Atlantic, and presumably the north-south oscillation of the ITCZ.

Reasonably typical Holocene patterns persisted into the early twentieth century (see Figure IV.14). Warming global and northern temperatures in the 1850s to the 1860s matched a trough in El Niño activity. A cooler northern hemisphere from the late 1860s to the 1890s seems to have been part of the system that fed the strong El Niños of these decades, and apparently the sporadic failure of Asian and West African monsoons. Throughout the First Great Super-Cycle Expansion (the Second Industrial Revolution) from the 1870s to the 1910s, solar input declined and global temperatures cooled; all of these factors seem to have been pretty typical of the natural Holocene system, which may have been operating coherently for the last time, despite the growing levels of human emissions.

Then during the First Great Interruption of 1910–45, the world wars and the Depression, temperature rose significantly. A warmer northern

---

[46] Robert K. Kaufman, "Reconciling Anthropogenic Climate Change with Observed Temperature 1998–2008," *PNAS* 108 (2011), 11790–3. An alternative explanation for the recent warming stasis was published as this book went to press: Yu Kosaka and Shang Ping Xie, "Recent Global-Warming Hiatus Tied to Equatorial Pacific Surface Cooling," *Nature* 501 (2013), 403–7.

hemisphere seems to have suppressed El Niño and contributed to good monsoon rainfall in West Africa and in India (though Indian rainfall tapered off in the 1930s). The central factor at work may have been a rising solar input. But sulfur dioxide emissions slowed during these decades, and this clearing of industrial pollution may have contributed to raising these temperatures.[47] In any event, the general Holocene patterns seem to have been still the dominant players in the climate system.

The first signs that things were getting seriously out of norm may have come in the late 1930s. At the peak of the climbing global and Atlantic temperatures around 1939–41 there was an abnormal El Niño spike in 1941, coinciding with the great snows that helped stall the German advance into Russia, as the Dalton Minimum had stopped Napoleon.[48] There was also a brief but intense drought period in West Africa.

This early World War II aberration may well have been the first sign of things to come. But during the massive increase of industrial emissions of the 1950s and 1960s global temperatures stabilized and even cooled (see Figure IV.14). With an historically high solar intensity, this halt in global warming seems to have been due to the burden of sulfate aerosols injected into the northern hemisphere. With northern hemisphere temperatures cooling somewhat, there was a corresponding rise in El Niños peaking in the 1960s. Generally, through 1970, West Africa had abundant rain for twenty years; and the monsoons over India were strong.[49]

[47] For ENSO, see David E. Black et al., "An 8-Century Tropical Atlantic SST Record from the Cariaco Basin: Baseline Variability, Twentieth-Century Warming, and Atlantic Hurricane Frequency," *Paleoceanography* 22 (2007), PA4204; L. G. Thompson et al., "A 1500 Year Record of Tropical Precipitation Recorded in Ice Cores from the Quelccaya Ice Cap, Peru," *Science* 229 (1985), 971–3; Global-SST ENSO index, 1817 – November 2008; and the Puerto Chicama Perú (8°S) SST (C) datasets, Joint Institute for the Study of the Atmosphere and Ocean (JISAO) Web site, http://jisao.washington.edu/data_sets/ (accessed August 8, 2012); Mike Davis, *Late Victorian Holocausts: El Niño Famines and the Making of the Third World* (New York, 2001); for West Africa: T. M. Shanahan, "Atlantic Forcing of Persistent Drought in West Africa," *Science* 324 (2009), 377–80; Sahel rainfall index (20–10N, 20W–10E), 1900 – March 2009, JISAO; for India: Jayendra Singh and Ram R. Yadav, "Spring Precipitation Variations over the Western Himalaya, India, since A. D. 1731, as Deduced from Tree Rings," *JGR* 110 (2005), D01110; Nerilie J. Abram et al., "Recent Intensification of Tropical Climate Variability in the Indian Ocean," *NatGeosc* 1 (2008), 849–53.

[48] The 1941 El Niño coincided with a year of poor rainfall in India, but it does not seem to have been directly responsible for the 1943 Bengal Famine.

[49] Williams et al., "The Response of the Climate System"; Black et al., "An 8-Century Tropical Atlantic SST Record"; Leon D. Rotstayn and Ulrike Lohmann, "Tropical Rainfall Trends and the Indirect Aerosol Effect," *JClim* 15 (2002), 2103–16; Xin Wang et al., "Decadal Variability of Twentieth-Century El Niño and La Niña Occurrence from Observations and IPCC AR4 Coupled Models," *GRL* 36 (2009), L11701; Robert J. Allan and Rosanne D. D'Arrigo, "'Persistent' ENSO Sequences: How Unusual was the 1990–1995 El Niño?" *The Holocene* 9 (1999), 101–8; Robert J. Allan, "ENSO and Climatic Variability in the Past 150 Years," in Henry F. Diaz and Vera Markgraf, eds., *El Niño: Historical and Paleoclimatic Aspects of the Southern Oscillation* (New York, 1992), 6–11.

Then, in the 1970s, as anthropogenic warming began, the true consequences of the growing greenhouse gases began to be felt, with the masking effects of sulfate aerosols stabilizing and then declining (see Figure IV.14). Global temperatures increased sharply, especially in the northern hemisphere: the North Atlantic Oscillation shifted to a dominantly positive mode, shifting the winter westerlies north, and bringing increasing levels of drought to the Mediterranean, Anatolia, and points east. But there was an anomalous surge in El Niño activity, which should not have happened with positive NAO. Drought overwhelmed the Sahel, and the monsoon shifted erratically over South Asia, increasingly untethered from its ancient link to ENSO and events in the eastern Pacific. The central causal element seems to have been the anomalous heating of the tropics by the net effects of anthropogenic forcing of climate change; the Hadley Cells making up the tropical climate systems on either side of the Intertropical Convergence Zone are widening, shifting jet streams toward the poles. As the northern hemisphere has warmed so has the southern, especially the eastern Pacific and the Indian Ocean, apparently explaining both the anomalous rising number of El Niños and the growing independence of the Indian monsoons from the El Niño-La Niña oscillation.[50]

In the first decade of the new century, the two systems apparently have continued to move together anomalously: a pattern of positive NAO and El Niño shifted toward negative NAO and La Niña. At the same time, massive monsoon flooding struck Pakistan, China, the Philippines, and Australia, while the La Niña condition is being linked to an increasing number and greater velocity of hurricanes and tornados in the Atlantic and North America. Of course the indeterminacies of very recent time in a volatile system make any definitive predictions of the future problematic. It is certainly possible that NAO and ENSO will soon return to their "normal" relationship if third super-cycle sulphur emissions continue to keep global temperatures from rising. But there will be no immediate return to the temperatures of around 1970, or more remotely the nineteenth century. The system has changed. What may also be playing a role is the increasingly strength of

[50] James W. Hurrell et al., "North Atlantic Climate Variability: The Role of the North Atlantic Oscillation," *Journal of Marine Systems* 78 (2009), 28, 41, figure 10; Heidi M. Cullen et al., "Impact of the North Atlantic Oscillation on Middle-Eastern Climate and Streamflow," *ClimCh* 55 (2002), 315–38; Dian J. Seidel et al., "Widening of the Tropical Belt in a Changing Climate," *NatGeosc* 1 (2008), 21–4; Qiang Fu and Pu Lin, "Poleward Shift of Subtropical Jets Inferred from Satellite-Observed Lower-Stratospheric Temperature," *JClim* 24 (2011), 5597–603; Bin Wang and Soon-Il An, "Why the Properties of El Niño Changed during the Late 1970s," *GRL* 28 (2001), 3709–12; C. P. Cheng et al., "Possible Roles of Atlantic Circulation on the Weakening Indian Monsoon-Rainfall Relationship," *JClim* 14 (2001), 2376–80; F. Kucharski et al., "Low-Frequency Variability of the Indian Monsoon-ENSO Relationship and the Tropical Atlantic: The Weakening of the 1980s and 1990s," *JClim* 20 (2007), 4255–66; K. N. Krishnakumar et al., "Rainfall Trends in the Twentieth Century over Kerala, India," *Atmospheric Environment* 43 (2009), 1940–4.

the global water cycle, moving moisture from oceans into the lower tropo-sphere and back again – quite simply increasing the volume and intensity of storms and precipitation, a key dimension of predictions for the impacts of climate change. Quite simply, the weather is getting more extreme as the planet warms. Perhaps, as atmospheric CO_2 and average temperature approach and exceed that of the Miocene, so too will the intensity of global weather.[51]

Thus, while we begin to measure the impact of a general global warm-ing on sea levels, the geography of natural biomes, arable land, and disease, there seems to be evidence for important alterations in the structure of the earth's climate system. The present and future climate system is and will be a strange fusion of natural systems and anthropogenic influences. Our influ-ence may – if William Ruddiman is right – run back thousands of years, in a climatic stabilization, deflecting of the trajectory toward a future glacial period. But the enhancement of that influence has been extremely rapid, over the past century and a half, and most powerfully in the past six to seven decades. With a sudden warming has come the beginnings of fun-damental alterations in the global system itself. Of course, if we compare our atmospheric impacts with those that have occurred in geological times, they perhaps pale by comparison; left to its own devises the earth system would revert to reasonably "normal" circumstances in a few millennia. But it will not be left to its own devises, given the press of human numbers and their aspirations for a seemingly more secure and gratifying life grounded in the energy-intensive economy of the Third Great Super-Cycle. Here we confront a series of paradoxes: if recent climate changes have been slight, expanded global populations and degraded natural services have seriously narrowed the margin for civilizational error.[52] More minor disasters are having a larger impact. And then there is the scale of the latent change built into the new atmospheric system: if we have already matched or exceeded greenhouse gas levels of the Miocene, millions of years ago, temperature levels and climate effects are just beginning to respond. We are like the stone in the slingshot, pulled back and on the verge of release into a fundamen-tally different reality.

[51] Paul J. Durack et al., "Ocean Salinities Reveal Strong Water Cycle Intensification during 1950 to 2000," *Science* 336 (2012), 455–8; Seung-Ki Min et al., "Human Contributions to More-Intense Precipitations Extremes," *Nature* 470 (2011), 378–81; Alexey V. Federov, "Tropical Cyclones and Permanent El Niño in the Early Pliocene Epoch," *Nature* 463 (2010), 1067–70; Christopher B. Field et al., eds., *Managing the Risks of Extreme Events and Disasters to Advance Climate Change Adaption: A Special Report of the Intergovernmental Panel on Climate Change* (New York, 2012).
[52] Johan Rockström et al., "A Safe Operating Space for Humanity," *Science* 461 (2009), 472–5. See also the work of the Stockholm Resilience Center, at http://www.stockholmresilience. org/planetary-boundaries (accessed August 8, 2012).

Coda

A Rough Journey into an Uncertain Future

The emergence of the modern economy has made humanity an agent in abrupt climate change and, more broadly, abrupt planetary change. In a flash of either geological or human evolutionary time, human populations have doubled and redoubled to more than 7 billion, twenty-four times the number inhabiting the earth 1,000 years ago; six times the number two centuries ago. In just the past sixty years, human populations have more than doubled, and in a great burst of creative energy and economic and technological transformation, our role in building greenhouse gases has tripled, and we have begun to disrupt the natural systems and services that have sustained us for millions of years. Projections put global population in the year 2100 at 10 billion, long since seen as the outer carrying capacity of the earth. We now stand facing an uncertain future, and hope that our wits, which brought us to a precarious place, will suffice to ensure the sustainability of future generations.[1]

Behind the trajectories that have suddenly launched us out of premodernity lies a tangled paradox of human numbers, prosperity, and earth system stability. On one hand, the evidence of the demographic transition is clear and unequivocal: economic development and a general improvement of human well-being slows population growth by reducing fertility. The decline in fertility that marks the closing of the demographic transition, long completed in the developed world, is advancing significantly in the developing world. But the achieving this goal will require massive resources and energy production – inevitably producing massive quantities of greenhouse gases and further contributing to global warming. The prospect of an irreversible tipping point to a new regime of planetary ecology taking us into a very hostile future lies just over the horizon. Resolving this paradox while

---

[1] Joel E. Cohen, *How Many People Can the Earth Support?* (New York, 1995); Johan Rockström et al., "Planetary Boundaries: Exploring the Safe Operating Space for Humanity," *Ecology and Society* 14/2/32 (2009); Will Steffen, "Observed Trends in Earth System Behavior," *WIREs Climate Change* 1 (2010), 428–49.

we forestall this tipping point, if it can be done, will take all the intellectual, political, and material resources that we can bring to bear.

* * *

Malthus Vindicated?

The future of modern humanity began to be a subject of heated public debate during the 1960s, when the world began to recover from the horrors of world war, and to consider the consequences of that recovery. The pessimistic view of the human future was presented most dramatically after Rachel Carson's 1962 *Silent Spring* by ecologist Paul Ehrlich's 1968 *The Population Bomb* and the Club of Rome's 1972 *Limits to Growth*. These volumes sounded the alarm of a looming global crisis of population and resources, in which shortages of oil, food, and water on an overpopulated planet would lead to famine and war. The optimistic response came from economist Julian Simon, whose 1981 *The Ultimate Resource* argued that growing numbers would inexorably drive beneficent economic growth. Building on Ester Boserup's arguments about agricultural intensification driven by population growth, Simon was certain that limited resources would never be a problem in human history, because human ingenuity would find a constant flow of solutions.[2] During the 1980s and 1990s, Simon's cornucopian vision seemed to prevail over Ehrlich and Meadows' Malthusianism, with the success of the Green Revolution in averting famine, discoveries of new oil reserves, and the constant flow of technological innovation.

Despite the failure of Ehrlich's predictions to materialize in the short term of the late twentieth century, concerns about resource shortages over the long term are matters of serious anxiety for the global future. The catastrophic failure and meltdown at the Fukushima nuclear facility following the 2011 Japanese tsunami has undermined hopes that nuclear power is a viable option for meeting massively growing demands for electricity.[3] In

---

[2] Rachel Carson, *Silent Spring* (Boston, MA, 1962); Paul R. Ehrlich, *The Population Bomb* (New York, 1968); Donna H. Meadows et al., *Limits to Growth: A Report for the Club of Rome's Project on the Predicament of Mankind* (New York, 1972); Julian L. Simon, *The Ultimate Resource* (Princeton, NJ, 1981); Simon's precursors include H. Barnett and C. Morse, *Scarcity and Growth: The Economics of Natural Resource Availability* (Baltimore, MD, 1963); and V. K. Smith, ed., *Scarcity and Growth Reconsidered* (Baltimore, MD, 1979). See the useful commentaries in R. Davis Simpson et al., "Introduction: the 'New Scarcity,'" in Simpson et al., *Scarcity and Growth Revisited: Natural Resources and the Environment in the New Millennium* (Washington, DC, 2005), 1–11; and Pierre Desrochers and Christine Hoffbauer, "The Post War Intellectual Roots of the Population Bomb: Fairfield Osborn's 'Our Plundered Planet' and William Vogt's 'Road to Survival' in Retrospect," *Electronic Journal of Sustainable Development* 1 (2009).
[3] Hiroko Tabuchi, "Inquiry Declares Fukushima Crisis a Man-Made Disaster," *NYT*, July 5, 2012.

India, an electricity blackout in the summer of 2012, apparently caused by competition for a limited supply, impacted a tenth of the world's population. The 2012 Indian blackout has drawn attention to one of the most perilous contradictions of the modern condition: economic productivity requires reasonably cool and dry working conditions, putting enormous strain on the electrical systems in rapidly growing equatorial countries, and adding huge volumes of greenhouse gases into the atmosphere.[4] Technological development may have lifted the threat of an imminent decline in oil production, but the press of demand requires constant innovation and access to increasingly remote, ecologically fragile, and politically volatile corners of the world. Oil production will eventually peak and decline, and global supplies of coal are realistically measured in centuries. New technologies involving hydraulic fracturing for shale gas and the exploitation of off-shore methane hydrate deposits may lead the way toward an energy transition, but one still very much locked into fossil carbon fuels. As important as energy, key industrial metals, vital to the new technologies of the Third Industrial Revolution, are in limited supply, and are being used as a strategic weapon in the world economy. Most important, however, Malthusian concerns focus less on the supply of fuel for developed economies than on the supply of fresh water and arable land in the less developed world. Thus there are real concerns about a classical endogenous Malthusian overload: by one estimate the earth was 30 percent overpopulated in the year 2000; another series of estimates suggests that humanity consumes somewhere between 16 percent and 23 percent of the total annual net primary productivity of the earth.[5]

---

[4] Garnder Harris and Vikas Bajaj, "As Power is Restored to India, the 'Blame Game' Begins," *NYT*, August 1, 2012; Elisabeth Rosenthal, "The Cost of Cool," *NYT*, August 19, 2012.

[5] On oil production see, among others, Daniel Yergin, *The Quest: Energy, Security, and the Remaking of the Modern World* (New York, 2011), 227–41, and *The Joint Forces Environment* (United States Joint Forces Command, Suffolk, VA, 2010), 24–9. Kenneth S. Deffeyes, *Hubbert's Peak: The Impending World Oil Shortage*, rev. ed. (Princeton, NJ, 2008) and Richard Heinberg, *The Party's Over: Oil, War and the Fate of Industrial Societies* (Gabriola Is., Can., 2003) paint a pessimistic picture, but for a critique, see Vaclav Smil, *Global Catastrophes and Trends: The Next Fifty Years* (Cambridge, MA, 2008), 77–82. On shale gas and methane hydrates, see Charles Mass, "What if We Never Run Out of Oil?" *Atlantic Monthly* 311/4 (May 2013), 48–63. On emerging resource issues, see R. Davis Simpson et al., "Introduction: the 'New Scarcity,'" Christian Azar, "Emerging Scarcities: Bioenergy-Food Competition in a Carbon Constrained World," Partha Dasgupta, "Sustainable Economic Development in the World of Today's Poor," in Simpson et al., *Scarcity and Growth Revisited*, 1–33, 98–120, 267–82; and the discussions of resource conflict in note 23. On overpopulation and net primary productivity, see Tony McMichael, *Human Frontiers, Environments and Diseases: Past Patterns, Uncertain Futures* (Cambridge, 2001), 218; Fridolin Krausmann et al., "Global Patterns of Socioeconomic Biomass Flows in the Year 2000: A Comprehensive Assessment of Supply, Consumption and Constraints," *EcolEcom* 65 (2007), 471–87; Helmut Haberl et al., "Quantifying and Mapping the Human Appropriation of Net Primary Productivity in Earth's Terrestrial Ecosystems," *PNAS* 104 (2007), 12942–7.

By the late 1980s, however, the focus of immediate concern had shifted from sources to sinks, as an awareness of the global reach of the emissions and impacts of the modern economy began to emerge. Rather than running out of oil, the primary concern became that we might kill planetary sustainability by overloading its sinks long before we run out of resources to drive the economy. If climate change now occupies center stage in public concern about the future of humanity and the earth, the cumulative weight of environmental impacts is an equally important dimension of this modern endogenous Malthusian overload. Both the 2011 Fukushima meltdown and the 2010 British Petroleum Deep Horizon oil well rupture in the Gulf of Mexico have revived realistic concerns about the environmental hazards of advanced but unregulated energy systems. The sudden expansion of gas production throughout the United States has raised justifiable concerns about the hazards that new hydraulic fracturing technologies pose to water supplies. These classic environmental concerns are now amplified by the less obvious impact of consumer and industrial electronics, which have put an enormous and growing load of toxic metals into an increasingly globalized garbage stream. Urban and suburban sprawl has spread with global development, and as increasing fractions of the landscape in the United States, Europe, and now Latin America, India, and China are built or paved over, natural systems of drainage and water control are disrupted and destroyed. The result has been increasing volumes of toxic runoff – from agricultural fertilizers as much as urban sprawl – and the sudden weakening of natural buffers against floods and storm surges, as was so dramatically demonstrated in the 2005 destruction of much of the city of New Orleans in Hurricane Katrina, and the impact of Hurricane Sandy on the New York metropolitan region in 2012. Throughout the world, but now most obviously in the developing world, this rapid urbanization is taking place on river estuaries and delta environments. Ironically, these were the environments that attracted postglacial Mesolithic peoples, given their extremely high net primary productivity. The consequences of this modern development are the loss of both valuable farm land and the contributions that the natural productivity of these deltaic regions make to marine ecosystems.[6]

The massive and increasing use of synthetic nitrogen in agriculture, the essential engine of the Green Revolution of the 1970s, is having increasing impacts in both the ocean and the atmosphere. On one hand, as much as 60 percent of agricultural nitrogen fertilizer runs off into river systems, which eventually deposit this excess in the ocean, causing blooms of algae and anoxic "dead zones," which appear annually in the Gulf of Mexico, off the northeast United States and northern Europe, the Mediterranean

---

[6] Vikas Bajaj, "As Mumbai Spills Over, Floodwater Creeps Closer," *NYT*, July 14, 2009; Mark Fischetti predicted the devastation by Katrina in "Drowning New Orleans," *SA* (October 2001), 76–85.

and the Black Sea, and the water off Japan and China. The production and application of nitrogen fertilizers also contribute to photochemical smog, has incorporated nitrogen forms into precipitation, and is a growing component of greenhouse gases. If the emission of CFCs has been successfully curbed since the Montreal accord of 1990, it now appears that nitrous oxide is the leading source of stratospheric ozone depletion.[7]

More generally, the demands of a globalized economy contribute in different ways to the erosion of the biotic complexity of the earth. Rapidly advancing deforestation in the tropics is pushing unknown numbers of species to extinction, while the global spread of insects, microbes, and invasive plant species threaten the integrity of many temperate ecosystems.[8]

Then there are the vectors of global change that directly threaten the human body. On one hand, the globalization that carries invasive species also carries disease. Worldwide anxieties about another sudden pandemic coming from Ebola, AIDs, SARs, bird flu, and now swine flu are not unrealistic. If we think that we are more distant from nature, the reality is that human and animal vectors are even more perilously interwoven than they were in the ancient past. Populations lacking the immunities of constant animal-human interaction are nonetheless exposed to viruses and infections spreading from vast pig and poultry farms, from wild animal transfer to hunters and hikers, and even from patterns of bird migration. In addition, since World War II, modern medicine – like modern agriculture – has been conducting a worldwide experiment in biochemistry; the same antibiotics that have saved countless lives are driving a microbial evolutionary response in the form of antibiotic resistance, and there is the real danger that the microbes will win. Finally, there is the global experiment that involves volatile synthetic chemicals, including PCBs, which mimic the behavior of hormones. Like mercury, these chemicals have entered the global food stream; among other potential impacts, they may be contributing to metabolic disorders such as obesity and type 2 diabetes and to gendering disorders in animals and perhaps humans. Not a pretty picture.[9]

---

[7] Vaclav Smil, *Enriching the Earth: Fritz Haber, Carl Bosch, and the Transformation of World Food Production* (Cambridge, MA, 2001), 133–99; A. R. Ramishankara et al., "Nitrous Oxide (N2O): The Dominant Ozone-Depleting Substance Emitted in the 21st Century," *Science* 326 (2009), 123–5.

[8] Edward O. Wilson, *The Diversity of Life* (New York, 1992), 215–80; –, *The Future of Life* (New York, 2002), 42–102; Smil, *Global Catastrophes and Trends*, 203–8.

[9] David Quammen, *Spillover: Animal Infections and the Next Human Pandemic* (New York, 2012). Andrew Price-Smith, *Contagion and Chaos: Disease, Ecology, and National Security in the Era of Globalization* (Cambridge, MA, 2009), 117–59; Smil, *Global Catastrophes and Trends*, 209–12; Karen P. Phillips and Warren G. Foster, "Key Developments in Endocrine Disruptor Research and Human Health," *Journal of Toxicology and Environmental Health, Part B* 11 (2008), 322–44; Sarah M. Zala and Dustin J. Penn, "Abnormal Behaviors Induced by Chemical Pollution: A Review of the Evidence and New Challenges," *Animal Behavior* 68 (2004), 649–4; for the history of the first decade of the endocrine debate, see Sheldon

Then there are the observed and predicted regional ecological impacts of changing global climate. First, warming is and will be most pronounced on the land masses and across the high northern latitudes. Every summer unprecedented passages open up through the Arctic Sea ice and continental ice sheets on Greenland are melting more rapidly in the summer than they reaccumulate during the winter. There are ominous signs of the impending collapse of continental ice shelves around Antarctica. Tropical glaciers are also melting at a rapid rate, in many cases exposing land glaciated since the Mid-Holocene. The significant melting of glacial ice would contribute to a rise in sea level unprecedented since the end of the Pleistocene, perhaps led by the catastrophic sudden collapse of ice shelves around Antarctica. At present, however, rising sea levels are mainly the result of the thermal expansion of warming ocean water, which is now at record high temperatures and climbing every year. Given the effect of currents and regional wind flow increasing evaporation, sea levels will not rise uniformly, but vary around the world. Over land, precipitation has been declining and will continue to decline in the arid and semiarid regions of the tropics, while it is increasing in the northern latitudes, often in violent summer storm events. At the same time, there are serious questions about the impact of heating tropical waters on large climatic systems, most importantly the monsoon forces driving hurricanes and typhoons, and the forces operating across the Pacific that shape the El Niño/Southern Oscillation. One scenario might be a Pliocene-like permanent El Niño, another – perhaps more likely – is a permanent La Niña similar to the warm conditions of the Early Holocene or the Medieval Climate Anomaly.[10]

Many of the emerging environmental hazards and impacts summarized here are deeply interconnected with this recent process of global warming

Krimsky, *Hormonal Chaos: The Scientific and Social Origins of the Environmental Endocrine Hypothesis* (Baltimore, MD, 2000); for an early overview, see Theo Colborn et al., *Our Stolen Future: Are We Threatening Our Fertility, Intelligence, and Survival?* (New York, 1996).

[10] IPCC, "Summary for Policy Makers," in Core Writing Team, Rajendra K. Pachauri, and Andy Reisinger, eds., *Climate Change 2007: Synthesis Report. Contribution of Working Groups I, II and III to the Fourth Assessment Report of the Intergovernmental Panel on Climate Change* (Geneva, 2007), 7–14; IPCC, "Summary for Policy Makers," in M. L. Parry et al., eds., *Climate Change, 2007: Impacts, Adaptation and Vulnerability. Contribution of Working Group II to the Fourth Assessment Report of the Intergovernmental Panel on Climate Change* (Cambridge, 2007), 7–22; Nathaniel L. Bindoff et al., "Chapter 5: Observations: Oceanic Climate Change and Sea-Level," in *Climate Change 2007: The Physical Science Basis*, 410–21; Lonnie G. Thompson et al., "Abrupt Tropical Climate Change: Past and Present," *PNAS* 103 (2006), 10536–43; James Hansen et al., "Global Temperature Change," *PNAS* 103 (2006), 14288–93, esp. 14390–1; Matthew Collins and CMIP Modelling Groups, "El Niño or La Niña-Like Climate Change?" *ClimDyn* 24 (2005), 89–104; Cornelia Dean, "Ocean Temperatures are Highest on Record," *NYT*, August 15, 2009, reporting http://www.noaanews.noaa.gov/stories2009/20090814_julyglobalstats.html accessed August 8, 2012; for a useful overview, see Smil, *Global Catastrophes and Trends*, 171–95.

and climate change. Synthetic nitrogen and CO_2 emitted from tropical deforestation make important contributions to greenhouse gas buildup, and thus to rising temperatures. The threats of the destruction of marshland and estuary buffers by urbanization and agriculture will combine with projected rising sea levels and increased storm intensity to put coastal cities at even greater risk of future flooding. And as global warming drives the expansion of tropical biomes to the north and the south away from the equator, these shifting ecologies are already adding new complexities to the rise of new diseases and the spread of invasive plant and animal species, driven independently by the wider process of economic globalization and population growth. At the same time, the increased volume of atmospheric CO_2, added to longer growing seasons in a warming northern hemisphere, is resulting in an increase in net primary productivity, as plant life responds to changing environmental conditions. In the oceans, a similar increased drawdown of CO_2 is having a different effect, increasing the acidity of sea water. Both rising acidity and water temperature are adversely affecting tropical coral reefs, which are critical habitats for a vast array of ocean life forms.[11]

The central question about the sudden surge toward a warmer planet is how far and fast the warming will be. In particular, there is great concern that the warming launched by human population growth and industrialization is already triggering a natural accelerator in the irreversible warming of the Arctic regions, where a release of CO_2 and methane frozen in the tundra since the beginning of the Pleistocene will double the greenhouse pressures and throw the earth into an entirely new condition. While the tundra is already releasing CO_2 and methane, there are particular concerns about methane hydrates, methane gas trapped in icebeds under the seafloor. Destabilized by warming or by drilling for energy, the sudden release of massive volumes of methane from hydrate gas deposits could trigger a runaway warming such as occurred 50 million years ago during the Late Paleocene Thermal Maximum event. Plumes of methane rising from Arctic Sea hydrate beds have been detected since 2009.[12]

[11] Ramakrishna R. Nemani et al., "Climate-Driven Increases in Global Terrestrial Net Primary Productivity from 1982 to 1999," *Science* 300 (2003), 1560–3; Katharina E. Fabricius et al., "Losers and Winners in Coral Reefs Acclimatized to Elevated Carbon Dioxide Concentrations," *Nature Climate Change* 1 (2011), 165–9; R. Rodolpho Metalpa et al., "Coral and Mollusc Resistance to Ocean Acidification Adversely Affected by Warming," *Nature Climate Change* 1 (2011), 308–12; Smil, *Global Catastrophe and Trends*, 185–7. It remains to be seen how much natural solar variation might offset anthropogenic warming forces: a new projection based on the past 9,400 years of variation suggests that the sun will enter a period of lower activity during this century, rising during the next two centuries. Friedhelm Steinhilber and Jurg Beer, "Prediction of Solar Activity for the Next 500 Years," *Journal of Geophysical Research: Space Physics* 118 (2013), 1861–7.

[12] K. M. Walter et al., "Methane Bubbling from Siberian Thaw Lakes as a Positive Feedback to Climate Warming," *Nature* 443 (2006), 71–5; Michael Marshall, "As Arctic Ocean Warms, Megatonnes of Methane Bubble Up," *New Scientist*, August 17, 2009.

Such a runaway warming is one of the worse-case scenarios that increasingly haunt scientists and scholars considering our global future. Another that has caused some concern, but is now seen as unlikely in the immediate future, is the threat of a "Youngest Dryas": a sudden freshening of the waters off Greenland caused by rapid ice melt might shut down the North Atlantic thermohaline pump, sending the earth into a millennium of glaciation.[13] But there are other concerns about abrupt nonlinear changes – regime shifts – not just regarding climate but in entire natural ecosystems, and human social and political systems. And if we are concerned about the endogenous, human-driven sources of "regime shift," there are still exogenous natural forces that could by themselves seriously impact our condition. Among these the next solar Hallstatt/Siberian High event, if they are even vaguely cyclical, is far in the distance – perhaps AD 3600–4000 – and the least of our worries. More immediately, the tectonic impacts of volcanic eruptions, earthquakes, and tsunamis are recurrent realities, as are hurricanes and cyclones: an unfortunate clustering of these events could severely stress our capacity to cope. Beyond these earthly forces lie more distant possibilities: the reversal of the earth's magnetic field – perhaps already under way – or a meteor impact.[14]

If we set aside the more exotic of these potential threats, and the simple discomfort of a hotter planet, the most pervasive and serious of the impacts of either gradual or abrupt climate change on the human condition will involve changes in patterns of precipitation and water distribution, rising sea levels, and how shifting biomes will contribute to new disease regimes. Economies and people who are directly and primarily dependent on rain- or glacial-fed agriculture will suffer most dramatically from drought and water shortage. Highly populated coastal districts and cities throughout the world will be directly impacted by rising sea levels. And warming temperatures will make new and established diseases, often tropical in origin, much more pervasive. But global climate change is already having very different scales of adverse impact on different global regions. Unfortunately, the impacts of warming already are falling disproportionately on peoples who had little role in their causes, while those who collectively have been most responsible for these changes – and who have the capacity to possibly correct them – will

[13] Walter Gibbs, "Scientists Back Off Theory of a Colder Europe in a Warming World," *NYT*, May 15, 2007; William Calvin, "The Great Climate Flip-Flop," *Atlantic Monthly*, January 1998. A potential future "Youngest Dryas" event was wildly overdramatized in the feature film *The Day after Tomorrow*.

[14] Marten Scheffer, *Critical Transitions in Nature and Society* (Princeton, NJ, 2009); Thomas F. Homer-Dixon, *The Upside of Down: Catastrophe, Creativity, and the Renewal of Civilization* (Washington, DC, 2006); A. J. McMichael, *Planetary Overload: GEC and the Health of the Human Species* (Cambridge, 1993). Smil, *Global Catastrophes and Trends*, esp. 9–70, suggests that fears of megadisaster are overblown.

suffer the least. Very broadly, these circumstances once again pit a wealthier, temperate north against a poorer, arid, and tropical south.

The most dramatic and perhaps unfortunate irony may be that much of the United States, which has for more than a century led the world in economic growth and carbon emission, will probably escape the very worst impacts of global warming. This is not to say that there will be no impacts. As part of the wider Arctic circuit, Alaska has already begun to experience serious impacts of global warming. Arctic Sea pack ice is retreating, and disappearing totally along the Alaskan and Siberian coasts during summers that are melting the permafrost, undermining Inuit villages and oil rigs alike, and destabilizing vast stretches of coniferous taiga forest.[15]

Across the lower forty-eight of the United States, rising temperatures are already setting off more frequent and persistent heat waves, increasing demand for electricity across American cities and suburbs, fueling wildfires, spring tornadoes, and drought that has the signature of the megadroughts that toppled the city-state of Cahokia at the end of the Medieval Climate Anomaly. La Niña drought in 2012 fed forest fires and buckled roads while scorching the agricultural heartland, putting more than half of the nation's counties onto federal disaster relief, raising the threat of increased food prices and energy costs.[16] Rising seas will soon threaten both coasts, but especially the overbuilt Atlantic shoreline; seawalls have been proposed to protect New York Harbor from storm surges. Global tropical diseases like malaria and dengue fever, suppressed by public health measures for a century, will make inroads from the Caribbean; West Nile Fever is already entrenched.[17]

---

[15] Peter Lemke et al., "Ch. 4: Changes in Snow, Ice and Frozen Ground," in *Climate Change, 2007: The Physical Science Basis*, 339, 344, 357–9, 369–74; Timothy Egan, "Alaska, No Longer So Frigid, Starts to Crack, Burn and Sag," *NYT*, June 16, 2002.

[16] Justin Gillis, "Climate Change Seen as Posing Risk to Food Supplies," *NYT*, November, 1, 2013; "July 2012: Hottest Month on Record for Contiguous United States," State of the Climate, National Oceanic and Atmospheric Administration, National Climatic Data Center, available at http://www.ncdc.noaa.gov/sotc/?fbState, accessed August 8, 2012; FSA Disaster Designation Information, August 8, 2012 available at http://www.fsa.usda.gov/FSA/webapp?area=home&subject=diap&topic=landing, accessed August 9, 2012; Anne Lowrety and Ron Nixon, "Severe Drought Seen as Driving Cost of Food Up," *NYT*, July 25, 2012; Michael A. Webber, "Will Drought Cause the Next Blackout?" *NYT*, July 25, 2012; Kate Galbraith, "Assessing Climate Change in a Drought Stricken State," *NYT*, August 26, 2011.

[17] IPCC, "Summary for Policy Makers," *Climate Change, 2007: Synthesis Report*, 7–13; IPCC, "Summary for Policy Makers," in M. L. Parry et al., eds., *Climate Change, 2007: Impacts, Adaptation and Vulnerability. Contribution of Working Group II to the Fourth Assessment Report of the Intergovernmental Panel on Climate Change* (Cambridge, 2007), 8–18; Julienne C. Stroeve et al., "The Arctic's Rapidly Shrinking Sea Ice Cover: Research Synthesis," *ClimCh* 110 (2012), 1005–27; Samuel S. Myers and Jonathan A. Patz, "Emerging Threats to Human Health from GEC," *Annual Review of Environment and Resources* 34 (2009), 223–52.

Beyond these favored regions bordering the North Atlantic, which launched the modern economy, the world's more populated regions will feel or are already feeling the adverse effects of global warming much more severely. The droughts that started in the Sahel in the 1970s are probably the leading edge of these effects that are projected to encompass southern Europe, northern Africa, Southwest and South Asia, China, and large parts of Australia and Latin America. The impact of these shifts is already apparent in Spain and Greece, where droughts have set the stage for massive wildfires in recent years, and across Europe in general, where unprecedented heat waves beginning in the mid-1990s have killed thousands of people.[18] Declining snowfall in Anatolia – driven by a strong positive mode of the North Atlantic Oscillation – is projected to dry up the spring and summer flow of the Tigris, the Euphrates, and the Jordan River basin. South Asia and Andean South America will be affected by the melting of tropical glaciers; after a burst of melted water there will be permanently restricted and insufficient volumes of spring runoff. In China generally, warming will increase demand for irrigation from already overutilized rivers. The densely populated great river deltas in Bangladesh, Southeast Asia, and China will be threatened by rising sea levels and storm surges; China, Pakistan, and the Philippines have been severely impacted by strong La Niña flooding. These events can be clearly connected to the advancing global temperatures of the past three decades, which reached a record high during the summer of 2012. In sum, where the U.N. classified thirty-two countries as suffering from water scarcity or water stress; by 2050 this number will rise to sixty, encompassing nearly one half of the population of the world.[19] These conditions will obviously be exacerbated by deforestation, which will encourage evaporation and runoff, and obviously by increasing demands for water from growing populations. Even without any climate change, the increasing populations of the developing world would put huge pressures on water supplies, to say nothing of soils and timber. More broadly, the combined pressures of population growth and climate change will put enormous burdens on the wider less-developed tropics, further limiting economic progress for this world majority.[20]

[18] Anthee Carassava, "Thousands Flee Athens Fires, *NYT*, August 24, 2009; Araine Bernard, "Europe Bakes under a Heat Wave," *NYT*, July 26, 2006; John Tagliabue, "Scorching Heat around Europe Causes Deaths and Droughts," *NYT*, July 19, 2005; Andrew C. Revkin, "Europe: 2003 Summer was Hottest in 500 Years," *NYT*, March 6, 2004; Craig R. Whitney, "Europe Wilts, Records Fall in Heat Wave," *NYT*, August 3, 1994; "Forest Fires Blackening Acres of 'Green Spain,'" *NYT*, September 10, 1989.

[19] James E. Hansen et al., "Perceptions of Climate Change," *PNAS* Early Edition, August 6, 2012, doi: 10.1073/pnas.120527; "Summary for Policy Makers," Rex Victor Cruz, "Chapter 10: Asia," in Parry et al., eds., *Climate Change, 2007: Impacts, Adaptation and Vulnerability*, 479–85, 493–5; Smil, *Global Catastrophes and Trends*, 198–9.

[20] Melissa Dell et al., "Climate Change and Economic Growth: Evidence from the Last Half Century," N.B.E.R. Working Paper 14132, June 2008; Jeffrey D. Sachs et al., "The

The next several decades, at the least, will see large generations coming of age in impoverished economies with limited prospects. In broad outline, their circumstances bear some similarity to those of the Siberian High millennia of the Holocene past: climate shifts toward drought, often abrupt, contributing to failing economies and failing states, set the stage for migrations, civil violence, and war. Such is the pattern I have suggested for the key breaks in Old World histories since the Mid-Holocene Crisis and the rise of the state in 3000 BC, and the pattern that scholars have found for China and globally over the past millennium.[21] Recent work has suggested the same for modern societies: warming climate slows economic growth disproportionately in poorer, tropical countries, and drought is already an aspect of the causal factors in civil wars around the world, such as in Darfur, Liberia, Somalia, and northern Nigeria. Water may well contribute to conflict in the Middle East, where water flow in Israel, Jordan, and Iraq is controlled by dams in Syria and Turkey. Connections between drought in China, rising food prices during "agflation," and emerging regional water stresses are suggesting that climate change is a key part of the background to the wider Middle Eastern "Arab Spring." Rising resource stress may not necessarily be the direct cause of conflict, but it will certainly intensify and accelerate preexisting national, ethnic, and class animosities.[22]

Geography of Poverty and Wealth," *SA* (March 2001), 71–4; Andrew D. Mellinger et al., "Climate, Coastal Proximity, and Development," in Gregory L. Clark et al., eds., *The Oxford Handbook of Economic Geography* (New York, 2000), 169–94; Jack A. Goldstone, "The New Population Bomb," *Foreign Affairs* 89 (2010), 31–43.

[21] David D. Zhang et al., "Global Climate Change, War, and Population Decline in Recent Human History," *PNAS* 104 (2007), 19214–19; David D. Zhang et al., "Climate Change and War Frequency in Eastern China over the Last Millennium," *HumEcol* 35 (2007), 403–14, esp. 413; David D. Zhang et al., "Climatic Change, Wars, and Dynastic Cycles in China over the Last Millennium," *ClimCh* 76 (2006), 459–77. See also Solomon M. Hsiang et al., "Quantifying the Influence of Climate on Human Conflict," *Science* 341, (2013), DOI:10.1126/science.1235367.

[22] John D. Steinbrunner et al., eds., *Climate and Social Stress: Implications for Security Analysis* (Washington, DC, 2012); –, *Turn down the Heat: Why a 4° Warmer World Must Be Avoided* (Washington, DC, 2012); Diane Raines Ward, *Water Wars: Droughts, Flood, and the Politics of Thirst* (New York, 2002), 187–209; Michael T. Klare, *Resource Wars: The New Landscape of Global Conflict* (New York, 2001), 138–89; Thomas F. Homer-Dixon, *Environment, Scarcity, and Violence* (Princeton, NJ, 1999); Parth S. Dasgupta, "Population, Poverty, and the Local Environment," *SA* (Feb. 1995), 40–5; Jeffrey Sachs, "Land, Water and Conflict," *Newsweek* July 7–14, 2008; Elizabeth Rosenthal, "An Amazon Culture Withers as Food Dries Up," *NYT*, July 25, 2009; Campbell Robertson, "Iraq, a Land between 2 Rivers, Suffers as One of Them Dwindles," *NYT*, July 14 2009; Nicholas D. Kristof, "Extended Forecast: Bloodshed," *NYT*, April 13, 2008; Stephen Faris, "The Real Roots of Darfur," *The Atlantic Monthly*, April 2007; Caitlin E. Werrell and Francesco Femia, eds., *The Arab Spring and Climate Change: A Climate and Security Correlations Series* (Center for American Progress, Feb. 2013) http://climateandsecurity.files.wordpress.com/2012/04/climatechangearabspring-ccs-cap-stimson.pdf, accessed April 25, 2013. For a very qualified statement of the current social science literature, see Ragnhild Nordås and Nils Petter Gleditsch, "Climate Change

If climate change can raise the threat of civil war, the press of population and technology on resources is driving its own dynamic for conflict. Rare minerals essential for advanced technology will be increasingly the focus of competition in the coming decades, as they are now to different degrees in the Congo, South America, and China. China itself has been seeking to command new resources on near and far frontiers. Its efforts to control Tibet and the eastern Uighur autonomous region have explicitly been efforts to settle ethnically Han people, particularly military veterans, outside the Chinese core, and the Chinese government has launched a series of efforts to secure resources in sub-Saharan Africa. And on the other hand, despite arguments that oil supplies are plentiful, the industrial West has been extremely aggressive in securing access to oil; protecting the global flow of oil from the Persian Gulf has been a central tenet of United States foreign and military policy since the close of World War I.[23]

* * *

Deniers, Pessimists, and Pragmatists

On a broad front, then, climate change, population growth, and energy resources all are already directly shaping the context of global struggle in the decades to come. Some already claim that the wider impact of climate change is the vehicle of a genocide by the north being perpetrated against the global south.[24] Put more scientifically, or more delicately, by E. O. Wilson and William McKibben, we are at a "bottleneck" or a "special moment."[25] The question is how to get through this bottleneck. Answers to this question run across a wide gamut of public opinion. In the end they lead us to domains beyond the formal purview of this book: politics and governance.

and Conflict," *Political Geography* 26 (2007), 627–38; Jon Barnett and W. Neil Adgerb, "Climate Change, Human Security, and Violent Conflict," *Political Geography* 26 (2007), 639–55 offer an overview of a research agenda. See also the essays in Paul F. Diehl and Nils Petter Gleditsch, eds., *Environmental Conflict: An Anthology* (Boulder, CO, 2000).

[23] Jeffrey Gettleman, "Rwanda Stirs Deadly Brew of Troubles in Congo," *NYT*, Dec. 3, 2008; William J. Broad, "Plan to Carve Up Ocean Floor Riches Nears Fruition," *NYT*, March 29, 1994; David Barbosa, "China Starts Investing Globally," *NYT*, February 21, 2009; Edward Wong, "Clashes in China Shed Light on Ethnic Divide," July 8, 2009; Daniel Yergin, *The Prize: The Epic Quest for Oil, Money and Power* (New York, 1992), 396–403, 430–98, 588–613, 633–52, 769–79; Klare, *Resource Wars*, 27–137; Carolyn Pumphrey, ed., *Global Climate Change: National Security Implications* (Carlisle, PA, 2008); John M. Broder, "Climate Change Seen as Threat to U.S. Security," *NYT*, Aug. 9, 2009.

[24] Gideon Polya, "Climate Criminals and Climate Genocide," July 2, 2007 at http://www.countercurrents.org/polya010807.htm, accessed August 8, 2012. See also Naomi Klein, *The Shock Doctrine: The Rise of Disaster Capitalism* (New York, 2007).

[25] Wilson, *The Future of Life*, 22–49; Bill McKibben, "A Special Moment in History," *Atlantic Monthly* (May 1998), 55–78.

Until recently, public opinion on the ecological future of the earth and its people has been described in the terms framed by the debate between Paul Ehrlich and Julian Simon, alarmist Malthusians and optimistic Cornucopians. With the shift of the center of the debate from resources to climate change, new frameworks and positions have emerged. Simon's cornucopianism, with its fundamental free-market-driven assumption that a business-as-usual pursuit of economic growth could continue forever, has shifted toward a posture of denial. The active "deniers," about 7 percent of the American public according to surveys, simply refuse to accept any of the evidence that human activity has had an impact on natural climate systems. Strongly conservative and individualistic in their worldview, deniers call the evidence of climate change "junk science," "a false theory," a conspiracy, or media hype, or they argue that any changes are simply driven by natural forces. The deniers are supported by extremely powerful and wealthy interests entrenched in an old technology, especially the oil industry, which had its origins more than a century ago in the Second Industrial Revolution. And their voices have been wildly amplified by a small group of well-financed and well-connected right-wing ideologues who have worked assiduously to move public opinion against scientific evidence on cancer and tobacco, acid rain, and the ozone layer, before ginning up the campaign against climate change science.[26]

At the other end of the spectrum, separated from the deniers by a broad body of the public inclined to see climate change as a significant if somewhat abstract issue, the environmental "alarmists" have divided into two camps. The time for sounding the alarm is over, and environmentalists and their allies have had to decide on the best course of action. Very broadly they have divided into positions of angry pessimism and concerned pragmatism.

A mood of angry pessimism hangs like a dark cloud over the scientific world. For decades, scientists have been increasingly concerned about the planetary future, and frustrated by the roadblocks to mitigation thrown up by the partisans of denial in the political arena. With politicians and entrenched interests standing in the way of change, the evidence about the deep past and the unfolding present has mounted to support the premise that the earth is on the brink of nonlinear catastrophic change.[27] At this late juncture, the pessimists fear, intervention is just too little too late. This angry pessimism does not often find its way into the scientific literature, but it has found its most powerful expression in the words of James Lovelock, whose

---

[26] Anthony A. Leiserowitz, "American Risk Perceptions: Is Climate Change Dangerous?" *Risk Analysis* 25 (2005), 1433–42; Naomi Oreskes and Erik M. Conway, *Merchants of Doubt: How a Handful of Scientists Obscured the Truth in Issues from Tobacco Smoke to Global Warming* (New York, 2010).

[27] A recent poll indicates the massive consensus among climate scientists on the human causes of recent climate change and their probable consequences: http://visionprize.com/results, accessed August 8, 2012.

insights forty years ago about the interconnections of life, atmosphere, and the solid, moving earth have underpinned the earth systems approach that drives modern environmental science. In *The Revenge of Gaia*, published in 2006, Lovelock describes the future of the earth in apocalyptic terms:

[N]ow the evidence coming in from watchers around the world brings news of an imminent shift in our climate toward one that could easily be described as Hell: so hot, so deadly that only a handful of the teeming billions now alive will survive. We have made this appalling mess of the planet, and mostly rampant liberal good intensions. Even now, when the bell has started tolling to mark our ending, we still talk of sustainable development and renewable energy as if these feeble offerings would be accepted by Gaia as an appropriate and affordable sacrifice.[28]

Lovelock closes his book with the image of future survivors on camelback making their way through horrific deserts to refuges north of the Arctic Circle. But Lovelock cannot help but toy with the technological solutions that have captured the attention and efforts of many of his environmentalist peers and their new allies among the ranks of economists. This new body of pragmatists, all concerned and some hopeful, are poised on the classic pivot between Malthus and Boserup: Will the press of human numbers overwhelm the planet, or will it drive another technological revolution bringing those numbers into balance with the earth system? Can economic growth be detached from demographic numbers, attached as it has been for millennia? And can growth be detached from the environmental impacts that have followed from human activity for those same millennia?

Paltry as they might seem to Lovelock and the pessimists, the efforts of the pragmatists seeking a way through the bottleneck at times have seemed to fill the news. Fully aware of the timeline of predictions of tipping points and points of no return and the threats of abrupt change, the pragmatic approach is driven by a calculation that many discrete efforts will add up to the necessary course correction in the trajectory of the earth and its people. They are increasingly attuned to the idea that the earth will have to be managed by human action for a sustainable future, and that this will require the acceptance of a certain level of risk. And they are self-consciously thinking through a model of human social resilience in the face of sudden climatic change.[29]

---

[28] James Lovelock, *The Revenge of Gaia: Earth's Climate Crisis & the Fate of Humanity* (New York, 2006), 147–8, 159; see also Tim Dyson, "On Development, Demography and Climate Change: The End of the World as We Know It?" *Population and Environment* 27 (2005), 117–49; John D. Cox, *Climate Crash: Abrupt Climate Change and What It Means for Our Future* (Washington, DC, 2005), 177–90; Eugene Linden, *The Winds of Change: Climate, Weather, and the Destruction of Civilizations* (New York, 2006), 247–69; Anthony Barnofsky, *Heatstroke: Nature in an Age of Global Warming* (Washington, DC, 2009), Naomi Oreskes and Erik M. Conway, "The Collapse of Western Civilization: A View from the Future," *Daedalus* 142 (2013), 40–58.

[29] Smil, *Global Catastrophe and Trends*, 219–53; Scheffer, *Critical Transitions*, 265–325; Andrew C. Revkin, "Middle Stance Emerges in Debate over Climate," *NYT*, January 1,

The best established of these pragmatic programs, and perhaps the model for others in other arenas, is the effort to improve living conditions in the developing world. In a line that runs back to the nineteenth-century reformers and responding to the consequences of the control of mortality, the first pragmatist turn came in response to the earliest Malthusian concerns about population in the postwar years. In this effort they had after 1945 a ready-made global institution, the United Nations, which since its founding has devoted a large percentage of its budget to addressing pressures on the developing world, through programs and agencies devoted to population, health, economic development, food, refugees, women and children, and human settlements. Outside of the U.N., institutions such as the World Bank and the International Monetary Fund have also had a global reach, though often with the effect of advancing the interests of the developed world. Private philanthropic foundations established by the beneficiaries of the Second and Third Industrial Revolutions have also played a increasingly important role, the long-established Rockefeller and Ford Foundations now overshadowed by the Bill and Melinda Gates Foundation, which is putting vast resources into innovative development projects aimed at the world's poorest populations, and especially into health initiatives involving malaria, AIDs, and childhood diseases. The U.N.'s Millennium Development Goals, adopted in 2001, establish well-articulated plans to move aggressively to help the poorest countries, and the poorest billion of the world's population, out of poverty, challenging the world's richest nations to fund this effort with .7 percent of their GDP, less than what has been promised – but not delivered – in international aid.[30]

Over the past ten to twenty years, entrepreneurs and engineers have joined climate scientists in a similar pragmatic coalition to address global warming

2007; Stephen Pacala and Robert Socolow, "Stabilization Wedges: Solving the Climate Problem for the Next 50 Years with Current Technologies," *Science* 305 (2004), 968–72. For an early manifesto of the need for pragmatic earth system management, see Daniel B. Botkin, *Discordant Harmonies: A New Ecology for the Twenty-First Century* (New York, 1990); –, *Shaping Climate-Resilient Development: A Framework for Decision-Making* (The Economics of Climate Adaptation Working Group, 2009); Rob Atkinson et al., *Climate Pragmatism: Innovation, Resilience, and No Regrets* (The Hartwell Group, 2011). The rise of the environmental pragmatists has attracted the attention of certain skeptics (if not hardcore deniers), who advocate action or adaptation: Gregg Easterbrook, "Some Convenient Truths," *Atlantic Monthly* (September 2006), 29–30; Bjorn Lomborg, *Cool It: The Skeptical Environmentalist's Guide to Global Warming* (New York, 2007). For a very optimistic pragmatism, see Ramez Naam, *The Infinite Resource: The Power of Ideas on a Finite Planet* (Hanover, NH, 2013).

[30] Jeffrey D. Sachs, *Commonwealth: Economics for a Crowded Planet* (New York, 2008); –, *The End of Poverty: Economic Possibilities for our Time* (New York, 2005), esp. 288–308; Paul Collier, *The Bottom Billion: Why the Poorest Countries are Failing and What Can Be Done about It* (New York, 2007); Jean Strouse, "How to Give Away $21.8 Billion," *NYT*, April 16, 2000.

and the energy systems that have driven it. The technology required to reduce greenhouse gases is advancing, driven by patriotic and pocketbook concerns about energy independence, energy efficiency, and potential profit as much as environmental impact. Efforts to bring this transition to the private automobile are now advancing, with hybrid gasoline-electric vehicles well established in the market, and electric cars beginning to hit the streets.[31] Bus fleets are being converted to cleaner-burning natural gas, and hydrogen fuel systems could be in cost-effective production in a decade or two. Solar and wind energy have suddenly emerged as real possibilities. While Europe and particularly Germany are now the world leaders in solar energy supply, solar panel arrays are being installed throughout the hotter regions of the United States, and China has begun to dominate the world solar market through a major, heavily subsidized campaign.[32] Enormous fields of wind turbines are an increasingly common sight across the United States, and are becoming a significant part of the employment picture in some rural regions. Whether these weather-dependent systems can provide the steady high volume of sustained electric power remains to be seen, however.

These efforts to limit emissions may well come up short, too little too late, or simply fail. The result is a growing if contested interest in more aggressive interventions into the workings of the earth system. One idea being developed is to literally scrub CO_2 out of the air with chemical machinery that would convert the carbon to quicklime. Such CO_2 scrubbers have been constructed in laboratories, and efforts are under way to see if they can be manufactured on a real-world scale.[33] Other approaches are more controversial, because they involve more radical geoengineering interventions that might well lead to widely ramifying unintended consequences. One solution would be to dump many tons of iron fillings into the south Pacific to encourage blooms of algae that would ingest and sequester

---

[31] The transition to new automotive fuels may – or not – be driven by new resources shortages. If the weight of the environmental debate shifted from sources to sinks in the 1980s and 1990s, the sudden entry of China and India into the world economy after the year 2000 drove the massive spike in oil prices that ran from the summer of 2007 into 2008. This price increase clearly drove the biofuels enthusiasm that has diverted huge volumes of corn from foodstocks to fuel, driving a worldwide increase in food prices. But the price of oil fell in 2008 as the financial crisis began to unfold, and has been held down by the recession. As the world economy recovers, oil prices should rise again, and the eagerness of American consumers to dump "clunkers" for fuel-efficient Toyotas in the summer of 2009 seems to have been a strategic hedge against a projected price increase. But if indeed oil supplies themselves are not really limited, the constriction point is refinery capacity.

[32] Keith Bradsher, "China Racing Ahead of U.S. in the Drive to Go Solar," *NYT*, August 25, 2009; Associated Press, "GM Rolls Past 1 Million Miles in Fuel Cell Demo," reported in the *NYT*, Sept. 11, 2009.

[33] Nicola Jones, "Sucking it Up," *Nature* 458 (2009), 1094–7; Wallace S. Broecker and Robert Kunzig, *Fixing Climate: What Past Climate Changes Reveal about the Current Threat – and How to Counter It* (New York, 2008), 198–233.

CO_2. Another proposal is to inject sulfate aerosols into the stratosphere to simulate the effect of volcanic eruptions, thus cooling the earth; another would have special ships spraying seawater to whiten stratospheric clouds. Yet another involves positioning enormous reflectors above the atmosphere, which would deflect solar radiation. The most extreme model so argues that the hiatus in warming in the 1950s and 1960s was not caused by industrial sulfates but by pulverized rock put into the atmosphere by surface testing of nuclear weapons; the article quantifies the cost of sending daily flights to the top of the atmosphere to spread tons of powdered limestone. The first objection to these concepts, some of which are seen as borderline feasible, are the unintended consequences. Overshooting the dumping of iron filings could cool the earth climate suddenly, while imitating volcanic emissions runs the risk of further interfering with global precipitation patterns. As important, these technological interventions could well encourage global powers to accept a solution of continuing high greenhouse emissions offset by technological fixes. Such a "solution" would require century after century of careful maintenance because shutting down such technologies while inflated levels of greenhouse gases remain in the atmosphere would indeed set off a hellish surge of catastrophic warming. On the other hand, having these technologies in reserve might well be a prudent policy, because they could be deployed in a worst-case scenario.[34]

Policy, however, requires politics. Shaping these technical fixes are the political decisions that will direct the flow and structuring finances necessary to effect change. These involve complex negotiations between global institutions and sovereign nations, which have as yet not arrived at a workable solution, given the deeply entrenched interests at stake. As in development and population, the center of efforts to address questions of global environment and climate change are institutions framed by the United Nations. First, the Intergovernmental Panel on Climate Change was established in 1988, the hot year that suddenly brought the question of global warming to public attention, as a global consortium of scientists assessing the evidence for climate change. Formed on the initiative of the World Meteorological Organization and the U.N. Environmental Programme, which dated back to 1873 and 1972 respectively, the IPCC thus has roots in the late nineteenth-century institutionalization of science and the launch of the environmental movement after the first Earth Day. Publishing its first report in 1995, the IPCC was formally made the advisory arm to the U.N.'s negotiating body,

---

[34] William J. Broad, "How to Cool a Planet (Maybe)," *NYT*, June 27, 2006. For skeptical views, see the articles by Stephen Schneider and James Lovelock in Brian Launder and J. Michael T. Thompson, eds., *Geo-Engineering Climate Change: Environmental Necessity or Pandora's Box?* (New York, 2010), 3–26, 84–92; Gabriele C. Hegerl and Susan Solomon, "Risks of Climate Engineering," *Science* 325 (2009), 955–6. For the nuclear model, see Yoshiaki Fugii, "The Role of Atmospheric Nuclear Explosions on the Stagnation of Warming in the Mid-20th Century," *Journal of Atmospheric and Solar-Terrestrial Physics* 73 (2011), 643–52.

the Framework Convention on Climate Change (UNFCCC), established at the Earth Summit at Rio de Janeiro in 1992. The Framework convention has met annually since 1995, but the negotiations have never reached on a consensus on how the leading and established economies might disproportionately cut their emissions, leading toward green technology while developing countries continue energy- and emission-intensive economic development. The Kyoto Protocol of 1997 established a global plan to bring greenhouse emissions 6 percent to 8 percent below 1990 levels by 2008–12; the U.S. target of 7 percent was blocked by the U.S. Senate during the Democratic Clinton administration and explicitly rejected by the Republican Bush administration in 2001. In June 2009, the U.S. House of Representatives passed the Waxman-Markey Clean Energy and Security Act, which established a cap-and-trade system aimed at reducing U.S. greenhouse emissions by 17 percent (from 2005) in 2020, and 80 percent in 2050, mandated the modernization and increased efficiency of electrical systems, and advanced support for renewable energy and electric vehicles. Under the relentless pressure of the economic recession and a drumbeat of opposition from the American Republican Party, this bill has disappeared from the national agenda, as the debate over health care and then the slow economic recovery from the 2008 crash have stifled any political momentum toward action on climate.[35]

The central and obvious roadblock to a comprehensive global agreement lies in the perceived trade-off between economy and environment. As we have seen, the modern history of economic expansions and interruptions has demonstrated so far that flourishing economies – producing and consuming increasing volumes of electricity – produce equivalent emissions. The United States has refused to control emissions if that would interfere with an "American lifestyle," and developing countries such as China have been equally unwilling to slow their development for the sake of the environment. While the evidence from the 1987 Montreal Protocol, which banned CFCs, has shown how effective global controls can be implemented without serious economic consequences, the largest greenhouse contributors stand against decisive action.

Thus a worldwide debate on practical, pragmatic solutions for the next century hinges on the balance between economic growth and projected climate change. The Fourth Assessment Report of the IPCC, issued early in 2007, stands at the institutional and intellectual center of this debate. Working Group III of IPCC was assigned the task of assessing the range of mitigation strategies, and presenting a graduated series of options for the Framework Convention and its member nations to consider and act upon. The core of their report is a review of the costs of investments in technology,

---

[35] Weart, *The Discovery of Global Warming*, 32–3, 142–59, 168–9, 174–5, 187–90; John M. Broder, "House Passes Bill to Address Threat of Climate Change," *NYT*, June 27, 2009.

infrastructure, and behavior modification that would be required to bring greenhouse gas emissions to within certain stabilization targets. They estimate that keeping CO_2 concentrations in 2030 in the 440–485 ppm range might shave off perhaps 1 percent of global GDP, and keeping it within 350–440 ppm range might cost 2 to 3 percent. Estimates for the years 2050 are considerably higher, as much as 5.5 percent. On the other hand, the Working Group does not assess the costs of *not acting*, but suggests that action might even *increase* GNP slightly, by as much as 1 percent by 2050. New estimates posit that the costs of inaction against global warming are much higher than previously expected; it remains to be demonstrated directly that they would be much higher than those of action.[36]

The IPCC Report, and the Stern Review issued by Nicholas Stern, climate adviser to the United Kingdom in 2006, both present relatively cost-free plans for addressing climate change. As revised in a 2009 book, the Stern report is now the core of a pragmatic solution. He proposes a 50 percent cut in 1990 emissions by 2050, with a target of ~450 ppm CO_2 (or 500 ppm CO_2 in total greenhouse gas equivalents). Developed countries would agree immediately to reductions by 2020 and 2050, totally 80 percent of 1990 emissions; developing countries would agree to reductions in 2020. The entire process would be governed by a global system of cap and trade in "carbon credits" that would grow increasingly costly through time, driving emitters to adopt improved technologies. Essential elements include success in stopping tropical deforestation, subsidies by developed countries for the necessary technology, and serious efforts to provide a wide range of assistance to the developing world.[37]

The Stern position is the essence of pragmatism. It addresses the deniers by arguing that the costs of climate mitigation would not be too high, and it warns the pessimists to not "disrupt the possibility of agreement in the very near future."[38] But its premises have been strongly challenged. James

[36] IPCC, "Summary for Policy Makers," and Brian Fisher et al., "Ch. 3: Issues Related to Mitigation in the Long-Term Context," in B. Metz et al., eds., *Climate Change 2007: Mitigation: Contribution of Working Group III to the Fourth Assessment Report of the Inter-governmental Panel on Climate Change* (Cambridge, 2007), 11, 18; 197–200, 203–6, 231–3. For an assessment of the literature on the costs of inaction, see Richard S. J. Tol, "The Social Cost of Carbon: Trends, Outliers and Catastrophes," *Economics: The Open-Access, Open-Assessment E-Journal* 2 (2008); and –, "Why Worry about Carbon? A Research Agenda," *Environmental Values* 17 (2008), 437–70; Martin Parry et al., *Assessing the Costs of Adaptation to Climate Change: A Review of the UNFCCC and other Recent Estimates* (London, 2009).

[37] Nicholas Stern, *The Global Deal: Climate Change and the Creation of a New Era of Progress and Prosperity* (New York, 2009), 144–80. Originally published in the United Kingdom as *A Blueprint for a Safer Planet*. See also Fred Krupp and Miriam Horn, *Earth the Sequel: The Race to Reinvent Energy and Stop Global Warming* (New York, 2008). Fred Krupp is the president of the Environmental Defense Fund.

[38] Stern, *The Global Deal*, 150–1.

Hansen, the director of the NASA Goddard Institute for Space Science and one of the leading climate scientists in the United States, opened the public climate change debate in his 1988 report to Congress. He earned his spurs as a pragmatist during the last decade, arguing that a low-cost mitigation could be achieved through focusing on reducing methane and black soot emissions to zero, while allowing CO_2 emissions to continue relatively unabated for several decades.[39] But in the past few years, following his own review of the entire sweep of Cenozoic climate history, he has rejected the 450 ppm target advanced by the IPCC and the Stern report, and strongly advocated for a goal of reducing CO_2 to 350 ppm as soon as possible. His position is supported by new studies focusing on the long-range impacts of highly persistent atmospheric CO_2. Hansen's analysis hinges on the "tipping point" toward a glaciated planet 35 million years ago during the late Eocene, when he argues that CO_2 dropped below a range of 450–600 ppm. In this analysis, a planet with an atmospheric CO_2 count of higher than 450 ppm, "if long maintained would push Earth toward an ice-free state," the extreme, apocalyptic picture of the "angry pessimists." Thus Hansen – with a distinguished group of coauthors – argues strenuously that we need to return as soon as possible to a "safe" 350 ppm level. To achieve this goal, he reiterates his recommendations on eliminating methane and black soot emissions, recommends serious efforts at reforestation, the elimination of biomass burning, and demands that all coal emissions be sequestered or phased out. Then he takes an initial step toward geoengineering, proposing the industrial production of the CO_2 air scrubbers that now exist as prototypes. His fellow NASA scientist Drew Shindell has advanced the argument for black carbon reductions, combining the evidence for its unique greenhouse impact with its adverse effects on agricultural productivity and human health.[40]

In the final analysis, our current circumstance needs to be seen both as a crisis in the relation of humanity and the earth system, and as a moment in the long-term transformation of economic systems on a scale with any of the

---

[39] James Hansen et al., "Global Warming in the Twenty-First Century: An Alternative Scenario," *PNAS* 97 (2000), 9875–80; James Hansen and Larissa Nazarenko, "Soot Climate Forcing via Snow and Ice Albidos," *PNAS* 101 (2004), 423–8; James Hansen and Makiko Sato, "Greenhouse Growth Rates," *PNAS* 101 (2004), 16109–14; James Hansen, "Defusing the Global Warming Time Bomb," *SA* (March 2004), 70–7.

[40] James Hansen et al., "Target Atmospheric CO_2: Where Should Humanity Aim?" *The Open Atmospheric Science Journal* 2 (2008), 217–31, and suppl. i–xxi. See also Myles R. Allen et al., Warming Caused by Cumulative Carbon Emissions toward the Trillionth Tonne," *Nature* 458 (2009), 1163–6; J. A. Lowe, "How Difficult Is It to Recover from Dangerous Levels of Global Warming?" *Environmental Research Letters* 4 (2009), 014012; Malte Meinshausen, "Greenhouse-Gas Emission Targets for Limiting Global Warming to 2°C," *Nature* 458 (2009), 1158–62; Susan Solomon et al., "Irreversible Climate Change Due to Carbon Dioxide Emissions," *PNAS* 106 (2009), 1704–9; Drew Shindell et al., "Simultaneously Mitigating Near-Term Climate Change and Improving Human Health and Food Security," *Science* 335 (2012), 183–9.

great ruptures of the human past. Scientists, engineers, and entrepreneurs, the core of the pragmatic coalition, are mapping a possible path to a sustainable future. Quite simply, it can go one way or another. What is needed is a new legal framework to shape the transition to a new system of energy and the market. If an earth system crisis is averted, it will be because the politics of economic transformation was able to unfold quickly enough to make a difference.

Over the past 500 years, all significant epochs of economic transformation have had a fundamentally political dimension. In each case, the state's role in the determination of the course of economic action made the decisive difference. European states set the conditions that launched the age of empire; the resolution of the English Revolution in 1689 and eventually British victories over Napoleon framed the conditions of the First Industrial Revolution; the legal, institutional, and financial initiatives of European governments and the United States set the conditions for the Second Industrial Revolution.[41] In each of these transitions there was a heated political struggle between the established order and the advocates of change. It can be argued that we currently sit stalled in the midst of the Third Industrial Revolution, but that the tools needed to address the earth system crisis are those of that third revolution: an explosion of innovation and investment in an energy-technology economy that will drive the human condition forward while maintaining the essential integrity of the earth system. The critical lever to launch and sustain this transformation must be the collective action of democratic governance at the national and the international levels. There are strong indications that the American public is beginning to understand the case for action.[42]

What is necessary, what all of the pragmatists are working for, what the pessimists despair of, and what the deniers reject in antihistorical, antiscientific ideological animus, entrenched interest, and a good bit of wishful thinking, is a global solution. We hold it in our collective capacity to address the earth system crisis that is now upon us. That capacity must be mobilized by an informed political will.

---

[41] Here see Carlota Perez on the role of politics and law in the turning points of long waves, in *Technological Revolutions and Financial Capital: The Dynamics of Bubbles and Golden Ages* (Cheltenham, UK, 2002), 52–3, 120–1; and Robert U. Ayres, "Resources, Scarcity, Technology, and Growth," in Simpson et al., *Scarcity and Growth Revisited*, 144–54.

[42] The public support for taking climate change seriously is stronger than much of the media coverage would indicate. See Anthony Leiserowitz et al., *Climate Change in the American Mind: Public Support for Climate & Energy Policies in March 2012: Yale University and George Mason University* (New Haven, CT, 2012); University of Texas Energy Poll, reported in Mark Drajem, "Record Heat Wave Pushes U.S. Belief in Climate Change to 70%," *Bloomberg News*, July 18, 2012.

Data Bibliography: Full Citations for Data Used in Figures and Tables

Allen, Robert, C. "Prices and Wages in London & Southern England, 1259–1914," Consumer price indices, nominal / real wages and welfare ratios of building craftsmen and labourers, 1260–1913, International Institute of Social History data files, available at http://www.iisg.nl/hpw/data.php#europe, accessed August 8, 2012.

Angel, J. Lawrence. "Health as a Crucial Factor in the Changes from Hunting to Developed Farming in the Eastern Mediterranean," in Mark N. Cohen and George J. Armelagos, eds., *Paleopathology at the Origins of Agriculture* (New York, 1984), 51–73; 137–67.

Bar-Matthews, M., A. Ayalon, M. Gilmour, A. Matthews, and C. J. Hawkesworth. "Sea-Land Oxygen Isotopic Relationships from Planktonic Foraminifera and Speleothems in the Eastern Mediterranean Region and Their Implication for Paleorainfall during Interglacial Intervals," *Geochimica et Cosmochimica Acta* 67/17 (2003), 3181–99.

Belfer-Cohen, A., L. A. Schepartz, and B. Arensburg. "New Biological Data for the Natufian Populations of Israel," in Ofer Bar-Yosef and Francois R. Valla, eds., *The Natufian Culture in the Levant* (Ann Arbor, MI, 1991), 411–24, at 413 and 421–2.

Berger, A. and M. F. Loutre. "Insolation Values for the Climate of the Last 100 Million Years," *QSR* 10 (1991), 297–317.

Bergman, Noam M., Timothy M. Lenton, and Andrew J. Watson. "COPSE: A New Model of Biogeochemical Cycling over Phanerozoic Time," *American Journal of Science* 304 (2004), 421. COPSE **fig 1.2.

Binford, Lewis L. *Constructing Frames of Reference: An Analytical Method for Archaeological Theory Building Using Hunter-Gatherer and Environmental Data Sets* (Berkeley, CA, 2001), 142–4.

Biraben, Jean-Nöel. "Essai sur l-Évolution du Nombre des Hommes," *Population* 34 (1979), 13–24.

Bird, Broxton W., M. B. Abbott, M. Vuille, D. T. Rodbell, N. D. Stansell, and M. F. Rosenmeier. "A 2,300-Year-Long Annually Revolved Record of the South American Summer Monsoon from the Peruvian Andes," *PNAS* 108 (2011), 8583–8.

Bocquet-Appel, Jean-Pierre. "Paleoanthropological Traces of a Neolithic Demographic Transition," *Current Anthropology* 43 (2002), 637–50.

"Estimates of Upper Paleolithic Meta-Population Size in Europe from archaeological data," *JArchS* 32 (2005), 1656–68.

Bocquet-Appel, Jean-Pierre, and Stephan Naji. "Testing the Hypothesis of a Worldwide Neolithic Demographic Transition: Corroboration from American Cemeteries," *Current Anthropology* 47 (2006), 341–65.

Boden, Tom, Gregg Marland, and Bob Andres. "Global CO_2 Emissions from Fossil-Fuel Burning, Cement Manufacture, and Gas Flaring: 1751–2008" (June 10, 2011), Carbon Dioxide Information Analysis Center, Oak Ridge National Laboratory, Oak Ridge, Tennessee 37831–6290, data file at http://cdiac.ornl.gov/ftp/ndp030/global.1751_2008.ems, accessed August 8, 2012.

Bond, Gerard, Bernd Kromer, Juerg Beer, Raimund Muscheler, Michael N. Evans, William Showers, Sharon Hoffmann, Rusty Lotti-Bond, Irka Hajdas, and Georges Bonani. "Persistent Solar Influence on North Atlantic Climate during the Holocene," *Science*, New Series, 294 (2001), 2130–6.

Bottema, Sytze. "The Use of Palynology in Tracing Early Agriculture," in R. T. J. Cappers and S. Bottema, eds., *The Dawn of Farming in the Near East* (Berlin, 2002), 27–38 (Huleh Oak sequence).

BP Statistical Review of World Energy. June 2011, available at http://www.bp.com/statisticalreview, accessed August 8, 2012.

Brooks, E. J., et al., "Rapid variation in atmospheric methane concentration during the past 110,000 years," *Science* 273 (1996), 1087–91.

Casting, James F. "When Methane Made Climate," *Scientific American* 291 (July 2004), 78–85.

Chalié, Françoise and Françoise Gasse. "Late-Glacial-Holocene Diatom Record of Water Chemistry and Lake Level Change from the Tropical East African Rift Lake Abiyata (Ethiopia)," *PPP* 187 (2002), 259–83.

Chen, F. H., J. H. Chen, J. Holmes, I. Boomer, P. Austin, J. B. Gates, N. L. Wang, S. J. Brooks, and J. W. Zhang. "Moisture Changes over the Last Millennium in Arid Central Asia: A Review, Synthesis and Comparison with Monsoon Region," *QSR* 29 (2010), 1055–68.

Chesnais, Jean-Claude. *The Demographic Transition: Stages, Patterns, and Economic Implications* (Oxford, 1992), 58–60 (infant mortality), 118–19 (crude birth rate).

Chu, G., Q. Sun, X. Wang, and J. Sun. "Snow Anomaly Events from Historical Documents in Eastern China during the Past Two Millennia and Implication for Low-Frequency Variability of AO/NAO and PDO," *GRL* 25 (2008), L14806, doi:10.1029/2008GL034475.

Cinnirella, Francesco. "Optimists or Pessimists? A Reconsideration of Nutritional Status in Britain, 1740–1865," *EREconHist* 12 (2008), 339.

Clark, Gregory. "The Long March of History: Farm Wages, Population, and Economic Growth, England 1209–1869," *EconHistR* 60 (2007), 97–135, at 99–100 (wages), 120 (population).

Cook, Edward R. et al., "Megadroughts in North America: Placing IPCC Projections of Hydroclimatic Change in a Long-Term Palaeoclimate Context," *JQS* 25 (2010), 48–61.

Crafts, N. F. R. and C. K. Harley. "Output Growth and the British Industrial Revolution: A Restatement of the Crafts-Harley View," *EconHistR* 45 (1992), 703–30 ("revised best guess," 725–7).

Cullen, H. M. "Climate Change and the Collapse of the Akkadian Empire: Evidence from the Deep Sea," *Geology* 28 (2000), 379–82.

de Vries, Jan. *European Urbanization, 1500–1800* (Cambridge, MA, 1984), 30 (urban population).

deMenocal, Peter B. "Abrupt Onset and Termination of the African Humid Period: Rapid Climate Responses to Gradual Insolation Forcing," *QSR* 19 (2000), 347–61.

"African Climate Change and Faunal Evolution during the Pliocene-Pleistocene," *EPSL* 220 (2004), 3–24 (Figure 11).

Dykoski, Carolyn A., R. Lawrence Edwards, Hai Cheng, Daoxian Yuan, Yanjun Cai, Meiliang Zhang, Yushi Lin, Jiaming Qing, Zhisheng An, and Justin Revenaugh. "A High-Resolution, Absolute-Dated Holocene and Deglacial Asia Monsoon Record from Dongge Cave, China," *EPSL* 233 (2005), 71–86.

Earth Impact Database, University of New Brunswick, at http://www.passc.net/EarthImpactDatabase/Diametersort.html (all craters from 40 km in diameter), accessed August 8, 2012.

Ellenblum, Ronnie. *The Collapse of the Eastern Mediterranean: Climate Change and the Decline of the East, 950–1072* (Cambridge, 2012) (Nile drought list at p. 31).

Ellison, Rosemary. "Diet in Mesopotamia: The Evidence of the Barley Ration Tests (c. 3000–1400 BC)," *Iraq* 45 (1981), 35–45.

"Some Thoughts on the Diet of Mesopotamia from c. 3000–600BC," *Iraq* 45 (1983), 146–50.

Etheridge, D. M., L. P. Steele, R. J. Francey, and R. L. Langenfelds. "Atmospheric Methane between 1000 A.D. and Present: Evidence of Anthropogenic Emissions and Climatic Variability," *JGR* 103 (1998), D13, pp. 15,979 (98JD00923).

Etheridge, D. M., L. P. Steele, R. L. Langenfelds, R. J. Francey, J.-M. Barnola, and V. I. Morgan. "Natural and Anthropogenic Changes in Atmospheric CO_2 over the Last 1000 Years from Air in Antarctic Ice and Firn," *JGR* 101 (1996), 4115–28.

Fleitman, Dominik, Stephen J. Burns, Augusto Mangini, Manfred Mudelsee, Jan Kramers, Igor Villa, Ulrich Neff, Abdulkarim A. Al-Subbary, Annett Buettner, Dorothea Hippler, and Albert Matter. "Holocene ITCZ and Indian Monsoon Dynamics Recorded in Stalagmites from Oman and Yemen (Socotra)," *QSR* 26 (2007), 170–88.

Flinn, Michael W. *History of the British Coal Industry, Vol. 2, 1700–1830: The Industrial Revolution* (Oxford, 1984), 26.

Floud, Roderick, Kenneth Wacher, and Annabel Gregory. *Height, Health and History: Nutritional Status in the United Kingdom, 1750–1880* (Cambridge, 1990), 240.

Ford, David and Jan Golonka. "Phanerozoic Paleography, Paleoenvironment and Lithofacies Maps of the Circum-Atlantic Margins," *Marine and Petroleum Geology* 20 (2003), 249–85.

Formicola, Vincenzo and Monica Giannecchini. "Evolutionary Trends of Stature in Upper Paleolithic and Mesolithic Europe," *JHumEv* 36 (1999), 319–33.

Garnsey, Peter. *Food and Society in Classical Antiquity* (Cambridge, 1999), 57–9.

Gerhards, Guntis. "Secular Variations in the Body Stature of the Inhabitants of Latvia (7th millennium BC – 20th c. AD)," *Acta Medica Lituanica* 12 (2005), 33–9.

Glikson, Andrew. "Asteroid/Comet Impact Clusters, Flood Basalts and Mass Extinctions: Significance of Isotopic Age Overlaps," *EPSL* 236 (2005), 933–7.

Greene, Kevin. *The Archaeology of the Roman Economy* (London, 1986), 60–1.

Grootes, P. M. and M. Stuiver. "Oxygen 18/16 Variability in Greenland Snow and Ice with 10^3 to 10^5-Year Time Resolution," *JGR* 102 (1997), 26455–70.

Guerrero, Emma, Stephen Naji, and Jean-Pierre Bocquet-Appel. "The Signal of the Neolithic Demographic Transition in the Levant," in Jean-Pierre Bocquet-Appel and Ofer Bar-Yosef, eds., *The Neolithic Demographic Transition and Its Consequences* (New York, 2008), 57–80.

Gupta, Anil K., David M. Anderson, and Jonathan T. Overpeck. "Abrupt Changes in the Asian Southwest Monsoon during the Holocene and Their Links to the North Atlantic Ocean," *Nature* 421 (2003), 354–7.

Hassan, Fekri A. "Extreme Nile Floods and Famines in Medieval Egypt (A.D. 930–1500) and Their Climatic Implications," *QuatInt* 173–4 (2007), 101–12.

Hatcher, John. *The History of the British Coal Industry, Vol. I, Before 1700: Towards the Age of Coal* (Oxford, 1993), 68.

Haug, G. H., K. A. Hughen, L. C. Peterson, D. M. Sigman, and U. Röhl. "Southward Migration of the Intertropical Convergence Zone through the Holocene," *Science* 293 (2001), 1304–8.

Henry, Donald O. "Models of Agricultural Origins and Proxy Measures of Prehistoric Demographics," in R. T. J. Cappers and S. Bottema, eds., *The Dawn of Farming in the Near East* (Berlin, 2002), 15–25.

Hershkovitz, Israel and Avi Gopher. "Demographic, Biological, and Cultural Aspects of the Neolithic Revolution: A View from the Southern Levant," in Jean-Pierre Bocquet-Appel and Ofer Bar-Yosef, eds., *The Neolithic Demographic Transition and its Consequences* (New York, 2008), 441–75.

Hillson, Simon W., Clark Spencer Larsen, Başak Boz, A. Pilloud, Joshua W. Sadvari, Sabrina C. Agarwal, Bonnie Glencross, Patrick Beauchesne, Jessica Pearson, Christopher B. Ruff, Evan M. Garofalo, Lori Hager, and Scott D. Haddow. "The Human Remains I: Interpreting Community Structure, Health, and Diet in Neolithic Çatalhöyük," in Ian Hodder, ed., *Humans and Landscapes of Çatalhöyük* (Los Angeles, CA, 2013).

Hist. Stat.: Susan B. Carter, Scott Sigmund Gartner, Michael R. Haines, Alan L. Olmstead, Richard Sutch, and Gavin Wright, eds., *Historical Statistics of the United States: Millennium Edition Online* (New York, 2012).

Hist. Stat.: Table Aa 699–715 Urban and rural territory – population, by size of place: 1790–1990. Contributor: Michael Haines.

Hist. Stat.: Table Bd 653–87. Selected anthropometric measurements – height, weight, and body mass index: 1710–1989. Contributor: Richard Steckel.

Hist. Stat.: Table Aa 9–14 – National population and the demographic components of change: 1790–2000 (annual estimates) Contributors: Michael R. Haines and Richard Sutch.

Hist. Stat.: Table Db 164–71 – Energy consumption, by energy source: 1850–2001. Contributor: Gavin Wright.

Hist. Stat.: Table Db 218–27 – Electric utilities power generation and fossil fuel consumption, by energy source: 1920–2000. Contributor: Gavin Wright.

Hodell, D. A., M. Brenner, and J. H. Curtis. "Terminal Classic Drought in the Northern Maya Lowlands Inferred from Multiple Sediment Cores in Lake Chichancanab (Mexico)," *QSR* 24 (2005), 1413–27.

Hole, Frank. "Burial Patterns in the Fifth Millennium," in Elizabeth F. Henrickson and Ingolf Thuesen, eds., *Upon This Foundation: The 'Ubaid Reconsidered* (Copenhagen, 1989), 149–80.

Hong, Y. T., B. Hong, Q. H. Lin, Y. Shibata, M. Hirota, Y. X. Zhu, X. T. Leng, Y. Wang, H. Wang, and L. Yi. "Inverse Phase Oscillations between the East Asian and Indian Ocean Summer Monsoons during the Last 12000 Years and Paleo-El Niño," *EPSL* 231 (2005), 337–46.

Houghton, R. A. "Carbon Flux to the Atmosphere from Land-Use Changes: 1850–2005," (2008), in *TRENDS: A Compendium of Data on Global Change*. Carbon Dioxide Information Analysis Center, Oak Ridge

National Laboratory, available at: http://cdiac.ornl.gov/trends/landuse/houghton/houghton.html, accessed August 8, 2012.

Indermühle, A., T. F. Stocker, F. Joos, H. Fischer, H. J. Smith, M. Wahlen, B. Deck, D. Mastroianni, J. Tschumi, T. Blunier, R. Meyer, and B. Stauffer. "Holocene Carbon-Cycle Dynamics Based on CO_2 Trapped in Ice at Taylor Dome, Antarctica," *Nature* 398 (1999), 121–6.

IPCC Box 6.4: Regional temperature proxies (c. 800–present) developed by Timothy Osborn and Keith Briffa for Box 6.4, Ch. 6, Paleoclimate, in Susan Solomon et al., eds., *Climate Change 2007 – The Physical Science Basis: Working Group I Contribution to the Fourth Assessment Report of the Intergovernmental Panel on Climate Change* (Cambridge and New York, 2007), available at http://www.ncdc.noaa.gov/paleo/pubs/ipcc2007/ipcc2007.html and http://www.cru.uea.ac.uk/~timo/datapages/ipccar4.htm, accessed August 8, 2012. See also Timothy A. Osborn and Keith R. Briffa, "The Special Extent of 20th-Century Warmth in the Context of the Past 1200 Years," *Science* 311 (2006), 841–4.

IPCC Figure 6.10: Northern Hemisphere temperature tree-ring synthesis (B2000: AD 1–present) developed by Keith Briffa and Timothy Osborn for figure 6.10, chapter 6, Paleoclimate, in *Climate Change 2007 – The Physical Science Basis*.

JISAO/ENSO: "Global-SST ENSO index, 1817 – February 2011," Joint Institute for the Study of the Atmosphere and Ocean, University of Washington, available at http://jisao.washington.edu/data/globalsstenso/, accessed August 8, 2012.

Jones P. D., T. J. Osborn, and K. R. Briffa. "The Evolution of Climate over the Last Millennium," *Science* 292 (2001), 662–7 (NAO index).

Jones, P. D., D. H. Lister, T. J. Osborn, C. Harpham, M. Salmon, and C. P. Morice. "Hemispheric and Large-Scale Land-Surface Air Temperature Variations: An Extensive Revision and an Update to 2010," *JGR*, 117 (2012), D05127.

Khalil, M. A. K., M. J. Shearer, and R. A. Rasmussen. "Methane Sources in China: Historical Current Emissions," *Chemosphere* 26 (1993), 127–42, at 142. Data before 1900 is extrapolated from the ratio of Chinese population in 1900 and Chinese methane emissions estimated for 1900.

Khalil, M. Aslam Kahn, Christopher L. Butenhoff, and Reinhold A. Rasmussen. "Atmospheric Methane: Trends and Cycles of Sources and Sinks," *Environmental Science and Technology* 41 (2007), 2131–7.

King, Anthony. "Diet in the Roman World: A Regional Inter-Site Comparison of the Mammal Bones," *JRomArch* 12 (1999), 168–202.

Koepke, Nikola and Joerg Baten. "The Biological Standard of Living in Europe during the Last Two Millennia," *EREconHist* 9 (2005), 61–95.

Kuijt, Ian. "People and Space in Early Agricultural Villages: Exploring Daily Lives, Community Size, and Architecture in the Late Pre-Pottery Neolithic," *JAnthArch* 19 (2000), 75–102.

Kuzucuoğlu, Catherine et al., "Mid- to Late-Holocene Climate Change in Central Turkey: The Tecer Lake Record," *Holocene* 21 (2011), 173–88.

Law, C. M. "The Growth of Population in England and Wales, 1801–1911," *Transactions of the Institute of British Geographers* 41 (1967), 142 (urban population).

Lindsay, J. F. and D. M. Brazier. "Evolution of the Precambrian Atmosphere: Carbon Isotopic Evidence from the Australian Continent," in Patrick G. Eriksson et al., eds., *The Precambrian Earth: Tempo and Events* (Amsterdam, 2004), 400; Patrick G. Eriksson et al., "Patterns of Sedimentation in the Precambrian," *SedGeol* 176 (2005), 23.

Ljungqvist, Frederik C. "A New Reconstruction of Temperature Variability in the Extra-Tropical Northern Hemisphere during the Last Two Millennia," *Geografiska Annaler: Series A* 92 (2010), 339–51.

Loulergue, L., A. Schilt, R. Spahni, V. Masson-Delmotte, T. Blunier, B. Lemieux, J.-M. Barnola, D. Raynaud, T. F. Stocker, and J. Chappellaz. "Orbital and Millennial-Scale Features of Atmospheric CH4 over the Past 800,000 Years," *Nature* 453 (2008), 383–6.

Lukacs, John R. and J. N. Pal. "Skeletal Variation among Mesolithic People of the Ganga Plains: New Evidence of Habitual Activity and Adaptation to Climate," *Asian Perspective* 42 (2003), 329–51.

Lüthi, D., M. Le Floch, B. Bereiter, T. Blunier, J.-M. Barnola, U. Siegenthaler, D. Raynaud, J. Jouzel, H. Fischer, K. Kawamura, and T. F. Stocker. "High-Resolution Carbon Dioxide Concentration Record 650,000–800,000 Years before Present," *Nature* 453 (2008), 379–82.

Maddison, Angus. "Historical Statistics of the World Economy: 1–2008 AD," March 2010 data file at http://www.ggdc.net/maddison/Maddison.htm, accessed August 8, 2012 (population since 1870; GDP).

The World Economy: A Millennial Perspective (Paris, 2001), 29–30 (life expectancy).

Mauna Loa CO$_2$ Annual Mean Data, 1959–2011. Dr. Pieter Tans, NOAA/ESRL and Dr. Ralph Keeling, Scripps Institution of Oceanography. Dataset at http://www.esrl.noaa.gov/gmd/ccgg/trends/#mlo_data, accessed August 8, 2012.

Mayewski, P. A., L. D. Meeker, M. S. Twickler, S. I. Whitlow, Q. Yang, W. B. Lyons, and M. Prentice. "Major Features and Forcing of High-Latitude Northern Hemisphere Atmospheric Circulation Using a 110,000-Year-Long Glaciochemical Series," *JGR* 102 (1997), 26345–66.

McEvedy, Colin and Richard Jones. *Atlas of World Population History* (New York, 1978).

Meadows, John. "The Younger Dryas Episode and the Radiocarbon Chronologies of the Lake Huleh and Ghab Valley Pollen Diagrams, Israel and Syria," *The Holocene* 15 (2005), 631–6.

Mitchell B. R., with Phyllis Deane. *Abstract of British Historical Statistics* (Cambridge, 1971), 225–6.

British Historical Statistics (Cambridge, 1988), 258 (coal), 370, 373, 375 (horsepower).

International Historical Statistics: Europe, 1750–1993, fourth edition (New York, 1998), 79–85, 87 (UK population), 426, 428, 431–2, 477, 480, 482, 484 (coal), 562–3 (electrical generation).

Monnin, Eric, Andreas Indermühle, André Dällenbach, Jacqueline Flückiger, Bernhard Stauffer, Thomas F. Stocker, Dominique Raynaud, and Jean-Marc Barnola. "Atmospheric CO_2 Concentrations over the Last Glacial Termination," *Science* 291 (2001), 112–14.

Moy, Christopher M. "Variability of El Niño-Southern Oscillation Activity at Millennial Timescales during the Holocene Epoch," *Nature* 420 (2002), 162–5.

Munoz, Samuel E., Konrad Gajewski, and Matthew C. Peros. "Synchronous Environmental and Cultural Change in the Prehistory of the Northeastern United States," *PNAS* 107 (2010), 22008–13.

Museum of London Center for Bioarchaeology Web site: http://www.museumoflondon.org.uk/Collections-Research/LAARC/Centre-for-Human-Bioarchaeology/Database/Medieval+cemeteries/, accessed August 8, 2012.

Musson, A. E. "Industrial Motive Power in the United Kingdom, 1800–70," *Economic History Review* NS 29 (1976), 415–39, at 423.

Nef, Joseph U. *The Rise of the British Coal Industry* (London, 1932), 1:19–20.

Oppo, Delia W., Yair Rosenthal, and Braddock K. Linsley. "2,000-Year-Long Temperature and Hydrology Reconstruction from the Indo-Pacific Warm Pool," *Nature* 460 (2009), 1113–16.

Parker, A. J. *Ancient Shipwrecks of the Mediterranean and the Roman Provinces* (London, 1992), 10ff.

Parker, Geoffrey. *The Global Crisis: War, Climate and Catastrophe in the Seventeenth-Century World* (New Haven, CT, 2013) (Nile droughts at 193, 470).

Rein, Bert et al., "El Niño Variability off Peru during the Last 20,000 Years," *Paleoceanography* 20 (2005), PA403, 1–17.

Robb, J., R. Bigazzi, L. Lazzarini, C. Scarsini, and F. Sonego. "Social 'Status' and Biological 'Status': A Comparison of Grave Goods and Skeletal Indicators from Pontecagnano," *AJPA* 115 (2001), 213–22.

Roberts, Charlotte and Margaret Cox. "The Impact of Economic Intensification and Social Complexity on Human Health in Britain from 6000 BP (Neolithic) and the Introduction of Farming to the

Mid-Nineteenth Century AD," in Mark Nathan Cohen and Gillian M. M. Crane-Kramer, eds., *Ancient Health: Skeletal Indicators of Agricultural and Economic Intensification* (Gainesville, FL, 2007), 149–63.

Rohling, E. J., K. Braun, K. Grant, M. Kucera, A. P. Roberts, M. Siddall, and G. Trommer. "Comparison between Holocene and Marine Isotope Stage-11 Sea-Level Histories," *EPSL* 291 (2010) 97–105.

Rohling, E. J., P. A. Mayewski, R. H. Abu-Zied, J. S. L. Casford, and A. Hayes. "Holocene Atmosphere-Ocean Interactions: Records from Greenland and the Aegean Sea," *ClimDyn* 18 (2002), 587–93 (Gisp2k+).

Royer, Dana L., Robert A. Berner, Isabel P. Montañez, Neil J. Tabor, and David J. Beerling. "CO_2 as a Primary Driver of Phanerozoic Climate," *GSA Today* 14/3 (March 2004), 4–10.

Ruff, Christopher B., Brigitte M. Holt, Vladimir Sládek, Margit Berner, William A. Murphy Jr., Dieter zur Nedden, Horst Seidler, and Wolfgang Recheis. "Body Size, Body Proportions, and Mobility in the Tyrolean 'Iceman'," *JHumEv* 51 (2006), 91–101.

Russell, J. M., T. C. Johnson, and M. R. Talbot. "725 yr Cycle in the Climate of Central Africa during the Late Holocene," *Geology* 31 (2003), 677–80.

Shanahan, T. M., J. T. Overpeck, K. J. Anchukaitis, J. W. Beck, J. E. Cole, D. L. Dettman, J. A. Peck, C. A. Scholz, and J. W. King. "Atlantic Forcing of Persistent Drought in West Africa," *Science* 324 (2009), 377–80.

Shapiro, A. I., W. Schmutz, E. Roazanov, M. Schoall, M. Haberreiter, A. V. Shapiro, and S. Nyeki. "A New Approach to Long-Term Reconstruction of the Solar Irradiance Leads to Large Historical Forcing," *Astronomy and Astrophysics* 529 (2011), A67.

Siegenthaler, U., E. Monnin, K. Kawamura, R. Spahni, J. Schwander, B. Stauffer, T. F. Stocker, J.-M. Barnola, and H. Fischer. "Supporting Evidence from the EPICA Dronning Maud Land Ice Core for Atmospheric CO_2 Changes during the Past Millennium," *Tellus* 57B (2005), 51–7.

Sinha, Ashish, Max Berkelhammer, Lowell Stott, Manfred Mudelsee, and Hai Chang. "The Leading Mode of Indian Summer Monsoon Precipitation Variability during the Last Millennium," *GRL* 38 (2011), L15703.

Smith S. J., J. van Aardenne, Z. Klimont, R. J. Andres, A. Volke, and S. Delgado Arias. "Anthropogenic Sulfur Dioxide Emissions: 1850–2005," *Atmospheric Chemistry and Physics* 11 (2011), 1101–16.

Staubwasser, M., F. Sirocko, P. M. Grootes, and H. Erlenkeuser. "South Asian Monsoon Climate Change and Radiocarbon in the Arabian Sea during Early and Middle Holocene," *Paleoceanography* 17 (2002), 1063, doi:10.1029/2000PA000608.

Steckel, Richard H. "New Light on the 'Dark Ages': The Remarkably Tall Stature of Northern European Men during the Medieval Era," *Social Science History* 28 (2004), 211–29.

Stock, J. T., S. K. Pfeiffer, M. Chazan, and J. Janetski. "F-81 Skeleton from Wadi Mataha, Jordan, and Its Bearing on Human Variability in the Epipaleolithic of the Levant," *AJPA* 128 (2005), 453–65.

Stott, L. D., K. Cannariato, R. Thunell, G. H. Haug, A. Koutavas, and S. Lund. "Decline of Surface Temperature and Salinity in the Western Tropical Pacific Ocean in the Holocene Epoch," *Nature* 431 (2004), 56–9.

Szreter, Simon and Graham Mooney. "Urbanization, Mortality, and the Standard of Living Debate: New Estimates of the Expectation of Life at Birth in Nineteenth-Century British Cities," *EconHistR* 51 (1998), 84–112, at 104 (life expectancy).

Tan, L. et al., "Climate Patterns in North Central China during the Last 1800 y and Their Possible Driving Forces," *Climates of the Past* 7 (2011), 685–92.

Tett, Simon F. B., Richard Betts, Thomas J. Crowley, Jonathan Gregory, Timothy C. Johns, Andy Jones, Timothy J. Osborn, Elisabeth Öström, David L. Roberts, and Margaret J. Woodage. "The Impact of Natural and Anthropogenic Forcings on Climate and Hydrology since 1550," *ClimDyn* 28 (2007), 25, 27.

Thompson, L. G., E. Mosley-Thompson, M. E. Davis, K. A. Henderson, H. H. Brecher, V. S. Zagorodnov, T. A. Mashiotta, and P. N. Lin et al., "Kilimanjaro Ice Core Records: Evidence of Holocene Climate Change in Tropical Africa," *Science* 298 (2002): 589–93.

Thompson, L. G., 1992, Quelccaya Ice Core Database. IGBP PAGES/World Data Center-A for Paleoclimatology Data Contribution Series # 92–008. NOAA/NGDC Paleoclimatology Program, Boulder CO, USA.

Thompson, L. G., E. Mosley-Thompson, M. E. Davis, P-N. Lin, K. A. Henderson, J. Cole-Dai, J. F. Bolzan, and K-b. Liu. "Late Glacial Stage and Holocene Tropical Ice Core Records from Huascaran, Peru," *Science* 269 (1995), 46–50.

UN: *World Population Prospects: The 2010 Revision*. File 1: Total population (both sexes combined) by major area, region and country, annually for 1950–2100 (thousands) United Nations Population Division Department of Economic and Social Affairs, April 2011 (POP/DB/WPP/Rev.2010/02/F01) available at http://esa.un.org/wpp/Excel-Data/population.htm, accessed August 8, 2012.

von Rad, Ulrich, Michael Schaaf, Klaus H. Michels, Hartmut Schulz, Wolfgang H. Berger, and Frank Sirocko. "A 5000-Yr Record of Climate Change in Varved Sediments from the Oxygen Minimum Zone off Pakistan, Northeastern Arabian Sea," *QuatRes* 51 (1999), 39–53.

Weber, Adna F. *The Growth of Cities in the Nineteenth Century: A Study in Statistics* (New York, 1899), 144–5 (European urban population in 1890).

Whitmore, Thomas M., B. L. Turner II, Douglas L. Johnson, Robert W. Kates, and Thomas R. Gottschang. "Long Term Population Change," in B. L. Turner et al., *The Earth as Transformed by Human Action:*

Global and Regional Changes in the Biosphere over the Past 300 Years (Cambridge, 1990), 27–30.

Wick, Lucia, Genry Lencke, and Michael Sturm. "Evidence of Lateglacial and Holocene Climatic Change and Human Impact in Eastern Anatolia: High-Resolution Pollen, Charcoal, Isotopic and Geochemical Records from the Laminated Sediments of Lake Van, Turkey," *Holocene* 13 (2003), 665–75.

Wignall, Paul B. "Large Igneous Provinces and Mass Extinctions," *Earth-Science Reviews* 53 (2001), 1–33, esp. 18–20, 24–6.

Wrigley, E. A., R. S. Davies, J. E. Oeppen, and R. S. Schofield. *English Population History from Family Reconstitution, 1580–1837* (Cambridge, 1997), 614.

Yancheva, G., N. R. Nowaczyk, J. Mingram, P. Dulski, G. Schettler, J. F. Negendank, J. Liu, D. M. Sigman, L. C. Peterson, and G. H. Haug. "Influence of the Intertropical Convergence Zone on the East Asian Monsoon," *Nature* 445 (2007), 74–7.

Zachos, James, Mark Pagani, Lisa Sloan, Ellen Thomas, and Katherina Billups. "Trends, Rhythms, and Aberrations in Global Climate 65 Ma to Present," *Science* 292 (2001), 686–93 (figure 2).

Zakrzewski, Sonia R. "Variations in Ancient Egyptian Stature and Body Proportions," *AJPA* 121 (2003), 219–29.

Zielinski, G. A., P. A. Mayewski, L. D. Meeker, S. Whitlow, M. S. Twickler, M. Morrison, D. A. Meese, A. J. Gow, and R. B. Alley. "Record of Volcanism since 7000 B.C. from the GISP2 Greenland Ice Core and Implications for the Volcano-Climate System," *Science* 264 (1994), 948–52.

Index

31738752R00359

Printed in Great Britain
by Amazon